World History
THE HUMAN EXPERIENCE

THE EARLY AGES

NATIONAL
GEOGRAPHIC
SOCIETY

Mounir A. Farah
Andrea Berens Karls

Glencoe
McGraw-Hill

New York, New York   Columbus, Ohio   Woodland Hills, California   Peoria, Illinois

About the Authors

The **National Geographic Society**, founded in 1888 for the increase and diffusion of geographic knowledge, is the world's largest nonprofit scientific and educational organization. Since its earliest days, the Society has used sophisticated communication technologies and rich historical and archival resources to convey knowledge to a worldwide membership. The Educational Media Division supports the Society's mission by developing innovative educational programs—ranging from traditional print materials to multimedia programs including CD-ROMs, videodiscs, and software.

Mounir A. Farah, Ph.D. is a research historian and Associate Director of the Middle East Studies Program at the University of Arkansas, Fayetteville. Dr. Farah taught history and social science at New York University and Western Connecticut State University and has lectured at many teachers' conferences and workshops in the United States and abroad. He was a consultant to the Ministry of Education in Jordan and served as Coordinator of Social Studies in the Monroe, Connecticut public schools. Named Outstanding History Scholar-Teacher in New England and a recipient of the Connecticut Social Studies Annual Award, Dr. Farah is a past president of the Connecticut Council for the Social Studies and of the Middle East Outreach Council and a board member of the Arkansas Council for Social Studies. He is a contributing writer to several books and has authored numerous articles and reviews. Dr. Farah also is coauthor of Glencoe's *Global Insights.*

Andrea Berens Karls is an educator and coauthor of Glencoe's *Global Insights.* Educated at Wellesley College and Harvard University, she has taught at both the elementary and secondary levels. Ms. Karls was formerly Program Associate at Global Perspectives in Education, Inc., where she edited and wrote curriculum materials and worked with teachers. She is a member of the National Council for the Social Studies and the American Historical Association.

About the Cover

The mask of the Egyptian pharaoh Tutankhamen was created c. 1342 B.C. The mask is made of gold, and is decorated with gems and precious stones. It was discovered in 1924 by the archaeologist Howard Carter during his exploration of Tutankhamen's tomb.

The cathedral of Saint Basil the Blessed was built in Moscow between 1554 and 1560. Ivan the Terrible ordered the cathedral's construction to give thanks to God for Russia's recent military victories. Two Russian architects, Posnik and Barma, designed the church, which is located on Red Square. It has ten colorful domes and is a magnificent example of the Byzantine architectural style.

Glencoe/McGraw-Hill

A Division of The **McGraw·Hill** Companies

Design and Production: DECODE, Inc.
Cover photograph: Mask of Tutankhamen: Eqyptian National Museum, Cario, Egypt/Superstock; Cathedral of Basil the Blessed: Superstock

Send all inquiries to:
Glencoe/McGraw-Hill, 936 Eastwind Drive, Westerville, Ohio 43081

ISBN 0-02-664151-8 (Student Edition) ISBN 0-02-664152-6 (Teacher's Wraparound Edition)

Printed in the United States of America.
1 2 3 4 5 6 7 8 9 10 071 01 00 99 98

Academic Consultants

Teacher Reviewers

TABLE OF CONTENTS

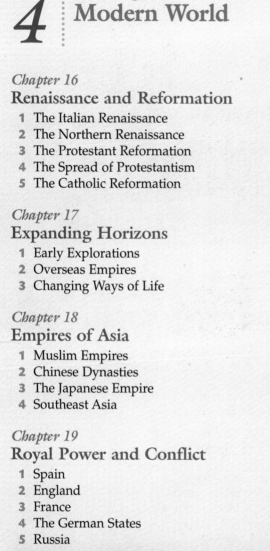

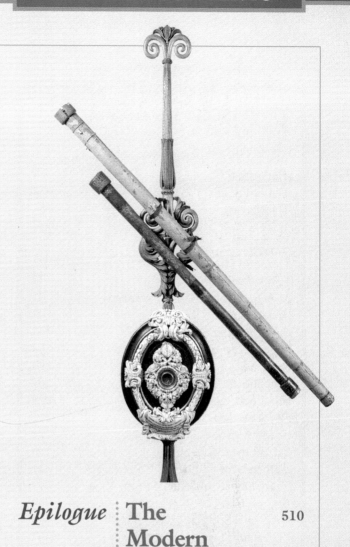

TABLE OF CONTENTS

TURNING POINT

The Spread of Ideas

Bridge to the Past — Literature

CONNECTIONS To...

TABLE OF CONTENTS

Footnotes to History

Around the World

Multimedia Activity

SKILLS

Maps

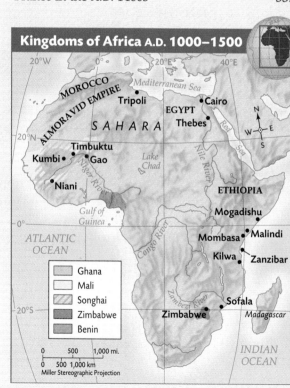

Kingdoms of Africa A.D. 1000–1500

TABLE OF CONTENTS

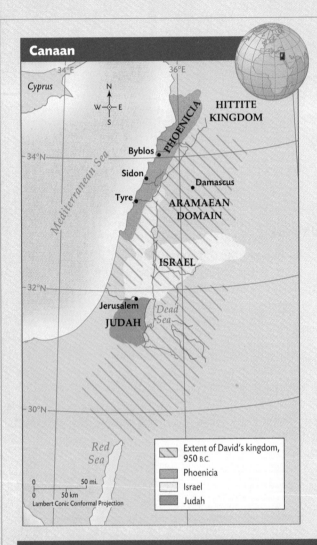

Canaan

Cyprus

Mediterranean Sea

HITTITE
KINGDOM

PHOENICIA

Byblos

Sidon

Tyre

Damascus

ARAMAEAN
DOMAIN

ISRAEL

Jerusalem

JUDAH

Dead
Sea

Red
Sea

Extent of David's kingdom,
950 B.C.

Phoenicia

Israel

Judah

0   50 mi.

0   50 km

Lambert Conic Conformal Projection

Charts, Graphs, and Diagrams

Early India's Social System

Brahmans Priests
Study and teach the Vedas, perform religious ceremonies
to please Aryan deities and ensure welfare of people

Kshatriyas Warriors, rulers
Study the Vedas, lead government, and head army

Vaisyas Common people: merchants, artisans, farmers
Tend herds, care for land; make and sell useful products

Sudras Unskilled laborers, servants
Serve other varnas

Pariahs Slaves
Perform tasks considered unclean

**Each group as a proportion
of the total population**

Varnas   Group outside varnas

Reference Atlas

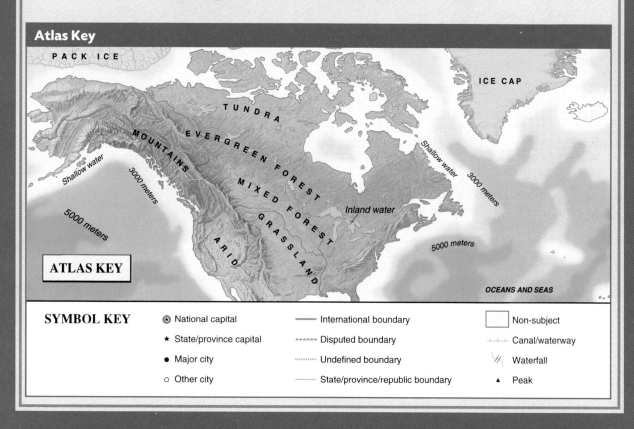

Atlas Key

PACK ICE

ICE CAP

TUNDRA

EVERGREEN FOREST

MOUNTAINS

Shallow water

Shallow water

3000 meters

3000 meters

5000 meters

MIXED FOREST

Inland water

GRASSLAND

ARID

5000 meters

ATLAS KEY

OCEANS AND SEAS

SYMBOL KEY

◎ National capital	—— International boundary	☐ Non-subject
★ State/province capital	----- Disputed boundary	⊥⊥⊥ Canal/waterway
● Major city	.... Undefined boundary	⁄⁄⁄ Waterfall
○ Other city	—— State/province/republic boundary	▲ Peak

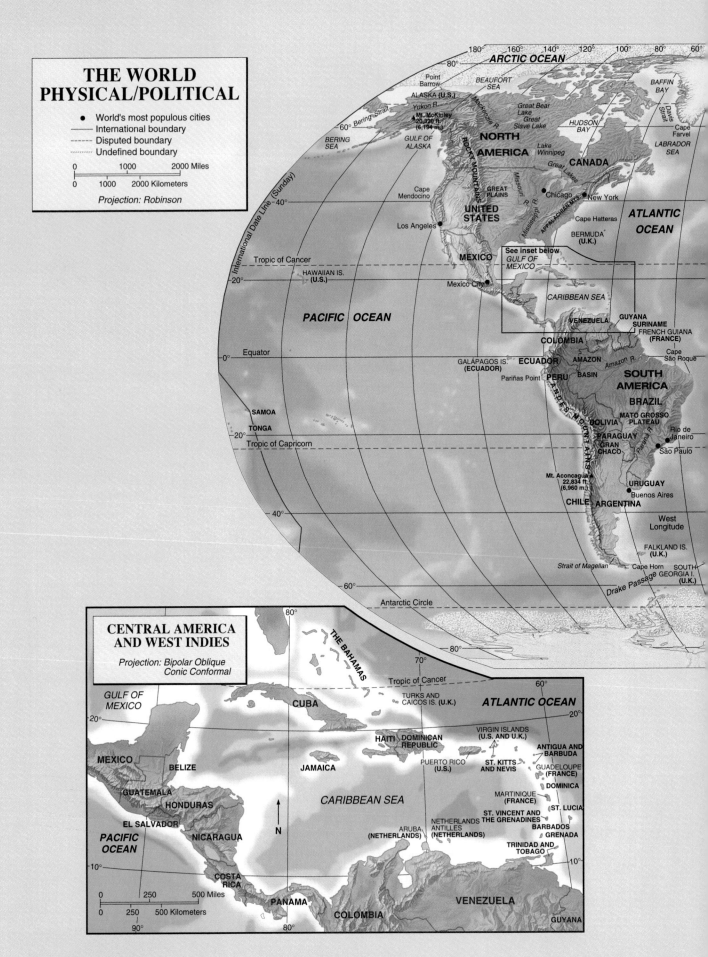

THE WORLD
PHYSICAL/POLITICAL

- ● World's most populous cities
- —— International boundary
- ------ Disputed boundary
- ········· Undefined boundary

| 0 | 1000 | 2000 Miles |
| 0 | 1000 | 2000 Kilometers |

Projection: Robinson

CENTRAL AMERICA AND WEST INDIES

Projection: Bipolar Oblique Conic Conformal

| 0 | 250 | 500 Miles |
| 0 | 250 | 500 Kilometers |

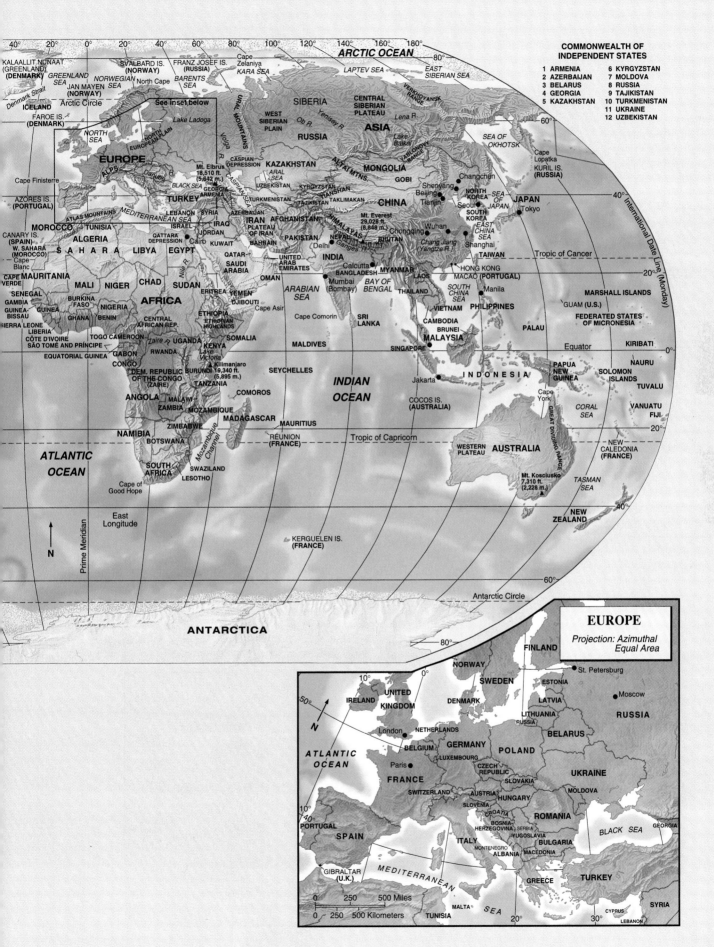

ARCTIC OCEAN

COMMONWEALTH OF
INDEPENDENT STATES

1	ARMENIA	6	KYRGYZSTAN
2	AZERBAIJAN	7	MOLDOVA
3	BELARUS	8	RUSSIA
4	GEORGIA	9	TAJIKISTAN
5	KAZAKHSTAN	10	TURKMENISTAN
		11	UKRAINE
		12	UZBEKISTAN

KALAALLIT NUNAAT
(GREENLAND)
(DENMARK)
GREENLAND
SEA
JAN MAYEN
(NORWAY)
NORWEGIAN
SEA
North Cape
SVALBARD IS.
(NORWAY)
FRANZ JOSEF IS.
(RUSSIA)
Cape
Zelaniya
KARA
SEA
LAPTEV SEA
EAST
SIBERIAN SEA
VERKHOYANSK RANGE
Denmark Strait
ICELAND
FAROE IS.
(DENMARK)
Arctic Circle
North Cape
BARENTS
SEA
URAL MOUNTAINS
SIBERIA
CENTRAL
SIBERIAN
PLATEAU
Lena R.
60°
See Inset below
NORTH
SEA
Lake Ladoga
WEST
SIBERIAN
PLAIN
Yenisey R.
Ob R.
RUSSIA
ASIA
Lake
Baikal
SEA OF
OKHOTSK
Cape
Lopatka
KURIL IS.
(RUSSIA)
EUROPE
ALPS
EUROPEAN PLAIN
Danube R.
Volga R.
CASPIAN DEPRESSION
Mt. Elbrus
18,510 ft.
(5,642 m.)
CASPIAN SEA
ARAL
SEA
KAZAKHSTAN
ALTAI MTNS.
MONGOLIA
GOBI
Changchun
Shenyang
NORTH
KOREA
SEA
OF
JAPAN
JAPAN
40°
Cape Finisterre
BLACK SEA
GEORGIA
ARMENIA
UZBEKISTAN
TURKMENISTAN
KYRGYZSTAN
TIANSHAN
TAJIKISTAN
TAKLIMAKAN
CHINA
Beijing
Tianjin
Seoul
SOUTH
KOREA
EAST
CHINA
SEA
Tokyo
AZORES IS.
(PORTUGAL)
TURKEY
MEDITERRANEAN SEA
LEBANON
SYRIA
IRAQ
ISRAEL
JORDAN
AZERBAIJAN
IRAN
AFGHANISTAN
PLATEAU
OF IRAN
PAKISTAN
HIMALAYAS
Mt. Everest
29,028 ft.
(8,848 m.)
NEPAL
Ganges R.
BHUTAN
Chongqing
Wuhan
Chang Jiang
(Yangtze R.)
Shanghai
TAIWAN
Tropic of Cancer
20°
MOROCCO
TUNISIA
ATLAS MOUNTAINS
QATTARA
DEPRESSION
Cairo
KUWAIT
BAHRAIN
Delhi
INDIA
HONG KONG
MACAO (PORTUGAL)
International Date Line (Monday)
CANARY IS.
(SPAIN)
W. SAHARA
(MOROCCO)
Cape
Blanc
ALGERIA
LIBYA
EGYPT
Nile R.
SAHARA
QATAR
UNITED
ARAB
EMIRATES
SAUDI
ARABIA
OMAN
Calcutta
BANGLADESH
MYANMAR
LAOS
THAILAND
SOUTH
CHINA
SEA
Manila
MARSHALL ISLANDS
GUAM (U.S.)
CAPE
VERDE
MAURITANIA
MALI
NIGER
CHAD
SUDAN
ERITREA
YEMEN
DJIBOUTI
ARABIAN
SEA
Mumbai
(Bombay)
BAY OF
BENGAL
VIETNAM
PHILIPPINES
FEDERATED STATES
OF MICRONESIA
SENEGAL
GAMBIA
GUINEA-
BISSAU
GUINEA
BURKINA
FASO
NIGERIA
BENIN
AFRICA
CENTRAL
AFRICAN REP.
ETHIOPIA
ETHIOPIAN
HIGHLANDS
SOMALIA
Cape Asir
Cape Comorin
SRI
LANKA
CAMBODIA
BRUNEI
MALAYSIA
PALAU
SIERRA LEONE
LIBERIA
CÔTE D'IVOIRE
SÃO TOMÉ AND PRÍNCIPE
GHANA
TOGO
CAMEROON
Zaire R.
UGANDA
KENYA
Lake
Victoria
MALDIVES
SINGAPORE
KIRIBATI
Equator
0°
EQUATORIAL GUINEA
GABON
CONGO
RWANDA
BURUNDI
Kilimanjaro
19,340 ft.
(5,895 m.)
SEYCHELLES
INDONESIA
PAPUA
NEW
GUINEA
SOLOMON
ISLANDS
NAURU
DEM. REPUBLIC
OF THE CONGO
(ZAIRE)
TANZANIA
INDIAN
OCEAN
Jakarta
Cape
York
TUVALU
ANGOLA
MALAWI
ZAMBIA
MOZAMBIQUE
COMOROS
MADAGASCAR
MAURITIUS
GREAT DIVIDING RANGE
CORAL
SEA
VANUATU
FIJI
ATLANTIC
OCEAN
NAMIBIA
ZIMBABWE
BOTSWANA
Mozambique Channel
RÉUNION
(FRANCE)
Tropic of Capricorn
WESTERN
PLATEAU
AUSTRALIA
NEW
CALEDONIA
(FRANCE)
20°
SOUTH
AFRICA
SWAZILAND
LESOTHO
Cape of
Good Hope
Mt. Kosciusko
7,310 ft.
(2,228 m.)
TASMAN
SEA
NEW
ZEALAND
40°
N
Prime Meridian
East
Longitude
KERGUELEN IS.
(FRANCE)
60°
ANTARCTICA
Antarctic Circle
80°

40° 20° 0° 20° 40° 60° 80° 100° 120° 140° 160° 180° 80° 60° 40° 20° 0° 20° 40° 60°

EUROPE

*Projection: Azimuthal
Equal Area*

FINLAND
NORWAY
St. Petersburg
SWEDEN
ESTONIA
Moscow
IRELAND
UNITED
KINGDOM
DENMARK
LATVIA
LITHUANIA
RUSSIA
RUSSIA
London
NETHERLANDS
BELGIUM
GERMANY
POLAND
BELARUS
ATLANTIC
OCEAN
Paris
FRANCE
LUXEMBOURG
CZECH
REPUBLIC
SLOVAKIA
UKRAINE
SWITZERLAND
AUSTRIA
HUNGARY
MOLDOVA
SLOVENIA
CROATIA
ROMANIA
PORTUGAL
BOSNIA
HERZEGOVINA
SERBIA
YUGOSLAVIA
SPAIN
ITALY
MONTENEGRO
ALBANIA
MACEDONIA
BULGARIA
BLACK SEA
GEORGIA
GREECE
TURKEY
GIBRALTAR
(U.K.)
MEDITERRANEAN
SEA
SYRIA
CYPRUS
LEBANON
MALTA
TUNISIA

0   250   500 Miles
0   250   500 Kilometers

50°
10°
0°
40°
10°
20°
30°

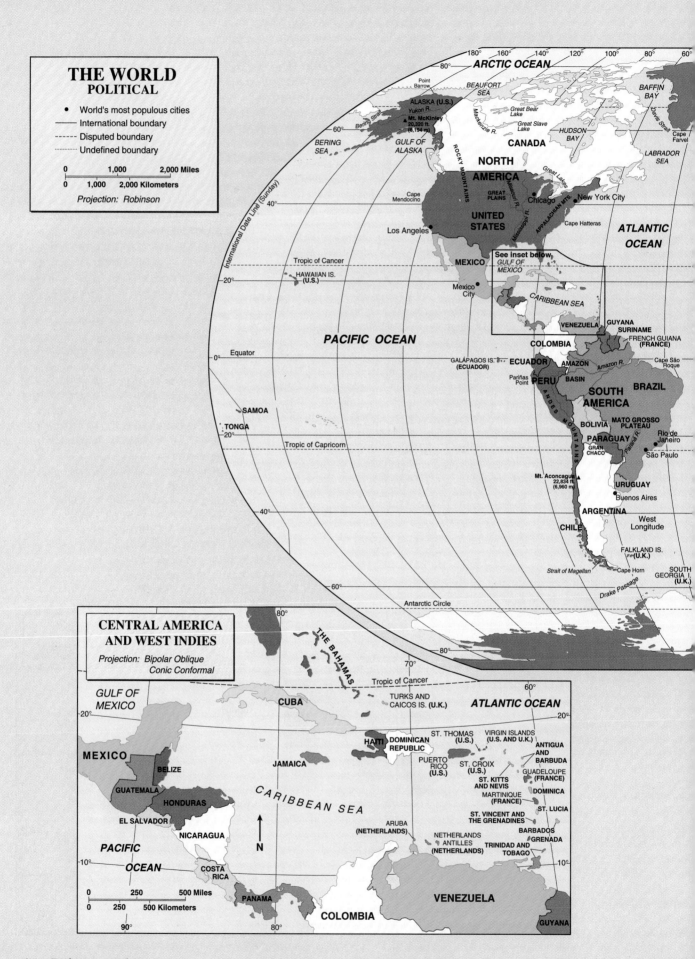

THE WORLD
POLITICAL

- • World's most populous cities
- —— International boundary
- – – – Disputed boundary
- ········· Undefined boundary

| 0 | 1,000 | 2,000 Miles |
| 0 | 1,000 | 2,000 Kilometers |

Projection: Robinson

ARCTIC OCEAN

Point Barrow

BEAUFORT SEA

ALASKA (U.S.)
Yukon R.
▲ Mt. McKinley 20,320 ft. (6,194 m)

Bering Strait

BERING SEA

GULF OF ALASKA

Great Bear Lake

Mackenzie R.

Great Slave Lake

HUDSON BAY

BAFFIN BAY

Davis Strait

Cape Farvel

CANADA

NORTH AMERICA

ROCKY MOUNTAINS

GREAT PLAINS

Missouri R.

Great Lakes

LABRADOR SEA

Mississippi R.

APPALACHIAN MTS.

Chicago

New York City

Cape Mendocino

UNITED STATES

Cape Hatteras

ATLANTIC OCEAN

Los Angeles

MEXICO

See inset below
GULF OF MEXICO

Tropic of Cancer

HAWAIIAN IS. (U.S.)

Mexico City

CARIBBEAN SEA

VENEZUELA

GUYANA
SURINAME
FRENCH GUIANA (FRANCE)

PACIFIC OCEAN

COLOMBIA

Equator

GALÁPAGOS IS. (ECUADOR)

ECUADOR

AMAZON

Amazon R.

Cape São Roque

Pariñas Point

PERU

BASIN

BRAZIL

SOUTH AMERICA

SAMOA

ANDES MOUNTAINS

BOLIVIA

MATO GROSSO PLATEAU

TONGA

PARAGUAY

Rio de Janeiro

Tropic of Capricorn

GRAN CHACO

Paraná R.

São Paulo

Mt. Aconcagua 22,834 ft. (6,960 m) ▲

URUGUAY

Buenos Aires

ARGENTINA

West Longitude

CHILE

FALKLAND IS. (U.K.)

Strait of Magellan

Cape Horn

SOUTH GEORGIA I. (U.K.)

Drake Passage

Antarctic Circle

International Date Line (Sunday)

CENTRAL AMERICA AND WEST INDIES

Projection: Bipolar Oblique Conic Conformal

GULF OF MEXICO

THE BAHAMAS

Tropic of Cancer

CUBA

TURKS AND CAICOS IS. (U.K.)

ATLANTIC OCEAN

MEXICO

BELIZE

HAITI

DOMINICAN REPUBLIC

ST. THOMAS (U.S.)

VIRGIN ISLANDS (U.S. AND U.K.)

ANTIGUA AND BARBUDA

JAMAICA

PUERTO RICO (U.S.)

ST. CROIX (U.S.)

GUADELOUPE (FRANCE)

GUATEMALA

ST. KITTS AND NEVIS

DOMINICA

HONDURAS

CARIBBEAN SEA

MARTINIQUE (FRANCE)

ST. LUCIA

EL SALVADOR

ST. VINCENT AND THE GRENADINES

N

NICARAGUA

ARUBA (NETHERLANDS)

BARBADOS

GRENADA

PACIFIC OCEAN

NETHERLANDS ANTILLES (NETHERLANDS)

TRINIDAD AND TOBAGO

COSTA RICA

| 0 | 250 | 500 Miles |
| 0 | 250 | 500 Kilometers |

PANAMA

VENEZUELA

COLOMBIA

GUYANA

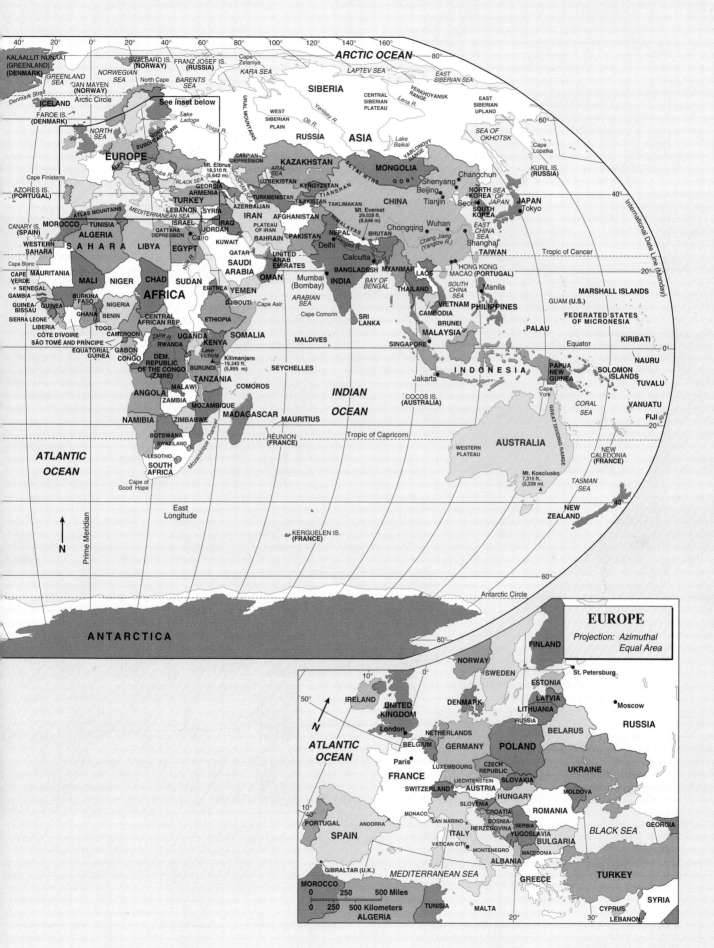

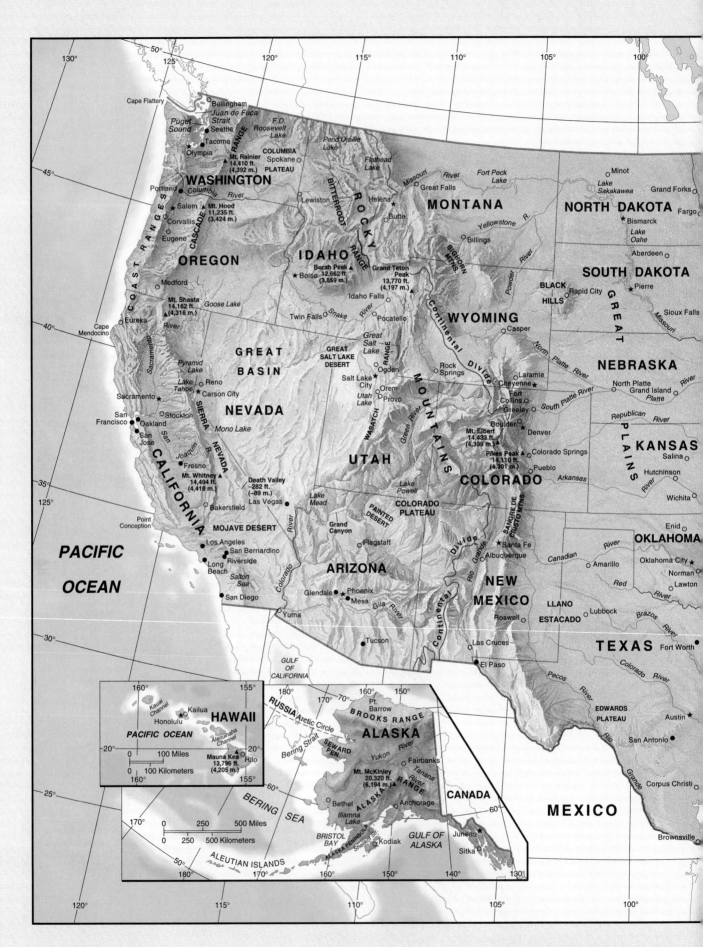

Cape Flattery
Bellingham
Juan de Fuca Strait
Puget Sound
Seattle
Tacoma
Olympia
Mt. Rainier 14,410 ft. (4,392 m.)
F.D. Roosevelt Lake
COLUMBIA
Spokane
Pend Oreille Lake
Flathead Lake
Fort Peck Lake
Minot
Lake Sakakawea
Grand Forks
Fargo

WASHINGTON
PLATEAU
Portland
Columbia River
Lewiston
Helena
Great Falls
Missouri River
MONTANA
NORTH DAKOTA
Bismarck

Salem
Mt. Hood 11,235 ft. (3,424 m.)
Corvallis
Eugene
CASCADE RANGE
Butte
Billings
Yellowstone
Lake Oahe
Aberdeen

OREGON
IDAHO
ROCKY
BITTERROOT
Borah Peak 12,662 ft. (3,859 m.)
Boise
Grand Teton Peak 13,770 ft. (4,197 m.)
BIGHORN MTS.
Powder River
SOUTH DAKOTA
Pierre

Medford
Mt. Shasta 14,162 ft. (4,316 m.)
Goose Lake
Idaho Falls
RANGE
BLACK HILLS
Rapid City
Sioux Falls

Eureka
Cape Mendocino
Twin Falls
Snake River
Pocatello
Continental Divide
WYOMING
Casper
North Platte River
GREAT
NEBRASKA

Sacramento River
GREAT BASIN
GREAT SALT LAKE DESERT
Great Salt Lake
Ogden
Rock Springs
Laramie
Cheyenne
North Platte
Grand Island
Platte
KANSAS

Pyramid Lake
Lake Tahoe
Reno
Carson City
Salt Lake City
Orem
Provo
Utah Lake
Fort Collins
Greeley
South Platte River
Republican River

Sacramento
NEVADA
RANGE
WASATCH
Green River
MOUNTAINS
Boulder
Mt. Elbert 14,433 ft. (4,399 m.)
Denver
PLAINS

San Francisco
Oakland
San Jose
Stockton
Mono Lake
UTAH
Pikes Peak 14,110 ft. (4,301 m.)
COLORADO
Colorado Springs
Salina
Hutchinson

San Joaquin R.
Fresno
Mt. Whitney 14,494 ft. (4,418 m.)
Death Valley -282 ft. (-89 m.)
Las Vegas
Lake Powell
Pueblo
Arkansas River
Wichita

CALIFORNIA
SIERRA NEVADA
Bakersfield
Lake Mead
PAINTED DESERT
COLORADO PLATEAU
SANGRE DE CRISTO MTS.
Enid
OKLAHOMA

Point Conception
MOJAVE DESERT
Grand Canyon
Flagstaff
Santa Fe
Albuquerque
Canadian River
Amarillo
Oklahoma City
River

Los Angeles
San Bernardino
Riverside
Long Beach
Salton Sea
Colorado River
ARIZONA
Continental Divide
Rio Grande
NEW MEXICO
LLANO ESTACADO
Lubbock
Red River
Norman
Lawton

San Diego
PACIFIC OCEAN
Glendale
Phoenix
Mesa
Gila River
Roswell
Brazos River

Yuma
Tucson
Las Cruces
El Paso
TEXAS
Fort Worth

GULF OF CALIFORNIA
Pecos River
Colorado River
EDWARDS PLATEAU
Austin

MEXICO
Rio Grande
San Antonio
Corpus Christi
Brownsville

A6   Reference Atlas

HAWAII inset:
Kauai Channel
Kailua
Honolulu
HAWAII
PACIFIC OCEAN
Alenuihaha Channel
Mauna Kea 13,796 ft. (4,205 m.)
Hilo
0   100 Miles
0   100 Kilometers

ALASKA inset:
RUSSIA
Arctic Circle
Pt. Barrow
BROOKS RANGE
ALASKA
SEWARD PEN.
Bering Strait
Yukon River
Fairbanks
Tanana River
ALASKA RANGE
Mt. McKinley 20,320 ft. (6,194 m.)
Bethel
Iliamna Lake
Anchorage
CANADA
BERING SEA
BRISTOL BAY
ALASKA PENINSULA
Shelikof Str.
Kodiak
GULF OF ALASKA
Juneau
Sitka
ALEUTIAN ISLANDS
0   250   500 Miles
0   250   500 Kilometers

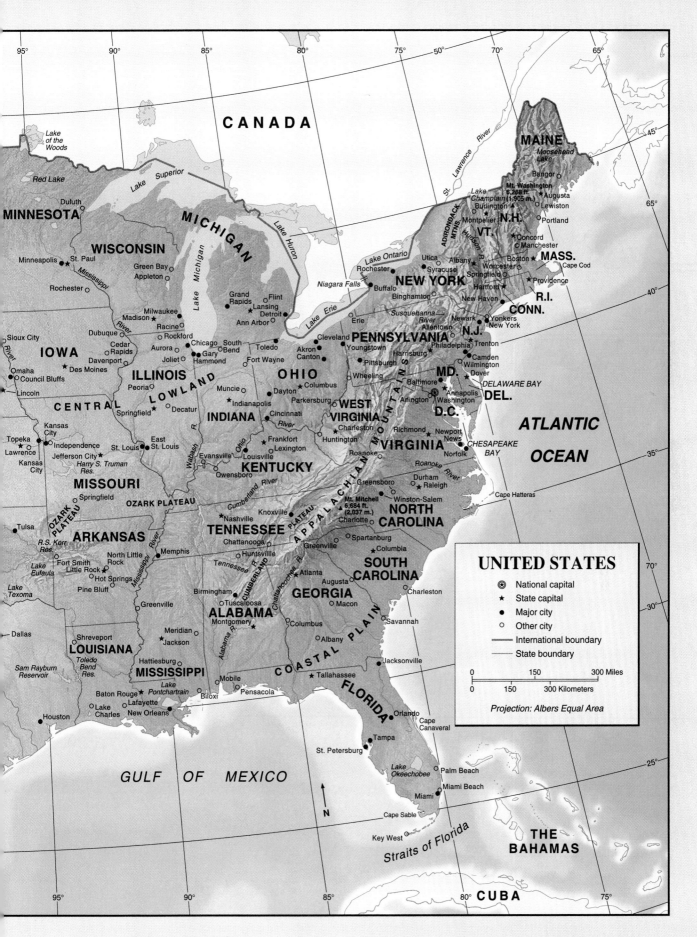

CANADA

MINNESOTA

Lake of the Woods

Red Lake

Duluth

WISCONSIN

Lake Superior

MICHIGAN

Lake Michigan

Lake Huron

MAINE

Moosehead Lake

Bangor

Mt. Washington 6,288 ft. (1,905 m.)

Lake Champlain

Augusta
Lewiston

St. Lawrence River

Portland

Montpelier

N.H.

VT.

Concord
Manchester

Hudson R.

Minneapolis
St. Paul

Mississippi River

Green Bay
Appleton

Lake Ontario

Rochester

Utica
Syracuse
Albany

Boston

MASS.

Cape Cod

Rochester

Milwaukee
Madison
Racine

Grand Rapids
Flint
Lansing
Detroit
Ann Arbor

Niagara Falls
Buffalo

NEW YORK

Binghamton

Springfield
Worcester
Hartford

Providence

R.I.

New Haven

CONN.

Sioux City

Dubuque

Rockford

Chicago
South Bend

Toledo

Lake Erie
Erie

Cleveland
Youngstown

Susquehanna River

Newark
Allentown

N.J.

Yonkers
New York

IOWA

Cedar Rapids
Davenport

Aurora
Joliet

Gary
Hammond

Fort Wayne

Akron
Canton

PENNSYLVANIA

Harrisburg

Philadelphia

Trenton

Des Moines

Omaha
Council Bluffs

ILLINOIS

Peoria

LOWLAND

Muncie

OHIO

Dayton
Columbus

Pittsburgh
Wheeling

Camden
Wilmington
Dover

Lincoln

Springfield
Decatur

INDIANA

Indianapolis
Cincinnati

Parkersburg

WEST VIRGINIA

Baltimore

MD.

Annapolis
Washington

DEL.

DELAWARE BAY

CENTRAL

Wabash R.

Ohio River

Frankfort
Lexington

Charleston
Huntington

D.C.

Arlington

Richmond
Newport News

ATLANTIC

Kansas City

Topeka
Lawrence

Independence

Jefferson City

St. Louis
East St. Louis

Evansville
Louisville

KENTUCKY

Roanoke

VIRGINIA

CHESAPEAKE BAY
Norfolk

OCEAN

Kansas City

Harry S. Truman Res.

Owensboro

Cumberland River

Roanoke River

MISSOURI

Springfield

OZARK PLATEAU

Nashville
Knoxville

Greensboro
Durham
Raleigh

Tulsa

OZARK PLATEAU

Mississippi River

ARKANSAS

TENNESSEE

Chattanooga

Tennessee River

PLATEAU

Mt. Mitchell 6,684 ft. (2,037 m.)

Charlotte

Winston-Salem

NORTH CAROLINA

Cape Hatteras

R.S. Kerr Res.

Fort Smith

North Little Rock
Little Rock

Memphis

Huntsville
Greenville

Spartanburg

Cape Hatteras

Lake Eufaula

Hot Springs
Pine Bluff

APPALACHIAN MOUNTAINS

CUMBERLAND

Columbia

SOUTH CAROLINA

Lake Texoma

Greenville

Birmingham

Atlanta

Augusta

Dallas

Shreveport

LOUISIANA

Meridian
Jackson

Tuscaloosa

ALABAMA

Montgomery

GEORGIA

Columbus

Chattahoochee R.

Macon

Charleston

Savannah

	UNITED STATES
⊛	National capital
★	State capital
●	Major city
○	Other city
	International boundary
	State boundary

Sam Rayburn Reservoir

Hattiesburg

MISSISSIPPI

Alabama R.

Tallahassee

Jacksonville

Lake Pontchartrain

Toledo Bend Res.

Baton Rouge

Biloxi

Mobile

Pensacola

FLORIDA

0   150   300 Miles

0   150   300 Kilometers

Lafayette
Lake Charles

New Orleans

COASTAL PLAIN

Projection: Albers Equal Area

Houston

Orlando

Cape Canaveral

GULF   OF   MEXICO

Tampa

St. Petersburg

Lake Okeechobee

Palm Beach

Miami Beach

Miami

N

Cape Sable

Key West

Straits of Florida

THE BAHAMAS

CUBA

95°   90°   85°   80°   75°   50°   70°   65°

45°

65°

40°

35°

70°

30°

25°

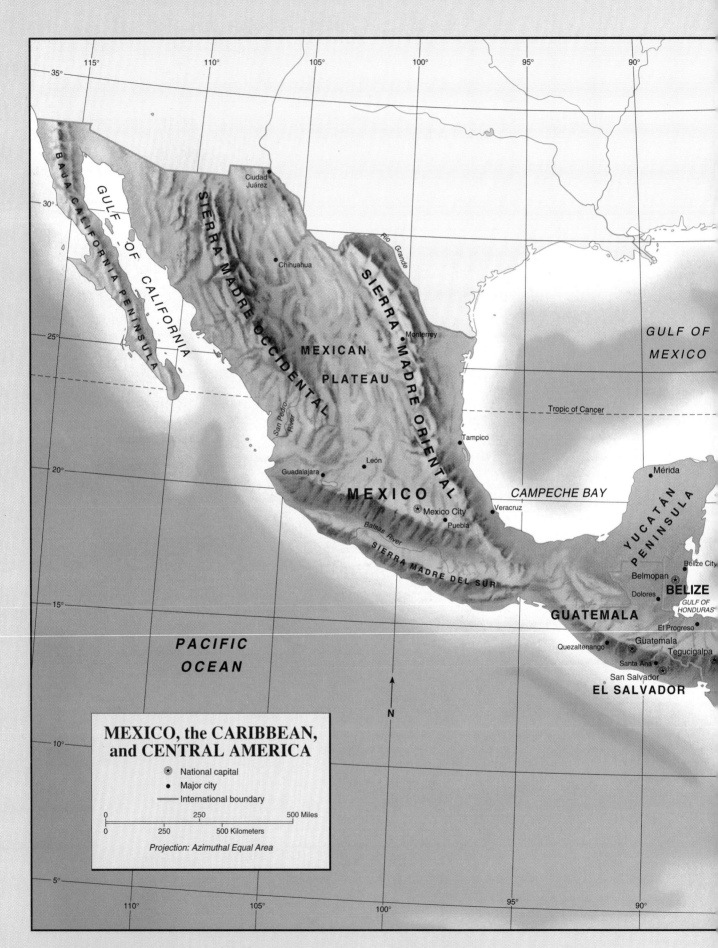

MEXICO, the CARIBBEAN, and CENTRAL AMERICA

- ⊛ National capital
- • Major city
- ── International boundary

0   250   500 Miles
0   250   500 Kilometers

Projection: Azimuthal Equal Area

GULF OF CALIFORNIA

BAJA CALIFORNIA PENINSULA

PACIFIC OCEAN

SIERRA MADRE OCCIDENTAL

MEXICAN PLATEAU

SIERRA MADRE ORIENTAL

MEXICO

SIERRA MADRE DEL SUR

GULF OF MEXICO

CAMPECHE BAY

YUCATÁN PENINSULA

GUATEMALA

BELIZE

GULF OF HONDURAS

EL SALVADOR

Ciudad Juárez

Chihuahua

Monterrey

Río Grande

Tropic of Cancer

Tampico

León

Guadalajara

Mexico City

Puebla

Veracruz

Balsas River

San Pedro River

Mérida

Belize City

Belmopan

Dolores

El Progreso

Quezaltenango

Guatemala

Tegucigalpa

Santa Ana

San Salvador

N

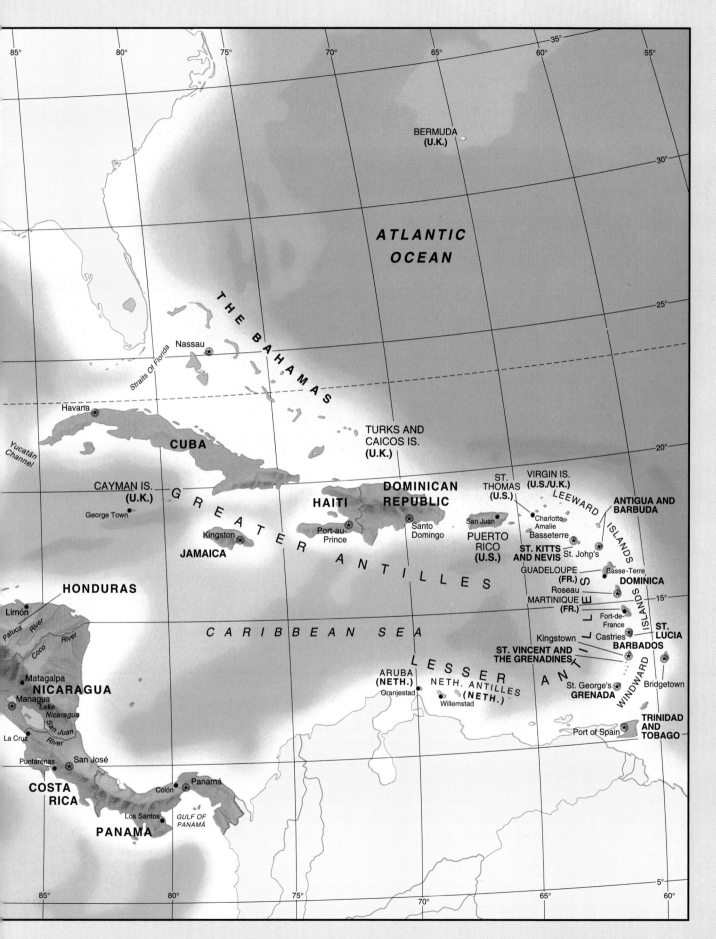

BERMUDA
(U.K.)

ATLANTIC
OCEAN

THE BAHAMAS

Nassau

Straits Of Florida

Havana

Yucatán
Channel

CUBA

TURKS AND
CAICOS IS.
(U.K.)

CAYMAN IS.
(U.K.)

George Town

GREATER ANTILLES

DOMINICAN
REPUBLIC

HAITI

Port-au-
Prince

Santo
Domingo

Kingston

JAMAICA

PUERTO
RICO
(U.S.)

San Juan

ST.
THOMAS
(U.S.)

VIRGIN IS.
(U.S./U.K.)

Charlotte
Amalie

Basseterre

ST. KITTS
AND NEVIS

St. John's

LEEWARD ISLANDS

ANTIGUA AND
BARBUDA

GUADELOUPE
(FR.)

Basse-Terre

DOMINICA

Roseau

MARTINIQUE
(FR.)

Fort-de-
France

ANTILLES

ST.
LUCIA

Castries

BARBADOS

Bridgetown

HONDURAS

Limón

Patuca River

Coco River

Matagalpa

NICARAGUA

Managua

Lake
Nicaragua

La Cruz

San Juan River

Puntarenas

San José

COSTA
RICA

Los Santos

PANAMA

Colón

Panamá

GULF OF
PANAMÁ

CARIBBEAN SEA

LESSER ANTILLES

ARUBA
(NETH.)

Oranjestad

NETH. ANTILLES
(NETH.)

Willemstad

Kingstown

ST. VINCENT AND
THE GRENADINES

WINDWARD ISLANDS

St. George's

GRENADA

Port of Spain

TRINIDAD
AND
TOBAGO

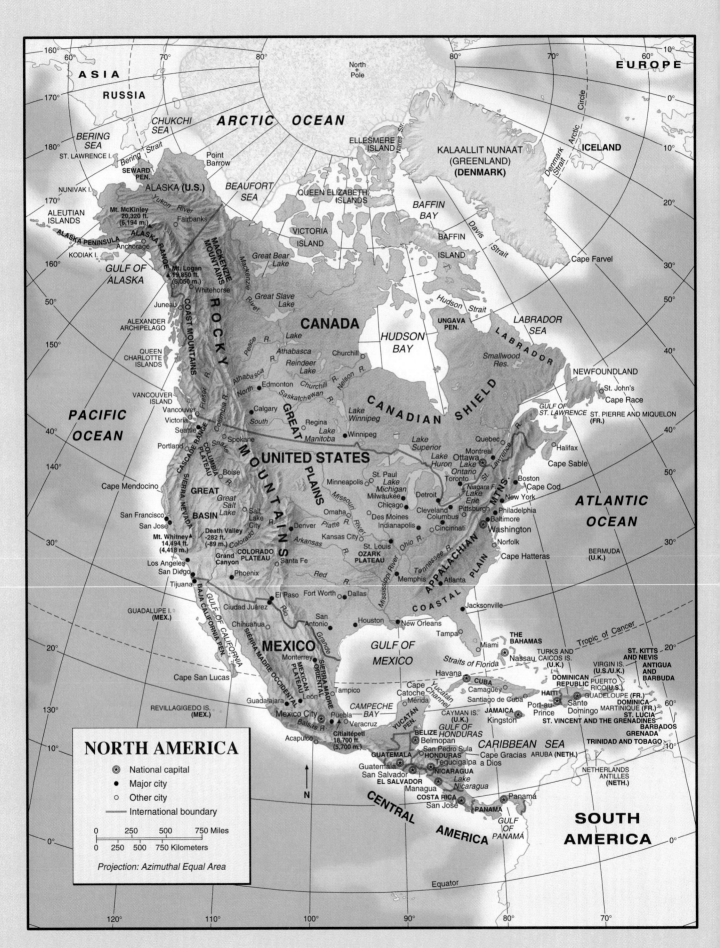

NORTH AMERICA

⊛ National capital
● Major city
○ Other city
— International boundary

0   250   500   750 Miles
0   250   500   750 Kilometers

Projection: Azimuthal Equal Area

SOUTH AMERICA

- ⊛ National capital
- • Major city
- ○ Other city
- International boundary

0   250   500 Miles
0   250   500 Kilometers

Projection: Azimuthal Equal Area

EUROPE

- ⊛ National capital
- ● Major city
- ○ Other city
- International boundary
- Republic boundary
- Canal

0   100   200   300 Miles
0   100   200   300 Kilometers

Projection: Azimuthal Equal Area

ICELAND
Reykjavik

Arctic Circle

NORWEGIAN SEA

FAROE IS. (DEN.)

SHETLAND IS. (U.K.)

Trondheim

NORWAY
Bergen
Oslo

Galdhøpiggen 8,097 ft. (2,468 m.)

SCANDINAVIAN HIGHLANDS

GULF OF BOTHNIA

SWEDEN
Uppsala
Stockholm

ÅLAND I.

HIIUMAA I.
SAAREMAA I.
GOTLAND I.

OUTER HEBRIDES IS.
Cape Wrath
ORKNEY ISLANDS

SCOTLAND
Glasgow
Edinburgh

NORTHERN IRELAND (U.K.)
Belfast

PENNINE RANGE

UNITED KINGDOM

NORTH SEA

Skagerrak

Göteborg

Kattegat

Lake Vänern

Lake Vättern

OLAND I.

BALTIC SEA

RUSSIA

IRISH SEA
Dublin
IRELAND
Cork

ISLE OF MAN
Manchester
Liverpool
Leeds
Sheffield
ENGLAND
Birmingham

JUTLAND
Copenhagen
DENMARK
Odense
Malmö
BORNHOLM I.

Kiel Canal
Rostock
Szczecin

Gdańsk

NORTH

POLAND

Vistula

Cape Clear
St. George's Channel
WALES
Cardiff
Bristol

London

NETHERLANDS
Amsterdam
The Hague
Rotterdam

Hamburg
Bremen
Mittelland Canal

Elbe R.

Hannover
Magdeburg

Berlin

Poznań
Warsaw

Łódź

ATLANTIC OCEAN

GUERNSEY I. (U.K.)
JERSEY I. (U.K.)

BRETON PEN.

English Channel
Strait of Dover

Le Havre

Antwerp
BELGIUM
Brussels
Liège

Essen
Cologne
Bonn
LUXEMBOURG
Luxembourg

Dortmund

GERMANY
Frankfurt

Leipzig
Dresden

Chemnitz

Prague

CZECH REPUBLIC

Brno

Ostrava

Wrocław

Katowice

Kraków

SLOVAKIA

Nantes

Paris
Marne R.
Marne-Rhine Canal

Seine River
Rhine R.

Stuttgart

Strasbourg

Danube River

Munich

Vienna
Linz

Bratislava

Miskolc

Loire

FRANCE

Loire River

Bordeaux

CENTRAL MASSIF

Garonne R.
Midi

PYRENEES

Aneto Peak 11,168 ft. (3,404 m.)

Toulouse

Montpellier

Rhône R.
Lyon

Bodensee
Zürich
Bern
SWITZERLAND
Lausanne
Geneva
Geneva

LIECHTENSTEIN
Vaduz
Innsbruck

AUSTRIA

Salzburg

Graz

Ljubljana

SLOVENIA

Budapest
L. Balaton

HUNGARY

Pécs

Tisza

Zagreb

CROATIA

Novi Sad

Belgrade

Sava R.

DINARIC ALPS

Cape Finisterre

BAY OF BISCAY

Bilbao

CANTABRIAN MTNS.

Mt. Blanc 15,771 ft. (4,807 m.)

Mt. Rosa 12,203 ft. (4,634 m.)

Milan
Turin
PO VALLEY
Genoa
Venice
Po R.

ALPS

Bologna

SAN MARINO
San Marino

APENNINES

BOSNIA-HERZEGOVINA
Sarajevo

Split

MONTENEGRO

ADRIATIC SEA

Porto

Valladolid

Duero River

Ebro River

ANDORRA
Andorra la Vella

Marseille
GULF OF LION

Nice

Monaco
MONACO

Florence

VATICAN CITY
Rome

ITALY

MACEDONIA

Tirané

ALBANIA

PORTUGAL
Lisbon
Setúbal

IBERIAN PENINSULA

Zaragoza
Madrid

Tagus River

Guadiana River

Barcelona

Valencia

CORSICA (FR.)

SARDINIA (IT.)

Naples

Bari

SIERRA MORENA
SPAIN
Seville

Granada

Murcia

Palma
BALEARIC IS. (SP.)

TYRRHENIAN SEA

G. OF TARANTO

IONIAN SEA

KEFALLINIA I.

Cape St. Vincent
Málaga

Strait of Gibraltar
GIBRALTAR (U.K.)

MEDITERRANEAN

Cagliari

Palermo
SICILY
Catania

Strait of Sicily

PANTELLERIA (IT.)

MALTA
Valletta

AFRICA

SEA

North
Cape
30°   40°   70°
50°
BARENTS
SEA
Murmansk
KOLA
PENINSULA
WHITE
SEA
White Sea-
Baltic
Waterway
FINLAND
Lake
Onega
Tampere
Lake
Saimaa
Lake
Ladoga
Turku
Helsinki
Espoo
Volga-Baltic
Waterway
Tallinn
St. Petersburg
GULF OF FINLAND
ESTONIA
Rybinsk
Reservoir
Chudskoye
Lake
Yaroslavl
GULF
OF
RIGA
LATVIA
Riga
Volga River
Volga-Baltic
Waterway
Moscow
BALTIC
PLAIN
W. Dvina
River
River
Oka
Tula
LITHUANIA
Kaunas
Vilnius
Minsk
BELARUS
CENTRAL RUSSIAN UPLAND
Kursk
Pripet   River
Desna
Desna
R.
RUSSIA
Voronezh
Don
Don
Kiev
Kremenchug
Reservoir
Kharkov
Lugansk
UKRAINE
Lvov
DNIEPER UPLAND
Dniester
R.
Dnepropetrovsk
Krivoy Rog
Zaporozhye
Donetsk
Don River
Rostov
MOLDOVA
Prut River
Chisinau
DNIEPER LOWLAND
Dniep.
River
Kakhovka
Res.
SEA
OF
AZOV
CARPATHIAN MTNS.
Odessa
Debrecen
Cluj-Napoca
CRIMEA
Krasnodar
ROMANIA
Timisoara
Brasov
Bucharest
WALLACHIA
PLAIN
Danube
Ruse
Constanta
BLACK   SEA
SERBIA
Nis
Varna
BULGARIA
Sofia
Burgas
Skopje   Plovdiv
Musala Peak
9,536 ft.
(2,926 m.)
Bosporus
TURKEY
PENINSULA
Salonika
BALKAN
Dardanelles
SEA OF
MARMARA
Larissa
AEGEAN
SEA
GREECE
Patras   Athens
Piraeus
PELOPONNESE
PEN.
RHODES
CRETE (GR.)
Iraklion
30°
40°

60°
Pechora
R.
TIMAN   RIDGE
N.
Dvina
River
Vychegda
River
URAL
Mt. Konzhakovskiy
5,147 ft.
(1,569 m.)
Kama
R.
Sukhona River
Perm
MOUNTAINS
70°
50°
Kazan
Kama River
Ufa
Nizhniy
Novgorod
Kuybyshev
Reservoir
Samara
Orenburg
Ural River
VOLGA UPLAND
Volga River
Saratov
Volgograd
Reservoir
KAZAKHSTAN
Volgograd
Volga
River
Ural River
Tsimlyansk
Reservoir
DEPRESSION
Astrakhan
CASPIAN
Delta of
the Volga
CASPIAN
SEA
Grozny
CAUCASUS MTNS.
Mt. Elbrus
18,510 ft.
(5,642 m.)

ASIA
70°   60°   80°

70°
50°

40°

60°

ARAL
SEA

30°

ASIA

50°

Reference Atlas   A13

ARCTIC OCEAN

FRANZ JOSEF ISLANDS

Cape Zelaniya

BARENTS SEA

KARA SEA

EUROPE

BALTIC SEA

GULF OF FINLAND

Murmansk

KOLA PENINSULA

WHITE SEA

NOVAYA ZEMLYA

Kara Strait

YAMAL PEN.

GYDAN PENINSULA

(RUSSIA)

St. Petersburg

Lake Ladoga

Baltic-White Sea Canal

Arkhangel'sk

Lake Onega

Volga-Baltic Waterway

TIMAN RIDGE

Yenisey River

VALDAI HILLS

N. Dvina R.

Vychegda

River

Urengoy

Minsk

BELARUS

Rybinsk Res.

Vologda

Sukhona R.

Pechora

URAL

Ob

WEST

Lvov

DNIEPER UPLAND

Dnieper R.

Yaroslovl

NORTHERN HILLS

River

River

Ob

SIBERIAN

Kiev

UKRAINE

DNIEPER LOWLAND

Moscow

Ivanovo

Volga

MOUNTAINS

Mt. Konzhakovskiy
5,147 ft.
(1,569 m.)

PLAIN

MOLDOVA

Tula

Ryazan'

Nizhniy Novgorod

Kamsk Res.

Chisinau

Kharkov

Voronezh

R.

Kazan

Izhevsk

Perm

R.

Yekaterinburg

Vakh

R.

Odessa

Nikolayev

Krivoy Rog

Dnepropetrovsk

Don

River

Kuybyshev Res.

Ul'yanovsk

Kama

Ufa

Vologda

Penza

Tol'yatti

Samara

Chelyabinsk

Tobol

Irtysh

River

Tomsk

Zaporozh'ye

Donetsk

Lugansk

VOLGA UPLAND

Saratov

R.

Orenburg

R.

Omsk

L. Chany

Kemerovo

Mariupol

Rostov

Volgograd Reservoir

KYRGYZ

TURGAY

Ishim

Novosibirsk

Novosibirsk Res.

SEA OF AZOV

BLACK SEA

Krasnodar

Tsimlyansk Res.

Volga

Volgograd

CASPIAN DEPRESSION

Astrakhan

Ural R.

STEPPE

PLATEAU

KAZAK

Novokuznetsk

Barnaul

Mt. Belukha
14,783 ft.
(4,506 m.)

CAUCASUS

Mt. Elbrus
18,510 ft.
(5,642 m.)

KAZAKHSTAN

UPLAND

Karaganda

Semipalatinsk

GEORGIA

MTNS.

Tbilisi

ARMENIA

Yerevan

AZERBAIJAN

CASPIAN

ARAL SEA

BETPAK-DALA

L. Zaysan

Lake Balkhash

AZERBAIJAN

Baku

SEA

USTYURT PLATEAU

Syr

Kzyl-Orda

DESERT

Ili R.

L. Alakol

KARA BOGAZ GOL GULF

PLAINS OF TURAN

Darya

ASIA

TURKMENISTAN

KARAKUM

UZBEKISTAN

Amu

Almaty

Bishkek

KYRGYZSTAN

L. Issyk-Kul

Ashkhabad

DESERT

Samarkand

Tashkent

Darya

ALAY MOUNTAINS

Dushanbe

TAJIKISTAN

Communism Pk.
24,590 ft.
(7,495 m.)

ARCTIC
OCEAN

+ North Pole

CHUKCHI
SEA

Bering Strait

BERING   SEA

WRANGEL
ISLAND

Long Strait

Cape
Navarin

CHUKOTSK
PEN.

EAST SIBERIAN
SEA

Cape Arkticheski

SEVERNAYA
ZEMLYA

NEW SIBERIAN
ISLANDS

Sannikov Strait

Laptev Strait

Cherskiy

Anadyr R.

KORYAK
MTNS.

KOLYMA
PLAIN

KOLYMA RANGE

KARAGIN
ISLAND

Vil'kitskiy Strait

LAPTEV SEA

Evensk

SHELIKHOV
GULF

SREDINNY RA.

KOMANDORSKIY
ISLANDS

TAYMYR
PEN.

BYRRANGA
MTNS.

L. Taymyr

Kolyma

River

KAMCHATKA

Mt. Klyuchevsk
15,584 ft.
(4,750 m.)

CHERSKIY RANGE

Indigirka

VERKHOYANSK

Verkhoyansk

River

Magadan

PENINSULA

Petropavlovsk-
Kamchatskiy

Noril'sk

Katuy R.

Olenёk

SIBERIA

RANGE

SEA OF OKHOTSK

Cape Lopatka

160°

CENTRAL SIBERIAN

Lena

River

Markha

Vilyuy

R.

Vilyuy

River

Yakutsk

KURIL

Tura

Tunguska

River

Vilyuysk
Reservoir

LENA PLATEAU

Aldan

Cape Yelizavety

ISLANDS

Lowet

PLATEAU

RUSSIA

ALDAN
MTNS.

River

STANOVOY RANGE

DZHUGDZHUR RA.

Uda R.

SAKHALIN

Tatar

Strait

ISLAND

Terpeniya Point

Yenisey

River

Angara

R.

Lena

Vitim

STANOVOY
UPLAND

Komsomol'sk

River

La Pérouse
Strait

Bratsk

Lake
Baikal

YABLONOVY RANGE

R.

Amur

Khabarovsk

SIKHOTE-ALIN RA.

Krasnoyarsk

Bratsk
Reservoir

Chita

Krasnoyarsk
Reservoir

Irkutsk

Ulan-Ude

Shilka

R.

Ussuri River

L. Khanka

SAYAN
MOUNTAINS

ALTAI MTNS.

ASIA

Vladivostok

SEA OF JAPAN

RUSSIA AND
THE EURASIAN REPUBLICS

⊛ National capital

● Major city

○ Other city

── International boundary

0   250   500 Miles

0   250   500 Kilometers

Projection: Two-Point Equidistant

North Pole 80° 70° 60° 170° 180° 170° 50° 40° 140° 30° 90° 100° 110° 120° 130° 160° 150°

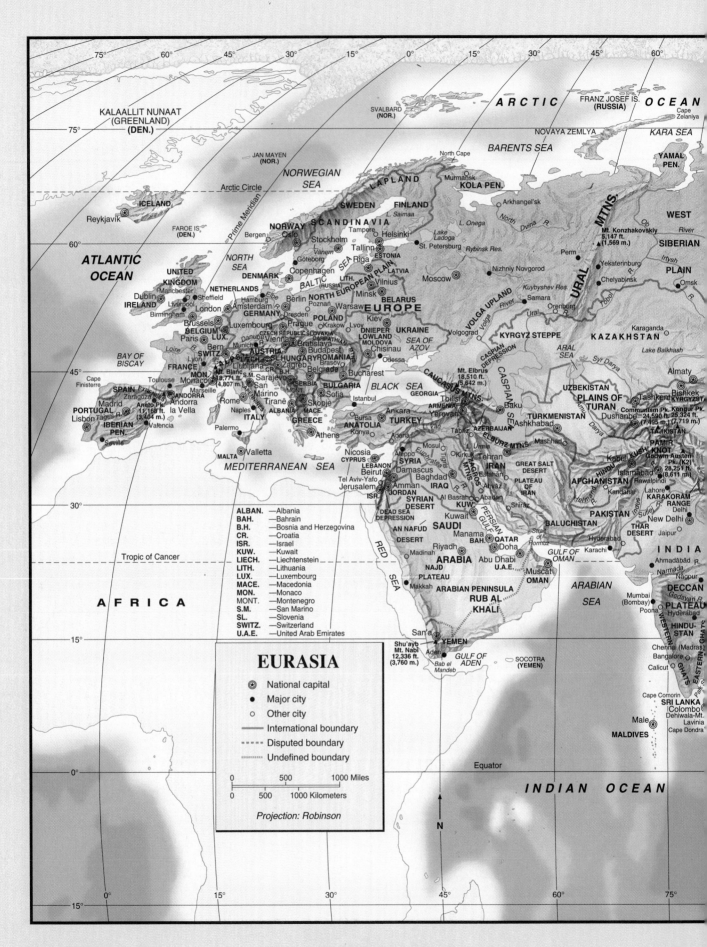

EURASIA

- ⊛ National capital
- ● Major city
- ○ Other city
- International boundary
- Disputed boundary
- Undefined boundary

0   500   1000 Miles

0   500   1000 Kilometers

Projection: Robinson

ALBAN. —Albania
BAH. —Bahrain
B.H. —Bosnia and Herzegovina
CR. —Croatia
ISR. —Israel
KUW. —Kuwait
LIECH. —Liechtenstein
LITH. —Lithuania
LUX. —Luxembourg
MACE. —Macedonia
MON. —Monaco
MONT. —Montenegro
S.M. —San Marino
SL. —Slovenia
SWITZ. —Switzerland
U.A.E. —United Arab Emirates

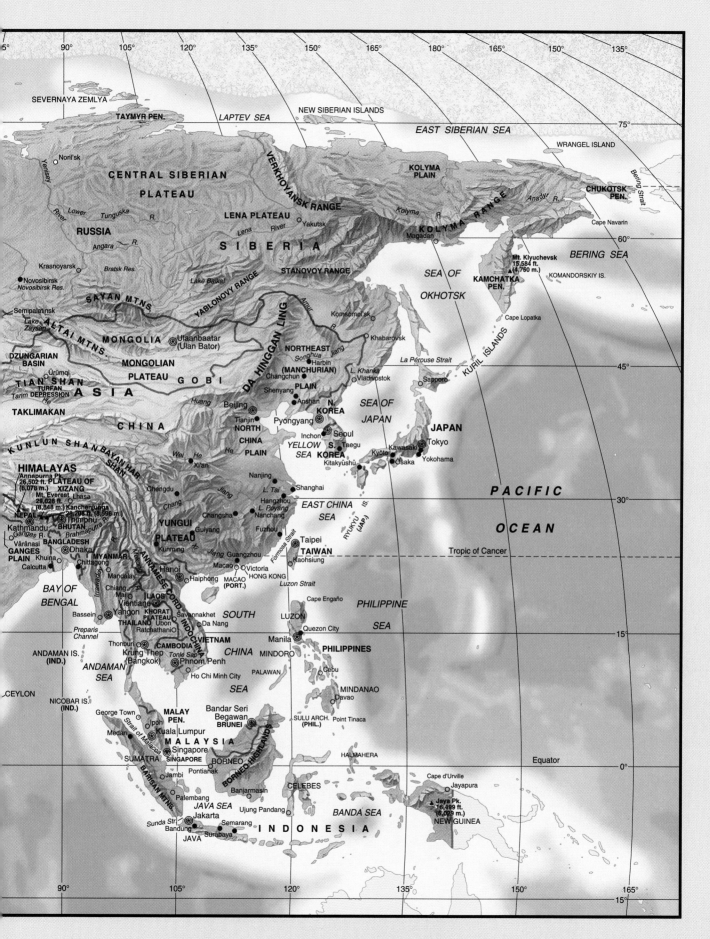

5° 90° 105° 120° 135° 150° 165° 180° 165° 150° 135°

SEVERNAYA ZEMLYA

TAYMYR PEN. *LAPTEV SEA* NEW SIBERIAN ISLANDS

EAST SIBERIAN SEA 75°

CENTRAL SIBERIAN **KOLYMA** WRANGEL ISLAND

Noril'sk **PLATEAU** **PLAIN**

VERKHOYANSK RANGE Kolyma R **KOLYMA RANGE** **CHUKOTSK** *Bering Strait*

LENA PLATEAU Yakutsk **PEN.**

Lower *Tunguska* R. Magadan Cape Navarin

RUSSIA Lena River **KOLYMA RANGE** 60°

River *Angara* R. **S I B E R I A** Anadyr R.

Krasnoyarsk *Bratsk Res.* **STANOVOY RANGE** *SEA OF* Mt. Klyuchevsk **BERING SEA**

Novosibirsk Lake Baikal *OKHOTSK* 15,584 ft. KOMANDORSKIY IS.

Novosibirsk Res. **KAMCHATKA** (4,750 m.)

SAYAN MTNS. **YABLONOVY RANGE** Komsomol'sk **PEN.**

Semipalatinsk Amur Cape Lopatka

Lake **ALTAI MTNS.** Khabarovsk *La Pérouse Strait* **KURIL ISLANDS**

Zaysan **MONGOLIA** **DA HINGGAN LING** *L. Khanka*

DZUNGARIAN Ürümqi Ulaanbaatar **NORTHEAST** Songhua Harbin Vladivostok Sapporo

BASIN (Ulan Bator) **(MANCHURIAN)** Changchun *Jiang*

TIAN SHAN **MONGOLIAN** **PLAIN** Shenyang Anshan

TURFAN **PLATEAU** **GOBI** Beijing **N.** *SEA OF* **JAPAN**

Tarim DEPRESSION **A S I A** Huang **KOREA** *JAPAN* Kyōto Kawasaki Tokyo

TAKLIMAKAN **C H I N A** Tianjin Pyongyang Osaka Yokohama

NORTH Inchon Seoul Kitakyūshū

KUNLUN SHAN **BAYAN HAR** **CHINA** Wei He Xi'an *YELLOW* **S.** Taegu

HIMALAYAS **SHAN** **PLAIN** *SEA* **KOREA**

Annapurna Pk. Nanjing

26,502 ft. **PLATEAU OF** Chengdu *L. Tai* Shanghai

(8,078 m.) **XIZANG** *Jiang* Hangzhou *EAST CHINA* **PACIFIC**

Mt. Everest Lhasa Chang *L. Poyang* Nanchang

29,028 ft. Kanchenjunga Changsha *SEA* **RYUKYU IS.** 30°

NEPAL Thimphu Guiyang Fuzhou **(JAP.)** **O C E A N**

Kathmandu **BHUTAN** **YUNGUI** Kunming Taipei

Ganges R. Brahmaputra **PLATEAU** *Jiang* Guangzhou **TAIWAN**

Vārānasi **BANGLADESH** Macao Kaohsiung *Formosa Strait*

GANGES Khulna Dhaka Hanoi Macao Victoria Tropic of Cancer

PLAIN Calcutta Chittagong **MYANMAR** Haiphong **MACAO** **HONG KONG**

Mandalay **(PORT.)** *Luzon Strait*

Chiang **ANNAMESE CORD.** **INDOCHINA** Cape Engaño *PHILIPPINE*

BAY OF Mai Mekong **SOUTH** **LUZON** *SEA*

BENGAL **LAOS** R. Savannakhet Da Nang

Bassein Vientiane Yangon **KHORAT** **CHINA** Quezon City 15°

Preparis **THAILAND** **PLATEAU** Ubon **VIETNAM** Manila

Channel Ratchathani **CAMBODIA** Ho Chi Minh City **PHILIPPINES**

ANDAMAN IS. Thonburi **Krung Thep** *Tonle Sap* **CHINA** **MINDORO**

(IND.) **(Bangkok)** Phnom Penh *SEA* **PALAWAN** Cebu

ANDAMAN **MINDANAO**

SEA Davao

CEYLON **MALAY** Bandar Seri

NICOBAR IS. George Town **PEN.** Begawan **SULU ARCH.** Point Tinaca

(IND.) Ipoh **BRUNEI** **(PHIL.)**

Medan Kuala Lumpur **BORNEO HIGHLANDS** *HALMAHERA*

Strait of Malacca **M A L A Y S I A**

SUMATRA Singapore Cape d'Urville

Singapore **BORNEO** Jayapura

Pontianak Equator 0°

BARISAN MTNS. Jambi Banjarmasin **CELEBES**

Palembang Jaya Pk.

JAVA SEA Ujung Pandang *BANDA SEA* 16,499 ft.

Sunda Str. Jakarta Semarang **I N D O N E S I A** (5,029 m.)

Bandung Surabaya **NEW GUINEA**

JAVA

15°

90° 105° 120° 135° 150° 165°

15°

Reference Atlas   A17

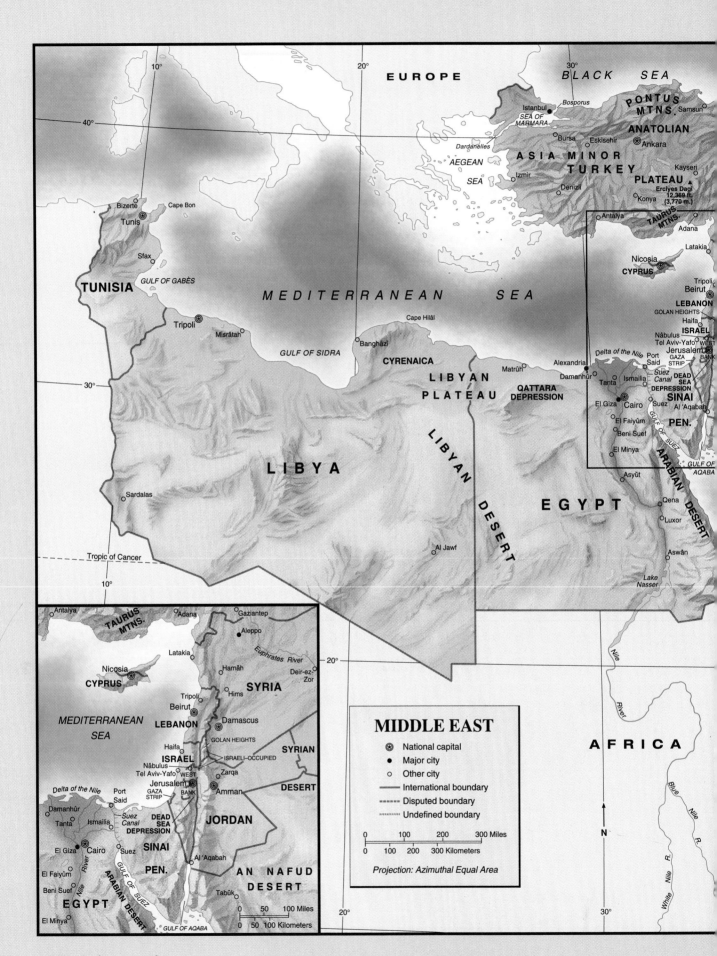

EUROPE

BLACK SEA

PONTUS MTNS. · Samsun
· Bosporus
Istanbul · SEA OF MARMARA
ANATOLIAN
· Bursa · Eskisehir · Ankara
Dardanelles
ASIA MINOR
AEGEAN SEA
TURKEY
· Izmir
· Kayseri
PLATEAU
· Denizli
Konya · Erciyes Dagi 12,369 ft. (3,770 m.)

TAURUS MTNS.
· Antalya
· Adana
· Latakia
Nicosia ·
CYPRUS
Tripoli · Beirut ·
LEBANON
GOLAN HEIGHTS
Haifa ·
Nâbulus · ISRAEL
Tel Aviv-Yafo · WEST
Jerusalem · BANK
GAZA STRIP
· Bizerte · Cape Bon
Tunis ·

· Sfax
TUNISIA
GULF OF GABÈS
Tripoli ·
· Misrâtah

MEDITERRANEAN SEA

· Cape Hilâl
Banghâzi ·
CYRENAICA
· Matrûh
Alexandria ·
Delta of the Nile
Port Said
Damanhûr · Tanta · Ismailia
Suez Canal
DEAD SEA DEPRESSION
LIBYAN PLATEAU
QATTARA DEPRESSION
El Giza · Cairo ·
· Suez
SINAI PEN.
· El Faiyûm
· Beni Suef
Al 'Aqabah
GULF OF AQABA
30°

LIBYA
EGYPT
· El Minya

· Sardalas
LIBYAN DESERT
· Asyût
ARABIAN DESERT
· Qena
· Luxor
Tropic of Cancer
10°
· Al Jawf
· Aswân
Lake Nasser

Nile River

AFRICA

Blue Nile R.
White Nile R.
N
20°
30°

Inset map

· Antalya
TAURUS MTNS.
· Adana
· Gaziantep
Aleppo ·
Euphrates River
· Latakia
· Hamâh
Deir-ez-Zor
Nicosia ·
CYPRUS
Tripoli ·
· Hims
SYRIA
Beirut ·
· Damascus
MEDITERRANEAN SEA
LEBANON
GOLAN HEIGHTS
Haifa ·
ISRAEL
ISRAELI-OCCUPIED
SYRIAN
Nâbulus ·
Tel Aviv-Yafo · WEST
· Zarqa
Jerusalem · BANK
GAZA STRIP
· Amman
DESERT
Delta of the Nile
Port Said
DEAD SEA DEPRESSION
JORDAN
Damanhûr ·
Tanta · Ismailia
Suez Canal
El Giza · Cairo ·
· Suez
SINAI
Al 'Aqabah
· El Faiyûm
PEN.
AN NAFUD
· Beni Suef
ARABIAN DESERT
GULF OF SUEZ
· Tabûk
DESERT
EGYPT
· El Minya
GULF OF AQABA

0   50   100 Miles
0   50 100 Kilometers

Legend

MIDDLE EAST

⊛ National capital
● Major city
○ Other city
— International boundary
----- Disputed boundary
······· Undefined boundary

0   100   200   300 Miles
0 100 200 300 Kilometers

Projection: Azimuthal Equal Area

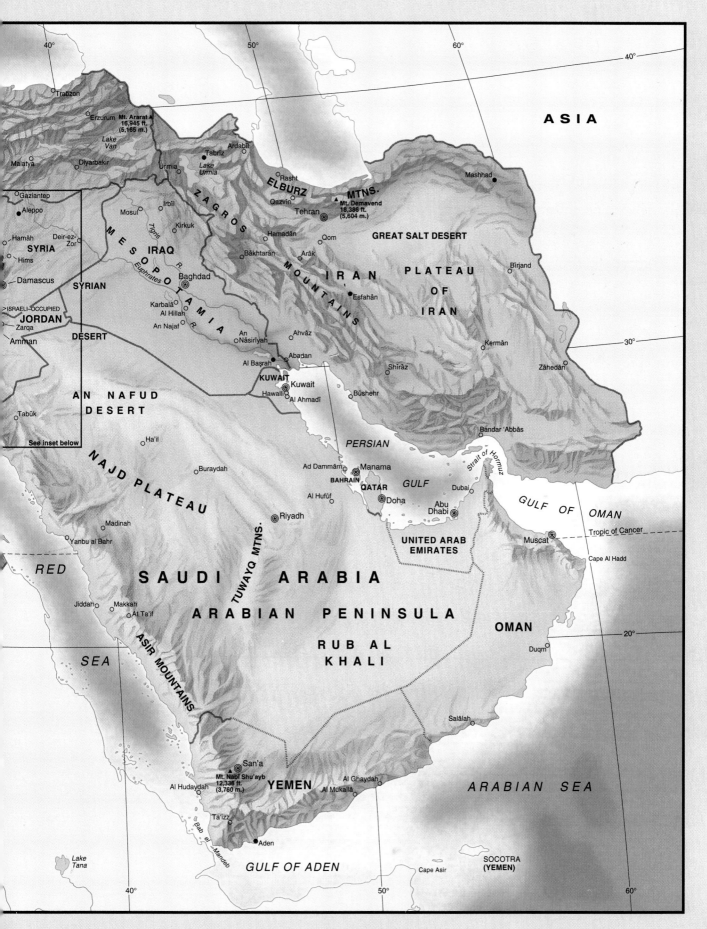

ASIA

Trabzon

Erzurum Mt. Ararat ▲
16,945 ft.
(5,165 m.)

Malatya   Lake
Van   Ardabīl
Diyarbakir   Urmia   Tabrīz   Lake   Rasht   Mashhad
                                Urmia   ELBURZ   MTNS.
Gaziantep   Qazvin   ▲ Mt. Demavend
Aleppo   Mosul   Irbīl   Kirkuk   Tehran   18,386 ft.
                                                              (5,604 m.)
Hamāh   Hamadān   GREAT SALT DESERT
Deir-ez-   IRAQ   Qom
SYRIA   Zor   Bīrjand
Hims   Baghdad   Bākhtarān   Arāk   PLATEAU
                    Karbalā   OF
Damascus   SYRIAN   Al Hillah   Esfahān   IRAN
ISRAELI-OCCUPIED   An Najaf   Kermān
JORDAN   An
Zarqa   DESERT   Nāsirīyah   Ahvāz   Shīrāz   Zāhedān
Amman   Al Baṣrah   Abadan   Bandar 'Abbās

           AN NAFUD   KUWAIT   Kuwait
           DESERT   Hawalli   Al Ahmadī   Būshehr
Tabūk   PERSIAN
                                                                      Strait of Hormuz
           Ha'il   GULF
See inset below   Ad Dammām   Manama
           NAJD   Buraydah   BAHRAIN   Dubai   GULF OF OMAN
                                    QATAR   Doha
           PLATEAU   Al Hufūf   Abu   Tropic of Cancer
Madinah   Dhabi
           Riyadh   UNITED ARAB   Muscat
Yanbu al Bahr   EMIRATES   Cape Al Hadd

RED   SAUDI   ARABIA
                                              OMAN
           ARABIAN   PENINSULA
Jiddah   Makkah   Duqm
At Ta'if   RUB AL
SEA   KHALI

                                    Salālah
                 San'a
           Mt. Nabi Shu'ayb
           12,336 ft.   Al Ghaydah   ARABIAN   SEA
Al Hudaydah   (3,760 m.)   YEMEN   Al Mukallā

           Ta'izz
Lake   Aden   SOCOTRA
Tana   GULF OF ADEN   Cape Asir   (YEMEN)

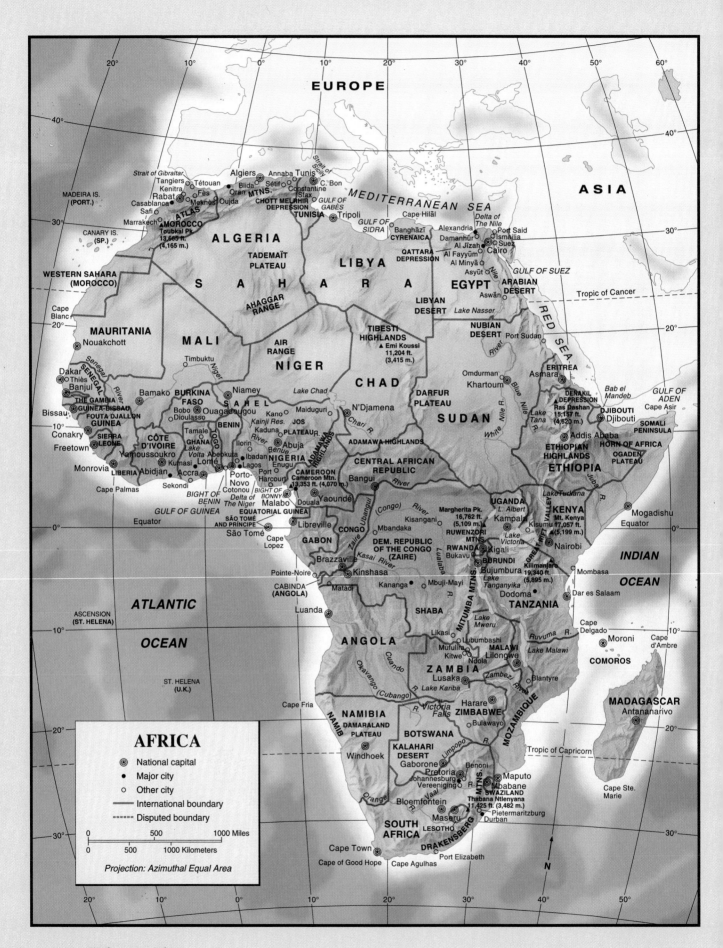

AFRICA

- ⊛ National capital
- ● Major city
- ○ Other city
- —— International boundary
- ----- Disputed boundary

0   500   1000 Miles

0   500   1000 Kilometers

Projection: Azimuthal Equal Area

EUROPE

ASIA

MEDITERRANEAN SEA

Strait of Gibraltar
Tangiers Tétouan
Kenitra Blida Sétif
Rabat Fès Oujda Constantine
Casablanca Meknès Oran MTNS.
Safi CHOTT MELRHIR Sfax
Marrakech DEPRESSION TUNISIA
MOROCCO GULF OF GABÈS Tripoli
Toubkal Pk. ALGERIA GULF OF
13,665 ft. SIDRA
(4,165 m.)

Algiers Annaba Tunis
C. Bon

Cape Hilâl

Delta of
The Nile
Banghāzī Alexandria Port Said
CYRENAICA Damanhūr Ismailia
Al Jīzah Suez
QATTARA Al Fayyūm Cairo
DEPRESSION Al Minyā

LIBYA EGYPT ARABIAN
DESERT

GULF OF SUEZ

Tropic of Cancer

MADEIRA IS.
(PORT.)

CANARY IS.
(SP.)

WESTERN SAHARA
(MOROCCO)

Cape
Blanc

MAURITANIA
Nouakchott

TADEMAÏT
PLATEAU

AHAGGAR
RANGE

S A H A R A

MALI

AIR
RANGE

NIGER

LIBYAN
DESERT Lake Nasser

Aswān

TIBESTI
HIGHLANDS
▲ Emi Koussi
11,204 ft.
(3,415 m.)

NUBIAN
DESERT Port Sudan

RED SEA

Dakar SENEGAL
Thiès
Banjul
THE GAMBIA Bamako BURKINA
GUINEA-BISSAU FASO
Bissau FOUTA DJALLON Bobo Ouagadougou
GUINEA Dioulasso
Conakry BENIN
SIERRA Tamale
Freetown LEONE GHANA
Yamoussoukro CÔTE Lake
D'IVOIRE Kumasi Volta Abeokuta
Monrovia Abidjan Lomé
LIBERIA Accra
Cape Palmas Sekondi

Timbuktu

Niger

SAHEL

Kano
Maiduguri
Niamey Kaduna
Kainji Res. JOS
Ilorin PLATEAU
Ibadan Enugu
NIGERIA Benue
Port CAMEROON
Harcourt Cameroon Mtn.
13,353 ft. (4,070 m.)

Lake Chad

N'Djamena
Chari R.

CHAD

DARFUR
PLATEAU

SUDAN

Omdurman
Khartoum

White Nile Blue Nile

ERITREA
Asmara

DENAKIL
DEPRESSION
Ras Dashan
15,157 ft.
(4,620 m.)

Lake
Tana

Bab el
Mandeb GULF OF
ADEN
Cape Asir

DJIBOUTI
Djibouti
SOMALI
PENINSULA

Addis Ababa
ETHIOPIAN
HIGHLANDS HORN OF AFRICA
OGADEN
PLATEAU

ETHIOPIA

ADAMAWA HIGHLANDS

CENTRAL AFRICAN
REPUBLIC
Bangui

River

Lake Turkana

ABUJA

Porto-
Novo BIGHT OF
Cotonou BENNY
Malabo Douala
EQUATORIAL GUINEA
SÃO TOMÉ
AND PRÍNCIPE
São Tomé Cape
Lopez

Delta of
The Niger
BIGHT OF
BONNY

Yaoundé
Libreville

GABON

CONGO

Brazzaville

Equator

ATLANTIC

OCEAN

ASCENSION
(ST. HELENA)

ST. HELENA
(U.K.)

Pointe-Noire

CABINDA
(ANGOLA)
Matadi

Kinshasa

(Congo) River

Mbandaka

DEM. REPUBLIC
OF THE CONGO
(ZAIRE)

Kasai River

Kisangani

Margherita Pk.
16,762 ft.
(5,109 m.)
RUWENZORI
MTNS.

Kananga Mbuji-Mayi

SHABA

Lualaba

L. Albert
UGANDA Kampala
Lake
Victoria
RWANDA Kisumu
Bukavu Kigali
BURUNDI
Bujumbura Lake
Tanganyika Dodoma

Mt. Kenya
17,057 ft.
(5,199 m.)

KENYA
Nairobi

Kilimanjaro
19,340 ft.
(5,895 m.)

Mombasa

Dar es Salaam

TANZANIA

Equator

INDIAN

OCEAN

Luanda

ANGOLA

Likasi
Mufulira
Lubumbashi
Kitwe Ndola

ZAMBIA
Lusaka

Lake
Mweru

Lake Malawi
MALAWI
Lilongwe

Ruvuma R. Cape
Delgado
Moroni Cape
d'Ambre

COMOROS

Cape Fria

NAMIBIA

NAMIB

DAMARALAND
PLATEAU

Okavango
(Cubango)
Cuando

Zambezi River
Lake Kariba
Victoria Harare
Falls ZIMBABWE

Bulawayo

MOZAMBIQUE

Blantyre

MADAGASCAR
Antananarivo

KALAHARI
DESERT

BOTSWANA
Gaborone
Limpopo

Windhoek

Benoni
Pretoria
Johannesburg
Vereeniging MTNS.
Orange Vaal R.
Bloemfontein

SOUTH
AFRICA DRAKENSBERG

Cape Town Cape of Good Hope Cape Agulhas

Maseru
LESOTHO

Thabana Ntlenyana
11,425 ft. (3,482 m.)

Maputo
Mbabane
SWAZILAND

Pietermaritzburg
Durban

Port Elizabeth

Tropic of Capricorn

Cape Ste.
Marie

N

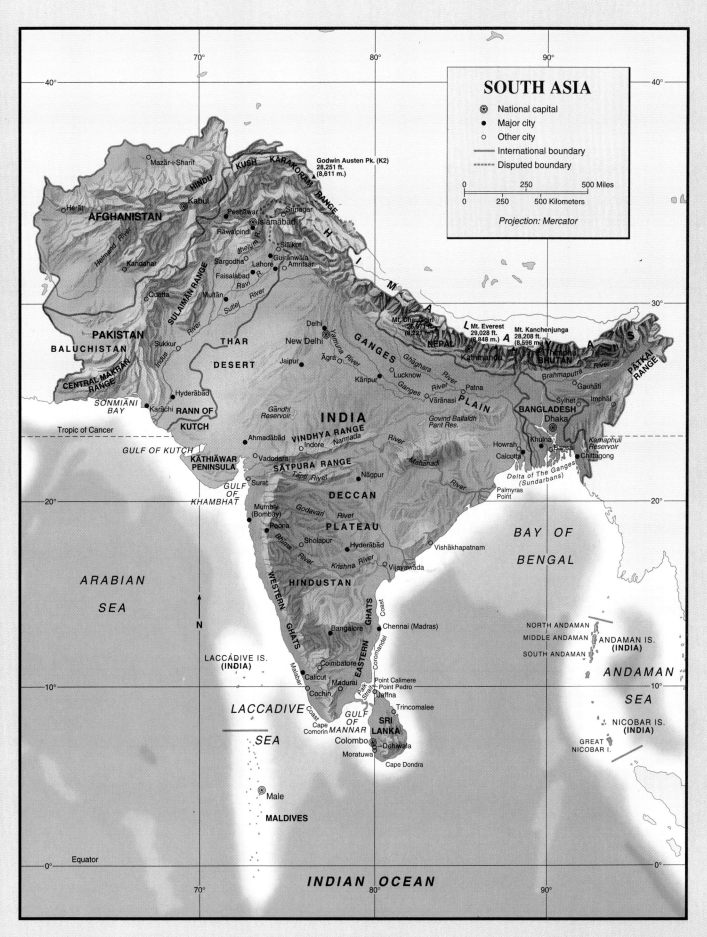

SOUTH ASIA

⊛ National capital
● Major city
○ Other city
— International boundary
---- Disputed boundary

| 0 | | 250 | | 500 Miles |
| 0 | 250 | | 500 Kilometers | |

Projection: Mercator

40° — 40°

30° — 30°

20° — 20°

10° — 10°

0° — 0°

70° — 80° — 90°

Mazār-i-Sharīf

KUSH

HINDU

KARAKORAM RANGE

Godwin Austen Pk. (K2)
28,251 ft.
(8,611 m.)

Herāt

Kabul

AFGHANISTAN

Peshāwar
Srīnagar

Islāmābād

Rāwalpindi

Jhelum
Siālkot

Gujrānwāla
Sargodha
Lahore
Amritsar

Faisalabad
Ravi R.

Helmand River

Kandahar

Quetta

Multān

SULAIMAN RANGE

Sutlej River

H

I

M

A

L

A

Y

A

S

PAKISTAN

BALUCHISTAN

Indus River

Sukkur

THAR

DESERT

Delhi

Mt. Dhaulagiri
26,971 m.
(8,221 m.)

Mt. Everest
29,028 ft.
(8,848 m.)

Mt. Kanchenjunga
28,208 m.
(8,598 m.)

New Delhi

NEPAL

Kathmandu

BHUTAN

Thimphu

PATKAI RANGE

River

CENTRAL MAKRAN RANGE

Jaipur

Āgra

Yamuna River

GANGES

Ghāghara River

Lucknow

Kānpur

Ganges River

Patna

Vārānasi

Brahmaputra

Gauhāti

Sylhet

Imphāl

SONMIANI BAY

Karāchi

Hyderābād

RANN OF KUTCH

Gāndhi Reservoir

INDIA

VINDHYA RANGE

Indore

Narmada

Govind Ballaldh Pant Res.

River

BANGLADESH

Dhaka

Tropic of Cancer

GULF OF KUTCH

KĀTHIĀWAR PENINSULA

Ahmadābād

Vadodara

SĀTPURA RANGE

Tāpti River

Mahanadi

Howrah

Calcutta

Khulna

Barisāl

Karnaphuli Reservoir

Chittagong

GULF OF KHAMBHAT

Surat

Nāgpur

DECCAN

River

Delta of The Ganges
(Sundarbans)

Palmyras Point

Mumbai
(Bombay)

Godavari

PLATEAU

River

Poona

Bhīma

Sholapur

Hyderābād

River

Krishna River

Vishākhapatnam

Vijayawāda

BAY OF

BENGAL

ARABIAN

SEA

WESTERN

GHATS

HINDUSTAN

Bangalore

EASTERN GHATS

Coast

Chennai (Madras)

Coromandel Coast

NORTH ANDAMAN

MIDDLE ANDAMAN

SOUTH ANDAMAN

ANDAMAN IS.
(INDIA)

ANDAMAN

LACCADIVE IS.
(INDIA)

Coimbatore

Calicut

Madurai

Cochin

Malabar Coast

Palk Strait

Point Calimere
Point Pedro
Jaffna

Trincomalee

SEA

NICOBAR IS.
(INDIA)

Cape Comorin

GULF OF MANNAR

SRI LANKA

Colombo
Dehiwala
Moratuwa

Cape Dondra

GREAT NICOBAR I.

LACCADIVE

SEA

N

Male

MALDIVES

Equator

INDIAN OCEAN

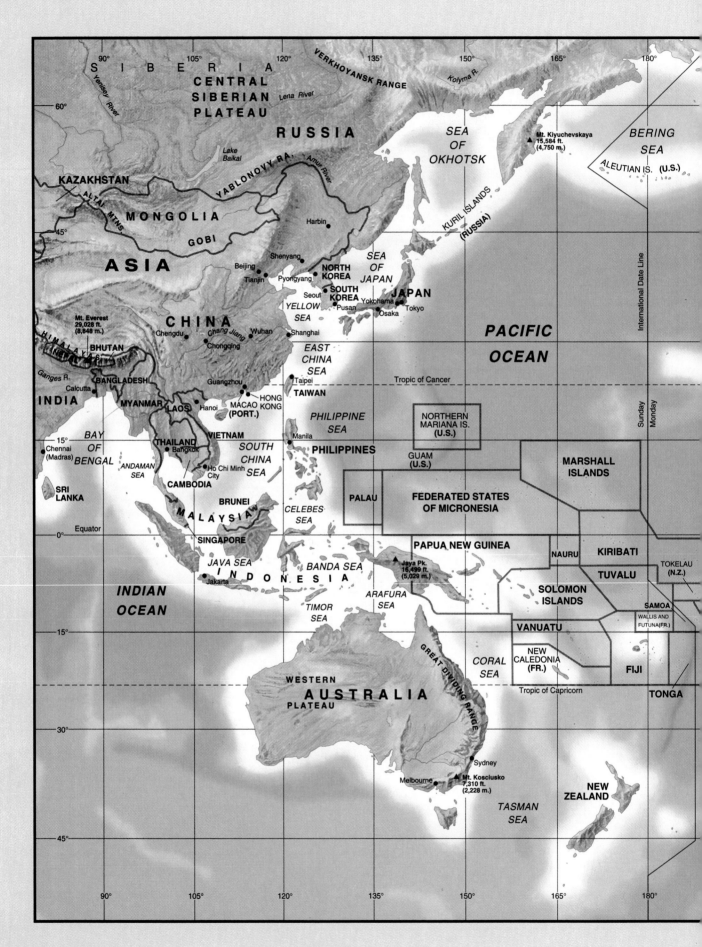

SIBERIA

CENTRAL
SIBERIAN
PLATEAU

Yenisey River

VERKHOYANSK RANGE

Lena River

Kolyma R.

RUSSIA

SEA
OF
OKHOTSK

▲ Mt. Kiyuchevskaya
15,584 ft.
(4,750 m.)

BERING
SEA

ALEUTIAN IS. (U.S.)

KAZAKHSTAN

ALTAI MTNS

MONGOLIA

GOBI

Lake
Baikal

YABLONOVY RA.

Amur River

Harbin

KURIL ISLANDS
(RUSSIA)

ASIA

Shenyang

Beijing

Tianjin

Pyongyang

NORTH
KOREA

SEA
OF
JAPAN

Seoul

SOUTH
KOREA

Pusan

Yokohama

JAPAN

Tokyo
Osaka

PACIFIC
OCEAN

International Date Line

Mt. Everest
29,028 ft.
(8,848 m.)

HIMALAYAS

BHUTAN

NEPAL

CHINA

Chengdu

Chang Jiang

Chongqing

Wuhan

Shanghai

YELLOW
SEA

EAST
CHINA
SEA

Tropic of Cancer

Ganges R.

BANGLADESH

Calcutta

INDIA

MYANMAR

Guangzhou

LAOS

Hanoi

MACAO
(PORT.)

HONG
KONG

Taipei

TAIWAN

PHILIPPINE
SEA

NORTHERN
MARIANA IS.
(U.S.)

Sunday

Monday

BAY

OF

BENGAL

Chennai
(Madras)

VIETNAM

THAILAND

Bangkok

Ho Chi Minh
City

SOUTH
CHINA
SEA

Manila

PHILIPPINES

GUAM
(U.S.)

MARSHALL
ISLANDS

ANDAMAN
SEA

CAMBODIA

PALAU

FEDERATED STATES
OF MICRONESIA

SRI
LANKA

BRUNEI

MALAYSIA

CELEBES
SEA

Equator

SINGAPORE

PAPUA NEW GUINEA

▲ Jaya Pk.
16,499 ft.
(5,029 m.)

NAURU

KIRIBATI

TOKELAU
(N.Z.)

INDIAN
OCEAN

JAVA SEA

INDONESIA

Jakarta

BANDA SEA

TUVALU

SOLOMON
ISLANDS

SAMOA

ARAFURA
SEA

TIMOR
SEA

WALLIS AND
FUTUNA(FR.)

VANUATU

WESTERN

AUSTRALIA

PLATEAU

GREAT DIVIDING RANGE

CORAL
SEA

NEW
CALEDONIA
(FR.)

FIJI

Tropic of Capricorn

TONGA

Sydney

▲ Mt. Kosciusko
7,310 ft.
(2,228 m.)

Melbourne

NEW
ZEALAND

TASMAN
SEA

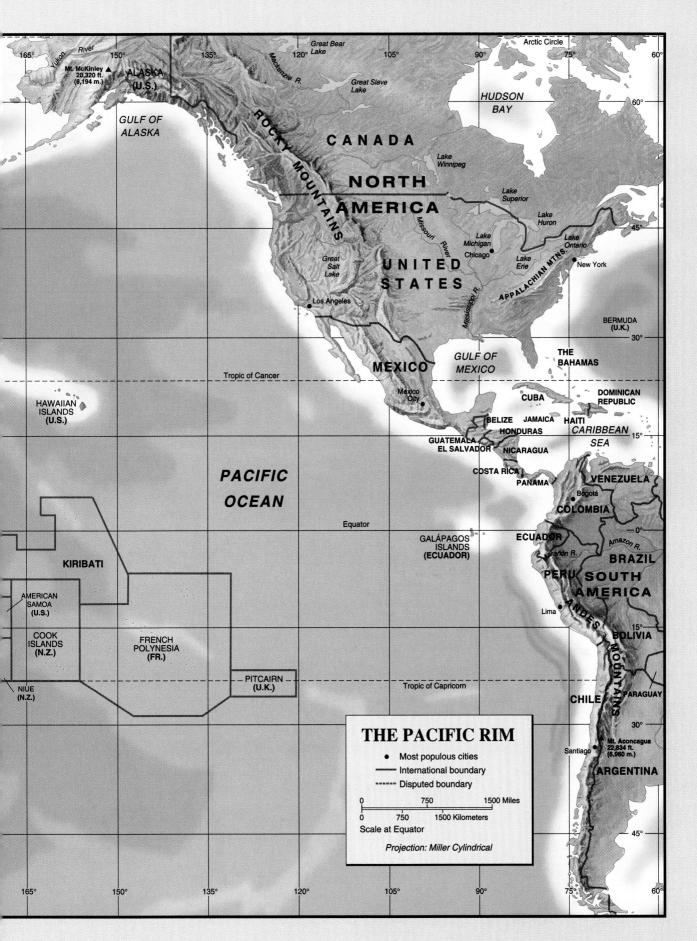

THE PACIFIC RIM

- Most populous cities
— International boundary
----- Disputed boundary

| 0 | 750 | 1500 Miles |
| 0 | 750 | 1500 Kilometers |

Scale at Equator

Projection: Miller Cylindrical

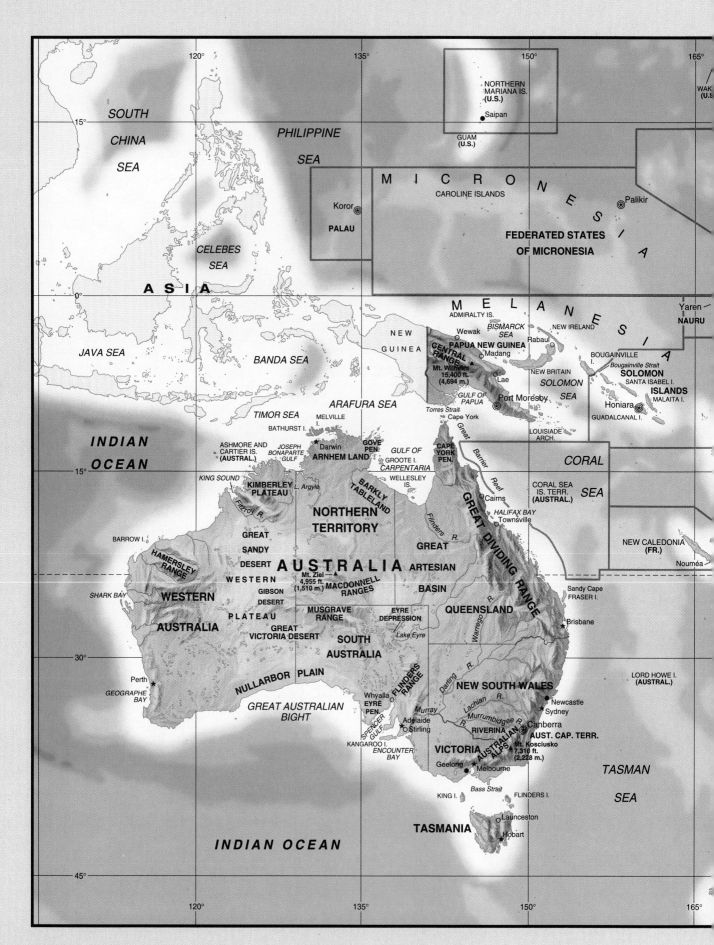

SOUTH CHINA SEA

PHILIPPINE SEA

NORTHERN MARIANA IS. (U.S.)
• Saipan

GUAM (U.S.)

WAKE (U.S.)

ASIA

CELEBES SEA

MICRONESIA

CAROLINE ISLANDS

Koror ⊚
PALAU

Palikir ⊚

FEDERATED STATES OF MICRONESIA

Yaren
NAURU

MELANESIA

JAVA SEA

BANDA SEA

NEW GUINEA

ADMIRALTY IS.

Wewak
BISMARCK SEA

NEW IRELAND

INDIAN OCEAN

TIMOR SEA

ARAFURA SEA

PAPUA NEW GUINEA
CENTRAL RANGE
Mt. Wilhelm 15,400 ft. (4,694 m.)
Madang •

Rabaul •

BOUGAINVILLE I.
Bougainville Strait

SOLOMON
SANTA ISABEL I.

Lae •
GULF OF PAPUA
Port Moresby
SOLOMON SEA
Honiara ⊚
GUADALCANAL I.
MALAITA I.
ISLANDS

MELVILLE I.

BATHURST I.

Torres Strait
Cape York
LOUISIADE ARCH.

CORAL SEA IS. TERR. (AUSTRAL.)

CORAL SEA

ASHMORE AND CARTIER IS. (AUSTRAL.)

JOSEPH BONAPARTE GULF

★ Darwin
GOVE PEN.
ARNHEM LAND

GULF OF CARPENTARIA

GROOTE I.

CAPE YORK PEN.

Great Barrier Reef

KING SOUND

KIMBERLEY PLATEAU

L. Argyle

WELLESLEY IS.

• Cairns

HALIFAX BAY
Townsville

NEW CALEDONIA (FR.)

Nouméa •

Fitzroy R.

BARKLY TABLELAND

BARROW I.

GREAT SANDY DESERT

NORTHERN TERRITORY

GREAT DIVIDING RANGE

GREAT ARTESIAN

Flinders R.

HAMERSLEY RANGE

AUSTRALIA
Mt. Ziel 4,955 ft. (1,510 m.) ▲
MACDONNELL RANGES

WESTERN

GIBSON DESERT

BASIN

Sandy Cape
FRASER I.

SHARK BAY

WESTERN AUSTRALIA

PLATEAU

MUSGRAVE RANGE

EYRE DEPRESSION

QUEENSLAND

Warrego R.

• Brisbane

GREAT VICTORIA DESERT

SOUTH AUSTRALIA

Lake Eyre

LORD HOWE I. (AUSTRAL.)

NULLARBOR PLAIN

Perth ★

GEOGRAPHE BAY

FLINDERS RANGE

Darling R.

NEW SOUTH WALES

• Newcastle

Lachlan R.

GREAT AUSTRALIAN BIGHT

Whyalla •
EYRE PEN.

SPENCER GULF

Murray R.

Murrumbidgee R.
RIVERINA

Sydney

Canberra
AUST. CAP. TERR.

KANGAROO I.

Adelaide •
• Stirling

ENCOUNTER BAY

R.

VICTORIA
AUSTRALIAN ALPS
Mt. Kosciusko 7,310 ft. (2,228 m.)

TASMAN SEA

Geelong •
• Melbourne

KING I.

Bass Strait

FLINDERS I.

TASMANIA

Launceston •
Hobart •

INDIAN OCEAN

15°

0°

15°

30°

45°

120°

135°

150°

165°

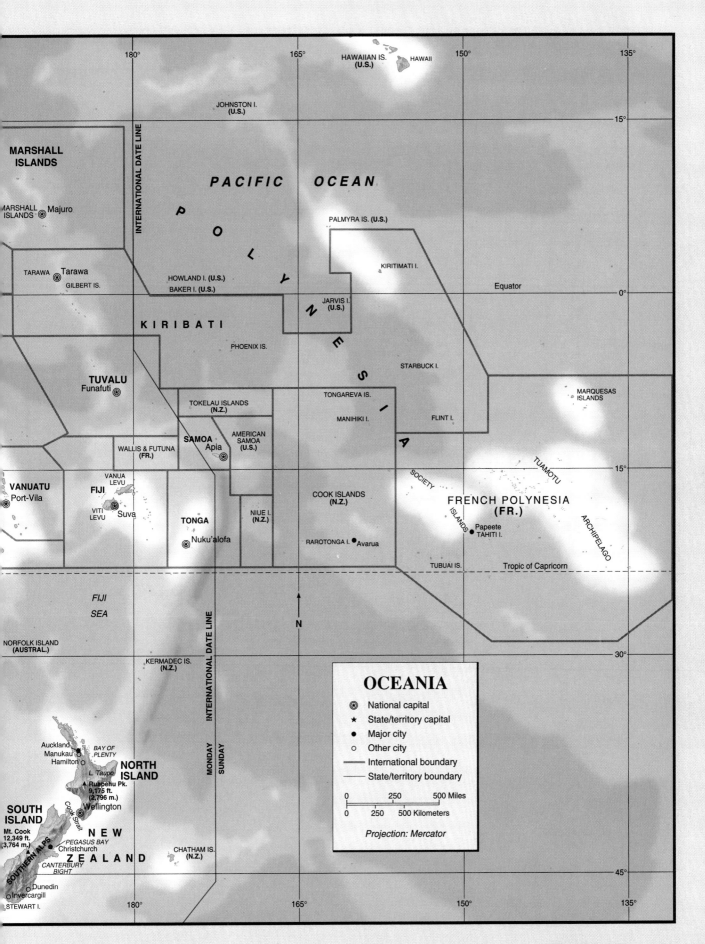

180°   165°   HAWAIIAN IS. 150°   135°
                (U.S.)   HAWAII

JOHNSTON I.   15°
(U.S.)

MARSHALL
ISLANDS   PACIFIC   OCEAN

MARSHALL   Majuro
ISLANDS   PALMYRA IS. (U.S.)

P   KIRITIMATI I.

TARAWA   Tarawa   O   Equator   0°
            GILBERT IS. HOWLAND I. (U.S.) L
                         BAKER I. (U.S.)
                                     JARVIS I.
K I R I B A T I   Y (U.S.)

                         PHOENIX IS.   N

                                              STARBUCK I.
TUVALU   E
Funafuti   TOKELAU ISLANDS   MARQUESAS
                         (N.Z.)   TONGAREVA IS. S   ISLANDS

                         AMERICAN   MANIHIKI I.   I FLINT I.
         SAMOA Apia   SAMOA   A
WALLIS & FUTUNA   (U.S.)
(FR.)   SOCIETY   TUAMOTU   15°
VANUA
VANUATU LEVU   ISLANDS FRENCH POLYNESIA ARCHIPELAGO
Port-Vila FIJI   COOK ISLANDS   (FR.)
                         (N.Z.)   Papeete
VITI   NIUE I.   TAHITI I.
LEVU Suva   TONGA   (N.Z.)
                         RAROTONGA I. Avarua
             Nuku'alofa
                                              TUBUAI IS. Tropic of Capricorn

FIJI

SEA

NORFOLK ISLAND
(AUSTRAL.)   30°
         KERMADEC IS.
         (N.Z.)

                         INTERNATIONAL DATE LINE

                                   N

                         MONDAY SUNDAY

                              OCEANIA

                              ⊛ National capital
Auckland   ★ State/territory capital
Manukau   BAY OF   ● Major city
Hamilton PLENTY   ○ Other city
         L. Taupo NORTH   — International boundary
         Ruapehu Pk. ISLAND ---- State/territory boundary
         9,175 ft.
SOUTH   (2,796 m.)   0   250   500 Miles
ISLAND   Wellington   0   250   500 Kilometers
Mt. Cook N E W
12,349 ft. PEGASUS BAY   Projection: Mercator
(3,764 m.) Christchurch CHATHAM IS.
         CANTERBURY   (N.Z.)
         BIGHT
Z E A L A N D

Dunedin
Invercargill
STEWART I.
         180°   165°   150°   135°

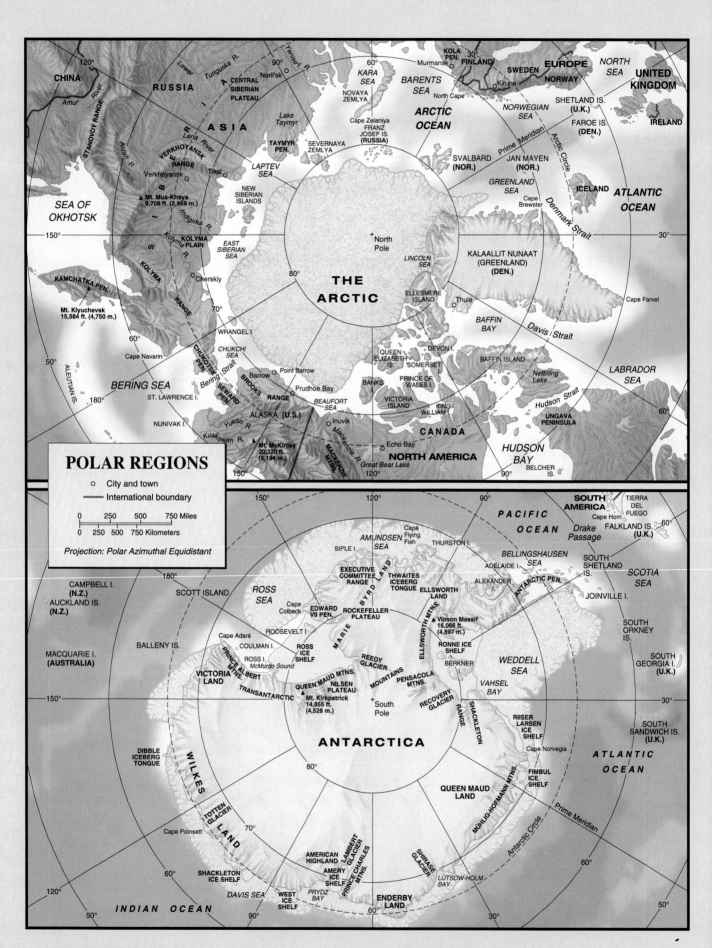

POLAR REGIONS

○ City and town
— International boundary

| 0 | 250 | 500 | 750 Miles |
| 0 | 250 | 500 | 750 Kilometers |

Projection: Polar Azimuthal Equidistant

THE ARCTIC

CHINA
RUSSIA
CENTRAL SIBERIAN PLATEAU
ASIA
STANOVOY RANGE
Amur
Lower
Tunguska R.
Noril'sk
Yenisey R.
KARA SEA
NOVAYA ZEMLYA
FRANZ JOSEF IS. (RUSSIA)
Cape Zelaniya
BARENTS SEA
KOLA PEN.
Murmansk
FINLAND
SWEDEN
NORWAY
EUROPE
Kiruna
NORTH SEA
UNITED KINGDOM
IRELAND
North Cape
ARCTIC OCEAN
NORWEGIAN SEA
SHETLAND IS. (U.K.)
FAROE IS. (DEN.)
Prime Meridian
Arctic Circle
VERKHOYANSK RANGE
Lake Taymyr
TAYMYR PEN.
SEVERNAYA ZEMLYA
SVALBARD (NOR.)
JAN MAYEN (NOR.)
ICELAND
ATLANTIC OCEAN
Aldan R.
Lena River
Verkhoyansk
Tiksi
LAPTEV SEA
NEW SIBERIAN ISLANDS
GREENLAND SEA
Cape Brewster
Denmark Strait
SEA OF OKHOTSK
Mt. Mus-Khaya 9,708 ft. (2,959 m.)
Indigirka R.
EAST SIBERIAN SEA
North Pole
80°
LINCOLN SEA
KALAALLIT NUNAAT (GREENLAND) (DEN.)
Kolyma R.
KOLYMA PLAIN
Cherskiy
70°
THE ARCTIC
ELLESMERE ISLAND
Thule
Cape Farvel
KAMCHATKA PEN.
KOLYMA RANGE
WRANGEL I.
CHUKCHI SEA
60°
BAFFIN BAY
Davis Strait
LABRADOR SEA
Mt. Klyuchevsk 15,584 ft. (4,750 m.)
50°
CHUKOTSK PEN.
Cape Navarin
Bering Strait
SEWARD PEN.
Barrow
Point Barrow
BEAUFORT SEA
Prudhoe Bay
BANKS
QUEEN ELIZABETH IS.
DEVON I.
SOMERSET I.
PRINCE OF WALES I.
BAFFIN ISLAND
Nettilling Lake
BERING SEA
ST. LAWRENCE I.
BROOKS RANGE
ALASKA (U.S.)
Yukon R.
VICTORIA ISLAND
KING WILLIAM I.
Hudson Strait
UNGAVA PENINSULA
ALEUTIAN IS.
NUNIVAK I.
Kuskokwim R.
Mt. McKinley 20,320 ft. (6,194 m.)
Inuvik
Mackenzie R.
MACKENZIE MTS.
Echo Bay
Great Bear Lake
NORTH AMERICA
CANADA
HUDSON BAY
BELCHER IS.
120°
90°
60°
30°
150°
180°

ANTARCTICA

PACIFIC OCEAN
SOUTH AMERICA
TIERRA DEL FUEGO
Cape Horn
Drake Passage
FALKLAND IS. (U.K.)
AMUNDSEN SEA
Cape Flying Fish
THURSTON I.
SIPLE I.
BELLINGSHAUSEN SEA
ADELAIDE I.
SOUTH SHETLAND IS.
SCOTIA SEA
CAMPBELL I. (N.Z.)
AUCKLAND IS. (N.Z.)
SCOTT ISLAND
ROSS SEA
EXECUTIVE COMMITTEE RANGE
BYRD LAND
THWAITES ICEBERG TONGUE
ELLSWORTH LAND
ALEXANDER I.
ANTARCTIC PEN.
JOINVILLE I.
MACQUARIE I. (AUSTRALIA)
BALLENY IS.
Cape Colbeck
EDWARD VII PEN.
ROCKEFELLER PLATEAU
ELLSWORTH MTS.
Vinson Massif 16,066 ft. (4,897 m.)
SOUTH ORKNEY IS.
Cape Adaré
ROOSEVELT I.
COULMAN I.
ROSS ICE SHELF
RONNE ICE SHELF
BERKNER I.
WEDDELL SEA
SOUTH GEORGIA I. (U.K.)
PRINCE ALBERT MTS.
ROSS I.
McMurdo Sound
MARIE
REEDY GLACIER
PENSACOLA MTS.
VAHSEL BAY
VICTORIA LAND
QUEEN MAUD MTS.
NILSEN PLATEAU
MOUNTAINS
RECOVERY GLACIER
RIISER LARSEN ICE SHELF
SOUTH SANDWICH IS. (U.K.)
TRANSANTARCTIC
Mt. Kirkpatrick 14,855 ft. (4,528 m.)
South Pole
RANGE
SHACKLETON
Cape Norvegia
ATLANTIC OCEAN
ANTARCTICA
FIMBUL ICE SHELF
DIBBLE ICEBERG TONGUE
WILKES LAND
80°
QUEEN MAUD LAND
MÜHLIG-HOFMANN MTS.
TOTTEN GLACIER
Cape Poinsett
70°
Prime Meridian
Arctic Circle
SHACKLETON ICE SHELF
AMERICAN HIGHLAND
LAMBERT GLACIER
AMERY ICE SHELF
PRINCE CHARLES MTS.
SHIRASE GLACIER
LÜTZOW-HOLM BAY
60°
INDIAN OCEAN
DAVIS SEA
WEST ICE SHELF
PRYDZ BAY
ENDERBY LAND
50°
60°
30°

Historical Atlas AND World Data Bank

Early Civilizations 3500 B.C –1700s B.C.

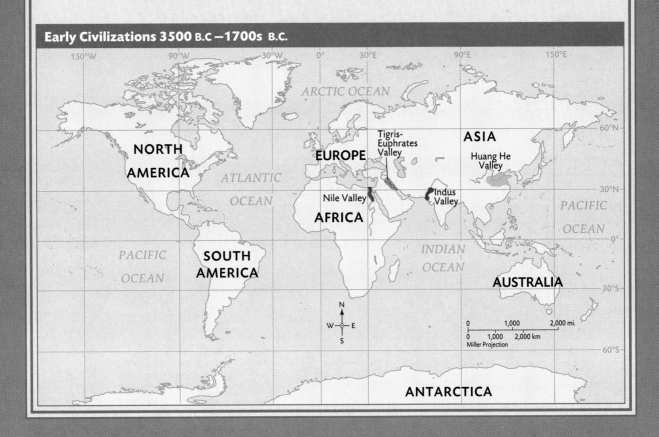

A27

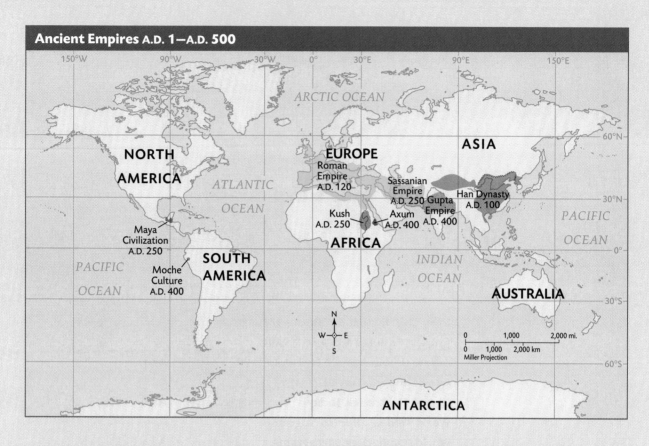

A.D. 1—A.D. 500 map showing:
- NORTH AMERICA
- SOUTH AMERICA
- EUROPE
- ASIA
- AFRICA
- AUSTRALIA
- ANTARCTICA
- Roman Empire A.D. 120
- Sassanian Empire A.D. 250
- Han Dynasty A.D. 100
- Gupta Empire A.D. 400
- Axum A.D. 400
- Kush A.D. 250
- Maya Civilization A.D. 250
- Moche Culture A.D. 400
- ARCTIC OCEAN
- ATLANTIC OCEAN
- PACIFIC OCEAN
- INDIAN OCEAN
- Miller Projection

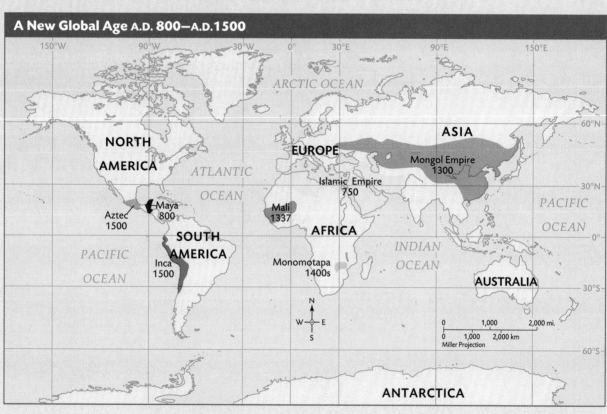

A.D. 800—A.D. 1500 map showing:
- NORTH AMERICA
- SOUTH AMERICA
- EUROPE
- ASIA
- AFRICA
- AUSTRALIA
- ANTARCTICA
- Mongol Empire 1300
- Islamic Empire 750
- Mali 1337
- Monomotapa 1400s
- Aztec 1500
- Maya 800
- Inca 1500
- ARCTIC OCEAN
- ATLANTIC OCEAN
- PACIFIC OCEAN
- INDIAN OCEAN
- Miller Projection

Age of Imperialism 1870–1914

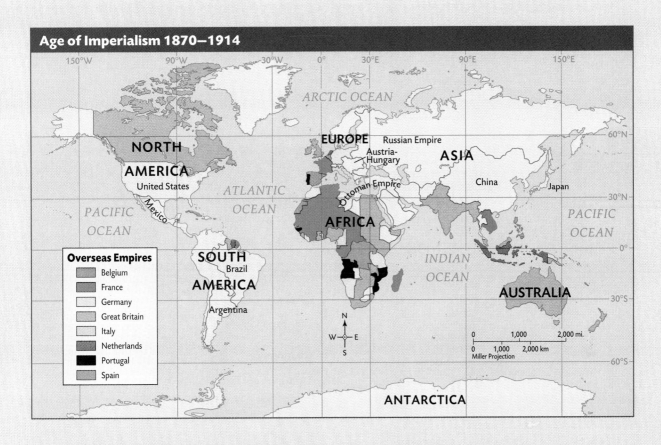

Overseas Empires
- Belgium
- France
- Germany
- Great Britain
- Italy
- Netherlands
- Portugal
- Spain

0   1,000   2,000 mi.
0   1,000   2,000 km
Miller Projection

Global Civilization Today

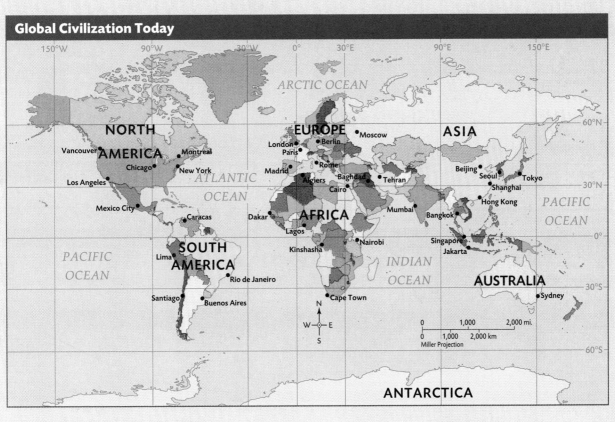

0   1,000   2,000 mi.
0   1,000   2,000 km
Miller Projection

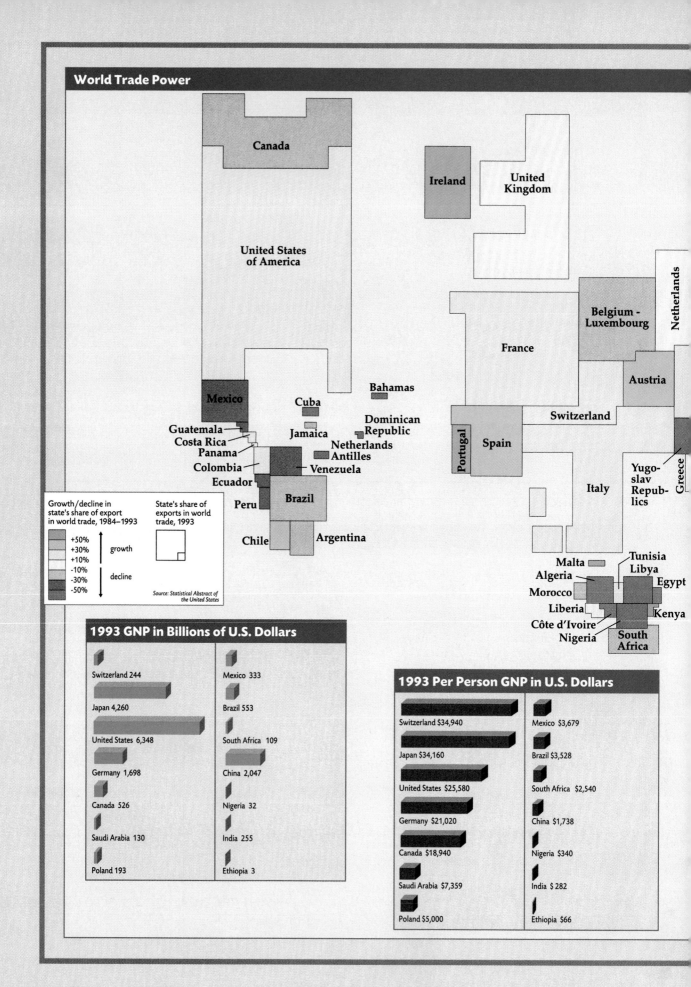

World Trade Power

Canada

Ireland   United Kingdom

United States of America

Belgium - Luxembourg

Netherlands

France

Austria

Bahamas

Mexico

Cuba

Dominican Republic

Switzerland

Guatemala
Costa Rica
Panama

Jamaica

Netherlands Antilles

Portugal   Spain

Colombia

Venezuela

Ecuador

Peru   Brazil

Yugo-slav Repub-lics

Italy

Greece

Chile   Argentina

Malta   Tunisia
Libya
Algeria   Egypt
Morocco
Liberia   Kenya
Côte d'Ivoire
Nigeria   South Africa

Growth/decline in state's share of export in world trade, 1984–1993

State's share of exports in world trade, 1993

+50%
+30%   growth
+10%
-10%
-30%   decline
-50%

Source: *Statistical Abstract of the United States*

1993 GNP in Billions of U.S. Dollars

Switzerland 244

Mexico 333

Japan 4,260

Brazil 553

United States 6,348

South Africa 109

Germany 1,698

China 2,047

Canada 526

Nigeria 32

Saudi Arabia 130

India 255

Poland 193

Ethiopia 3

1993 Per Person GNP in U.S. Dollars

Switzerland $34,940

Mexico $3,679

Japan $34,160

Brazil $3,528

United States $25,580

South Africa $2,540

Germany $21,020

China $1,738

Canada $18,940

Nigeria $340

Saudi Arabia $7,359

India $282

Poland $5,000

Ethiopia $66

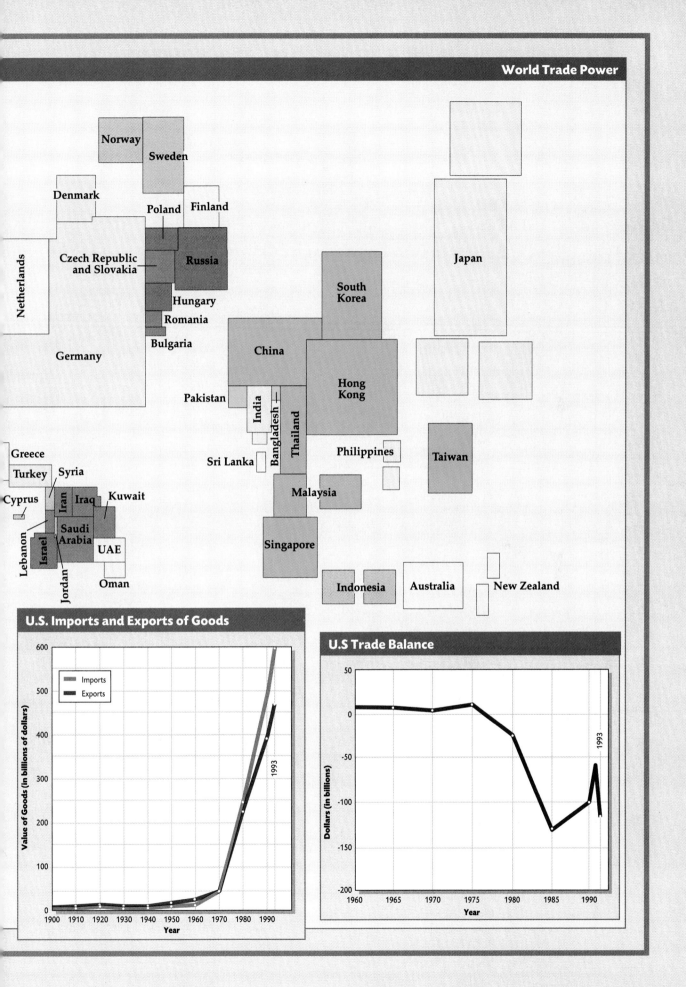

Norway

Sweden

Denmark

Poland Finland

Netherlands

Czech Republic and Slovakia

Russia

Hungary

Romania

Bulgaria

Germany

Japan

South Korea

China

Hong Kong

Pakistan

India

Bangladesh

Thailand

Sri Lanka

Philippines

Taiwan

Greece

Turkey Syria

Cyprus

Iran Iraq Kuwait

Lebanon

Israel

Saudi Arabia

UAE

Jordan

Oman

Malaysia

Singapore

Indonesia

Australia

New Zealand

U.S. Imports and Exports of Goods

Imports

Exports

Value of Goods (in billions of dollars)

600

500

400

300

200

100

1900 1910 1920 1930 1940 1950 1960 1970 1980 1990

Year

1993

U.S Trade Balance

Dollars (in billions)

50

0

-50

-100

-150

-200

1960 1965 1970 1975 1980 1985 1990

Year

1993

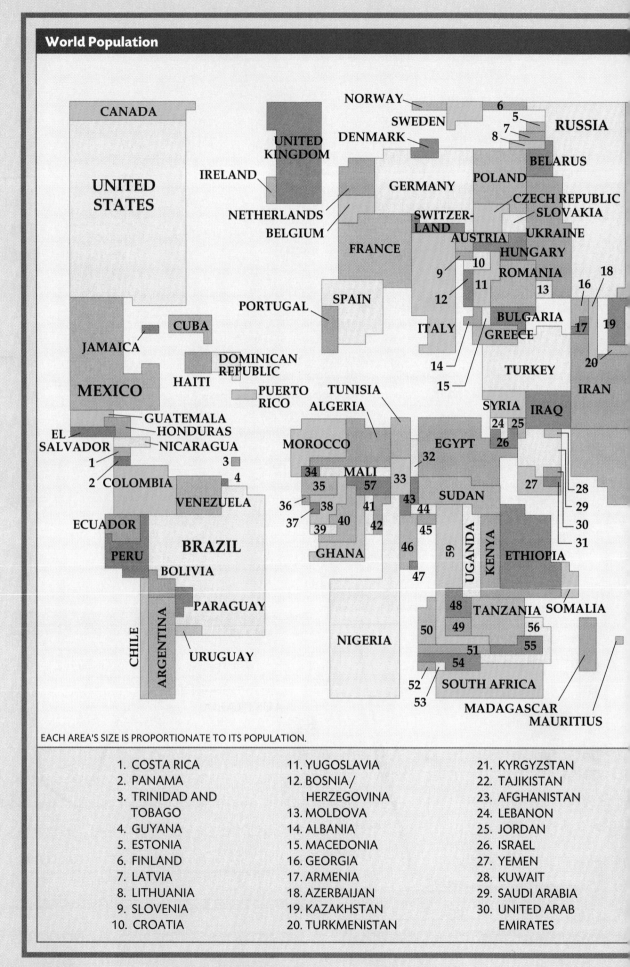

EACH AREA'S SIZE IS PROPORTIONATE TO ITS POPULATION.

1. COSTA RICA	11. YUGOSLAVIA	21. KYRGYZSTAN
2. PANAMA	12. BOSNIA/	22. TAJIKISTAN
3. TRINIDAD AND	HERZEGOVINA	23. AFGHANISTAN
TOBAGO	13. MOLDOVA	24. LEBANON
4. GUYANA	14. ALBANIA	25. JORDAN
5. ESTONIA	15. MACEDONIA	26. ISRAEL
6. FINLAND	16. GEORGIA	27. YEMEN
7. LATVIA	17. ARMENIA	28. KUWAIT
8. LITHUANIA	18. AZERBAIJAN	29. SAUDI ARABIA
9. SLOVENIA	19. KAZAKHSTAN	30. UNITED ARAB
10. CROATIA	20. TURKMENISTAN	EMIRATES

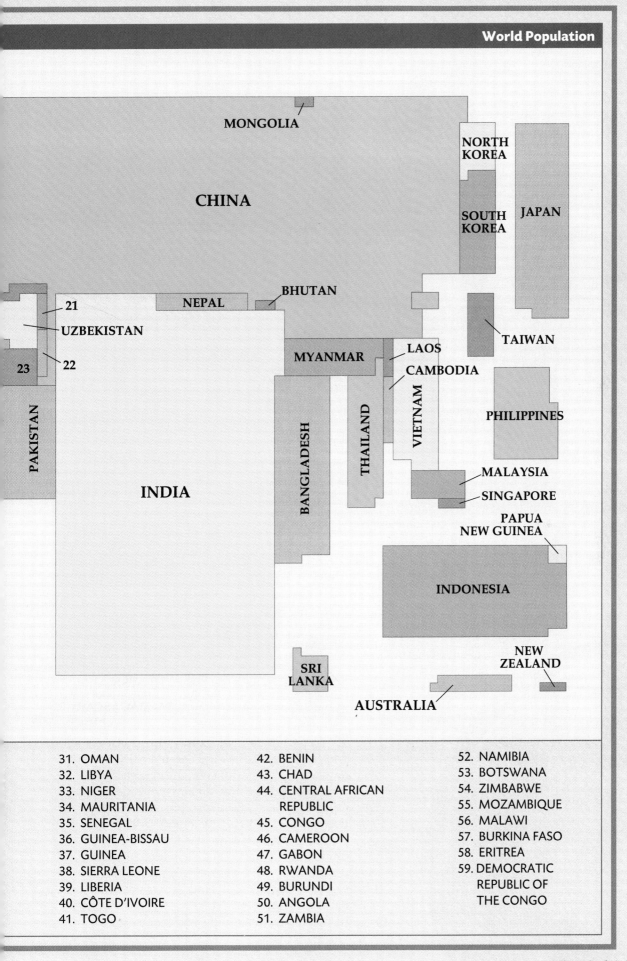

MONGOLIA

CHINA

NORTH
KOREA

SOUTH
KOREA

JAPAN

BHUTAN

21

NEPAL

UZBEKISTAN

23

22

TAIWAN

LAOS

MYANMAR

CAMBODIA

PAKISTAN

THAILAND

VIETNAM

PHILIPPINES

INDIA

BANGLADESH

MALAYSIA

SINGAPORE

PAPUA
NEW GUINEA

INDONESIA

NEW
ZEALAND

SRI
LANKA

AUSTRALIA

31. OMAN
32. LIBYA
33. NIGER
34. MAURITANIA
35. SENEGAL
36. GUINEA-BISSAU
37. GUINEA
38. SIERRA LEONE
39. LIBERIA
40. CÔTE D'IVOIRE
41. TOGO

42. BENIN
43. CHAD
44. CENTRAL AFRICAN
    REPUBLIC
45. CONGO
46. CAMEROON
47. GABON
48. RWANDA
49. BURUNDI
50. ANGOLA
51. ZAMBIA

52. NAMIBIA
53. BOTSWANA
54. ZIMBABWE
55. MOZAMBIQUE
56. MALAWI
57. BURKINA FASO
58. ERITREA
59. DEMOCRATIC
    REPUBLIC OF
    THE CONGO

What Is Geography?

The story of humanity begins with **geography**—the study of the earth in all of its variety. Geography concerns the earth's land, water, and plant and animal life. It also tells you about the people who live on the earth, the places they have created, and how these places differ. The earth is a planet of diverse groups of people. A study of geography can help you see why the people of the earth are so diverse.

The Five Themes of Geography

The study of geography can be organized around five themes: **location**, **place**, **human/environment interaction**, **movement**, and **region**. Geographers use these five themes to study and classify all parts of the earth and its variety of human activity.

Geography and World History

World geography is especially important to the study of world history. Historians use geography to explain connections between the past and the present. They study how places

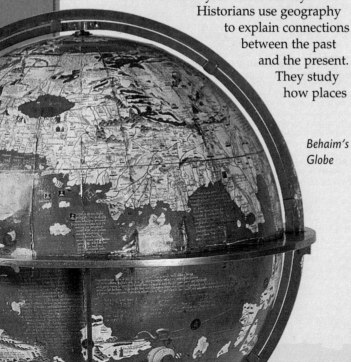

Behaim's Globe

looked in the past, how places and patterns of human activity have changed over time, and how geographic forces have influenced these changes.

GLOBES AND MAPS

Globes

Photographs from space show the earth in its true form—a great ball spinning around the sun. The only accurate way to draw the earth is as a globe, or a round form. A globe gives a true picture of the earth's size and the shape of the earth's landmasses and bodies of water. Globes also show the true distances and true directions between places.

Maps

A map is a flat drawing of the earth's surface. People use maps to locate places, plot routes, and judge distances. Maps can also display useful information about the world's peoples.

What advantages does a map have over a globe? Unlike a globe, a map allows you to see all areas of the world at the same time. Maps also show much more detail and can be folded and more easily carried.

Maps, however, have their drawbacks. As you can imagine, drawing a round object on a flat surface is very difficult. Cartographers, or mapmakers, have drawn many **projections**, or kinds of maps. Each map projection is a different way of showing the round earth on a flat map. This is because it is impossible to draw a round planet on a flat surface without distorting or misrepresenting some parts of the earth. As a result, each kind of map projection has some distortion. Typical distortions involve distance, direction, shape, and/or area.

The Hemispheres

To determine location, distance, and direction on a map or globe, geographers have developed a network of imaginary lines that crisscross the earth. One of these lines, the **Equator**, circles the earth midway between the **North Pole** and the **South Pole**. It divides the earth into "half spheres," or **hemispheres**. The Northern Hemisphere includes all of the land and water between the Equator and the North Pole. The Southern Hemisphere includes all of the land and water between the Equator and the South Pole.

Another imaginary line running from north to south divides the earth into half spheres in the other direction. This line is called the **Prime Meridian**. Every place east of the Prime Meridian is in the Eastern Hemisphere. Every place west of the Prime Meridian is in the Western Hemisphere.

Latitude and Longitude

The Equator and the Prime Meridian are the starting points for two sets of lines used to find any location. The two sets measure distances north or south of the Equator, and east and west of the Prime Meridian.

One set of lines called **parallels** circle the earth and show **latitude**, which is distance measured in degrees (°) north and south of the Equator at 0° latitude. The letter *N* or *S* following the degree symbol tells you if the location is north or south of the Equator. The North Pole is at 90° North (*N*) latitude, and the South Pole is at 90° South (*S*) latitude.

Two important parallels in between the poles are the **Tropic of Cancer** at 23 1/2°N latitude and the **Tropic of Capricorn** at 23 1/2°S latitude. You can also find the **Arctic Circle** at 66 1/2°N latitude and the **Antarctic Circle** at 66 1/2°S latitude.

The second set of lines called **meridians** run north to south from the North Pole to the South Pole. These lines signify **longitude**, which is distance measured in degrees east (*E*) or west (*W*) of the Prime Meridian at 0° longitude. On the opposite side of the earth is the International Date Line, at about the 180° meridian.

The Grid System

Lines of latitude and longitude cross one another in the form of a **grid system**. You can use the grid system to find where places are exactly located on a map or globe. Each place on Earth has an address on the grid. This grid address is the place's **coordinates**—its degrees of latitude and longitude. For example, the coordinates of the city of San Francisco are 38°N latitude and 122°W longitude. This means that San Francisco lies about 38 degrees (°) north of the Equator and 122 degrees (°) west of the Prime Meridian. Where those two lines cross is called the **absolute location** of the city.

Map Symbols

Maps can direct you down the street, across the country, or around the world. There are as many different kinds of maps as there are uses for them. Being

Hemispheres

NORTHERN HEMISPHERE
North Pole
NORTH AMERICA
Equator
SOUTH AMERICA
South Pole
SOUTHERN HEMISPHERE

WESTERN HEMISPHERE
EASTERN HEMISPHERE
North Pole
NORTH AMERICA
EUROPE
AFRICA
SOUTH AMERICA
Prime Meridian
South Pole
ANTARCTICA

NORTHERN HEMISPHERE
North Pole
AFRICA
ASIA
Equator
AUSTRALIA
ANTARCTICA
South Pole
SOUTHERN HEMISPHERE

EASTERN HEMISPHERE
WESTERN HEMISPHERE
North Pole
ASIA
NORTH AMERICA
180°
PACIFIC OCEAN
AUSTRALIA
ANTARCTICA
South Pole

GEOGRAPHY HANDBOOK

able to read a map begins with learning about its parts.

The **map key** explains the symbols used on the map. On a map of the world, for example, dots mark cities and towns. On a road map, various kinds of lines stand for paved roads, dirt roads, and interstate highways. A pine tree symbol may represent a state park, while an airplane is often the symbol for an airport.

An important first step in reading any map is to find the direction marker. A map has a symbol that tells you where the **cardinal directions**—north, south, east, and west—are positioned. Sometimes all of these directions are shown with a **compass rose**.

A measuring line, often called a **scale bar**, helps you find distance on the map. The map's **scale** tells you what distance on the earth is represented by the measurement on the scale bar. For example, 1 inch on a map may represent 100 miles on the earth. Knowing the scale allows you to visualize how large an area is, as well as to measure distances. Map scales are usually given in both miles and kilometers, a metric measurement of distance.

purpose maps are physical maps and political maps. **Physical maps** show natural features, such as rivers and mountains. **Political maps** show places that people have created, such as cities or the boundaries of countries and states.

Special Purpose Maps

Special purpose maps show information on specific topics, such as climate, land use, or vegetation. Human activities, such as exploration routes, territorial expansion, or battle sites, also appear on special purpose maps. Colors and map key symbols are especially important on this type of map.

LANDSAT Maps

LANDSAT maps are made from photographs taken by camera-carrying LANDSAT satellites in space. The cameras record millions of energy waves invisible to the human eye. Computers then change this information into pictures of the earth's surface. With LANDSAT images, scientists can study whole mountain ranges, oceans, and geographic regions. Changes to the earth's environment can also be tracked using the satellite information.

TYPES OF MAPS

Maps of many different kinds are used in this text to help you see the connection between world geography and the history of humanity.

General Purpose Maps

Maps that show a wide range of general information about an area are called **general purpose maps**. Two of the most common general

LANDSAT map of
San Francisco Bay area

San Francisco

San Francisco
(38°N, 122°W)

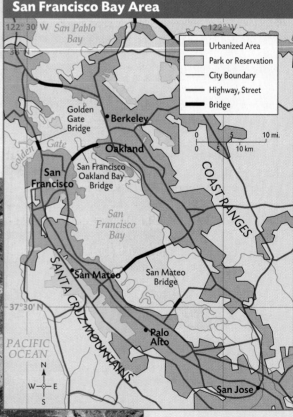

San Francisco Bay Area

CONTINENTS

Geographers divide most of the earth's land surface into seven large landmasses called **continents**. The continents are North America, South America, Europe, Africa, Asia, Australia, and Antarctica. Asia is the largest continent in size, and Australia is the smallest.

LANDFORMS

Landforms cover about 30 percent of the surface of the earth. **Landforms**, or the natural features of the earth's surface, include **mountains**, **hills**, **plateaus**, and **plains**. Geographers describe each landform by its **elevation**, or height above sea level, and by its **relief**, or changes in height.

Mountains

Mountains are the highest of the world's landforms. They rise from about 2,000 feet (610 m) to more than 20,000 feet (6,100 m) above sea level. One of the peaks in the Himalaya mountain ranges of central Asia is Mount Everest, the world's highest mountain. It towers 29,028 feet (8,848 m) above sea level. Other mountains, such as the Appalachians in eastern North America, are not as high. Mountains generally have high relief.

Hills, Plateaus, and Plains

Hills are lower than mountains and generally rise from about 500 to 2,000 feet (152 to 610 m) above sea level. They generally have moderate relief.

Plateaus are raised areas of flat or almost flat land. Most plateaus have low relief and vary in elevation from about 300 to 3,000 feet (91 to 914 m) above sea level. The world's largest plateau area is the Tibetan Plateau in central Asia. It covers about 715,000 square miles (1,852,000 sq. km) and has an average altitude of 16,000 feet (4,877 m) above sea level.

Plains are large areas of flat or gently rolling land that generally rise less than 1,000 feet (305 m) above sea level and have low relief. The world's largest plain is the North European Plain, which stretches for more than 1,000 miles (1,609 km) from the western coast of France to the Ural Mountains in Russia.

BODIES OF WATER

About 70 percent of the earth's surface is covered with water. Geographers identify bodies of water by their shapes and sizes. The major types include oceans, seas, bays, gulfs, lakes, and rivers.

Oceans and Seas

The largest bodies of water in the world are the four saltwater **oceans**—the Pacific, the Atlantic, the Indian, and the Arctic. The Pacific Ocean is the largest ocean, covering about 64 million square miles (165,760,000 sq. km)—more than all the land areas of the earth combined.

Seas are smaller bodies of salt water that are usually in part surrounded by land. The world's largest sea is East Asia's South China Sea, with an area of 1,148,500 square miles (2,975,000 sq. km).

Bays and Gulfs

Still smaller bodies of salt water are gulfs and bays. **Bays** are extensions of a sea usually smaller than a **gulf.** The largest bay in the world measured by shoreline is Hudson Bay, Canada, with a shoreline of 7,623 miles (12,265 km) and an area of 476,000 square miles (1,233,000 sq. km). Measured by area, the Bay of Bengal, in the Indian Ocean and bordering South Asia and part of Southeast Asia, is larger at 839,000 square miles (2,173,000 sq. km).

Lakes and Rivers

Other water features of the earth include lakes and rivers. A **lake** is a body of water completely surrounded by land. The world's largest freshwater lake is Lake Superior, one of the five Great Lakes between the United States and Canada. It has an area of 31,820 square miles (82,414 sq. km). The world's largest inland body of water, however, is the Caspian Sea, often considered a saltwater lake. Lying between Europe and Asia and east of the Caucasus Mountains, the Caspian Sea has a total area of 143,550 square miles (371,795 sq. km).

A **river** is a waterway flowing through land and emptying into another body of water. The world's longest river is the Nile River in Africa, which flows into the Mediterranean Sea from the highlands of East Africa. The Nile's length is about 4,160 miles (6,690 km).

GEOGRAPHY HANDBOOK

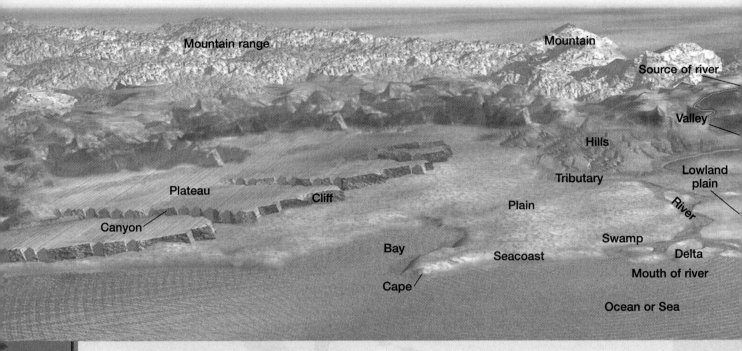

Mountain range • Mountain • Source of river • Valley • Hills • Lowland plain • Plateau • Cliff • Tributary • Plain • River • Canyon • Swamp • Bay • Seacoast • Delta • Cape • Mouth of river • Ocean or Sea

GEOGRAPHIC DICTIONARY

As you read about the world's geography and history, you will discover most of the terms listed and explained below. Many of the terms are pictured in the diagram above. Others you learned earlier in this Geography Handbook.

absolute location–exact location of a place on the earth described by global coordinates

basin–area of land drained by a given river and its branches; area of land surrounded by lands of higher elevations

bay–part of a large body of water that extends into a shoreline

canyon–deep and narrow valley with steep walls

cape–point of land surrounded by a body of water

channel–deep, narrow body of water that connects two larger bodies of water; deep part of a river or other waterway

cliff–steep, high wall of rock, earth, or ice

continent–one of the seven large landmasses on the earth

cultural feature–characteristic that humans have created in a place, such as language, religion, and history

delta–land built up from soil carried downstream by a river and deposited at its mouth

divide–stretch of high land that separates river basins

downstream–direction in which a river or stream flows from its source to its mouth

elevation–height of land above sea level

Equator–imaginary line that runs around the earth halfway between the North and South Poles; used as the starting point to measure degrees of north and south latitude

glacier–large, thick body of slowly moving ice, found in mountains and polar regions

globe–sphere-shaped model of the earth

gulf–part of a large body of water that extends into a shoreline, larger than a bay

harbor–a sheltered place along a shoreline where ships can anchor safely

highland–elevated land area with sloping sides such as a hill, mountain, or plateau, smaller than a mountain

island–land area, smaller than a continent, completely surrounded by water

isthmus–narrow stretch of land connecting two larger land areas

lake–a sizable inland body of water

latitude–distance north or south of the Equator, measured in degrees

longitude–distance east or west of the Prime Meridian, measured in degrees

lowland–land, usually level, at a low elevation

map–drawing of all or part of the earth shown on a flat surface

meridian–one of many lines on the global grid

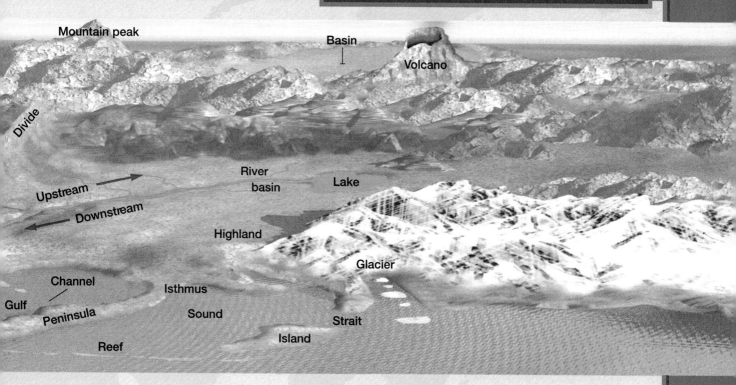

Mountain peak

Basin

Volcano

Divide

River basin

Lake

Upstream

Downstream

Highland

Glacier

Channel

Isthmus

Gulf

Peninsula

Sound

Strait

Reef

Island

running from the North Pole to the South Pole, used to measure degrees of longitude

mesa–area of raised land with steep sides; smaller than a plateau

mountain–land with steep sides that rises sharply from surrounding land; larger and more rugged than a hill

mountain peak–pointed top of a mountain

mountain range–a series of connected mountains

mouth–(of a river) place where a stream or river flows into a larger body of water

ocean–one of the four major bodies of salt water that surrounds a continent

ocean current–stream of either cold or warm water that moves in a definite direction through an ocean

parallel–one of many lines on the global grid that circle the earth north or south of the Equator; used to measure degrees of latitude

peninsula–body of land almost surrounded by water

physical feature–characteristic of a place occurring naturally, such as a landform, body of water, climate pattern, or resource

plain–area of level land, usually at a low elevation

plateau–area of flat or rolling land at a high elevation

Prime Meridian–line of the global grid running from the North Pole to the South Pole at Greenwich, England; used as the starting point for measuring degrees of east and west longitude

relative location–position of a place on the earth in relation to other places

relief–changes in elevation, either few or many, that occur over a given area of land

river–large stream of water that runs through the land

sea–large body of water completely or partly surrounded by land

seacoast–land lying next to a sea or ocean

sea level–average level of an ocean's surface

sound–body of water between a shoreline and one or more islands off the coast

source–(of a river) place where a river or stream begins, often in high lands

strait–narrow stretch of water joining two larger bodies of water

tributary–small river or stream that flows into a large river or stream; a branch of the river

upstream–direction opposite the flow of a river; toward the source of a river or stream

valley–area of low land between hills or mountains

volcano–mountain created as liquid rock or ash are thrown up from inside the earth

CLIMATE

Climate is the usual pattern of weather events that occurs in an area over a long period of time. Climate is determined by distance from the Equator, by location near large bodies of water, and sometimes by positions near mountain ranges

The world's climates can be organized into four major regions: **tropical**, **mid-latitude**, **high latitude**, and **dry**. Some of these regions are determined by their latitude; others are based on the vegetation that grows in them.

Tropical Climates

Tropical climates get their name from the tropics, the areas along the Equator. Temperatures in the tropics change little from season to season. The warm tropical climate region can be separated into two types: tropical rain forest and tropical savanna.

The tropical rain forest climate region is wet in most months, with up to 100 inches (254 cm) of rain a year. In these areas, rain and heat produce lush vegetation and **rain forests**, dense forests that are home to millions of kinds of plant and animal life. The Amazon River basin in South America is the world's largest rain forest area.

The tropical **savanna** climate has two seasons—one wet and one dry. Savannas, or grasslands with few trees, occur in this region. Among the leading tropical savanna climate areas are southern India and eastern Africa.

Mid-Latitude Climates

Mid-latitude, or moderate, climates are found in the middle latitudes of the Northern and Southern Hemispheres. Most of the world's people live in this climate region. The mid-latitude region has a greater variety of climates than other regions. This variety results from the mix of air masses—warm air coming from the tropics and cool air coming from the polar regions. In most places, temperatures change with the seasons.

High Latitude Climates

High latitude, or polar, climate regions lie in the high latitudes of each hemisphere. Climates are cold everywhere in the high latitude regions, some more severe than others.

High latitude climate regions also include highland or mountainous regions even in lower

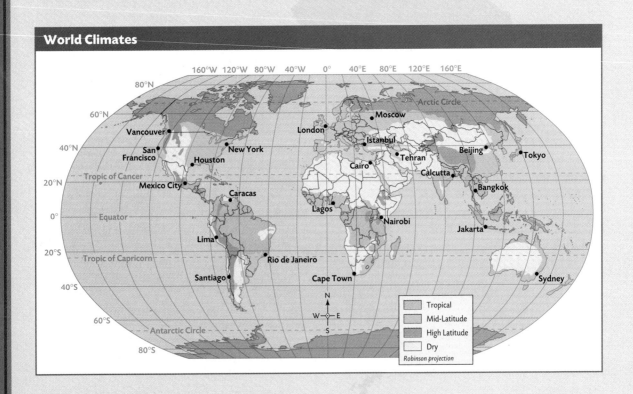

World Climates

World Land Use and Resources

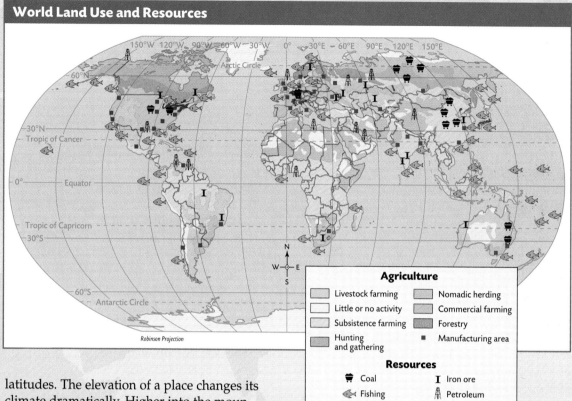

Robinson Projection

Agriculture

- Livestock farming
- Little or no activity
- Subsistence farming
- Hunting and gathering
- Nomadic herding
- Commercial farming
- Forestry
- ■ Manufacturing area

Resources

- Coal
- Fishing
- Iron ore
- Petroleum

latitudes. The elevation of a place changes its climate dramatically. Higher into the mountains, the air becomes thinner. It cannot hold the heat from the sun, so the temperature drops. Even in the tropics, snow covers the peaks of high mountains.

Dry Climates

Dry climate refers to dry or partially dry areas that receive little or no rainfall. Temperatures can be extremely hot during the day and cold at night. Dry climates can also have severely cold winters.

Nearly an eighth of the world's land surface is dry, with a rainfall of less than 10 inches (25 cm) per year. The Sahara in North Africa is the largest desert in the world. The area covered by the Sahara—3,579,000 square miles (9,270,000 sq. km)—is about the size of the United States.

NATURAL RESOURCES

Natural resources refer to anything from the natural environment that people use to meet their needs. Natural resources include fertile soil, clean water, minerals, trees, and energy sources. Human skills and labor are also valuable natural resources.

Renewable Resources

Some natural resources can be replaced as they are used up. These renewable resources can be replaced naturally or grown fairly quickly. Forests, grasslands, plant and animal life, and rich soil all can be renewable resources if people manage them carefully. A lumber company concerned about future growth can replant as many trees as it cuts. Fishing and whaling fleets can limit the number of fish and whales they catch in certain parts of the ocean.

Nonrenewable Resources

Metals and other minerals found in the earth's crust are nonrenewable resources. They cannot be replaced because they were formed over millions of years by geologic forces within the earth.

One important group of nonrenewable resources is fossil fuels—coals, oil, and natural gas. Industries and people depend on these fuels for energy and as raw materials for plastics and other goods. We also use up large amounts of other metals and minerals, such as iron, aluminum, and phosphates. Some of these can be reused, but they cannot be replaced.

When people use natural resources to make a living, they affect the environment. The unmanaged use of resources is a threat to the environment. Many human activities can cause pollution—putting impure or poisonous substances into the land, water, and air.

Land and Water

Only about 11 percent of the earth's surface has land good enough for farming. Chemicals that farmers use may improve their crops, but some also may damage the land. Pesticides, or chemicals that kill insects, can pollute rivers and groundwater, or water that fills tiny cracks in the rock layers below the earth's surface.

Other human activities also pollute soil and water. Oil spills from tanker ships threaten ocean coastal areas. Illegal dumping of dangerous waste products causes problems. Untreated sewage reaching rivers pollutes lakes and groundwater as well. Salt water can also pollute both soil and groundwater.

Air

Industries and vehicles that burn fossil fuels are the main sources of air pollution. Throughout the world, fumes from cars and other vehicles pollute the air. The chemicals in air pollution can seriously damage people's health.

These chemicals combined with precipitation may fall as acid rain, or rain carrying large amounts of sulfuric acid. Acid rain eats away the surfaces of buildings, kills fish, and can destroy entire forests.

Energy

All of the world nations need safe, dependable sources of energy. Fossil fuels are most often used to generate electricity, heat buildings, run machinery, and power vehicles. Fossil fuels, however, are non-renewable resources. In addition, they contribute to air pollution. So today many countries are trying to discover new ways of using renewable energy sources. Two of these ways are hydroelectric power, the energy generated by falling water, and solar energy, or energy produced by the heat of the sun.

Geographic factors have shaped the outcome of historical events. Landforms, waterways, climate, and natural resources all have helped or hindered human activities. In many cases, people have learned either to adapt to their environment or to transform it to meet their needs.

Throughout the units of your text, you will discover how geography has shaped the course of events in world history. Here are some examples of the role that geographic factors have played in the story of humanity.

Unit 1 The Rise of Civilizations

Rivers contributed to the rise of many of the world's early civilizations. By 3000 B.C. the Sumerians of the Middle East had set up 12 prosperous city-states in the Tigris-Euphrates River valley. The Fertile Crescent, as the area is often called because of its relatively rich topsoil and its curved shape, was able to support city-state populations ranging from 20,000 to 250,000 people.

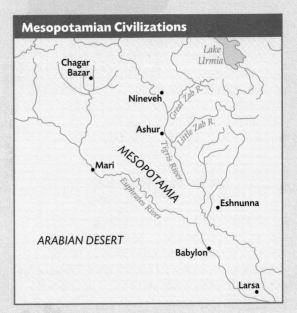

Mesopotamian Civilizations

Aegean Civilizations 1400 B.C.

Unit 2 Flowering of Civilizations

Landforms and waterways also affected the political relationships of the world's ancient peoples. For example, the rugged landscape of Greece divided the ancient Greeks into separate city-states instead of uniting them into a single nation. Furthermore, closeness to the sea caused the Greek city-states to expand their trade, culture, and sense of civic pride to other parts of the Mediterranean world.

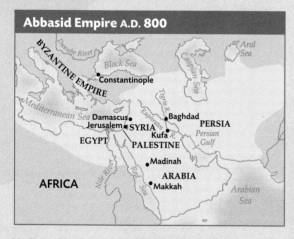

Abbasid Empire A.D. 800

Unit 3 Regional Civilizations

From about A.D. 400 to A.D. 1500, regional civilizations developed at the crossroads of trade between different areas of the world. The city of Makkah (Mecca), in the Middle East's Arabian Peninsula, was a crossroads for caravans from North Africa, Palestine, and the Persian Gulf. The religion of Islam established a firm base in Makkah, from which it spread to other areas of the Middle East, North Africa, South Asia, and Southeast Asia.

Unit 4 Emergence of the Modern World

The desire to control or to obtain scarce natural resources has encouraged trade and stimulated contact among the world's peoples. At the dawn of the modern era, Asians and Europeans came into contact with one another partly because Europeans wanted Asia's spices and silks. When the Asiatic people known as the Mongols could no longer guarantee safe passage for traders on overland routes, Europeans were forced to consider new water routes to Asia. This opened a new global age that brought the peoples of Europe, Asia, Africa, and the Americas into closer contact with each other.

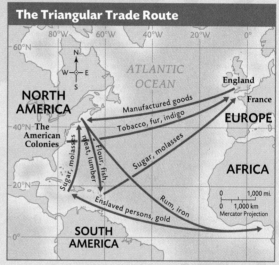

The Triangular Trade Route

Geography and History Journal

You are about to journey to the past to learn about the people and events that have shaped the world you live in today. Throughout your course of study, keep a record of the events discussed above and any other events in world history that have been affected by geography. When you come to the last unit, you may also want to explore how geography impacts current events or issues: For example, how has geography influenced peacekeeping missions in Bosnia and other parts of the world, or what would happen to Canada geographically if the province of Quebec were to separate and form an independent nation? On a world map locate the places where these historical events have occurred, and identify the units of study in your text in which they are discussed.

THE *Five* THEMES OF GEOGRAPHY

To help illustrate the link between history and geography, geographers have identified five themes that can be used to examine the role that geography plays.

1 **Location** serves as a starting point by asking, "Where is it?" To be more specific, there are two types of location. **Absolute location** refers to the exact location on the earth's surface as measured by latitude (lines north and south of the Equator) and longitude (lines east and west of the Prime Meridian). Every location on the earth can be found in this way.

    Relative location is less precise. It helps you orient yourself to a location that is relative to something else. Relative location has been important historically as people decided where to build their cities and establish their civilizations.

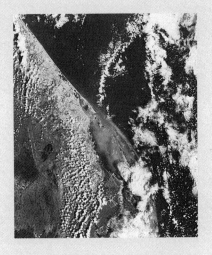

Modern mapmaking uses photography as a tool. A LANDSAT satellite provided data for this image of Miami, Florida.

2 The idea of **Place** includes more than just where something is located. It includes those features and characteristics that give an area its own identity or personality. These can be *physical* characteristics—such as landforms, weather, plants, and animals—or *human* characteristics—language, religion, architecture, music, politics, and way of life.

This village in Tunisia, North Africa, is at the northern edge of the Sahara. Stone and mud brick buildings give the village and its surroundings a sense of place.

3 **Human/Environment Interaction** focuses on how people respond to and alter their environment. To live comfortably or even to survive in many parts of the world, people must make changes in the environment or adapt to conditions they cannot change, or both.

How people choose to change their environment depends on their attitude toward the natural setting and on the technology they have available to change it.

Fishing is a major industry in Denmark, a small European nation nearly surrounded by water.

4 The **Movement** of people and things between places means that events in other places can have an impact on you personally. Transportation routes, communication systems, and trade connections link people and places throughout the world. Products, ideas, and information are sent around the globe, either slowly by ship or almost instantaneously by electronics.

The movement of people is particularly important because they can spread ideas and cultural characteristics from one place to another. Sometimes those ideas or characteristics are accepted in the new location, and the culture is changed by that linkage.

On the southern coast of China is Hong Kong, one of Asia's busiest ports.

Street signs and buildings in a historical area of Montreal reveal the French character of the Canadian province of Quebec.

5 A **Region** is an area that is unified by some feature or a mixture of features. It is used to generalize about parts of the earth's surface in either physical or human terms. A neighborhood is an example of a small region, while a cultural region that shares a common language would be a larger region. Other regions could be economic, where a particular economic activity is dominant, or political, where the same type of political system is followed.

Geography's Impact on History

While studying the history of the world, you will be learning about the people and events that have shaped the past and provide the framework for the future. As you read *World History: The Human Experience*, pay special attention to the ways in which geography has influenced history and fashioned the world in which you live.

Relation to Environment
The ancient Egyptians develop a civilization in northeastern Africa's Nile River Valley.

Bust of infant sun god

Uniformity
Early Chinese dynasties establish and maintain a strong central government in East Asia.

Terra-cotta warriors—Qin dynasty

Change
Early modern Europe enjoys a cultural awakening based on ancient Greek and Roman ideas as well as on Christianity and Judaism.

Renaissance musicians

Plato's School

Cultural Diffusion
Greek philosophy spread throughout the Mediterranean and is still influential in Europe and America today.

Movement
In order to find a route to China, Europeans explore the world.

Discovery of Magellan Strait

*W*orld history is a record of the adventures of humankind—both the famous and the ordinary—throughout thousands of years. By studying world history—by gazing across time—you can understand the past and recognize its contribution to the present and the future. World history tells of significant people and events. It also encompasses broad historical themes that happen again and again, providing meaning for events in the past and showing how they affect contemporary life.

World History: The Human Experience introduces 9 key historical themes. Each chapter highlights and develops several of these themes that demonstrate the interconnectedness of ideas and events. These events help organize your study of world history and make connections across time.

Cooperation/Conflict focuses on how people relate to each other throughout history—sometimes in cooperation, working together to accomplish a common goal, at other times in conflict, struggling against one another.

Revolution/Reaction deals with revolution, or the sudden overthrow of long-established ideas and organizations, contrasted with reaction, or the efforts to oppose new ideas and preserve traditional ways.

Change includes political, social, religious, cultural, and economic transformations that influence human activities throughout the centuries.

Diversity/Uniformity focuses on the diversity or variety of world peoples and customs, contrasted with the desire for uniformity or commonality in some societies.

Regionalism/Nationalism deals with a sense of loyalty and belonging, expressed in ties to a region, to a nation, or to the world as a whole—to the global community.

Innovation includes cultural, scientific, and technical breakthroughs that increase knowledge and impact the way people live and think.

Cultural Diffusion focuses on the spread of cultural expressions through a variety of means across nations, regions, and the world.

Movement involves the movement of people throughout history, including patterns of migration, exploration, and colonization as well as imperialism—people in one place on the globe exercising control over people in another place.

Relation to Environment emphasizes human-environment interchange—how people are affected by their environment and, in turn, how they affect that same environment.

Horn player, Benin

Rise of Civilizations

Then & Now *Scholars have divided history into periods according to environmental changes on Earth and cultural developments of humanity. The Paleolithic period or Old Stone Age began about 2 million years ago and lasted until about 12,000 B.C. The earliest evidence of human cultural development was discovered by four teenagers, quite by accident. Jacques Marshal and three young friends entered a cave near Lascaux, France, in 1940 and found the most spectacular cave paintings from Ice Age Europe, created some 17,000 years ago. Cave paintings have been discovered in many parts of the world, but the Lascaux paintings provide the most dramatic and best preserved "snapshots" of early human life yet to be discovered.*

A Global Chronology

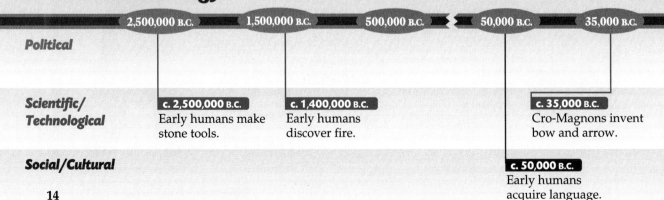

	2,500,000 B.C.	1,500,000 B.C.	500,000 B.C.	50,000 B.C.	35,000 B.C.
Political					
Scientific/ Technological	**c. 2,500,000 B.C.** Early humans make stone tools.	**c. 1,400,000 B.C.** Early humans discover fire.			**c. 35,000 B.C.** Cro-Magnons invent bow and arrow.
Social/Cultural				**c. 50,000 B.C.** Early humans acquire language.	

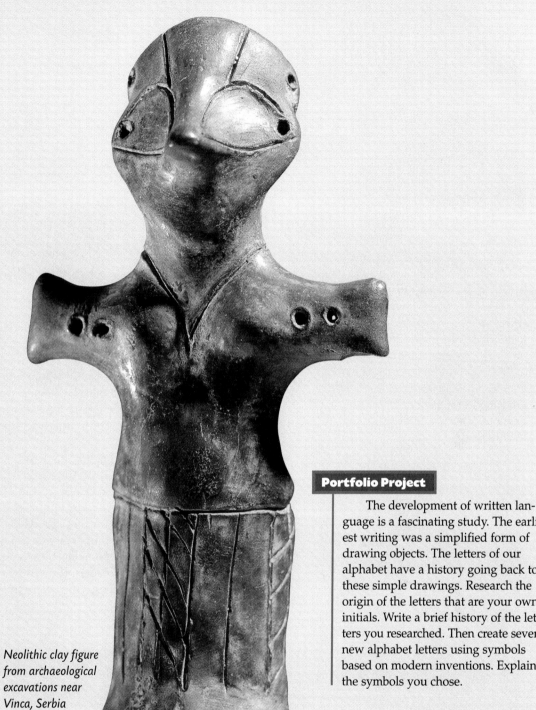

Neolithic clay figure from archaeological excavations near Vinca, Serbia

4000 B.C.   3000 B.C.   2000 B.C.   1000 B.C.

c. 3500 B.C.
Sumerians build
first cities.

c. 3000 B.C. Narmer
unites Upper Egypt
and Lower Egypt.

c. 1150 B.C. Olmec
civilization begins
in Mexico.

c. 3400 B.C. Corn
and beans cultivated
in the Americas.

c. 1700 B.C.
Stonehenge
monument is built.

c. 2000 B.C. Chinese
write on oracle bones.

The Spread of Ideas

Farming and Civilization

etween 8,000 and 10,000 years ago, a quiet revolution took place. In scattered pockets of the Middle East, Asia, Africa, and the Americas, people learned to cultivate food-producing plants for the first time. As knowledge of farming gradually spread, it dramatically changed human culture. Farming encouraged the growth of permanent communities, which in turn became the seedbeds for the world's first civilizations.

The Middle East
Breadbasket of the Ancient World

Today only sparse vegetation covers the foothills of Iran's Zagros Mountains. Erosion and overgrazing by sheep and goats have taken their toll. Around 8000 B.C., however, wild wheat known as emmer covered the hills. Experts believe it was here that the world's first farmers may have watched seeds fall to earth and sprout. This observation led these ancient wanderers to plant seeds.

Over time, knowledge of farming spread in a broad arc of fertile land that curved from the Persian Gulf to the Mediterranean Sea. Farmers gradually added other foods to their diets—barley, chickpeas, lentils, figs, apricots, pistachios, walnuts, and more. A hunger for these foods kept people in one place. Hunting and gathering lifestyles changed as people began to develop new ideas and skills. Slowly—very slowly—farming settlements grew into cities. Known by names such as Ur, Babylon, and Jericho, these cities were the centers of Earth's oldest civilizations.

Greek grain storage jar

Foothills of the Zagros Mountains

The Americas
Mexico and Peru: Farming and Diversity

For much of world history, distance separated the Americas from the rest of the world. But the independent invention of farming in the areas of present-day Mexico and Peru created cities as sophisticated as those in other regions. The crops that spurred their growth, however, differed from crops elsewhere. Few of the wild grains found on other continents grew in the Americas. The first farmers in the Americas used the seeds of other plants, especially squash and beans. They also developed two high-yield foods unknown to the rest of the world—potatoes and maize (corn). When distant civilizations made contact, ideas about agriculture accompanied the wide distribution of foods that early peoples had developed and cultivated.

Corn Dance by Frank Reed Whiteside

Asia and Africa
Expansion of Earth's Gardens

The farming revolution did not happen just once. It occurred several times in widely separated regions. More than 6,000 years ago, farmers along the upper Huang He in present-day northern China started planting millet. About 5,000 years ago, farmers near the mouth of the Chang Jiang in southern China learned to grow rice. At roughly the same time, farmers along the Nile River in the northern part of Africa harvested their first crops of wheat and barley.

Like the gardens of the Middle East, the gardens of China and northern Africa grew more diverse. By 3000 B.C., farmers cultivated soybeans, bananas, and sugarcane. Supported by the harvests, people had more time to think and dream. Soon they created things that were used by the civilizations of the Middle East—calendars, systems of writing, forms of art and government.

Wood relief of farming activities, Yoruba peoples

LINKING THE IDEAS

1. How do experts think farming probably began?
2. Why is farming considered one of the most important inventions of human history?

Critical Thinking

3. **Cause and Effect** What is the connection between farming and the rise of ancient civilizations?

Human Beginnings

Chapter Themes

▶ **Movement** Migrations of prehistoric peoples result in their spread throughout the world. *Section 1*

▶ **Innovation** Early humans produce tools and domesticate animals and crops. *Section 2*

▶ **Change** The earliest civilizations begin with the evolution of farming settlements into the first cities. *Section 3*

The Storyteller

On the coast of southern Africa, in caves and rock shelters, lived some of the world's first communities of prehistoric people. The region enjoyed a mild climate and abundant food from both the land and the sea. Women gathered supplies, while men made longer journeys inland, hunting for big animals such as antelope, buffalo, and wildebeest. Both men and women searched the coast at each low tide for small sea animals.

The cave dwellers preserved food for times of scarcity by drying leftover meat in smoke from fires. They did not know that more than 70,000 years later scientists and other people exploring the same area would uncover the remains of their long-vanished way of life.

Historical Significance

How did early peoples develop skills that became the basic elements of human ways of life? What developments led to the rise of the world's first civilizations?

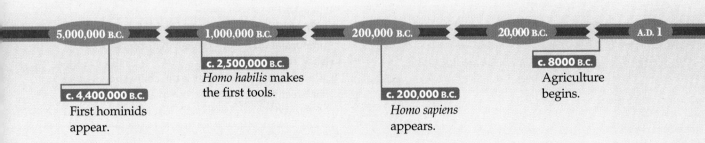

| 5,000,000 B.C. | 1,000,000 B.C. | 200,000 B.C. | 20,000 B.C. | A.D. 1 |

c. 4,400,000 B.C.
First hominids appear.

c. 2,500,000 B.C.
Homo habilis makes the first tools.

c. 200,000 B.C.
Homo sapiens appears.

c. 8000 B.C.
Agriculture begins.

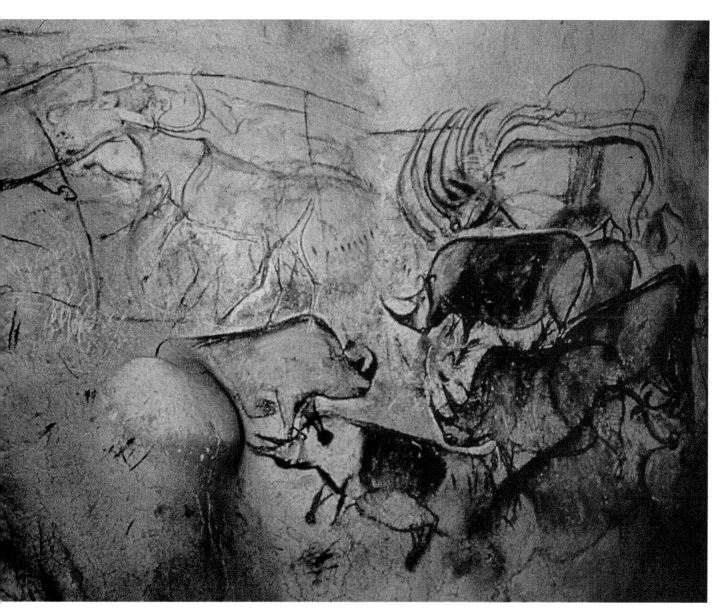

Cro-Magnon cave paintings from Vallon-Pont-d'Arc
near Avignon, France

Your History Journal

Imagine that you and a friend are stranded on a large uninhabited island. You have no tools except a pocket knife. There are many species of small animals, a stream of fresh water, a sandy beach, and a dense forest. You must survive until rescued, perhaps a month later. Write a journal account of your first seven days.

5,000,000 B.C.		3,000,000 B.C.		1,000,000 B.C.

c. 4,400,000 B.C.
Earliest known human ancestor lives in East Africa.

c. 2,500,000 B.C.
Homo habilis develops first stone tools.

c. 1,700,000 B.C.
Homo erectus reaches Asia.

Section 1

Discovery of Early Humans in Africa

Setting the Scene

▶ **Terms to Define**
prehistory, hominid, anthropologist, paleontologist, archaeologist, artifact, radiocarbon dating, nomad, culture, technology

▶ **People to Meet**
Gen Suwa, Tim D. White, Donald C. Johanson, Louis Leakey, Mary Leakey

▶ **Places to Locate**
Aramis, Hadar, Olduvai Gorge

 **ind Out** How have recent archaeological finds contributed to our understanding of human origins?

Storyteller

On the slab lies the shriveled corpse of a man.... Alongside him lies a long wooden stave with a fibrous end. Laid out on the slab ... are the other finds—the axe with its elbow-shafting and metal blade, a stone bead with a strange tassel of twisted hide thongs, the small dagger ... a wooden stick with holes in it, a scrap of leather, and a nut-sized stone.... Archaeologist Konrad Spindler's assessment: 'Roughly four thousand years old ... [or] even earlier.'

—adapted from *The Man in the Ice*, Konrad Spindler, 1994

Excavation of an ancient site in Lake Kinneret, Galilee

History tells the story of humankind. Because historians mostly use written records to gather information about the past, history is said to begin with the invention of writing about 5,500 years ago. But the story of humankind really begins in the time *before* people developed writing—the period called prehistory.

Using the best available evidence, scientists have traced the existence of the first humanlike creatures back to about 4.4 million years ago in Africa. Human beings and the humanlike creatures that preceded them together belong to a group of beings named hominids (HAH•muh•nuhds). The scientific study of hominids—their physical features, development, and behavior—is called anthropology. Physical anthropologists (AN•thruh•PAH•luh•jihsts) compare hominid bones and other fossil remains, looking for changes in such features as brain size and posture. Anthropologists work closely with other scientists. Paleontologists (PAY•lee•AHN •TAH•luh•jihsts), for example, study fossil remains to determine the characteristics of various prehistoric periods. Archaeologists (AHR•kee•AH•luh •jihsts) investigate prehistoric life by unearthing and interpreting the objects left behind by prehistoric people. These artifacts include any objects that were shaped by human hands—tools, pots, and beads—as well as other remains of human life, such as bits of charcoal.

Dating Early Artifacts

As they carefully unearth the remains of prehuman and human settlements, archaeologists and physical anthropologists face the additional problem of dating what they find. It is easy to determine the relative sequence in which events happened.

More recent remains are usually found above older ones. The problem lies in assigning a definite age to fossil bones, tools, and other remains.

Among the techniques for determining age is radiocarbon dating. Once-living things contain small amounts of radioactive carbon. Because radioactive carbon decays at a known rate, archaeologists can measure how much the radioactive carbon has decayed in organic remains and figure out when the animal or plant died. In recent years, they also have used a dating technique that measures the rate of decay for chemical elements other than carbon.

Scientists have increased our understanding of the age of prehistoric peoples through the use of genetic evidence. They obtain genetic material called DNA from living people and compare it with DNA from other people and from living animals. Using computers, they calculate and analyze the rate of change in DNA over time. Although not error free, these studies have produced valuable information about the links between people today and their prehistoric ancestors.

Prehistoric Finds in Africa

On December 17, 1992, a paleontologist from Japan named **Gen Suwa** walked across the rugged desert landscape of Ethiopia in East Africa. At a site called **Aramis**, an object in the ground caught Suwa's eye. It turned out to be one of the oldest hominid teeth ever found—a link to the origins of our human ancestors!

The Oldest Human Ancestor

Over the next two years, Suwa, his colleague **Tim D. White** of the University of California, and a 20-person team uncovered additional remains. They came up with teeth, arm bones, and parts of a skull and jaw that belonged to 17 individuals. Analyzing the fossils, the scientists determined that they were about 4.4 million years old and came from the oldest direct human ancestor known. The small creatures would have weighed about 65 pounds (30 kg) and stood 4 feet (1.2 m) tall. Scientists have yet to determine whether they walked upright.

Discovery of Lucy

About 45 miles (73 km) north, at **Hadar**, two scientists—**Donald C. Johanson** and Tom Gray—in 1974 had uncovered the 3.2 million-year-old skeleton of a hominid nicknamed "Lucy." Lucy received her name from a popular Beatles song of the period,

Visualizing History Mary Leakey, a noted paleoanthropologist, follows a trail of hominid footprints fossilized in volcanic ash. *What are hominids?*

"Lucy in the Sky with Diamonds." Hers was the most nearly complete skeleton of any erect-walking prehuman found up to that time.

Since then, Johanson and his team of researchers have made further discoveries. In 1994 they assembled, from other fossils found at the Hadar site, the first reasonably complete skull of a Lucy-like hominid. The scientists claimed that the skull provided evidence that males and females in this early hominid group were of significantly different sizes. The evidence also indicated that Lucy-like hominids spent some time climbing in trees and could also walk upright.

The earliest known direct evidence of upright walking comes from Kenya, where archaeologists in 1995 discovered a fossilized hominid shinbone about 4 million years old. The shape and size of the bone indicate upright walking.

Human Origins

Scientists disagree about many aspects of the story of human beginnings. As scientists unearth more clues, newer evidence may require them to reinterpret older evidence.

The First Hominids

According to one of the generally accepted theories, the first prehuman hominids, of whom the discoveries in Ethiopia are an example, date back about 4.4 million years. Known as *Australopithecus* (aw•STRAY•loh•PIH•thuh•kuhs), or "southern ape," they stood about 3.5 to 5.0 feet (1.1 to 1.6 m) tall and walked on two legs. They had large faces that jutted out. The brain was small, the nose flat, and the teeth large. The back teeth were suitable for grinding food.

Australopithecus lived in the humid forests of eastern and southern Africa, where they fed on fruits, leaves, and nuts. They probably also ate fish caught in streams and meat from animals killed by lions or other predators. *Australopithecus* were most likely nomads—moving constantly in search of food. They probably had few, if any, possessions and may have shared food with one another. Fossil evidence shows that family groups lived in temporary camps. Perhaps they lived together for protection from large animals. No evidence exists showing that *Australopithecus* made or used tools. They may have used grass stems and twigs as tools and sticks or bones to dig roots, however.

Hominid Groups

Scientists use the Latin word *Homo*, which means "human," to name these hominids and all later human beings as well. Anthropologists today are still not certain whether a direct relationship connected *Australopithecus* and human beings or exactly when hominids became truly human. Scientists divided *Homo*—the genus of humans—into three species that differ somewhat in body structures. These three human or humanlike species arose at different times in prehistory. The earliest of the three was *Homo habilis*, or "person with ability," who lived until about 1.5 million years ago. After *Homo habilis* lived the second type

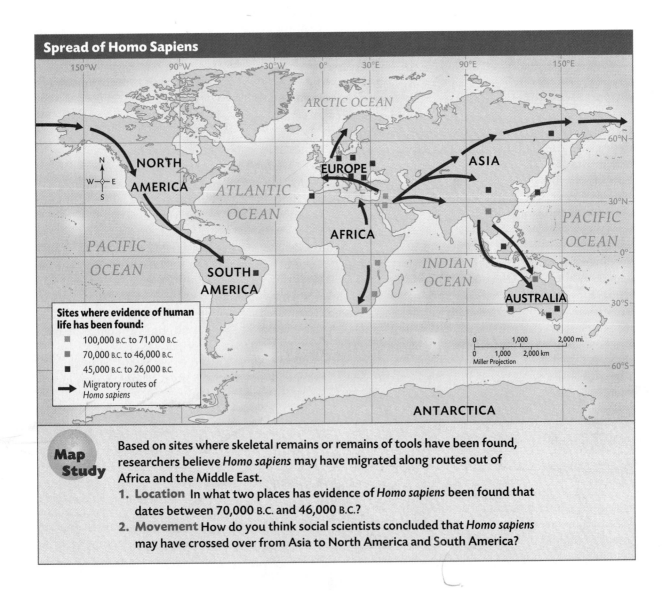

Spread of Homo Sapiens

Sites where evidence of human life has been found:
- 100,000 B.C. to 71,000 B.C.
- 70,000 B.C. to 46,000 B.C.
- 45,000 B.C. to 26,000 B.C.
- → Migratory routes of *Homo sapiens*

Map Study Based on sites where skeletal remains or remains of tools have been found, researchers believe *Homo sapiens* may have migrated along routes out of Africa and the Middle East.

1. **Location** In what two places has evidence of *Homo sapiens* been found that dates between 70,000 B.C. and 46,000 B.C.?
2. **Movement** How do you think social scientists concluded that *Homo sapiens* may have crossed over from Asia to North America and South America?

© Bob Campbell

Hominid Hunter

Kenneth Garrett

Meave Leakey, daughter-in-law of famed fossil hunters Mary and Louis Leakey, sifts through the soil near Lake Turkana in northern Kenya, a site in the East African Rift System famous for its treasury of the fossils of early humans. In recent years a wide range of scholars have continued to push back the date for the origin of the earliest humans. Molecular biologists, through the study of human, chimpanzee, and gorilla genes and blood proteins, speculate that hominids, or early humans, originated somewhere between five and seven million years ago. One of a number of scientists influenced by this research, Meave Leakey and her team began exploring for new evidence. They now theorize that a jawbone found near Lake Turkana in 1994 may be 4.1 million years old. Before that discovery there was little evidence of hominids older than 3.6 million years. Some researchers believe that a 5.6 million-year-old jaw fragment (left) discovered in 1967 may be the oldest hominid fossil yet found. ⊕

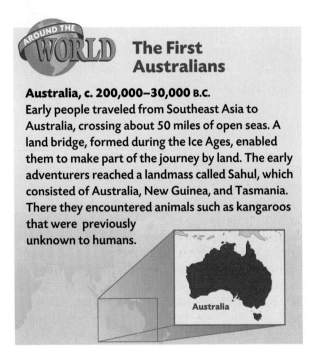

AROUND THE WORLD — The First Australians

Australia, c. 200,000–30,000 B.C.
Early people traveled from Southeast Asia to Australia, crossing about 50 miles of open seas. A land bridge, formed during the Ice Ages, enabled them to make part of the journey by land. The early adventurers reached a landmass called Sahul, which consisted of Australia, New Guinea, and Tasmania. There they encountered animals such as kangaroos that were previously unknown to humans.

Australia

of early human—*Homo erectus*, or "person who walks upright"—who was, in turn, followed between 100,000 and 200,000 years ago by *Homo sapiens*, or "person who thinks." All people living today belong to the species *Homo sapiens*.

The Ice Ages

Climatic changes played an important part in the development of early humankind. Between 2 million and 10,000 years ago, Earth experienced four long periods of cold climate, known as the Ice Ages. During each such period, average temperatures in many parts of the world fell to below freezing, and massive glaciers spread out from the Poles, scarring the landforms over which they crept. The northern glaciers covered large portions of Europe, Asia, and North America, and the ice fields of Antarctica stretched over wide regions in the Southern Hemisphere. Only the middle latitudes remained warm enough to support human and animal life. Between glacial periods, Earth's climate warmed overall, and abundant rains brought lush plant growth—until the next glacial period began.

As the sheets of ice formed, the level of the oceans dropped more than 300 feet (90 m). As a result, some areas that are now separated by water were connected then by bridges of land. One such land bridge joined Japan and mainland Korea, another connected Great Britain and Ireland to western Europe, a third led from the Malay Peninsula through the Indonesian islands almost all the way to Australia, and a fourth connected Asia and North America at the Bering Strait.

Early human beings responded to the environmental changes of the Ice Ages in several ways. Some migrated to warmer places. Others found strategies for keeping warm, such as clothing and fire. Those who could not adapt died from starvation or exposure.

Human Culture

Clothing and fire had become part of the culture, or way of life, of prehistoric people. Culture also includes the knowledge a people have, the language they speak, the ways in which they eat and dress, their religious beliefs, and their achievements in art and music.

Toolmaking

One of the earliest aspects of culture that people formed was the use of tools. At first they dug roots and tubers out of the ground with wooden digging sticks. Later, they made crude tools of stone, which enabled them to skin small animals and cut off pieces of meat. Improving their technology—the skills and useful knowledge available to them for collecting material and making the objects necessary for survival—early people began to create specialized tools, such as food choppers, skin scrapers, and spear points.

The Stone Age

The use of stone tools by early people led historians to apply the name Stone Age to the period before writing became established. Scholars divided the Stone Age into three shorter periods, depending on differences in toolmaking techniques. The earliest period, the Paleolithic (PAY•lee •uh•LIH•thihk) or Old Stone Age, began about 2.5 million years ago with the first toolmaking by *Homo habilis* and lasted until about 12,000 B.C. The Mesolithic (MEH•zuh•LIH•thihk) period or Middle Stone Age is usually dated from 12,000 B.C. to about 8000 B.C. The Neolithic (NEE•uh•LIH•thihk) period or New Stone Age lasted from about 8000 B.C. to 5000 B.C.

Paleolithic Hunter-Gatherers

Archaeologists as yet do not know a great deal about the culture of the early humans called *Homo habilis* and *Homo erectus*. Their knowledge, however, widens as new discoveries are made.

Homo Habilis

Homo habilis lived during the first quarter of the Paleolithic period. It seems probable, however, that these prehistoric people are the oldest hominids known to manufacture tools. They lived in Africa from about 2.5 million to 1.5 million years ago, alongside *Australopithecus*. Their larger brains indicate that they were more physically and mentally advanced. Much of the evidence for *Homo habilis* has come from research by **Louis and Mary Leakey**, and later their son Richard, at **Olduvai** (OHL•duh•VY) **Gorge** in Tanzania and other sites in the eastern part of Africa.

Homo Erectus

Scientists have gathered much more information about *Homo erectus* than about *Homo habilis*. *Homo erectus* first appeared in Africa and lived from 1.8 million years ago to about 30,000 years ago. Their living areas covered a variety of environments from woodlands and grasslands in Africa to forests and plains in Europe and Asia.

Homo erectus at first were mostly food gatherers. Scientists think the females gathered fruits, nuts, and seeds, and the males scavenged for meat—either searching for an animal that had died of natural causes or yelling and waving their arms to frighten carnivores away from a kill. By about 500,000 years ago, however, the males had become hunters, using spears and clubs to kill such small prey as deer, pigs, and rabbits. The females, whose movements were restricted by the constant demands of child care, continued to forage close to home for vegetable food.

Meanwhile, these early humans also had learned how to make fire. This discovery allowed them to keep warm, cook food, and scare away threatening animals. It also enabled them to live in caves. Before, they had protected themselves from the weather by digging shallow pits and covering these with branches. Now, they could drive animals out of caves and use the caves themselves.

Homo erectus by this time not only had fire but also made clothing. Initially they simply wrapped themselves in animal skins, having first scraped hair and tissue off the inner side of the skins. Later, they laced the skins together with strips of leather.

Migrations

Scientists disagree on when prehistoric peoples left Africa and moved to other parts of the world. Some experts believe that *Homo habilis* may have been the earliest to migrate to Europe and Asia; however, clear evidence to support this view is lacking. Scientists do know, however, that *Homo erectus* migrated from their native Africa to Europe and Asia. Skeletal remains found in Java have led anthropologists to conclude that *Homo erectus* reached the Indonesian islands about 1.6 to 1.8 million years ago. *Homo erectus* was clearly well established in China by 460,000 years ago, and the earliest skeletal traces in Europe may also date back around 400,000 years.

Language

To communicate, *Homo erectus* may have used little more than gestures and grunts. By 50,000 B.C., however, prehistoric peoples had developed speech. Language was one of humanity's greatest achievements. It enabled individuals to work with one another—to organize a hunting group, for example, or to give specific instructions about where to find a spring of fresh water. It allowed individuals to exchange ideas, such as how the world began or what caused animals to migrate across the plains. Individuals could sit around a hearth fire, eat together, and talk about the day's events. They could talk about the best way to fell a tree or build a shelter. Perhaps most significantly, spoken language made it possible for the older generation to pass its culture on to the younger generation, enabling new generations to build upon the knowledge of the past.

SECTION I REVIEW

Recall

1. **Define** prehistory, hominid, anthropologist, paleontologist, archaeologist, artifacts, radiocarbon dating, nomad, culture, technology.
2. **Identify** Gen Suwa, Tim D. White, Donald C. Johanson, Louis Leakey, Mary Leakey.
3. **Locate** each of these prehistoric sites and explain their importance: Aramis, Hadar, Olduvai Gorge.

Critical Thinking

4. **Making Comparisons** Compare and contrast the culture of *Homo habilis* and *Homo erectus*. Consider housing, technology, and mobility.

Understanding Themes

5. **Movement** How did changes in climate affect the migration of early peoples from one part of the world to another?

c. 100,000 B.C. Neanderthals spread from Africa into Europe and Asia.

c. 50,000 B.C. Modern humans originate in Africa.

c. 15,000 B.C. World population reaches about 2 million.

Section 2

The Appearance of *Homo Sapiens*

Setting the Scene

▶ **Terms to Define**
   domesticate, deity

▶ **People to Meet**
   Neanderthals, Cro-Magnons

▶ **Places to Locate**
   Neander Valley, Lascaux, Vallon-Pont-d'Arc, Jericho, Çatal Hüyük

Find Out What were the achievements of the earliest humans?

The Storyteller

The first sign of animal domestication we have discovered, at some of the earliest human settlements, is not of something that pulled a plow, or was eaten; it is the dog. This creature, which willingly chooses a human as the leader of its life-long pack, was humankind's first friend, it seems, as well as its best. Certain species began to thrive under human care; and humans rearranged their lives to care for the animals that now came to depend on them.

—adapted from *Women's Work: The First 20,000 Years,* Elizabeth Wayland Barber, 1994

Paleolithic scraper

Homo erectus discovered, used, and improved upon numerous aspects of culture that are basic to present-day life. These accomplishments occurred extremely slowly, however, taking place over many thousands of years. When *Homo sapiens,* the modern human species, appeared, cultural changes began occurring with much greater frequency and took on greater sophistication. In 1995 archaeologists uncovered in the Democratic Republic of the Congo, a number of 80,000-year-old barbed points and blades. This find indicates that humans made the first sophisticated tools in Africa and at a much earlier date than had been believed.

The Neanderthals

Evidence of early *Homo sapiens* dates back about 200,000 years. The first *Homo sapiens* probably were the **Neanderthals** (nee•AN•duhr•TAWLZ). Anthropologists named them after the **Neander Valley** in Germany where their remains were first discovered in the A.D. 1850s. Fossil evidence indicates that Neanderthal people may have originated in Africa and began spreading into Europe and Asia about 100,000 years ago.

Neanderthals stood about 5.5 feet (1.7 meters) tall. Their brains were slightly larger than those of modern human beings, and their bodies were stocky, with thick bones and very muscular necks and shoulders. Some scientists today believe that these distinctive physical characteristics enabled Neanderthals to adapt to colder climates.

Technological Skills

Like their predecessors, Neanderthals were nomadic hunter-gatherers who used fire for warmth and for cooking their food, but their toolmaking ability was more sophisticated than that of *Homo erectus*. Neanderthals skillfully crafted stone knives, spear points, and bone tools. Hide-cleaning and food-preparing tools were made of flakes struck from flint or whatever other kind of stone was available. The flakes were delicately shaped by chipping away small pieces from one or more edges of the stone.

Ways of Life

Most Neanderthals lived in small groups of 35 to 50 people. Because they were nomads, Neanderthals did not live in permanent homes. In good weather or warm climates, they lived in open-air camps along the shores of lakes or rivers. In several places, archaeologists have found the remains of Neanderthal shelters built of branches and animal skins. In colder climates, Neanderthals lived together in caves or under the overhangs of cliffs. Heavy clothing made from animal skins must have been worn to fight off the cold.

Culture and Beliefs

The Neanderthals were advanced culturally. They cared for their sick and aged, and may have been the first to practice medicine. A number of Neanderthal fossils show signs of serious injuries that had completely healed before death. Neanderthals also apparently had a belief in life after death. They covered the bodies of their dead with flowers and buried them in shallow graves with food, tools, and weapons.

Homo Sapiens Sapiens

Most scientists believe that modern humans, or *Homo sapiens sapiens*, originated in Africa about 50,000 years ago. Within 20,000 years, this new group dominated almost every continent in the world, including Australia and North America and South America. Many scientists believe that as *Homo sapiens sapiens* appeared in various places, they may have come into contact with Neanderthals and even *Homo erectus*. With the extinction of the Neanderthals and *Homo erectus*, *Homo sapiens sapiens* became the only hominids left on Earth.

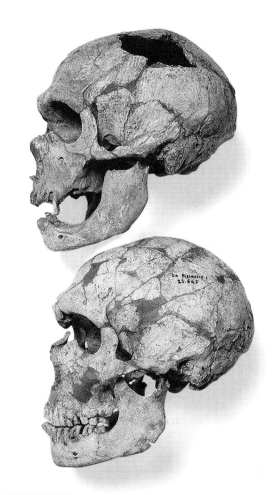

Visualizing History *Homo neanderthalensis* fossil skulls found in caves in France resemble the original fossil skull from the Neander Valley in Germany. Neanderthals were short, sturdy hunter-gatherers. *How did Neanderthals adapt to cold weather?*

The Cro-Magnons

The earliest *Homo sapiens sapiens* in Europe are called **Cro-Magnons**, after the rock shelter in France where their remains were first found in the A.D. 1860s. Since then, a wealth of Cro-Magnon remains have been found in other parts of Europe and in eastern and central Asia. Similar forms of modern humans have been discovered in Russia, China, Southeast Asia, and all over Africa.

The Cro-Magnons were taller but less robust than the Neanderthals. They brought with them improved technology and a more sophisticated

Footnotes to History

The First Razors
Archaeologists have unearthed evidence that prehistoric men were shaving as early as 18,000 B.C. Some Cro-Magnon cave paintings portray beardless men, and early Cro-Magnon grave sites contain sharpened shells that were the first razors. Later, people hammered razors out of bronze, and eventually, out of iron.

culture. Although they still made their living by hunting and gathering, their methods of food gathering were more efficient, and their hunting techniques were more effective than those of earlier groups.

Cro-Magnon Technology

The many advances the Cro-Magnons made in their toolmaking technology transformed human life. Their blades were thinner and had sharper cutting edges than those of the Neanderthals. The Cro-Magnons used bone, antler, and ivory to make new kinds of tools—hammers, hoes, and pincers. Soon they were fishing with bone fishhooks and using bone needles to sew fitted leather clothes.

With the invention of the stone ax, Cro-Magnons could chop down trees and shape them into canoes. Soon they were traveling down rivers and along seacoasts. They may have used rafts to cross 50 miles (80 km) of sea to reach Australia.

Cro-Magnon hunters also invented long-distance weapons—the spear-thrower and the bow and arrow. Now they could hunt several animals at once and larger animals, too, such as woolly mammoths and bison. The food supply increased and with it the number of people on Earth. Anthropologists estimate that by 15,000 B.C., the world population of human beings stood at a little more than 2 million.

Social Life

The Cro-Magnons' increased food supply had political and social consequences as well. Because it was not possible for a lone band of Cro-Magnons to carry out a big-game hunt, it became necessary for four or five unrelated bands to cooperate, often for weeks at a time. The cooperating bands probably needed formal rules in order to get along, giving rise in turn to leaders who devised and enforced the rules. The evidence for Cro-Magnon leaders consists of high-status burials. Archaeologists have discovered certain Cro-Magnons buried with ivory daggers, amber beads, and other signs of high rank.

Cro-Magnons at first lived in a variety of temporary structures. Some lived inside cave

Images *of the* Times

Early Human Technology

Although they are difficult to date precisely, ancient artifacts provide important clues to early human life.

Discovered in France, this bison licking its flank was carved from bone during the Mesolithic period–12,000–8000 B.C.

A Paleolithic scraper, c. 70,000–50,000 B.C., flaked by repeated blows, helped ancient people dig up roots, shape wood, and cut meat.

entrances, while others built huts in forested areas. As better hunting methods developed, Cro-Magnons built more permanent homes. Long houses holding many families were made of stone blocks. There is archaeological evidence that communities of 30 to 100 people lived together.

Cave Paintings

To their technological advances, the Cro-Magnons added accomplished artistry. They created cave paintings like those found at **Lascaux** (la •SKOH) and **Vallon-Pont-d'Arc** (vah•YOHN pohn DAHRK), both in France, as well as those at numerous other cave sites in Spain and Africa. Researchers so far can only speculate on the purpose behind the mysterious wall images. Perhaps the hunting scenes were educational, designed to teach young hunters how to recognize prey. On the other hand, the Cro-Magnon painters may have been reaching out to the spiritual world, creating images meant to have mystical powers that would help the hunters.

Archaeologists have discovered some Cro-Magnon figures sculpted from clay or carved from reindeer antlers. They have also found figures of ivory and bone decorated with animal drawings and abstract designs. Some of these artifacts may well have been used in magic rituals.

The Neolithic Revolution

During the Neolithic period and immediately after, humanity made one of its greatest cultural advances. New environments had developed with the end of the last Ice Age, and forests and grasslands appeared in many areas. Over some 5,000 years, people gradually shifted from gathering and hunting food to producing food. Because new agricultural methods led to tremendous changes in peoples' lifestyles, this period is usually called the Neolithic Revolution.

Sumerian cuneiform laid the foundation of writing about 3000 B.C.

REFLECTING ON THE TIMES

1. What clue to early human life does the bison licking its flank provide?
2. How did people store information about the past before writing began?

In a sense, the Mesolithic period was a forerunner of the Neolithic Revolution. Most of the cultural changes of the Mesolithic period came in methods of obtaining food. People domesticated, or tamed for human purposes, the dog and used it to help them hunt small game. They also domesticated the goat to use for meat and milk. Early farmers invented the sickle for cutting wild grains so that they could eat the seeds. Pottery, made from sun-hardened clay, was far more effective for carrying and storing food and water than the pouches of animal skin people had used previously.

The Dawn of Agriculture

The Neolithic Revolution not only took place slowly, but also began at different times in different parts of the world. Archaeologists have found evidence of agriculture in the Middle East dating as far back as 8000 B.C. In contrast, China and the Americas did not have agriculture until between 5000 B.C. and 4000 B.C.

The crops that Neolithic people domesticated varied from place to place, depending on the varieties of wild plants and on the crops best adapted to the region's climate—wheat and barley in the Middle East, rice in Southeast Asia, and corn in the Americas. Farmers in Africa cultivated bananas and yams, and farmers in South America grew potatoes. Neolithic people also domesticated animals. They used cattle, pigs, and sheep for meat and sometimes milk. Chickens provided eggs as well as meat.

Farming in many ways made life easier. It brought a steady food supply and enabled people to stay longer in one place. However, farmers had to work harder and longer than earlier hunters and gatherers.

Early Humans				
	Homo Habilis	**Homo Erectus**	**Homo Sapiens**	
Years B.C.	**2.5–1.5 million**	**1.8 million–30,000**	**200,000–35,000**	**40,000–8,000**
			Neanderthal	**Cro-Magnon**
TECHNOLOGICAL INNOVATIONS	• Crude stone tools	• Hand axes and other flaked stone tools • Caves used and pits dug • Clothing of animal skins • Fire controlled for warmth, protection, and cooking	• Spear points and hide scrapers • Shelters built or caves improved • Skins laced for clothing	• Knives, chisel, spear-thrower, bow and arrow • Bone tools: needle, fish hook, harpoon • Fish nets, canoes • Sewed leather clothing • Sun-hardened pottery
SOCIAL BEHAVIORS	• Limited speech • Food gathering and scavenging	• Beginnings of language • Nomadic bands • Hunting-gathering	• Planned burials of dead • Care for disabled members of the community	• Cooperative big-game hunts • Status burials for leaders • Possible magic rituals with cave painting and carved, sculpted artifacts

Chart Study The category "Technological Innovations" describes items found in archaeological digs and dated to a specific period. Interpretation of likely prehistoric social behaviors, however, depends mostly on inferences made by archaeologists and anthropologists.

What evidence do researchers have to support the theory that the social behaviors listed above really existed?

The First Villages

Now that they could produce food, many more people survived. Anthropologists estimate that by 4000 B.C. the world population had risen to 90 million. Once they had agriculture, people could also settle in communities instead of wandering as nomads. Soon, agricultural villages of about 200 or so inhabitants began to develop where soil was fertile and water abundant. Archaeologists date one of the earliest such villages—**Jericho**, in the modern West Bank—back to 8000 B.C. Another village, **Çatal Hüyük** (CHAH•tuhl hoo• YOOK), in present-day Turkey, dates from 7000 to 6300 B.C.

Çatal Hüyük is one of the largest Neolithic villages that archaeologists have so far discovered. Its people built rectangular, flat-roofed houses of mud bricks placed in wooden frames. Houses of several related families made up a compound with shared walls. People had to walk across roofs. The villagers of Çatal Hüyük also painted the interior walls of their windowless houses with vivid scenes of hunting and other activities.

Technological Advances

Neolithic farmers eventually made their agricultural work easier and more productive by inventing the plow and by training oxen to pull it. They also learned how to fertilize their fields with ashes, fish, and manure.

The relatively steady food supply quickened the pace of technological advance. Neolithic villagers invented the loom and began weaving textiles of linen and wool. They invented the wheel and used it for transportation. They found a way to bake clay bricks for construction. They learned how to hammer the metals copper, lead, and gold to make jewelry and weapons. In 1991, for example, the frozen body of a late Neolithic Age man was discovered in the Italian Alps. The 5,000-year-old "Iceman" wore well-made fur and leather clothing and shoes stuffed with grass. He carried a wooden backpack, a copper ax, a bow, and arrows.

The agricultural way of life led to many other changes. People created calendars to measure the seasons and determine when to plant crops. Because their food supply depended on land ownership, people now cared about such matters as boundary lines and rules of inheritance. Warfare probably came into being as villages competed for land and water.

Neolithic people also believed in many deities, or gods and goddesses. The spirits that supposedly surrounded them throughout nature were transformed into humanlike gods and goddesses with the power to help or hurt people. The people of Çatal Hüyük, for example, set up shrines at which they offered gifts in honor of their deities.

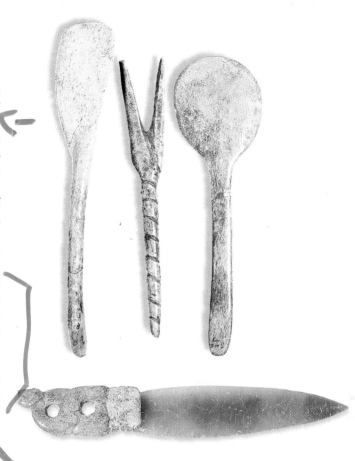

Visualizing History This Neolithic flint knife and these cooking utensils are from Çatal Hüyük. *What evidence tends to show that these people enjoyed art?*

SECTION 2 REVIEW

Recall
1. **Define** domesticate, deity.
2. **Identify** Neanderthals, Cro-Magnons, Neolithic Revolution.
3. **List** the innovations made during the Neolithic period.

Critical Thinking
4. **Evaluating Information** Does the use of agriculture by Neolithic peoples deserve to be called a revolution? Give reasons.

Understanding Themes
5. **Innovation** Discuss how technological developments affected the food supplies of early peoples in various parts of the world.

c. 10,000 B.C.
Last Ice Age ends.

c. 8000 B.C.
Agriculture begins
in various places.

c. 3500 B.C.
Cities develop
along the Tigris
and Euphrates Rivers.

c. 1500 B.C.
First urban
communities in
East Asia appear.

Section 3

Emergence of Civilization

Setting the Scene

▶ **Terms to Define**
civilization, economy, artisan, cultural
diffusion, myth

▶ **People to Meet**
the Sumerians

▶ **Places to Locate**
Nile, Tigris-Euphrates, Indus, and Huang
River valleys

 **Find Out** What economic, political, and social
changes resulted from the rise of cities?

The Storyteller

*Archaeological evidence leaves little doubt
that women played key roles in every aspect of life
in Old Europe. "In the temple workshops …
females made and decorated quantities of various
pots appropriate to different rites. Next to
the altar of the temple stood a vertical loom on which were probably
woven the sacred garments…. The
most sophisticated creations of Old
Europe—the most exquisite vases,
sculptures, etc. now extant—were
women's work."*

—from *The Early
Civilizations of Europe*,
(Monograph for Indo-
European Studies,
UCLA, 1980), Marija
Gimbutas

Mohenjo-Daro mother goddess

Over thousands of years, some of the
early farming villages evolved slowly
into complex societies, known as
civilizations. The people of a civilization lived in a
highly organized society with an advanced knowledge of farming, trade, government, art, and science. The word *civilization* comes from the Latin
word *civitas*, meaning "city," and most historians
equate the rise of civilizations with the rise of cities.
Because most city dwellers learned the art of writing, the development of cities also marks the beginning of history.

River Valley Civilizations

As with agriculture, cities formed at different
times in different parts of the world. Many of the
earliest civilizations, however, had one thing in
common: They rose from farming settlements in
river valleys like that of the **Nile** River in northeastern Africa. The earliest cities that archaeologists
have uncovered so far lie in the valley of the **Tigris
and Euphrates** (yoo•FRAYT•eez) Rivers in present-
day Iraq and date back to about 3500 B.C. Cities
arose in the **Indus** River valley in South Asia some
1,000 years later. The first urban communities in
East Asia appeared about 1500 B.C. in the **Huang
He** (HWONG HUH) valley. By about 1000 B.C.
cities were flourishing in Europe and in the
Americas, and by 750 B.C. in East Africa.

Early river valley civilizations also shared several other basic features. People's labor was specialized, with different men and women doing different jobs. The civilization depended on advanced
technology, such as metalworking skills. Each civilization always had some form of government to
coordinate large-scale cooperative efforts such as
building irrigation systems. The people in each

Behind high baked-brick walls the people of the ancient city of Mohenjo-Daro, near the Indus River in Pakistan, used four-wheeled carts to carry grain to a large granary. *What was the value of surplus food to the development of a civilization?*

civilization also shared a complex system of values and beliefs.

Not all societies formed civilizations, however. Some people continued to live in small agricultural villages, while others lived by hunting and gathering. Some nomadic people built a specialized culture that relied on moving herds of domesticated animals in search of good pasture.

The Economy of a Civilization

The ways in which people use their environment to meet their material needs is known as an economy. The economy of early civilizations depended on their farmers' growing surplus food. With extra food, fewer men and women had to farm and more could earn their living in other ways.

First Irrigation Systems

A major reason that farmers could produce surpluses of grain crops was that early civilizations built massive irrigation systems. Neolithic farmers had relied at first on rainfall to water their crops. Later, farmers transported water to grow the crops by digging ditches from a nearby river to their fields. Then they began building small canals and simple reservoirs.

Farmers also built earthen dikes and dams to control flooding in their valley by the river itself. They could now count on a reasonably steady flow of water and prevent destructive flooding.

Specialization of Labor

As men and women continued to specialize in ways of earning a living, artisans—workers skilled in a craft—became increasingly productive and creative. The longer they worked at one task, such as producing storage vessels, the more they learned about how to handle available materials, such as different types of clay. Gradually they turned out larger quantities of goods and improved the quality of their products.

Jewelry, eating utensils, weapons, and other goods were made by hammering copper, lead, and gold. Later, metalworkers in the early civilizations learned to make alloys, or mixtures of metals. The most important alloy was bronze, a reddish-brown metal made by mixing melted copper and tin. Historians refer to the period that followed the Stone Age as the Bronze Age, when bronze replaced flint and stone as the chief material for weapons and tools.

Bronze, harder than either copper or tin alone, took a sharper cutting edge. Artisans also found it much easier to cast bronze, or shape the liquid metal by pouring it into a mold to harden. Because the copper- and tin-containing ores needed to make bronze were scarce, however, the metal was expensive and therefore used only by kings, priests, and soldiers.

Long-Distance Trade

The search for new sources of copper and tin is an example of the long-distance trade that accompanied the rise of early civilizations. At first farmers and artisans traded within their own communities. They eventually began traveling to nearby areas to exchange goods. After a while merchants, a specialized class of traders, began to handle trade, and expeditions soon were covering longer routes.

Some long-distance trade moved overland by means of animal caravans. Some goods were transported by water. People made rafts and boats for travel on rivers. After a time, people learned how to harness the force of the wind, and rivers and seacoasts became filled with sailing ships.

Along with goods, ideas were actively shared. This exchange of goods and ideas when cultures come in contact is known as cultural diffusion. Although early civilizations developed many similar ideas independently, other ideas arose in a few areas and then spread throughout the world by cultural diffusion. When ancient peoples learned about the technology and ideas of different civilizations, the new knowledge stimulated them to improve their own skills and way of life.

The Rise of Cities

Civilizations grew both more prosperous and more complex. Early cities had from 5,000 to 30,000 residents. A population of this size could not function in the same way that a Neolithic village of 200 inhabitants had.

Planning and Leadership

Ancient cities faced several problems unknown in the Neolithic period. Because city residents depended on farmers for their food, they had to make certain that farmers regularly brought their surplus food to city markets. At the same time, farmers could not build dams, dig irrigation ditches, and maintain reservoirs on their own. As civilizations prospered, they drew the envy of nomadic groups, who would repeatedly raid and pillage farms and attack caravans. In short, the first cities needed a way of supervising and protecting agriculture and trade.

The early city dwellers found two solutions to these problems. First, ancient cities organized a group of government officials whose job it was to oversee the collection, storage, and distribution of farming surpluses. These officials also organized and directed the labor force needed for large-scale construction projects, such as irrigation systems and public buildings. Second, ancient cities hired professional soldiers to guard their territory and trade routes.

Government leaders, military officials, and priests belonged to a ruling class often led by a king, although women also held positions of authority. The ruling class justified its power by means of religion. According to ancient beliefs, the land produced food only if the gods and goddesses looked on the people with favor. One of the king's main functions, therefore, was to assist priests in carrying out religious ceremonies to ensure an abundant harvest. The first kings were probably elected, but in time they inherited their positions.

Levels of Social Standing

Archaeological evidence for the position of the ruling class can be found both in the treasures with which they were buried and in the physical layout of the ancient cities. At the city's center was an area that held the most imposing religious and government buildings. Nearby stood the residences of the ruling class. Next to these came the houses of the merchants. Farther out, the shops and dwellings of specific groups of artisans—such as weavers or smiths—were established in special streets or quarters. Farmers, as well as sailors and fishers, lived on the city's outskirts. Archaeological evidence suggests too that slaves, who were probably captured in battle, lived in many parts of the city.

Invention of Writing

Many archaeologists think that writing originated with the records that priests kept of the wheat, cloth, livestock, and other items they received as religious offerings. At first the priests used marks and pictures, called pictograms, to represent products. After a time they used the marks and pictures to represent abstract ideas and, later still, to represent sounds. Priestly records listed the individual men and women who were heads of households, landowners, and merchants. Soon the priests were also recording such information as the king's battle victories, along with legal codes, medical texts, and observations of the stars.

Systems of Values

Among the materials recorded by the priesthoods in early civilizations were myths, traditional stories explaining how the world was formed, how people came into being, and what they owed their creator. The priests of **the Sumerians** in the Tigris-Euphrates River valley wrote their myth of creation, for example, on seven clay tablets.

According to the Sumerian story, before creation there were two gods, Apsu the First Father and Tiamat the First Mother. They married and had many children. "But each generation of gods grew taller than its parents … [and] the younger gods could do things their parents had never tried to do." Eventually Apsu's great-grandson Ea made a magic spell and killed Apsu. Ea's son Marduk killed Tiamat. Then:

> Marduk turned again to the body of
>   Tiamat.
> He slit her body like a shellfish into two parts.
> Half he raised on high and set it up as sky.…
> He marked the places for the stars.…
> He planned the days and nights, the months
>   and years.
> From the lower half of Tiamat's body, Marduk
>   made the earth.
> Her bones became its rocks.
> Her blood its rivers and oceans.…
> 'We need creatures to serve us,' he said.
> 'I will create man and woman who must
>   learn to plow land to plant, and make the
>   earth bring forth food and drink for us.
> I will make them of clay.'…
>
> —"Enuma Elish," Sumerian account
> of creation from *The Seven Tablets
> of Creation*, date unknown

After relating how the people drained marshes

Geography

Migrations Then and Now

One of the land bridges that formed during the Ice Ages joined Siberia, the easternmost part of Asia, with Alaska, the westernmost part of the Americas. Modern historians have named this land bridge Beringia, after the shallow Bering Strait that covers it today.

Approximately 40,000 years ago, groups of Cro-Magnons may have crossed Beringia from Asia to the Americas. According to some anthropologists, these groups were nomadic hunting bands in search of migrating herds of animals. We do not know whether the migrants crossed all at once or in successive waves.

From the north the migrants gradually moved south into new territory. Anthropologists estimate that their journey all the way to the southernmost tip of South America took about 600 generations. This equals a rate of migration of about 18 miles (29 kilometers) per generation, over 18,000 years.

Today, the availability of fast, safe, and mechanized transportation—by air and by water—makes migration easier and quicker from one place to another. As in the past, war, persecution, and disasters—such as famines and epidemics—have forced people to flee their homelands. At the same time, people have also been attracted to new places by economic opportunity—a better job and higher standards of living.

Little Diomedes Island, Bering Strait

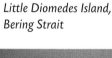

Linking Past and Present ACTIVITY

Research and write a brief essay comparing and contrasting prehistoric and modern migrations. Focus on methods and routes of travel, reasons for migrating, and the challenges faced in the new homeland.

Statue of the god Abu and his consort from the temple at Tel Asmar. *What god was worshiped by the ancient Sumerians as creator of the earth?*

for farmland, built walled cities, learned to make bricks, and built a great temple at the center of their biggest city, the myth continues:

> ❝ Daily they sang praises to Marduk,
>   supreme among the gods
> He who created the vast spaces and fashioned
>   earth and men;
> He who both creates and destroys; who is god
>   of storms and of light;
> He who directs justice; a refuge for those in
>   trouble;
> From whom no evil doer can escape;
> His wisdom is broad. His heart is wide. His
>   sympathy is warm. ❞

Creation myths have been found in every civilization. Because these myths vary from place to place, historians often examine them for evidence of a people's customs and values. For example, the seven Sumerian clay tablets could easily imply information about Sumer's values and beliefs. The clay tablets reveal that Marduk, though not the first god, had become—at the time the tablets were recorded—the leading one by supplanting the goddess Tiamat. The Sumerians seemed to believe too that evil should—and would—be punished. Apparently they also thought it was effective to praise and worship Marduk. Of course, the inferences an archaeologist can reasonably make from a myth are often limited and leave many unanswered questions.

SECTION 3 REVIEW

Recall
1. **Define** civilization, economy, artisan, cultural diffusion, myth.
2. **Identify** the Sumerians.
3. **Name** the four river valleys in which the world's earliest civilizations developed.

Where are these river valleys located?

Critical Thinking
4. **Synthesizing Information** Imagine that you rule a city in an early civilization. What instructions would you give to your government officials to

improve the living conditions of your people?

Understanding Themes
5. **Change** How did technological changes of the first civilizations improve toolmaking skills and the transportation of trade goods?

Understanding Map Projections

Greenland appears to be a larger landmass than Australia on some maps, yet Australia actually has a larger land area than Greenland. Have you ever wondered why?

Learning the Skill

When mapmakers attempt to transfer the three-dimensional surface of Earth to a flat surface, some inaccuracies occur. To accomplish this mapmakers use *projections*—an image produced when light from within the globe projects the globe's surface on a flat paper. These projections may stretch or shrink Earth's features, depending on the map's intended use.

Projections create two major kinds of maps. A *conformal map* shows land areas in their true shapes, while distorting their actual size. An *equal-area map* shows land areas in correct proportion to one another, but distorts shapes.

The map on this page is a *Cylindrical Projection (Mercator)*. Imagine wrapping a paper cylinder around the globe. A light from within projects the globe's surface on the paper. The resulting conformal projection makes Alaska appear larger than Mexico. Distortion is greatest near the Poles.

A *Conic Projection* is formed by placing a cone of paper over a lighted globe. This produces a cross between a conformal and an equal-area map. This projection is best to show areas in middle latitudes.

To understand map projections use the following steps:
- Compare the map to a globe.
- Determine the type of projection used.
- Identify the purpose of the projection.

Practicing the Skill

Turn to the map of the world in the Atlas. Compare the sizes and shapes of the features on this map to those on a globe. Based on this comparison, answer the following questions:

1. What is the map's projection?
2. How does the map distort Earth's features?
3. In what way does the map accurately present Earth's features?
4. Why did the mapmaker use this projection?

Applying the Skill

Compare the size of Antarctica as it appears on a map with Antarctica on a globe.

For More Practice

Turn to the Skill Practice in the Chapter Review on page 43 for more practice in understanding map projections.

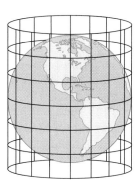

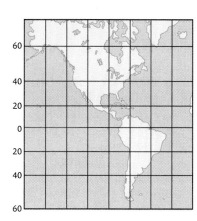

Cylindrical Projection (Mercator): This projection is accurate along the line where the cylinder touches the globe, with great distortions near the Poles.

Sygma

The Iceman

On September 19, 1991, Helmut and Erika Simon, a German couple hiking near the border between Austria and Italy, wandered slightly off the trail. Suddenly Erika Simon caught sight of a small head and pair of shoulders emerging from the ice. The Simons thought they had stumbled across a discarded doll. In fact, they had found the solitary prehistoric traveler now known around the world as the Iceman.

At first the Iceman was thought to be 4,000 years old—which would have made the discovery remarkable enough. Scientists later discovered that the Iceman was at least 5,000 years old! In comparison, Tutankhamen, Egypt's boy-king, was born some 2,000 years later.

The Iceman is the oldest body ever retrieved from an Alpine glacier; the next-oldest was only 400 years old. At 10,530 feet (3,210 m),

Overcome by fatigue and cold, a mountaineer (above) lies down to die high in the Alps. Some 5,000 years later, the discovery of his well-preserved body, along with clothes and a copper ax, offers startling clues about how humans greeted the metal age in Europe.

The Iceman (top) emerges from under a melting glacier.

Greg Harlin/Wood Ronsaville Harlin, Inc.

Sygma

NGS Cartographic Division

0 5 FEET
NGS CARTOGRAPHIC DIVISION

DAGGER AND SHEATH

ICEMAN

GRASS CAPE FRAGMENT

QUIVER

BIRCH-BARK CONTAINER

AX

BOW

BACKPACK FRAME

AUSTRIA

SWITZ.

SITE ENLARGED

ITALY

the site where the Iceman lay is the highest elevation in Europe in which prehistoric human remains have been found. Not even traces of a campfire have ever been discovered at that height.

The body of the Iceman was preserved through sheer luck. Shortly after he died, the rocky hollow where he lay filled with snow. For thousands of years a glacier covered this pocket of snow, only a few yards over the Iceman's head. More commonly, a body caught in a glacier would be crushed and torn by the movement of the ice. Instead, the Iceman was naturally mummified.

In the four days following the discovery, many well-meaning hikers and officials tried to free the Iceman from the glacier. They took turns hacking and prodding around the body with ice axes and ski poles. Unfortunately, they damaged the Iceman and the artifacts found with him—in ways that 5,000 years of glaciation had not. One of the "rescuers" seized a stick to dig with, breaking it in the process; the stick turned out to be part of the hazel-wood-and-larch frame of the Iceman's backpack, a type of ancient artifact never seen before. Workers also snapped off the top

The local coroner (above) and an assistant remove the corpse from his icy grave.

The Iceman was found at an elevation of 10,530 feet (3,210 m) on the Austrian-Italian border. His tools and backpack frame were located near his body.

end of the Iceman's six-foot-long bow. What remained of the Iceman's clothing was torn off, as were parts of his body, and an officer using a jackhammer left a gaping hole in the Iceman's hip. To be sure, none of the salvagers suspected how old the Iceman was.

Not until five days after the discovery did an archaeologist examine the Iceman's body. Basing his estimate on the style of the ax found with the body, the archaeologist guessed that the Iceman was 4,000 years old.

Once officials knew the Iceman's approximate age, a rigorous effort to stabilize his condition began. The mummy was placed in a freezer, where the temperature was kept at a constant 21°F (-6°C) and the humidity at 98 percent—conditions much the same as those of the ice in which he had lain. The Iceman was not removed from the freezer for more than 20 minutes at a time, and then only for the most important scientific research. Part of that research was carbon-dating the Iceman to verify how old he was. Further chemical analysis revealed that the blade of his ax was not bronze, but nearly pure copper. He was, in fact, unique: a mummy from the Copper Age, which lasted in central Europe roughly from 4000 to 2200 B.C. Two different laboratories concluded that he was 5,000 to 5,500 years old.

THE ICEMAN'S DOMAIN was the Alps, stretching from southeast France to the Swiss-German border, and from Austria to northern Italy. Five thousand years ago these mountains were a vast wilderness. In the Copper Age, hardy voyagers trekked these ranges, and the goods they traded traveled even farther. We know from his tools and clothes that the Iceman was one of these

Iceman's artifacts photographed by Kenneth Garrett

rugged mountaineers.

The first half of the Copper Age was an era of climatic warming, when humans penetrated higher than ever into the Alps. The tree line climbed during the warming, game followed the forests, and hunters followed the game. Meadows above the tree line offered the best pastures for sheep, goats, and cattle and contained great green veins of a newly valued metal—which today we call copper. Copper changed the Alpine world forever, leading to the development of major trade routes between isolated valleys. Earlier, wealth was made through cattle or wheat. Copper was not only a form of portable wealth but also a stimulus for the development of specialized occupations. Men became smelters, axmakers, possibly even salesmen. The world's earliest known man-made copper objects—beads, pins,

◼ *A fragment of the Iceman's plaited-grass cape (above) was found next to his head.*

◼ *This stone disk threaded with a leather thong (inset, top right) may have been worn to protect against evil.*

◼ *The Iceman's copper ax is the oldest ever found in Europe with its bindings and handle intact (inset, bottom right).*

◼ *A fungus on a string may have been a first-aid kit (inset, above left).*

and awls—were made about 8000 B.C. in Turkey and Iran. There is evidence of copper mining in the Balkans by 5000 B.C. From there the technology spread west, reaching the Alps a thousand years later.

The work of many researchers over the past 30 years tells us much about life during the Copper Age. Excavations have yielded bones that indicate that by around 5000 B.C. Alpine people had domesticated five animals: dogs, which were originally more important for food than companionship, cattle, sheep, goats, and pigs. Horses and chickens were still unknown in the Alps. Villagers grew wheat and barley and made linen clothes from flax. They had only recently discovered how to milk a cow and how to make cheese and butter. Their sheep may have been used for meat but not yet for wool. Many staple foods of today were still unknown, including potatoes, onions, and oats.

EVENTUALLY, THE ICEMAN'S possessions may tell us more than his body will. Of those possessions, his copper ax may tell us most. Its yew-wood handle ends in a gnarled joint, where a notch holds the blade. Dark birch gum held the blade firmly in position beneath a tightly wrapped thong of rawhide. It is a ribbed ax, rather than the more primitive flat ax that archaeologists would have expected to find.

Researchers who reconstructed what remained of the Iceman's clothing observed that his garment had been skillfully stitched together with sinew. Cruder repairs had been made, probably by the Iceman himself on his travels. This led researchers to believe that the Iceman had been part of a community, although he was used to fending for himself. Also, tiny pieces of a wheat that grew only at low altitudes, and bits of charcoal from a variety of trees found throughout the Alps were discovered with the Iceman, indicating that he may have come from southern Tirol (in Austria).

Included among the Iceman's possessions were a stick with a tip of antler used to sharpen flint blades; a deerskin quiver that contained 14 arrows; and an unfinished bow. His small flint dagger was similar to those found at other Copper Age sites, but no one had ever seen the kind of delicately woven sheath that held the dagger.

Central Europe's oldest known plow is more than a thousand years younger than the Iceman. Yet Copper Age artists cut images of plows on rocks. Rows of furrows have been found preserved at a major Copper Age religious complex excavated in northwest Italy, though experts believe plowing was ritualistic rather than agricultural.

The Iceman also had tattoo-like marks that might imply something about his spiritual life. Located on normally hidden places—his lower back, behind his knee, and on his ankle—the marks were not for

Kenneth Garrett

The Iceman's head was reconstructed by John Gurche, an anthropologically trained artist. He first sculpted a replica of the skull by using computer images, X rays, and CT scans of the Iceman. Gurche then added clay to duplicate the Iceman's mummified face, complete with smashed nose and lip. Next, he added muscles and fatty tissue, nasal cartilage, and glass eyes. Finally he made a new model of the head with soft urethane, tinted to suggest wind-burned skin. He completed the replica of the Iceman's head by adding human hair.

show. Perhaps they were meant to confer supernatural power or protection. So might the pair of fungi he carried, each pierced by a leather thong. Archaeologists have never seen anything like this artifact from that period. The fungi contain chemical substances now known to be antibiotic. If the Iceman used them to counteract illness, perhaps they also seemed magical to him.

We may never know what drew the Iceman to the mountain pass where he died. Perhaps he was a shepherd, a trader, or an outcast. But, in the late 20th century, it is our good fortune to have the opportunity to learn from this ambassador of the Copper Age.

Historical Significance Prehistoric people created the basics of human culture—for example, tools, language, and religious belief. In time, increased food supplies and a diverse labor force led to the rise of cities and civilizations. In ancient times, cities enabled large numbers of people to live together, to cooperate with each other, and to carry out many cultural activities. Today the populations of many cities are more than 100 times that of these first cities. Modern cities serve as complex economic, cultural, and political centers in a world that has become, in many ways, one global civilization.

Using Key Terms

Write the key term that completes each sentence. Then write a sentence for each term not chosen.

a. technology
b. artisan
c. myth
d. civilization
e. nomad
f. economy
g. anthropologist
h. prehistory
i. radiocarbon dating
j. archaeologist
k. artifact
l. cultural diffusion
m. culture

1. The period of time before people developed writing is called _____.
2. Among the techniques used by scientists for determining the age of organic remains is _____.
3. Over thousands of years, some of the early agricultural villages evolved into highly complex societies, known as _____ .
4. The exchange of goods and ideas when different peoples come in contact is known as _____.
5. _____ includes the skills and useful knowledge available to people for collecting materials and making objects necessary for survival.

Technology Activity

Using a Word Processor Search the Internet for information on recent discoveries about early humans. Narrow your search by using words such as *archaeology* and *anthropology*. On your word processor, create a chart to organize your information. Include headings such as location, date of discovery, results of discovery, and approximate time period of remains. Then in a paragraph, theorize about what caused the extinction of early humans.

Using Your History Journal

Evaluate your journal account of being stranded on a deserted island. What skills and knowledge, known to early humans but not to you, may have helped you survive?

Reviewing Facts

1. **Geography** Name the four land bridges used by prehistoric people during the Ice Ages.
2. **Geography** Locate the two places in which Cro-Magnons seem to have originated before spreading into other parts of the world.
3. **Culture** Explain why language is one of humanity's greatest achievements.
4. **Technology** Describe how the invention of the spear-thrower and the bow and arrow changed the Cro-Magnons' food supply.
5. **Culture** Explain the social, economic, and geographic factors that led to the rise of the world's first civilizations.
6. **History** State the ways archaeologists, anthropologists, historians, and geographers analyze limited evidence.

Critical Thinking

1. **Apply** What do you think are the three basic characteristics of a civilization?
2. **Analyze** What were the major cultural features of each period in the Stone Age?
3. **Synthesize** How do you think the invention of the stone ax might have changed the culture of a people who lived along the banks of a navigable river?

4. **Evaluate** What do you think was the most valuable skill that prehistoric people learned during the Paleolithic period? What was the most valuable skill learned during the Neolithic period?

Geography in History

1. **Location** Refer to the map below. What is the relative location of Mesopotamia?
2. **Human/Environment Interaction** Where in this area would ancient peoples have likely begun farming?
3. **Human/Environment Interaction** Why did early farmers build dikes and dams in the river valleys where they raised their crops?

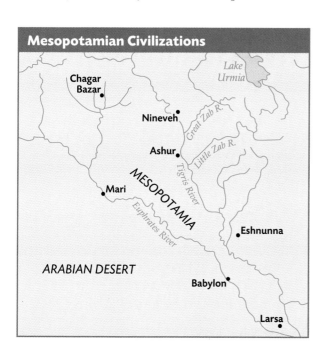

Mesopotamian Civilizations

Understanding Themes

1. **Movement** Describe the migrations of human beings from their places of origin to other parts of the world.
2. **Innovation** How did improvements in tool-making affect the way in which prehistoric people lived?
3. **Change** How did city life differ from village life in early civilizations?

Linking Past and Present

1. Many aspects of human culture are passed down from generation to generation. What cultural achievements of *Homo erectus*—from more than 200,000 years ago—do people still use today?
2. Government officials 5,000 years ago directed large-scale building projects, such as irrigation systems, and oversaw the collection, storage, and distribution of agricultural surpluses. Evaluate the effectiveness of their activities. How do government officials' activities in early civilizations compare with those of government officials in your community?

Skill Practice

Using a small tennis ball, place a dot on each side directly opposite one another to represent the North and South Poles. Cut paper strips in such a way that they could completely cover this "globe." (See the example below.)

1. Why are the cut strips shown on the example below wider at the middle than at each of the ends?
2. If the strips are laid side-by-side on a flat surface, what object do they resemble or what pattern do they form?
3. What does this show about the problem of creating an accurate map of a round object on a flat surface?
4. The earth is a sphere, but it is somewhat pear-shaped—not a perfect sphere. What additional problem does this create for the cartographer who wants to make a very accurate map of the world?

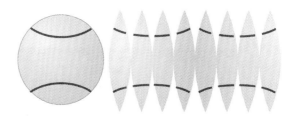

Chapter

2

4000–1000 B.C.
Early Civilizations

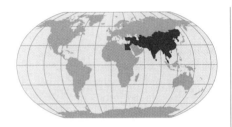

Chapter Themes

▶ **Relation to Environment** The Egyptians learn to control the floodwaters of the Nile River upon which their agriculture relies. *Section 1*

▶ **Cooperation** The peoples of the Fertile Crescent work together to build irrigation systems and cities. *Section 2*

▶ **Cultural Diffusion** Cities in early India develop close trading and cultural ties with the Fertile Crescent area. *Section 3*

▶ **Innovation** Early Chinese civilization excels in metal-casting skills. *Section 4*

𝒮toryteller

Under the blazing sun, a gigantic stone structure began to take shape on the desert sands of Egypt in northeastern Africa. A hundred thousand men toiled together, building a burial pyramid for Khufu, a king of Egypt about 2500 B.C. Gangs of laborers dragged huge blocks of limestone up winding ramps of dirt and brick to pile layer upon layer of stone. Farmers during the rest of the year, these laborers were compelled to work for the 3 or 4 months during which the annual flooding of the Nile River made farming impossible. It would take 20 years of their forced labor and more than 2 million blocks of stone before the Egyptians completed the massive pyramid. Today, the Great Pyramid built almost 5,000 years ago still stands at Giza, near the city of Cairo.

Historical Significance

In what ways were each of the early civilizations unique? How were they different? How did the river valley civilizations lay the foundations for the global civilization that we know today?

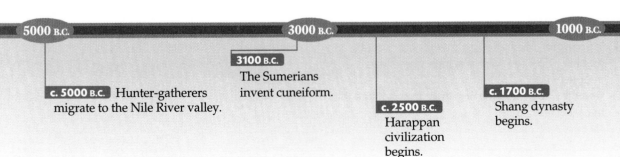

5000 B.C.

3000 B.C.

1000 B.C.

3100 B.C.
The Sumerians invent cuneiform.

c. 5000 B.C. Hunter-gatherers migrate to the Nile River valley.

c. 2500 B.C.
Harappan civilization begins.

c. 1700 B.C.
Shang dynasty begins.

History & Art Fowling scene from a tomb at Thebes along the Nile River, Egypt

3000 B.C.	2000 B.C.	1000 B.C.

c. 3000 B.C.
King Narmer unifies Egypt.

c. 1700s B.C.
The Hyksos invade Egypt.

c. 1480 B.C.
Queen Hatshepsut comes to power.

c. 945 B.C.
Egypt enters long period of foreign rule.

Section 1

The Nile Valley

Setting the Scene

▶ **Terms to Define**
monarchy, dynasty, theocracy, bureaucracy, pharaoh, empire, polytheism, hieroglyphics

▶ **People to Meet**
Narmer, Hatshepsut, Thutmose III, Akhenaton, Ramses II

▶ **Places to Locate**
Nile River valley, Memphis, Thebes

 Find Out Why was Egypt called the "gift of the Nile"?

The Storyteller

Live for today; the afterlife will come soon enough! The following message about the brief pleasures of this life demonstrates that Egyptian poets sometimes sang what their wealthy patrons liked to hear:

"The pharaohs, those ancient gods, rest now in their pyramids. The people who built houses; their walls have crumbled, as if they had never been! Listen! Put perfume upon your head, wear fine linen. Make holiday! … No one who has died has ever returned."

—freely adapted from "Song of the Harper," *Journal of Near Eastern Studies* 4, 1945, translated by Miriam Lichtheim

King Narmer

One of the world's first civilizations developed along the banks of the Nile River in northeastern Africa. The **Nile River valley**'s early inhabitants called their land *Kemet*, meaning "black land," after the dark soil. Later, the ancient Greeks would name the Nile area *Egypt*. Of the four early river valley civilizations, people today probably know the most about the ancient Egyptian civilization. People still marvel at its remains in modern Egypt—especially the enormous Sphinx, the wondrous pyramids, and the mummies buried in lavish tombs.

A River Valley and Its People

Running like a ribbon through great expanses of desert, the Nile River for thousands of years has shaped the lives of the Egyptians. The land of Egypt receives little rainfall, but its people have relied instead on the Nile's predictable yearly floods to bring them water.

At 4,160 miles (6,690 km) in length, the Nile River is the world's longest river. Several sources in the highlands of East Africa feed the Nile. The river then takes a northward route to the Mediterranean Sea. On its course through Egypt the Nile crosses six cataracts, or waterfalls. Because of the cataracts the Nile is not completely navigable until it reaches its last 650 miles (1,040 km). Before emptying into the Mediterranean, the Nile splits into many branches, forming a marshy, fan-shaped delta.

The Gifts of the River

The green Nile Valley contrasts sharply with the vast desert areas that stretch for hundreds of miles on either side. Rich black soil covers the river's banks and the Nile Delta. From late spring through summer, heavy tropical rains in central Africa and melting mountain snow in East Africa add to the Nile's volume. As a result the river overflows its banks and floods the land nearby. The floodwaters recede in late fall, leaving behind thick deposits of silt.

As early as 5000 B.C., nomadic hunter-gatherers of northeastern Africa began to settle by the Nile. They took up a farming life regulated by the river's seasonal rise and fall, growing cereal crops such as wheat and barley. The Nile also provided these Neolithic farmers with ducks and geese in its marshlands and fish in its waters. The early Egyptians harvested papyrus growing wild along the banks of the Nile, using the long, thin reeds to make rope, matting, sandals, baskets, and later on, sheets of paperlike writing material.

Uniting Egypt

Protected from foreign invasion by deserts and cataracts, the early farming villages by the Nile prospered. In time a few strong leaders united villages into small kingdoms, or monarchies, each under the unrestricted rule of its king. The weaker kingdoms eventually gave way to the stronger. By 4000 B.C. ancient Egypt consisted of two large kingdoms: Lower Egypt in the north, in the Nile Delta, and Upper Egypt in the south, in the Nile Valley.

Around 3000 B.C., **Narmer**, also known as Menes (MEE•neez), a king of Upper Egypt, gathered the forces of the south and led them north to invade and conquer Lower Egypt. Narmer set up the first government that ruled all of the country. He governed both Lower Egypt and Upper Egypt from a capital city he had built at **Memphis**, near the border of the two kingdoms.

Narmer's reign marked the beginning of the first Egyptian dynasty, or line of rulers from one family. From 3000 B.C. until 332 B.C., a series of 30 dynasties ruled Egypt. Historians have organized the dynasties into three great periods: the Old Kingdom, the Middle Kingdom, and the New Kingdom.

The Old Kingdom

The Old Kingdom lasted from about 2700 B.C. to 2200 B.C. During the first centuries of the unified kingdom, Upper Egypt and Lower Egypt kept their separate identities as kingdoms. In time, however, Egypt built a strong national government under its kings. It also developed the basic features of its civilization.

CONNECTIONS

Geography

Stemming the Flood

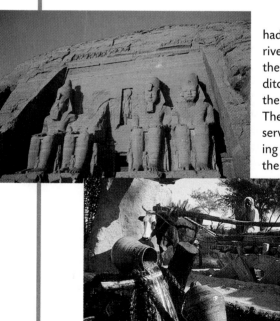

Ancient Egyptians had to take control of their river environment. Over the years farmers built ditches and canals to carry the floodwaters to basins. There the silt settled and served as fertilizer for planting crops. Machines, such as the shadoof, lifted water to cultivated land. Farmers eventually built dams and reservoirs, making year-round irrigation possible.

Built in the 1960s, the Aswan High Dam in southeastern Egypt trapped the waters of the Nile in a huge reservoir for later irrigation. When the rising waters of the Nile behind the dam threatened to destroy statues of Ramses II, engineers had to move the statues to higher ground. Today, the dam generates electrical power and protects against flooding. Because the dam prevents the Nile from flowing over the valley land, however, the floodwaters no longer deposit fertile silt annually. Farmers must add expensive chemical fertilizers to their fields. The absence of silt has also increased land erosion along the Nile.

Linking Past and Present ACTIVITY

Describe ancient ways of controlling rivers. How are the Nile and other rivers "tamed" today? Why might people object to some modern methods of river control?

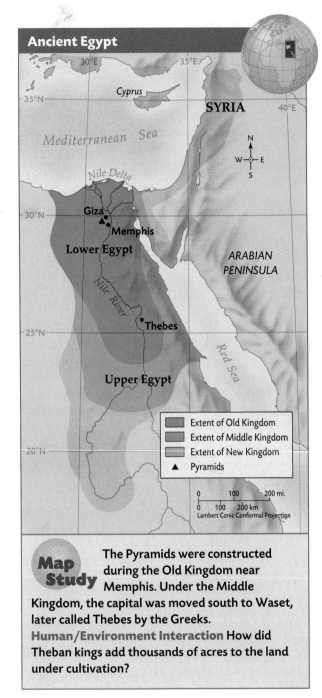

SYRIA

Mediterranean Sea

Cyprus

Nile Delta

Giza ▲
• Memphis

Lower Egypt

ARABIAN PENINSULA

Nile River

• Thebes

Red Sea

Upper Egypt

Extent of Old Kingdom
Extent of Middle Kingdom
Extent of New Kingdom
▲ Pyramids

0   100   200 mi.
0   100   200 km
Lambert Conic Conformal Projection

Map Study The Pyramids were constructed during the Old Kingdom near Memphis. Under the Middle Kingdom, the capital was moved south to Waset, later called Thebes by the Greeks.
Human/Environment Interaction How did Theban kings add thousands of acres to the land under cultivation?

The Egyptian Monarchy

The Egyptian people regarded their king as a god who ruled over all Egyptians. Such a government, in which the same person is both the religious leader and the political leader, is called a theocracy. As a god, the king performed many ritual acts believed to benefit the entire kingdom, such as cutting the first ripe grain to ensure a good harvest. As political leader, the king wielded absolute power, issuing commands regarded as the law of the land.

Unable to carry out all official duties himself,

the king delegated many responsibilities to a bureaucracy, a group of government officials headed by the king's vizier, or prime minister. Through the vizier and other bureaucrats the king controlled trade and collected taxes. He also indirectly supervised the building of dams, canals, and storehouses for grain—all crucial to survival for an agriculture-based civilization.

The Pyramids: A Lasting Legacy

To honor their god-kings and to provide them with an eternal place of rest, the Egyptians of the Old Kingdom built lasting monuments—the Pyramids. The Step Pyramid was built for King Djoser in the mid-2600s B.C. Overlooking Memphis, it was the first large, all-stone building in the world. Later the Egyptians constructed the three Pyramids at Giza, which stand today as testimony to Egyptian engineering skills. The Great Pyramid, the largest of the three, stands 481 feet (147 m) high. Long, narrow passageways lead to the king's burial chamber deep within the pyramid.

The Egyptians believed that a king's soul continued to guide the kingdom after death. Before entombing a dead king in his pyramid, they first preserved the king's body from decay by a procedure called embalming. Next they wrapped the dried, shrunken body—called a mummy—with long strips of linen and placed it in an elaborate coffin. Only then could the coffin lie in the burial chamber of the pyramid along with the king's clothing, weapons, furniture, and jewelry—personal possessions the king could enjoy in the afterlife.

The Middle Kingdom

Around 2200 B.C., the kings in Memphis began to lose their power as ambitious nobles fought each other for control of Egypt. The stable, ordered world of the Old Kingdom entered a period of upheaval and violence. Then, around 2050 B.C., a new dynasty reunited Egypt and moved the capital south to **Thebes**, a city in Upper Egypt. This new kingdom, known as the Middle Kingdom, would last until after 1800 B.C.

In time Theban kings became as powerful as the rulers of the Old Kingdom and brought unruly local governments under their control. They supported irrigation projects that added thousands of acres to the land already under cultivation. The Theban dynasty seized new territory for Egypt, setting up fortresses along the Nile to capture Nubia (part of modern Sudan) and launching military campaigns against Syria. Theban kings also ordered construction of a canal between the Nile and the Red Sea, and as a result, Egyptian ships traded along the coasts of the Arabian Peninsula and East Africa.

In the 1700s B.C., local leaders began to challenge the kings' power again, shattering the peace and prosperity of the Middle Kingdom. At the same time, Egypt also faced its first serious threat—invasion by the Hyksos (HIHK•SAHS), a people from western Asia. The Hyksos swept across the desert into Egypt with new tools for war—bronze weapons and horse-drawn chariots. So armed, they easily conquered the Egyptians, who fought on foot with copper and stone weapons. The Hyksos established a new dynasty that ruled for about 110 years.

The New Kingdom

The Egyptians despised their Hyksos masters. To overthrow Hyksos rule, the Egyptians learned to use Hyksos weapons and adopted the horse-drawn chariots of their conquerors. About 1600 B.C. Ahmose (ah•MOH•suh), an Egyptian prince, raised an army and drove the Hyksos out.

Visualizing History The Great Pyramid (left), built for King Khufu (Cheops), rises on the Nile River's west bank in northern Egypt. The smaller pyramid (right) was constructed for King Khafre (Chephren). *Why did the Egyptians build pyramids for their kings?*

Pharaohs Rule an Empire

Ahmose founded a new Egyptian dynasty—the first of the New Kingdom. He and his successors assumed the title pharaoh, an Egyptian word meaning "great house of the king." Ahmose devoted his energies to rebuilding Egypt, restoring abandoned temples, and reopening avenues of trade. The pharaohs who followed him, however, used large armies to realize their dreams of conquest. They pressed farther to the east and into the rest of Africa than had the kings of the Middle Kingdom.

Around 1480 B.C. Queen **Hatshepsut** (hat•SHEHP•soot) came to power in Egypt. She first ruled with her husband and then ruled on behalf of her stepson **Thutmose** (thoot•MOH•suh) **III**, who was too young to govern. Finally she had herself crowned pharaoh. Hatshepsut assumed all the royal trappings of power, including the false beard traditionally worn by Egyptian kings. Hatshepsut carried out an extensive building program, which included a great funeral temple and a tomb built

into the hills of what is now called the Valley of the Kings.

Thutmose III did reclaim the throne at Hatshepsut's death and soon after marched with a large army out of Egypt toward the northeast. He conquered Syria and pushed the Egyptian frontier to the northern part of the Euphrates River. In a short time, Thutmose III had conquered an empire for Egypt, bringing many territories under one ruler.

The Egyptian Empire grew rich from commerce and tribute from the conquered territories. The capital of Thebes, with its palaces, temples, and carved stone obelisks, reflected the wealth won by conquest. No longer isolated from other cultures, Egyptians benefited from cultural diffusion within their empire.

Akhenaton Founds a Religion

A new ruler, Amenhotep (AH•muhn•HOH•TEHP) IV, assumed power about 1370 B.C. Supported by his wife, Nefertiti, Amenhotep broke with the Egyptian tradition of worshiping many

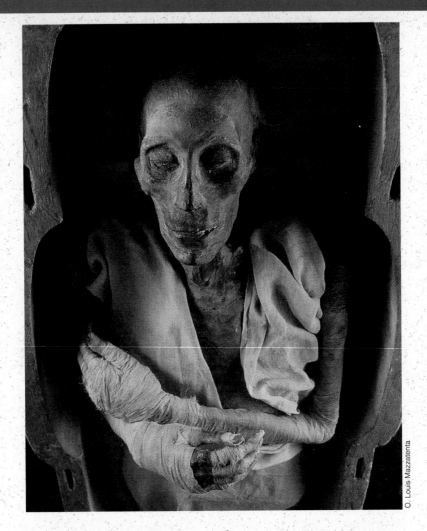

O. Louis Mazzatenta

Ramses the Great

O. Louis Mazzatenta

The mummy of Ramses the Great (above) lies in a display case on the second floor of the Egyptian Museum in Cairo. For many centuries before Ramses was brought to Cairo, the great pharaoh lay in his tomb near Luxor in a richly decorated coffin (left), embellished with symbols of Osiris, god of the afterlife. Ramses was nearly 90 when he died in 1237 B.C. His mummy has remained intact for the last 3,000 years.

Egyptians believed strongly in the afterlife and took great care to preserve the bodies of their pharaohs. Embalmers spent 70 days preparing the corpse of Ramses the Great. First they removed the internal organs and placed them in sacred jars. The heart was sealed in the body because Egyptians believed that it was the source of intellect as well as feeling and was needed in the afterlife. The brain, on the other hand, was thought to be useless, and embalmers drew it out through the nose and threw it away. The body was then dried with salt, washed, coated with preserving resins, and wrapped in hundreds of yards of linen. Recent medical tests show that Ramses suffered from arthritis, dental abscesses, gum disease, and poor circulation. ⊕

deities. He declared that Egyptians should worship only Aton, the sun-disk god, as the one supreme deity. Claiming to be Aton's equal, Amenhotep changed his royal name to **Akhenaton** (AHK •NAH•tuhn), which means "spirit of Aton." To stress the break with the past, Akhenaton moved the capital from Thebes to a new city in central Egypt dedicated to Aton.

These controversial changes had an unsettling effect on Egypt. Many of the common people rejected the worship of Aton, a god without human form, and continued to believe in many deities. The priests of the old religion resented their loss of power. At the same time, the army was unhappy about Egypt's loss of territories under Akhenaton's weak rule.

After Akhenaton's death, the priests restored the old religion. They also made Akhenaton's successor, Tutankhamen, move the capital back to Thebes. Shortly thereafter, the head of the Egyptian army overthrew the dynasty and created a new one.

Recovery and Decline

During the 1200s B.C., the pharaohs worked to restore Egypt's prestige. Under **Ramses II**, or Ramses the Great, the Egyptians fought their neighbors, the Hittites, for control of Syria. The conflict, however, led to a standoff at the Battle of Kadesh in 1285 B.C. Later the two empires concluded a treaty—unique for its time—pledging to keep permanent peace with each other and to fight as allies against any enemy.

In Egypt, Ramses, who ruled for 67 years, erected large statues of himself and built many temples and tombs. In A.D. 1995, archaeologists uncovered one of the most significant Egyptian discoveries: a vast underground tomb believed to be the burial place of 50 of Ramses' 52 sons.

After the death of Ramses II in 1237 B.C., Egypt weakened under the attacks of Mediterranean sea raiders, and entered a period of decline. Beginning in 945 B.C., it came under the rule of foreigners—among them the Libyans from the west and the Kushites from the south.

Life in Ancient Egypt

At the height of its glory, ancient Egypt was home to some 5 million persons, most of whom lived in the Nile Valley and the Nile Delta. Even though Egyptian society was divided into classes, ambitious people in the lower classes could improve their social status somewhat.

Levels of Egyptian Society

Royalty, nobles, and priests formed the top of the social order. They controlled religious and political affairs. Members of the wealthy upper class lived in the cities or on estates along the Nile River. There they built large, elaborately decorated homes surrounded by magnificent gardens, pools, and orchards.

Below the upper class in social rank was the middle class. Its members—artisans, scribes, merchants, and tax collectors—carried out the business activities of Egypt. Middle-class homes—mostly in the cities—were comfortable but not elegant.

The majority of Egyptians belonged to the poor lower class. Many were farmers. For the land they farmed, they paid rent to the king—usually a large percentage of their crop. Farmers also worked on building projects for the king, and some members of the lower class served the priests and the nobles. They lived in small villages of simple huts on or near the large estates along the Nile.

Egyptian Families

In the cities and in the upper class the husband, wife, and children made up the family group.

Visualizing History Ramses II holds an offering table—one of many great monuments erected to honor the pharaoh and Queen Nefertari. *What recent discovery yielded more information about the reign of Ramses II?*

Outside the cities, especially among farmers and laborers, a family also included grandparents and other relatives, who took an active part in the life of the household. An Egyptian child was taught great respect for his or her parents, with a son particularly expected to maintain his father's tomb.

The status of Egyptian women changed somewhat as the centuries passed. Literature of the Old Kingdom portrayed women as the property of their husbands and as valued producers of children. Wise men reminded children to cherish their mothers for bearing them, nourishing them, and loving and caring for them. By the time of the empire, documents indicate that women's legal rights had improved. Women could buy, own, and sell property in their own names, testify in court, and start divorce and other legal proceedings. The lives of Hatshepsut and some of the queens of the later pharaohs, like Nefertiti, suggest that privileged women of the royalty could attain prominence.

Worshiping Many Deities

Religion guided every aspect of Egyptian life. Egyptian religion was based on polytheism, or the worship of many deities, except during the controversial rule of Akhenaton. Gods and goddesses were often represented as part human and part animal—Horus, the sky god, had the head of a hawk. The Egyptians in each region worshiped local deities, but rulers and priests promoted the worship of specific gods and goddesses over all of Egypt. These deities included Ra, the sun god, whom the Theban pharaohs joined with their favorite god Amon to make one god, Amon-Ra.

The popular god Osiris, initially the powerful god of the Nile, became the god responsible for the life, death, and rebirth of all living things. The Egyptians worshiped Osiris and his wife, the goddess Isis, as rulers of the realm of the dead. They believed that Osiris determined a person's fate after death.

Because their religion stressed an afterlife, Egyptians devoted much time and wealth to preparing for survival in the next world. At first they believed that only kings and wealthy people could enjoy an afterlife. By the time of the New Kingdom, however, poor people could also hope for eternal life with Osiris's help.

Writing With Pictures

In their earliest writing system, called hieroglyphics, the Egyptians carved picture symbols onto pieces of slate. These picture symbols, or hieroglyphs, stood for objects, ideas, and sounds. For everyday business, however, the Egyptians used a cursive, or flowing, script known as hieratic, which simplified and connected the picture symbols.

Few people in ancient Egypt could read or write. Some Egyptians, though, did prepare at special schools for a career as a scribe in government or commerce. Scribes learned to write hieratic script on paper made from the papyrus reed.

Visualizing History The falcon god Horus served both as a protector and symbol of the pharaoh. Horus was the son of the deities Osiris and Isis. *What was the major role of Osiris and Isis?*

After the decline of ancient Egypt, hieroglyphs were no longer used, and their meaning remained a mystery to the world's scholars for nearly 2,000 years. Then in A.D. 1799 French soldiers in Egypt found a slab of stone dating to the 200s B.C. near the town of Rosetta. The stone was carved with Greek letters and two forms of Egyptian writing. In A.D. 1822 a French archaeologist named Jean-François Champollion (shahn•pawl•YOHN) figured out how the Greek text on the Rosetta stone matched the Egyptian texts. Using the Greek version, he was able to decipher the Egyptian hieroglyphics.

Some of the oldest writings from the Old Kingdom were carved on the inner walls of the Pyramids. Scribes also copied many prayers and hymns to deities. The Book of the Dead collected texts telling how to reach a happy afterlife, recording more than 200 prayers and magic formulas.

The ancient Egyptians also wrote secular, or nonreligious, works such as collections of proverbs. One vizier gave this advice: "Do not repeat slander; you should not hear it, for it is the result of hot temper. Repeat a matter seen, not what is heard." The Egyptians also enjoyed adventure stories, fairy tales, and love stories, as this excerpt shows:

> 66 Now I'll lie down inside
>   and act as if I'm sick.
> My neighbors will come in to visit,
>   and with them my girl.
> She'll put the doctors out,
>   for she's the one to know my hurt. 99
>
> –a love poem by a young Egyptian,
> date unknown

Achievements in Science

Pyramids, temples, and other monuments bear witness to the architectural and artistic achievement of Egyptian artisans. These works, however,

Stonehenge Religious Site

Salisbury Plain, England, c. 1700 B.C.
Ancient people created a religious monument in southwestern England by dragging huge stones from miles away and arranging them in giant circles. The work probably took hundreds of years to complete. The layout of stones suggests that they were used in ceremonies linked to the rising of the sun on the longest day of the year.

ENGLAND
Stonehenge

would not have been possible without advances in disciplines such as mathematics. The Egyptians developed a number system that enabled them to calculate area and volume, and they used principles of geometry to survey flooded land.

The Egyptians worked out an accurate 365-day calendar by basing their year not only on the movements of the moon but also on Sirius, the bright Dog Star. Sirius rises annually in the sky just before the Nile's flood begins.

Egyptians also developed medical expertise, having first learned about human anatomy in their practice of embalming. Egyptian doctors wrote directions on papyrus scrolls for using splints, bandages, and compresses when treating fractures, wounds, and diseases. Other ancient civilizations would acquire much of their medical knowledge from the Egyptians.

SECTION 1 REVIEW

Recall
1. **Define** monarchy, dynasty, theocracy, bureaucracy, pharaoh, empire, polytheism, hieroglyphics.
2. **Identify** Narmer, the Hyksos, Ahmose, Hatshepsut, Thutmose III, Akhenaton, Ramses II.
3. **Explain** how a bureaucracy

became part of government in ancient Egypt.

Critical Thinking
4. **Evaluate**
Which pharaoh—Thutmose III or Ramses II—was more successful in handling conflict with neighboring peoples? Support your opinion.

Understanding Themes
5. **Relation to Environment**
How did geography and climate affect where people lived in ancient Egypt? How did the ancient Egyptians make use of the environment to meet their economic and cultural needs?

The Egyptians

The Valley of the Kings has seen more than its share of visitors. For thousands of years, travelers, warriors, and more recently, archaeologists have descended on this area on the outskirts of what is now Luxor to marvel at the magnificence of ancient Egypt. It was thought that most of what there was to discover had been found after British explorer Howard Carter opened up the tomb of Tutankhamen in 1922.

Then in 1988, plans were made to build a parking lot over the site of Tomb 5, which had been discovered—and looted—years earlier. Wanting to make sure that the parking facility would not seal off anything important, Egyptologist Kent Weeks of the American University of Cairo decided to make one last exploration of the tomb. To his surprise, beyond a few debris-choked rooms, he opened a door that led to the mostly unexcavated tomb of perhaps 50 of the sons of Ramses II, the powerful pharaoh who ruled Egypt from 1279 to 1212 B.C.

Though the tomb was emptied of valuables long ago, archaeologists consider Weeks's discovery a major find. Scientists and researchers hope

Illustration by C.F. Payne

Kenneth Garrett

that artifacts found in the tomb will provide clues about Egyptian civilization during Egypt's last golden age.

For students of Judeo-Christian history, any information on Ramses' oldest son, Amen-hir-khopshef, would be a most important discovery. Ramses was in power when, in retribution for the enslavement of the Israelites, according to the Book of Exodus, the Lord "...smote all the firstborn in the land of Egypt, from the firstborn of Pharaoh that sat on his throne unto the firstborn of the captive that was in the dungeon."

The tomb and pyramids of

ancient Egypt hold many answers: These stone monuments have certainly established the immortality of the pharaohs. But what about the commoners, who vastly outnumbered the royalty? What of the men and women who gave their strength, sweat, and lives to create Egypt's lasting monuments? The widespread fame of the Sphinx and the Pyramids at Giza make it easy to forget that basic questions about Egyptian history have remained unanswered. Only recently have Egyptologists begun to fill in those gaps.

SEVERAL YEARS AGO, archaeologists began to excavate two sites—located about half a mile from the Sphinx—searching for signs of the

Offerings of food are carved in relief on an official's tomb (left).

Another pyramid nears completion about 2500 B.C. (above). Limestone facing blocks were quarried across the Nile and ferried to the work site. Teams then dragged the blocks to ramps made of rubble that were built around the pyramid during construction. Some experts believe that it took only 10,000 men—far below earlier estimates of up to 100,000—and 25 years to lay 5 million tons of rock. Half lion, half pharaoh, the Sphinx (in the foreground) is carved from an outcropping left unexcavated in a U-shaped quarry.

ordinary people who built the pyramids. Within months they uncovered the remains of many mud-brick buildings, including the oldest bakery yet discovered in Egypt.

This was a significant find. While the pyramids built Egypt by drawing its provinces together in a unified effort, it can be said that bread built the pyramids. For thousands of workers, a loaf of emmer–wheat bread—washed down with beer—was most likely the dietary staple.

At about the time the bakery was discovered, searchers also unearthed a cemetery of 600 graves of workers. Their skeletons revealed years of hard labor: Vertebrae were compressed and damaged from years of carrying heavy loads. Some skeletons were missing fingers and even limbs. A few of the tombs were adorned with mini-pyramids several feet high, made of mud brick. Nothing like these tiny pyramids had been found before. In the past, scholars believed that the pyramid form was invented as the shape for a royal tomb. However, Zahi Hawass, director general of the Giza Pyramids, thinks that the pyramid form actually may have arisen among the common people. He believes that the mini-pyramids evolved from sacred rectangular mounds found in tombs even older than the pharaohs' pyramids.

Life for most ancient Egyptians was hard. Society was built around a preoccupation with the pharaohs' immortality. But perhaps there were spiritual rewards for the common people in this devotion to their pharaohs. Some scholars think that ancient Egyptians believed not so much that the pharaoh was divine,

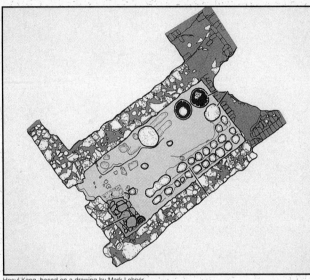

Hosul Kang, based on a drawing by Mark Lehner

Kenneth Garrett

■ *A drawing of an ancient bakery (top) was used to build this replica of an ancient Egyptian bakery near Saqqara, Egypt (bottom).*

but that through the pharaoh the divine nature of their society was expressed. Building a pyramid might have been an act of faith much as building a cathedral was in the Middle Ages.

Such recent discoveries about the life of the common people may lead to a new way of seeing ancient Egypt: not only as a brilliant civilization of the elite trickling down to the masses but also as a culture built

from the bottom up—a culture that stood on the daily toil of the workers and the beliefs of ordinary men and women.

Much of the emerging picture of daily life in ancient Egypt is one of arduous toil. The villages were crowded and dirty. Huts were made of thatch and mud brick. Men wore loincloths; women dressed in long sheaths with wide shoulder straps; and children went naked. On wooden sledges workers hauled the giant granite blocks that built the pyramids. Egypt created a vast agricultural empire, yet all the irrigation was done by hand. Farmers filled two heavy jars from the canals, then hung them from a yoke over their shoulders. Oxen dragging wooden plows tilled the fertile soil along the Nile, followed by lines of sowers who sang in cadence as they cast grains of emmer wheat from baskets.

There is much still to be learned and understood about daily life in ancient Egypt. The discovery of the bakery has provided insight into what sustained the masses; the bones in the commoners' graveyard tell us that life was not easy; the mini-pyramids illustrate that art, culture, and faith may have developed up from the average man and woman, rather than down from the royalty. For years Egyptologists have focused on the grandiose—and thereby disregarded most of Egyptian society. Eventually, however, our view of ancient Egyptian culture is broadening to encompass those responsible for creating it.

Kenneth Garrett

Kenneth Garrett

Kenneth Garrett

⊠ A potter was hired to make replicas of the old baking pots. A local worker (top left) heats the tops in a wood fire in preparation for baking.

⊠ A kind of wheat known as emmer was supplied by a Californian who collects and grows ancient grains. The wet flour made from the emmer was left outside to collect free-floating native yeast spores and bacteria. (Store–bought yeast was not known to ancient Egyptians.) On baking day, the dough was placed into the pot bottoms and allowed to rise (bottom left). A hole for each pot was dug in the hot coals. The heated pot tops were then placed on the heated bottom halves and were placed in the coals to bake.

⊠ Success! For perhaps the first time in more than 4,000 years, a loaf of emmer bread popped out of an Old Kingdom-style pot. Edward Wood (above), who has been baking ancient breads for 50 years, holds up a perfect loaf.

Chapter 2 *Early Civilizations* **57**

3000 B.C.	2000 B.C.	1000 B.C.

c. 3000 B.C.
Sumerians set up city-states.

c. 2300 B.C.
Akkadian king Sargon I begins conquests.

c. 1700 B.C.
Hammurabi develops code of laws.

Section 2

The Fertile Crescent

Setting the Scene

▶ **Terms to Define**
city-state, cuneiform

▶ **People to Meet**
the Sumerians, Sargon I, the Akkadians, Hammurabi

▶ **Places to Locate**
Fertile Crescent, Mesopotamia, Tigris and Euphrates Rivers

 **Find Out** How did Sumer's achievements enrich the early culture of the Middle East?

The Storyteller

Sumerians honored the sun god Shamash as a defender of the weak, giver of life, and even as a judge of business deals, as in this hymn:
"The whole of mankind bows to you,
Shamash the universe longs for your light….
As for him who declines a present, but
nevertheless takes the part of the weak,
It is pleasing to Shamash, and he will prolong
his life….
The merchant who practices trickery as he holds the balances…
He is disappointed in the matter of profit and loses his capital.
The honest merchant who holds the balances and gives good weight—
Everything is presented to him in good measure."

Sumerian board game

—from *Babylonian Wisdom Literature*, W. B. Lambert, in *Readings in Ancient History* (2nd ed.), N. Bailkey

round 5000 B.C.—at about the same time as Egyptian nomads moved into the Nile River valley—groups of herders started to journey north from the Arabian Peninsula. Rainfall in the area had declined over the years, and the lakes and grasslands had begun to dry up. Other peoples—from the highlands near present-day Turkey—moved south at this time. Driven by poor weather, they also fled war and overpopulation.

Both groups of migrants headed into the crescent-shaped strip of fertile land that stretched from the Mediterranean Sea to the Persian Gulf, curving around northern Syria. Called the **Fertile Crescent**, this region included parts of the modern nations of Israel, Jordan, Lebanon, Turkey, Syria, and Iraq.

Many of the peoples migrating from the north and south chose to settle in **Mesopotamia** (MEH •suh•puh•TAY•mee•uh), the eastern part of the Fertile Crescent. Located on a low plain lying between the **Tigris and Euphrates Rivers**, the name *Mesopotamia* means "land between the rivers" in the Greek language. The two rivers begin in the hills of present-day eastern Turkey and later run parallel to each other through present-day Iraq on their way to the Persian Gulf. In this region, the newcomers built villages and farmed the land.

The Twin Rivers

Beginning with Neolithic farmers, people used the Tigris and Euphrates Rivers to water their crops. Unlike the Nile River, however, the twin rivers did not provide a regular supply of water. In the summer no rain fell, and the Mesopotamian plain was dry. As a result, water shortages often coincided with the fall planting season. By the spring harvest season, however, the rivers swelled with rain and melting snow. Clogged with deposits of silt, the Tigris and Euphrates Rivers often overflowed onto the plain. Strong floods sometimes swept away whole villages and fields. The time of year of such flooding, however, was never predictable, and the water level of the rivers often varied from year to year.

The early Mesopotamian villages cooperated in order to meet the rivers' challenges. Together they first built dams and escape channels to control the seasonal floodwaters and later constructed canals and ditches to bring river water to irrigate their fields. As a result of their determined efforts, Mesopotamian farmers were producing food, especially grain crops, in abundance by 4000 B.C.

The Sumerian Civilization

Around 3500 B.C. a people from either central Asia or Asia Minor—the Sumerians—arrived in Mesopotamia. They settled in the lower part of the Tigris-Euphrates river valley, known as Sumer. Sumer became the birthplace of what historians have considered the world's first cities.

The Sumerian City-States

By 3000 B.C. the Sumerians had formed 12 city-states in the Tigris-Euphrates valley, including Ur, Uruk, and Eridu. A typical Sumerian city-state consisted of the city itself and the land surrounding it.

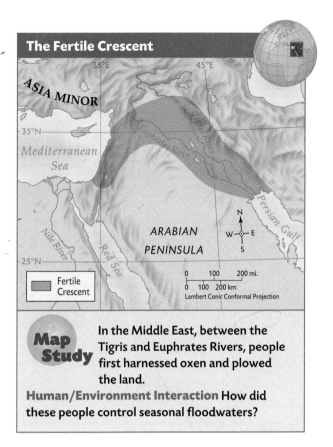

The Fertile Crescent

ASIA MINOR

Mediterranean Sea

ARABIAN PENINSULA

Nile River

Red Sea

Persian Gulf

Euphrates River

Tigris River

Fertile Crescent

0   100   200 mi.
0 100 200 km
Lambert Conic Conformal Projection

Map Study

In the Middle East, between the Tigris and Euphrates Rivers, people first harnessed oxen and plowed the land.
Human/Environment Interaction How did these people control seasonal floodwaters?

Visualizing History

Restored ziggurat at Ur, c. 2100 B.C.
What was the purpose of a ziggurat?

The population of each city-state ranged from 20,000 to 250,000.

The people of Sumer shared a common culture, language, and religion. Sumerian city-states also shared some physical features. A ziggurat (ZIH•guh•RAT), or temple, made of sun-dried brick and decorated with colored tile, was built in each city-state. Sumerians built a ziggurat as a series of terraces, with each terrace smaller than the one below. A staircase climbed to a shrine atop the ziggurat. Only priests and priestesses were allowed to enter the shrine, which was dedicated to the city-state's chief deity. In form a ziggurat resembled a pyramid—both being massive stepped or peaked structures—but the feeling and emphasis of the two differed. A pyramid hid an inner tomb reachable only through passageways. A ziggurat raised a shrine to the sky, reached by mounting outer stairs.

Sumerian Government

Each Sumerian city-state usually governed itself independently of the others. In the city-state of Uruk, for example, a council of nobles and an assembly of citizens ran political affairs at first. But later, as city-states faced threats of foreign invaders and began to compete for land and water rights, the citizens of each city-state typically chose a military leader from among themselves. By 2700 B.C. the

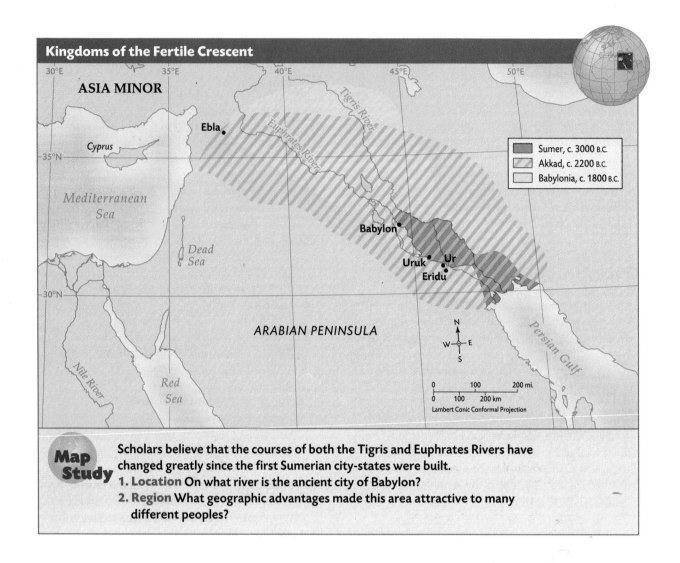

ASIA MINOR

Ebla

Cyprus

Mediterranean Sea

Dead Sea

Babylon

Uruk • Ur
Eridu

ARABIAN PENINSULA

Nile River

Red Sea

Persian Gulf

Sumer, c. 3000 B.C.
Akkad, c. 2200 B.C.
Babylonia, c. 1800 B.C.

N
W—E
S

0   100   200 mi.
0   100   200 km
Lambert Conic Conformal Projection

Map Study

Scholars believe that the courses of both the Tigris and Euphrates Rivers have changed greatly since the first Sumerian city-states were built.
1. **Location** On what river is the ancient city of Babylon?
2. **Region** What geographic advantages made this area attractive to many different peoples?

leaders of several city-states ruled as kings. Soon after, the kingships became hereditary.

A Sumerian king served not only as military leader but as the high priest, who represented the city-state's deity. Thus the governments of the city-states were not only monarchies but theocracies. Because the Sumerians believed that much of the land belonged to a city-state's god or goddess, a king and his priests closely supervised farming. A king also enforced the law and set penalties for law-breakers. Most punishments consisted of fines and did not involve bodily injury or loss of life.

The Roles of Men and Women

Sumerian law extensively regulated family life and outlined the roles of men and women. As the heads of households, men exercised great authority over their wives and children. According to Sumerian law codes, a man could sell his wife or children into slavery if he needed the money to pay a debt. He could also divorce his wife for the slightest cause. For a Sumerian woman, in contrast, the law codes made divorce much more difficult. Women did enjoy some legal rights, however. Like Egyptian women, they could buy and sell property. They could also operate their own businesses and own and sell their own slaves.

Writing on Clay Tablets

Commerce and trade dominated the Sumerian city-states. The Sumerians developed a system of writing so they could keep accounts and prepare documents. Archaeologists believe that the writing system the Sumerians invented is the oldest in the world, dating to about 3100 B.C. The cuneiform (kyoo•NEE•uh•FAWRM) system began with pictograms—as did Egyptian hieroglyphics—and consisted of hundreds of wedge-shaped markings made by pressing the end of a sharpened reed on wet clay tablets. Then the Sumerians dried or baked the tablets until they were hard. Eventually the pictograms developed into symbols representing complex ideas. In this way, cuneiform influenced later Mesopotamian writing systems.

Medical remedies are inscribed on this Sumerian clay tablet—a cuneiform writing tablet that was baked until hard. *How did cuneiform develop as a writing system?*

Sumerians wishing to learn cuneiform and become scribes studied for many years at special schools called *eddubas*. As educated professionals, scribes rose to high positions in Sumerian society. They produced business records, lists of historical dates, and literary works.

One of these literary works, the epic poem *Gilgamesh*, was written down about 1850 B.C. Scholars believe that the *Gilgamesh* epic may be the oldest story in the world. The scribes probably based the stories of Gilgamesh, a godlike man who performs heroic deeds, on an actual king of the city-state of Uruk.

Sumer's Many Deities

The Sumerians, like the Egyptians, practiced a polytheistic religion. Each Sumerian deity presided over a specific natural force—rain, moon, air—or over a human activity—plowing or brick making, for example. An, the highest Sumerian deity, was responsible for the seasons. Another important god—Enlil, god of winds and agriculture—created the hoe. Although Sumerians honored all the deities, each city-state claimed as its own one god or goddess, to whom its citizens prayed and offered sacrifices.

The Sumerians pictured their gods and goddesses as unpredictable, selfish beings who had little regard for human beings. The Sumerians believed that if deities became angry, they would cause misfortunes such as floods or famine. To appease their temperamental gods and goddesses, Sumerian priests and priestesses performed religious ceremonies and rituals.

Unlike the Egyptians, the Sumerians felt that humans had little control over their daily lives and could not look forward to a happy life after death. Only a grim underworld, without light or air, awaited them—an afterlife where the dead were only pale shadows.

Sumerian Inventions

Historians credit the Sumerians with numerous technological innovations. The Sumerians developed the wagon wheel, for example, to better transport people and goods, the arch to build sturdier buildings, the potter's wheel to shape containers, and the sundial to keep time. They developed a number system based on 60 and devised a 12-month calendar based on the cycles of the moon. The Sumerian civilization also was the first to make bronze out of copper and tin and to develop a metal plow. They produced an abundance of finely crafted metal work, some of which has been discovered in the Royal Cemetery at Ur. These and other Sumerian achievements have prompted one scholar to observe that "history begins at Sumer."

First Mesopotamian Empires

After a long period of conquest and reconquest, the Sumerian city-states eventually fell to foreign invaders in the 2000s B.C. The invaders of Sumer, like the Egyptians of the New Kingdom, were inspired by dreams of empire.

Footnotes to History

The Umbrella

1400 B.C.—Umbrellas actually originated under the sunny skies of Mesopotamia. Sumerians used palm fronds or feather umbrellas to shield their heads from the harsh rays and scorching heat of the Middle Eastern sun.

Sargon Leads the Akkadians

The first empire builder in Mesopotamia—**Sargon I**—may have been born a herder or a farmer's son. According to legend his mother abandoned him as a baby, setting him out on the Euphrates River in a reed basket. Downstream a farmer irrigating his fields pulled Sargon ashore and raised him as his own.

Sargon's people, **the Akkadians**, were Semites, one of the nomadic groups that had migrated from the Arabian Peninsula to the Fertile Crescent around 5000 B.C. The Akkadians established a kingdom called Akkad (AH•KAHD) in northern Mesopotamia. When Sargon assumed power in Akkad around 2300 B.C., he immediately launched a military campaign of expansion. Sargon's conquests united all of the city-states of Mesopotamia in one empire, which predated the empire of the Egyptian New Kingdom by more than 800 years.

Under Sargon's rule the people of Mesopotamia began to use the Akkadian language instead of Sumerian. But the Akkadians adopted various Sumerian religious and farming practices. After Sargon's death and the successful rule of his grandson, however, the Akkadian Empire disintegrated.

The Kingdom of Ebla

No one really knows how far Sargon's empire extended. Historians do know, however, that Ebla, a kingdom located in what is now northern Syria, fought unsuccessfully against Sargon for control of the Euphrates River trade. When Sargon's grandson captured Ebla, he burned the royal archives. Yet fire did not destroy the thousands of clay tablets stored there. These tablets and other finds from Ebla have convinced historians that highly developed Semitic civilizations prospered in that area of Syria earlier than previously believed.

The overland trade that passed between Egypt and Mesopotamia made Ebla a wealthy and powerful city-state. Ebla controlled a number of neighboring towns, from which it exacted tribute.

The kings of Ebla were elected for seven-year terms. In addition to their political role, they looked

Images
of the Times

Mesopotamia

For many centuries, beginning about 4000 B.C., enterprising civilizations rose and fell in the fertile valley of the Tigris and Euphrates Rivers.

The Royal Standard of Ur is an oblong decorated box with panels that represent scenes of war and peace. The war panel celebrates a military victory by the Sumerian city of Ur.

after the welfare of the poor. If the kings failed, they could be removed by a council. After 2000 B.C., Ebla declined and eventually was destroyed by the Amorites, a Semitic people from western Syria.

Hammurabi's Babylonian Empire

The Amorites also expanded beyond Syria. Their military forces poured into Mesopotamia, which was in decline after a short period of prosperity under the kings of Ur. The Amorites overran many Sumerian centers, including Babylon. The dynasty that they founded at Babylon later produced a ruler who would dominate Mesopotamia: **Hammurabi**.

Hammurabi used his might to put down other Mesopotamian rulers. He eventually brought the entire region under his control, reorganizing the tax system and ordering local officials to build and repair irrigation canals. Hammurabi organized a strong government and worked to increase the economic prosperity of his people. Under Hammurabi's rule, Babylon became a major trade center. Merchants from as far away as India and China paid gold and silver for the grain and cloth the Babylonians produced.

POINT

Hammurabi's Law Code

Historians consider Hammurabi's greatest achievement his effort "to make justice appear in the land." Hammurabi collected laws of the various Mesopotamian city-states and created a law code covering the entire region. When completed, Hammurabi's code consisted of 282 sections dealing with most aspects of daily life. It clearly stated which actions were considered violations and assigned a specific punishment for each. Hammurabi's code penalized wrongdoers more severely than did the old Sumerian laws. Instead of fining violators, it exacted what the Bible later expressed as "an eye for an eye, and a tooth for a tooth." According to the harsh approach of Hammurabi's code:

This goddess, one of many similar preserved relics, along with discovered temple sites, reveals the significance of religion in early Mesopotamian civilizations.

The Kassite stela fragment shows animals that were important to a vigorous agricultural people, the Kassites, who emerged as a dominant force after 2000 B.C.

REFLECTING ON THE TIMES

1. What evidence reveals the importance of religion in Mesopotamian cities?
2. What role might gods and goddesses have in times of war?

Other sections of Hammurabi's code covered the property of married women, adoption and inheritance, interest rates on loans, and damage to fields by cattle. Some laws were attempts to protect the less powerful—for example, protecting wives against beatings or neglect by their husbands. The development of written law in Mesopotamia was a major advance toward justice and order. Before this achievement, people who had been offended or cheated often acted on their own and used violence against their opponents. Now, crimes against people or property became the concern of the whole community. Government assumed the responsibility of protecting its citizens in return for their loyalty and service.

Babylonian Society

Historians have been able to infer from Hammurabi's code a threefold division of Babylonian social classes—the kings, priests, and nobles at the top; the artisans, small merchants, scribes, and farmers next; and slaves as the lowest group. His laws varied according to the class of the person offended against, with more severe penalties for assaulting a landowner than for hurting a slave. Most slaves had been captured in war or had failed to pay their debts.

The Babylonians borrowed heavily from Sumerian culture. They used the cuneiform script for their Semitic language and wrote on clay tablets. Babylonian literature was similar to that of Sumer.

Decline and Fall

After Hammurabi's death, the Babylonian Empire declined, and Mesopotamia was again divided into a number of small states. Hammurabi's dynasty finally ended and his empire fell apart when the Hittites, a people from Asia Minor, raided Babylon about 1600 B.C. Babylon, however, would again play a role in Mesopotamian civilization in the 600s B.C. as the capital of a new empire under the Chaldeans.

Visualizing History King Hammurabi stands in front of the sun god Shamash at the top of the stone slab upon which is inscribed Hammurabi's code of laws. Shamash—the supreme judge—delivers the laws to the king. *Why were Hammurabi's laws carved in stone for public display?*

❝ If a builder has built a house for a man and has not made his work sound, so that the house he has made falls down and causes the death of the owner of the house, that builder shall be put to death. If it causes the death of the son of the owner of the house, they shall kill the son of that builder. ❞

SECTION 2 REVIEW

Recall
1. **Define** city-state, cuneiform.
2. **Identify** the Sumerians, Gilgamesh, Sargon I, the Akkadians, Hammurabi.
3. **Explain** the purpose of the religious ceremonies and rituals performed by Sumerian priests and priestesses.

Critical Thinking
4. **Making Comparisons** Contrast Hammurabi's code with modern American law. Which do you think serves justice better? Explain your answer.

Understanding Themes
5. **Cooperation** Identify an economic or cultural achievement of one of the civilizations of the Fertile Crescent region that must have required skillful planning and organization of many people.

Classifying Information

Imagine shopping in a store where shoes, rugs, dishes, and books are all mixed together in piles. To find the item you need, you would have to comb through each pile. How frustrating!

Dealing with large quantities of information about a subject likewise can be frustrating. It is easier to understand information if you put it into groups, or classify it.

Learning the Skill

In classifying anything, we put together items with shared characteristics. Department stores group items according to their uses. For example, shoes and boots are in the footwear department, while pots and pans are in the kitchen department.

We can classify written information in the same way.

1. As you read about a topic, look for items that have similar characteristics. List these items in separate columns or on separate note cards.
2. Label these categories with an appropriate heading.
3. Add facts to the categories as you continue reading.
4. Review the groups. If necessary, subdivide the categories into smaller groups or combine categories that overlap.

Once you have classified the material, look for patterns and relationships in the facts. Make comparisons, draw conclusions, and develop questions or hypotheses for further study.

Practicing the Skill

Use the information in the following passage to answer these questions:

1. The passage describes two groups of children in ancient Egypt. What are these groups?
2. Classify the educational opportunities available to each group.

3. Classify the occupations available to each group.
4. From your classifications, what conclusions can you draw about Egyptian society?

  ❝ The royal children ... were privately tutored ... frequently joined by the sons of great noble families.... The most sought-after profession in Egypt was that of scribe.... The most important subjects were reading and writing ... history, literature, geography, [and] ethics. Arithmetic was almost certainly part of the curriculum.... Boys who were to specialize in medicine, law or religious liturgy would perhaps have devoted some of their time to elementary studies in these fields.

Formal education for [a son from] the lower classes ... was not selected for him because he wished to become an artist or goldsmith or a farmer ... he entered a trade because it was his father's work. The sons of artists and craftsmen were apprenticed and went to train at one of the temples or state workshops ... the sons of peasants would have joined their fathers in the field at an early age. **❞**

—A. Rosalie David,
The Egyptian Kingdoms, 1975

Applying the Skill

Find two newspaper or magazine articles about a topic that interests you. Classify the information on note cards or in a chart.

For More Practice

Turn to the Skill Practice in the Chapter Review on page 77 for more practice in classifying information.

c. 2500 B.C.
Settlements develop in
the Indus River valley.

c. 2300 B.C. Harappan people
trade with Mesopotamia.

c. 1500 B.C.
Indus Valley
civilization
declines.

Section 3

Early South Asia

Setting the Scene

▶ **Terms to Define**
subcontinent, monsoon

▶ **People to Meet**
the Harappans

▶ **Places to Locate**
Indus River valley, Harappa, Mohenjo-Daro

Find Out How did people of the Indus River valley civilization build cities?

The Storyteller

For a long time, it had been known that the mounds of Mohenjo-Daro and Harappa contained archaeological remains. But neighborhood construction workers actually used the ancient mounds as sources for bricks, until practically none remained above ground. As Sir Alexander Cunningham, the first Director General of the Archaeological Survey records, "Perhaps the best idea of the extent of the ruined brick mounds of Harappa may be formed from the fact that they have more than sufficed to furnish brick ballast for about 100 miles of Lahore and Multan Railway."

—adapted from *Indus Valley Civilization*, Ashim Kumar Ron N.N. Gidwani (Cunningham, 1875), 1982 and *Harappan Civilization*, Gregory Possehl, 1982

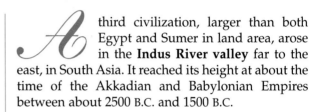

Harappan jar lid

A third civilization, larger than both Egypt and Sumer in land area, arose in the **Indus River valley** far to the east, in South Asia. It reached its height at about the time of the Akkadian and Babylonian Empires between about 2500 B.C. and 1500 B.C.

The Subcontinent

Three modern nations—India, Pakistan, and Bangladesh—trace their roots to the Indus Valley civilization. These countries lie on the subcontinent of South Asia, a large, triangular-shaped landmass that juts into the Indian Ocean.

Bounded by Mountains

Natural barriers separate the South Asian subcontinent from the rest of Asia. Water surrounds the landmass on the east and west. To the north rise two lofty mountain ranges—the Himalayas and the Hindu Kush. Throughout history, invaders entering the subcontinent by land have had to cross the few high mountain passes of the Hindu Kush.

Plains sweep across the landscape to the south of the mountains. Across the plains flow three rivers, fed by rain and melting mountain snows. The Indus River drains into the Arabian Sea, and the Ganges (GAN•JEEZ) and Brahmaputra (BRAH •muh•POO•truh) Rivers join and empty into the Bay of Bengal, forming a wide delta. The Ganges-Brahmaputra Delta and the Indus-Ganges plain are formed from soils left by the rivers. Like the Nile Valley and Delta and the Tigris-Euphrates plains, fertile river areas of South Asia have supported vast numbers of people over the ages.

Seasonal Winds

The northern mountains ensure generally warm weather in South Asia. Like a wall, they block blasts of cold air from central Asia. Two seasonal winds called monsoons affect the climate,

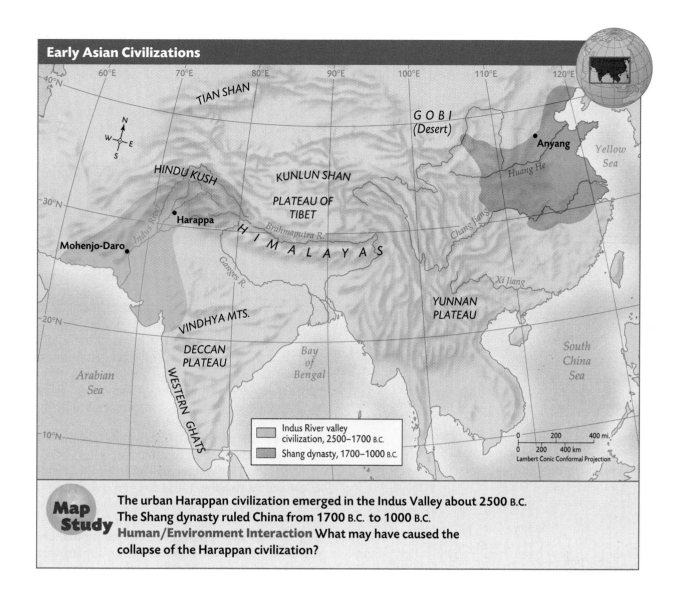

Map Study The urban Harappan civilization emerged in the Indus Valley about 2500 B.C. The Shang dynasty ruled China from 1700 B.C. to 1000 B.C. **Human/Environment Interaction** What may have caused the collapse of the Harappan civilization?

however, and shape the pattern of life on the subcontinent.

The northeast, or winter, monsoon blows from November to March; the southwest, or summer, monsoon from June to September. The northeast wind brings dry air from the mountains, and the average winter temperatures of the Indus-Ganges plain remain mild—about 70°F (21°C). By June, temperatures have soared, sometimes exceeding 100°F (38°C), and South Asians welcome the rain-bearing southwest wind blowing off the ocean.

Because of the heavy downpours of the southwest monsoon, the rivers swell rapidly, then widen across the flat plains and rush to the sea. The flooding enriches the soil, but in some years unusually heavy rains drown people and animals and destroy whole villages. In other years the monsoon arrives late or rainfall is light; then crops are poor and people go hungry. The people of the plains are dependent on the monsoons.

The Indus Valley Civilization

Less than a century ago, archaeologists working in the Indus River valley first identified an ancient civilization in South Asia. They dated this early civilization to about 2500 B.C.

Centrally Planned Cities

Archaeologists named the Indus Valley settlements "the Harappan civilization" after one of its major cities, **Harappa** (huh•RA•puh), located in present-day Pakistan. **Mohenjo-Daro** (moh •HEHN•joh DAHR•oh), another important Harappan city, lay nearer the Arabian Sea.

The ruins of Harappa and Mohenjo-Daro are outstanding examples of urban planning. A citadel, or fortress, built on a brick platform overlooked each city—possibly serving as a government and religious center. Below the citadel Harappan engineers skillfully laid out each city in a grid pattern of

Some fine jewelry crafted by Harappan artisans has survived. These pieces are now in the National Museum at New Delhi, India. *Why is less known about Harappan civilization than about Egypt and Mesopotamia?*

grew wheat, barley, rice, and cotton. Farmers planted at the beginning or end of the flood season and relied on the drenched land to provide the necessary water for their crops.

Supported by a food surplus, Harappan city dwellers engaged in industry and commerce. Some artisans worked bronze and copper into tools, while others made silver vessels and gold, shell, and ivory jewelry. The Harappans also mass-produced clay pots, and they spun and wove cotton cloth. Merchants who handled these goods used soapstone seals to identify bundles of merchandise. The discovery by archaeologists of Harappan seals in Mesopotamia indicates that Indus Valley people traded with the people of Mesopotamia as early as 2300 B.C.

Language and Religion

The Harappans inscribed pictograms on the seals they placed on packages of goods. Scientists have yet to decipher these inscriptions—almost the only known examples of the written language of the Harappan civilization. Some believe that the Harappans made their pictograms after adopting the idea of writing from the people of Mesopotamia.

The lack of written records has made it difficult to learn as much about the Harappan civilization as is known about Egypt and Mesopotamia. Artifacts found in the ruins, however, have provided archaeologists with some clues. For example, animal and humanlike figures suggest that the Harappans worshiped gods associated with natural forces.

Collapse of a Civilization

By 1500 B.C. the Harappan civilization had disappeared. Historians have many theories for what caused this collapse. Evidence of floods, for example, suggests possible climate changes. In the Mohenjo-Daro ruins are signs that some of its people may have met a violent end, possibly at the hands of invaders.

straight streets crossing each other at right angles. **The Harappans** used oven-baked bricks to build houses with flat wooden roofs, and some houses rose to several stories and enclosed courtyards. Almost every house had at least one bathroom, with drains and chutes connected to a brick sewer system beneath the streets.

Harappan Life

Most of the Harappan people worked the land. In the fields of the Indus Valley floodplain they

---

SECTION 3 REVIEW

Recall
1. **Define** subcontinent, monsoon.
2. **Identify** the Harappans.
3. **Name** three modern nations of South Asia that trace their roots to the Indus Valley civilization. In what present-day nation were the cities of Harappa and Mohenjo-Daro located?

Critical Thinking
4. **Analyzing Information** What do archaeological clues suggest about the decline and collapse of the Indus Valley civilization?

Understanding Themes
5. **Cultural Diffusion** How might the Indus Valley civilization at Mohenjo-Daro and the civilization at Harappa have been influenced by the Mesopotamian city-states and empires?

2500 B.C.	2000 B.C.	1500 B.C.	1000 B.C.

c. 2500 B.C. Lung-shan culture begins in China.

c. 2000 B.C. Yu founds the legendary Xia dynasty.

c. 1700 B.C. Tang establishes the Shang, the first historical dynasty.

c. 1000s B.C. The Zhou dynasty comes to power.

Section 4

Early China

Setting the Scene

▶**Terms to Define**
　mandate

▶**People to Meet**
　Yu the Great

▶**Places to Locate**
　Huang He valley, Anyang

Find Out What were the major contributions of early Chinese civilization?

The Storyteller

What would the oracle say this time? Tang tried not to lean too far forward to watch as the fortune-teller began to apply red-hot coals to the turtle shell. A man of his station should not appear too anxious: his confidence in divine support should be seen by all. On the shell was inscribed a question known only to him: "Shall I attack before harvest?" So much depended on the answer. There was nothing to do now but wait for the fire to work on the brittle shell covered with scratchings, containing the destiny of China.

—adapted from *Ancient Records of Assyria and Babylon,* Volume 1, edited by Daniel David Luckenbill, 1968

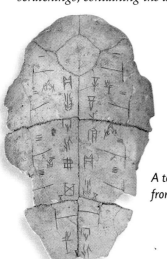

A tortoise shell oracle bone from the Shang Dynasty

Even as the Harappans were meeting their mysterious fate, China's first dynasty had begun to assert its power over another river valley. This fourth river valley civilization has endured to the present day.

For many centuries the Chinese lived in relative isolation from the rest of the world. They called their homeland *Zhong Guo* (JOONG GWAH), or "the Middle Kingdom." To them it was the center of the whole world and the one truly supreme civilization. The lack of outside contacts allowed the Chinese to develop one culture across many regions and a strong sense of national identity as well. As a result, China has the oldest continuous civilization in the world.

China's Geography

China's varied geography has affected its historical development. Mountains make up about one-third of China's area. The Himalayas close off China to the southwest, and on the western border rise the Kunlun Shan and Tian Shan ranges. To the east of the Tian Shan lie the vast desert wastes of the Gobi. These rugged physical features hindered cultural diffusion both into and out of China for many centuries.

On the east, China's coastline touches the Pacific Ocean. Although some Chinese became devoted seafarers, they mostly focused on developing the agriculture of eastern China's fertile river valleys and plains. Unlike the land to the west with its forbidding terrain, the east welcomed life. For centuries large numbers of Chinese have farmed in the region's North China Plain.

Three major rivers drain eastern China: the Huang He (HWONG HUH); the Chang Jiang (CHAHNG JYAHNG), known also as the Yangtze (YANG•SEE); and the Xi Jiang (SHEE JYAHNG), also called the West River. The Huang He flows more than 2,900 miles (4,640 km) from the northern

Oracle bones used to obtain advice about military campaigns were often inscribed with the question and answer and preserved as part of the king's records. *Why were such oracle bones stored by the rulers?*

highlands eastward to the Yellow Sea. On its way it cuts through thick layers of loess (LEHS), a rich yellow soil. The river carries away large amounts of loess, which it deposits farther downstream. The abundance of yellow soil in the Huang's waters gives it its name—Yellow River. The Chinese sometimes call the Huang He "the Great Sorrow" because of the tragedy brought by its floods. However, the silt deposits brought by the flooding river have made the North China Plain a rich agricultural area.

A favorable climate also contributes to successful farming on the North China Plain. Melting snow from the mountains and the monsoon rains between July and October feed the Huang He. Farmers of the region have long depended on the seasonal rhythm of temperature and rainfall.

The Shang Dynasty

Very little is known about the origins of Chinese civilization. In the A.D. 1920s, archaeologists in the Huang He valley uncovered traces of Neolithic life in China. The magnificent painted pots of the Yang-shao (YAHNG•SHOW) culture found by the archaeologists date back to 3000–1500 B.C. Archaeologists have discovered that the Lung-shan culture, from about 2500–2000 B.C., used a potter's wheel to make delicate pots and goblets. These and other Neolithic finds dated to earlier than 5000 B.C. make it clear that the **Huang He valley**, like the river valleys of Egypt, the Fertile Crescent, and South Asia, invited settlement from very early times.

Chinese Myths

Over the centuries the Chinese developed many myths to explain their remote past. One myth tells how the universe was created from the body of a giant named Pan Gu (PAHN GOO), who hatched from an egg. Other legends celebrate the deeds of hero-kings. These larger-than-life rulers included Yao (YOW), a person in the form of a mountain, and Shun, the master of elephants. Another, **Yu the Great**, was a miraculous engineer. According to a myth about Yu:

> 66 When widespread waters swelled to Heaven and serpents and dragons did harm, Yao sent Yu to control the waters and to drive out the serpents and dragons. The waters were controlled and flowed to the east. The serpents and dragons plunged to their places. 99

The myth about Yu—written much later than the first oral tellings—may reflect stories about the attempts of one or many early rulers to channel the floodwaters of the Huang He.

According to tradition, Yu the Great founded China's first dynasty, named Xia (SYAH), around 2000 B.C. Archaeologists, however, have yet to find evidence of the legendary Xia. The first dynasty to be dated from written records in China is the Shang (SHAHNG). The Shang ruled China from about 1700 B.C. to 1000 B.C.

Early Religion

Though the Shang kings were political leaders, they also performed religious duties. As high priests, they could communicate with nature deities on behalf of the people. They prayed, made offerings, and performed sacrifices to gain a good harvest, a change in the weather, or victory in battle. Kings also had special powers for calling upon their ancestors. To do so, they had a priest scratch a question on an animal bone or sometimes on a

tortoise shell. The priest then applied intense heat to the bone. The bone would crack, and the priest would interpret the splintered pattern of cracks as the answer to the king's question. The bones helped the kings to predict the future. The scratchings on the oracle bones, as they are called, are the first known examples of writing in China.

Important Achievements

The priests writing on the oracle bones used a script with many characters. These characters represented objects, ideas, or sounds and were written in vertical columns. To use the script with ease, a writer had to memorize each character. Because only a small percentage of the population could master all the characters, few people in ancient China could read and write.

Not only did the Chinese of the Shang period develop a written script, but they also perfected their metal-casting skills and produced some of the finest bronze objects ever made. These included bronze daggers, figurines, and ritual urns. They built massive ceremonial cauldrons that stood on legs. Bronze fittings adorned hunting chariots, and warriors carried bronze daggers. Artisans also carved beautiful ivory and jade statues. They wove silk into elegantly colored cloth for the upper class and fashioned pottery from kaolin, a fine white clay.

The Chinese built their first cities under the Shang. Archaeologists today have identified seven capital cities, including the city of **Anyang** (AHN•YAHNG). Their excavations reveal the general layout of Anyang. A palace and temple stood at the center of the city, as in the cities of other early civilizations, and public buildings and homes of government officials circled the royal sanctuary. Beyond the city's center stood various workshops and other homes.

Expansion and Decline

Shang kings at first ruled over a small area in northern China. Later, their armies, equipped with bronze weapons and chariots, conquered more distant territories and finally took over most of the Huang He valley.

The Shang dynasty lacked strong leaders, however, and in time grew weak. Around 1000 B.C., Wu, a ruler of a former Shang territory in the northwest, marshaled his forces and marched on the capital. Wu killed the Shang king and established a new dynasty. Wu's dynasty, known as the Zhou (JOH), ruled China for 800 years.

Many Centuries of Dynasties

From the beginning of its recorded history until the early 1900s, dynasties ruled China. When writing about China's past, Western historians have followed the Chinese practice of dividing Chinese history into periods based on the reigns of these ruling families.

The Chinese believed that their rulers governed according to a principle known as the Mandate of Heaven. If rulers were just and effective, they received a mandate, or authority to rule, from heaven. If rulers did not govern properly—as indicated by poor crops or losses in battle—they lost the mandate to someone else who then started a new dynasty. The principle first appeared during the Zhou dynasty. Indeed the Zhou, as did later rebels, probably found the Mandate of Heaven a convenient way to explain their overthrow of an unpopular dynasty.

SECTION 4 REVIEW

Recall
1. **Define** mandate.
2. **Identify** Yu the Great, Xia dynasty, Shang dynasty, Mandate of Heaven.
3. **Use** the map on page 67 to list the major physical features of China. Explain how these physical features affected the development of Chinese civilization.

Critical Thinking
4. **Making Comparisons** Compare the Mandate of Heaven with the way Egyptian kings justified their rule.

Understanding Themes
5. **Innovation** Explain the basic features of the Chinese writing system as it developed in early times. How widespread was the use of this method of writing in China under the early dynasties?

Literature

from

Gilgamesh

retold by Herbert Mason

Like people today, ancient Sumerians loved adventure tales featuring extraordinary heroes battling the forces of evil. Many Sumerian myths featured a king, Gilgamesh, who lived around 2700 B.C. The earliest known written accounts of Gilgamesh's adventures date from about 1850 B.C., making them the oldest surviving examples of epic poetry. An epic is a long poem recalling the exploits of a legendary hero. Gilgamesh, after the death of his friend Enkidu, searched for the secret of eternal life, which he hoped to share with his departed friend. In the following excerpt, Gilgamesh, hoping to learn how to escape death, listens to a mysterious elderly man, Utnapishtim, recount how he survived a great flood.

There was a city called Shurrupak
   On the bank of the Euphrates.
It was very old, and so many were the gods
Within it. They converged in their complex
   hearts
On the idea of creating a great flood.
There was Anu, their aging and weak-minded
   father,
The military Enlil, his adviser,
Ishtar, the sensation-craving one,
And all the rest. Ea, who was present
At their council, came to my house
And, frightened by the violent winds that filled
   the air,
Echoed all that they were planning and had said.
Man of Shurrupak, he said, tear down your
   house
And build a ship. Abandon your possessions
And the works that you find beautiful and crave,
And save your life instead. Into the ship
Bring the seed of all living creatures.

I was overawed, perplexed,
And finally downcast. I agreed to do
As Ea said, but I protested: What shall I say
To the city, the people, the leaders?

Tell them, Ea said, you have learned that Enlil
The war god despises you and will not
Give you access to the city anymore.
Tell them for this Ea will bring the rains.

This is the way gods think, he laughed. His tone
Of savage irony frightened Gilgamesh
Yet gave him pleasure, being his friend.
They only know how to compete or echo.
But who am I to talk? He sighed as if
Disgusted with himself; I did as he
Commanded me to do. I spoke to them,
And some came out to help me build the ship
Of seven stories, each with nine chambers.
The boat was cube in shape, and sound; it held
The food and wine and precious minerals
And seed of living animals we put
In it. My family then moved inside,
And all who wanted to be with us there:
The game of the field, the goats of the steppe,
The craftsmen of the city came, a navigator
Came. And then Ea ordered me to close
The door. The time of the great rains had come.
O there was ample warning, yes, my friend,
But it was terrifying still. Buildings
Blown by the winds for miles like desert brush.
People clung to branches of trees until
Roots gave way. New possessions, now debris,
Floated on the water with their special
Sterile vacancy. The riverbanks failed
To hold the water back. Even the gods
Cowered like dogs at what they had done.
Ishtar cried out like a woman at the height
Of labor: O how could I have wanted
To do this to my people! They were *hers*,
Notice. Even her sorrow was possessive.
Her spawn that she had killed too soon.
Old gods are terrible to look at when
They weep, all bloated like spoiled fish.
One wonders if they ever understand

That they have caused their grief. When the
    seventh day
Came, the flood subsided from its slaughter
Like hair drawn slowly back
From a tormented face.
I looked at the earth and all was silence.
Bodies lay like alewives [a type of fish], dead
And in the clay. I fell down
On the ship's deck and wept. Why? Why did they
Have to die? I couldn't understand. I asked
Unanswerable questions a child asks
When a parent dies—for nothing. Only slowly
Did I make myself believe—or hope—they
Might all be swept up in their fragments
Together
And made whole again
By some compassionate hand.
But my hand was too small
To do the gathering.
I have only known this feeling since
When I look out across the sea of death,
This pull inside against a littleness—myself—
Waiting for an upward gesture.

O the dove, the swallow and the raven
Found their land. The people left the ship.
But I for a long time could only stay inside.
I could not face the deaths I knew were there.
Then I received Enlil, for Ea had *chosen* me;
The war god touched my forehead; he blessed
My family and said:
Before this you were just a man, but now
You and your wife shall be like gods. You
Shall live in the distance at the rivers' mouth,
At the source. I allowed myself to be
Taken far away from all that I had seen.
Sometimes even in love we yearn to leave mankind.
Only the loneliness of the Only One
Who never acts like gods
Is bearable.

Visualizing History Gilgamesh subdues a lion. By the 700s B.C. Gilgamesh had become a mythological hero. The real Gilgamesh ruled over ancient Uruk. *What blessing did the war god give Gilgamesh and his family?*

I am downcast because of what I've seen,
Not what I still have hope to yearn for.
Lost youths restored to life,
Lost children to their crying mothers,
Lost wives, lost friends, lost hopes, lost homes,
I want to bring these back to them.
But now there is you.
We must find something for you.
How will you find eternal life
To bring back to your friend?
He pondered busily, as if
It were just a matter of getting down to work
Or making plans for an excursion.
Then he relaxed, as if there were no use
In this reflection. I would grieve
At all that may befall you still,
If I did not know you must return
And bury your own loss and build
Your world anew with your own hands.
I envy you your freedom.

As he listened, Gilgamesh felt tiredness again
Come over him, the words now so discouraging,
The promise so remote, so unlike what he sought.
He looked into the old man's face, and it seemed changed,
As if this one had fought within himself a battle
He would never know, that still went on.

RESPONDING TO LITERATURE

1. How did Utnapishtim of Shurrupak survive the great flood?
2. How were the reactions of the gods and of Utnapishtim similar?
3. What questions would you ask Utnapishtim if you could meet him?
4. **Applying Information** What aspects of this tale about the great flood in Mesopotamia might apply to other cultures in other places and at other times?

Connections Across Time

Historical Significance The world's first civilizations developed along the banks of river valleys—the Nile, Tigris-Euphrates, Indus, and Huang. They faced similar challenges in explaining the mysteries of nature, using their resources, and providing for defense. They all sought answers through cooperation, government, technology, and religion. They built cities, created dynasties, developed writing systems, and devised laws. Their political ideas, social institutions, and cultural achievements were inherited by later peoples and became the foundation of the civilization we know today.

Using Key Terms

Write the key term that completes each sentence. Then write a sentence for each term not chosen.

a. bureaucracy
b. city-state
c. cuneiform
d. dynasty
e. empire
f. hieroglyphics
g. mandate
h. monarchy
i. monsoon
j. pharaoh
k. polytheism
l. theocracy

1. In ancient China, the first historical _____, or line of rulers from one family, was called the Shang.
2. The ancient Egyptians carved onto pieces of slate a variety of picture symbols, or _____, that stood for objects, ideas, and sounds.
3. The Sumerian form of writing, _____, consisted of hundreds of wedge-shaped markings made by pressing the end of a sharpened reed on wet clay tablets.
4. A typical Sumerian ____ included the city itself and surrounding land.
5. Sargon I united all of the Mesopotamian city-states in a single ____, which consisted of many different territories under one ruler.

Technology Activity

Using E-mail Search the Internet for the E-mail address of an Egyptologist from an international museum or university. Compose a letter requesting information about various aspects of ancient Egyptian culture such as architecture, religion, hieroglyphics, or medicine. From your response, write a short report of your findings. Share your report with the class.

Using Your History Journal

Choose one event from this chapter. Describe the event in picture-writing (cuneiform). Exchange your description with other students and try to guess what each person's event is.

Reviewing Facts

1. **Technology** Explain how the early Mesopotamians controlled the Tigris and Euphrates Rivers.
2. **Culture** Describe the major difference between the pyramids of Egypt and the ziggurats of Mesopotamia.
3. **Economics** Explain why archaeologists believe that there was contact between Mesopotamian and Harappan cultures.
4. **Culture** List the achievements of the ancient Chinese that show their artistic innovation.
5. **Geography** Describe how the Himalayas affected two early river valley civilizations.
6. **History** Identify one event from each of the following periods: the Old Kingdom, the Middle Kingdom, and the New Kingdom.
7. **Government** Name the capital of Upper Egypt that was established in 2050 B.C.
8. **Government** Explain why Amenhotep changed his royal name to Akhenaton.
9. **Government** Describe the main powers and responsibilities of a typical king of a Sumerian city-state around 2700 B.C.
10. **Government** List four examples of the kinds of laws found in Hammurabi's code. Explain why the code was a significant development.

Critical Thinking

1. **Apply** What clues do artifacts found in the ruins at Harappa and Mohenjo-Daro provide about the Harappan religion?
2. **Compare** How did the powers of the Egyptian kings differ from those of the Shang kings? How were their powers the same?
3. **Synthesize** What reaction would you have had to Akhenaton's reforms if you had been a priest of Amon-Ra?
4. **Compare** How did life along the Tigris and Euphrates Rivers in Mesopotamia differ from life along the Nile River in Egypt?

Geography in History

1. **Location** Refer to the map below. What is the relative location of the Sinai Peninsula? Find this peninsula on the Middle East map in the Atlas. What is its absolute location?
2. **Place** Why was most agricultural production in ancient Egypt and in that nation today found along the Nile River?
3. **Movement** Why would travel in ancient Egypt have been easier for a person who was going from south to north than for a person going from east to west? What might make travel from east to west less difficult today?

Skill Practice

Read about life in Harappan civilization in the Indus River valley on pages 67 and 68 in Section 3. Use this information to complete the following chart.

Harappan Life		
Occupations	**Artifacts**	**Theories of Decline**

Understanding Themes

1. **Relation to Environment** What flood-control methods of the ancient Egyptians and other river valley peoples are still in use today?
2. **Cooperation** In what areas of city life today is cooperation as important as it was when the Sumerians built the earliest cities?
3. **Cultural Diffusion** What advances in the twentieth century have made cultural diffusion easier and faster than in ancient times?
4. **Innovation** Why would you consider each of the following developments in ancient China an innovation: a writing script with many characters, bronze vessels and tools, pottery, and silk cloth?

Linking Past and Present

1. Examine Hatshepsut's role as a ruler of Egypt. How does her position and its influence compare with those of modern women holding high political office?
2. Why was early China largely isolated from the rest of the world? Do these same factors still affect modern China? In what ways have the modern Chinese increased contacts with other cultures? To what extent are they still isolated?

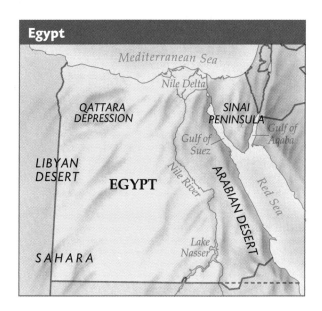

Egypt

Mediterranean Sea
Nile Delta
QATTARA DEPRESSION
SINAI PENINSULA
Gulf of Aqaba
Gulf of Suez
LIBYAN DESERT
EGYPT
Nile River
ARABIAN DESERT
Red Sea
Lake Nasser
SAHARA

2000–400 B.C.

Kingdoms and Empires in the Middle East

Chapter Themes

▶ **Cultural Diffusion** Aramaean and Phoenician merchants spread ideas throughout the Middle East. *Section 1*

▶ **Innovation** The Israelites contribute to the world the concept of monotheism. *Section 2*

▶ **Conflict** A series of empires—Hittite, then Assyrian, then Chaldean, then Persian—each conquers the previous one. *Section 3*

The Storyteller

Ashurbanipal, the last great Assyrian king, reigned in the mid-600s B.C. The dim rooms were almost still in Ashurbanipal's great palace at Nineveh, the splendid capital of his empire. Men with shoulder-length hair and squared-off beards glided in their tunics and sandals through the vast hallways. But the stone reliefs that decorated the palace walls told a less peaceful story. In intricately carved scenes, the impassive hunter in his chariot lets fly with a volley of arrows into a staggering lion, and the valiant general on the battlefield proudly waves his sword above the defeated enemy legions. Ashurbanipal followed a long line of ruthless Assyrian conquerors who boasted of their military exploits and cruelty.

Historical Significance

How did traders, religious thinkers, and empire builders shape the development of the ancient Middle East? How have their achievements influenced cultural and religious life today?

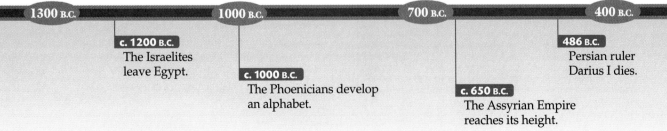

1300 B.C.	1000 B.C.	700 B.C.	400 B.C.

c. 1200 B.C.
The Israelites leave Egypt.

c. 1000 B.C.
The Phoenicians develop an alphabet.

c. 650 B.C.
The Assyrian Empire reaches its height.

486 B.C.
Persian ruler Darius I dies.

Ashurbanipal hunting on horseback. Relief from the NW Palace at Nineveh, c. 640 B.C.

Your History Journal

Early Middle Eastern accounts deal with the themes of peace and justice. Read the quotes on pages 86 and 93, and write similar verses describing events in the chapter that relate to these themes.

1200 B.C.   1000 B.C.   800 B.C.   600 B.C.

c. 1200 B.C.
Aramaeans settle
in central Syria.

c. 1100 B.C.
Phoenicians reach Spain and
western Africa.

c. 600s B.C.
Lydians develop a
wealthy kingdom
in Asia Minor.

Section 1

Trading Peoples

Setting the Scene

▶ **Terms to Define**
confederation, alphabet, colony, barter

▶ **People to Meet**
the Aramaeans, the Phoenicians, the Lydians

▶ **Places to Locate**
Syria, Damascus, Tyre

Find Out How did trading peoples influence
the development of the Middle East?

The Storyteller

*King Hiram was pleased. Tyre, his capital city,
was a bustling seaport: sophisticated, cosmopoli-
tan, and rich. Not only did the kings of Egypt and
Babylon send ambassadors to Hiram's court, they
also brought business to his land. Gold, copper,
ivory, and linen from Egypt; precious stones from
Babylon; silver from Asia Minor; and pottery from
Crete enriched Tyre. In return, Tyre exchanged
cedar, cut from the nearby mountains, and a vivid
purple dye, harvested from murex shells found in
the seas near the rocky coast. Hiram's people were
Phoenicians, the people of the purple, the color—
beautiful, costly, and rare—which throughout the
ancient world marked an individual as one of
immense wealth and high rank.*

—adapted from
*The Bible as
History*, Werner
Keller, translated
by William Neil,
1969

Phoenician ship

The magnificent civilizations of
Mesopotamia and Egypt greatly influenced neighboring peoples in the
Fertile Crescent—among them **the Aramaeans**
(AR•uh•MEE•uhnz) and **the Phoenicians** (fih
•NEE•shuhnz). In turn, these trading peoples
helped to spread their own cultures throughout the
region and into much of the ancient world.
Traveling on sailing ships and by caravan, traders
from the Fertile Crescent brought languages, customs, and ideas along with their trade goods.

The Aramaeans

One of the most active peoples in early Middle
Eastern trade, the Aramaeans settled in central
Syria around 1200 B.C. Although Aramaean kings
established a capital at **Damascus**, provincial leaders frequently challenged their authority. Despite
political weaknesses, the Aramaeans gained control
of the rich overland trade between Egypt and
Mesopotamia.

Because Aramaean caravans crossed and
recrossed the Fertile Crescent on business, people
throughout the region learned Aramaic, the language of the Aramaeans. Until the A.D. 800s, the
majority of the people living in the Fertile Crescent
spoke Aramaic, a language closely related to
Hebrew and Arabic. In addition, some parts of the
Bible were written in Aramaic.

The Phoenicians

Between ancient Egypt and Syria lay the land of
Canaan, today made up of Lebanon, Israel, and
Jordan. The Phoenicians, one of the Semitic groups
that migrated from the Arabian Peninsula about
3000 B.C., settled in the northern part of Canaan.
Their neighbors in Canaan, the Philistines, came
from the eastern Mediterranean. The Romans would

Lloyd K. Townsend

Merchants of the Mediterranean

In this illustration sturdy cargo boats dock in their North African home port of Carthage, and war galleys in the harbor lie in wait for any rivals caught in Phoenician waters. A captain bargains over the price of a bale of purple cloth for the next voyage as his crew unloads grain from Sardinia and cedar logs from North Africa. Above deck sit clay jars of olive oil and wine; below, silver, tin, gold, and ivory are stored. Departing vessels take on terra-cotta figurines, decorated ostrich eggshells, metal utensils, and perfume vials.

From their cities nestled along the coast of the eastern Mediterranean Sea, Phoenicians launched a trading empire. They soon became middlemen for their neighbors in Mesopotamia, Arabia, and Egypt. By 800 B.C., Phoenician trade had spread into the western Mediterranean. From Carthage and other Mediterranean cities, the Phoenicians manned supply depots, guarded sea lanes, and expanded their trading empire. ⊕

later call southern Canaan *Palestine,* meaning "land of the Philistines."

In contrast to the Aramaeans, who trekked overland to reach their markets, the Phoenicians sailed the seas. On a narrow strip of land between the mountains of western Syria and the Mediterranean Sea, Phoenicia lacked enough arable land for farming, and many Phoenicians turned to the sea to earn a living. They harvested timber from the cedar forests on nearby slopes to build strong, fast ships.

By 1200 B.C. the Phoenicians had built a string of cities and towns along their coast. Many of these scattered ports grew to become city-states, the largest of which were **Tyre**, Byblos, Sidon, and Berytus (modern Beirut). The city-state of Tyre often provided the leadership for what remained a confederation, or loose union, of independent Phoenician city-states. According to the Bible:

> ❝Who was like Tyre.... In the midst of the sea? When your wares were unloaded from the seas, You satisfied many peoples; With your great wealth and merchandise You enriched the kings of the earth. ❞
> —Ezekiel 27:32-33

The Phoenicians sailed from their coastal city-states throughout the Mediterranean. Expert navigators, they learned to plot their voyages with great accuracy by means of the sun and the stars. By 1100 B.C. Phoenicians reached the southern coast of Spain and the western coast of Africa. Some historians believe they even ventured as far as the British Isles in northwestern Europe.

Astute traders and businesspeople, the Phoenicians soon took charge of Mediterranean shipping and trade. At ports of call, they exchanged cedar logs, textiles dyed a beautiful purple, glass objects, and elegant jewelry for precious metals. They also brought new business practices, such as bills of sale and contracts.

An advantage that Phoenician merchants held over their competitors when keeping track of complex business deals was an improved alphabet—a series of written symbols that represent sounds. Phoenicians developed their efficient alphabet about 1000 B.C. from earlier, more complicated systems from southern Canaan and northwest Syria. The concise Phoenician alphabet used just 22 characters, each character representing a consonant sound. Readers mentally supplied vowels in the proper places.

The Phoenician system later became the foundation of several alphabets, including Greek, which in turn became the basis of all Western alphabets. Because the Phoenician alphabet did not require years of study to master, merchants no longer needed the services of specially trained scribes to keep records.

To protect and resupply their ships, Phoenician sailors and traders set up along the coasts of the Mediterranean a network of temporary trading posts and colonies, or settlements of Phoenician emigrants. For example, about 814 B.C., people from Tyre founded a colony named Carthage on the coast of present-day Tunisia. Carthage eventually became the most powerful city in the western Mediterranean.

The Lydians

The Lydians (LIH•dee•uhnz) lived in Asia Minor—the peninsula jutting westward between the Mediterranean, Aegean, and Black Seas. Lydian merchants and artisans were well situated to prosper in the growing regional trade. By the late 600s B.C., the Lydians had developed a wealthy and independent kingdom famous for its rich gold deposits.

Most traders from neighboring cultures still relied on a system of barter for their transactions, exchanging their wares for other goods. The Lydians, however, began to set prices and developed a money system using coins as a medium of exchange. Soon Greek and Persian rulers began to stamp their own coins, and the concept of money spread beyond Lydia.

SECTION I REVIEW

Recall
1. **Define** confederation, alphabet, colony, barter.
2. **Identify** the Aramaeans, the Phoenicians, the Lydians.
3. **Describe** the bodies of water bordering the regions of Canaan and Asia Minor.

Critical Thinking
4. **Evaluating Information** What geographic factors enabled the Phoenician city-states to remain independent and to prosper?

Understanding Themes
5. **Cultural Diffusion** Why was the Phoenician alphabet a significant development?

c. 1900 B.C.
Abraham settles in Canaan.

c. 1200 B.C.
The Israelites first celebrate Passover.

c. 1000 B.C.
David sets up capital at Jerusalem.

c. 530s B.C.
Jews rebuild the Temple in Jerusalem.

Section 2

Early Israelites

Setting the Scene

▶ **Terms to Define**
monotheism, prophet, covenant, exodus, Diaspora

▶ **People to Meet** the Israelites, Abraham, Moses, Deborah, David, Solomon

▶ **Places to Locate** Canaan, Jerusalem

ind Out   What part do slavery, exile, and return play in the history of the Israelites?

The Storyteller

This battle would be decisive, Jael was certain. Before the sun set, the Israelites would be recognized as Yahweh's chosen people. Unlike the nomads who had passed through Canaan for generations, the 12 tribes of Israel now sought permanent settlement. However, to remain and prosper, the Israelites had to join together and defeat the threatening Canaanites. Several tribes of Israel, held together only by their common covenant with Yahweh, were sending armed men to battle. Jael, resolving to take action herself, if necessary, was sure that Yahweh would muster the heavens themselves to confound the enemies of the covenant, give victory to the Israelites, and bring peace to the land.

—adapted from the *Holy Bible,* Judges

Mount Sinai

Most cultures of the ancient world worshiped many deities. The Phoenicians, for example, worshiped a chief god known as El, Baal, or Melqart; an earth-mother goddess called Astarte; and a young god of rebirth named Adonis.

The Israelites—another people living in **Canaan**—were an exception. They adhered to monotheism, the belief in one all–powerful God whose commands were revealed by prophets, or holy messengers. The Israelites believed that God, whom they called Yahweh, determined right and wrong and expected people to deal justly with each other and to accept moral responsibility for their actions. The teachings of the Israelites exist today as the religion of Judaism, which shares many beliefs with two other monotheistic religions— Christianity and Islam.

The Land of Canaan

The Bible remains one of the main sources of ancient history in the Fertile Crescent. As a record of the early Israelites, the Bible traces their origins to **Abraham**, a herder and trader who lived in the Mesopotamian city of Ur. Around 1900 B.C. Abraham and his household left Ur and settled in Canaan at the command of Yahweh, or God. The Israelites believed that God made a covenant, or agreement, with Abraham at this time. "I will make of you a great nation" was God's promise to bless Abraham and his descendants if they would remain faithful to God.

According to the Bible, once in the land of Canaan, the descendants of Abraham shared the land with other peoples, such as the Phoenicians and Philistines. Canaan contained rocky hills and desert, fertile plains and grassy slopes, with the best farming in the valley of the Jordan River. Many people lived as nomads herding sheep and goats.

The Exodus From Egypt

Abraham's grandson Jacob, also known as Israel, raised 12 sons in Canaan, and each son led a separate family group, or tribe. These groups became the 12 tribes of Israel. To escape a severe famine, the Israelites migrated to Egypt. There they lived peacefully for several generations, until the Egyptians decided to enslave them.

In the 1200s B.C., the Israelite prophet **Moses** led his people out of Egypt in an exodus, or departure, into the Sinai Desert. Every year during the festival of Passover, Jews today retell the story of the Exodus from Egypt.

According to the Bible, during the long trek across the desert of the Sinai Peninsula, God renewed the covenant made with Abraham. Moses and the Israelites pledged to reject all gods other than the one true God and to obey God's laws, the most important of which would be called the Ten Commandments:

> ❝ I the Lord am your God who brought you out of the land of Egypt, the house of bondage: You shall have no other gods beside Me.
>
> You shall not make for yourself a sculptured image....
>
> You shall not swear falsely by the name of the Lord your God....
>
> Remember the sabbath day and keep it holy....
>
> Honor your father and your mother, that you may long endure on the land that the Lord your God is giving you.
>
> You shall not murder.
>
> You shall not commit adultery.
>
> You shall not steal.
>
> You shall not bear false witness against your neighbor.
>
> You shall not covet ... anything that is your neighbor's. ❞
>
> —Exodus 20:2–14

In return for their loyalty, God promised the Israelites a safe return to the land of Canaan.

Settling the Land

Moses died before reaching Canaan, but his successor, Joshua, led the Israelites across the Jordan River into Canaan. For about 200 years, the

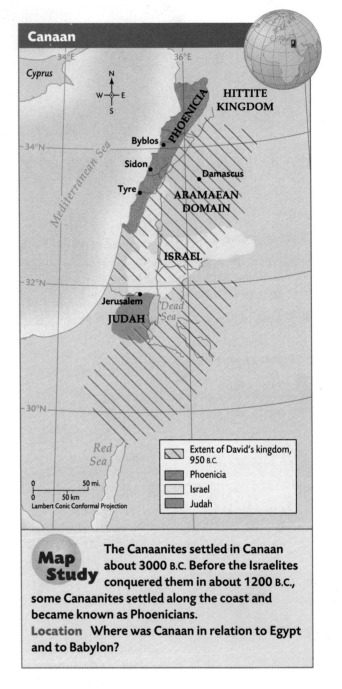

Canaan

The Canaanites settled in Canaan about 3000 B.C. Before the Israelites conquered them in about 1200 B.C., some Canaanites settled along the coast and became known as Phoenicians.

Location Where was Canaan in relation to Egypt and to Babylon?

Israelites fought the Philistines and the Canaanites who now occupied the land.

The Fighting Judges

Lack of unity among the 12 tribes of Israel prolonged the campaign to acquire Canaan. Leaders known as "judges" ruled each tribe. Serving as both judicial and military leaders, some of the judges attempted to rally the Israelites. The Bible relates how **Deborah**, a judge widely admired for her wisdom, planned an attack on a Canaanite army camped near Mount Tabor. The Israelites believed that through God's help, they won the battle.

The Davidic Monarchy

Around 1020 B.C. continual warfare led most of the Israelite tribes to unite under one king, Saul. Although he was popular at first, Saul's power waned when he proved unable to defeat the Philistines. **David**, who had once fought the Philistine Goliath on Saul's behalf, took the throne in 1012 B.C. and ruled for the next 40 years. King David set up a capital at **Jerusalem**, organized a central government, and enlarged his kingdom's borders. During his reign, the Israelites enjoyed economic prosperity.

David's son **Solomon** succeeded his father in 961 B.C. Solomon founded new cities and lavished money on the construction of a magnificent temple to God in Jerusalem. The Israelites resented Solomon's high taxes and harsh labor requirements. After Solomon's death in 922 B.C., the 10 northern tribes broke away from the 2 tribes in the south. The northern tribes continued to call their kingdom Israel. The 2 southern tribes called their kingdom Judah, and kept Jerusalem as their capital. The word *Jew* comes from the name *Judah*.

Exile and Return

Although split politically, the people of Israel and Judah continued to share one religion. The 2 kingdoms, however, were too weak to resist invasions by powerful neighbors. In 722 B.C. the Assyrians of Mesopotamia swept in and conquered Israel, scattering the people of the 10 northern tribes throughout the Assyrian Empire. Then, in 586 B.C., another Mesopotamian people, the Chaldeans (kal•DEE•uhnz), gained control of Judah and destroyed the Temple in Jerusalem. They enslaved some of the city's residents and carried them off to exile in the Chaldean capital city of Babylon.

Exile in Babylon

During this difficult period, a series of prophets arose among the Israelites, who were called Jews after the Babylonian exile. Some prophets, such as Jeremiah, condemned abuses in society and blamed the exile on the Jews' forgetting their duties to God and to one another. The prophets also helped the Jews retain their religious culture during the exile.

CONNECTIONS

Science and Technology

Counting the Days

How many days are there in a week? Different ancient peoples had more than one answer to this question. The Assyrians used a five-day week, while the Egyptians favored groupings of seven.

The modern week may trace its origins to the Jewish custom of observing a Sabbath day every seven days. Alternatively, our week may have originated in the Babylonian belief in the sacredness of the number seven—a belief probably linked either to the four seven-day phases of the moon or to the seven planets then visible in the heavens.

Ancient peoples often developed lunar calendars, based on the length of time it takes the moon to circle Earth, about 29 days. Of course, the lunar year of about 354 days did not correspond to the solar, or agricultural, year of 365 days. To solve this problem, Babylonian rulers added an extra month to certain years by royal decree.

Astronomers continued to try to adjust calendars to match the annual cycle of seasons. In 46 B.C. the Roman ruler Julius Caesar decreed that months should be longer than a lunar month. He also introduced January 1 as the first day of a new year. But not until A.D. 1582 were errors in the Julian calendar corrected by Pope Gregory XIII, who formalized a self-correcting system of leap years. The Gregorian calendar used today by most people in the Western world closely matches the solar year.

Linking Past and Present ACTIVITY

Describe how our modern calendar differs from the ancient Babylonian calendar. Then, research current proposals for calendar reform. Would you support any of the proposed changes? Why or why not?

A modern sundial

While in Babylon, the Jews no longer had a temple in which to worship God. Instead, small groups of Jews began to meet on the Sabbath, the holy day of rest, for prayer and study. The rise of local synagogues developed from these gatherings.

Rebuilding Jerusalem

Many Jews continued to hope for a return to Jerusalem. Finally, in 539 B.C., the Persians conquered the Chaldeans. The Persian king, Cyrus II, allowed the Jewish exiles to return to Judah and to rebuild the Temple in Jerusalem. In the 400s B.C., Jewish holy writings were collected and organized into the Torah, made up of the first five books of the Bible: Genesis, Exodus, Leviticus, Numbers, and Deuteronomy.

Although a new Jewish community arose in Jerusalem, many Jews chose to remain in Babylon, and some migrated to other areas in the Middle East. Ever since this time, communities of Jews have existed outside their homeland in what has become known as the Diaspora, a Greek word meaning "scattered."

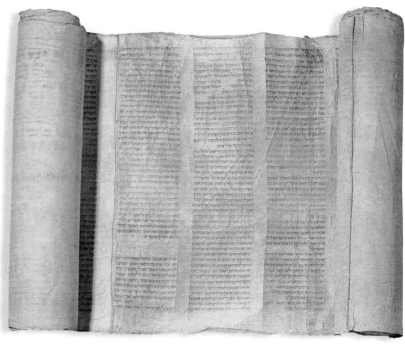

Visualizing History Scribes recopied the Torah carefully, comparing each letter and word to the original copy. *What was the prophet Micah's vision for the world?*

A Lasting Legacy

Their troubled history—with cycles of slavery, exile, and return—made the Jews keenly aware of their past. Seeing events as having a God-directed purpose, the Jews recorded their history and examined it for meaning. The Jewish Scriptures begin with the Torah and include the writings of the prophets. As the Jews scattered beyond Canaan, they took the Torah with them, and its teachings spread around the world.

From the Torah has come the concept that every human being, made in the image of God, has infinite worth. Further, humans work in partnership with God, striving to achieve a

perfect world, and this link makes people accountable for what happens in the world. The Jewish prophet Micah expressed his vision for the world as follows:

❝ And they shall beat their swords
 into plowshares,
And their spears into pruning hooks.
Nation shall not take up
Sword against nation;
They shall never again know war;
But every man shall sit
Under his grapevine or fig tree
With no one to disturb him. ❞

—Micah 4:3–4

SECTION 2 REVIEW

Recall
1. **Define** monotheism, prophet, covenant, exodus, Diaspora.
2. **Identify** the Israelites, Abraham, Moses, Deborah, David, Solomon.
3. **Locate** Jerusalem on the map on page 84. What was the significance of Jerusalem to Jews in exile in Babylon?

Critical Thinking
4. **Analyzing Information** Create a chronology of the migrations of the Israelites.

Understanding Themes
5. **Innovation** What religious beliefs set the Israelites apart from other ancient peoples? How have these beliefs helped the Jews to survive in spite of exile and persecution?

Problem Solving

You have just done poorly on a geography exam. You wonder why you can't do better since you always go to class, take notes, and study for exams. In order to improve your grades, you need to identify the specific problem, and then take actions to solve it.

Learning the Skill

There are six key steps you should follow that will help you through the problem-solving process.

1. Identify the problem. In this case, you know that you are not doing well on geography exams.

2. Gather information. You know that you always go to class and take notes. You study by yourself for about two hours each day for two or three days before the exam. You also know that as you are taking the exam, you sometimes forget details or get confused about things.

3. List and consider options. For example, instead of studying by yourself, you might try a study group, or study with a friend.

4. Consider the advantages and disadvantages of each option.

5. Choose and implement a solution to the problem. Now that you have listed and considered the options, you need to choose the best option.

6. Evaluate the effectiveness of the solution. This will help you determine if you've solved the problem. If, on the next few geography exams, you earn better scores, you know that you have solved your problem.

Practicing the Skill

Reread the material in Section 1 on pages 80–82 about the trading peoples of the Middle East. Use that information to answer the following questions.

1. What problem did the Phoenicians encounter as they tried to farm the land of Phoenicia?

2. Summarize information the Phoenicians might have gathered after finding that they couldn't rely on farming as a means of survival.

3. List some of the options available to the Phoenicians. What were the advantages? What were the disadvantages?

4. Explain the solution the Phoenicians implemented to solve their problem.

5. Evaluate the effectiveness of their solution. Was it successful? How do you determine this?

Applying the Skill

The conservation club at your school has no money to continue its recycling project. The school district allocated money to the club at the beginning of the year, but that money has been spent. As a member of the club, you have been asked to join a committee to save the conservation club and its projects. Write an essay describing the problem, the list of options and their advantages and disadvantages, a solution, and an evaluation of the chosen solution.

For More Practice

Turn to the Skill Practice in the Chapter Review on page 95 for more practice with problem solving.

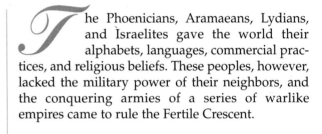

| 2000 B.C. | 1500 B.C. | 1000 B.C. | 500 B.C. |

c. 1600 B.C.
Hittite Empire reaches
its height.

c. 605 B.C.
Nebuchadnezzar
begins reign in
Babylon.

525 B.C.
Persian armies
conquer Egypt.

Section 3

Empire Builders

Setting the Scene

▶ **Terms to Define**
satrap

▶ **People to Meet**
the Hittites, the Assyrians, the Chaldeans,
Nebuchadnezzar, the Persians, Cyrus II,
Darius I, Zoroaster

▶ **Places to Locate** Anatolia, Babylon, Nineveh,
Persepolis

 How did a series of powerful
empires extend their rule throughout the
Middle East?

The Storyteller

*The scribe carefully recorded King
Ashurbanipal II's proclamation. The royal
archives would preserve an accurate
account of the actions taken against
the cities that had dared to revolt.
The king dictated: "With the
fury of my weapons I stormed
the city. I flayed all the chief
men who had revolted, and I
covered a pillar with their skins.
Some I impaled on the pillar on
stakes.... I fashioned a heroic
image of my royal self, my
power and my glory I inscribed
thereon...." Ashurbanipal called
the gods to destroy all who
opposed him, overthrowing their
kingdoms and blotting out their
names from the land.*

Giant winged bull

—from *Ancient Records of Assyria and
Babylonia,* Volume 1, edited by Daniel
David Luckenbill, 1968

The Phoenicians, Aramaeans, Lydians,
and Israelites gave the world their
alphabets, languages, commercial prac-
tices, and religious beliefs. These peoples, however,
lacked the military power of their neighbors, and
the conquering armies of a series of warlike
empires came to rule the Fertile Crescent.

The Hittites

Around 2000 B.C., **the Hittites**—perhaps coming from areas beyond the Black Sea—conquered
the local people of Asia Minor. The Hittites set up
several city-states on a central plateau called
Anatolia, and by about 1650 B.C., they had built a
well-organized kingdom. Archaeologists have deci-
phered the writing on some of the clay tablets
found in the ruins of Hattusas, the Hittite capital.
Other information about the Hittites comes from
records of peoples they confronted as they expanded their empire. An Egyptian source, for example,
described the Hittites' custom of wearing their hair
in a long, thick pigtail that hung down in the back.

Hittite kings assembled a fearsome army—the
first in the Middle East to wield iron weapons
extensively. The army used light, spoked-wheel
chariots that could carry two soldiers and a driver.
This gave the Hittites a decided advantage in battle,
because they were able to field twice as many
troops as their foes in two-person chariots.
Overwhelming any army that stood in their way,
the Hittites pushed eastward and conquered the
city of **Babylon** about 1595 B.C. The Hittite
Empire—spanning Asia Minor, Syria, and part of
Mesopotamia—lasted until about 1200 B.C.

The Hittites largely borrowed their culture
from Mesopotamia and Egypt. However, they did
contribute to Middle Eastern civilization a legal
system considered less harsh than Hammurabi's
code. Hittite law emphasized payments for damages rather than harsh punishments.

The Assyrians

The **Assyrians**, a people living in northern Mesopotamia, had faced constant invasions from adjoining Asia Minor—including those by the Hittites. About 900 B.C. the Assyrians finally became strong enough to repel attacks from the west. They also began to launch their own military campaigns to subdue their Mesopotamian neighbors.

A Powerful Army

The Assyrian army earned a reputation as the most lethal fighting force in the Middle East. The Assyrians organized their warriors into units of foot soldiers, charioteers, and fast-moving cavalry fighting on horseback. They were described as fighters "whose arrows were sharp and all their bows bent, the horses' hooves were like flint, and their [chariot] wheels like a whirlwind." The Assyrians fought with iron weapons and used battering rams against the walls of the cities they attacked.

The Assyrians treated conquered peoples cruelly. They burned cities and tortured and killed thousands of captives. The Assyrians routinely deported entire populations from their homelands. Resettling the land with people from other parts of the empire, the Assyrians forced these settlers to pay heavy taxes.

The Assyrian Empire

By about 650 B.C., the Assyrian kings governed an empire stretching from the Persian Gulf to Egypt and into Asia Minor. They divided their empire into provinces, each headed by a governor directly responsible to the king. Officials sent from the central government collected taxes to support the army and to fund building projects in **Nineveh**, the Assyrian capital. To improve communication, the Assyrians built a network of roads linking the provinces. Government messengers and Aramaean

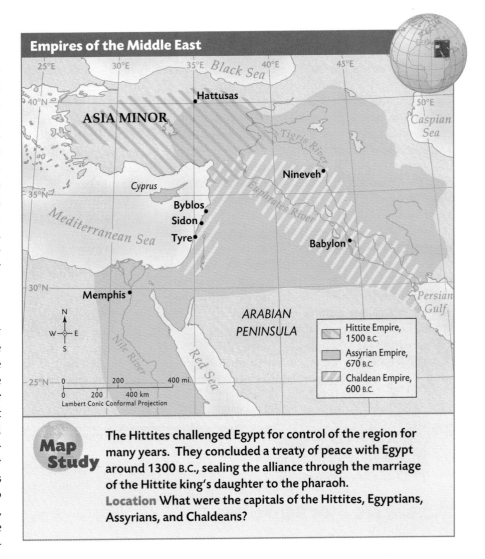

Empires of the Middle East

Hittite Empire, 1500 B.C.

Assyrian Empire, 670 B.C.

Chaldean Empire, 600 B.C.

Map Study

The Hittites challenged Egypt for control of the region for many years. They concluded a treaty of peace with Egypt around 1300 B.C., sealing the alliance through the marriage of the Hittite king's daughter to the pharaoh.
Location What were the capitals of the Hittites, Egyptians, Assyrians, and Chaldeans?

merchants traveled these roads, protected by soldiers from bandits.

In spite of these links, the Assyrian Empire eventually began to fracture as conquered peoples continually rebelled. In 612 B.C. **the Chaldeans**, who lived in the ancient city of Babylon, formed an alliance with the Medes from the east. The alliance captured Nineveh and brought down the Assyrian Empire.

The Chaldeans

Soon after the Assyrians fell, the Chaldean Empire succeeded in dominating the entire Fertile Crescent. Most of the Chaldeans—sometimes called the New Babylonians—were descended from people of Hammurabi's Babylonian Empire of the 1700s B.C.

The Chaldeans reached the height of their power during the reign of one of their greatest rulers, King **Nebuchadnezzar** (NEH•byuh•kuhd•NEH•zuhr), from 605 B.C. to 562 B.C. He extended the boundaries of the Chaldean Empire as far west as Syria and Canaan, conquering the city of Jerusalem and the Phoenician city-state of Tyre and forcing the people of the kingdom of Judah into a Babylonian exile in 586 B.C. Nebuchadnezzar also amassed great wealth and rebuilt Babylon into one of the most beautiful cities of the ancient world.

Historians of the time counted a feature of Babylon among the so-called Seven Wonders of the World—its Hanging Gardens. Nebuchadnezzar created the Hanging Gardens for his wife. Constructed on several levels and designed to be visible from any point in Babylon, the elaborate park was fed by water pumped from a nearby river. Another landmark of Babylon was an immense wall that snaked around the city, stood 50 feet (15 km) high, and bristled with watchtowers every 100 yards (90 m).

The Chaldeans were also noted for their interest in astrology. They recorded their observations of the stars and made maps that showed the position of the planets and the phases of the moon. Their studies laid the foundations for the science of astronomy.

After Nebuchadnezzar's death, a series of weak kings held the throne. Poor harvests and slow trade further sapped the strength of an empire whose people had been severely taxed and plundered. Then, in 539 B.C., **the Persians** under **Cyrus II** came from the mountains to the northeast, seized Babylon, and then conquered the rest of the Chaldean Empire.

The Persians

The Persians originated from a larger group of people now called Indo-Europeans. As warriors and cattle herders in search of new grasslands, the Persians and the Medes, another Indo-European group, left central Asia about 2000 B.C. They settled on a plateau between the Persian Gulf and the

Ancient Persepolis

The most luxurious palace of Darius was built at Persepolis. Completed by Xerxes, the palace was a monument to the king's power.

Alexander the Great destroyed most of the palace in 331 B.C., but the stone monumental gateways and terraces survived.

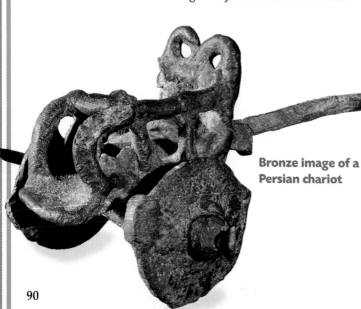

Bronze image of a Persian chariot

90

Caspian Sea, in the area of present-day Iran.

Cyrus's Conquests

During the 540s B.C., Cyrus had developed a strong army, conquered the Medes, and advanced into neighboring lands. He added northern Mesopotamia, Syria, Canaan, and the Phoenician cities to his empire. Cyrus also took over the kingdom of Lydia and the Greek city-states in Asia Minor. In 525 B.C. Cyrus's son Cambyses (kam•BY•seez) conquered Egypt, bringing all of the Middle East under Persian control.

The Persian Empire, then second to none, stretched from the Nile River to the Indus River, a distance of 3,000 miles (4,800 km). Within this immense empire, the Persians ruled more than 50 million people.

Darius's Empire

The best organizer among the Persian kings was **Darius I**, who reigned from 522 B.C. to 486 B.C. To administer his empire, Darius effectively divided the realm into provinces and assigned satraps, or provincial governors, to rule. Military officials and tax inspectors, chosen by the king from among the conquered people themselves, assisted the satraps in carrying out the king's decrees in the provinces. In addition, inspectors called "Eyes and Ears of the King" made unannounced tours of the provinces and reported directly to the king on the activities of officials. In this way, the king's court was able to keep watch on local government.

In contrast to the Assyrians, the Persians were tolerant rulers who allowed conquered peoples to retain their own languages, religions, and laws. The Persians won the loyalty of conquered peoples by respecting local customs. They believed that this loyalty could be won more easily with fairness than by fear or force. When faced with rebellion, however, the Persians did not hesitate to take extreme military measures.

Commerce and Roads

Darius brought artisans from many of his

Persian god and goddess protecting a palm tree

More than 1,000 years after Alexander destroyed Persepolis, the first curious travelers rediscovered the impressive remains of the city. The Apadana hall at the northern end of the palace contains stairways with beautiful reliefs of Persian nobles, guards, and tribute bearers.

REFLECTING ON THE TIMES

1. About what year did travelers rediscover Persepolis?
2. What ruins reveal the wealth of Persian kings?

91

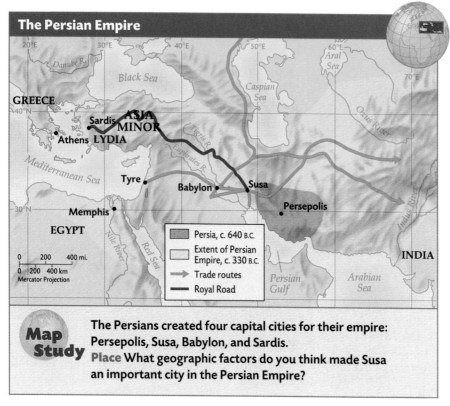

The Persian Empire

The Persians created four capital cities for their empire: Persepolis, Susa, Babylon, and Sardis.

Map Study

Place What geographic factors do you think made Susa an important city in the Persian Empire?

conquered lands to build **Persepolis**, the most magnificent city in the empire. The Persians themselves did not engage in trade, which they considered an indecent occupation. However, they did encourage trade among the peoples of their empire. To advance trade throughout the empire and aid the movement of soldiers, Darius had Persian engineers improve and expand the network of roads first laid down by the Assyrians. Royal messengers also journeyed on the roads allowing "neither snow, nor rain, nor heat, nor the darkness of night to hinder them in the prompt completion of their ... tasks."

The Royal Road, the most important thoroughfare in the Persian Empire, stretched more than 1,500 miles (2,400 km) from Persia to Asia Minor. Every 14 miles (22.4 km), stations along the Royal Road provided travelers with food, water, and fresh horses. Royal messengers could travel the length of the road in just seven days, a journey that had taken three months before the road was built.

A Persian Disaster

During his reign, Darius waged war against the Greeks over the control of city-states in Asia Minor. After Darius died, his son Xerxes (ZUHRK •SEEZ) led the forces of Persia in a disastrous campaign to conquer Greece in 480 B.C. Xerxes' defeat stopped Persian expansion into Europe.

Persian Religion and Culture

The Persians followed a strict moral code that stressed bravery and honesty. They taught their sons to "ride horses, to draw a bow, and to speak the truth." Before the 500s B.C., the Persian people worshiped many deities associated with the sky, sun, and fire. Then, about 570 B.C., a prophet named **Zoroaster** (ZOHR•uh•WAS •tuhr) began to call for reform of the Persian religion. Zoroaster preached that the world was divided by a struggle between good and evil. The god Ahura Mazda led the forces of good, and a lesser deity, Ahriman, represented the spirit of darkness. At the end of time, Ahura Mazda would triumph over Ahriman.

Zoroaster also taught that humans were caught up in this struggle and had to choose between good and evil. All humans who fought on the side of Ahura Mazda against evil would be rewarded with eternal life. Those who chose Ahriman would be condemned after death to eternal darkness and

Spread of Celtic Culture

Central Europe, c. 600 B.C.
The Hallstatt Celts spread their influence from Austria to the British Isles. They were among the first people in northern Europe to make iron. Their warlike chieftains relied on horses and slept on animal skins in crude houses. Their weapons and artifacts, however, were decorated with elaborate patterns. Celtic art featured highly stylized plants and animals.

This relief of King Darius and Xerxes is one of many at the palace of King Darius. *What do you think the appearance of these figures reveals about the Persian royal court?*

misery. These teachings were contained in a book called the Avesta.

Persian rulers believed that they ruled by the power of Ahura Mazda and were responsible to him alone. Darius I had the following statement carved on a cliff:

66 On this account Ahura Mazda brought me health.... Because I was not wicked, nor was I a liar, nor was I a tyrant, neither I nor any of my line. We had ruled according to righteousness. 99

Zoroaster's teachings were eventually linked to the glorification of the Persian monarchy. Because the monarchy was viewed as a sacred institution, Persian kings commanded great respect and were surrounded by pomp and pageantry. This style of kingship later shaped the development of monarchies in the Western world.

Zoroaster's beliefs also may have shaped beliefs in the Mediterranean world. Some scholars believe that Zoroaster's teachings about paradise, hell, and the Last Judgment—or the separation of good and evil at the end of time—may have influenced Judaism, Christianity, and Islam. Other aspects of Persian culture lived on as well, and mixed with Greek culture when Alexander the Great absorbed the Persians into his own empire in the 300s B.C.

SECTION 3 REVIEW

Recall
1. **Define** satrap.
2. **Identify** the Hittites, the Assyrians, the Chaldeans, Nebuchadnezzar, the Persians, Cyrus II, Darius I, Zoroaster.
3. **Locate** the Hittite, Assyrian, Chaldean, and Persian Empires on the maps on pages 89 and 92. Rank them in order of approximate size.

Critical Thinking
4. **Evaluating Information** Why might other religions have adopted features of the Zoroastrian religion?

Understanding Themes
5. **Conflict** How did the military exploits of the Hittites and the Assyrians both change the way peoples of the time fought military battles and the way in which they dealt with conquered peoples?

Connections Across Time

Historical Significance Trading peoples and empire builders both enriched the culture of the ancient Middle East and strongly influenced later civilizations. One of the most significant innovations, for example, was the concise and easy-to-learn Phoenician alphabet, which spread communication, enhanced trade, and eventually evolved into the alphabet used to spell the words on this page.

Spiritual life also evolved dramatically, through the adherence of the Israelites to a belief in one God, who required people to live justly. The concepts of monotheism and ethical laws have endured in the modern religions of Judaism, Christianity, and Islam.

Using Key Terms

Write the key term that completes each sentence. Then write a sentence for each term not chosen.

a. alphabet	f. satraps
b. monotheism	g. exodus
c. colony	h. prophets
d. covenant	i. Diaspora
e. barter	j. confederation

1. In the 1200s B.C., the Israelite leader Moses rallied his people and led them out of Egypt in a(n)_____ into the Sinai Desert.
2. The Phoenicians were organized into a(n) _____ of independent city-states along the coast of northern Canaan.
3. Israelite _____ condemned abuses in society and urged people not to forget their duties to God and to one another.
4. Persian kings appointed a number of a(n)_____ to govern the provinces of the Persian Empire.
5. Jewish communities existing outside of their homeland have become known as the _____, after a Greek word meaning "scattered."

Using Your History Journal

Choose one of the verses that you have written for your journal dealing with an event mentioned in the chapter. After research expand the verse into an epic poem about the event.

Reviewing Facts

1. **Culture** Explain how Aramaic came to be spoken throughout the Fertile Crescent.
2. **Technology** Identify the practices that the Phoenicians introduced to business and trade. What advantage did the Phoenicians have over their competitors?
3. **Culture** Describe how the Israelites interpreted and applied monotheism.
4. **History** List the peoples with whom the Israelites came into conflict after the Exodus from Egypt and the return to Canaan.
5. **Culture** Describe the role of Deborah in helping the Israelites settle Caanan.

Critical Thinking

1. **Apply** What natural resource supported the Lydians' development of a money system to replace the barter system?
2. **Analyze** How were the deities and beliefs of the Phoenicians, the Israelites, and the Persians different from one another?
3. **Analyze** What actions taken by Darius I made his rule so effective?

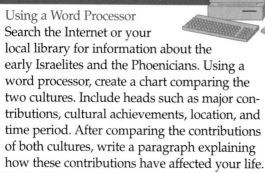

Technology Activity

Using a Word Processor
Search the Internet or your local library for information about the early Israelites and the Phoenicians. Using a word processor, create a chart comparing the two cultures. Include heads such as major contributions, cultural achievements, location, and time period. After comparing the contributions of both cultures, write a paragraph explaining how these contributions have affected your life.

4. Evaluate Why was the Exodus important to the Israelites? In what way did it shape the development of religion in the Western world?

Geography in History

1. Movement What event led to the establishment of a large Jewish community in Babylon after 586 B.C.?

2. Human/Environment Interaction How did the people of Babylon provide water to various locations inside the city walls?

3. Human/Environment Interaction How did the people of Babylon fortify the city against attack from outsiders?

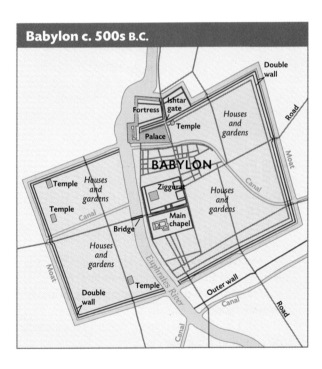

Understanding Themes

1. Cultural Diffusion Based on your knowledge of the ancient trading peoples of the Middle East, what kinds of ideas might people be likely to adopt from other cultures?

2. Innovation From a modern perspective, do you see any advantages or disadvantages to the development of a religious belief system based on monotheism?

3. Conflict Make a list of what aims might have motivated conquerors such as the Hittites, Assyrians, Chaldeans, and Persians to incorporate their neighbors into empires.

1. Does the legal system of our country parallel Hittite law or Hammurabi's code? Provide a brief explanation of your view.

2. The Persian Empire was made up of many different peoples. Evaluate the ways in which the Persians ruled their empire. How does the Persian experience compare or contrast with that of modern nations, such as the United States, that have diverse populations?

3. Solomon built a magnificent temple at Jerusalem. The last Jewish temple on the Temple Mount was destroyed in A.D. 70. What building stands on that site now?

Skill Practice

Reread pages 91-92 in Section 3 about Darius and his empire. Use that information to answer the following questions about the Persian Empire.

1. What problem hindered the expansion of the Persian Empire?

2. Write a short summary of the information the Persians might have gathered after deciding that trade was an indecent occupation in which to engage.

3. List the options that were available to the Persians. What were the advantages? What were the disadvantages?

4. What kind of solution did the Persians find to help in the expansion of the empire?

5. Evaluate and discuss the effectiveness of the solution. Why do you think it was, or was not, successful?

ABCNEWS INTERACTIVE™

Turning Points in World History

The Rise of Cities

Setting up the Video

Work with a group of your classmates to view "The Rise of Cities" on the videodisc *Turning Points in World History*. Many historians believe that the Sumerians arrived in Mesopotamia around 3500 B.C. They settled in the lower part of the Tigris-Euphrates river valley, known as Sumer. Scholars credit the Sumerians with being the first to create cities. This program highlights the contributions and innovations of the people of Sumer.

Side One, Chapter 3

View the video by scanning the bar code or by entering the chapter number on your keypad and pressing Search. (Also available in VHS format.)

Hands-On Activity

Design a bulletin board illustrating Sumerian technological advances and contributions to culture and government. Include examples of what Sumerian innovations have evolved into today. Write captions to go with the illustrations.

Surfing the "Net"

Ancient Cultures

To honor their god-kings and to provide them with an eternal place of rest, the Egyptians of the Old Kingdom built lasting monuments called pyramids. To learn about other ancient cultures and their monuments, look on the Internet.

Getting There

Follow these steps to gather information.

1. Go to a search engine. Type in the phrase *ancient cultures*.
2. After typing in the phrase, enter words like those below to focus your search:
   - *monuments*
   - *temples*
   - *structures*
   - *pyramids*

3. The search engine should provide you with a number of links to follow. Links are "pointers" to different sites on the Internet and commonly appear as blue underlined words.

What to Do When You Are There

Click on the links to navigate through the pages of information and gather your findings. Use a word processor to create an information pamphlet about your findings. Include information such as the purpose of the monument, its location and the time period it was created, illustrations, and the culture of the people. Draw a world map and indicate the location of each monument.

The bones of early human beings as well as other fossil remains, archaeological artifacts, and written records hold many clues for researchers studying the past. Although historians consider history to have begun about 5,500 years ago, when early peoples began writing, the human story extends much further into the past—into millions of years of prehistory.

Chapter 1
Human Beginnings

Using research techniques such as radiocarbon dating to date plant and animal matter, anthropologists and archaeologists have been able to establish a time frame for prehistoric human life. Scientists do not agree about all aspects of how or when the first human beings became truly human, but fossil evidence suggests that the first prehuman hominids lived about 4.4 million years ago. Over the next few million years, hominids gradually migrated to other areas and adapted to changes in their environment, such as a colder climate, in various ways. Some hominids evolved larger brains.

Early Humans

Two large-brained hominids, *Homo habilis* and *Homo erectus*, as well as all modern human beings, are scientifically classified in the genus, or group, *Homo*—human. Around 200,000 years ago, the modern human species, *Homo Sapiens*, appeared. Two major groups of early *Homo Sapiens* were the Neanderthals and the Cro-Magnons.

In prehistoric times, early human beings set many cultural patterns that continued into historic times. They cooperated with one another to obtain food and came into conflict over land and water. They developed techniques for staying warm, for hunting, and for defense and attack. Clothing and fire became part of the culture of prehistoric people, as did the use of stone tools and weapons. Prehistoric peoples also developed many social skills, including spoken language, and adopted from one another new methods and ideas.

Civilizations

Between 8,000 and 10,000 years ago, early peoples in various parts of the world shifted from hunting and food gathering to farming. The development of agriculture was an essential stepping-stone to civilization. Initially farming allowed people to give up their nomadic life and settle in communities. Eventually, with a relatively steady food supply, many men and women could devote their time to economic activities other than farming. As time passed, some of the early agricultural villages grew into the first cities, which were home to highly organized societies, or civilizations.

All early civilizations shared some basic features. They had specialized labor; cooperative methods for producing surplus food, such as irrigation; and metalworking technology. Under an organized government they formed social classes and maintained an army. They undertook long-distance trade. With a system of values and religious beliefs, they were sophisticated enough to have written records.

Visualizing History **Archaeologist working at a grave site in Jerusalem.** *What allowed people to give up their nomadic life and settle in cities?*

Chapter 2
Early Civilizations

Cities and civilizations arose at different times in different parts of the world. Many of the earliest civilizations had one thing in common, however: they grew out of agricultural settlements in river valleys. Civilization appeared around 3500 B.C. in the Tigris-Euphrates River valley in the Fertile Crescent, but it also arose soon thereafter in the Nile River valley of Egypt, and again later in the Indus River valley of the South Asia and in the Huang He valley in China.

Ancient Egypt and Mesopotamia

In northeastern Africa, villages along the Nile banded together in small kingdoms, which were later united under a king. The ruling monarch was a religious and political leader and head of a government bureaucracy, or a group of government officials.

With innovative irrigation and flood control methods, the Egyptians used the seasonally fluctuating Nile waters and the river's rich soil deposits to grow crops. They undertook ambitious building projects, such as the Pyramids, which required new engineering skills. The writing system that early Egyptians invented as well as the script that was later formed from it were used both for everyday purposes and for decorating their massive monuments.

Egypt's prosperity encouraged later Egyptian rulers, or pharaohs, to expand the frontiers of their country and to build an empire, or group of territories under a single ruler or government. The Egyptian Empire led to an exchange of ideas, goods, and customs among different cultures. This cultural diffusion further enriched Egyptian civilization.

In Mesopotamia, the land between the Tigris and Euphrates Rivers, peoples fleeing war and overpopulation, as well as poor climate, settled on the fertile river plain. Although the early Mesopotamians, unlike the Egyptians, could not depend on a regular supply of water, they managed to meet the challenges of the twin rivers by cooperating with one another and devising methods of irrigation and flood control. An innovative Mesopotamian people known as the Sumerians built city-states, invented the wheel, and created cuneiform, perhaps the world's oldest writing system. The prosperous Sumerians eventually fell to empire-builders, first the Akkadians and later the Babylonians.

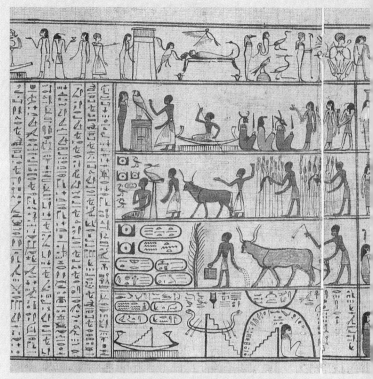

Visualizing History **A funeral papyrus from the *Book of the Dead*, Egypt.** *Along what river are most ancient Egyptian monuments found?*

South Asian and East Asian Civilizations

While empires rose and fell in Mesopotamia, a third river valley civilization to the east, the Harappans, reached its peak. Adapting to the unique seasonal wind and floods patterns of their environment, the people of the South Asian subcontinent prospered in the Indus River valley. They produced a surplus of food and various goods, which they traded with the Mesopotamians, among others. Although the remains of Harappan cities such as Mohenjo-Daro indicate that people of the Indus Valley were expert urban planners, why the cities were destroyed and what caused the end of their civilization remains a mystery.

The fourth river valley civilization, which began in ancient China, has continued to the present day. Isolated from other cultures for many centuries by formidable landforms, the Chinese formed a strong sense of national identity. From late prehistoric times, people settled and flourished in the Huang He valley. The Shang dynasty, or ruling family controlled the river valley from about 1700 B.C. to 1000 B.C. Under Shang rule, the Chinese built their first cities, created a complex writing system, and perfected their skill in casting bronze. The replacement of the Shang dynasty by the Zhou dynasty was the first of many transitions between the dynasties that successively governed China.

Visualizing History **Shang ritual vessel in the form of a tiger protecting a man.** *In what river valley did the Shang dynasty flourish?*

Chapter 3
Kingdoms and Empires in the Middle East

A region of the Middle East known as the Fertile Crescent continued to be home for diverse peoples after the earliest river valley civilizations fell. Many people in the Fertile Crescent were active in trade and made lasting cultural and economic contributions to later civilizations.

Traders and Herders

Prominent among the trading peoples of the Middle East were the Phoenicians. They navigated the Mediterranean Sea and beyond, founded overseas settlements, and created an alphabet that became a model for later alphabets. Among the other trading peoples in the region, the Aramaeans spread their Aramaic language, making it the primary language of trade and everyday speech in the Middle East. The Lydians left a lasting mark on the economies of other civilizations by using coins as a medium of exchange.

The Israelites also made lasting cultural contributions. Foremost among these was monotheism—the belief in one all-powerful, merciful, and just God—an idea that formed the basis of Judaism, Christianity, and Islam. During their long history, the Israelites several times came into conflict with neighboring peoples. Although they were enslaved and exiled, they kept close ties to their homeland.

Empire Builders

Many peoples in the Fertile Crescent suffered as warlike empires successively dominated the region and neighboring regions as well. In spite of their emphasis on war, these empires also advanced trade, created new methods of government, and carried out building projects. The Hittites were the first of the empire builders, coming to Asia Minor from Europe or central Asia. With many advantages in military tactics, the Hittites conquered an empire spanning Asia Minor, Syria, and part of Mesopotamia.

The Assyrians, a Mesopotamian people, were the next conquerors in the Middle East. They too had powerful armies, and cruelly treated the peoples they conquered. They controlled an empire stretching from the Persian Gulf to Egypt and into Asia Minor.

The well-organized and extensive Assyrian Empire fell to the Chaldeans (descendants of the Babylonians). The Chaldeans built their capital, Babylon, into one of the largest, most stunning cities of the ancient world. In less than 100 years, however, the Chaldean Empire was in turn overthrown by the Persians.

The Persians, who originated in central Asia and settled in the area of present-day Iran, built an empire that stretched from the Nile River to the Indus River. The Persians surpassed their predecessors in governing a vast area and in tolerating the languages, religions, and customs of subject peoples. When faced with rebellion, however, they did not hesitate to use military force. Persian rulers, such as Cyrus and Darius I, developed a well-organized government and surrounded themselves with pomp and pageantry. Their style of kingship later shaped the development of monarchies in the Middle East and the Western world.

SURVEYING UNIT I

1. **Chapter 1** Why was the development of agriculture a stepping-stone to the rise of the first civilizations?
2. **Chapter 2** How did early river valley civilizations, such as the Egyptian and the Sumerian, meet the challenges of their environments?
3. **Chapter 3** What major contribution was made by each of the following peoples: the Phoenicians, the Israelites, and the Persians?

2

Flowering of Civilizations

Then & Now

As people developed agricultural technology, nomadic life gave way to living in communities. Emerging cities became centers of trade and commerce, characterized by highly organized social structures and governments. Commerce brought wealth that allowed more people time for leisure and study. Ancient civilizations contributed much that remains in the modern world. China developed a civil service system based on merit. The city of Alexandria in Egypt had a great library. The Greeks refined geometry to calculate the size of the earth. Architecture, theater, and education all have their roots in ancient civilizations.

* In A.D. 532, a Christian monk started a system of dating events, beginning with the year he believed Jesus was born. The years before Jesus' birth were called *B.C.* (before Christ). The years after this event were called *A.D.*, an abbreviation for *anno Domini*, which is Latin for "in the year of the Lord." Today, some publications use *B.C.E.* (before the common era) instead of *B.C.*, and *C.E.* (common era) instead of *A.D.* Note that unlike *A.D.*, *C.E.* follows the year.

A Global Chronology

2000 B.C.	1500 B.C.	1000 B.C.
Political	c. 1500 B.C. Aryans cross the Hindu Kush into South Asia.	
Scientific/ Technological	c. 1700 B.C. Babylonian Empire adopts Sumerian calendar.	
Social/Cultural		c. 1200 B.C. Vedic Age begins in India.

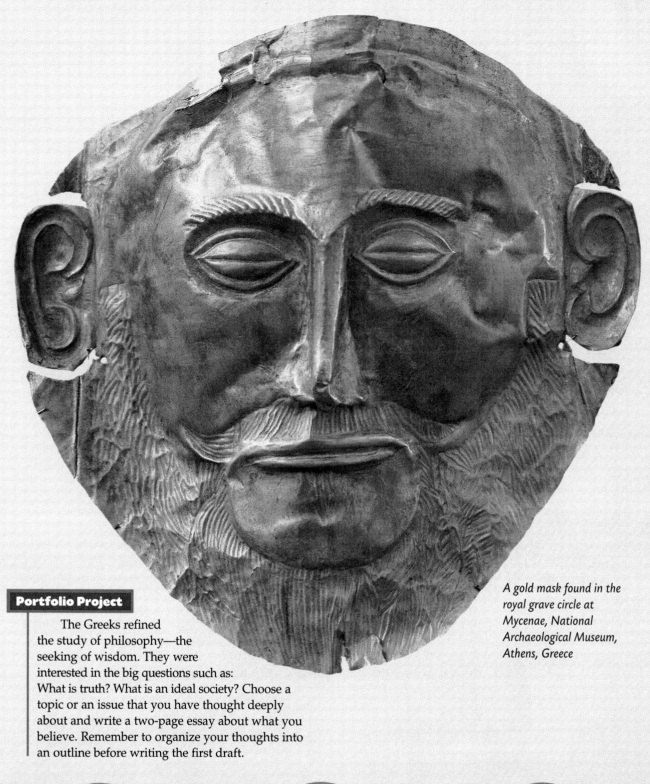

A gold mask found in the royal grave circle at Mycenae, National Archaeological Museum, Athens, Greece

Portfolio Project

The Greeks refined the study of philosophy—the seeking of wisdom. They were interested in the big questions such as: What is truth? What is an ideal society? Choose a topic or an issue that you have thought deeply about and write a two-page essay about what you believe. Remember to organize your thoughts into an outline before writing the first draft.

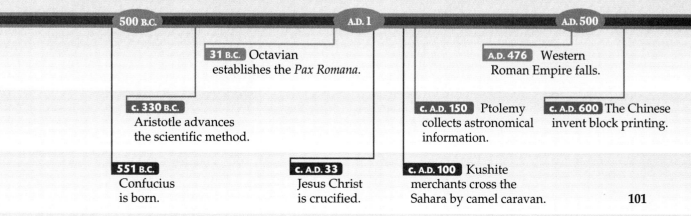

500 B.C.   **A.D. 1**   **A.D. 500**

31 B.C. Octavian establishes the *Pax Romana*.

A.D. 476 Western Roman Empire falls.

c. 330 B.C. Aristotle advances the scientific method.

c. A.D. 150 Ptolemy collects astronomical information.

c. A.D. 600 The Chinese invent block printing.

551 B.C. Confucius is born.

c. A.D. 33 Jesus Christ is crucified.

c. A.D. 100 Kushite merchants cross the Sahara by camel caravan.

101

The Spread of Ideas

Systems of Law

*L*aw is a code of conduct and rights accepted or formally recognized by a society. Law provides social control, order, and justice. It enables people to know their rights and responsibilities. Law also forms the cornerstone of constitutional government. A constitutional government based upon law helps ensure justice, or the fair treatment of all citizens. "Where law ends, tyranny begins," said William Pitt, an English leader, in A.D. 1770.

Roman Empire
Laying the Foundation

Sometime around 451-450 B.C., a group of judges posted 12 tablets in Rome's main forum, or marketplace. According to legend, the common people of Rome had demanded that the laws be written down for all to see. People would then know their rights. The tablets listed the unwritten laws that guided judges. They also included penalties imposed on people who broke the law.

Although a group of invaders smashed the so-called Twelve Tables in 390 B.C., the basic code of law remained in effect for almost 1,000 years. When Roman armies marched out to conquer a huge empire, they carried their belief in law with them. By A.D. 120 Roman law governed the entire Mediterranean world and much of western Europe.

In theory, Roman law applied to all people, regardless of wealth or power. Not everyone honored Roman legal ideals. Nonetheless, the Romans developed an important democratic principle. They believed people should be ruled by law rather than by the whims of leaders. In A.D. 533-534 the Byzantine emperor Justinian consolidated all Roman law into a single written code. The Justinian Code became the foundation of the present civil law system. Civil law and common law, which originated in England, are two of the major legal systems in the world today.

Cicero

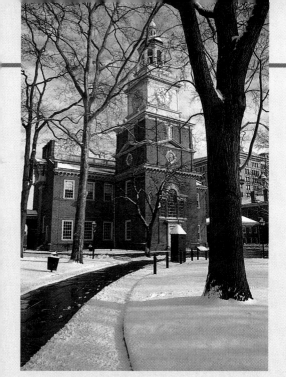

Independence Hall, Philadelphia

The United States
A Model for Constitutional Government

The Founders of the United States knew about and admired the Romans. They understood what the Roman orator Cicero meant when he spoke of the need to limit the power of government. When it came time to draw up a plan of government, they wrote a constitution that balanced the powers of government among three branches.

To ensure that rulers did not place themselves above the law, the Framers included a provision that made the Constitution "the supreme law of the land." The Framers used the example of Rome to defend the Constitution. "The Roman republic attained ... the utmost height of human greatness," declared Alexander Hamilton. He then explained how government under the Constitution would do the same.

A second system of legal justice, common law, evolved in England. Trial by jury, the right to petition the government, and many other rules governing trials originated in this system. Common law is not a written code but rather is based on written judicial decisions. Common law was established in the American colonies and continued to develop when the colonies became states of the United States.

France
Unifying the Law

In A.D. 1799 a French general named Napoleon Bonaparte set out to build an empire even larger than Rome's. By A.D. 1802 he had conquered much of Europe. Napoleon then tried to extend his reach into the Americas.

In seeking to rule this empire, Napoleon followed the Roman example. He took part in a commission to draw up a uniform code of laws. This code, known as the Napoleonic Code, was completed in A.D. 1804.

Although Napoleon ruled as emperor, the code named in his honor reaffirmed the principle that the same laws should be used to govern all people. In drafting these laws, Napoleon drew upon many of the legal precedents first introduced by the Romans. Under Napoleon, this code became applied in lands as far-flung as present-day Belgium, Quebec, Spain, and some Latin American nations.

Assemblée Nationale, Paris

LINKING THE IDEAS

1. What important democratic principle did the Romans develop?

Critical Thinking

2. How did the United States hope to ensure that rulers would not place themselves above the law?

Chapter

4

2500–350 B.C.

The Rise of Ancient Greece

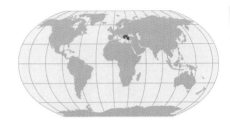

Chapter Themes

▶ **Relation to Environment** Closeness to the sea helps make the early Greeks seafarers. *Section 1*

▶ **Movement** The Greeks establish colonies throughout the area of the Mediterranean and Black Seas. *Section 2*

▶ **Regionalism** Two leading Greek city-states—Athens and Sparta—differ greatly from each other in their values, cultures, and achievements. *Section 3*

▶ **Conflict** Greek city-states together fight the Persians; then the city-states, led by rivals Athens and Sparta, fight each other. *Section 4*

Storyteller

An eager crowd gathered in the sun-drenched sports arena just outside King Minos's palace at Knossos on the Aegean island of Crete. According to legend, Minos ruled over the Minoan civilization in the 2000s B.C. The Minoans' favorite event—bull leaping—was about to begin. The crowd gasped as a raging bull, representing the earthquakes that shook Crete, charged a young male gymnast who stood motionless. Just before the collision, the gymnast grabbed the bull's horns and somersaulted onto the bull's back. Then his body arched into the air, and he completed a back flip, landing in the arms of his female partner waiting nearby. The crowd cheered at the end of this spectacle, part sport and part religious ritual. By leaping over the bull, the gymnast had shown that no matter how much the earth trembled, the Minoans would stay on Crete.

Historical Significance

What kinds of governments and societies developed in ancient Greece? How have Greek political ideas shaped the development of Western civilization?

1600 B.C.	1200 B.C.	800 B.C.	400 B.C.

c. 1600 B.C. Minoan civilization reaches its peak.

c. 1100 B.C. Dorians invade Greece.

c. 700 B.C. Greeks found colonies in the Mediterranean area.

c. 460 B.C. Golden Age of Athens begins.

e Aegean Area: -mild climate, rainy winters.
                  - Greeks became fishers, traders, and
                  pirates, since they live near the ocean.
                  · Mountains protected, isolated Greeks on
                  mainland.
                  -They spent lots of time in the outside,
                  actors would perform outside.

e gean Civilizations - early Greek the civilization on island of Crete.
                                    - Southeast of Greek mainland.

                  The Minoans
                          - on crete, archeologists uncovered palace of
                  King Minos.
                          - passages twist and turn forming a
                                   maze
                  labyrinth in palace.
                          - Minoans, men and women, both curled
                  their hair, wear gold, wore large belts.
                          - Minoans had more goddesses

 History & Art Minoan wall painting (fresco) of bull leaping.
Archaeological Museum, Heraklion, Crete, Greece

Your History Journal

Athens laid the foundation for the Western concept of democratic government. After reading about Athenian democracy, write an essay entitled "What Democracy Means to Me."

Section 1

Beginnings

Setting the Scene

▶ **Terms to Define**
labyrinth, bard

▶ **People to Meet**
Sir Arthur Evans, the Minoans, the Mycenaeans, Homer, Heinrich Schliemann

▶ **Places to Locate**
Crete, Mycenae

Find Out   Where and how did the early civilizations of Greece develop?

The Storyteller

The hero Sarpedon was a son of Zeus, but destined to die in the Trojan War. He held before him the perfect circle of his shield, a lovely thing of beaten bronze, which the bronze-smith had hammered out for him. On its inward side were stitched ox-hides in close folds with golden staples all around the circle.... And now Sarpedon spoke to Glaukos, son of Hippolochos: "Glaukos, why are we honored before others with the best seats, choice cuts of meat, brimming wine cups, and the best plots of land? Because we stand in the front line of blazing battle. Friend, if we could escape, and live forever ageless and immortal, I would not go on fighting, or encourage you to fight. But now, since the spirits of death stand close by us, let us go win glory for ourselves, or yield it to others."

Entrance to the ancient silver mines at Siphnos, Greece

—adapted from *The Iliad of Homer*, translated by Richmond Lattimore, 1951

The ancient Greeks became the people who set their stamp on the Mediterranean region and who also contributed greatly to the way we live today. Every time you go to the theater or watch the Olympic Games on television, you enjoy an activity that has its roots in ancient Greece. Modern public buildings often reflect Greek architectural styles. Above all, the ancient Greeks developed the Western concept of democracy.

The Aegean Area

Ancient Greece included the southern part of Europe's Balkan Peninsula and a group of small, rocky islands, most of which dot the Aegean (ih•JEE•uhn) Sea near Asia Minor. Low-lying, rugged mountains make up about three-fourths of the Greek mainland. Between the mountain ranges and along the coast lie fertile plains suitable for farming. Short, swift rivers flow from the interior to the sea, and the long, indented coastline provides many fine harbors. The climate is mild, with rainy winters. Afternoon breezes carrying cooler air from the sea offset the hot, dry summers.

The mountains both protected and isolated Greeks on the mainland. Besides making attacks by foreigners difficult, the mountains limited travel and communication between communities. The Greek people, therefore, never united under one government, although they spoke one language and practiced the same religion.

Because of the numerous harbors and since no place in Greece is more than 50 miles (80 km) from the coast, many Greeks turned to the sea to earn their living. They became fishers, traders, and even pirates.

In addition, the mild climate allowed the ancient Greeks to spend much of their time outdoors. People assembled for meetings in the public square, teachers met their students in public gardens, and actors performed plays in open-air theaters.

Chalices such as these are evidence that Mycenaean kings were rich and powerful.

What evidence suggests that these kings were meticulous about collecting taxes?

Aegean Civilizations

Greek myths referred to an early civilization on the island of **Crete**, southeast of the Greek mainland, but for a long time historians disputed this claim. Then, about A.D. 1900, British archaeologist **Sir Arthur Evans** unearthed remains of the Minoan civilization, which flourished from about 2500 B.C. to 1450 B.C.

The Minoans

At Knossos (NAH•suhs) on Crete, Evans uncovered the palace of legendary King Minos. Throughout the palace, passageways twist and turn in all directions to form a labyrinth, or maze. Brightly colored murals that decorate palace walls show that **the Minoans**—both men and women—curled their hair, bedecked themselves with gold jewelry, and set off their narrow waists with wide metal belts. The murals also show that they were fond of dancing and sporting events, such as boxing matches.

Minoan women apparently enjoyed a higher status than women in other early civilizations. For example, Minoan religion had more goddesses than gods. The chief deity of Crete was the Great Goddess, or Earth Mother, whom the Minoans believed caused the birth and growth of all living things.

The Minoans earned their living from sea trade. Crete's oak and cedar forests provided wood for ships. In addition, the island's location enabled Minoan traders to reach Egypt and Mesopotamia. By 2000 B.C., Minoan fleets dominated the eastern Mediterranean, carrying goods and keeping the seas free from pirates. The ships also guarded Crete

against outside attack, which explains why the Minoans did not build walls around their cities.

Minoan civilization reached its peak around 1600 B.C. About 250 years later it collapsed. Some historians think its cities were destroyed by huge tidal waves resulting from an undersea earthquake. Others think that a people from the Greek mainland, **the Mycenaeans** (MY•suh•NEE•uhnz), succeeded in invading Crete.

The Mycenaeans

The Mycenaeans originated among the Indo-European peoples of central Asia. About 2000 B.C., as a result of the rapid growth of their population, the Mycenaeans began moving out from their homeland. Upon entering the Balkan Peninsula, they gradually intermarried with the local people——known as Hellenes (HEH•leenz)—and set up a group of kingdoms.

Each Mycenaean kingdom centered around a hilltop on which was built a royal fortress. Stone walls circled the fortress, providing a shelter for the people in time of danger. Nobles lived on their estates outside the walls. They would turn out in armor when the king needed them to supply horse-drawn chariots. The slaves and tenants who farmed the land lived in villages on these estates.

Aegean Civilizations 1400 B.C.

Map Study The Greek civilization grew out of the Minoan and Mycenaean civilizations that thrived in the Aegean area from about 2500 B.C. to 1100 B.C.
1. Location The remains of the Minoan civilization were discovered on what island?
2. Location Where did the Mycenaeans originate before settling in the Aegean area?

Heinrich Schliemann discovered six tombs at the royal grave circle near the lion gate at Mycenae. They contained 16 skeletons and a large hoard of gold. *What events ended Mycenaean civilization?*

The palaces in the city of **Mycenae** served as centers of both government administration and production. Inside, artisans tanned leather, sewed clothes, fashioned jars for storing wine and olive oil, and made bronze swords and ox-hide shields. To help in collecting taxes, government officials kept records of the wealth of every person in the kingdom. They collected taxes in the form of wheat, livestock, and honey, which were stored in the palace.

Minoan traders visited the Greek mainland soon after the Mycenaeans set up their kingdom. Gradually, the Mycenaeans adopted many elements of Minoan culture—metalworking and shipbuilding techniques and navigation by the sun and stars. The Mycenaeans worshiped the Minoan Earth Mother as well.

By the mid-1400s B.C., the Mycenaeans had conquered the Minoans and controlled the Aegean area. By 1100 B.C., however, fighting among the Mycenaeans had destroyed the great hilltop fortresses. Soon after, a new wave of invaders, the Greek-speaking Dorians, entered Greece from the north. Armed with iron weapons, the Dorians easily overran the mainland.

Historians call the next 300 years of Greek history a "dark age." During this period, overseas trade stopped, poverty increased, and people lost skills such as writing and craft making. Thousands of refugees fled the mainland and settled in Ionia—the west coast of Asia Minor and its adjoining islands.

By 750 B.C. the Ionians had reintroduced culture, crafts, and skills to their homeland, including the alphabet used by Phoenician traders. The "dark age" of the Dorians ended, and a new Greek civilization with Mycenaean elements emerged. The new civilization—called Hellenic, after the original people of Greece—flourished from about the 700s B.C. until 336 B.C.

Poets and Heroes

During the "dark age," bards, or singing storytellers, had kept alive Mycenaean traditions. With their new ability to write, the Greeks began to record the epic poems that the bards had passed from generation to generation.

The *Iliad* and the *Odyssey*

According to tradition, a blind poet named **Homer** who lived during the 700s B.C. composed the two most famous Greek epics—the *Iliad* and the *Odyssey*. Homer set the *Iliad* and the *Odyssey* during and after the legendary Trojan War. The Mycenaeans had supposedly fought the people of Troy in the mid-1200s B.C. In A.D. 1870 **Heinrich Schliemann**, a German archaeologist, claimed that Troy actually existed and was a major trading city in Asia Minor.

The *Iliad* begins when a Trojan prince named Paris falls in love with Helen, the wife of a Mycenaean king, and takes her with him to Troy. To avenge Helen's kidnapping, the Mycenaeans lay siege to Troy for 10 years, but they cannot capture the city. Finally, they trick the Trojans by building a huge, hollow wooden horse. The best Mycenaean soldiers hide inside the horse, while the rest board their ships and pretend to sail away. The joyful Trojans, thinking themselves victorious, bring the gift horse into the city. That night, the Greeks creep out of the horse, slaughter the Trojan men, enslave

Erich Lessing, Magnum

Trojan Horse

O n this Greek vase from the 600s B.C. the Trojan horse of myth and epic stands tall. According to the Greek poet Homer—who described the Trojan War in his epic poem the *Iliad*—for ten long years the Mycenaeans of Greece battled their enemies who lived within the walls of the Turkish city of Troy. The two sides were so well matched that only a clever strategy of war could produce victory. So the Greeks came up with one: They built a great wooden horse, so large that a cargo of soldiers could hide in its belly. Then they set the horse on wheels and gave it to Troy as a "gift." Having tricked their way into Troy, the Greek soldiers leapt out of the horse and conquered their foe.

While time has blurred the line between historic fact and Homeric epic (written centuries after the struggle), an important war did take place in which a loose federation of Greek kings set out to conquer the city-state of Troy. Homer's epic reveals that piracy and plunder were part of that era's commerce. Archaeologists have uncovered the ruins of a mighty Turkish fortress that once commanded the narrows of the Hellespont. Modern opinions, however, differ as to whether or not this was the site of Homer's Troy. ⊕

the women and children, and burn the city to the ground.

The *Odyssey* describes the homeward wanderings of the Mycenaean king Odysseus after the fall of Troy. Because it took him 10 years to return to Greece, people refer to any long, adventure-filled journey as an *odyssey*.

Teaching Greek Values

Eventually, schools in ancient Greece used the *Iliad* and the *Odyssey* to present to students many of the values of Hellenic civilization. For example, in an exciting description of men marching to war, the *Iliad* taught students to be proud of their Greek heritage and their heroic ancestors:

> ❝ As a ravening fire blazes over a vast forest and the mountains, and its light is seen afar, so while they marched the sheen from their forest of bronze [spears] went up dazzling into high heaven.
>
> As flocks of wildfowl on the wing, geese or cranes or long-necked swans fly this way and that way over the Asian meadows, proud of the power of their wings, and they settle on and on honking as they go until they fill the meadow with sound: flocks of men poured out of their camp onwards over the Scamandrian plain, and the ground thundered terribly under the tramp of horses and of men. ❞
>
> --Homer, from the *Iliad*, mid-700s B.C.

The *Iliad* and the *Odyssey* also represented other values of Hellenic civilization, such as a love for nature, the importance of husband-wife relationships and tender feelings, and loyalty between friends. Hellenic schools also used the two epics to teach students to always strive for excellence and to meet with dignity whatever fate had in store.

A Family of Deities

In Greek religion, the activities of gods and goddesses explained why people behaved the way they did and why their lives took one direction rather than another. The Greeks also believed that their powerful deities caused the events of the physical world to occur—such as the coming of spring or violent storms with thunder and lightning.

Most ancient peoples feared their deities. They believed that people were put on the earth only to obey and serve the gods and goddesses. The Greeks were the first people to feel differently. They placed importance on the worth of the individual. Because they believed in their own value, the Greeks had a great deal of self-respect. This allowed them to approach their gods with dignity.

Much more than other civilizations did, the Greeks humanized their deities. Unlike the half-animal gods and goddesses of Egypt, Greek deities had totally human forms. They behaved like humans, too—marrying, having children, lying, and murdering. Frequently jealous of one another, the Greek deities quarreled and sometimes played tricks on one another. They also possessed superhuman powers. Since the Greeks saw their deities as sources of power, both physical and mental, they tried to be like them by doing everything to the best of their ability.

Gods and Goddesses

The gods and goddesses of ancient Greece combined features of both Minoan and Mycenaean deities. For example, different Greek goddesses took over different aspects of the Earth Mother. Athena became the goddess of wisdom and art, Demeter became the goddess of agriculture, and Aphrodite became the goddess of love and beauty. Each community chose a particular god or goddess as its patron and protector, but all Greeks worshiped as their chief deity the Mycenaean god Zeus.

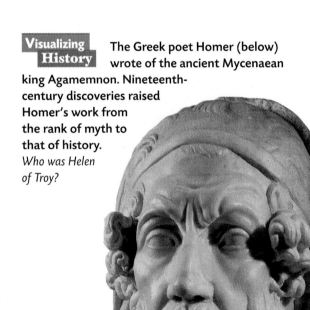

Visualizing History **The Greek poet Homer (below) wrote of the ancient Mycenaean king Agamemnon. Nineteenth-century discoveries raised Homer's work from the rank of myth to that of history.** *Who was Helen of Troy?*

Dionysus shown riding a leopard. Greek tragedy was developed from the odes sung by choruses in honor of the god Dionysus. *Where were Greek dramas performed?*

Greeks believed that the 12 most important Greek deities lived on high Mount Olympus, an actual mountain in Greece. Each of the deities controlled a specific part of the natural world. For example, Zeus, the chief god, was thought to rule the sky, weather, and thunderstorms. His brother Pluto was thought to rule the underworld, where the dead spent eternity.

Zeus's son Apollo, the god of light, drove the sun across the sky every day in his chariot. Because the Greeks also considered Apollo to be the god of prophecy, they would bring gifts to the oracle at Delphi—a holy place to honor Apollo—and ask to have hidden knowledge revealed. Like the Shang in ancient China, the Greeks believed that oracles could predict the future. At the Delphic oracle, they would ask questions, and the priests and priestesses would interpret Apollo's replies.

Festivals

As Hellenic civilization developed, certain religious festivals became an important part of Greek life. Every four years the Greeks held a series of athletic contests "for the greater glory of Zeus." Because these contests held at the city of Olympia, they were called the Olympic Games. The Greeks also originated the play—a celebration in honor of Dionysus, the god of wine and fertility. At these events, the audience sat on a hillside around an open space, where a chorus chanted a story about Dionysus and danced to the sound of a flute. As the years passed, cities began building permanent theaters, carving a hillside into a semicircle, adding rows of stone seats, and paving the stage area. Actors began to recite poems explaining the songs and dances of the chorus. The words they recited eventually evolved into dialogue.

SECTION I REVIEW

Recall
1. **Define** labyrinth, bard.
2. **Identify** Sir Arthur Evans, the Minoans, the Mycenaeans, Homer, Heinrich Schliemann.
3. **Describe** the routes the Mycenaeans would have taken to reach Troy and Knossos from their home city of Mycenae.

Critical Thinking
4. **Applying Information** Using Zeus, Athena, and Apollo, illustrate how the Greeks viewed their gods and goddesses.

Understanding Themes
5. **Relation to Environment** How did the geography and climate of Greece and the Aegean islands affect the development of the Minoan and Mycenaean civilizations?

c. 700s B.C. Greek kings lose power to aristocrats.

c. 600s B.C. Greeks learn coinage from the Lydians.

c. 500 B.C. The rule of tyrants in Greek city-states ends.

Section 2

The Polis

Setting the Scene

▶ **Terms to Define**
polis, citizen, aristocrat, phalanx, tyrant, oligarchy, democracy

▶ **Places to Locate**
Athens, Sparta

Find Out How did economic prosperity bring significant political and social changes to the Greek city-states?

The Storyteller

An Athenian ruler had to be careful of plots hatched by jealous nobles. The tyrant Hippias, the once-mild ruler of Athens, learned this lesson. He was with his bodyguard, arranging a citywide parade, when two assassins approached. Pretending to take part in the procession, they had daggers ready, hidden behind their shields. Suddenly, seeing one of their accomplices casually talking with Hippias, they halted, thinking that he had betrayed the plot to the tyrant. Turning, they rushed within the gates, met Hippias's brother, and killed him. Afterward, Athenians found Hippias harsher, ever fearful of revolt.

The Parthenon on the Acropolis

—adapted from *The Peloponnesian War*, Thucydides, Crawley translation revised by T.E. Wick, 1892

The English language offers evidence of how ancient Greeks have influenced modern life. Words such as *police* and *politics*, for example, derive from the Greek word *polis*. The polis, or city-state, was the basic political unit of Hellenic civilization. Each polis developed its own pattern of life independently but shared certain features with other city-states.

The Typical Polis

A typical polis included a city and the surrounding villages, fields, and orchards. At the center of the city on the top of an acropolis (uh•KRAH•puh•luhs), or fortified hill, stood the temple of the local deity. At the foot of the acropolis the agora, or public square, served as the political center of the polis. Citizens—those who took part in government—gathered in the agora to carry out public affairs, choose their officials, and pass their laws. Artisans and merchants also conducted business in the agora.

The citizens of a polis had both rights and responsibilities. They could vote, hold public office, own property, and speak for themselves in court. In return, the polis expected them to serve in government and to defend the polis in time of war.

Citizens, however, made up only a minority of the residents of a polis. In Athens, slaves and those who were foreign-born were excluded from citizenship, and before 500 B.C. so were men who did not own land. Greek women had no political or legal rights.

Greek Colonies and Trade

The return of prosperity after the "dark age" led to an increase in Greece's population. By 700 B.C. Greek farmers no longer grew enough grain to feed everyone. As a result, each polis sent out groups of people to establish colonies in coastal areas around the Mediterranean and Black Seas.

Colonies

Each colony kept close ties with its metropolis, or "parent city." A colony supplied its metropolis with grain—wheat and barley. Farmers on the Greek mainland produced wine, olive oil, and other cash crops for export. Because vineyards and olive groves needed fewer workers than did grain fields, many farmers moved to the cities, where they learned crafts. With more goods to sell, Greek merchants began trading throughout the Mediterranean region.

Economic Growth

During the 600s B.C. the Greeks replaced their barter system with a money economy, and their overseas trade expanded further. Merchants issued their own coins, but eventually individual city-states took over this responsibility.

The cities of Ionia in Asia Minor assumed leadership in a growing textile industry. Sheep in the interior of Asia Minor furnished the raw material. Purple dye obtained from mollusks, a type of shellfish, gave the woven materials color.

Pottery developed as a local industry wherever sufficient clay was found. Pottery made in Ionia was the earliest Greek pottery to be exported. Ionian pottery styles were based on Mycenaean and Middle Eastern influences. The artists who made and decorated the vases painted figures of birds and humans interspersed with line or geometric decorations.

Political and Social Change

Economic growth changed Greek political life. Greek communities at first were ruled by kings. By the 700s B.C., however, the kings had lost power to landholding aristocrats, or nobles, who as members of the upper class provided cavalry for the king's military ventures.

By 650 B.C. disputes arose between the aristocrats and the common people. Farmers often needed credit until harvest time. To obtain loans from the wealthy aristocrats, they had to pledge their fields as security. When they could not repay the loans, many farmers lost their land to the aristocrats and became either sharecroppers or day laborers in the cities. Some even had to sell themselves into slavery. In protest, farmers demanded political reforms.

Geography

Sailing the Aegean

Because of their many natural harbors, the Greeks transported most goods by sea. Sea travel made good sense, given the rugged mountains of the Greek mainland. Besides, pack animals could carry only small loads short distances. Merchants found sea transport of bulky cargo—grain, timber, and even jugs of olive oil—to be practical and inexpensive.

Greek sailors could sail easily only when the wind was behind them. The prevailing northerly winds made the voyage from Athens to the Black Sea slow and difficult, but the return trip was quick and easy. Likewise, Greek ships could coast to Egypt, but they had to struggle to get home. Most ships managed only one round-trip per year.

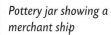

Pottery jar showing a merchant ship

The typical Greek freighter was broad—about 25 feet (7.5 m) wide compared to a length of 80 feet (24 m). Rigged with a large square sail, this sturdy ship averaged only about 5 knots with the wind. Merchant ships usually sailed in fleets escorted by warships—galleys propelled by oarsmen.

Compare the ancient ships with today's diesel-driven giants. A container ship makes the round-trip between the United States and Europe in 21 days. It holds cargo in 1,000 containers—four of which are the size of one Greek freighter. Some things have not changed, however. The Greek merchant fleet of today ranks among the largest in the world.

Linking Past and Present **ACTIVITY**

Explain why the ancient Greeks relied on the sea for the transport of goods. In what kind of vessels did they sail? How has cargo transport changed since ancient times?

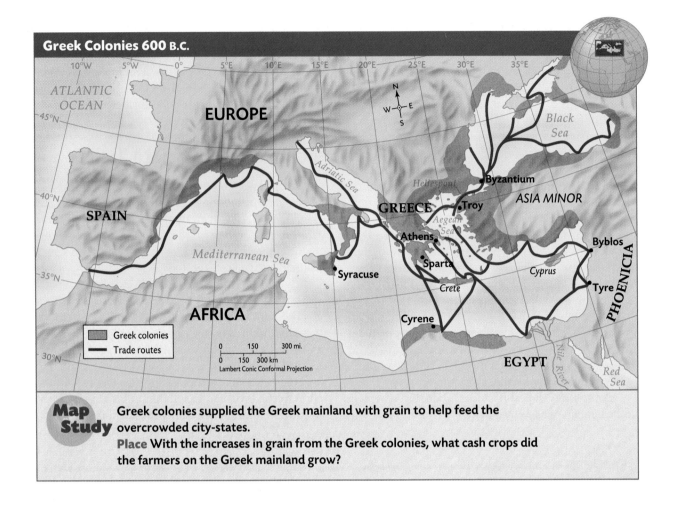

Greek Colonies 600 B.C.

Map Study Greek colonies supplied the Greek mainland with grain to help feed the overcrowded city-states.
Place With the increases in grain from the Greek colonies, what cash crops did the farmers on the Greek mainland grow?

The farmers, who were foot soldiers, were becoming more valuable to Greek armies than the aristocrats, who were cavalry. As Greek armies came to rely on the phalanx—rows of foot soldiers closely arrayed with their shields forming a solid wall—aristocrats began to lose influence. Middle-class, non-landowning merchants and artisans, thus far excluded from citizenship, wanted a voice in the government and joined the farmers in their demands. Merchants and artisans also wanted the polis to advance their interests by encouraging industry and by protecting profitable overseas trade routes.

As a result of the unrest, tyrannies arose. A tyranny was created when one man, called a tyrant, seized power and ruled the polis single-handedly. Although most tyrants ruled fairly, the harshness of a few gave *tyranny* its present meaning—rule by a cruel and unjust person.

Tyrants ruled various Greek city-states until about 500 B.C. From then until 336 B.C., most city-states became either oligarchies or democracies. In an oligarchy, a few wealthy people hold power over the larger group of citizens. In a democracy, or government by the people, power lies in the hands of all the citizens. The democracy of **Athens** and the oligarchy of **Sparta** became the most famous of the Greek city-states.

SECTION 2 REVIEW

Recall
1. **Define** polis, citizen, aristocrat, phalanx, tyrant, oligarchy, democracy.
2. **Identify** Athens, Sparta.
3. **Describe** the social and politi-cal functions of an acropolis and an agora in a Greek polis.

Critical Thinking
4. **Synthesizing Information** What arguments might a citi-zen of a polis present for or against changing citizenship?

Understanding Themes
5. **Movement** What kind of rela-tionship existed between a Greek colony and its metropo-lis on the Greek mainland?

650 B.C.		600 B.C.		550 B.C.		500 B.C.

c. 650 B.C.
Slaves revolt
in Sparta.

621 B.C.
Draco enacts code
of laws in Athens.

594 B.C. Solon becomes
leader of Athens.

507 B.C.
Athens becomes
a democracy.

Section 3

Rivals

Setting the Scene

▶ **Terms to Define**
   constitution, rhetoric

▶ **People to Meet**
   Draco, Solon, Peisistratus, Cleisthenes

▶ **Places to Locate**
   Peloponnesus, Attica

Find Out ▶ What different Greek values did
Athens and Sparta each represent?

The Storyteller

*Pausanias darted among the bushes to avoid
the moonlight. Finally, stumbling, he plunged
behind a large rock, his lungs heaving. Having
managed to steal just one loaf of fresh bread, he
knew that he must ration it out for at least two
days. The ephors had declared that those caught
with stolen food would be beaten severely. But, if
he could just survive for two more days, he
would finish the initiation and join the
other young men in the barracks. He
shivered quietly, trying to imagine
where he might spend the next two
cold nights.*

—adapted from *The Ancient
World,* edited by Esmond
Wright, 1979

Spartan female athlete

The two leading city-states in ancient
Greece—Sparta and Athens—stood in
sharp contrast to each other. Though
citizens of both Sparta and Athens participated in
polis government, the two city-states differed greatly
from each other in their values, cultures, and accomplishments.

Sparta

The descendants of the Dorian invaders of the
dark age founded Sparta. It was located in the
Peloponnesus (peh•luh•puh•NEE•suhs), a peninsula
of southern Greece. Like other city-states, Sparta
based its economy on agriculture.

Instead of founding overseas colonies, the
Spartans invaded neighboring city-states and
enslaved the local people. The polis of Sparta owned
many slaves, known as helots (HEH•luhts), who
farmed the estates of individual Spartans. In addition,
a group of free individuals called *perioeci*
(peh•REE•ee•sy)—artisans and merchants from the
conquered territories—worked for the Spartans.
Helots and *perioeci* together outnumbered Spartans
by about 200,000 to 10,000.

Around 650 B.C., the helots revolted against their
Spartan masters. It took 30 years, but the Spartans
managed to suppress the revolt. They then decided
that the only way they could maintain power was to
establish a military society.

A Military Society

All life in Sparta revolved around the army.
Spartan men strove to become first-rate soldiers, and
Spartan women aspired to become mothers of soldiers.
Spartans despised the other Greeks who lived
behind city walls, believing that a city defended by
Spartan soldiers did not need walls.

In Sparta, government officials examined newborn
infants to see if they were healthy. If not, an official
left the sickly infant on a hillside to die. At the age
of 7, Spartan boys were taken away from their homes

Chapter 4 *The Rise of Ancient Greece* **115**

and placed in military barracks. Their training included learning to read, write, and use weapons.

At age 20, Spartan men became soldiers and were sent to frontier areas. At age 30, they were expected to marry. But Spartan men could not closely supervise their family affairs. Instead, they spent their days in military drill until age 60, when they could retire from the army.

The Role of Women

The Spartans brought up women to be, like the Spartan men, as healthy and strong as possible. Female infants received as much food as their brothers, which was not the case elsewhere in Greece. Young Spartan girls trained in gymnastics, wrestling, and boxing. The women in Sparta married at age 19 rather than at 14—the average marrying age in most of Greece—which increased the likelihood that their children would be healthy.

Sparta gave its women more personal freedoms than the women of other Greek city-states received.

Spartan women could go shopping in the marketplace, attend dinners at which nonfamily members were present, own property, and express opinions on public issues. They could not, however, take part in government.

Sparta's Government

According to tradition, Sparta's government was set up by a lawmaker named Lycurgus during the 800s B.C. Two kings, who ruled jointly, officially governed Sparta. Except for leading the army and conducting religious services, however, Spartan kings had little power. The Assembly, made up of all male citizens over the age of 30, passed laws and made decisions concerning war and peace. Each year the Assembly elected five overseers, or ephors (EH•fuhrs), to administer public affairs. The ephors could also veto legislation. A Council of Elders, consisting of 28 men over the age of 60, proposed laws to the Assembly and served as a supreme court.

Images of the Times

The Glory of Greece

Archaeological treasures and architectural remains remind the world of the achievements of Greek civilization.

The Parthenon crowns the Acropolis at Athens.

Greek sculptors in the classical period depicted living and moving people in natural poses.

Results of Militarism

The Spartans succeeded in maintaining control over their subject peoples for nearly 250 years. They paid a price, however. Suspicious of any new ideas that might bring change, the Spartans lagged far behind other Greek city-states in economic development. For example, Sparta used heavy iron bars instead of coins as currency. In this way, it hoped to discourage trade and to remain self-reliant. The Spartans also shunned philosophy, science, and the arts, while Athens and other city-states advanced in these fields. The Spartans, however, were exceptional Olympic athletes, and their soldiers played key roles in defending Greece against invaders.

Athens

Northeast of the Peloponnesus—on a peninsula of central Greece named **Attica**—people descended from the Mycenaeans established the city-state of Athens. They named their polis after the goddess Athena. Like the early rulers of the other city-states, Athenian kings and aristocrats in the 600s B.C. faced demands by small farmers, merchants, and artisans for economic and political reforms.

Around this time, the governing methods of Athens and Sparta diverged. Athens gradually expanded its definition of citizenship to encompass more people. Initially, only a man whose father and maternal grandfather had been citizens could be a citizen; however, non-landowning citizens could not participate in Athens's Assembly. Athenians called the many free (non-enslaved) foreigners who lived in Athens *metics*. These people could not own land or participate in government. By 507 B.C., however, the constitution, or plan of government, of Athens stated that all free, Athenian-born men were citizens regardless of what class they belonged to, and that they could participate in the Assembly regardless of whether they owned land. This political change reduced much of the friction between social classes and enabled Athens to forge ahead.

The goddess Athena, according to Greek tradition, won the contest for control of Athens over the sea god Poseidon.

REFLECTING ON THE TIMES

1. What innovation did Greek sculptors introduce in the classical period?
2. Why was Athena's name rather than Poseidon's given to the city of Athens?

Draco

Four successive leaders brought most of the changes in Athenian government. **Draco**, the first of these leaders, issued an improved code of laws in 621 B.C. The penalties given to offenders were extremely harsh. Even minor offenses, like stealing a cabbage, were punishable by death.

Over time, the word *draconian* has come to describe something that is very cruel and severe. On the other hand, because Draco's laws were written down, everyone knew exactly what the laws were. Aristocrats could no longer dictate what was legal and what was not.

Solon

The next series of reforms took place under the poet-lawmaker **Solon**, who became the leader of Athens in 594 B.C. To improve economic conditions, Solon canceled all land debts and freed debtors from slavery. He also placed limits on the amount of land any one individual could own. By urging farmers to grow cash crops rather than grain, Solon promoted trade. He also promoted industry by ordering fathers to teach their sons a skill and by extending citizenship to foreigners who would settle in Athens as skilled artisans.

Next, Solon introduced political reforms that moved Athens toward democracy while preserving some aristocratic control. He allowed citizens of all classes to participate in the Assembly and public law courts. An aristocratic Council of 400 was also established to draft measures that then went to the Assembly for approval.

Peisistratus

In 546 B.C. **Peisistratus** (pih•SIHS•truh•tuhs) took over the government of Athens. Peisistratus pushed reforms in an even more radical direction than had Solon. He divided large estates among landless farmers and extended citizenship to men who did not own land. Peisistratus provided the poor with loans and put many of them to work building temples and other public works.

Athenian Democracy

Cleisthenes (KLYS•thuh•NEEZ), the fourth leader to help reform Athens, came to power in 508 B.C. The following year he introduced a series of laws that established democracy for Athens. Through his reforms, Cleisthenes sought to end local rivalries, break the power of the aristocracy, and reorganize the structure of Athenian government.

Under Cleisthenes' constitution, the Assembly won increased powers and fully emerged as the major political body. All citizens could belong to the Assembly, in which they were considered equal before the law and guaranteed freedom of speech. In addition to passing laws, the Assembly served as a supreme court and appointed generals to run the military. A Council of 500, whose membership was open to any citizen, carried out daily government business.

Each year in a lottery, Athenian citizens chose members of the Council. They favored a lottery over a ballot, believing that all citizens were capable of holding public office. Elections, in their view, would unfairly favor the rich, who had the advantage of fame and training in public speaking. Besides, all citizens were supposed to take part in government.

Athenian democracy included a jury system to decide court cases. Juries contained from 201 to

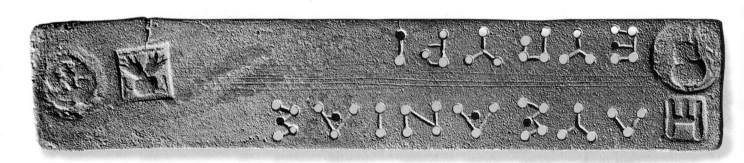

Visualizing History A juror's token is shown above. Athenian courts demonstrated faith in the ordinary man's ability. Groups of hundreds of citizens sat on panels called *dicasteries* and decided cases by majority vote. *Why were juries so large?*

1,001 members, with a majority vote needed to reach a verdict. The Athenians reasoned that the large size of their juries would keep jurors from being influenced by threats and bribes.

Athenian democracy also included a system called ostracism. Each year, citizens could write the name of an undesirable politician on a piece of baked clay called an ostracon. If a person's name appeared on 6,000 ostraca, he could be exiled.

Cleisthenes' democracy transformed Athens, but it affected only those 20 percent of Athenians who were citizens. Non-citizens—women, foreign-born males, and slaves—were still excluded from political life. In spite of these limitations, ancient Athens nevertheless laid the foundation for the Western concept of democratic government.

Athenian Education

The training an Athenian received depended on social and economic status. About a week after being born, a male child received a name and was enrolled as a citizen. Because Athens expected every citizen to hold public office at some time in his life, it required Athenian citizens to educate their sons. With few exceptions, Athenian girls—who would not participate in governing the democracy of Athens—did not receive a formal education. Instead, a girl learned household duties, such as weaving and baking, from her mother.

Private tutors educated the boys from wealthy upper-class families, while other students paid a small fee to attend a private school. Much of their education was picked up in the agora, through daily conversations and debates in the Assembly.

Athenian boys entered school at age 7 and graduated at age 18. Their main textbooks were the *Iliad* and the *Odyssey*, and students learned each epic by heart. They studied arithmetic, geometry, drawing, and music in the morning and gymnastics in the afternoon. When boys reached their teens, they added rhetoric, or the art of public speaking, to their studies. Because lawyers did not represent

Zapotec Temple Complex at Monte Albán

Mexico, c. 500 B.C.
Monte Albán in the valley of Oaxaca in southern Mexico became an important center of Zapotec culture. The Zapotecs flattened the mountaintop to create a large plaza, around which they designed a temple complex. They carved the slopes of the mountain into terraces for agriculture and housing. An estimated 5,000 people, or about 50 percent of the valley's population, lived at Monte Albán.

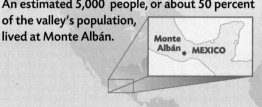

participants in a court case, an Athenian needed to be accomplished in rhetoric to argue his own position.

When young Athenian men reached 18, they left for two years of military service. Before entering the army, however, they went with their fathers to the temple of Zeus, where they swore the following oath:

    ❝ I will not bring dishonor upon my weapons nor desert the comrade by my side. I will strive to hand on my fatherland greater and better than I found it. I will not consent to anyone's disobeying or destroying the constitution but will prevent him, whether I am with others or alone. I will honor the temples and the religion my forefathers established. ❞

        —oath of enrollment in Epheboi corps, early 400s B.C.

SECTION 3 REVIEW

Recall
1. **Define** constitution, rhetoric.
2. **Identify** Draco, Solon, Peisistratus, Cleisthenes.
3. **Locate** Athens and Sparta on the map on page 121. In which peninsula was each located?

Critical Thinking
4. **Evaluating Information**
   Do you think the reasons the Athenians gave for choosing government officials by lottery were good reasons? What other method would you

propose if you were an Athenian reformer?

Understanding Themes
5. **Regionalism** Contrast Athens and Sparta in their idea of citizenship, type of education, and position of women.

546 B.C.
Persian armies
conquer Ionia.

490 B.C. Athenians
and Persians fight
the Battle of Marathon.

447 B.C. Pericles
begins rebuilding
of Athens.

431 B.C.
Peloponnesian
War begins.

Section 4

War, Glory, and Decline

Setting the Scene

▶ **Terms to Define**
   symposium, mercenary

▶ **People to Meet**
   Darius I, Xerxes, Themistocles, Leonidas,
   Pericles, Aspasia

▶ **Places to Locate**
   Marathon, Thermopylae, Salamis, Delos

Find Out How did the Persian Wars and the
Peloponnesian War affect democracy in the
Greek city-states?

The Storyteller

*The Greek historian Herodotus reported that
during the Persian Wars, some Greek deserters
approached the Persian king Xerxes. Questioned
about what the Greeks were about to do, they told
him the truth: The Olympic Games were being held.
They were going to watch the athletic competitions
and chariot races. When asked what the prize
was for such contests, they responded that the
Olympic prize was an olive wreath. Upon
hearing this, a Persian noble cried out
in fear: "What kind of men are
these? How can we be expected to
fight against men who compete
with each other for no material
reward, but only for honor!"*

—adapted from *The Histories,*
Herodotus, translated by
Aubrey de Selincourt

Themistocles

As the 400s B.C. opened, the Persian Empire—then the strongest military power in the ancient world—stood poised to extend its influence into Europe. Surprisingly, the Greek city-states not only cooperated with each other in resisting the Persian attack, but they also succeeded in throwing Persia's armed forces back into Asia.

After their victory against Persia, the Greeks—especially the Athenians—enjoyed a "golden age" of remarkable cultural achievements. Then, the Greek city-states began to fight among themselves. This bitter and devastating war lasted for more than 27 years.

The Persian Wars

In 546 B.C. the Persian armies, led by Cyrus II, conquered the Greek city-states of Ionia, in Asia Minor. Despite the mildness of Persian rule, the Ionians disliked the conquerors. The Ionians considered the non-Greek-speaking Persians to be barbarians. In addition, an all-powerful king ruled the Persian Empire, whereas the Greek population of Ionia believed that citizens should choose their own government.

Finally, in 499 B.C., the Ionians revolted against the Persians. Even though Athens and another mainland polis sent some warships to help the Ionians, **Darius I** of Persia soon defeated the Ionians. Darius then decided to punish the mainland Greeks for helping the rebels.

Marathon

Darius first tried to send an army around the northern coast of the Aegean Sea. However, a storm destroyed his supply ships, forcing him to turn back. Two years later, in 490 B.C., Darius tried again.

This time he sent his fleet directly across the Aegean to the coastal plain of **Marathon**, about 25 miles (40 km) north of Athens. For several days the Persians awaited the Athenians. However, the Athenians, outnumbered 20,000 to 10,000, did nothing. Finally, the Persians decided to attack Athens directly. They loaded their ships with the cavalry—the strongest part of their army—and then began loading the infantry.

Not waiting for the Persians to take the offensive, the Athenians struck. The Athenian general ordered his well-disciplined foot soldiers to charge down the hills above Marathon at the Persian infantry, which stood in shallow water waiting to board the ships. This tactic astounded the Persians, who believed that infantrymen would fight only with the support of horsemen and archers. Marathon was a terrible defeat for the Persians, who reportedly lost 6,400 men compared to only 192 Greek casualties.

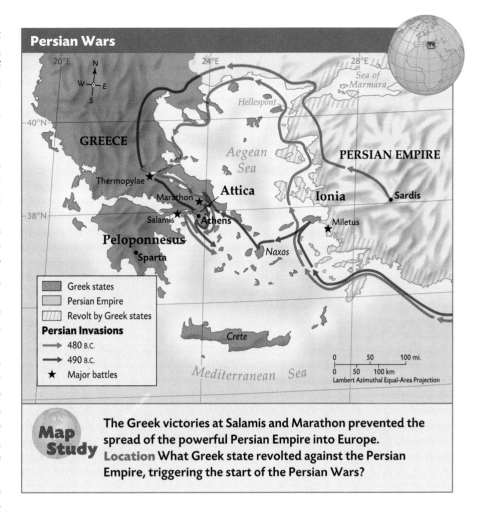

Persian Wars

Greek states

Persian Empire

Revolt by Greek states

Persian Invasions

→ 480 B.C.

→ 490 B.C.

★ Major battles

0   50   100 mi.

0   50   100 km

Lambert Azimuthal Equal-Area Projection

Map Study The Greek victories at Salamis and Marathon prevented the spread of the powerful Persian Empire into Europe.
Location What Greek state revolted against the Persian Empire, triggering the start of the Persian Wars?

Salamis

After Marathon, the Persians withdrew to Asia Minor, but they returned 10 years later. In 480 B.C. Darius's son and successor, **Xerxes**, invaded Greece from the north, this time with 200,000 soldiers. Because so huge an army could not live off the land, offshore supply ships accompanied them.

Once again the Greeks, this time under the leadership of Sparta, faced the Persians. A few years before, the oracle at Delphi had said that Greece would be safe behind a "wooden wall." The Athenian general **Themistocles** (thuh•MIHS•tuh •KLEEZ) tried to convince his Greek allies that a "wooden wall" meant a fleet of ships and that the way to defeat the Persians was to challenge them at sea.

To do this, the Greek army had to set up a delaying action on land. They chose **Thermopylae** (thuhr•MAH•puh•lee) as the place—a mountain

pass north of Athens. There, 7,000 Greeks led by King **Leonidas** of Sparta stood firm against the Persians for three days. Then a Greek traitor showed the enemy a trail over which they could attack the Greeks from the rear. Realizing that he would soon be surrounded, Leonidas sent off most of his troops. But he and 300 fellow Spartans remained obedient to the law of their polis—never

Marathon
According to legend, a messenger named Pheidippides (fy•DIH•puh•DEEZ) carried the news of the victory at Marathon back to Athens. Because Pheidippides had previously run 280 miles (448 km) in four days, he barely managed to reach the city and deliver his message before he fell to the ground, dead from exhaustion. Ever since, people have used the word *marathon* to describe a long-distance race.

surrender on the battlefield, but fight until victory or death.

> 66 They [the Spartans] defended themselves to the last, such as still had swords using them, and the others resisting with their hand and teeth; till the barbarians [Persians] … overwhelmed and buried the remnant left beneath showers of missile weapons. 99
>
> —Herodotus, from *History*, 400s B.C.

The heroic stand of Leonidas and the Spartans gave Themistocles time to carry out his plan. He drew the Persian fleet into the strait of Salamis, a narrow body of water between Athens and the island of **Salamis**. Themistocles reasoned that the heavy Persian ships would crowd together in the strait and make easy targets for the lighter but faster and more maneuverable Greek ships. The plan worked, and the outnumbered ships of the Greek navy destroyed almost the entire Persian fleet.

After the battle at Salamis, the Greeks gained the upper hand. By 479 B.C., the Persians had once again retreated to Asia Minor, this time for good. With the end of the Persian Wars, Athens emerged as a powerful and self-confident city-state, ready to embark on a new age of expansion.

The Golden Age of Athens

Greek culture reached its peak after the Persian Wars. Most historians refer to the period from 461 B.C. to 429 B.C. as the Golden Age of Athens because most Greek achievements in the arts and sciences took place in Athens during this time.

Pericles in Charge

The Athenian general **Pericles**, beginning in the 450s B.C., led Athens through its Golden Age. The Persians had burned Athens during the Persian Wars, but beginning in 447 B.C., Pericles was determined to rebuild the city. When the rebuilt temples and palaces crowned its acropolis, Athens became the most beautiful city in Greece. The most famous structure built under Pericles, the Parthenon (the temple of Athena), still stands.

Pericles wanted the polis of Athens to stand for all that was best in Greek civilization. A persuasive speaker, he expressed his ideas in a famous funeral oration quoted by the Greek historian Thucydides (thoo•SIH•duh•DEEZ):

> 66 We are called a democracy [because power] is in the hands of the many and not the few.… When it is a question of putting one person before another in positions of public responsibility, what counts is not membership of a particular class, but the actual ability which the man possesses.… We are prevented from doing wrong by respect … for the laws.… We are lovers of the beautiful, yet simple in our tastes, and we cultivate the mind without loss of manliness.… To avow poverty with us is no disgrace; the true disgrace is in doing nothing to avoid it.… Athens is the school of Hellas [Greece]. 99

Athenian Daily Life

Athenians lavished money on public buildings, but they kept their individual homes simple. The typical Athenian house contained two main rooms and several smaller ones built around a central courtyard. In one main room, the dining room, the men entertained guests and ate while reclining on couches. An Athenian woman joined her husband for dinner only if company was not invited. In the other main room, the wool room, the women spun and wove cloth. In the courtyard stood an altar, a wash basin, and sometimes a well. The courtyard also contained the family's chickens and goats.

Athenian men usually worked in the morning as farmers, artisans, and merchants. Then they spent the afternoon attending the Assembly or exercising in the gymnasium. Slaves—who were mostly foreigners and prisoners of war and who made up one-third of the population—did most of

Visualizing History Pericles held virtual control over Athenian affairs for the last 15 years of his life, being elected each year as one of the 10 city generals. *How did Pericles identify his faith in democracy?*

the heavy work in craft production and mining. Many slaves also worked as teachers and household servants. Most Athenian women spent their time at home, cooking and making wool cloth, but poor women worked in the open-air markets as food sellers and cloth weavers.

Upper-class Athenian men—as well as citizens from other city-states—enjoyed the symposium as a form of recreation. Wives were excluded from a symposium, which was a drinking session following a banquet. The men at a symposium were entertained by female dancers and singers as well as by acrobats and magicians. The guests also spent much of the evening entertaining each other, telling riddles and discussing literature, philosophy, and public issues.

Athenian Women

In spite of restrictions, many Athenian women were able to participate in public life—especially in city festivals—and learned to read and write. Public opinion allowed greater freedom to women of the *metic* class than to those of other groups. The most famous of *metic* women was **Aspasia**, who was known for her intelligence and personal charm. To her house came many of the women of Athens, and she apparently gave advice on home life while attempting to gain more education and greater freedom for Athenian women. Her views aroused great opposition among some Athenians of both sexes, and she was prosecuted on a charge of "impiety," or disloyalty to the gods. Aspasia was finally acquitted after an impassioned plea to the jury by Pericles himself.

The Peloponnesian War

Even after the Persian Wars ended, the Persian threat remained. Athens persuaded most of the city-states—but not Sparta—to ally against the enemy. This alliance became known as the Delian League because the treasury was kept on the sacred island of **Delos**. Athens provided the principal naval and land forces, while the other city-states furnished money and ships. Over the next several decades, the Delian League succeeded in freeing Ionia from Persian rule and sweeping the Aegean free of pirates. Overseas trade expanded, and Greece grew richer.

The Athenian Empire

Athens gradually began to dominate the other city-states. Pericles, for example, used part of the Delian League's treasury to build the Parthenon.

A Spartan soldier poised for battle. The Spartans developed a chain of orders to be shouted above the din of battle. *How did Sparta attain a navy?*

He insisted that criminal cases be tried only in Athens and that other city-states adopt the Athenian coinage system. He also sent Athenian troops to support revolts by commoners against aristocrats in other city-states. In short, the policies of Pericles more or less transformed the Delian League from what had been an anti-Persian defense league into an Athenian empire.

As Athens's trade and political influence grew, several city-states reacted by forming an alliance opposed to Athens. Sparta, a long-standing Athenian rival, became the leader of the anti-Athens alliance. Since Sparta was located in the Peloponnesus, historians have called the war against Athens and its allies the Peloponnesian War.

The Conflict

The Peloponnesian War lasted from 431 B.C. to 404 B.C., excluding one brief period of peace. At first it seemed as if Athens could hold out indefinitely, since Sparta had no navy. Sparta's fear and jealousy of Athens, however, were so strong that the Spartans made a deal with the Persians to return Ionia to Persian control. In exchange, Sparta received gold to build its own fleet. Then, in 430 B.C., a disastrous plague—probably typhus—weakened Athens. More

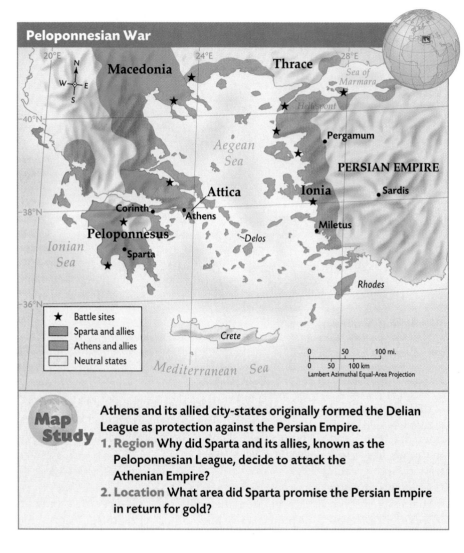

Peloponnesian War

Macedonia

Thrace

Sea of Marmara

Hellespont

Aegean Sea

• Pergamum

PERSIAN EMPIRE

Attica

Ionia

• Sardis

Corinth •

• Athens

• Miletus

Peloponnesus

Ionian Sea

• Sparta

~ Delos

Rhodes

★ Battle sites

Sparta and allies

Athens and allies

Neutral states

Crete

Mediterranean Sea

0   50   100 mi.

0 50 100 km

Lambert Azimuthal Equal-Area Projection

Map Study

Athens and its allied city-states originally formed the Delian League as protection against the Persian Empire.
1. **Region** Why did Sparta and its allies, known as the Peloponnesian League, decide to attack the Athenian Empire?
2. **Location** What area did Sparta promise the Persian Empire in return for gold?

fleet. After the Spartans laid siege to Athens itself, the Athenians finally surrendered in 404 B.C.

Effects of the War

The Peloponnesian War brought disaster to the Greek city-states, both victors and vanquished. Many city-states declined in population. Fighting had destroyed many fields and orchards. Unemployment became so widespread that thousands of young men emigrated and became mercenaries, or hired soldiers, in the Persian army.

Worst of all, the Greeks lost their ability to govern themselves. The length and cost of the war made people forget about the common good of their polis and think only about making money. Feelings between aristocrats and commoners grew increasingly bitter. Many Greeks, losing faith in democracy, even came to look down on free political discussion and began to believe that

than a third of its population died, including Pericles.

After Pericles died in 429 B.C., some Athenians wanted to make peace with Sparta and its allies, while other Athenians wanted to keep on fighting. No decision was made, and the war continued deadlocked for many more years. Eventually, several allies of Athens switched sides and joined the Spartan-led alliance. Then, with their Persian-financed navy, the Spartans destroyed the Athenian

might makes right.

For a time, Sparta tried to rule the other city-states. Then, in 371 B.C., a new alliance of city-states led by Thebes overthrew the harsh, incompetent Spartan rulers. The Thebans, however, also made poor rulers and were also overthrown. As a result of almost continual fighting, the city-states became weaker than ever. When a new invader, the Macedonians, threatened Greece in the 350s B.C., the city-states were unable to resist.

SECTION 4 REVIEW

Recall
1. **Define** symposium, mercenary.
2. **Identify** Ionia, Darius I, Marathon, Xerxes, Themistocles, Thermopylae, Leonidas, Salamis, Pericles, Aspasia.

Critical Thinking
3. **Compare** the daily activities of an Athenian husband with those of an Athenian wife.
4. **Evaluating Information** Judge whether Pericles' rule

was a "golden age" for Athens. Support your answer.

Understanding Themes
5. **Conflict** What was the significance of the outcome of the Persian Wars?

Making Comparisons

In shopping for athletic shoes, you have narrowed your selection to two pairs. Which pair should you buy? To decide this question, you must make a comparison.

Learning the Skill

Making comparisons means finding similarities and differences. In the above example, you might first notice the similarities between the shoes. Both pairs are the same price and the same color. Then, you would look for differences. One pair extends above the ankle, the other pair does not. One pair is designed for jogging, the other for aerobics. Once you have compared the shoes, you can draw a conclusion about which pair will best suit your needs.

Apply the same method in comparing any two objects, groups, or concepts. First, determine the purpose of your comparison. What question do you want to answer? Then determine the bases for comparison. In the shoe example, we compared on the bases of price, color, style, and athletic function. Then identify similarities and differences in each of these categories. Finally, use the comparison to draw conclusions or to answer your question.

Practicing the Skill

The excerpts on this page discuss the military strength of Sparta and Athens. Read the excerpts and answer the questions below.

1. Identify three bases for comparing the military strength of Athens and Sparta.
2. Do both city-states have armies and navies?
3. What are two differences in the military strength of Athens and Sparta?
4. Based on this comparison, which city-state has greater military strength? Why?

“ We [Spartans] have many reasons to expect success,—first, superiority in numbers and in military experience, and second, our general and unvarying obedience in the execution of orders. The naval strength which they [Athens] possess shall be raised by us from ... the monies at Olympia and Delphi. A loan from these enables us to seduce their foreign sailors by the offer of higher pay.... A single defeat at sea is in all likelihood their ruin. ”

—Thucydides, account of a Corinthian envoy to the Congress at Sparta, 432 B.C.

“ Personally engaged in the cultivation of their land, without funds either private or public, the Peloponnesians [Spartans] are also without experience in long wars across the sea.... Our naval skill is of more use to us for service on land, than their military skill for service at sea. Even if they were to ... try to seduce our foreign sailors by the temptation of higher pay ... none of our foreign sailors would consent to become an outlaw from his own country, and to take service with them. ”

—Pericles, account to Athenian Ecclesia, 432 B.C.

Applying the Skill

Choose a topic or activity that interests you, such as baseball, rock music, politics, etc. Research and compare two individuals, groups, or organizations involved in this activity. Write a short essay or make a chart outlining at least five similarities and five differences.

For More Practice

Turn to the Skill Practice in the Chapter Review on page 127 for more practice in making comparisons.

Connections Across Time

Historical Significance Ancient Greece provided the world with its first example of democratic government. Because the limited number of citizens in a Greek polis permitted direct participation by all citizens, Athens can be described as a *direct* democracy. In the United States today, where we elect senators and representatives who are responsible to us, the form of government is called a *representative* democracy. In contrast to citizenship in ancient Greece, United States citizenship has broadened to include women and people of all races, as well as naturalized foreign-born citizens.

Using Key Terms

Write the key term that completes each sentence. Then write a sentence for each term not chosen.

a. aristocrats
b. citizen
c. democracy
d. oligarchy
e. mercenary
f. polis
g. rhetoric
h. tyrant
i. symposiums
j. labyrinth
k. phalanx
l. bards
m. constitution

1. The _____, the basic political unit of ancient Greece, included a city and the surrounding villages, fields, and orchards.
2. A woman in ancient Greece was not considered to be a full _____ with the right to take part in political affairs.
3. By the 700s B.C., kings in Greece had lost power to landholding members of the upper class known as _____.
4. Athenian men entertained each other at _____, telling riddles and discussing literature, philosophy, and public issues.
5. _____, or singing storytellers, kept alive Mycenaean literary traditions during Greece's "dark age."

Technology Activity

Using a Spreadsheet Search the Internet or your local library for additional information about Greek gods and goddesses. Organize your findings by creating a spreadsheet. Include headings such as name of god or goddess, purpose of their existence, types of powers, and relationships to other gods or goddesses. Research further to find out and list the corresponding Roman names for Greek gods and goddesses.

Using Your History Journal

Democracy is not easy to achieve or to maintain. Make a list of the issues that challenge democracy in America. Write a paragraph entitled "Maintaining Democracy" or "Achieving Democracy" that responds to this issue.

Reviewing Facts

1. **Culture** List the elements of Minoan culture that were adopted by the Mycenaeans.
2. **Culture** State the values of the *Iliad* and the *Odyssey*.
3. **Culture** Explain how Greek attitudes toward their deities differ from those of the Egyptians.
4. **History** Explain how Sparta's response to the problems of increased population and a shortage of arable land differed from the response of most other Greek city-states.
5. **Citizenship** Trace the development of democracy in Athens, and describe citizens' rights and responsibilities. What groups were excluded from citizenship?

Critical Thinking

1. **Apply** How did Sparta's values affect its educational system?
2. **Analyze** How did the reforms of Cleisthenes in Athens affect the future development of government in the Western world?
3. **Synthesize** What might have been the outcome of the Persian Wars if Themistocles had not convinced the Greeks to build a fleet of ships?

4. Analyze Shown below, the south porch of the Erechtheum near the Parthenon has figures of maidens in place of conventional columns. The buildings on the Acropolis are examples of early classical architecture and sculpture. What might these figures suggest about the role of women in Athenian life?

Understanding Themes

1. **Relation to Environment** What aspects of Crete's environment enabled the Minoans to become skilled seafarers?
2. **Movement** What role did trade play in the development of Greek civilization?
3. **Regionalism** What effect did Sparta's emphasis on military values have on its development as a city-state?
4. **Conflict** How did the Peloponnesian War affect Athens, Sparta, and the other Greek city-states?

Linking Past and Present

1. Why did tyrants seize power in ancient Athens during times of unrest? Do you think a tyrant could establish a dictatorship today in the United States in a time of crisis? Explain your answer.
2. Why might students at the United States Naval Academy study the Persian Wars?

Skill Practice

Reread Section 3 and compare the two leading city-states in ancient Greece.

1. What are two similarities in the education of young people in Athens and Sparta?
2. What are two differences in their educations in these two city-states?
3. What are two similarities in the political structure of Athens and Sparta?
4. What are two differences that can be identified in the political structure of these two Greek city-states?
5. What are two differences in the roles of women in Athens and Sparta?
6. What are two similarities in women's roles in these two city-states?

Geography in History

1. **Place** Although it is a small island without much land area, Crete contains what two distinct, but neighboring, landforms?
2. **Location** Refer to the map on page 124. What is the relative location of Crete? What is Crete's absolute location?
3. **Location** Where was the palace of the legendary king Minos?
4. **Human/Environment Interaction** Geography has an impact on how people live from day to day. How did the early people of Crete earn their living?

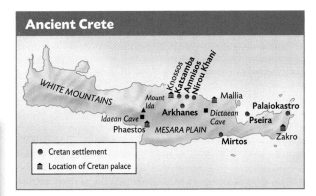

Ancient Crete

WHITE MOUNTAINS · Mount Ida · Knossos · Katsamba · Ammisos · Nirou Khani · Mallia · Palaiokastro · Idaean Cave · Arkhanes · Dictaean Cave · Pseira · Phaestos · MESARA PLAIN · Mirtos · Zakro

● Cretan settlement
🏛 Location of Cretan palace

750–150 B.C.

The Height of Greek Civilization

Chapter Themes

▶ **Innovation** The ancient Greeks develop a culture that becomes one of the foundations of Western civilization. *Section 1*

▶ **Innovation** Ancient Greek thinkers believe in reason and the importance of the individual. *Section 2*

▶ **Cultural Diffusion** Alexander's empire brings about a mix of Greek and Middle Eastern cultures. *Section 3*

The Storyteller

An outwardly unimpressive man, Socrates was nonetheless an intellectual giant in the Athens of the late 400s B.C. One of his devoted followers described Socrates' day: "At early morning he was to be seen betaking himself to one of the promenades or wrestling grounds; at noon he would appear with the gathering crowds in the marketplace; and as day declined, wherever the largest throng might be encountered, there was he to be found, talking for the most part, while anyone who chose might stop and listen." Socrates was a supreme questioner who succeeded in getting people to analyze their own behavior. Today, Socrates' reputation lives on as one of the greatest teachers of all time.

Historical Significance

What were the principal beliefs and values of the ancient Greeks? How did their achievements in art, philosophy, history, and science shape the growth of Western civilization?

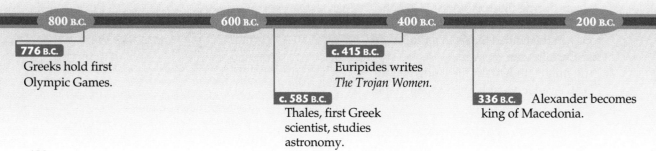

800 B.C.	600 B.C.	400 B.C.	200 B.C.

776 B.C.
Greeks hold first
Olympic Games.

c. 585 B.C.
Thales, first Greek
scientist, studies
astronomy.

c. 415 B.C.
Euripides writes
The Trojan Women.

336 B.C. Alexander becomes
king of Macedonia.

Plato's School, a mosaic from the Hellenistic period. National Museum Naples, Italy

Your History Journal

The word thespian, *meaning "actor," derives from the Greek dramatist Thespis. Many Greek innovations in staging productions are still used today. Research the history of early Greek drama. Write a comparison with modern theater.*

600 B.C.

c. 600 B.C.
Greeks perform
the earliest plays.

500 B.C.

459 B.C. Aeschylus
writes the *Oresteia*.

400 B.C.

432 B.C. Athenians
finish building the
Parthenon.

Section 1

Quest for Beauty and Meaning

Setting the Scene

▶ **Terms to Define**
classical, sanctuary, perspective, amphora, tragedy, comedy

▶ **People to Meet**
Myron, Phidias, Praxiteles, Aeschylus, Sophocles, Euripides, Aristophanes

▶ **Places to Locate**
Olympia

 **Find Out** How did the Greeks express their love of beauty and meaning?

The Storyteller

An early Greek actor remembers performing in his first tragedy: "I put on the robe of Zeus for the prologue, a lovely thing, purple worked with golden oak leaves.... The next thing I remember is sitting enthroned down center on the god-walk, eagle on left fist, scepter in right hand ... and all the eyes of Athens skinning me to the bone." The actor felt as though he had sleepwalked into the scene. Gripped by fear, he tried to remember his lines: "My father would die of shame.... He was twice the artist I am. At once my lines came back to me. I started my speech...."

—adapted from *The Mask of Apollo*, Mary Renault, 1974

Vase depicting actors preparing for a play

During the mid-400s B.C., Greek civilization reached its cultural peak, particularly in the city-state of Athens. This period of brilliant cultural achievement has been called ancient Greece's Golden Age. Artists of the Golden Age excelled in architecture, sculpture, and painting. They created works characterized by beautiful simplicity and graceful balance, an artistic style now called classical.

Classical Greek art, copied soon after in Roman artistic styles, set lasting standards of beauty still admired today. The writers and thinkers of ancient Greece also made enduring achievements in literature and drama, creating works read through the centuries and still considered classics today. Many cultural traditions of Western civilization—the civilization of Europe and those parts of the world influenced by Europeans—began with Greece's Golden Age.

Building for the Gods

The Greeks, wrote the Athenian leader Pericles, were "lovers of the beautiful." Each Greek city-state tried to turn its acropolis into an architectural treasure.

The Parthenon—the temple to Athena built on the summit of the Acropolis in Athens—best exemplified classical Greek architecture. It was begun in 447 B.C. and finished in 432 B.C., under the rule of Pericles. Because the Greeks worshiped either in their homes or at outdoor altars, they did not need large sanctuaries, or places of worship. Instead, they built temples as places where their deities would live.

The Parthenon has an ingeniously simple design. It is a rectangle surrounded by 46 fluted columns. At the same time, the Parthenon is extremely beautiful. In the right light, because of

An ancient Greek krater (vase) illustrates a scene from Odysseus and the Sirens. *What kinds of vases did the Greeks decorate with scenes from mythology?*

iron in its white marble, the Parthenon gleams a soft gold against the blue sky.

The Parthenon's graceful proportions perfectly balance width, length, and height. To the Greeks the Parthenon represented the ideal of "nothing to excess," an ideal sometimes called the "golden mean," or the midpoint between two extremes.

The architects of the Parthenon also understood optical illusions and perspective, or the artistic showing of distances between objects as they appear to the eye. Thus, they made the temple's columns thicker in the middle and thinner at the top so that the columns appeared straight when viewed from a distance. The steps leading up to the Parthenon, actually lower in the center than at either end, likewise appear straight. The Athenians wanted to create the impression of perfection—and they succeeded.

Greek Arts

The Greek love of beauty was expressed in the fine arts as well as in architecture. In both painting and sculpture, the Greeks—because they emphasized the individual—excelled at portraying the human form.

Painting on Vases

Although the Greeks painted murals, as had the Minoans, no originals have survived. We know of Greek murals only from written descriptions or Roman copies. But today we can still see examples of their work in the paintings on Greek vases.

The Greeks designed their pottery with different shapes that were suited for different functions. For example, Greek potters gave the *krater*—a small two-handled vase—a wide mouth in which it was easy to mix wine with water. On the other hand, they gave the *leythos* a narrow neck so that oil could be poured out slowly and in small quantities.

Most pottery remaining from ancient Greece is either red on a black background or black on a red background. The varied subjects of the paintings depended on the size and use of the vase. Potters usually decorated an amphora—a large vase for storing oil and other bulk supplies—with scenes from mythology. In contrast, a *kylix*—a wide, shallow two-handled drinking cup—showed scenes of everyday life: children attending school, shoemakers and carpenters plying their trades, a farmer guiding the plow behind a team of oxen, a merchant ship braving the winds. Greek potters skillfully adapted their designs and decorations to the curves and shape of the vase.

Sculpting the Human Body

Greek sculpture, like Greek architecture, reached its height in Athens during the time of Pericles. **Myron**, one of the greatest sculptors of Greece's Golden Age, portrayed in his statues idealized views of what people *should* look like rather than actual persons. When Myron sculpted his *Discus Thrower* poised to hurl the discus, he carved the lines of the body to indicate an athlete's excellent physical condition as well as his mental control over what he was doing.

The great sculptor **Phidias** (FIH•dee•uhs) was in charge of the Parthenon's sculptures. Phidias himself carved the towering statue of Athena that was placed inside the Parthenon. The statue, made of gold and ivory plates attached to a wooden framework, showed the goddess in her warlike aspect, carrying a shield, spear, and helmet.

Palace of Persepolis

The Persians completed a notable palace complex in their religious capital of Persepolis. Because Zoroastrianism did not require temples, the Persians built a group of adjoining buildings that included palaces, halls, chambers, and courtyards. Persian kings used a huge room, called the Hall of One Hundred Columns, as a reception area for visitors. The room was 250 feet (76 meters) square. Its vast beamed ceiling was supported by columns 60 feet (18 meters) high.

A hundred years after the Golden Age of Athens, the work of another famous Greek sculptor—**Praxiteles** (prak•SIH•tuhl•EEZ)—reflected the changes that had occurred in Greek life. The sculptures of Myron and Phidias had been full of power and striving for perfection, as befitted a people who had defeated the mighty Persian Empire. By the time of Praxiteles, the Greeks had suffered through the Peloponnesian War and had lost their self-confidence. Accordingly, Praxiteles and his colleagues favored life-sized statues rather than massive works. They emphasized grace rather than power. The sculptors of the Golden Age had carved only deities and heroes, but the sculptors of the 300s B.C. carved ordinary people too.

Drama and Theater

The Greeks also explored the human condition through theatrical dramas. They were the first people to write and perform plays, which they presented twice a year at festivals to honor Dionysus, the god of wine and fertility.

Aeschylus

The earliest Greek plays were tragedies. In a tragedy, the lead character struggles against fate only to be doomed—after much suffering—to an unhappy, or tragic, ending. **Aeschylus** (EHS•kuh •luhs), the first of the great writers of tragedies in the 400s B.C., wrote 90 plays. Seven have survived. His *Oresteia* is a trilogy—a set of three plays with a related theme—and is famous for the grandeur of its language.

The *Oresteia* shows how the consequences of one's deeds are carried down from generation to generation. The first play in the trilogy tells about the return of King Agamemnon from the Trojan War and his murder by his wife Clytemnestra in revenge for Agamemnon's sacrifice of their daughter Iphigenia before the Greeks sailed for Troy. The second play describes how Agamemnon's son Orestes in turn avenges his father's death by killing his mother. The third play has Orestes standing trial in Athens for his bloody deed. When the jury splits six to six, the goddess Athena intervenes and casts the deciding vote in favor of mercy. The moral of the trilogy is that the law of the community, not personal revenge, should decide punishment.

Sophocles

The next great tragedian, **Sophocles** (SAH•fuh •KLEEZ), had served as a general in the Athenian army and had lived through most of the Peloponnesian War. Sophocles accepted human suffering as an unavoidable part of life. At the same time, he stressed human courage and compassion.

In one of his most famous plays, *Oedipus Rex*, Sophocles deals with the plight of Oedipus, a king who is doomed by the deities to kill his father and marry his mother. Despite Oedipus's efforts to avoid his fate, the deities' decree comes true. When Oedipus discovers what he has done, he blinds himself in despair and goes into exile.

Euripides

The last of the three great Greek tragedians—**Euripides** (yu•RIH•puh•DEEZ)—rarely dealt with the influence of the gods and goddesses on human lives. Instead, he focused on the qualities human beings possess that bring disaster on themselves.

Euripides also hated war, and many of his 19 surviving plays show the misery war brings. In *The Trojan Women*, the Trojan princess Cassandra explains why the Greeks, despite their victory, are not better off than the Trojans:

    “ And when [the Greeks] came to the banks
        of the Scamander those thousands died.
        And why?
    No man has moved their landmarks or
        laid siege to their high-walled towns.
    But those whom war took never saw their
        children.
    No wife with gentle hands shrouded them
        for their grave.
    They lie in a strange land. And in their

Fulvio Rizzo

Liberto Perugi

Greek Soldier

A Greek warrior, sculpted in bronze, gazes at the world with a determined stare. For more than 1,500 years, the soldier rested under the waters of the Mediterranean Sea. Then in 1972 an Italian chemist from Rome, diving off the coast of southern Italy, found this statue and a companion bronze of an older Greek soldier. The statues were probably lost at sea en route to Rome—perhaps thrown overboard to lighten a storm-tossed ship. Rescued by divers (upper left) and carefully restored, the statues now stand guard in an Italian museum.

The Greeks began casting statues in bronze in the mid-500s B.C. Within a century ancient Greek civilization entered its Golden Age, the era in which Plato (427–347 B.C.) and Aristotle (384–322 B.C.) laid the foundations of Western philosophy; Sophocles (495–405 B.C.) wrote tragedies; Thucydides (471–c. 400 B.C.) recorded Greek history; and Phidias of Athens (500–431 B.C.) created statues—perhaps even these rare examples. It was an age in which sculptors created new modes of artistic expression and began to depict the human body with precision. ⊕

Chapter 5 *The Height of Greek Civilization* **133**

The Greek sculptor Myron honored the Olympic discus thrower, shown here in a Roman marble copy. *How did the Greeks honor winners of the Olympic Games?*

about issues of his day. In his play *The Clouds*, Aristophanes had a character named Strepsiades ask where Athens was on a map. When the polis's location was pointed out to him, Strepsiades replied: "Don't be ridiculous, that can't be Athens, for I can't see even a single law court in session."

The Olympic Games

Believing that healthy bodies made the best use of nature's gifts, the ancient Greeks stressed athletics in their school curriculum. Greek men who could afford the leisure time usually spent all or part of their afternoons practicing sports in their polis's gymnasiums.

The ancient Greeks held the Olympic Games—their best-known sporting event—in **Olympia** every four years. Because the Olympic Games were a religious festival in honor of Zeus, trading and fighting stopped while they were going on. The Greek calendar began with the supposed date of the first Olympic Games: 776 B.C.

Athletes came from all over the Greek-speaking world to compete in the Olympics. Only male athletes, however, were allowed to take part, and women were not permitted even as spectators. Games that honored the goddess Hera were held at a different location than Olympia and gave Greek women an opportunity to participate in races.

In line with the Greek emphasis on the individual, Olympic competition took the form of individual rather than team events. These consisted at first of only a footrace. Later other events—the broad jump, the discus throw, boxing, and wrestling—were added. An activity called the pentathlon (pehn•TATH•luhn) combined running, jumping, throwing the discus, wrestling, and hurling the javelin.

The Greeks crowned Olympic winners with wreaths of olive leaves and held parades in their honor. Some city-states even excused outstanding athletes from paying taxes.

homes are sorrows, too, the very same.
Lonely women who died, old men who
waited for sons that never came—no
son left to them to make the offering at
their graves.
That was the glorious victory they won. 🙾

——Euripides, from his tragedy
The Trojan Women, c. 415 B.C.

A Comedy Tonight

Eventually the Greeks also wrote comedies, plays with humorous themes and happy endings. **Aristophanes** (ar•uh•STAH•fuh•NEEZ), the most famous writer of comedies, created imaginative social satire. In his works he made witty comments about leading figures—such as Euripides—and

---

SECTION 1 REVIEW

Recall
1. **Define** classical, sanctuary, perspective, amphora, tragedy, comedy.
2. **Identify** Myron, Phidias, Praxiteles, Aeschylus, Sophocles, Euripides, Aristophanes.
3. **Describe** how worship of

Greek deities influenced architecture, art, and athletics.

Critical Thinking
4. **Applying Information** Show how the Greek emphasis on the individual was demonstrated both in the Olympic Games and in the fine arts.

Understanding Themes
5. **Innovation** How was the ancient Greeks' emphasis on reason and individuality revealed in their arts? Cite examples from architecture, sculpture, and drama.

c. 500s B.C.
Pythagoras develops mathematical theories.

435 B.C.
Herodotus writes history of the Persian Wars.

399 B.C.
Athenians try Socrates for treason.

335 B.C.
Aristotle opens the Lyceum in Athens.

Section 2

The Greek Mind

Setting the Scene

▶ **Terms to Define**
philosopher, logic, hygiene

▶ **People to Meet**
Sophists, Socrates, Plato, Aristotle, Herodotus, Thucydides, Thales, Pythagoras, Hippocrates

Find Out What did the ancient Greeks achieve in philosophy, history, and science?

The Storyteller

Socrates was on trial for his life, for crimes against religion and for corrupting the youth of Athens. He spoke in his own defense: "I have done nothing but try to persuade you all, young and old, not to be concerned with body or property first, but to care chiefly about improvement of the soul. I tell you that virtue does not come from money, but that money comes from virtue, as does every other good of man, public and private. This is my teaching, and if this corrupts the youth, then I am a mischievous person. O men of Athens, either acquit me or convict me; but whichever you do, understand that I shall never alter my ways, not even if I have to die many times."

—adapted from
The Apology of Socrates, Plato

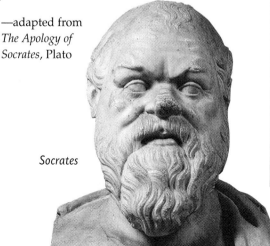

Socrates

The Greeks believed the human mind capable of understanding everything. As a result, the philosophers, or thinkers, of ancient Greece produced some of the most remarkable ideas the world has ever known. Through philosophy—which means "the seeking of wisdom"—they laid the foundations for such disciplines as history, political science, biology, and logic, or the science of reasoning.

The Sophists

In the 400s B.C. higher education was provided by professional teachers known as **Sophists**. Although Sophists traveled from polis to polis, many gathered in Athens, possibly for the freedom of speech allowed there. Sophists, meaning "knowers," claimed that they could find the answers to all questions.

Many Sophists rejected the belief that the gods and goddesses influenced human behavior. They also did not believe in absolute moral and legal standards. Instead, they asserted that "man is the measure of all things" and that truth is different for each individual.

Not only did Sophists challenge certain traditional Greek beliefs, they also took money for their teaching. Many of them seemed most intent on teaching young men how to win a political argument and get ahead in the world. Many Greeks, including two of Greece's greatest philosophers—**Socrates** (SAH•kruh•TEEZ) and his pupil **Plato**—criticized the Sophists severely.

Socrates

Socrates was born to a poor Athenian family in 470 B.C. Athough a sculptor by trade, he spent most of his time teaching. Unlike the Sophists, Socrates believed in absolute rather than relative truth. His main interest did not lie in teaching rhetoric or in imparting information. Rather, Socrates was attracted to the process by which people learned how to think for themselves.

To encourage his students to clear away mistaken ideas and discover the truth, Socrates developed a teaching technique known as the Socratic method. He would ask students pointed questions without giving them answers and then oppose the students' answers with clear logical arguments. Through this method, he forced his students to defend their statements and to clarify their thinking. For example, in discussing the topic of justice, Socrates proceeded as follows:

> 66 Socrates: Does falsehood then exist among mankind?
> Euthydemus: It does assuredly.
> Socrates: Under which head [justice or injustice] shall we place it?
> Euthydemus: Under injustice, certainly.
> Socrates: Well then … if a father, when his son requires medicine, and refuses to take it, should deceive him, and give him the medicine as ordinary food, and, by adopting such deception, should restore him to health, under which head must we place such an act of deceit?
> Euthydemus: It appears to me that we must place it under [justice].… I retract what I said before. 99
>
> —Xenophon, from *Memorabilia*,
> early 300s B.C.

Some prominent Athenians viewed Socrates' teachings as a threat to the polis. In 399 B.C. they accused him of "corrupting the young" and of "not worshiping the gods worshiped by the state" and had him brought to trial.

Socrates argued in his own defense that a person who *knew* what was right would always *do* what was right and that the intellectual search for truth was the most important thing in the world. "A man who is good for anything ought not to calculate the chance of living or dying; he ought only to consider whether … he is doing right or wrong."

Despite Socrates' eloquence, a jury of citizens found him guilty and sentenced him to death. Although Socrates had the right to ask for a lesser penalty, such as exile, he refused to do so. He had lived his life under the laws of his polis, and he would not avoid obeying them now.

Socrates carried out the sentence of his fellow citizens himself. He drank poisonous hemlock juice and died quietly among his grieving followers.

Plato

Born an Athenian aristocrat, Plato thought at first of entering politics. However, after Socrates' death, Plato—at age 40—became a teacher and opened his Academy, a school that remained in existence until A.D. 529.

From memory Plato recorded dialogues, or conversations, between Socrates and fellow Athenians, and he also wrote the earliest book on political science, *The Republic*. In this book, he presented a plan for what he considered would be the ideal society and government.

Plato disliked Athenian democracy and preferred the government of Sparta. He gave more importance to the state than to the individual. Like the Spartans, he believed that each person should place service to the community above strictly personal goals. Plato also believed that the result of people having too much freedom is social disorder. He distrusted the lower classes and wanted only the most intelligent and best-educated citizens to participate in government. As he explained in *The Republic*:

> 66 Until philosophers are kings, or the kings and princes of this world have the spirit and power of philosophy, and political greatness and wisdom meet in one, and those commoner natures who pursue either to the exclusion of the other are compelled to stand aside, cities will never have rest from their evils, no, nor the human race. 99

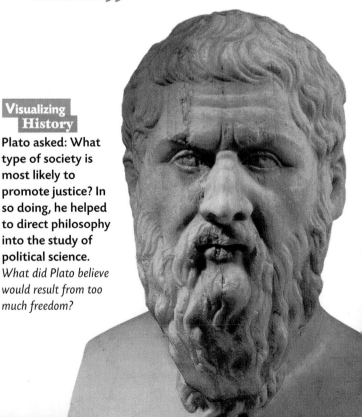

Visualizing History

Plato asked: What type of society is most likely to promote justice? In so doing, he helped to direct philosophy into the study of political science. *What did Plato believe would result from too much freedom?*

Plato's political views were part of an all-embracing philosophy by which he tried to search for "truth." Plato rejected the senses—seeing, hearing, touch, smell, and taste—as a source of truth, believing that the many things that could be perceived by these senses were only "appearance." Reality, the "real" world, was constructed from ideas, or ideal "forms," which could be understood through logical thought and reasoning.

Aristotle

The third great philosopher of ancient Greece was **Aristotle** (AR•uh•STAH•tuhl), who wrote more than 200 books on topics ranging from astronomy to political science. At his Athenian school known as the Lyceum, Aristotle taught the golden mean, an ethical principle that affirmed living moderately and avoiding extremes in one's actions.

Aristotle influenced later philosophers with his work on logic. He developed the syllogism, a means for presenting an argument in such a way that one can determine whether or not the conclusion follows logically from the premises, or basic statements.

Aristotle and Science

Aristotle also influenced scientific work. Unlike Plato, he stressed the value of knowledge gained through the senses. In his work *Physics*, Aristotle stated that the physical world's most striking feature is change, and that change basically consists of the same matter taking on new form. He was also the first person to observe facts, then classify them according to their similarities and their differences, and finally develop generalizations from his data. Some of his specific beliefs—notably, that Earth is the center of our solar system—were incorrect. Aristotle's views and his method of inquiry, however, would continue to dominate European scientific thinking for centuries.

Aristotle and Government

Many of Aristotle's writings focused on political science. Unlike Plato, he did not theorize about idealized principles of government. Instead, he examined the political structure of various city-states, analyzing their advantages and disadvantages. Only then did he spell out his conclusions in a book called *Politics*. Aristotle believed that the ideal form of government balanced monarchy, aristocracy, and democracy in one system. He preferred, however, to have power rest with the middle class, because they knew both how to command *and* obey.

Writers of History

The Greeks also used their intellectual skills in writing history. Until the 400s B.C. the Greeks had considered literary legends as history. **Herodotus** (hih•RAH•duh•tus), the first Greek historian, decided to separate fact from legend. Historians still consider him "the father of history."

Herodotus

Herodotus chose as his subject the Persian Wars and called his work the *Historia*, or "investigation." Herodotus traveled throughout the Persian Empire and also visited many Greek colonies. Everywhere he went, he asked questions, recorded answers, and checked the reliability of his sources. However, he accepted some statements that were not true, especially exaggerated numbers—such as how many Persians died at Marathon. He also sometimes offered supernatural explanations of events.

Herodotus did not limit himself to describing military and political events. He also wrote about outstanding individuals, social customs, and religious beliefs and practices. Later historians have learned a great deal from the *Historia* about the culture of the period and about the civilizations that Herodotus visited.

Thucydides

The second noted historian of ancient Greece, **Thucydides** (thoo•SIH•duh•DEEZ), wrote about the Peloponnesian War. Thucydides is regarded as the first scientific historian because he completely rejected the idea that the deities played a part in human history. Only human beings make history, Thucydides said. He also was as accurate and impartial as possible. He visited battle sites, carefully examined documents, and accepted only the evidence of actual eyewitnesses to events.

The Atom

The Greek thinker Democritus came up with the idea of a solid particle of matter so small that it was both invisible and not divisible. He named this particle *atom*, meaning "indivisible." Today scientists know that atoms are in fact divisible and include many separate and smaller types of matter. But the basic idea of atomic physics can be traced back to Democritus.

Visualizing History Greek physicians observed the many symptoms of disease and concluded that illnesses are not caused by evil spirits, but have natural causes. *What three prescriptions for health did Hippocrates suggest?*

guish mathematics as a pure science apart from everyday practical uses. They constructed systematic methods of reasoning to prove the truth of mathematical statements. Through the study of mathematics, Greek thinkers believed that they could find absolutely certain and eternal knowledge.

The first prominent Greek scientist was **Thales** (THAY•leez) of Miletus, a Greek city-state in Ionia. Born in the mid-600s B.C., Thales studied astronomy at Babylon and mathematics in Egypt and could foretell a solar eclipse. He also formulated a theory that water was the basic substance of which everything in the world is made.

During the 500s B.C., **Pythagoras** (puh •THA•guh•ruhs) tried to explain everything in mathematical terms. He explored the nature of numbers, especially whole numbers and their ratios. Students of geometry still learn the Pythagorean theorem about the relationship of sides of a right-angled triangle. Pythagoras also taught that the world was round and revolved around a fixed point.

Greek Medicine

Greek scientists also contributed to the field of medicine. Called "the father of medicine," the physician **Hippocrates** (hih•PAH•kruh•TEEZ) believed that diseases had natural, not supernatural, causes and that the body could heal itself. He was the first doctor to view medicine as a science separate from religious beliefs or mythological explanations.

Basing his work in the late 400s B.C. on observation, he traveled all over Greece diagnosing illnesses and treating sick people. He urged fellow doctors to keep records of their cases and to exchange information with one another. He strongly advocated proper hygiene, or health care, a sound diet, and plenty of rest.

According to tradition, Hippocrates drafted a code for ethical medical conduct that has guided the practice of medicine for more than 2,000 years. Many doctors today recite the Hippocratic oath when they receive their medical degree.

Thucydides did not simply recite facts, however. He also offered explanations for why events took place and what motivated political leaders. He believed that future generations could learn from the past.

The First Scientists

The ancient Greeks passed on a great scientific heritage. They believed that the world is ruled by natural laws and that human beings can discover these laws by using reason. Lacking scientific equipment, the Greek scientists made most of their discoveries by observation and thought. They then went on to develop general theories or statements about the workings of nature.

Greek Mathematicians

The Greeks became the first people to distin-

SECTION 2 REVIEW

Recall
1. **Define** philosopher, logic, hygiene.
2. **Identify** Sophists, Socrates, Plato, Aristotle, Herodotus, Thucydides, Thales, Pythagoras, Hippocrates.

3. **Explain** how Plato, Socrates, and Aristotle were related as philosophers.

Critical Thinking
4. **Making Comparisons** Compare the political views of Plato and Aristotle and their

attitudes regarding observations made through the senses.

Understanding Themes
5. **Innovation** How did Socrates and Hippocrates each contribute to the intellectual life of ancient Greece?

Finding Exact Location on a Map

Your new friend invites you to her house. In giving directions, she says, "I live at the northwest corner of Vine Street and Oak Avenue." She has pinpointed her exact location. We use a similar system to identify the exact location of any place on Earth.

Learning the Skill

Over many centuries, cartographers developed a grid system of imaginary lines—the lines of latitude and lines of longitude. Lines of latitude run east and west around the earth. Because they always remain the same distance from each other, they are also called parallels. The parallel lines of latitude measure distance north and south of the Equator, located at 0° latitude. Each line of latitude is one degree, or 69 miles (110 km), from the next. There are 90 latitude lines between the Equator and each Pole. For example, New York City lies 41° north of the Equator, or 41° N.

Lines of longitude, or meridians, run north and south from Pole to Pole. Unlike lines of latitude, lines of longitude are not always the same distance from each other. Lines of longitude are farthest apart at the Equator and intersect at each Pole. Longitude measures distance east and west of the Prime Meridian, located at 0° longitude. That line runs through Greenwich, England, in western Europe and through western Africa. Longitude lines increase east and west of the Prime Meridian to 180°. This meridian runs through the Pacific Ocean. New York City, for example, lies 74° west of the Prime Meridian, or 74° W.

With this system, we can pinpoint the "grid address" of any place on Earth. On a map, find the nearest line of latitude to the designated place. Then follow along this line until it crosses the nearest line of longitude. The point where the lines intersect is the grid address. For example, New York City has this grid address: 41° N, 74° W.

Practicing the Skill

Use the map below to answer the following questions:
1. What is the approximate grid address of Babylon?
2. What city is located at approximately 30° N, 31° E?
3. What is the approximate grid address of Nineveh?
4. What is the approximate grid address of Tyre?

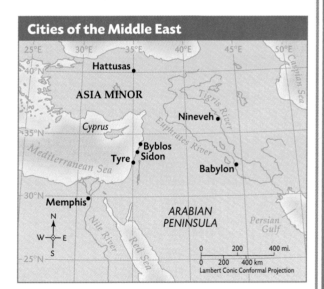

Cities of the Middle East

Applying the Skill

Create a travel itinerary for a tour of the ruins of ancient Egypt, Greece, or the Middle East. Choose at least 10 locations you would like to visit. Draw a map of the region, including grid lines. On the map, identify the approximate grid location of each place.

For More Practice

Turn to the Skill Practice in the Chapter Review on page 151 for more practice in finding exact location on a map.

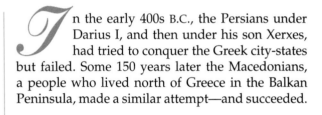

400 B.C.	300 B.C.	200 B.C.	100 B.C.

359 B.C. Philip II becomes king of Macedonia.

331 B.C. Alexander the Great defeats the Persians in the battle of Gaugamela.

250 B.C. Jewish scholars translate the Hebrew Bible into Greek.

c. 100 B.C. Roman Empire begins to conquer the Hellenistic world.

Section 3

Alexander's Empire

Setting the Scene

▶ **Terms to Define**
   domain

▶ **People to Meet**
   Philip II, Demosthenes, Alexander the Great, Zeno, Menander, Eratosthenes, Euclid, Archimedes

▶ **Places to Locate**
   Macedonia, Alexandria

 **Find Out** What were Alexander's goals for his empire, and how successful was he in achieving them?

The Storyteller

Hellenistic poets who lived in bustling cities loved to tell simple fables about love in a country-side setting:

A bee once stung the god of love [Cupid]
   as he was stealing honey.
His fingertips began to smart,
   and he blew upon his hand,
   stamped and danced.
When he showed his wound to his mother,
   she laughed. "Aren't you just like the bee,
      so small, yet inflicting great pain?"

—adapted from *The Idylls of Theocritus,* (no. 19, "The Honey-Thief"), in *Greek Pastoral Poetry,* Anthony Holden, 1974

Cupid, wall painting, Pompeii, Italy

In the early 400s B.C., the Persians under Darius I, and then under his son Xerxes, had tried to conquer the Greek city-states but failed. Some 150 years later the Macedonians, a people who lived north of Greece in the Balkan Peninsula, made a similar attempt—and succeeded.

Rise of Macedonia

The Macedonians, like the Spartans, were descended from the Dorians, and the Macedonian language incorporated many Greek words. The Greeks, however, looked down on the Macedonians as backward mountaineers.

In 359 B.C. **Philip II** became king of **Macedonia**. During his youth he had been a hostage for three years in the Greek city-state of Thebes. There he had learned to admire both Greek culture and military organization. As king, Philip determined to do three things: create a strong standing army, unify the quarreling Greek city-states under Macedonian rule, and destroy the Persian Empire.

Philip increased his army's fighting power by organizing his infantry into Greek-style phalanxes. Arrayed in close formation 16 rows deep, Philip's lance-bearing foot soldiers fought as a single unit.

For the next 23 years, Philip pursued his ambition. Sometimes he conquered a polis or bribed a polis's leaders to surrender. Sometimes he allied a polis through marriage; Philip had a total of six or seven wives.

The Greek city-states, weakened by the Peloponnesian War, would not cooperate in resisting Philip. The great Athenian orator **Demosthenes** (dih•MAHS•thuh•NEEZ) appealed to his fellow citizens to fight for their liberty. But Demosthenes' words were to no avail. By 338 B.C. Philip had conquered all of Greece except Sparta.

Philip then announced that he would lead the Greeks and Macedonians in a war against Persia. But in 336 B.C., just as he was ready to carry out his

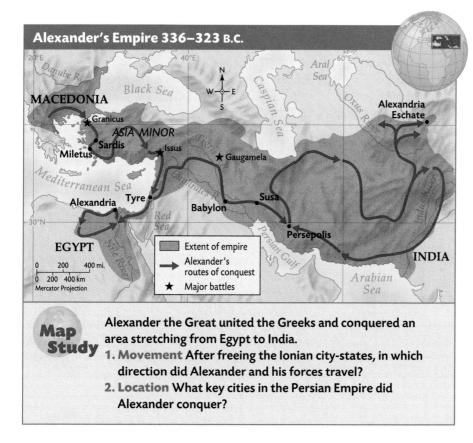

MACEDONIA

Granicus

ASIA MINOR

Sardis

Miletus

Issus

Gaugamela

Black Sea

Caspian Sea

Aral Sea

Oxus River

Alexandria Eschate

Mediterranean Sea

Alexandria

Tyre

Babylon

Susa

Persepolis

Red Sea

Persian Gulf

INDIA

Arabian Sea

EGYPT

Nile River

0   200   400 mi.
0 200 400 km
Mercator Projection

- Extent of empire
- → Alexander's routes of conquest
- ★ Major battles

Map Study

Alexander the Great united the Greeks and conquered an area stretching from Egypt to India.

1. **Movement** After freeing the Ionian city-states, in which direction did Alexander and his forces travel?
2. **Location** What key cities in the Persian Empire did Alexander conquer?

and Persians took place in 333 B.C. at Issus, Syria. Once again, Alexander's superb tactics resulted in victory, forcing the Persian king Darius III to flee.

Instead of pursuing Darius, Alexander and his troops moved south along the Mediterranean coast. First they captured the seaports of Phoenicia and cut off the Persian fleet from its main supply bases. The fleet soon surrendered. Next, turning west, they invaded Egypt where the people, discontented under Persian rule, welcomed them and declared Alexander a pharaoh. In Egypt, Alexander established a new city and named it **Alexandria** after himself.

Final Campaigns

In 331 B.C. Alexander again turned his attention eastward. He invaded Mesopotamia and smashed Darius's main army in the battle of Gaugamela near the Tigris River. He

plans, Philip was murdered—either by a Persian agent or by an assassin hired by his first wife, Olympias. Olympias' son Alexander, later known as **Alexander the Great**, became king.

Alexander's Conquests

Alexander was only 20 when he became the ruler of Macedonia and Greece. A commander in the Macedonian army since he was 16, Alexander was highly respected by his soldiers for his courage and military skill. He was also extremely well educated, for his father had him tutored by Aristotle.

Conflict With Persia

In 334 B.C. Alexander led 30,000 soldiers and 5,000 cavalry into Asia to open his campaign of "West against East." The first major encounter with the Persians took place at the Granicus River in western Asia Minor. Alexander's forces won, and he sent 300 suits of Persian armor to Athens as an offering to the goddess Athena. He then marched along the coast of Asia Minor, freeing the Ionian city-states from Persian rule.

The second major battle between the Greeks

Alexander the Great

went on to capture the key cities of the Persian Empire: Babylon, Persepolis, and Susa. When Darius was killed by one of his own generals, Alexander declared himself ruler of the Persian Empire.

Even this success was not enough for the young conqueror. In 327 B.C. he led his soldiers into India, and after three years they reached the Indus River valley. Alexander hoped to go farther yet, but his Macedonian veterans refused. Alexander therefore reluctantly turned around and went to Babylon, which he had made the capital of his empire. But the hardships of the journey had undermined his health, and he fell ill with a fever, probably malaria. In 323 B.C. Alexander the Great died at the age of 33.

Imperial Goals

When Alexander first set out with his army, his goal was to punish Persia for its invasion of Greece 150 years earlier. But as more and more territory came under his control, Alexander's views changed. His new vision was to create an empire that would unite Europe and Asia and combine the best of Greek and Persian cultures.

Alexander tried to promote this goal by example. He wore Persian dress and imitated the court life of Persian kings. He married a daughter of Darius III and encouraged 10,000 of his soldiers to marry Persian women. He enrolled 30,000 Persians in his army. He also founded about 70 cities that served both as military outposts and as centers for spreading the Greek language and culture throughout his empire.

Divided Domain

Following Alexander's death, three of his generals—Ptolemy (TAH•luh•mee), Seleucus (suh•LOO•kuhs), and Antigonus (an•TIH•guh•nuhs)—eventually divided his vast empire into separate domains, or territories. Ptolemy and his descendants ruled Egypt, Libya, and part of Syria. The most famous Ptolemaic ruler was Cleopatra VII, who lost her kingdom to the Romans in 31 B.C.

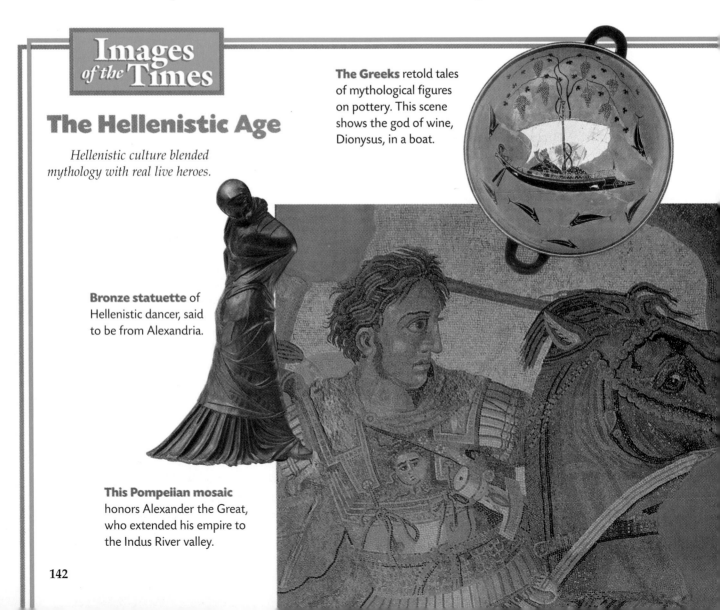

Images
of the Times

The Hellenistic Age

Hellenistic culture blended mythology with real live heroes.

The Greeks retold tales of mythological figures on pottery. This scene shows the god of wine, Dionysus, in a boat.

Bronze statuette of Hellenistic dancer, said to be from Alexandria.

This Pompeiian mosaic honors Alexander the Great, who extended his empire to the Indus River valley.

Seleucus and his descendants—the Seleucids (suh•LOO•suhds)—at first controlled the rest of Syria, as well as Mesopotamia, Iran, and Afghanistan. After a while, however, they were forced to give up their eastern territory and withdraw to Syria. In 167 B.C. Jewish guerrillas led by Judah Maccabee challenged the Seleucid control of Palestine. The Seleucid Antiochus IV had ordered the Jews to worship the Greek deities, but many Jews refused to abandon their religion. In 165 B.C. Judah Maccabee succeeded in reoccupying Jerusalem and rededicating the Temple, an event commemorated by the Jewish festival of Hanukkah. The kingdom of Judah would remain independent until its defeat by Rome in 63 B.C. The Seleucids likewise ruled in Syria until the Romans came.

The domain of Antigonus and his heirs consisted at first of Macedonia and Greece. But the Greek city-states soon declared their independence and once again began fighting with each other. In the 100s B.C., the growing Roman Empire would conquer Macedonia and Greece.

Hellenistic Culture

The political unity of Alexander's empire disappeared with his death, but the Greek language and culture continued to spread and flourish in the lands he had conquered. There, Hellenic ways of life mixed with elements of Middle Eastern culture to form a new culture, called Hellenistic.

City Life

Hellenistic culture was concentrated in cities. The largest and wealthiest of these was Alexandria in Egypt. Alexandria's straight streets intersected each other at right angles, in contrast to the crooked streets of older cities. Its white stucco stone palaces and temples gleamed brilliantly in the sun.

The city's economic position benefited from a double harbor that could hold 1,200 ships at a time. Another asset to trade was the city's lighthouse, which was visible from 35 miles (56 km) out at sea.

Alexandria also was a major intellectual center. Its museum was the first ever and included a

Woman and servant, a Hellenistic funerary stela from Kerameikos cemetery.

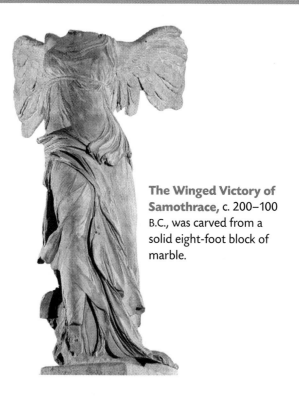

The Winged Victory of Samothrace, c. 200–100 B.C., was carved from a solid eight-foot block of marble.

REFLECTING ON THE TIMES

1. How did Greek pottery promote popular myths?
2. How are humans portrayed in Hellenistic art?

library of nearly a million volumes, an institute for scientific research, a zoo, and a botanical garden. Scientists came from all over the Hellenistic world. Around 250 B.C. Jewish scholars in Alexandria translated the Hebrew Bible into Greek. This translation, known as the Septuagint (sehp•TOO•uh•juhnt), was later used by the apostle Paul and is still used in the Eastern Orthodox Church.

During Hellenic times, the Greeks had been intensely involved with their particular polis. In Hellenistic society, however, the Greeks formed the upper class of Alexandria and other cities in the Middle East and Asia Minor that were ruled by kings. Rather than being loyal to their king or kingdom, professional Greek soldiers and bureaucrats moved from place to place, wherever job opportunities were best.

In Alexandria and other Hellenistic cities, the social status of upper-class Greek women improved over their traditional status in Athens. No longer secluded, women could move about freely. They learned how to read and write and entered such occupations as real estate, banking, and government. Such opportunities were not, however, available to commoners.

Hellenistic Philosophers

Hellenistic philosophers focused on personal behavior, especially the question of how to achieve peace of mind. Three systems of thought attracted most Hellenistic intellectuals: Cynicism, Epicureanism (EH•pih•kyu•REE•uh•NIH•zuhm), and Stoicism.

The best known Cynic was Diogenes (dy•AH•juh•NEEZ). He criticized materialism and asserted that people would be happy if they gave up luxuries and lived simply, in accord with nature. The scholar Epicurus started the philosophy of Epicureanism. He argued that people should avoid both joy and pain by accepting the world as it was, ignoring politics, and living simply and quietly with a few close friends.

Zeno founded Stoicism. The name *Stoicism* comes from the *Stoa Poikile*, or "painted porch," in which Zeno lectured. The Stoics believed that what happened to people was governed by natural laws. Accordingly, people could gain happiness by ignoring their emotions, and instead following their reason. In this way, they were able to accept even the most difficult circumstances of life and do their duty. Stoicism later affected both Roman intellectuals and early Christian thinkers.

Economics

An Economic Region

Geographers, historians, and economists often divide the world into regions based on economic factors, such as trade routes and uniform currency. The empire of Alexander the Great came to be one economic region.

Alexander and his successors used vast sums of gold and silver captured in Persia to finance public works projects, road construction, and harbor development. Extensive land routes helped maintain close economic links among the cities built by Alexander. A uniform currency also developed that held the empire together economically. International sea trade expanded greatly under Alexander's empire and its successor domains. Hellenistic sailors used monsoon winds to sail directly across the Indian Ocean between Africa and Asia

Coin bearing the face of Alexander the Great

instead of hugging the coast. As a result, luxury items from India and Arabia became common in Mediterranean cities. As in ancient times, the world today is made up of many different economic regions. For example, the American Midwest can be classified as an economic region because one of its economic characteristics is the production of corn, hogs, and cattle. Another example of an economic region is a large metropolitan area—such as that of Johannesburg, South Africa—in which a central urban area is joined to surrounding areas by transportation links, or by people's wants and needs, such as jobs, shopping, or entertainment.

Linking Past and Present ACTIVITY

List three economic characteristics of Alexander's empire. Then, identify an economic region in which you live and list its characteristics.

Actors preparing for a performance, a mosaic from the House of the Tragic Poet, Pompeii. National Museum, Naples, Italy *Why might people have had a work like this in their home?*

Hellenistic Art and Literature

During the Hellenistic era, artists departed from Hellenic styles. Instead of carving idealized individuals, Hellenistic sculptors showed people in the grip of powerful emotions. They also carved portrait heads, because art had become a business.

Hellenistic playwrights usually wrote comedies rather than tragedies. Like Hellenistic philosophers, they ignored the problems of the outside world as much as possible. **Menander**, the most renowned Hellenistic playwright, specialized in comedies about everyday life. Well-known lines from his works include "Whom the gods love die young" and "We live not as we will, but as we can."

Science, Medicine, and Mathematics

Although limited by their simple instruments, Hellenistic scientists performed many experiments and developed new theories. Aristarchus (AR•uh•STAHR•kuhs) of Samos concluded that the sun is larger than the earth, that the earth revolves around the sun, and that the stars lie at immense distances from both heavenly bodies. **Eratosthenes** (EHR•uh•TAHS•thuh•NEEZ) estimated the earth's circumference to within 1 percent of the correct figure. Hellenistic doctors dissected corpses in order to learn more about human anatomy. They discovered the body's nervous system, studied the brain and the liver, and learned how to use drugs to relieve pain.

The Hellenistic period also saw great developments and breakthroughs in mathematics and physics. **Euclid** of Alexandria wrote *The Elements of Geometry*, a book that organized all information about geometry. **Archimedes** (AHR•kuh•MEE•deez) invented the compound pulley, which moves heavy objects easily, and the cylinder-screw, which is still used to lift water for irrigation. He also discovered the principle of buoyancy and demonstrated the principle of the lever.

SECTION 3 REVIEW

Recall
1. **Define** domain.
2. **Identify** Philip II, Demosthenes, Alexander the Great, Zeno, Menander, Eratosthenes, Euclid, Archimedes.
3. **Locate** Macedonia and Alexandria on the map on page 141. What does Alexandria owe to the Macedonians?

Critical Thinking
4. **Making Comparisons** Compare and contrast Alexander the Great's original goal and the goal he finally chose for his empire. Why did his goals change?

Understanding Themes
5. **Cultural Diffusion** Explain how and why Hellenistic arts differed from Hellenic arts.

from

Antigone

by Sophocles

The Greek playwright Sophocles, who lived from about 495–405 B.C., wrote about the conflict between conscience and authority in his play Antigone. After Antigone's two brothers died battling each other for the throne of Thebes, her uncle, Creon, became king. Creon allowed one brother, Eteocles, an honorable burial. He declared, however, that the other brother, Polyneices, was a traitor whose body should be left for the "birds and scavenging dogs." Anyone attempting to bury Polyneices, he warned, would be stoned to death. Antigone's sister, Ismene, obeys Creon. Antigone, however, out of respect for her brother, buries him.

Creon [*slowly, dangerously*]. And you, Antigone, You with your head hanging—do you confess this thing?

Antigone. I do. I deny nothing.

Creon [*to* SENTRY].   You may go. [*Exit* SENTRY] [*To* ANTIGONE] Tell me, tell me briefly: Had you heard my proclamation touching this matter?

Antigone. It was public. Could I help hearing it?

Creon. And yet you dared defy the law.

Antigone.   I dared. It was not God's proclamation. That final justice That rules the world below makes no such laws. Your edict, King, was strong, But all your strength is weakness itself against The immortal unrecorded laws of God. They are not merely now: they were, and shall be, Operative forever, beyond man utterly.

I knew I must die, even without your decree: I am only mortal. And if I must die Now, before it is my time to die, Surely this is no hardship: can anyone Living, as I live, with evil all about me, Think death less than a friend? This death of mine Is of no importance; but if I had left my brother Lying in death unburied, I should have suffered. Now I do not.
                You smile at me. Ah Creon.

Think me a fool, if you like; but it may well be
That a fool convicts me of folly....
Creon, what more do you want than my death?

Creon.   Nothing.
That gives me everything.

Antigone.   Then I beg you: kill me.
This talking is a great weariness: your words
Are distasteful to me, and I am sure that mine
Seem so to you. And yet they should not seem so:
I should have praise and honor for what I have done.
All these men here would praise me
Were their lips not frozen shut with fear of you.
[*Bitterly*] Ah the good fortune of kings,
Licensed to say and do whatever they please!

Creon. You are alone here in that opinion.

Antigone. No, they are with me. But they keep their tongues
in leash.

Creon. Maybe. But you are guilty,
and they are not.

Antigone. There is no guilt in reverence for the dead.

Creon. But Eteocles—was he not
your brother too?

Antigone. My brother too.

Creon.   And you
insult his memory?

Antigone [*softly*]. The dead man
would not say that I insult it.

Creon. He would: for you honor a
traitor as much as him.

Antigone. His own brother, traitor or
not, and equal in blood.

Creon. He made war on his country.
Eteocles defended it.

Antigone. Nevertheless, there are
honors due all the dead.

History & Art Actors preparing for a performance
(detail), the House of the Tragic Poet,
Pompeii. National Museum, Naples, Italy
What is the theme of Antigone?

Wall painting of a Greek woman with flowers. National Museum, Naples, Italy

The Greeks admired beauty and virtue. *Does Ismene regain virtue by confessing a share in the crime?*

Creon. But not the same for the wicked as for the just.

Antigone. Ah Creon, Creon.
Which of us can say what the gods hold wicked?

Creon. An enemy is an enemy, even dead.

Antigone. It is my nature to join in love, not hate.

Creon [*finally losing patience*]. Go join them, then; if you must have your love,
Find it in hell!

Choragos [*leader of a group of 15 citizens*]. But see, Ismene comes:
[*Enter Ismene, guarded.*] Those tears are sisterly, the cloud
That shadows her eyes rains down gentle sorrow.

Creon. You too, Ismene,

Snake in my ordered house, sucking my blood
Stealthily—and all the time I never knew
That these two sisters were aiming at my throne!

                                           Ismene,
Do you confess your share in this crime, or deny it?
Answer me.

Ismene. Yes, if she will let me say so. I am guilty.

Antigone [*coldly*]. No, Ismene. You have no right to say so.
You would not help me, and I will not have you help me.

Ismene. But now I know what you meant; and I am here
To join you, to take my share of punishment.

Antigone. The dead man and the gods who rule the dead
Know whose act this was. Words are not friends.

Ismene. Do you refuse me, Antigone? I want to die with you:
I too have a duty that I must discharge to the dead.

Antigone. You shall not lessen my death by sharing it.

Ismene. What do I care for life when you are dead?

Antigone. Ask Creon. You're always hanging on his opinions.

Ismene. You are laughing at me. Why, Antigone?

Antigone. It's a joyless laughter, Ismene.

Ismene.   But can I do nothing?

Antigone. Yes. Save yourself. I shall not envy you.
There are those who will praise you; I shall have honor, too.

Ismene. But we are equally guilty!

Antigone.   No more, Ismene.
You are alive, but I belong to death.

RESPONDING TO LITERATURE

1. Explain what Antigone means when she says to Creon, "But all your strength is weakness itself against the immortal unrecorded laws of God."
2. Quote a passage that demonstrates Antigone's bravery.
3. Explain whether you would like to live in a society in which individuals followed only their consciences.
4. **Making Inferences** Predict whether Creon actually would have Antigone stoned to death.

Connections Across Time

Historical Significance Greek culture has influenced Western civilization in many ways. The ancient Greeks developed classical models on which later architects, artists, and playwrights have relied. Their thinkers also laid the foundation for the disciplines of history, political science, and logic.

The Founders of the United States took inspiration from ancient Greek ideals, such as belief in the worth and importance of the individual. The Founders' belief in a democratic form of government—as the one best suited to enabling people to enhance their abilities—also has its roots in ancient Greece.

Using Key Terms

Write the key term that completes each sentence. Then write a sentence for each term not chosen.

a. classical
b. comedies
c. logic
d. philosophers
e. tragedies
f. domains
g. hygiene
h. sanctuaries
i. amphora
j. perspective

1. The architects of the Parthenon in Athens understood _____, the artistic representation of distances between objects as they appear to the eye.
2. Greek potters usually decorated an _____—a large vase for storing bulk supplies—with scenes from their mythology and legends.
3. Greek artists and architects created works characterized by a _____ style known for its beautiful simplicity and graceful balance.
4. After Alexander's death in 323 B.C., his large multicultural empire was divided into several _____.
5. Greek thinkers, or _____, developed the foundations for disciplines such as history, political science, and logic.

Technology Activity

Building a Database Search the Internet or your local library for additional information about the Olympic Games. Build a database by collecting information about recent Olympic Game results of both summer and winter sporting events. Include headings such as name of the event, when it first became an event, if participated in by both sexes, and the number of medals each country obtained.

Using Your History Journal

The Greeks liked to relive historic events through drama. Each actor would wear a large mask to show the age, sex, and mood of each character. Write a short scene for a drama depicting an event from the chapter.

Reviewing Facts

1. **Geography** Locate where the Parthenon was built and explain for what purpose.
2. **Culture** Describe the main philosophical differences between the Sophists and Socrates.
3. **Science** Name the main steps in the scientific method of inquiry developed by Aristotle.
4. **History/Culture** Explain why Thucydides is considered the first scientific historian.
5. **History** Discuss the ways in which Alexander's conquests changed Greek life.
6. **Culture** Identify the two major cultural areas that contributed to Hellenistic civilization.
7. **Science** State the contributions of Pythagorus, Archimedes, and Eratosthenes.

Critical Thinking

1. **Apply** How did the Peloponnesian War affect Greek drama and philosophy?
2. **Evaluate** Whose political ideas does the United States government more closely follow, those of Plato or those of Aristotle?
3. **Analyze** Why did conflicts develop in Alexander's empire after his death? Could they have been resolved peacefully? Why or why not?

Geography in History

1. **Place** Refer to the map "Alexander's Empire Divided." Who controlled the area of Macedonia?
2. **Location** What present-day countries make up the part of Alexander's empire ruled by Ptolemy?
3. **Place** Which of the Hellenistic lands do you think was the most difficult to govern, based on geographic factors? Explain.

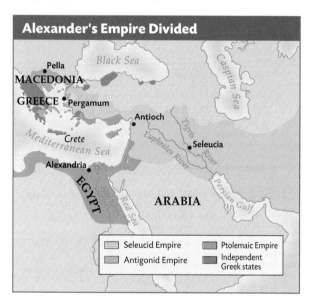

Alexander's Empire Divided

Pella
MACEDONIA
Black Sea
Caspian Sea
GREECE • Pergamum
Antioch
Mediterranean Sea
Crete
Tigris
Euphrates River
• Seleucia
Alexandria •
EGYPT
Red Sea
ARABIA
Persian Gulf

Seleucid Empire
Antigonid Empire
Ptolemaic Empire
Independent Greek states

Linking Past and Present

1. The Olympic Games were revived in 1896. In what ways do the modern Olympic Games resemble those of ancient Greece? In what ways do they differ?
2. The inclusion of diverse territories in Alexander the Great's empire led to widespread cultural diffusion. Besides military conquests, what factors promote cultural diffusion today?
3. Ideas of Greek civilization have affected much of American culture. Choose one area such as medicine, philosophy, politics, art, or architecture. Reread information about that area in your chapter. Then list as many examples of influences on American culture as you can. Ask friends, parents, or other family members to help complete the list.

Understanding Themes

1. **Innovation** What might contemporary theater be like if such great Hellenistic playwrights as Aristophanes and Menander had not lived and written about Greek society?
2. **Innovation** Do you think Herodotus deserves to be called the "father of history"? Explain your answer.
3. **Cultural Diffusion** How did Alexander the Great's founding of cities throughout his empire help spread Greek culture?

Skill Practice

Use the map "Greece and Persia" to answer the following questions.

1. What is the approximate location of Athens with regard to latitude and longitude?
2. Which body of water lies entirely north of 40° N latitude?
3. What is the approximate location of Sparta with regard to latitude and longitude?
4. What is the approximate location of Sardis with regard to longitude and latitude?
5. What is the relative location of Sardis?
6. What Mediterranean island lies along the 35th parallel?

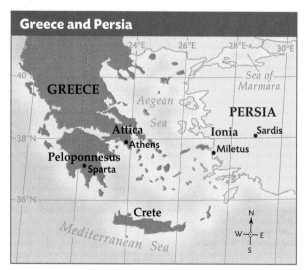

Greece and Persia

24°E 26°E 28°E 30°E
40°
GREECE
Sea of Marmara
Aegean Sea
PERSIA
Attica
Ionia • Sardis
38°N
• Athens
• Miletus
Peloponnesus
• Sparta
36°N
Crete
Mediterranean Sea
N
W—E
S

Ancient Rome and Early Christianity

Chapter Themes

▶ **Change** The Roman political system evolves as Rome allows more of its people to participate in government. *Section 1*
▶ **Conflict** Roman armies conquer most of the Mediterranean world. *Section 2*
▶ **Cultural Diffusion** The Romans build an empire and spread Latin culture. *Section 3*
▶ **Innovation** Christianity becomes the dominant religion in the West. *Section 4*
▶ **Change** Germanic invasions and cultural weaknesses destroy the Roman Empire. *Section 5*

The Storyteller

War trumpets rang over the cheers of the people of Rome who gathered to view the triumphal grand parade. Then sweating horses jerking at their harnesses rattled the victor's chariot over the paving stones, and the people's cries became louder. On this day in 146 B.C., the Romans were celebrating their conquest of the last of the free Greek city-states.

Ironically, however, over the next several centuries Greek culture would come to form the base of Roman culture and society. Texts written by Greeks would shape Roman knowledge in many areas of study. Even after years of Roman rule, the eastern Mediterranean world would retain Greek as its primary language.

Historical Significance

How did the small city-state of Rome become the center of a vast, diverse empire that spanned the Mediterranean world? What were Rome's last legacies to Europe, Africa, the Middle East, and other parts of the world?

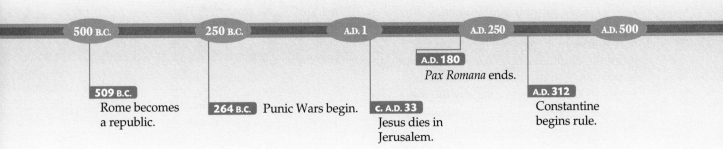

500 B.C.	250 B.C.	A.D. 1	A.D. 250	A.D. 500

509 B.C.
Rome becomes a republic.

264 B.C. Punic Wars begin.

C. A.D. 33
Jesus dies in Jerusalem.

A.D. 180
Pax Romana ends.

A.D. 312
Constantine begins rule.

Woman playing the cithera, painted on the east wall of a room in the villa of Publius Fannius Synistor, Pompeii, Italy

Your History Journal

The European cities of Bonn, Vienna, London, and Paris were each founded by the Romans. Research the early history of one of these cities and describe the Roman influence on its early architecture and lifestyle.

c. 753 B.C.	**c. 620 B.C.**	**451 B.C.**	**287 B.C.**
Romulus founds Rome.	Etruscans gain control of Rome.	The patricians of Rome enact the Twelve Tables.	The plebeians begin to make laws for Rome.

Section 1

The Roman Republic

Setting the Scene

▶ **Terms to Define**
patrician, republic, plebeian, consul, dictator, tribune

▶ **People to Meet**
the Etruscans, the Latins, Romulus, the Tarquins

▶ **Places to Locate**
Italy, Sicily, Rome

 **Find Out** How was Rome governed as a republic? How did the Roman Republic change over the years?

The Storyteller

The Forum

The city of Rome was besieged by Lars Porsena, king of Clusium, and the time had come for decisive action. One young Roman hoped to break the siege by killing Porsena. After laying his plan before the Senate, he set out alone toward enemy lines. However, he was seized as a spy and dragged by guards before the very man he had hoped to kill—Porsena. He spoke boldly: "I am a Roman, my name is Gaius Mucius. I came here to kill you—my enemy. I have as much courage to die as to kill. It is our Roman way to do and to suffer bravely."

—adapted from *Early History of Rome*, Titus Livy, in *The Global Experience, Readings in World History to 1500*, 1987

The peoples of **Italy** first came into contact with the Greeks around 900 B.C., when Greek traders sailed up both the east and west coasts of the Italian Peninsula. From about 750 B.C. to 500 B.C., the Greeks set up farming communities in southern Italy and in **Sicily**, an island southwest of the Italian Peninsula. These Greek colonists planted olive trees for the oil yielded and grapevines from which they could produce wine, thus introducing these two major products to Italy. The Greeks also introduced the Greek alphabet to the Italians.

The Italian Peninsula

The Greeks were interested in colonizing Italy for several reasons, one of which was Italy's central location in the Mediterranean. A narrow, boot-shaped peninsula, Italy extends from Europe toward the shores of Africa, dividing the Mediterranean almost in half. Thus, Italy was ideally situated to be the center of trade among three continents: Asia, Europe, and Africa. Italy's rich soil and mild, moist climate also attracted the Greek colonists. Beyond the mountains and foothills that covered three-quarters of the peninsula lay plains with soil enriched by the silt deposits of mountain streams.

However, the silt washing down Italy's short and shallow rivers blocked the mouths of many rivers, creating mosquito-infested swamps. The people of Italy suffered recurrent epidemics of malaria and other diseases carried by mosquitoes.

Because of Italy's mountains, the early inhabitants of the peninsula generally traded among themselves. Italy's only land connection—to the north—was cut off by the Alps. Furthermore, Italy's rocky and marshy coastline lacked good harbors. To increase trade, the Italians eventually turned to the sea, but until that time came, they remained attached to the land.

Early Peoples

Archaeological evidence suggests that people lived in Italy long before the Greeks arrived or Roman civilization began. The remains of human settlements reveal that Neolithic cultures may have begun to form in Italy as early as about 5000 B.C. Early peoples in the Italian Peninsula built villages and farms, moving on whenever they had exhausted the land around their settlements.

Indo-Europeans

Between 2000 B.C. and 1000 B.C., waves of Indo-European immigrants arrived and overwhelmed these Neolithic peoples. By the time Greek colonists came to Italy, many peoples inhabited the peninsula—including Umbrians in the north, Latins in the central plain called Latium (LAY•shee•uhm), and Oscans in the south. Like the Greeks, most of these people spoke Indo-European languages.

The Etruscans

From about 900 B.C. to 500 B.C., one of these peoples, **the Etruscans**, ruled northern Italy from the plains of Etruria. Little is known about their origins, although the Etruscans did not speak an Indo-European language as did many of the peninsula's other inhabitants. The Etruscan alphabet came from the Greeks, but modern scholars have been able to decipher only a few Etruscan words.

Although Etruscan writings still baffle our understanding, Etruscan art is expressive, needing no translation. In wall paintings, Etruscan figures dance and play music, enjoying a rich and pleasant life. In Etruscan sculpture, men and women feast and converse, triumphant soldiers revel in their victories, and hauntingly beautiful deities smile and gesture.

Such sculptures ornamented the homes of the Etruscan upper classes. Historians believe that Etruscan society probably consisted of wealthy overlords, aristocratic priests, and a slave labor force made up of conquered peoples. Wealthy overlords enslaved these peoples to provide themselves with comforts, and aristocratic priests sacrificed prisoners of war or forced them to duel to the death to appease angry gods.

After repeated revolts, the Etruscan lower classes and the other Italian peoples under

CONNECTIONS The Arts

Murals: Etruscan and Modern

Although archaeologists have unearthed the remains of some Etruscan cities, these tell little about Etruscan culture. Murals unearthed in burial chambers, however, have provided significant clues about the Etruscans.

Etruscan mural

The murals show colorful and lively scenes of Etruscan daily life. Particularly popular subjects are scenes of wrestling matches, religious ceremonies, and people enjoying music and feasts.

Today, the desire to beautify urban areas has produced many

striking murals in cities from Sydney, Australia, to Caracas, Venezuela. The boldly colored works appear on office, apartment, and supermarket walls. They usually are sponsored by municipal officials or businesses, and the artists employed draw inspiration from sources as varied as fashion magazines, cartoons, and modern art. Among their subjects are movie, TV, and sports celebrities as well as ordinary people involved in daily activities, such as shopping on a busy street or playing basketball at a neighborhood playground.

Linking Past and Present ACTIVITY

What subjects are popularly shown in Etruscan murals? Modern urban murals? What do Etruscan murals reveal about Etruscan life? What do urban murals today reveal about modern life?

Etruscan rule finally freed themselves from domination by these wealthy overlords and priests. Chief among those who overthrew the Etruscans were **the Latins**, whose center was the city of **Rome** in the central plain of Latium.

The Rise of Rome

According to legend, in 753 B.C., a stocky man named **Romulus** was building the wall of a city on a hill overlooking the Tiber River. His twin brother, Remus, came over from the hillside opposite, where he too had been laying the foundations for a city. The Roman historian Livy tells what happened next:

> ❝ Remus, by way of jeering at his brother, jumped over the half-built walls of the new settlement, whereupon Romulus killed him in a fit of rage, adding the threat, 'So perish whoever else shall over-leap my battlements.' ❞
>
> —Livy, *Ab Urbe Condita*, 29 B.C.

Setting more stone on the stains of his brother's blood, Romulus is said to have continued his building. In time, his namesake city—Rome—grew to include his brother's hill and the other nearby hills. Romulus was so effective a military ruler, the myth tells us, that Rome became the greatest city in that part of the peninsula.

In fact, the origins of Rome were probably much less violent. At some time between 800 B.C. and 700 B.C., the Latins huddled in straw-roofed huts in the villages on the seven hills apparently agreed to join and form one community. It was this community that came to be called Rome.

Etruscan Rule

About 620 B.C. the Etruscans gained control of Rome. A wealthy Etruscan family, **the Tarquins**, provided kings to rule over the Romans. The Tarquins taught the Latins to build with brick and to roof their houses with tile. They drained the marshy lowlands around Rome and laid out city streets. At the center of the city they created a square called the Forum, which became the seat of Roman government. The Tarquins also built temples, taught the Romans many of the Etruscans' religious rituals, and elevated Rome to a position among the wealthiest cities in Italy.

Then in 534 B.C. Tarquin the Proud came to the throne. This king's cruelties so angered the Romans that in 509 B.C. they drove the Tarquins out. Skilled Etruscan artisans stayed on in Rome, however, helping the city continue to prosper.

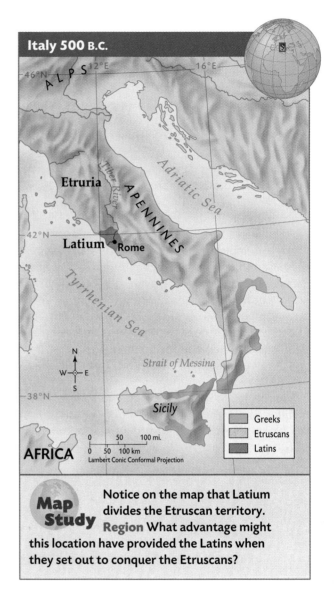

Italy 500 B.C.

Map Study Notice on the map that Latium divides the Etruscan territory. **Region** What advantage might this location have provided the Latins when they set out to conquer the Etruscans?

Social Groups

Under Etruscan rule, a new wealthy aristocratic class had come into being in Rome—Latin nobles called patricians. Once the Etruscan rulers were driven out, the patricians declared Rome a republic, a community in which the people elect their leaders.

Most of Rome's inhabitants, however, were plebeians (plih•BEE•uhns), who included wealthy, nonaristocratic townspeople and landowners as well as merchants, shopkeepers, small farmers, and laborers. As citizens, both the plebeians and the patricians had rights, such as the right to vote, and responsibilities, such as paying taxes and serving in the military. Plebeians, however, could not hold public office as patricians could.

The Roman Republic

The patricians organized Rome's government into executive and legislative branches. The

Roman legislative branch at first consisted of the Assembly of Centuries and the Senate, both under patrician control. Members of the Assembly of Centuries (named for a military formation of 100 soldiers) elected officials of the executive branch. However, the power of the Senate—a group of 300 patrician men who served for life—outweighed the Assembly of Centuries. The senators advised the consuls, debated foreign policy, proposed laws, and approved contracts for constructing roads, temples, and defenses.

The executive branch was headed by two patrician officials elected for one-year terms. These officials were called consuls because they had to consult each other before acting. They understood that either consul could veto the other's decisions. The word *veto* is Latin for "I forbid." The consuls oversaw other executive officials, such as praetors, or judges, and censors, or keepers of tax and population records. Only a dictator, a leader whose word was law, could overrule the consuls. But dictators were temporarily appointed to lead the Romans only in time of crisis.

The most admired Roman dictator was the legendary hero Cincinnatus (SIHN•suh•NA•tuhs). In 458 B.C., a powerful rival threatened Rome, and the Senate sent messengers to tell Cincinnatus that he had been named dictator to meet this emergency. The messengers found him plowing his fields. Always loyal to Rome, Cincinnatus immediately joined the army and led his forces into battle. He defeated the enemy, marched his army back to Rome, and then resigned as dictator. He returned to his plowing 16 days after taking command.

Plebeians Against Patricians

The plebeians resented their lack of power in the new republic—especially because they knew that the patricians could not maintain the republic without them. In 494 B.C., many plebeians refused to fight in the Roman army unless the patricians yielded to their demands for change.

Plebeian Victories

Frightened at the loss of their military forces, the patricians finally agreed to reforms. They recognized the plebeians' chosen representatives, the tribunes, granting them legal protections and the right to veto government decisions. The patricians also recognized the Assembly of Tribes, the body of plebeians who elected the tribunes. Eventually, the Assembly of Tribes even won the right to make laws.

In addition to political rights, the plebeians improved their social standing. Enslavement for debt was ended, and marriage between patricians and plebeians was allowed. In spite of these benefits for the common people, the republic's social structure was still dominated by a small group of powerful and wealthy citizens. However, through their struggles, the plebeians slowly moved Rome closer to democracy.

The Twelve Tables

The most significant plebeian victory was the creation of a written law code. Roman law rested largely on unwritten traditions that patrician judges often interpreted to favor their class. To make sure that the judges applied the laws fairly, the plebeians insisted that the government write down the laws.

In 451 B.C. the patricians finally engraved the laws on 12 bronze tablets and set them in the Forum for all to see. The Twelve Tables, as these tablets were called, became the basis for all future Roman law. Although sometimes harsh, the Twelve Tables established the principle that all free citizens had a right to the law's protection.

Religion

Early Romans worshiped nature spirits. Under Etruscan influence, they came to think of these spirits as gods and goddesses. They also adopted the practice of foretelling the future. Priests known as soothsayers believed that they could gain knowledge of future events by observing the flight of birds or the intestines of animals.

For almost 500 years, Rome thrived as a republic. During this time, the Romans were influenced by Greek culture. They borrowed Greek deities, giving them Roman names. Aphrodite, the Greek

A Roman Dinner Party
In ancient Rome, dinner guests of wealthy Romans would recline on couches while slaves served them delicacies. Main course dishes might include boiled stingray garnished with hot raisins; boiled crane with turnips; roast hare in white sauce; leg of boar; wood pigeon baked in a pie; or roast flamingo cooked with dates, onions, honey, and wine.

An Etruscan farmer and his animals, c. 300 B.C. Etruscan literature, music, painting, metalwork, and jewelry were admired by the Romans. *Why did the Romans drive the wealthy Etruscan family, the Tarquins, from the city?*

goddess of love, became the Roman goddess Venus. Ares, the Greek god of war, became Mars. They also made their old gods look Greek, giving the Etruscan god Jupiter the characteristics of the Greek Zeus.

Roman life remained distinctly Roman, however. Families privately worshiped their ancestral spirits and their storeroom guardians, as well as Vesta, goddess of the hearth.

Family

The family was the basic unit of Roman society. Roman households were large and close-knit. They included all unmarried children, married sons and their families, all dependent relatives, and household slaves.

In Roman families the father was absolute head of the household. He conducted the religious ceremonies, controlled property, and supervised the education of his sons. He also had the power to sell family members into slavery, or even kill them. However, fathers also felt a deep sense of responsibility for the welfare of all family members.

Roman wives had few legal rights, but they had more freedom than Greek women. They acted as hostesses for parties, did their marketing, and ran their households with little or no interference. Occasionally, however, they did acquire their own property and businesses. Wealthy women, with slaves to do their work, could study Greek literature, arts, and fashions. Lower-class women spent their time at household tasks and in family-run shops.

Roman children grew up with firm discipline and had to give complete loyalty to their family. In early Rome, parents taught their children reading, writing, and moral standards. Boys were trained by their fathers to be good farmers and soldiers. Mothers taught their daughters how to run households.

Rich or poor, most Romans held the same values: thrift, discipline, self-sacrifice, and devotion to the family and the republic. Long after the Roman Republic ended, nostalgic reformers saw these as traditional Roman values.

SECTION 1 REVIEW

Recall
1. **Define** patrician, republic, plebeian, consul, dictator, tribune.
2. **Identify** the Etruscans, the Latins, Romulus, the Tarquins.

3. **Locate** Etruria, Latium, and Rome on the map on page 156. How were the people of these three places connected?

Critical Thinking
4. **Evaluating Information** Did the struggle between patricians and plebeians strengthen or weaken Rome? Give examples to support your case.

Understanding Themes
5. **Change** Why did political change occur in the Roman Republic?

---

c. 264 B.C. Rome rules the entire Italian Peninsula.

202 B.C. Roman forces defeat Carthage at the battle of Zama.

133 B.C. The reformer Tiberius Gracchus becomes tribune.

44 B.C. Group of senators assassinate Julius Caesar.

Section 2

Expansion and Crisis

Setting the Scene

▶ **Terms to Define**
indemnity, triumvirate

▶ **People to Meet**
Hannibal, Scipio, Tiberius Gracchus, Gaius Gracchus, Marius, Sulla, Julius Caesar, Octavian, Marc Antony

▶ **Places to Locate**
Carthage

 **Find Out** How did economic and social problems bring down the Roman Republic?

The Storyteller

The government of Rome had become cumbersome and corrupt. Maecenas, the richest man in Rome, was about to propose a radical change.
Called before Mark Anthony, Marcus Lepidus, and Octavian, the most powerful men in Rome, he spoke persuasively. "Ever since we were led outside the peninsula, filling the whole earth with our power, nothing good has been our lot. Our city, like a great ship manned with a crew of every race and lacking a pilot, has been rolling and plunging as it has drifted in a heavy sea." Maecenas looked at his hearers. One of them must assume all authority. Rome had to cease being a republic.

Marc Antony

—from *Roman History*, Dio Cassius, in *Readings in Ancient History from Gilgamesh to Diocletian*, 1969

From about 500 B.C. to 300 B.C., Rome faced threats from its many neighbors in Italy. To protect their republic, the Romans either conquered these opponents or forced them to ally with Rome. In this way the Romans subdued one rival after another, until by 264 B.C. Rome ruled the entire peninsula.

Roman forces, however, had faced a tough challenge from the Greek colonies in southern Italy. In 282 B.C. the Greek colonists received help from Pyrrhus (PIHR•uhs), a ruler in western Greece. Twice Pyrrhus's armies threw back the Romans, but each time suffered terrible losses. In 275 B.C. Roman forces finally pushed Pyrrhus's exhausted troops back to Greece. Since then, a victory won at too great a cost has been called a "Pyrrhic victory."

Roman Legions

Rome's success in war was due to its strong army. In the early days of the republic, every male citizen had to serve in the military when needed. Early Roman armies also used the tactics of Greek phalanx warfare. Roman generals, however, learned that phalanxes were too large and slow to be effective. They reorganized their troops into legions of 6,000 men and divided these further into small, mobile units of 60 to 120 soldiers. With this new organization, the Romans could shatter the phalanxes of their enemies.

Roman soldiers—called legionaries—were well trained, and deserters were punished by death. With such iron discipline, the legionaries would conquer an empire. In a time when victors routinely slaughtered or enslaved whole cities, Rome treated conquered foes remarkably well. Some conquered peoples were allowed to keep their own governments if they helped fight Rome's wars.

Roman legionaries are shown in a mosaic, or picture made from bits of stone. *Why were legionaries so successful in their conquests?*

Rome gave other peoples partial rights, and to some peoples even granted citizenship.

The Romans set up permanent military settlements—called *coloniae*—throughout Italy to defend strategic heights and river crossings. To link these *coloniae*, the legions forged a chain of roads up and down the Italian Peninsula. As war yielded gradually to peace, some of these roads became major trade routes.

Rome Against Carthage

In Chapter 3 you read how **Carthage** became the Mediterranean area's wealthiest city. To expand their commerce, the Carthaginians had then gone on to conquer the Spanish coast and most of Sicily by about 300 B.C. The Romans decided to check the expansion of the Carthaginians—the *Punici*, as the Romans called them.

The First Punic War

In 264 B.C. Carthage threatened to seize the Strait of Messina, a narrow passage between Sicily and Italy. When the Romans sent a force to secure the strategic waterway, a full-scale war erupted.

The Romans' strong army conquered most of Carthage's colonies in Sicily. However, the Carthaginians lashed out at the Romans with their huge and powerful fleet. For a time this naval superiority gave Carthage the advantage.

Undaunted, the Romans built a larger fleet. In a battle off the African coast, they stunned the Carthaginians with a new tactic. They snared the enemy's ships with grappling hooks, boarded them, and defeated the enemy in hand-to-hand combat. This enabled the Romans to fight on sea as well as they did on land. Thus, they were able to force the Carthaginians to retreat.

The war raged on until 241 B.C., but the Carthaginians never regained control of Sicily or the sea. Threatened with invasion of their homeland, they agreed to hand the Romans a huge indemnity, or payment for damages.

The Second Punic War

In 221 B.C. a young soldier named **Hannibal** became general of the Carthaginian army in Spain. In 218 B.C. Hannibal grabbed one of Rome's allied cities in Spain. His next move was even more audacious—to take the war into Italy itself. Leading 40,000 soldiers and about 40 elephants, he marched out of Spain, crossed southern Gaul, and started up the Alps. His soldiers, however, were terrified by the sight of those chilly heights, and their fears were well-founded. Before they reached Italy, cold, snow, hunger, sickness, and attacks by mountain peoples killed half of Hannibal's army and most of the elephants.

Although outnumbered, Hannibal's troops defeated the Roman armies sent against them. By 216 B.C., in a battle at Cannae in southeastern Italy, Hannibal's soldiers had nearly destroyed the Roman army. But the Romans rallied, refusing to admit defeat, and raised dozens of new volunteer legions. Their general, **Scipio** (SIH•pee•OH), attacked Carthage and forced Hannibal's recall to Africa.

In 202 B.C. Scipio's forces defeated Hannibal's army at Zama, near Carthage. At Scipio's demand, the Carthaginians gave up their lands in Spain, handed over most of their warships, and agreed to another indemnity.

The Third Punic War

After 50 years of peace, Carthage regained its prosperity but posed no threat to Rome. The Romans, however, decided to force war on

Carthage. The most vindictive foe of Carthage was the Roman senator Cato, who always ended his speeches with the statement: *"Carthago delenda est"* (Carthage must be destroyed). In 146 B.C. the Romans burned Carthage, and sold its surviving population into slavery. Legend states that they even sowed salt in Carthage's soil so that no crops would grow. This victory gave Rome complete control of the western Mediterranean.

The Republic in Crisis

While Rome was fighting the Punic Wars in the west, its forces were also engaged in the east. Between 230 B.C. and 130 B.C., Rome brought the entire eastern Mediterranean area under its influence. As a result of this conquest, Romans began referring to the Mediterranean as *mare nostrum—* "our sea."

Rich, Poor, and Slavery

Although the Romans had triumphed militarily, they faced growing social discontent in their new empire. The conquered provinces, which paid tribute to Rome, complained of corrupt Roman officials stealing provincial wealth for personal gain. In Italy and throughout the empire, wealthy Romans acquired or seized land from war-ravaged small farmers who found it difficult to rebuild their farms, homes, and villages. Turning agriculture into a profitable business, these landowners created large estates called latifundia (LA•tuh•FUHN•dee •uh) that provided grain, sheep, olives, and fruits for urban markets. Labor for the latifundia was cheap because Rome's conquests brought thousands of captives and prisoners of war to work as slaves. By 100 B.C., slaves formed about 30 percent of Rome's people.

As slave labor replaced paid labor, thousands of small farmers and rural workers poured into the cities seeking employment. Jobs, however, were not readily available, and the new arrivals gradually formed into a class of urban, landless poor. Angry and without hope, the urban poor eked out a meager living and supported any politician who promised "bread and circuses," cheap food and free amusements.

As the gap between rich and poor steadily widened, upper-class Romans lived with the constant danger of revolts. To quell mounting unrest, Rome stationed legions in most provinces. Even Italy was not safe from uprisings. From 73 B.C. to 71 B.C., an army of 70,000 slaves led by the slave Spartacus plundered the Italian countryside in an effort to win freedom. With great difficulty, the Romans finally crushed the uprising and killed about 6,000 of Spartacus's followers. Putting down revolts cost Rome troops and money and placed a strain on its resources.

Visualizing History Rome's legions put down revolts in the provinces, but not without cost. Here, women funeral dancers mourn losses. *Why were the provinces not an endless source of wealth to Rome?*

Reformers and Generals

Feuding among Rome's leading families also weakened the republic. As violence increased, some Romans proposed reforms to narrow the social gap and to stabilize society. In 133 B.C. the tribune **Tiberius Gracchus** proposed limiting the size of the latifundia and distributing land to the poor. But the Senate, made up of the wealthiest Romans, opposed him, and Tiberius was killed in street fighting. Ten years later, his brother **Gaius Gracchus** proposed the same reforms and was also murdered.

Crowding the Cities

After the death of the Gracchi, army leaders came to power in Rome. The first, the general **Marius**, became a consul in 107 B.C. after saving Rome from attack by Germanic tribes. Because the dwindling number of small farmers had made a citizen army obsolete, Marius turned to the unemployed urban poor to build a new army. Unlike the citizen soldiers, Marius's recruits were paid, given uniforms and equipment, and promised land when they were discharged. As a result of Marius's action, Rome for the first time had a professional army in which soldiers owed allegiance to their commander, not to the republic.

To advance their political ambitions, rival military and political leaders formed their own separate armies and used them against each other. From 88 B.C. to 82 B.C., Marius and a rival general named **Sulla** fought for control of Rome. Sulla finally drove Marius into exile and had himself appointed dictator. This practice of using the army to gain political power was copied by a rising young politician named Julius Caesar.

Julius Caesar

Born in Rome in about 100 B.C. of an aristocratic family, **Julius Caesar** became one of Rome's greatest generals and political leaders. Skillfully maneuvering himself through Rome's tumultuous game of politics, Caesar gradually rose to power. In 60 B.C. the ambitious aristocrat allied himself with the general Pompey and the politician Crassus. A year later, with their help he was elected consul. For the next decade, the three men ruled Rome as a triumvirate, or group of three persons with equal power. Through force and bribery, the triumvirate silenced government critics, bending senators and tribunes alike to its will.

Caesar's Military Campaigns

While serving as consul, Caesar realized he needed military victories to advance his political career. In 59 B.C. he took a military command in Gaul, which was inhabited by Indo-Europeans known as Celts (KEHLTS). Caesar conquered the Celts and brought them under Roman rule. He also crossed the Rhine River to fight Germanic tribes and twice invaded Britain.

As a result of his victories, Caesar was hailed as a military hero by Rome's lower classes. But senators, alarmed at Caesar's growing popularity, regarded him as a political threat. By 50 B.C. the triumvirate itself had fallen apart: Crassus was dead, killed in battle while leading Roman forces in Asia, and Pompey had become Caesar's political rival.

In 49 B.C. the Senate, with Pompey's backing, ordered Caesar to give up his army and return to Rome. Caesar, however, had no intention of turning himself over to his enemies. He assembled 5,000 loyal troops and crossed the Rubicon, a stream that

Visualizing History Political strife following the murders of the Gracchi aided the rise of the young Julius Caesar, sculpted here in a heroic pose. *How do you think Roman sculpture differed from the Greek models on which it was based?*

divided his military provinces from Roman Italy. According to legend, Caesar had seen a vision that encouraged him to cross, and exclaimed to his troops, "Let us accept this as a sign from the gods, and follow where they beckon, in vengeance on our double-dealing enemies. The die is cast." By defying the Senate's order, Caesar realized there was no turning back; and a civil war was unavoidable. Ever since, "crossing the Rubicon" has meant making a decision that cannot be undone.

Caesar's army swiftly captured all of Italy and drove Pompey and his allies out of the country. The fighting eventually spread eastward, with Caesar's troops finally defeating Pompey's forces at Pharsalus, Greece, in 48 B.C.

Caesar in Power

In 45 B.C. Caesar took over the government as dictator for life, to rule very much like a monarch. As absolute ruler, Caesar granted Roman citizenship to many people in the provinces outside of Italy. He added to the Senate representatives from the provinces who were loyal to him. In making these reforms, Caesar not only made the central government more responsive to Rome's newly conquered territories, he also strengthened his own power at the expense of the old patricians.

Caesar also carried out social reforms aimed to benefit the poor. To provide jobs for the unemployed, he set up public works programs and ordered slave-owning landowners to hire more free laborers. Colonies were founded throughout Rome's territories to provide land for the city's landless poor. Under Caesar, the government also continued its long-standing practice of distributing free grain but reduced the number of people eligible for it.

Caesar's most lasting reform was a new calendar based on the work of scholars in Alexandria. Replacing the old Roman lunar calendar, this new solar calendar counted 365 days in a year and 1 extra day every fourth year. Caesar's calendar, later named Julian in honor of him, was used in western Europe until early modern times.

Caesar 's Death

Many Romans believed that Caesar was a wise ruler who had brought order and peace to Rome. Others, however, considered him to be a tyrant who meant to make himself a king. According to ancient Roman law, anyone who plotted to become king could be killed without trial. Acting on this law, a group of senators, led by the chief conspirators Brutus and Cassius, stabbed Caesar to death as he entered the Senate on March 15, 44 B.C.

End of the Republic

After the death of Julius Caesar, his 18-year-old grandnephew **Octavian** joined forces with **Marc Antony** and Marcus Lepidus, two of Caesar's top government officers. Together this second triumvirate defeated Caesar's assassins in 42 B.C. Then, while keeping up the appearance of republican government, these three generals divided the Roman world among themselves. Octavian took command in Italy and the west, Antony ruled in Greece and the east, and Lepidus took charge of North Africa.

The second triumvirate did not last long, however. Octavian forced Lepidus to retire from political life. When Antony married Cleopatra, the queen of Egypt, Octavian persuaded the Romans that Antony intended to rule them with his foreign queen by his side, and so Octavian declared war on Antony in Rome's name. In 31 B.C. Octavian scattered the forces of his enemies in a critical naval battle at Actium in Greece. A year later, to evade capture by Octavian, Antony and Cleopatra committed suicide in Egypt. With Antony dead, Octavian became the undisputed ruler of Rome. Octavian's period of rule would mark the beginning of the Roman Empire.

SECTION 2 REVIEW

Recall
1. **Define** indemnity, triumvirate.
2. **Identify** Hannibal, Scipio, Tiberius Gracchus, Gaius Gracchus, Marius, Sulla, Julius Caesar, Octavian, Marc Antony.
3. **Locate** Carthage and Gaul on the map on page 165. What was the importance of each place in the military history of the Roman Republic?

Critical Thinking
4. **Analyzing Information** How did Julius Caesar's crossing of the Rubicon help destroy the Roman Republic and create a dictatorship?

Understanding Themes
5. **Conflict** Explain how Roman conquests overseas affected Rome's development.

A.D. 1   A.D. 50   A.D. 100   A.D. 150   A.D. 200

A.D. 14
Augustus Caesar dies.

A.D. 79
Volcanic eruption destroys Pompeii.

A.D. 96 Rule of the Good Emperors begins.

A.D. 180
Pax Romana ends.

Section 3

The Roman Empire

Setting the Scene

▶ **Terms to Define**
  aqueduct

▶ **People to Meet**
  Augustus, Tiberius, Claudius, Nero, Marcus Aurelius, Galen, Ptolemy, Virgil, Livy

▶ **Places to Locate**
  Appian Way

 **Find Out** ➤ What was life like in the Roman Empire during the *Pax Romana*?

The Storyteller

The visitor, Aelius Aristides, an educated and well-travelled man, had never seen anything to rival Rome. And it was not just the city—it was everything that Rome represented: military might, sensible government, and an elegant lifestyle. Who could help but admire an empire that commanded vast territories and diverse peoples, a military that conquered both armed forces and selfish ambition, a government where officials ruled not through arbitrary power but by law. Romans "measured out the world, bridged rivers, cut roads through mountains, filled the wastes with posting stations, introduced orderly and refined modes of life." They were, he declared, natural rulers.

—adapted from *Oration on the Pax Romana*, Aelius Aristides, reprinted in *Sources of the Western Tradition*, Marvin Perry, 1991

Augustus Caesar

Under the Roman Republic, laws had proven too weak to control social changes, while generals had taken power away from elected officials. Thus, Octavian believed that Rome needed one strong leader. The Senate agreed and appointed Octavian consul, tribune, and commander in chief for life in 27 B.C. Octavian gave himself the title *Augustus*, or "Majestic One."

The First Emperors

Augustus claimed to support the republic, but he actually laid the foundation for a new state called the Roman Empire. In practice, he became Rome's first emperor, or absolute ruler.

Augustus Caesar

In the 40 years of his reign—from 27 B.C. to A.D. 14—Augustus rebuilt the city of Rome and became a great patron of the arts. He also introduced many reforms to the empire. Proconsuls could no longer exploit the provinces. Publican tax collectors were replaced with permanent government employees. Grain was imported from North Africa so that all in Rome would be fed. New roads were built and old ones repaired. Magnificent public buildings were constructed throughout the empire. Augustus boasted that he had "found Rome a city of brick and left it a city of marble."

In 31 B.C. there began the *Pax Romana*, or Roman Peace, which lasted about 200 years. The only major disturbances during those years occurred when new emperors came to power. For, although Augustus chose his own successor carefully, he failed to devise any law for the selection of later emperors.

The Julio-Claudian Emperors

Historians call the four emperors who ruled from A.D. 14 to A.D. 68 the Julio-Claudians because

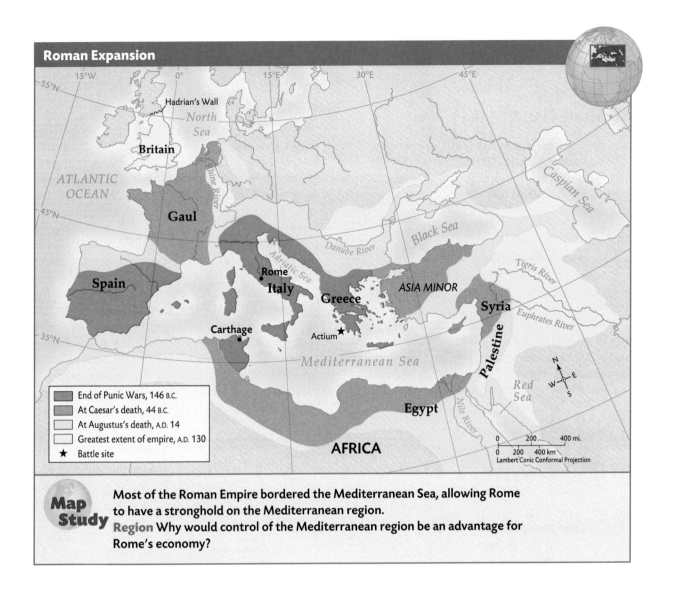

■	End of Punic Wars, 146 B.C.
■	At Caesar's death, 44 B.C.
☐	At Augustus's death, A.D. 14
☐	Greatest extent of empire, A.D. 130
★	Battle site

Map Study Most of the Roman Empire bordered the Mediterranean Sea, allowing Rome to have a stronghold on the Mediterranean region.
Region Why would control of the Mediterranean region be an advantage for Rome's economy?

each was a member of Augustus's family, known as the Julio-Claudians. Each showed promise when he became emperor, but later revealed great faults.

Augustus's adopted son **Tiberius**, who succeeded Augustus Caesar as emperor, spoiled his able leadership by accusing many innocent people of treason against him. Caligula, Tiberius's grand-nephew and successor in A.D. 37, became mentally disturbed and was killed by a palace guard in A.D. 41. Caligula's uncle, **Claudius**, was a renowned scholar, but as he grew older he had difficulty focusing on affairs of state.

Nero, Claudius's stepson, who became emperor in A.D. 54, was cruel and probably insane. Nero was willing to bankrupt Rome to pay for his twin pleasures—horse racing and music. Suspecting others of plotting against him, he killed his wife and his mother and executed many senators. In A.D. 68 the Senate sentenced Nero to death for treason. Before he committed suicide, reportedly he cried, "What a loss I shall be to the arts!"

The Good Emperors

For 28 years following Nero's death, Rome was governed by a number of emperors who were backed by the army. Then, in A.D. 96 the Senate chose its own candidate for emperor: Nerva. Historians consider Nerva the first of the so-called Good Emperors; the others were Trajan, Hadrian, Antoninus Pius, and **Marcus Aurelius** (aw•REE •lee•uhs). The Good Emperors were known for their skills as effective administrators and their support of large building projects.

The Emperor Trajan increased the empire to its greatest size. Hadrian then strengthened Rome's frontiers, building Hadrian's Wall in Britain and other defense positions. Antoninus Pius succeeded him, maintaining the empire's prosperity. The philosopher-ruler Marcus Aurelius brought the empire to the height of its economic prosperity. All of these Good Emperors lived by the principle of Stoic philosophy best expressed by Marcus Aurelius in *Meditations*: "Every moment think steadily as a

Roman and a human being how to do what you have in hand with perfect and simple dignity."

Roman Rule

By the time Augustus had come to power in 27 B.C., between 70 and 100 million people were living in the Roman Empire. To rule so many people effectively, Augustus had to make many changes in government.

Imperial Government

Augustus improved the working of the empire by carefully choosing professional governors rather than letting the Senate appoint inexperienced proconsuls every year. In some provinces, such as Judea, he left local kings in charge under his command. Augustus ordered new roads built so that he could keep in touch with all parts of the empire, and he personally inspected the provinces frequently.

Augustus also dignified his own position by serving as *pontifex maximus*, or chief priest of Rome. Thus he and each later emperor became the head of a national, unifying religion.

The Law

As the Romans won more provinces, they found that they needed a new kind of law that would apply to noncitizens. They therefore created the *jus gentium*, or law that dealt with noncitizens, as opposed to the *jus civile*, or citizen law. By the early A.D. 200s, however, emperors had granted citizenship to the peoples of so many nearby provinces that all free males in the empire had been made full citizens of Rome, and the two laws became one.

In their laws Romans generally stressed the authority of the state over the individual. They also accorded people definite legal rights, one of which was that an accused person should be considered innocent until proven guilty. The Roman system of law has formed the basis for the legal systems of many Western nations and of the Christian Church.

Images *of the* Times

Pompeii, A.D. 79

On August 23-25, A.D. 79, the volcano Vesuvius erupted in southern Italy. The city of Pompeii was buried in a single day.

A detail from the Villa of the Mysteries shows that life for many in Pompeii offered many comforts and pleasures.

An Imperial Army

Augustus and later emperors maintained the professional army. As conditions became more peaceful, however, Augustus reduced the number of legions and supplemented this fighting force with troops recruited from the provincial peoples. Even with forces combined, the emperor could count on having only about 300,000 troops, which was not enough to defend a border with a length of about 4,000 miles (6,440 km). Therefore, by A.D. 160, invasions by peoples outside the empire had become a continuing problem.

Roman Civilization

From about 31 B.C. to A.D. 180, the Roman world enjoyed a period of prosperity known as the *Pax Romana*, or Roman Peace. The stability of the *Pax Romana* boosted trade, raised standards of living, and generated many achievements in the arts. The Latin author Tertullian described this time:

“ Everywhere roads are built, every district is known, every country is open to commerce … the [fields] are planted; the marshes drained. There are now as many cities as there were once solitary cottages…. Wherever there is a trace of life, there are houses and human habitations, well-ordered governments, and civilized life. ”

—Tertullian, *Concerning the Soul*, c. A.D. 180

The Empire's Economy

Tertullian's description of economic growth under the empire was not exaggerated. In the first century A.D., artisans in Italy made pottery, woven cloth, blown glass, and jewelry for sale throughout the empire. The provinces in turn sent to Italy luxury items, such as silk cloth and spices, gathered in trade with China, India, and Southeast Asian countries. Dockworkers at Rome's harbor, Ostia, unloaded raw materials such as tin from Britain,

Citizens of Pompeii were almost instantly overwhelmed by volcanic ash and fire. A plaster cast of victims serves as a stern reminder of Vesuvius's power.

REFLECTING ON THE TIMES

1. Why were so many artifacts from Pompeii so well preserved?
2. What do Roman wall paintings in Pompeii reveal about the lifestyles of upper-class Romans?

167

iron from Gaul, and lead from Spain. Soon skillful Greek traders within the empire were doing business in distant areas, such as eastern Africa, Southeast Asia, and China.

Life During the *Pax Romana*

These economic changes brought changes in lifestyles. The family gradually became less significant than it had been during the republic. Romans had fewer children and were likely to divorce and remarry several times. Fathers lost some of the absolute power they had during the republic, and wives gained some legal rights. Society became less stable. Patricians might go bankrupt, wealthy military officers might sit in the Senate, and a poor man might even make a fortune in manufacturing.

Within each class, a consistent pattern of life formed. The wealthy often held public office, owned large farms outside the cities, ran factories, or directed trading firms. They lived comfortably in luxurious homes with marble walls, mosaic floors, running water, and baths.

The prosperity of the *Pax Romana* sometimes reached people of average means—shopkeepers and artisans. Although fewer people became very rich, more became moderately well off. The majority in Rome, however, were still poor. There were no private baths for them; instead they bathed at crowded public areas built under Augustus and later emperors. Most Romans lived in flimsy wooden apartment buildings of six or seven stories that readily collapsed or caught fire.

Public Amusements

Despite these trying conditions, the poor did not rebel against the government, because it offered them both free bread and free entertainment. By A.D. 160, Romans were celebrating 130 holidays a year. On some days, teams of charioteers competed in races in the Circus Maximus, an arena seating more than 150,000. On other holidays, crowds could watch gladiators fight each other to the death or battle wild animals in stadiums like the Colosseum.

Architecture, Engineering, and Science

The Romans erected many impressive buildings during the *Pax Romana* besides the Circus Maximus and the Colosseum. Between A.D. 118 and A.D. 128, Hadrian rebuilt the Pantheon, a temple for all the deities, with a soaring dome and a huge skylight. To build the Pantheon, the Romans mixed concrete—a new building material—with various kinds of stone.

The Romans also excelled in road building. The first major Roman road was the **Appian Way**. Constructed in the 300s B.C., it connected Rome and southeastern Italy. During the *Pax Romana*, a network of roads was built to link Rome with the provinces. Reaching a total length of 50,000 miles (80,000 km), the road network contributed to the empire's unity.

As they constructed public buildings and a vast network of roads, the Romans engineered aqueducts, or artificial channels for carrying water.

Visualizing History Entertainment at the giant arena Circus Maximus, depicted in this bas-relief, was free to Roman citizens. *What new building material did the Romans use to construct the Pantheon?*

© Sonia Halliday Photographs

Roman Forum

The ruins of the Roman Forum are a major tourist attraction of modern Rome. In ancient times, the Forum was the center of both politics and commerce. The Forum contained a number of separate buildings: In the foreground the Temple of Castor and Pollux, built in the 400s B.C., honored Roman gods. Behind is the Arch of Titus, the ruler whose military victory is enshrined in the arch built about A.D 80. Beyond the Arch stand the walls of the Colosseum. The largest amphitheater built in ancient Rome, the Colosseum took a decade to construct and could seat 50,000. Here the Romans watched gladiators battle lions and later vanquish Christians.

The rise of the Roman state began with the city of Rome itself hundreds of years before the birth of Christ. Slowly the Romans consolidated control over Italy and built a great army. By 200 B.C. Rome had become a vast empire. Power brought wealth and great monuments such as these in the Forum. ⊕

These lofty arches built out of stone enabled water to flow into Rome from as far away as 57 miles (about 92 km). One Roman-built aqueduct in Segovia, Spain, was so well constructed that it is still used today—nearly 1,900 years after it was completed.

The Romans excelled at adapting the discoveries of others and using them in new and more practical ways. They made use of the Etruscan arch and dome to build aqueducts and the Pantheon, and borrowed the Greek design for columns to support porches built around city squares.

Roman scientists also relied upon information that had been gathered from other cultures. The medical ideas of the ancient world compiled by the Greek physician **Galen** formed the basis of Roman medical science. Likewise, the observations of the Egyptian astronomer **Ptolemy** formed the foundation of Roman astronomy. Galen's works influenced medical science for many centuries, and Ptolemy's work made it possible for later astronomers to predict with accuracy the motion of the planets.

Roman Education

The Romans studied their borrowed knowledge avidly. Wealthy boys and girls received private lessons at home. Young men from wealthy families went on to academies—where former Greek slaves often taught—to learn geometry, astronomy, philosophy, and oratory. The daughters of the wealthy did not attend academies. Many upper-class women continued to study at home, however, and often became as well educated as Roman men. People in the lower classes usually had at least the basic knowledge of reading, writing, and arithmetic they needed to conduct business.

Language and Literature

Latin, Rome's official language, had a vocabulary far smaller than that of Greek or modern English; thus, many words expressed several meanings. Nevertheless, Latin remained the *lingua franca*, or common language, of Europe as late as the A.D. 1500s. Latin also forms the basis of the so-called Romance languages, such as Italian, French, Spanish, Portuguese, and Romanian, and supplies the roots for more than half of English words.

Although Romans learned from Greek literature, during the reign of Augustus Latin literature achieved an elegance and power of its own. Cicero, a Roman senator, published beautifully written speeches. Ovid wrote the *Metamorphoses*, verses based on Greek mythology. Horace, a poet, wrote about the shortness of life and the rewards of companionship in his *Odes*. Horace's friend **Virgil** wrote the *Aeneid*, an epic poem comparable to those of Homer. In one passage of this poem, Virgil expresses both the humility and pride of Romans:

❝ Others, no doubt, will better mould the bronze
To the semblance of soft breathing, draw, from marble,
The living countenance; and others plead
With greater eloquence, or learn to measure,
Better than we, the pathways of the heaven,
The risings of the stars: remember, Roman,
To rule the people under law, to establish
The way of peace, to battle down the haughty,
To spare the meek. Our fine arts, these, forever. ❞

—Virgil, the *Aeneid*, c. 20 B.C.

Livy, a later writer, wrote a monumental history of Rome that glorified the early Romans. The historian Tacitus, in contrast, condemned the tyranny of the Julio-Claudian emperors with subtle but scathing irony. In *Germania*, Tacitus contrasted the robust life of the Germans with what he felt was the weak and pleasure-loving life of the Romans.

SECTION 3 REVIEW

Recall
1. **Define** aqueduct.
2. **Identify** Augustus, *Pax Romana*, Tiberius, Claudius, Nero, Marcus Aurelius, Galen, Ptolemy, Virgil, Livy.
3. **Use** the map on page 165 to identify Roman expansion. When did the empire reach its greatest extent?

Critical Thinking
4. **Synthesizing Information** The expression "bread and circuses" has been used to describe hasty measures taken by a government to prevent discontent among the poor. Explain whether you believe this expression applies to any aspects of life in the modern United States. If so, to what aspects does it apply?

Understanding Themes
5. **Change** How did Roman family life change from the time of the republic to that of the *Pax Romana*?

A.D. 1	A.D. 150	A.D. 300	A.D. 450

c. A.D. 30
Jesus preaches in Palestine.

A.D. 70 Jews in Palestine unsuccessfully revolt against Roman rule.

A.D. 312
Constantine becomes Roman emperor.

A.D. 392
Christianity becomes Rome's official religion.

Section 4

The Rise of Christianity

Setting the Scene

▶ **Terms to Define**
sect, messiah, disciple, martyr, bishop, patriarch, pope

▶ **People to Meet**
Jesus, Paul, Peter, Constantine, Theodosius, Augustine

 What did Jesus of Nazareth teach, and how did the early Christians influence the later Roman Empire?

The Storyteller

How could Justin, a man well versed in philosophy and intellectual pursuits, explain to the emperor why he had embraced Christianity? He had opened a school to teach others about this religion, although most educated people dismissed it as a dangerous superstition. He had to convince the emperor that, just as the ancient philosophers had sought truth, Christians sought it too. Since both scholars and Christians shared this quest, following Christian teachings could only help in the search for understanding. He set his pen to paper and began to write a defense of the Christian faith.

—from *Apology,* Justin, reprinted in *Readings in Ancient History from Gilgamesh to Diocletian,* Nels M. Bailkey, 1969

Mosaic of Jesus as shepherd

The early Romans worshiped nature spirits. Under Etruscan influence they came to think of these spirits as deities. Later, the Romans adopted much of Greek religion, identifying Greek deities with their own. Beginning with Augustus, the government also expected people to honor the emperor as Rome's chief priest. Nevertheless, the empire's people were still allowed to worship freely, and a variety of religions flourished.

Meanwhile, a new monotheistic religion called Christianity began to be practiced by some of the Jews in the eastern Mediterranean. At first, both the Romans and the earliest Christians thought of the new religion as a sect, or group, within Judaism. As Christians won over non-Jewish followers, however, the faith diverged from its Jewish roots and became a separate religion.

Judaism and the Empire

In A.D. 6 the Emperor Augustus turned the kingdom of Judah into the Roman province of Judea. The Romans in Judea still allowed the Jews to practice their religion, but they treated them cruelly. Many Jews therefore strengthened their hope that a messiah, or a deliverer chosen by God, would help them regain their freedom. The coming of a messiah had long been foretold by Jewish prophets.

Believing that God would intervene on their behalf, some Jews took matters into their own hands. In A.D. 66 they rebelled against the Romans and overpowered the small Roman army in Jerusalem. But only four years later, in A.D. 70, the Romans retook Jerusalem, destroying the Temple and killing thousands of Jews.

Then, after another unsuccessful rebellion in A.D. 132, the Romans banned the Jews from living

Chapter 6 *Ancient Rome and Early Christianity* **171**

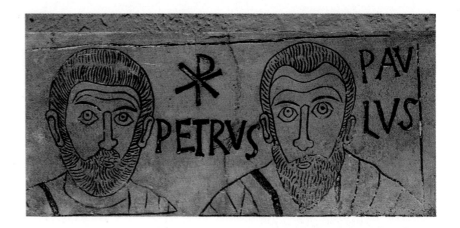

An engraving of the apostles Peter and Paul decorates the sepulchre of the child Asellus. *Why did the apostles form churches?*

in Jerusalem. The Jews were forced to live in other parts of the Mediterranean and the Middle East. In their scattered communities, the Jews continued to study the Torah, the entire body of Jewish religious law and learning. They set up special academies called yeshivas to promote its study. Furthermore, between A.D. 200 and A.D. 500, rabbis—scholars trained in the yeshivas—assembled their various interpretations of the Torah into a book known as the Talmud. To this day the Talmud remains an important book of Jewish law.

Jesus of Nazareth

A few decades before the Jewish revolts, a Jew named **Jesus** grew up in the town of Nazareth. With deep spiritual fervor, Jesus traveled through Galilee and Judea from about A.D. 30 to A.D. 33, preaching a new message to his fellow Jews and winning disciples, or followers.

Proclaiming that God's rule was close at hand, Jesus urged people to turn away from their sins and practice deeds of kindness. He said that God was loving and forgiving toward all who repented, no matter what evil they had done or how lowly they were. In his teaching, Jesus often used parables, or symbolic stories. With the parable below, Jesus urged his followers to give up everything so that they would be ready for God's coming:

❝ The kingdom of heaven is like treasure lying buried in a field. The man who found it, buried it again; and for sheer joy went and sold everything he had, and bought that field. **❞**

—Matthew 13:44-46

Jesus' disciples believed that he was the messiah; other Jews, believing that the messiah had yet to come, disputed this claim. The growing controversy over Jesus troubled Roman officials in Palestine. They believed that anyone who aroused such strong public feelings could endanger Roman rule in the region. In about A.D. 33, the Roman governor Pontius Pilate arrested Jesus as a political rebel and ordered that he be crucified—hung from a cross until dead. This was a typical Roman way of punishing criminals.

The Spread of Christianity

After Jesus' death, his disciples proclaimed that he had risen from the dead and had appeared to them. They pointed to this as evidence that Jesus was the messiah. His followers began preaching that Jesus was the Son of God and the way of salvation. Small groups in the Hellenistic cities of the eastern Mediterranean world accepted this message. Jews and non-Jews who accepted Jesus and his teachings became known as Christians— *Christos* was Greek for "messiah." They formed churches—communities for worship, fellowship, and instruction.

A convert named **Paul** aided Christianity's spread, especially among non-Jews. He traveled widely and wrote on behalf of the new religion. Paul's letters to various churches were later combined with the Gospels, or stories about Jesus, and the writings of other early Christian leaders. Together, these works form the New Testament of the Bible.

Meanwhile, other apostles, or Christian missionaries, spread Christianity throughout the Roman world. It is believed that **Peter**, the leader of the group, came to Rome and helped found a church in that city. Other churches were set up in Greece, Asia Minor, Egypt, and later in Gaul and Spain.

Persecution and Competition

Christians taught that their religion was the only true faith. They refused to honor the emperor as a god and rejected military service. As a result, many Romans accused them of treason.

The Romans feared that Christian rejection of their deities would bring divine punishment. Therefore, although they did not hunt out the Christians, if local officials thought Christians were causing trouble, they might have the Christians killed. The Romans frequently threw these Christian martyrs—people who chose to die rather than give up their beliefs—into the stadiums to be killed by wild beasts in front of cheering crowds.

Such persecution, which lasted until the early A.D. 300s, kept many people from becoming Christians. To win converts, Christians had to overcome this obstacle. Christianity also had to compete for followers with polytheistic religions and mystery religions—so named for their mythical heroes and secret rituals—and with Judaism.

During the A.D. 200s and 300s, Christianity flourished in the Mediterranean world along with these other religions. Like Judaism, Christianity was mainly a religion of the cities, while traditional Roman religions retained their hold in the countryside. Even though the number of Christians was relatively small during this period, their strength in the cities of the Roman Empire gave Christianity an influence that was far beyond its size.

POINT

Romans Adopt Christianity

According to legend, in A.D. 312, as the Roman general **Constantine** led his army into battle, a flaming cross appeared in the sky and beneath it in fiery letters appeared the Latin words *In hoc signo vinces*: "With this as your standard you will have victory." Apparently because of this vision, Constantine ordered his soldiers to paint the Christian symbol of the cross on their shields. When his army won the battle, Constantine credited the victory to the Christian God.

Named emperor of Rome in A.D. 312, Constantine thus became a protector of Christianity. That same year, he issued the Edict of Milan, which decreed that all religious groups in the empire, including Christians, were free to worship as they pleased. Constantine attended meetings of Christian leaders and ordered churches to be built in Rome and Jerusalem.

Because of effective missionary work and growing government support, Christianity further increased in size and influence throughout the entire Roman world. It became as important in the western part of the empire as it was in the eastern part. In A.D. 392 the Emperor **Theodosius** (THEE•uh •DOH•shuhs) made Christianity the official religion of the Roman Empire. At the same time, he banned the old Hellenistic and Roman religions.

The Early Church

From early times Christians recognized that their organization, the Church, would prosper only if it was united. They also felt that Christian teachings had to be stated clearly to avoid differences of opinion that might divide the Church. Consequently, Christians turned to important religious thinkers who attempted to explain many Christian beliefs. Between A.D. 100 and A.D. 500, various scholars known as Church Fathers wrote books explaining Christian teachings. They greatly influenced later Christian thinkers.

Teachings of Augustine

Christians in the western part of the empire especially valued the work of **Augustine**, a scholar born in North Africa in A.D. 354. Augustine is considered to have written one of the world's first great autobiographies. In this work called *Confessions*, Augustine describes how he was converted to Christianity:

“ I heard from a neighboring house a voice, as of a boy or girl, I know not, chanting, and oft repeating, 'Take up and read; Take up and read.'… So … I arose, interpreting it to be no other than a command from God, to open the book [the Bible], and read the first chapter I should find. ”

—Augustine, *Confessions*, c. A.D. 398

 Constantine became a defender of Christianity. *How did the status of Christians living in the Roman Empire change under the rule of Constantine?*

The walls of Roman catacombs host many depictions of Christian art such as the Eucharistic Banquet version of the Last Supper. *What kind of literature was the* City of God?

So powerful was Augustine's influence that he became a leading church official in North Africa. In this post he wrote books, letters, and sermons that shaped Christian thought during his own time and afterward. For instance, he wrote *City of God*—the first history of humanity from the Christian viewpoint.

Church Structure

By Augustine's time, Christian leaders had organized the Church as a hierarchy—into levels of authority, each level more powerful than the level below it. Local gatherings of Christians, called parishes, were led by priests. Priests conducted worship services and supervised parish activities. Several parishes together formed a diocese, each overseen by a bishop. Bishops interpreted Christian beliefs and administered regional church affairs. The most powerful bishops governed Christians in the empire's larger cities. The bishops of the five leading cities—Rome, Constantinople, Alexandria, Antioch, and Jerusalem—were called patriarchs.

The bishops of the Christian Church met in councils to discuss questions and disputes about Christian beliefs. The decisions they reached at these councils, such as that at Nicaea in A.D. 325, came to be accepted as doctrine, or official teachings. The points of view the council did not accept were considered heresy, or false doctrine.

During the A.D. 400s, the bishop of Rome began to claim authority over the other patriarchs. Addressed by the Greek or Latin word *papa*, his name today is rendered *pope* in the English language. Latin-speaking Christians in the West regarded the pope as head of all of the churches. Greek-speaking Christians in the East, however, would not accept the authority of the pope over their churches. The bishops of Alexandria and Antioch claimed to exercise a paternal rule equal to that of the pope. Eventually these churches and those of the Latin West separated from each other. In time, the Latin churches as a group became known as the Roman Catholic Church. The Greek churches as a group became known as the Eastern Orthodox Church.

Recall
1. **Define** sect, messiah, disciple, martyr, bishop, patriarch, pope.
2. **Identify** the Talmud, Jesus, Paul, Peter, Constantine, Theodosius, Augustine.
3. **Use** a chart to describe the hierarchy of the Christian Church by the time of Augustine. What were the functions of bishops? Of priests?

Critical Thinking
4. **Evaluating Information** Why might the Romans in Judea especially have responded harshly toward anyone arousing strong feelings among the Jewish people?

Understanding Themes
5. **Innovation** List some of the ways in which Christianity diverged from Judaism to become a distinct religion rather than a sect.

Section 5

Roman Decline

Setting the Scene

▶ **Terms to Define**
  inflation

▶ **People to Meet**
  Diocletian, Constantine, Theodosius I, Alaric, Attila

▶ **Places to Locate**
  Constantinople

Find Out What caused the decline of the western Roman Empire?

The Storyteller

The old world had ended. There was no longer any doubt of that. Gregory, whose family had for countless generations served Rome as Senators and consuls, looked out the window at the city which had once ruled the world. Now it was in the hands of warlike tribes who had no appreciation for Roman virtue, achievements, or culture.

"Cities are destroyed," he mused, "fortifications razed, fields devastated. Some men are led away captive, others are mutilated, others slain before our eyes." The pride of Rome was reduced to memories of a vanished glory.

—from *Homiliarum in Ezechielem*, Pope Gregory I, reprinted in *Sources of the Western Tradition*, Marvin Perry, Joseph Peden, and Theodore Von Laue, 1991

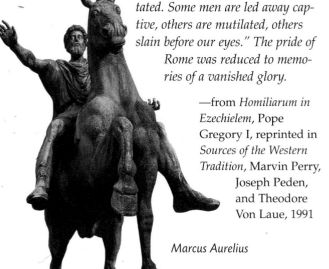

Marcus Aurelius

During the A.D. 200s, while Christianity was spreading through the Roman Empire, Germanic tribes began to overrun the western half of the empire. Many inhabitants in this area reported widespread devastation and chaos. The Germanic tribes had always been a threat to the empire. Why were they so much more successful now than they were during the times of Marcus Aurelius?

The Empire's Problems

The Romans had a brief rest from political violence during the reign of the five Good Emperors. When Marcus Aurelius died in A.D. 180, however, a new period of violence and corruption brought the *Pax Romana* to an end.

Political Instability

The time of confusion began with the installation of Emperor Commodus, Marcus Aurelius's son. Like Nero, he spent so much state money on his own pleasures that he bankrupted the treasury. In A.D. 192 Commodus's own troops plotted to kill him.

From A.D. 192 to A.D. 284, army legions installed 28 emperors, only to kill most of them off in rapid succession. During this time of political disorder, Rome's armies were busier fighting each other than they were defending the empire's borders. Germanic tribes such as the Goths, the Alemanni, the Franks, and the Saxons repeatedly and successfully attacked the empire.

Economic Decline

Political instability led to economic decline. Warfare disrupted production and trade. For artisans and merchants, profits declined sharply, forcing many out of business. Warfare also destroyed farmland, causing food shortages that sent food prices soaring.

Chapter 6 *Ancient Rome and Early Christianity* **175**

To cope with falling incomes and rising prices, the government minted more coins. It hoped the increase would make it easier to pay its soldiers. However, because the government had already drained its stores of gold and silver, the new coins contained less of the precious metals—cutting their value. To continue getting the same return for their goods, merchants raised prices. Thus, the government's policy sparked severe inflation—a rise in prices corresponding to a decrease in the value of money.

The spiraling decline in wealth affected almost all parts of the empire. To sustain a fighting force, the Roman government had to continually raise soldiers' wages. Taxing landowners heavily seemed the only way to meet this expense, but as increased taxes made farming less profitable, more and more farmers abandoned their lands. As a result, the output of crops shrank even more, worsening the food shortage.

Unsuccessful Reforms

During the late A.D. 200s and early A.D. 300s, two emperors—**Diocletian** (DY•uh•KLEE•shuhn) and later, **Constantine**—struggled to halt the empire's decline. Their reforms preserved the government in the eastern part of the empire for more than 1,000 years. In the west, they succeeded only in briefly delaying the Germanic tribes' invasion of Rome.

Diocletian

General Diocletian came to power in A.D. 284 by slaying the murderer of the preceding emperor. To hold back invasions, he raised the number of legions in the army and spent his time traveling throughout the empire to oversee defenses. Recognizing, however, that the empire was too large for one person to govern, Diocletian divided the empire into two administrative units. Diocletian set himself up as coemperor of the eastern provinces and set up General Maximian as coemperor of the western provinces.

Diocletian also tried to stop the empire's economic decline. To slow inflation, he issued an order called the Edict of Prices. In this edict, Diocletian froze wages and set maximum prices for goods. Yet, even though the penalty for breaking the law was death, his effort failed completely. Citizens merely sold their goods through illegal trade. To stop farmers from leaving their lands and heavily taxed people from changing their

As this relief sculpture shows, tax collectors in Roman times were very visible. *Why did the Roman government have to increase taxes?*

professions to avoid taxation, Diocletian required farmers who rented land never to leave their property and all workers to remain at the same job throughout their lives.

Constantine

When Diocletian retired in A.D. 305, civil wars broke out again. They continued until Constantine came to power in A.D. 312.

Constantine worked to stabilize the empire once more by reinforcing Diocletian's reforms. He made it legal for landowners to chain their workers to keep them on the farm. He declared most jobs hereditary; sons had to follow their fathers' occupations. In A.D. 330 he moved the capital of the eastern empire to the Greek town of Byzantium —an ideal site for trade and well protected by natural barriers—and renamed it **Constantinople**.

Theodosius

After Constantine's death in A.D. 337, civil war flared anew until **Theodosius I** succeeded Constantine. During Theodosius's rule, the empire still suffered internal problems, and again the western half suffered more. To lessen the problems, Theodosius willed upon his death that the eastern and western parts should be separate empires. In A.D. 395 this division came to pass. To distinguish the two, historians refer to the eastern empire as the Byzantine Empire—after Byzantium, the town that became the capital—and the western empire as the Roman Empire.

Barbarian Invasions

Germanic tribes entered the Roman Empire for many reasons. Beginning in the late A.D. 300s, large numbers of Germanic peoples migrated into the empire because they sought a warmer climate and

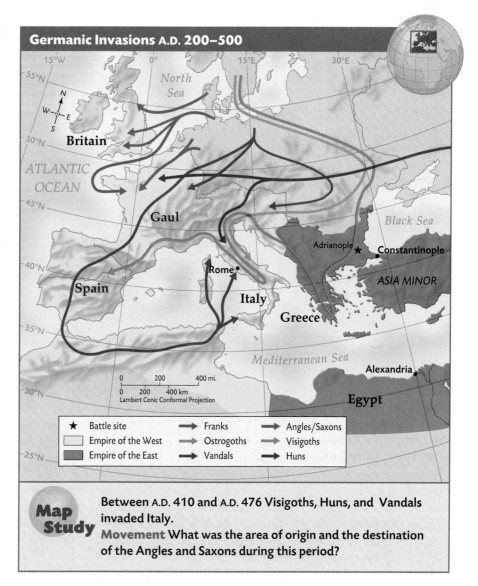

Germanic Invasions A.D. 200–500

Map Study Between A.D. 410 and A.D. 476 Visigoths, Huns, and Vandals invaded Italy.
Movement What was the area of origin and the destination of the Angles and Saxons during this period?

better grazing land. Others crossed the empire's borders wanting a share of Rome's wealth. Most, however, came because they were fleeing the Huns, fierce nomadic invaders from central Asia.

Warrior Groups

Germanic warriors lived mostly by raising cattle and farming small plots. Despite their interest in the empire's goods, they themselves had little surplus to trade and were poor compared to the Romans. Each warrior group consisted of warriors, their families, and a chief. This chief governed the group and also led the warriors into battle. As the bands of warriors were numerous, so too were the chiefs. Often the only unifying factor among these Germanic groups was their language, which to the Romans sounded like unintelligible babbling. The Romans labeled the Germanic peoples barbarians, a reference to the sounds they made.

Sassanids Establish an Empire

Persia, A.D. 200s

Ardashir I, king of Persis, defeated the Parthian army in a decisive victory, then entered the capital of Ctesiphon in triumph. There he was crowned King of Kings and established the Sassanid Empire, which lasted until A.D. 651. Ardashir founded or rebuilt many cities and made Zoroastrianism the state religion. A rock carving at Naqshi-Rustam shows Ardashir taking the symbol of royalty from the supreme Zoroastrian god.

Sassanid Empire

The Visigoths

During the late A.D. 300s and A.D. 400s, a variety of Germanic groups extended their hold over much Roman territory. They were the Ostrogoths, Visigoths, Vandals, Franks, Angles, and Saxons. The Visigoths, at first, were the most important of these groups. In A.D. 378 they rebelled against Roman rule and defeated a large Roman army at Adrianople in the Balkan Peninsula, killing the eastern Roman emperor. His successor managed to buy peace by giving the Visigoths land in the Balkans. Then in A.D. 410 the Visigothic chief, **Alaric**, led his people into Italy, capturing and sacking Rome. After Alaric's death the Visigoths retreated into Gaul.

The Huns

The next threat to the empire was invasion by the Huns. This nomadic group streamed westward from the grasslands of central Asia. Led by their chief, **Attila**, the Huns raided the eastern empire; then they moved north into Gaul. In A.D. 451 the Romans and the Visigoths combined to fight and stop the Huns in central Gaul. Foiled in the provinces, Attila turned upon Italy. There his horde plundered the larger cities and terrified the people. Eventually plague and famine took their toll on the Huns. After Attila died in A.D. 453, they retreated to eastern Europe.

The end of the empire of the Huns brought new troubles to the Romans. Wandering Germans, Persians, Slavs, and Avars battered continually at the Roman Empire's eastern frontier. Diplomacy, bribery, and warfare kept them at bay for only a short time.

End of the Western Empire

With the Huns gone and Italy devastated, nothing remained to prevent Germanic tribes from taking over. The Vandals raided and thoroughly sacked Rome in A.D. 455. Franks and Goths divided Gaul among themselves. Finally, in A.D. 476, a German soldier named Odoacer (OH•duh•WAY•suhr) seized control of Rome and overthrew the young emperor, Romulus Augustulus. Odoacer then named himself king of Italy.

Because Odoacer called himself king and never named a substitute emperor, people today refer to A.D. 476 as the year in which the Roman Empire "fell." However, this event no more signifies the collapse of the empire than any other event. Its end was caused by a complex interaction of events between A.D. 200 and A.D. 500.

More accurately, the western Roman Empire ended in the late A.D. 400s. Yet it did not mean the end of Roman culture, for the new Germanic rulers accepted the Latin language, Roman laws, and the Christian Church. In the Byzantine Empire, however, aspects of Roman culture were gradually supplanted by Hellenistic culture. By the A.D. 700s, Greek had even replaced Latin as the language of the Byzantine Empire.

SECTION 5 REVIEW

Recall
1. **Define** inflation.
2. **Identify** Diocletian, Constantine, Theodosius I, Alaric, Attila, Odoacer.
3. **Locate** Adrianople on the map on page 177. What significant event occurred there during the time of the "fall" of the Roman Empire?

Critical Thinking
4. **Synthesizing Information** Which do you think had a greater impact on the fall of the Roman Empire, internal difficulties or outside invaders? Why?

Understanding Themes
5. **Change** How did warfare both create and destroy the Roman Empire?

Decision Making

Suppose you have been given the choice of taking an art class or a music class during your free period at school. How will you decide which class to take?

Learning the Skill

When you make a decision, you are making a choice between alternatives. In order to make that choice, you must be informed and aware. There are five key steps you should follow that will help you through the decision-making process.

1. Identify the problem. What are you being asked to choose between?
2. Identify and consider various alternatives that are possible.
3. Determine the consequences for each alternative. Identify both the positive and the negative consequences.
4. Evaluate the consequences. Consider both the positive and negative consequences for each alternative.
5. Ask yourself: Which alternative seems to have more positive consequences? Which seems to have more negative consequences? Then make your decision.

Practicing the Skill

Decisions throughout history have affected the outcome of events, and defined history as we know it today. Identify the alternatives and describe their consequences for each of the following events that occurred during the time of ancient Rome. Each of these events took place as a result of a decision made by a person or a group of people.

1. The Twelve Tables became the basis for all future Roman law in 451 B.C.
2. During the Third Punic War, in 146 B.C., the Romans burned Carthage.
3. In 27 B.C., Augustus Caesar became Rome's first emperor.

4. The Emperor Theodosius made Christianity the official religion of the Roman Empire in A.D. 392.
5. Beginning in the late A.D. 300s, large numbers of Germanic peoples migrated into the Roman Empire.

Applying the Skill

Use a newspaper or magazine to find a current issue that directly affects your life. Identify the issue, and then review the facts and what you already know about the issue. Identify various alternatives, and then determine the consequences for each alternative. Use this information to evaluate both positive and negative consequences. Make a sound decision about which alternative would be best for you.

For More Practice

Turn to the Skill Practice in the Chapter Review on page 181 for more practice in decision making.

Connections Across Time

Historical Significance The Romans established a common culture among the diverse peoples of the Mediterranean world. Their legal system, forms of government, engineering feats, and arts formed the foundation of many provincial cities. Frequent civil wars triggered a chain of events that ultimately led to the Roman Empire's economic and political ruin.

The lasting legacies of the Roman Empire, however, are its Latin language, which provided the root of the Romance languages; its engineering skills; its transmission of Greek culture; and Christianity. Today, the city of Rome is still the center of the Roman Catholic Church.

Using Key Terms

Write the key term that completes each sentence. Then write a sentence for each term not chosen.

a. indemnity
b. bishop
c. plebeians
d. sect
e. inflation
f. aqueducts
g. republic
h. patricians
i. triumvirate
j. messiah
k. pope
l. consul
m. dictator

1. After years of rule by kings, the Romans declared their city-state a _____, a form of government in which people elect their leaders.
2. In 60 B.C. Pompey, Crassus, and Julius Caesar formed a _____, a group of three persons with equal power, to control the government.
3. After their defeat, the people of Carthage agreed to pay the Romans a huge _____, or payment for damages.
4. Early Christianity was thought of as a _____, or group, within Judaism.
5. The majority of people in the Roman Republic were _____ —nonaristocratic landowners, merchants, shopkeepers, small farmers, and laborers.

Technology Activity

Creating a Multimedia Presentation Search a computerized card catalog or the Internet for information about the early Etruscans. Using multimedia tools, create a short presentation about the Etruscan culture. Incorporate images from the Internet. Before you begin, plan the type of presentation you want to develop and the steps you will take to make the presentation successful. Indicate tools you will need and cite all electronic resources.

Using Your History Journal

Imagine that you are either a young Roman legionary stationed in a remote outpost of the empire in A.D. 130 or you are a friend of the legionary, awaiting his return to Rome. Write a letter describing what you have been doing in the past week.

Reviewing Facts

1. **Science** Identify Roman achievements in science and engineering, and discuss their impact.
2. **Government** Describe how Rome's political system changed under Augustus Caesar.
3. **Citizenship** Trace the development of Roman law and its influence on Western civilization.
4. **Government** Discuss how Roman governors made provincial cities more like Rome.
5. **Geography** Explain the geographic factors that helped Rome to dominate the Mediterranean.

Critical Thinking

1. **Apply** In what ways did the Roman Republic, in its structure and growth, affect later governments in western Europe and America?
2. **Analyze** What evidence suggests that Roman society was more stable during the republic than during the time of the empire?
3. **Evaluate** In what ways did the Romans' treatment of the peoples they conquered differ from the ways in which other victors usually treated the peoples they conquered? How might Roman attitudes have strengthened the empire?

4. **Analyze** The vase shown here incorporates the Etruscan alphabet. Why have scholars been unable to tell the full story of Etruscan history?

Geography in History

1. **Location** Refer to the map below. Which area (east or west) was more heavily influenced by Christianity by A.D. 200?
2. **Movement** What major body of water did many early missionaries cross in their efforts to spread Christianity?
3. **Place** According to the map below, which city in western Europe had the largest concentration of Christians by A.D. 200?

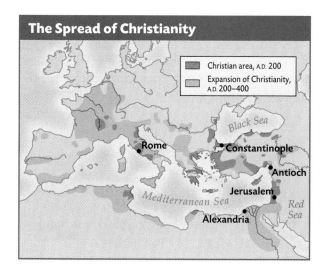

The Spread of Christianity

Christian area, A.D. 200
Expansion of Christianity, A.D. 200–400

Black Sea
Rome
Constantinople
Antioch
Jerusalem
Mediterranean Sea
Alexandria
Red Sea

Understanding Themes

1. **Change** How did the Roman government change from the time of the Etruscans to Augustus Caesar?
2. **Conflict** Evaluate a conflict between nations that has occurred in the recent past, and analyze the ways in which it is similar to conflicts between the Romans and other peoples of the Mediterranean region.
3. **Cultural Diffusion** How might Roman roads have helped to foster cultural diffusion?
4. **Innovation** In what way did Constantine's victory in battle in A.D. 312 change the religious life of the Roman Empire? How did his religious policies later shape the future course of religion in Western civilization?
5. **Change** How did Roman architecture reflect the political and social changes that transformed Rome from a republic into an empire?

Linking Past and Present

The United States government operates on the system of checks and balances, in which each branch of government limits the power of the other branches. Did this system operate in the Roman Republic? Why or why not? Use examples from Roman history to support your answer.

Skill Practice

Reread page 160 about the Punic Wars. For each of the three wars, identify the decision that affected the outcome of each. Explain the consequences of each decision, and how they affected the outcome. Examining the decisions and final outcomes of each war will help you see alternatives that might have been available to the decision makers at the time. Discuss some of the alternatives and their consequences for each war. How would history have changed if different decisions had been made?

Chapter

7

1500 B.C.–A.D. 1500

Flowering of African Civilizations

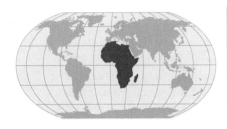

Chapter Themes

▶ **Movement** Migrations of Bantu-speaking people influence Africa's cultural development. *Section 1*
▶ **Cultural Diffusion** Africa's trade contacts with Europe and Asia affect African cultures. *Section 2*
▶ **Innovation** East African city-states develop a new culture based on African and Arab cultures. *Section 3*

The Storyteller

The Yoruba—West Africans living by the Niger River—gather each winter to hear storytellers recount a legend that tells of how their ancestors struggled to clear their land with tools made of wood and soft metal. Even orishas, or gods, could not cut through vines or trees with these tools until the god Ogun appeared, carrying his bush knife.

"He slashed through the heavy vines, felled the trees and cleared the forest from the land…. So [the people] made [Ogun] their ruler…. He built forges for them and showed them how to make spears, knives, hoes, and swords."

Legends such as this describe experiences that early people valued most. Early Africans built civilizations that have left rich traditions for today's peoples.

Historical Significance

How did early Africans use the natural resources of their environment to develop trade networks? What impact did their cultures have on other lands?

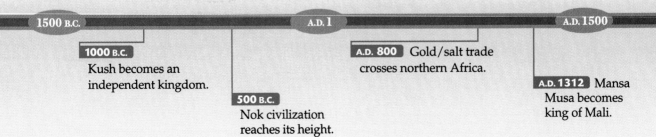

1500 B.C.

1000 B.C. Kush becomes an independent kingdom.

500 B.C. Nok civilization reaches its height.

A.D. 1

A.D. 800 Gold/salt trade crosses northern Africa.

A.D. 1312 Mansa Musa becomes king of Mali.

A.D. 1500

History & Art Prehistoric cave art from
Tassili N'Ajjer Plateau, Algeria

Your History Journal

Consult a historical atlas, and draw an outline map of Africa showing early African kingdoms, the dates when they existed, and major trade routes. Write and answer questions based on the map's data.

| 2000 B.C. | 1000 B.C. | A.D. 1 | A.D. 1000 |

c. 750 B.C.
Kushite kings
rule over Egypt.

c. 250 B.C. Merchants from
Egypt, Rome, Persia, and
India trade with Axum.

A.D. 330 Christianity
becomes Axum's
official religion.

Section 1

Early Africa

▶ **Terms to Define**
   oral tradition, plateau, savanna, matrilineal, age set

▶ **People to Meet**
   Piankhi, Ezana, the Nok

▶ **Places to Locate**
   Nubia, Kush, Axum

 **Find Out** What kinds of societies emerged in early Africa?

The Storyteller

African oral tradition contained stories full of wisdom, to be enjoyed by all. For example, where did death come from? A myth from Madagascar gave this answer. One day God asked the first couple what kind of death they wanted, one like that of the moon, or that of the banana? The couple was puzzled. God explained: The banana creates young plants to take its place, but the moon itself comes back to life every month. After consideration, the couple prayed for children, because without children they would be lonely, would have to do all the work, and would have no one to provide for. Since that time, human life is short on this earth.

—freely adapted from
The Humanistic Tradition,
Gloria K. Fiero, 1992

Kilimanjaro

Africa's earliest civilizations left few written records of their existence. It was through oral traditions—legends and history passed by word of mouth from one generation to another—that early African peoples communicated knowledge about their culture. Thus, archaeologists and historians have had to rely on legends and artifacts to learn about the culture of African civilizations between 1100 B.C. and A.D. 1500.

Archaeologists have discovered that early African cultures developed technologies and trade based on regional natural resources. Civilizations rose and declined, and were influenced by the movement of people and by the way in which natural resources were developed.

Geography and Environment

Africa's geography and climate are a study in contrasts. Africa, the world's second-largest continent, is three times larger than the United States. Within its huge expanse lie desolate deserts, lofty mountains, rolling grasslands, and fertile river valleys.

Regions of Africa

The African continent can be divided into five regions based on location and environment: North Africa, East Africa, West Africa, Central Africa, and Southern Africa.

North Africa consists of a thin coastal plain, bordering the Mediterranean Sea, and an inland desert area. Coastal North Africa has mild temperatures and frequent rainfall. In contrast, the area south of this green belt is a vast expanse of sand: the Sahara, the world's largest desert. Extending more than 3,500 miles (5,630 km) across the continent, the Sahara is a region of shifting dunes and jagged rock piles.

Wall painting from the Metropolitan Museum of Art, New York City, New York. **Four late Bronze Age Nubian princes offer rings and gold to an Egyptian ruler.** *In what ways did Nubian culture resemble Egyptian culture?*

The Sahel

South of the Sahara, the continent of Africa is dominated by a great central plateau—a relatively high, flat area known as the Sahel. This region receives moderate rainfall to sustain the savannas, or treeless grasslands, that cover the plateau. The savannas south of the Sahara constitute about 40 percent of Africa's land area.

In East Africa, the Sahel descends into a deep crack known as the Great Rift Valley. The valley extends 40 miles (65 km) in width and 2,000 feet (610 m) in depth. It runs 3,000 miles (4,827 km) from the Red Sea in the north all the way to Southern Africa. Rising above the Sahel plateau east of the valley are two mountain peaks—Mount Kenya and Kilimanjaro. Kilimanjaro is Africa's highest mountain, with an elevation of 19,340 feet (5,895 m).

In West Africa, the Sahel descends to a narrow coastal plain that has a relatively unbroken coastline. The major rivers that do flow through the coastal plain—the Niger and the Zaire (Congo)—are navigable only for short distances. The few natural harbors and limited river travel isolated early African civilizations and made foreign invasions difficult in some areas.

Central Africa near the Equator has lush tropical rain forests so thick that sunlight cannot reach the forest floor. Although the rain forest climate is hot and humid, 1,500 miles (2,413 km) farther south the land again turns into a desert—the Kalahari. Still farther south, the Kalahari gives way to a cool,

fertile highland in Southern Africa.

The African continent has provided rich resources for its people. Early cultures developed where rainfall was plentiful, or near lakes or along rivers like the Nile.

Nubia and Kush

By 3000 B.C., a people called the Nubians established a kingdom called **Nubia** in the southern part of the Nile River valley in present-day Sudan. The Nubian people mastered the bow and arrow and became warriors. With their military skills, they conquered smaller neighboring communities in the Nile Valley.

The Nubians maintained close contacts with Egypt to the north. Archaeologists have uncovered the tombs of Nubian kings, which contained precious stones, gold, jewelry, and pottery. These are as ornate as those found in Egypt from the same period. Some scholars believe that political ideas, such as monarchy, and various objects, like boats and eating utensils, reveal the early beginnings of the close cultural links between Nubia and Egypt.

By 2000 B.C., the Nubian river civilization had developed into the kingdom of **Kush**. After defeat in warfare, Kush was under Egyptian rule for 500 years. Egyptian pharaohs stationed soldiers in Kush to collect duties on goods moving through the region.

The people of Kush used their location along the Upper Nile River to develop a strong trade economy. The Kushite cities of Napata and Meroë stood where trade caravans crossed the Nile, bringing gold, elephant tusks, and timber from the African interior. This strategic location brought wealth to the merchants and kings of Kush.

Around 1000 B.C. Kush broke away from Egypt and became politically independent. In time Kush grew strong enough that a Kushite king named **Piankhi** (pee•AHNK•hee) in 724 B.C. led a powerful army from Kush into Egypt and defeated the Egyptians. After this victory, Kushite kings ruled over both Egypt and Kush from their capital at Napata. The city boasted white sandstone temples, monuments, and pyramids fashioned in styles similar to those of the Egyptians.

In 671 B.C. the Assyrians invaded Egypt, easily defeating the Kushites, whose bronze weapons were no match against Assyrian iron swords. The Kushites were forced to leave Egypt and return to their home territory at the bend of the Upper Nile. In spite of their defeat, the Kushites learned from their enemies the technology of making iron. They built a new capital at Meroë that became a major center for iron production. Kush merchants traded iron, leopard skins, and ebony for goods from the Mediterranean and the Red Sea regions. They also conducted business throughout the Indian Ocean area. Meroë's merchants used their wealth to construct fine houses built around a central courtyard and public baths modeled after ones they had seen in Rome.

For about 150 years, the Kushite kingdom thrived. Then a new power—**Axum**, a kingdom located near the Red Sea—invaded Kush and ended Kushite domination of northeastern Africa.

Axum

Because of its location along the Red Sea, Axum also emerged as a trading power. During the 200s B.C., merchants from Egypt, Greece, Rome, Persia, and India sent ships laden with cotton cloth, brass, copper, and olive oil to Axum's main seaport at Adulis. Traders exchanged their goods for cargoes of ivory that the people of Axum hauled from Africa's interior.

Through trade Axum absorbed many elements of Roman culture, including a new religion:

Visualizing History Church of St. Mary of Zion. According to tradition, this church contains the original tablets of Moses, brought by King Menelik I to Axum. Menelik, the legendary founder of Axum's monarchy, was reputed to be the son of the Israelite king Solomon and the Arabian queen of Sheba. *How did Christianity come to Axum?*

Christianity. A remarkable event led to the conversion of Axum's King **Ezana** to Christianity. Shipwrecked off the coast of Ethiopia, two Christians from Syria were picked up and brought to King Ezana's court, where they lived for several years. The young men convinced Ezana that he should become a Christian. About A.D. 330 the king made Christianity the official religion in Axum. During this time, Christianity also became dominant in other areas of northeastern Africa—Kush and Egypt.

Axum declined after the rise of the religion of Islam during the A.D. 600s. Its Red Sea ports lost their importance as links to the Mediterranean world, and Axum's rulers—confined to the remote interior of East Africa—set up the Christian kingdom of Ethiopia.

South of the Sahara

Between 700 B.C. and 200 B.C., during Axum's rise to power, a West African culture called **the Nok** had already established itself in the fertile Niger and Benue River valleys. In the 1930s archaeologists working in present-day central Nigeria found terra-cotta, or baked clay, figurines that provided evidence of the Nok culture. Working in the Nok sites and other areas of West Africa, archaeologists also unearthed iron hoes and ax-heads. This latter discovery provided evidence that metal production had enabled African cultures south of the Sahara to farm their land more effectively.

As West African farmers used their iron tools to produce more food, the population increased. In time, arable land became scarce, causing widespread food shortages. Small groups of Africans began to migrate from West Africa to less populated areas. Other groups followed. Over about a thousand years a great migration took place.

Bantu Migrations

Historians call this mass movement the Bantu migrations because descendants of the people who migrated throughout the continent share elements of a language group known as Bantu. The Bantu migrations did not follow a single pattern. Some villagers followed the Niger or other rivers, settling in one spot to farm for a few years and moving on as the soil became less fertile. Other groups penetrated the rain forests and grew crops along the riverbanks. Still others moved to the highland savannas of East Africa and raised cattle. Groups that settled on the

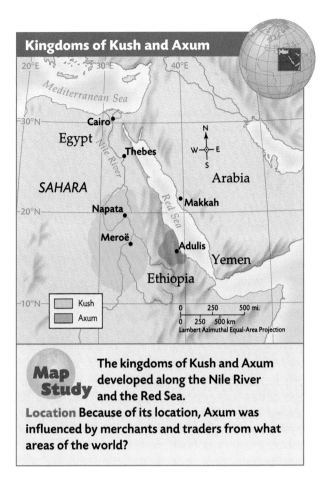

Kingdoms of Kush and Axum

Kush
Axum

0   250   500 mi.
0   250   500 km
Lambert Azimuthal Equal-Area Projection

Map Study The kingdoms of Kush and Axum developed along the Nile River and the Red Sea.

Location Because of its location, Axum was influenced by merchants and traders from what areas of the world?

eastern coastal plain grew new crops, such as bananas and yams that had been brought to East Africa by traders from Southeast Asia.

As people pushed into new areas, they met other African groups that adopted their ways of life. In time, Bantu-speaking peoples became the dominant group in Africa south of the Sahara.

Village Life

Africans who spoke Bantu languages became divided into hundreds of ethnic groups, each with its own religious beliefs, marriage and family customs, and traditions. Ethnic groups living around A.D. 1000 formed close-knit communities where most families were organized into large households that included descendants of one set of grandparents.

Many villages were matrilineal societies in which villagers traced their descent through mothers rather than through fathers. However, when a girl married, she became a member of her husband's family. To compensate the bride's family for the loss of a member, the husband's family gave the bride's family gifts of iron tools, goats, or cloth.

Even before marriage, specific jobs were assigned to groups of males and females of a similar

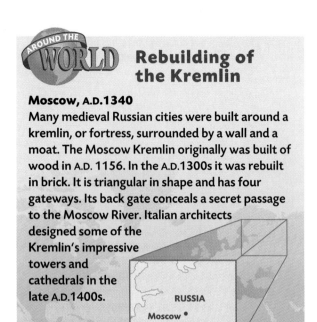

Around the World

Rebuilding of the Kremlin

Moscow, A.D.1340

Many medieval Russian cities were built around a kremlin, or fortress, surrounded by a wall and a moat. The Moscow Kremlin originally was built of wood in A.D. 1156. In the A.D.1300s it was rebuilt in brick. It is triangular in shape and has four gateways. Its back gate conceals a secret passage to the Moscow River. Italian architects designed some of the Kremlin's impressive towers and cathedrals in the late A.D.1400s.

RUSSIA

Moscow •

age, called age sets. Boys younger than 10 or 12 herded cattle; girls of the same age helped their mothers plant as well as tend and harvest crops. At about 12 years old, boys and girls took part in ceremonies initiating them into adulthood. A boy remained with his age set throughout his life. After marriage, a girl joined an age set in her husband's village.

Religious Beliefs

To most Africans, marriage customs and all other social laws and traditions were made by a single supreme god who created and ruled an orderly universe. The god rewarded those who followed social rules with abundant harvests and the birth of healthy children, and punished those who violated tradition with accidents, crop failures, or illness.

Beneath the supreme god were many lesser deities who influenced the daily affairs of men and women. These deities were present in natural phenomena such as storms, mountains, and trees.

Many Africans also believed that spirits of dead ancestors lived among the people of the village and guided their destiny.

The religious beliefs and family loyalties of most Africans maintained stability and support within villages. Most communities expected their members to obey the social rules they believed to have come from the supreme god.

Although African communities relied heavily on religious and family traditions to maintain a stable social structure, outside influences through trade and learning still affected them. North Africans absorbed influences from the Arab world, whereas African people south of the Sahara adapted to Persian, Indian, and later, European influences. From these outsiders, African communities adopted many new customs, ideas, and languages.

The Arts

Various arts developed throughout Bantu-speaking Africa. Sculpture was an important art form. African sculpture included figures, masks, decorated boxes, and objects for ceremonial and everyday use. Most of these items were made of wood, bronze, ivory, or baked clay. The wearing of masks at ceremonial dances symbolized the link between the living and the dead. Those wearing the masks and performing the dances called upon ancestral spirits to guide the community.

Music rich in rhythm was interwoven with the fabric of everyday African life. It included choral singing, music performed at royal courts, and songs and dances for ceremonies. In villages, where many activities were performed by groups, music often provided the motivation and rhythm for various tasks, such as digging ditches or pounding grain. African musicians used a variety of drums as well as harps, flutes, pipes, horns, and xylophones.

Early Africa excelled in oral literature passed down from one generation to another. The stories included histories, fables, and proverbs. Oral literature not only recorded the past but also taught traditions and values.

SECTION 1 REVIEW

Recall

1. **Define** oral tradition, plateau, savanna, matrilineal, age set.
2. **Identify** Sahel, Nubia, Kush, Piankhi, Axum, Ezana, the Nok, Bantu.
3. **Locate** the Nile River valley on

the map on page 187. Why did the Nubians settle in the Upper Nile Valley?

Critical Thinking

4. **Applying Information** Explain how Mediterranean trade influenced the economy

of the kingdom of Axum.

Understanding Themes

5. **Movement** How do the Bantu migrations in early Africa compare with the Aryan migrations in early South Asia?

A.D. 300 Ghana begins to build a trading empire.

c. A.D. 1275 Mali conquers surrounding territory.

A.D. 1493 Askia Muhammad begins rule in Songhai.

Section 2

Kingdoms in West Africa

Setting the Scene

▶ **Terms to Define**
monotheism, ghana, mosque

▶ **People to Meet**
Sundiata Keita, Mansa Musa, Askia Muhammad

▶ **Places to Locate**
Ghana, Mali, Timbuktu, Songhai

 ind Out   How was trade carried out in West Africa?

The Storyteller

The poets of Mali preserved the history of their people. Hear one speak: "I teach kings the history of their ancestors so that the lives of the ancients might serve them as an example, for the world is old, but the future springs from the past. My word is pure and free of all untruth…. Listen to my word, you who want to know, by my mouth, you will learn the history of Mali. By my mouth you will get to know the story of the ancestor of great Mali, the story of him who … surpassed even Alexander the Great…. Whoever knows the history of a country can read its future."

—from *Sundiata: An Epic of Old Mali* in *The Humanistic Tradition*, Gloria K. Fiero, 1992

Horn player, Benin

A diverse environment provided rich natural resources for the early kingdoms of West Africa. Africans living in this region between A.D. 300 and A.D. 1500 mined gold and other mineral resources. An active trade developed between them and peoples outside West Africa who practiced a religion called Islam. Islam preached monotheism, or the belief in one God, and spread throughout the Middle East, North Africa, and Spain during the A.D. 600s and A.D. 700s. Through their trade contacts with Muslims, the followers of Islam, African cultures gradually adopted Islamic cultural elements such as language and religion.

Kingdom of Ghana

The kingdom of **Ghana** became one of the richest trading civilizations in West Africa due to its location midway between Saharan salt mines and tropical gold mines. Between A.D. 300 and A.D. 1200 the kings of Ghana controlled a trading empire that stretched more than 100,000 square miles (260,000 sq. km). They prospered from the taxes they imposed on goods that entered or left their kingdom. Because the ghana, or king, ruled such a vast region, the land became known by the name of its ruler—Ghana.

There was two-way traffic by caravan between cities in North Africa and Ghana. Muslim traders from North Africa sent caravans loaded with cloth, metalware, swords, and salt across the western Sahara to northern settlements in Ghana. Large caravans from Ghana traveled north to Morocco, bringing kola nuts and farming produce. Ghanaian gold was traded for Saharan salt brought by Muslim traders.

Salt was an important trade item for the people of Ghana. They needed salt to preserve and flavor their foods. Using plentiful supplies of gold as a medium of exchange, Ghanaian merchants traded the precious metal for salt and other goods from Morocco and Spain.

Masudi, a Muslim traveler, writing about A.D. 950, described how trade was conducted:

> ❝ The merchants … place their wares and cloth on the ground and then depart, and so the people of [Ghana] come bearing gold which they leave beside the merchandise and then depart. The owners of the merchandise then return, and if they are satisfied with what they have found, they take it. If not, they go away again, and the people of [Ghana] return and add to the price until the bargain is concluded. ❞

Ghana reached the height of its economic and political power as a trading kingdom in the A.D. 800s and A.D. 900s. The salt and gold trade moving through Ghana brought Islamic ideas and customs to the kingdom. Muslim influence increased and many Ghanaians converted to Islam.

At the end of the A.D. 1000s, an attack on the Ghanaian trade centers by the Almoravids, a Muslim group from North Africa, led to the decline of Ghana as a prosperous kingdom. Groups of Ghanaians broke away to form many small Islamic states.

Kingdom of Mali

Mali, one of the small states to break away from Ghana, became a powerful kingdom that eventually ruled much of West Africa. The word *Mali* means "where the king resides" and is an appropriate name for a kingdom that gained much of its power and influence from its kings. **Sundiata Keita**, one of Mali's early kings, defeated his leading rival in A.D. 1235 and began to conquer surrounding territories. By the late A.D. 1200s, Mali's territory included the old kingdom of Ghana.

Images *of the* Times

Africa's Religious Heritage

Religion played a central role in the development of African cultures. Islam became the dominant religion in the north.

The Great Mosque at Timbuktu
Founded around A.D. 1100, the city of Timbuktu became a major center of trade and site of an important Islamic school.

Altar of the Hand, Benin
Beginning in the A.D. 1200s the kingdom of Benin emerged as a wealthy trading state. The *oba*, or king, became the political, economic, and spiritual leader of the people.

Sundiata worked to bring prosperity to his new empire. He restored the trans-Saharan trade in gold and salt that had been interrupted by the Almoravid attacks and he restored agricultural production. Sundiata ordered soldiers to clear large expanses of savanna and burn the grass that had been cleared to provide fertilizer for crops of peanuts, rice, sorghum, yams, beans, onions, and grains. With the benefit of rainfall, agriculture flourished in Mali. With larger tracts of land under cultivation, farmers produced surplus crops that Mali's kings collected as taxes.

Mali's greatest king was **Mansa Musa**, who ruled from A.D. 1312 to A.D. 1332. By opening trade routes and protecting trade caravans with a powerful standing army, Musa maintained the economic prosperity begun by Sundiata. He also introduced Islamic culture to Mali.

A Muslim himself, Musa enhanced the prestige and power of Mali through a famous pilgrimage to Makkah in A.D. 1324. Arab writers report that Musa traveled in grand style. He took with him 12,000 slaves, each dressed in silk or brocade and carrying bars of gold. Musa gave away so much gold on his journey that the world price of gold fell. At Makkah, Musa persuaded a Spanish architect to return with him to Mali. There the skilled architect built great mosques—Muslim houses of worship—and other fine buildings, including a palace for Musa in the capital of **Timbuktu** (TIHM•BUHK•TOO). Timbuktu became an important center of Muslim art and culture mainly through the efforts of Mansa Musa, who encouraged Muslim scholars to teach at his court. Two hundred years later, the North African scholar and traveler Hassan ibn Muhammad (known in the West as Leo Africanus) described Timbuktu's continuing intellectual brilliance:

“ Here are great store of doctors, judges, priests, and other learned men that are bountifully maintained at the king's cost and charges. And hither are brought diverse manuscripts or written books out of [North Africa], which are sold for more money than any other merchandise. ”

Terra-cotta heads, c. early 1600s, commemorate the deceased members of the royal family among the Akan peoples of southern Ghana.

REFLECTING ON THE TIMES

1. How did religion influence the arts and other aspects of culture in Africa?
2. In what ways did Africans honor royalty?

James L. Stanfield

West African Empire

This turreted mosque in Djenné, Mali, harks back to the A.D. 1300s, when the town thrived as a center of trade and Islamic learning. A masterpiece of African-Muslim architecture, the great mosque boasts massive mud ramparts broken by patterns of protruding beams. Its tall spires are crowned not with the traditional Islamic crescent but with ostrich eggs, symbol of fertility and fortune. Every year, after the rainy season, the town turns out 4,000 people to replaster the walls of the mosque with their bare hands. The job is done in a day.

Almost two centuries before Columbus set off for the Americas, an Arab traveler and author named Ibn Battuta began his travels in A.D. 1325 to the far corners of the Islamic world—from North Africa to China and back. He returned home three decades later as one of history's great travelers and travel writers. His journeys totaled 75,000 miles (121,000 km)— three times the distance logged by his European predecessor, Marco Polo. Ibn Battuta's final journey brought him here to the West African empire of Mali where he praised the piety of the Muslims. Battuta sought out the ruler, Mansa Sulayman, at his capital but was not impressed with the king's generosity. Mansa Sulayman, he wrote, "is a miserly king." Battuta also traveled to Timbuktu—about a hundred years before the city really started to prosper. At its height, in the A.D. 1500s, the city could boast three universities and perhaps 50,000 residents. ⊕

After Mansa Musa died in A.D. 1332, the empire came under attack by Berbers, a people living in the Sahara region to the north. They raided Mali and captured Timbuktu. From the south, warriors from the rain forest also attacked Mali. Inside the kingdom, people living in the **Songhai** region of the Niger River valley resented losing control over their region and rebelled against the empire. By the middle of the A.D. 1500s, Mali had split into several independent states.

Kingdom of Songhai

The rebellious Songhai, who were skilled traders, farmers, and fishers, were led by strong leaders. During the late A.D. 1400s their ruler, Sunni Ali, fought many territorial wars and managed to conquer the cities of Timbuktu and Djenné, expanding his empire to include most of the West African savanna. Sunni Ali was a Muslim ruler, but when he died, rule fell to his son, a non-Muslim. The Muslim population of Songhai overthrew Ali's son and brought a Muslim ruler to the throne.

Under the new ruler, **Askia Muhammad**, the Songhai Empire reached the height of its glory. Ruling from A.D. 1493 to A.D. 1528, Askia Muhammad divided Songhai into five huge provinces, each with a governor, a tax collector, a court of judges, and a trade inspector—very much like the government structure of China in the A.D. 1400s. The king maintained the peace and security of his realm with a cavalry and a navy. Timbuktu was a center of Muslim learning.

Devoted to Islam, Muhammad introduced laws based on the teachings of the holy book of Islam, the Quran (kuh•RAHN). Lesser crimes were sometimes overlooked, but those who committed major crimes such as robbery or idolatry received harsh punishments. Askia Muhammad appointed Muslim

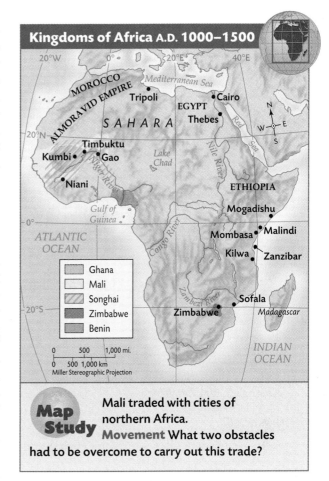

Kingdoms of Africa A.D. 1000–1500

Map legend:
Ghana
Mali
Songhai
Zimbabwe
Benin

0 500 1,000 mi.
0 500 1,000 km
Miller Stereographic Projection

Map Study Mali traded with cities of northern Africa.
Movement What two obstacles had to be overcome to carry out this trade?

judges, assuring that Islamic laws would be upheld.

In A.D. 1528 Askia Muhammad was overthrown by his son. A series of struggles for the throne followed, leading to a weakened central government. Around A.D. 1589 the rulers of Morocco sent an army across the Sahara to attack Songhai gold-trading centers. Moroccan soldiers, armed with guns and cannons, easily defeated the Songhai forces fighting with only swords, spears, and bows and arrows. By A.D. 1600 the Songhai Empire had come to an end.

SECTION 2 REVIEW

Recall
1. **Define** monotheism, ghana, mosque.
2. **Identify** the Almoravids, Sundiata Keita, Mansa Musa, Askia Muhammad.
3. **Locate** Timbuktu on the map on this page. How did Timbuktu become an important center of Islamic art and learning during the A.D. 1300s?

Critical Thinking
4. **Analyzing Information** Why was trade vital to the economies of the West African kingdoms?

Understanding Themes
5. **Cultural Diffusion** What goods were traded, and how did trade between West Africa and the Islamic world influence the development of West African cultures between A.D. 900 and A.D. 1500?

A.D. 900 Arab and Persian merchants trade in East Africa.

c. A.D. 1200 Kilwa thrives as East African coastal city-state.

c. A.D. 1300 People of Karanga build stone-walled fortresses.

Section 3

African Trading Cities and States

Setting the Scene

▶ **Terms to Define**
monopoly, multicultural

▶ **Places to Locate**
Kilwa, Malindi, Mombasa, Sofala, Zanzibar, Karanga, Great Zimbabwe

 **Find Out** How did areas in East, Central, and Southern Africa develop as a result of inland and overseas trade?

The Storyteller

The first trained engineer ever to see the ruins of the Great Zimbabwe reported: "For fifty miles I saw the ruins…. The ruins are principally terraces, which rise up continually from the base to the apex of all the hills…. The terraces are all made very flat and of dry masonry…. The way the ancients seem to have levelled off the contours of the various hills around which the water courses are laid is very astonishing, as they seem to have been levelled with as much exactitude as we can accomplish with our best mathematical instruments."

Ruins of the Great Zimbabwe

—from *The Mystery of the Great Zimbabwe,* Wilfrid Mallows, 1984

*D*uring the same time that West African kings ruled their empires, important trading communities developed along the coast of East Africa and in the interior of Central and Southern Africa. Inland African kingdoms mined copper and iron ore and traded these minerals and ivory with city-states that had developed along the East African coast. There Muslim traders brought cotton, silk, and Chinese porcelain from India and Southeast Asia to exchange for the products from Africa's interior. As in West Africa, trade contacts with the Muslim world enabled East African coastal areas to adopt the religion of Islam and Islamic cultural practices.

East Africa

As early as 500 B.C., coastal areas of East Africa were trading with the Arabian Peninsula and South Asia. Using dhows (Arab sailboats), East Africans sailed with the monsoon winds across the stretch of Indian Ocean separating Africa from India. By the A.D. 900s Arab and Persian merchants had settled on the East African coast and controlled the trade there. Traders from the interior of Africa brought ivory, gold, iron, and rhinoceros horn to the east coast to trade for Indian cloth and Chinese porcelain.

Coastal City-States

By A.D. 1200 small East African trading settlements had become thriving city-states taxing the goods that passed through their ports. The port of **Kilwa** had a virtual monopoly, or sole control or ownership, of the gold trade with the interior. **Malindi** and **Mombasa**, both ports farther north on the coast, were also important centers, as was **Sofala**, a port in what is present-day Mozambique. The iron mined in the surroundings of these three city-states was widely used in the Arabian Peninsula and South Asia.

The island of **Zanzibar** was also an important center of trade. Sailors from the islands of Southeast Asia as well as India and China came to Zanzibar in search of ivory and gold, which was brought to Zanzibar ports from the coastal city-states of East Africa.

Blending of Cultures

By the A.D. 1300s, the city-states of East Africa had reached the height of their prosperity. They had become truly multicultural centers—populated by a variety of cultural groups. Within each city-state, Islamic and African cultures blended. For the most part, Arab and Persian merchants ruled the trading states. They converted many Africans to Islam.

Arab merchants married local women who had converted to Islam. Families having members with African and Islamic cultural backgrounds began speaking Swahili, a Bantu language that included Arabic and Persian words. The people of the East African coastal city-states also developed an Arabic form of writing that enabled them to record their history.

East African rulers were either Arab governors or African chieftains. They used coral from Indian Ocean reefs to build mosques, palaces, and forts.

The Bantu Kingdoms

The Indian Ocean trade was not limited to the coastal trading states. It reached far inland, contributing to the rise of wealthy Bantu kingdoms in Central and Southern Africa. The inland kingdoms mined rich deposits of copper and gold. During the A.D. 900s, traders from the East African coast made their way to the inland mining communities in Central Africa and began an active trade among the people living there. The traders brought silk and porcelain from China, glass beads from India, carpets from Arab lands, and fine pottery from Persia. They traded these goods for minerals, ivory, and coconut oil. They also acquired enslaved Africans for export.

Great Zimbabwe

The people of **Karanga**, a Bantu kingdom located on a high plateau between the Zambezi and Limpopo Rivers, built nearly 300 stone-walled fortresses throughout their territory between A.D.

East African Trading Cities

In the A.D. 700s Arab immigrants arrived on East Africa's coast to set up a flourishing trade in gold, ivory, and tortoise shells. Descendants of the Arab immigrants and the local African inhabitants became known as the Swahili (an Arabic word for "people of the coast"). By the late A.D. 1100s, thriving Swahili port cities, such as Kilwa, Malindi, and Mombasa, served as trading links between the gold and ivory producers of East Africa's interior and traders from India, Ceylon (Sri Lanka), and China. Cotton, porcelain, and pottery were the major imports. By the 1500s China's withdrawal from foreign trade and the coming of European rule to East Africa contributed to a serious decline in East Africa's international trade.

Today, the East African coast has become an important link in the global trading network. While preserving its old town and traditions, the modern city of Mombasa ranks as one of Africa's busiest seaports and the second-largest city in the nation of Kenya. It handles most of the international shipping of Kenya as well as that of the neighboring, land-locked nations of Uganda, Rwanda, and Burundi, to which it is linked by rail. East African agricultural products, such as coffee, tea, sisal (a plant fiber used for twine), cotton, sugar, and coconuts are exported from Mombasa, as well as petroleum products produced from the foreign oil refined at Mombasa's refinery.

Port of Mombasa, Kenya

 **ACTIVITY**

Compare and contrast Mombasa's trade in the A.D. 1200s with that of the city today. What factors have contributed to any changes?

Visualizing History This view shows the circular stone ruins of the Great Zimbabwe with an exterior wall more than 800 feet in circumference.

What functions did this "stone house" serve?

1000 and A.D. 1500. The largest was called the **Great Zimbabwe**—meaning "stone house"—and served as the political and religious center of the kingdom. The oval stone wall of the Zimbabwe enclosure was 30 feet (9.15 m) high. Within the wall was a maze of interior walls and hidden passages that protected the circular house of the Zimbabwe chief. Near the house, archaeologists have uncovered a platform with several upright stones that may have been the place where the chief held court.

Territorial Divisions

For nearly five centuries, Karanga and the other Bantu states grew wealthy from their control of the chief routes between the gold mines and the sea. However, during the A.D. 1400s, Bantu states in Southern Africa struggled in civil wars that brought disorder to the kingdoms and disrupted trade.

The Changamire Empire became stronger than the Monomotapa Empire. Changamire rulers took over Great Zimbabwe and built the fortress's largest structures. At the same time, European explorers arrived along the African coasts. Eager to control the sources of gold, ivory, and copper, the Europeans threatened the survival of the African civilizations in the continent's interior.

SECTION 3 REVIEW

Recall
1. **Define** monopoly, multicultural.
2. **Identify** Kilwa, Malindi, Mombasa, Sofala, Zanzibar, Karanga, Great Zimbabwe.
3. **Explain** why the Bantu kingdoms of Central and Southern Africa prospered.

Critical Thinking
4. **Synthesizing Information** Imagine that you are an Arab merchant visiting an East African coastal city-state in the A.D. 1300s. What aspects of the people's culture would be familiar to you? What parts might seem different?

Understanding Themes
5. **Innovation** What new aspect of cultural life developed in the city-states of East Africa as a result of African and Middle Eastern contacts?

Interpreting Point of View

Suppose you are interested in seeing a new science fiction movie, but you are hearing mixed reviews from your friends. Opinions range from "terrific" to "boring." People often have different opinions about the same people, events, or issues because they look at them from different points of view.

Learning the Skill

A point of view is a set of beliefs and values that affects a person's opinion. Many factors affect an individual's point of view, including age, sex, racial or ethnic background, economic class, and religion. In order to determine the accuracy of a description or the objectivity of an argument, first you must identify the speaker's point of view.

To interpret point of view in written material, read the material to identify the general subject. Then gather background information on that author that might reveal his or her point of view. Identify aspects of the topic that the author chooses to emphasize or exclude. Look for emotionally charged words such as *cruel, vicious, heartrending, drastic.* Also notice metaphors and analogies that imply an opinion such as, "If this budget can work, then pigs can fly."

If you are uncertain of an author's point of view, read a selection on the same topic by another author with a different background. By comparing works on the same subject, both points of view may become clear. This may not always be an easy task.

Practicing the Skill

Read the following excerpt from Ross E. Dunn's book *The Adventures of Ibn Battuta* and then answer these questions.

1. What is the general subject of the excerpt?
2. What do you know about Ibn Battuta that might reveal his point of view?
3. What emotionally charged words and phrases indicate his point of view?
4. Which aspects of Islamic leadership are praised and which are not?

66 Sulayman came close to matching his brother's [Mansa Musa's] reputation for Islamic leadership and piety. Moreover, he ruled Mali in prosperity and peace. He was the sort of king from whom Ibn Battuta had come to expect an honorable and large-hearted reception. . . . Later, when Ibn Battuta had returned to his house, one of the scholars called to tell him that the sultan [Sulayman] had sent along the requisite welcoming gift.

'I got up, thinking that it would be robes of honor and money, but behold! It was three loaves of bread and a piece of beef fried in *gharti* [shea butter] and a gourd containing yoghurt. When I saw it I laughed, and was long astonished at their feeble intellect and their respect for mean things.' 99

According to Dunn, Ibn Battuta found Sulayman to be "a miserly king from whom no great donation is to be expected," while Mansa Musa had been "generous and virtuous."

Applying the Skill

In a newspaper, find an editorial, column, or a letter to the editor that expresses a point of view that conflicts with your own. Write a brief paragraph analyzing the author's point of view and compare it to your point of view. Explain why you agree or disagree with the viewpoint of the author.

The Columbus Dispatch
An Independent Newspaper Serving Ohio Since July 1, 1871
JOHN F. WOLFE, Publisher, President and CEO
MICHAEL F. CURTIN, Editor
EDITORIALS
Ballot issue
Workers' comp to steal thunder from schools

For More Practice

Turn to the Skill Practice in the Chapter Review on page 199 for more practice in interpreting point of view.

Connections Across Time

Historical Significance Throughout the early history of Africa, civilizations developed religious beliefs, agriculture, and trade networks in harmony with their environment. Some African peoples mined gold, iron, and other minerals from the land and then turned the raw ores into trade items. Others grew surplus crops to sell at local markets.

Trade networks brought Africa, Europe, the Middle East, South Asia, and East Asia into contact with each other and encouraged the exchange of ideas and practices. This set the stage for the later development of global trading links.

Using Key Terms

Write the key term that completes each sentence. Then write a sentence for each term not chosen.

a. multicultural
b. matrilineal
c. plateau
d. savanna
e. ghana

f. oral traditions
g. monopoly
h. age sets
i. monotheism
j. mosque

1. Africa south of the Sahara includes a large central _____—a relatively high, flat area called the Sahel.
2. Early African peoples communicated knowledge about their culture through _____ —legends and history passed by word of mouth from one generation to another.
3. Much of Africa's landscape is covered by ____, or treeless grasslands.
4. The city-state of Kilwa had a near _____, or sole control, of the gold trade along the East African coast.
5. A society is said to be _____ when it has people of many different cultural backgrounds.

Technology Activity

Using a Computerized Card Catalog Choose a modern-day African country to research. Use a computerized card catalog to find information on that country from its early history to the present. Then create a bulletin board about that country, including an illustrated time line of significant events of the country's history. Display current information about culture, national resources, demographics, and government.

Using Your History Journal

On your map of Africa draw in the modern states where each ancient kingdom that you identified was located. Use the map of Africa in the Atlas of your text.

Reviewing the Facts

1. **Geography** List the five major regions of Africa.
2. **History** Discuss how archaeologists and historians have learned about early Africa.
3. **Culture** Identify the Nok people, their location, and their major cultural achievements.
4. **Economics** Explain Ghana's wealth.
5. **History** Summarize the major accomplishments of Mansa Musa in Mali.
6. **Culture** Name the city that became a major center of trade and learning in Mali.
7. **Government** Explain how Askia Muhammad kept order and control over his huge empire.
8. **Economics** List the products traded in the coastal city-states of East Africa.
9. **Culture** State how the language of Swahili originated.
10. **Geography** Name the three areas of Africa that prospered from the Indian Ocean trade.
11. **Culture** Identify Great Zimbabwe and discuss its importance to Karanga.

Critical Thinking

1. **Apply** How do climate and geography affect the development of a civilization?

2. **Evaluate** The Bantu languages changed as people moved into central, eastern, and southern regions of Africa. Why do you think this happened?

3. **Making Comparisons** Compare the causes for the decline of each of the three West African kingdoms.

4. **Synthesize** Discuss how family and social life in a typical Bantu-speaking village was organized around A.D. 1000.

5. **Analyze** What two cultural values does this artifact of a West African horn player reveal?

Horn player, Benin

Understanding Themes

1. **Movement** How did population movements affect the development of early Africa?

2. **Cultural Diffusion** What were major political and cultural developments in each of the following early African territories: Nubia, Axum, Songhai, Kilwa, and Karanga?

3. **Innovation** What two examples can you give that illustrate how the peoples of coastal East Africa and of the interior of Central Africa and Southern Africa made creative use of their resources?

Linking Past *and* Present

1. Gold helped make Ghana a powerful empire. Name another natural resource that has made African countries wealthy today.

2. Ancient peoples adapted to their environments in order to survive. Explain ways we adapt today.

3. How do strong central governments affect a nation's economic and social structures? What factors often lead to a weakening of central governments?

Skill Practice

Read the following African proverbs carefully. Then answer the questions for each proverb.

- Familiarity breeds contempt; distance breeds respect.
- When you follow in the path of your father, you learn to walk like him.

1. What is the general subject of each proverb?
2. Describe the point of view expressed in each proverb.
3. Do you agree with the point of view? Make sure you are able to support your answer.

Geography in History

1. How does the continent of Africa compare with the United States in land area?
2. Refer to the map below. Why has communication and travel always been difficult between the northwest African interior and northeast Africa?
3. Why has Egypt had nearly continual contact with peoples of Asia and Europe?

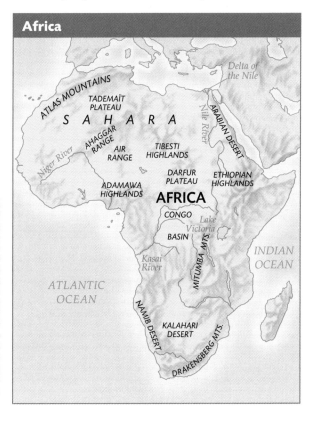

Africa

India's Great Civilization

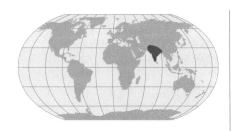

Chapter Themes

▶ **Movement** Aryans invade the Indian subcontinent and bring new ideas and practices. *Section 1*
▶ **Innovation** Hinduism and Buddhism emerge and become the dominant religions in much of Asia. *Section 2*
▶ **Cultural Diffusion** Mauryan and Gupta rulers bring unity to northern India and encourage cultural achievements. *Section 3*

The Storyteller

The Mahabharata, *an epic poem of ancient India, relates an amazing event. A battle raged, but the prince Arjuna did not want to fight. After all, among his foes were relatives. Arjuna took his case to the god Krishna: "O Krishna, when I see my own people ... eager for battle, my limbs shudder, my mouth is dry, my body shivers, and my hair stands on end.... I can see no good in killing my own kinsmen."*

Krishna answered, "As a [warrior], your duty is to fight a righteous battle.... Arise, O Arjuna, and be determined to fight. Get ready for battle without thought of pleasure and pain, gain and loss, victory and defeat."

As a warrior, Arjuna understood Krishna's words. A warrior must fight. It was his duty.

Historical Significance

What were the achievements of India's early civilization? What religions emerged from early India that have shaped the cultures of Asia and, in many ways, the rest of the world?

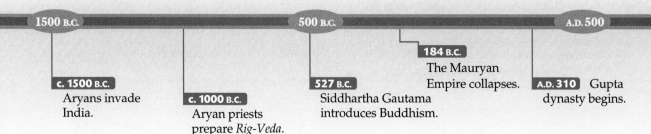

1500 B.C.	500 B.C.		A.D. 500
		184 B.C. The Mauryan Empire collapses.	
c. 1500 B.C. Aryans invade India.	**c. 1000 B.C.** Aryan priests prepare *Rig-Veda*.	**527 B.C.** Siddhartha Gautama introduces Buddhism.	**A.D. 310** Gupta dynasty begins.

Visualizing History Hindus communicated their beliefs through poems, tales, songs, and art. This painting of Vishnu on a bird honors one of the three main gods of Hinduism.

Your History Journal

Using a recent edition of an almanac, make a chart of the world's major religions, including the number of people who today are adherents of each religion.

c. 1200 B.C.
Vedic Age begins.

c. 1000 B.C.
Rig-Veda records
Aryan legends.

c. 700 B.C.
Religious thinkers
compile the *Upanishads.*

Section 1

Origins of Hindu India

Setting the Scene

▶ **Terms to Define**
rajah, epic, *varna*, *jati*, dharma, reincarnation, karma, ahimsa

▶ **People to Meet**
the Aryans

▶ **Places to Locate**
Hindu Kush, Ganges Plain

**ind Out** How did the cultures of the Aryans and the peoples they conquered develop into the culture of Hindu India?

The Storyteller

The bleeding warrior lay helpless with a broken arm. Only proper words and medicines could save him now. The priest, sprinkling him with water and herbs chanted: "He who drinks you, medicine, lives. Save the man. You are mender of wounds inflicted by club, arrow, or flame. Mend this man. O most beautiful one, go to the fracture." Next would come the grass and termite mud mixture to drink, then water in a cow's horn, and
pepper-corns to eat. The warrior breathed quietly, thankful that he had found a healer who knew the ritual.

—adapted from *Religious Healing in the Veda,*
Kenneth Zysk, 1985

Hindu Kush

Into the Indus River valley raced horse-drawn chariots carrying tall, light-skinned warriors. These warriors, known as **the Aryans**, were an Indo-European group from areas north of the Black and Caspian Seas. The invasion began around 1500 B.C. For several generations, waves of Aryans swept through passes in the mountains known as the **Hindu Kush** into the Indus River valley and from there into northern India.

Aryans

After conquering the people of the Indus River valley, the Aryans moved southeast into the **Ganges Plain**. There they subdued the local inhabitants and developed a new civilization that eventually spread over much of South Asia. Aspects of this civilization endure today.

Ways of Life

The Aryans were loosely organized into tribes of nomadic herders. Each tribe was led by a rajah, or chief. Ancient Aryan legends and hymns describe people who delighted in waging war, gambling on chariot races, and singing and dancing at festivals. Cattle were the basis of their diet and economy, even serving as money. Wealth was measured in cattle, and so the Aryans raided each other's herds. They were often at war.

The fertile Indus Valley was ideal for farming, and the Aryans soon settled down into an agricultural way of life. Dozens of Aryan words describe cattle, indicating their continued prominence in Aryan life. Cattle provided meat, fresh milk, and ghee, or liquid butter. The Aryans also hunted game and butchered sheep and goats from their herds. Later, their herds would be considered so sacred that a ban was placed on eating meat. The

Aryans also ate cucumbers, bananas, and barley cakes.

Men dominated the Aryan world. Although a woman had some say in choosing a husband, the man she married expected no challenge to his authority. Even so, women took part in religious ceremonies and social affairs, and they were allowed to remarry if they were widowed—freedoms they would lose in the centuries to come. Both girls and boys from families of high rank attended school, where they learned Aryan traditions.

Language and Traditions

As a nomadic people, the Aryans had no written language. Sanskrit, their spoken language, evolved slowly and became one of the major languages of India. As part of the great Indo-European language family, Sanskrit has many of the same root words as English, Spanish, French, and German. It also includes many words from the languages of the peoples living in India before the Aryan invasions.

The Aryan warrior-herders sang rousing hymns and recited epics, long poems celebrating their heroes. For centuries these hymns and poems were passed by word of mouth from generation to generation. Families of warriors and priests were responsible for preserving this oral heritage. Over and over they repeated the legends, striving for complete accuracy.

Eventually, the Aryans developed a written form of Sanskrit. Priests collected the hymns, poems, legends, and religious rituals into holy books known as Vedas (VAY•duhz), or "Books of Knowledge," which formed the basis of Aryan religious practices.

Indeed, the Vedas are extremely valuable sources of knowledge, for without them historians would know little about the Aryans. Unlike the Indus River valley people, the Aryans left no artifacts or structures. Whatever we know of their life and culture we know from the Vedas. Indeed, Indian history from 1200 B.C. to 500 B.C. is known as the Vedic Age. The oldest of the four Vedas, the *Rig-Veda*, dates from around 1000 B.C. It records legends that tell us about Aryan life. The *Rig-Veda* is one of the world's oldest religious texts still in use.

Social Structure

The Vedas reveal the complex social system of ancient India. The invading Aryans brought a system of four main social classes, or *varnas*. At first the warriors, called Kshatriyas (KSHA•tree•uhz), were the most honored *varna*. They were followed by the priests, or Brahmans; merchants, artisans, and farmers, called Vaisyas (VYSH•yuhz); and

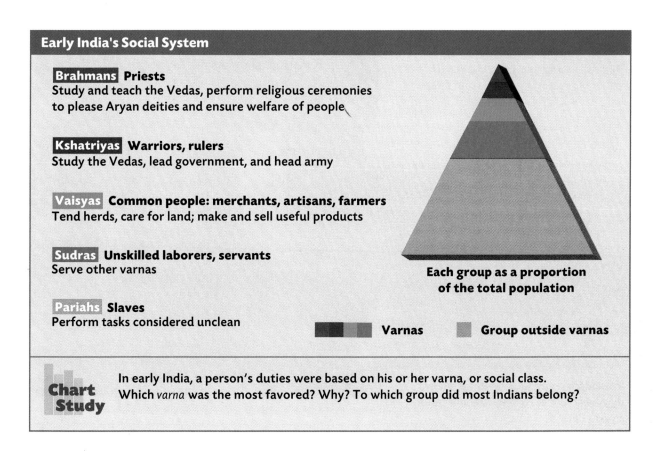

Early India's Social System

Brahmans Priests
Study and teach the Vedas, perform religious ceremonies to please Aryan deities and ensure welfare of people

Kshatriyas Warriors, rulers
Study the Vedas, lead government, and head army

Vaisyas Common people: merchants, artisans, farmers
Tend herds, care for land; make and sell useful products

Sudras Unskilled laborers, servants
Serve other varnas

Pariahs Slaves
Perform tasks considered unclean

Each group as a proportion of the total population

■ Varnas   ■ Group outside varnas

Chart Study In early India, a person's duties were based on his or her varna, or social class. Which *varna* was the most favored? Why? To which group did most Indians belong?

unskilled laborers and servants, known as Sudras (SHOO•druhz).

Only priests and warrior families were allowed to hear and recite the Vedas. Over the years, rituals grew more secret and complex, and priests replaced warriors as the most honored members of society. The priests alone knew how to make sacrifices properly and to repeat the appropriate hymns. The social system changed to reflect the importance of priests.

Each *varna* had its own duties and took pride in doing them well. The Brahmans performed the elaborate rituals and studied the Vedas; only they could teach the Vedas. As warriors, Kshatriyas took charge of the army and the government. They led the councils of elders who ran small villages. Kshatriyas could study the Vedas but were not allowed to teach them. Vaisyas had the important tasks of tending the cattle, lending money, trading goods, and caring for the land. The Sudras' job was to serve the other varnas. They worked in the fields and acted as servants.

By 500 B.C. the division among the four *varnas* had become more rigid. Varnas were divided into smaller groups known as *jati*. Jati were formed according to occupations: shoemakers, potters, farmers, and so on. Priests were higher than cultivators, and cultivators were higher than carpenters, for example. *Jati* had their own rules for diet, marriage, and social customs. Groups lived in separate neighborhoods and did not mix socially with others.

Centuries later, Europeans named the Indian system of *varnas* and *jati* the caste system. The word *caste* has no one definition, but how it worked is clear. Within the system people were always ranked. They were born into a group, and that group could not be changed. People married within their own group. Moreover, that group determined a great deal about people's everyday lives. Members of the group lived in the same neighborhoods and did not mix socially with those outside.

Outside the system of *varnas* and *jati* were a group later called the pariahs. They did work that

Images
of the Times

Hindu Beliefs

The three main gods of Hinduism are Brahma, Vishnu, and Siva. Brahma is creator of the world, Vishnu is preserver, and Siva is destroyer. These three are part of the same universal spirit.

Meeting to read holy writings such as the *Mahabharata* is a long-standing custom among Hindus in India.

was considered unclean, such as skinning animals and tanning their hides for leather. Sometimes called "outcastes" or "untouchables," the pariahs lived outside the villages and were shunned by most other people.

Concept of Duty

The Vedas outlined the dharma, or duties, of the males who belonged to each *varna*. Members of each *varna* were urged to do their duty. The epic poem called the *Mahabharata* (muh•HAH•BAH•ruh•tuh) makes the concept clear. One eloquent section, called the *Bhagavad Gita* (BAH•guh•VAHD GEE•tuh), or "Song of the Lord," includes the story you read at the beginning of this chapter. Arjuna's decision—to fight no matter what the personal cost—illustrates the importance of dharma in Indian life. As a warrior, Arjuna had to do his duty, even if it meant fighting against family.

The concept of dharma included doing what was proper for one's age. For instance, a male student would follow an occupation that was appropriate for his class. He then took a wife, and assumed responsibility for a family. In old age, he retired. As he neared death, he withdrew from his friends and family to pray. A woman was educated in household tasks. She married and served her husband and family until he died or retired, at which time she was expected to retire from active life and be taken care of by her sons and daughters-in-law. This concept of duty affected every member of society.

India's Two Epics

Two epics addressed the concepts of good and evil and became the spiritual forebears of India's main religions. The tale of Arjuna is a small part of the *Mahabharata*, which is 100,000 verses in length—as long as the first five books of the Bible. The epic—like the Bible—is a collection of writings by several authors. Some characters are historical, while others represent human ideals and various deities. Woven into the story of two families' struggle for power are discussions of religion and philosophy.

Much of India's fine art is related to its religions. Hindus built elaborate temples, such as this Mehsana Sun Temple (interior shown).

This sculpture of Ganesha, god of good fortune and auspicious beginnings, was done in the A.D. 1700s.

REFLECTING ON THE TIMES

1. How did Hinduism contribute to the development of fine art in India?
2. What epic describes the concept of duty that affects every member of Hindu society?

One passage tells of how the need for a king arose when dharma no longer guided people in everyday life:

> 66 Bhishma said: … Neither kingship nor king was there in the beginning, neither scepter nor the bearer of the scepter. All people protected one another by means of righteous conduct (dharma). Thus, while protecting one another by means of righteous conduct, O Bharata, men eventually fell into a state of spiritual lassitude [weariness]. Then delusion overcame them … their sense of righteous conduct was lost. When understanding was lost, all men … became victims of greed. 99

Later, the God Vishnu chooses "… that one person among mortals who alone is worthy of high eminence." A man named Virajas is brought forth, and he becomes the first king.

A second epic, the well-loved *Ramayana*, grew to 24,000 verses before it was written down. It presents the moving tale of Rama and Sita (SEE•tuh). Rama was the ideal king; Sita, his faithful wife. Vividly describing the struggle between good and evil, the *Ramayana* tells how the demon Ravana captures Sita. When Rama finds that she is missing, he cries:

> 66 Sita! Gentle Sita! If you have wanted to prove my love, if you are hiding from us, let the agony of my fear suffice. Come to me, my love, come to me!"
>
> He stood there, both his arms held wide, as though half hoping she might run forward to his embrace. The country lay very still around him. Only the old tree shivered in every leafy spray and seemed to wring its hands for pity.
>
> Slowly that gleam of hope quite faded, and his arms fell to his sides. 99

Rama at first doubts Sita; but later she is saved, and they reunite. Like other Indian epics, the *Ramayana* ends with good winning over evil.

Hinduism

The Aryan conquerors believed in many deities and thought their gods and goddesses had power over the forces of nature. They worshiped Agni, the god of fire; Indra, the god of thunder and war; and Usha, the goddess of dawn. Aryan priests created elaborate rituals and offered sacrifices to appease the gods and win their favor.

Over the centuries, as political and social organizations evolved, the Aryan religion slowly changed into Hinduism and became the national religion of India.

Universal Spirit

Hinduism was not founded on the teachings of one person, nor did it have one holy book. Instead it was based on different beliefs and practices, many of which had their roots in the Vedas and the Indian epics. As a result, Hinduism became a complex religion of many deities. Three gods, however, eventually emerged as the most important: Brahma, the Creator; Vishnu, the Preserver; and Siva, the Destroyer.

Other ideas that became part of Hinduism came from religious thinkers who looked for a single religious truth behind the many Hindu deities and rituals. Between 800 B.C. and 400 B.C., their personal searches and philosophies were reflected in the religious writings known as the *Upanishads* (oo•PAH•nih•SHAHDZ).

The *Upanishads* tell of a universal spirit present within all life, "a light that shines beyond all things on earth." According to these writings, all living things—including gods, humans, and animals—have souls. All souls, say the *Upanishads*, are part of the one eternal spirit, sometimes called Brahman Nerguna. Their bodies tie them to the material world, but only for a short time. To know true freedom, a soul must be separated from the material world and united with Brahman Nerguna: "As a lump of salt thrown in water dissolves, and cannot be taken out again as salt, though wherever we taste the water it is salt."

The authors of the *Upanishads* taught that forms of self-denial such as fasting helped people achieve union with the universal spirit. They encouraged the practice of yoga, a discipline that combines physical and mental exercises designed to help one achieve a state of tranquility.

Cycle of Rebirth

Another idea that came from the *Upanishads* was that of reincarnation, or the rebirth of the soul. Hindus believe the soul passes through many lifetimes before it finally achieves union with the universal spirit. The *Upanishads* offer this picture of rebirth:

> 66 As a caterpillar, having reached the end of a blade of grass, takes hold of another blade, then draws its body from the first,

so the Self, having reached the end of his body, takes hold of another body, then draws itself from the first. **99**

The cycle of rebirth is determined by a principle called karma. According to this principle, how a person lives his or her life determines what form the person will take in the next life. To move toward the universal spirit, one must live a good life and fulfill one's dharma. For example, a conscientious diplomat, a Kshatriya, might be reborn as a Brahman. The souls of those who fail to fulfill their dharma, however, might be reborn in a lower *varna*, or perhaps even as snakes or insects.

The concept of karma creates the desire to live a good life, for "By good deeds a man becomes what is good, by evil deeds what is bad." Out of that desire arose the practice of nonviolence toward all living things—still important to Hindus today. Called ahimsa (uh•HIHM•SAH), this practice requires the believer to protect humans, animals, and even insects and plants.

The cycle of reincarnation continues until a person reaches spiritual perfection. The ultimate aim of life is *moksha*, or release from the pain and suffering of rebirth after rebirth. In *moksha* a person finds freedom from reincarnation in a state of complete oneness with Brahman Nerguna. Hindus teach that a life committed to prayer, religious rituals, strict self-denial, and rejection of all worldly possessions will help a person to achieve the final goal of *moksha*.

Jainism

As Hinduism evolved, many holy people stressed different aspects of Hindu belief and practice. The teacher Mahavira (muh•hah•VEE•ruh) placed a special emphasis on the practice of ahimsa. Born a noble in northern India, Mahavira gave up his wealthy lifestyle and traveled for many years throughout the country. About 500 B.C. Mahavira founded Jainism, a new religion that rejected sacrifices and rigid Hindu social divisions. Believing in

History & Art Siva, ringed by a circle of flames, dances on the back of the dwarf Apasmara. *Why do Hindus regard animals as sacred?*

the sacredness of all life, the Jains, as Mahavira's followers were called, used brooms to sweep aside insects so they would not step on them. They refused to farm for fear of plowing under living things. Instead, they turned to commerce and gained great wealth and influence.

SECTION 1 REVIEW

Recall
1. **Define** rajah, epic, *varna, jati,* dharma, reincarnation, karma, ahimsa.
2. **Identify** the Aryans, Sanskrit, Vedas, *Mahabharata, Bhagavad Gita, Ramayana,* Hinduism, *Upanishads.*
3. **Explain** how geography affected the life of the Aryan groups that invaded India.

Critical Thinking
4. **Applying Information** Illustrate the Hindu concept of dharma by telling the story of the warrior-prince Arjuna.

Understanding Themes
5. **Movement** How did the Aryan invasion beginning about 1500 B.C. affect the development of Indian culture?

600 B.C.   550 B.C.   500 B.C.

c. 566 B.C.   c. 540 B.C.   c. 500 B.C.   Gautama
Siddhartha   Gautama begins   (the Buddha) dies.
Gautama is born.   spiritual search.

Section 2

Rise of Buddhism

Setting the Scene

▶ **Terms to Define**
   nirvana, stupa

▶ **People to Meet**
   Siddhartha Gautama

Find Out Why did Buddhism appeal to many people in India, Southeast Asia, and East Asia?

The Storyteller

Siddhartha stood still, as if a snake lay in his path. Suddenly the icy thought stole over him: he must begin his life completely afresh. "I am no longer what I was, … I am no longer a hermit, no longer a priest, no longer a Brahmin. How can I return home? What would I do at home with my father? Study? Offer sacrifices? Practice meditation? All this is over for me now." He realized how alone he was. Now he was Siddhartha, the awakened. He must begin his life afresh. He began to walk quickly, no longer homewards, no longer looking back.

—from *Siddhartha*, Herman Hesse, translated by Hilda Rosner, 1957

Gautama, the Buddha

During the 500s B.C., changes occurred in Indian religious life. Many devout Hindus became dissatisfied with external rituals and wanted a more spiritual faith. They left the towns and villages and looked for solitude in the hills and forests. Through meditation, many of these religious seekers developed new insights and became religious teachers. Their ideas and practices often led to the rise of new religions. The most influential of the new religions was Buddhism.

The Buddha

Siddhartha Gautama (sih•DAHR•tuh GOW •tuh•muh), the founder of Buddhism, began his life as a Kshatriya prince. Born around 566 B.C., Gautama was raised in luxury. As a young man he continued to live a sheltered life, shielded from sickness and poverty. Tradition states that one day Gautama's charioteer drove him around his estates, and for the first time Gautama saw sickness, old age, and death. Shocked at these scenes of misery, Gautama decided to find out why people suffered and how suffering could be ended. Around the age of 29, he left his wife and newborn son and wandered throughout India.

For seven years Gautama lived as a hermit, seeking the truth through fasting and self-denial. This did not lead him to the truth, however. One day, while meditating under a tree, Gautama gained a flash of insight that he felt gave him an answer to the problem of suffering. He began to share with others the meaning of his "enlightenment." Dressed in a yellow robe, he preached his message to people and began to gather followers. His closest friends began calling him the Buddha, or "Enlightened One."

Rajesh Bedi

The Buddha's First Sermon

From this stupa, or domed shrine, in Isipatana, a village in northern India, the Buddha is said to have delivered his first sermon. Once a small village, Isipatana is now Sarnath, a suburb of the city of Varanasi. Here, Buddhists believe, in the 500s B.C. the Buddha delivered his first sermon to five followers. A large monastery, which once housed 1,500 monks, was founded on this sacred spot. Today the shrine stands empty.

The Buddha began India's second religion, after the far older Hindu religion had become entrenched. He lived in a unique moment of history. The 500s B.C. gave birth not only to Buddhism in India but also to Confucianism in China and to new rationalist philosophies in Greece. Buddhism became one of the world's major religions and the Buddha one of the most notable spiritual leaders in the history of the world. ⊕

Four Noble Truths

The Buddha developed a new religious philosophy. He outlined his main ideas in the Four Noble Truths. First, as he had discovered, all people suffer and know sorrow. Next, said the Buddha, people suffer because their desires bind them to the cycle of rebirth. He told his followers:

> 66 The thirst for existence leads from rebirth to rebirth; lust and pleasure follow. Power alone can satisfy lust. The thirst for power, the thirst for pleasure, the thirst for existence; there, O monks, is the origin of suffering. 99

The third truth, said the Buddha, was that people could end their suffering by eliminating their desires. And according to the fourth truth, one could eliminate desire by following the Eightfold Path.

The Eightfold Path

The Buddha urged his disciples to do eight things: know the truth, resist evil, say nothing to hurt others, respect life, work for the good of others, free their minds of evil, control their thoughts, and practice meditation. By avoiding extremes and following the Eightfold Path, a person could attain nirvana, a state of freedom from the cycle of rebirth. Nirvana is not a place, like heaven, but a state of extinction. In fact, the root meaning of the word *nirvana* is a "blowing out," as of a candle. In nirvana, a person would be in a state of oneness with the universe.

The Buddha rejected the *varna* system. He taught that a person's place in life depended on the person, not on the person's birth. He taught that anyone, regardless of caste, could attain enlightenment. He did not believe in the Hindu deities. He believed in reincarnation but taught that one could escape the cycle of suffering and reach nirvana by following the Eightfold Path.

Spread of Buddhism

The Buddha spent 40 years teaching the Four Noble Truths and the Eightfold Path. He gathered thousands of disciples around him. After their master's death, traveling monks carried the new religion beyond India to other parts of Asia, especially to China, Japan, Korea, and the Middle East.

Architecture and the Arts

The rise of Buddhism led to a flowering of architecture and the arts. Buddhist architects built stupas, or large stone mounds, over the bones of Buddhist holy people. Stupas were known for their elaborately carved stone gateways. Paintings and statues of the Buddha, carved of polished stone or wood covered with gilt, adorned stupas and cave temples. Exquisite smaller statues were made from fine porcelain. Books about the Buddha's life and teachings were often beautifully illustrated.

Divisions

As Buddhism spread, disagreements developed among the Buddha's followers. Two distinct branches of Buddhism soon arose. One branch, known as Theravada, was established in South Asia and Southeast Asia. It remained fairly close in practice to the original teachings of the Buddha, regarding him as simply a teacher.

The other branch of Buddhism was known as Mahayana. It became dominant in China, Korea, and Japan. Mahayana encouraged the worship of the Buddha as a divine being and savior.

Today, only a few Indians are Buddhists. Most are Hindus. Muslims, Jains, Christians, and others make up the rest of the population. Recently, however, Buddhism has gained new followers in India, as well as in the West.

SECTION 2 REVIEW

Recall
1. **Define** nirvana, stupa.
2. **Identify** Siddhartha Gautama, Four Noble Truths.
3. **Locate** on a map in the Atlas the Asian countries to which monks and merchants carried the teachings of the Buddha: China, Japan, Korea, Myanmar, Malaysia, Indonesia. How did monks and merchants help to assure the survival of Buddhism as a worldwide religion?

Critical Thinking
4. **Synthesizing Information** Compare the religions of Hinduism and Buddhism, explaining which Hindu beliefs and practices the Buddha accepted and which he rejected in his teaching.

Understanding Themes
5. **Innovation** Decide how your own life and goals would be different if you tried to live by the Four Noble Truths and the Eightfold Path.

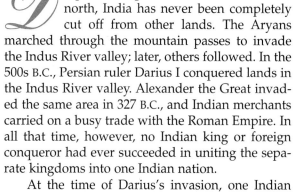
Section 3

Indian Empires

Setting the Scene

▸ **Terms to Define**
"Arabic numerals"

▸ **People to Meet**
Chandragupta Maurya, Asoka, Chandragupta I, Chandragupta II

▸ **Places to Locate**
Magadha

 What were the cultural achievements of the Mauryan and Gupta Empires?

The Storyteller

It troubled King Asoka that criminals continued their wrongdoing within his empire. Therefore he was proud of his latest merciful decree, carved on stone monuments: "Thus speaks the Beloved of the Gods.... This is my instruction from now on: Men who are imprisoned or sentenced to death are to be given three days respite. Thus their relations [relatives] may plead for their lives, or, if there is no one to plead for them, they may make their donations or undertake a fast for a better rebirth in the next life. For it is my wish that they should gain the next world."

—from *Asoka and the Decline of the Mauryas,* Romila Thapar, 1961

Lion-headed capital atop a Rock Edict pillar of Asoka

Despite the high mountain barriers in the north, India has never been completely cut off from other lands. The Aryans marched through the mountain passes to invade the Indus River valley; later, others followed. In the 500s B.C., Persian ruler Darius I conquered lands in the Indus River valley. Alexander the Great invaded the same area in 327 B.C., and Indian merchants carried on a busy trade with the Roman Empire. In all that time, however, no Indian king or foreign conqueror had ever succeeded in uniting the separate kingdoms into one Indian nation.

At the time of Darius's invasion, one Indian kingdom, **Magadha**, was expanding in the north. King Bimbisara, who ruled Magadha from 542 B.C. to 495 B.C., added to its territory by conquest and marriage. Although Magadha declined after Bimbisara's death, it was to become the center of India's first empire.

The Mauryan Empire

At the time of Alexander's invasion, Magadha was only one of many small warring states in northern India. Then, in 321 B.C., a military officer named **Chandragupta Maurya** (CHUHN•druh•GUP•tuh MAH•oor•yuh) overthrew the Magadhan king and proclaimed himself ruler.

Chandragupta Maurya was a skilled administrator whose achievements included the development of an efficient postal system. He kept control of his empire by maintaining a strong army and by using an extensive spy network. He founded a Mauryan kingdom that included most of northern and central India and lasted until 184 B.C.

Asoka's Enlightened Rule

Indian civilization blossomed during the reign of Chandragupta's grandson, **Asoka** (uh•SHOH•kuh). Asoka's rule began in 274 B.C. with fierce wars of conquest. His merciless armies swept

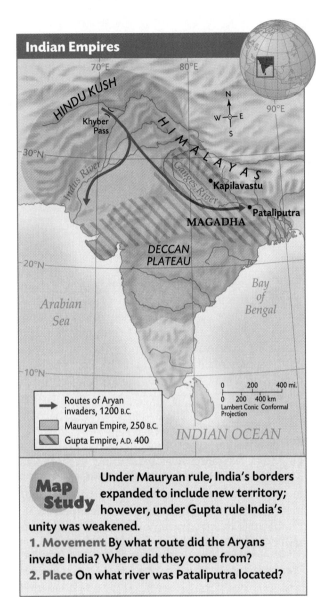

Indian Empires

HINDU KUSH
Khyber Pass
HIMALAYAS
Indus River
Ganges River
•Kapilavastu
•Pataliputra
MAGADHA
DECCAN PLATEAU
Arabian Sea
Bay of Bengal

→ Routes of Aryan invaders, 1200 B.C.
☐ Mauryan Empire, 250 B.C.
☐ Gupta Empire, A.D. 400

INDIAN OCEAN

0   200   400 mi.
0   200   400 km
Lambert Conic Conformal Projection

Map Study Under Mauryan rule, India's borders expanded to include new territory; however, under Gupta rule India's unity was weakened.
1. Movement By what route did the Aryans invade India? Where did they come from?
2. Place On what river was Pataliputra located?

today as the Rock Edicts, were carved on rocks and on tall stone pillars throughout the vast empire.

Asoka's public projects reflected the same care for people. He provided free hospitals and veterinary clinics. He built fine roads, with rest houses and shade trees for the travelers' comfort.

Although he promoted Buddhism, Asoka permitted his non-Buddhist subjects to continue to practice Hinduism if they wished. The Hindu caste system continued.

Collapse of Mauryan Empire

The Mauryan Empire declined after Asoka's death in 232 B.C. because his successors were not as enlightened as he was. They levied heavy taxes on the goods sold by merchants and seized large portions of the crops grown by peasants. Such harsh policies caused the people to turn against the Mauryas. When the last Mauryan ruler was murdered in 184 B.C., northern India again split into many small warring kingdoms.

The Gupta Empire

After the Mauryan Empire, 500 years passed before much of India was again united. About A.D. 310, **Chandragupta I** began to build an empire. He was not related to Chandragupta Maurya, but like that earlier ruler he made Magadha the base of his kingdom.

Chandragupta I introduced the Gupta dynasty, which ruled northern India for more than 200 years. The arts and sciences flourished, and the Gupta period would later be called India's Golden Age.

The Guptas governed a much smaller empire than the Mauryas. They never gained control of the Indus Valley or of the Deccan, the broad plateau that forms most of India's southern peninsula. The Guptas did manage to build a strong state, however, and worked to maintain unquestioned authority. They trained soldiers and used spies and political assassins. In short, they did whatever they felt had to be done to maintain power.

Gupta Religion

The Gupta rulers encouraged learning based on the ideas found in the *Upanishads*. They made Hinduism the religion of their empire. Hindu temples were built—elaborate structures with brightly painted sculptures depicting tales in the *Mahabharata* and the *Ramayana*. Although each temple had its presiding god or goddess, the Hindus viewed the many deities as different ways of worshiping Brahman Nerguna, the eternal spirit.

across the plains and into the forests and cities, hunting down and killing their enemies. He built an empire that covered two-thirds of the Indian subcontinent.

After one particularly brutal battle, Asoka rode out to view the battlefield. The experience changed his life. As he looked on the bloodied bodies of the dead and maimed, the Indian ruler was horrified. Determined never again to rule by force and terror, Asoka renounced war. Henceforth, he announced, he would follow the teachings of the Buddha and become a man of peace. Asoka kept his word. During his reign, missionaries spread Buddhism throughout India and other parts of Asia.

Asoka issued laws stressing concern for other human beings. To make sure these laws became widely known, Asoka wrote them in the local languages rather than in Sanskrit. The laws, known

The Arts

Indian Music

Like the other arts of India, Indian music has a long and rich history. It began in Hindu temples and the courts of Indian rulers centuries ago. Traditionally, Indian musicians play instruments and sing without using chords or other harmonies. A group of musicians starts out with a basic melody called a raga, which each player then develops with his or her own spontaneous arrangements. The musicians perform on a number of different instruments, including drums, flutes, and a stringed instrument known as a sitar. Their performances often go on for several hours at a time.

Probably the best-known modern Indian musician is Ravi Shankar, often called India's "sitar king" and the "godfather of world music." Shankar, almost as well known in the West as in India, has brought an appreciation of Indian music to Western audiences. He has worked with George Harrison of the Beatles and other musicians, such as violinist Yehudi Menuhin, flutist Jean-Pierre Rampal, and composer Philip Glass.

Ravi Shankar

Linking Past and Present ACTIVITY

Discuss the origins of Indian music and its major characteristics. What contribution has Ravi Shankar made to world music?

Gupta Life

The Gupta Empire reached its height under **Chandragupta II**, who ruled from A.D. 375 to A.D. 415. Faxian (FAH•SYEN), a Buddhist monk from China, traveled to India and recorded in his diary:

“ In the Gupta Empire, people are numerous and happy; only those who cultivate the royal land have to pay [in] grain.... If they want to go, they go; if they want to stay, they stay. The king governs without decapitation [cutting off heads] or corporal [bodily] punishment.... The leaders of Vaisya families have houses in the cities for dispensing charity and medicine. ”

Faxian may have exaggerated the benefits of Gupta rule, but he provided a useful glimpse into Indian life. By easing tax burdens, Chandragupta II gave people more freedom. Of all the Gupta monarchs, he was the most chivalrous and heroic. Though he expanded the empire, he is remembered for more than conquest. Gupta rulers believed they had reached a high level of civilization. They began to write down rules for everything, from grammar to drama to politics. The Sanskrit of the Gupta court became the major language in the north.

In one respect, though, daily life did not improve during the Gupta period. The status of Indian women had declined since Aryan times. Aryan women at first often had a say about whom they would marry. By Gupta times, parents were choosing mates for their children, and child marriages were common. Women and mothers were

Footnotes to History

Highway Rest Stops
Asoka's highway rest stops were marked by stone pillars engraved with Buddhist teachings. On one of these pillars, Asoka explained:

I have ordered banyan trees to be planted along the roads to give shade to men and animals. I have ordered mango groves to be planted. I have ordered wells to be dug every [half-mile], and I have ordered rest houses built.

—The Edicts of Asoka

Buddhist monks carved this 24-foot-long reclining Buddha on the wall of the Chai-tya-griha cave in the first century B.C. *What do the Ajanta carvings reveal about life in Gupta India?*

highly respected, but they had little power or independence.

Gupta Achievements

Learning flourished under the Guptas. The court welcomed poets, playwrights, philosophers, and scientists. Much of the writing was concentrated on religion, but folktales were also popular. A collection of tales called the *Panchatantra* presented moral lessons through animals who acted like humans. Many of these stories eventually spread to the Middle East and the West, where they were retold by other authors. Drama was also important during Gupta times. Kalidasa, the most famous playwright, wrote *Shakuntala*, a play about romantic love between a king and a forest maiden.

Gupta mathematicians contributed significantly to mathematics as it is today, making major advances in developing the principles of algebra. They also explained the concept of infinity and invented the concept of zero. The symbols they devised for the numbers 1 to 9 were adopted by traders from the Middle East and so came to be called "Arabic numerals" in the West.

Gupta astronomers used these mathematical discoveries to advance their understanding of the universe. They realized that the earth is round, and they had some knowledge of gravity. In medicine, Gupta doctors set bones, performed operations, and invented hundreds of medical instruments.

Many countries benefited from Gupta achievements, as both ideas and products traveled the land and sea trade routes that connected India to the rest of the world. Indian exporters traded such items as gems, spices, cotton, teak, and ebony for horses from Arabia and central Asia, silk from China, and gold from Rome.

The Golden Age Ends

After Chandragupta II's death in A.D. 415, the Gupta Empire began to fail. As the government weakened, the Guptas faced invasions along India's northwestern border. By A.D. 600, the Gupta Empire had dissolved into a collection of small states.

However, much of the culture that was uniquely Indian survived. Many aspects of India's life today grew out of the social structures and religions, the arts and sciences, that were born during the 2,000 years that followed the Aryan invasions.

SECTION 3 REVIEW

Recall
1. **Define** "Arabic numerals."
2. **Identify** Chandragupta Maurya, Asoka, Chandragupta I, Chandragupta II, *Panchatantra*, *Shakuntala*.
3. **Locate** the map on page 212, and find the Mauryan Empire and the Gupta Empire. Compare and contrast their sizes and features.

Critical Thinking
4. **Analyzing Information** How did the rulers of India's empires have an effect on the religious life of the Indian people?

Understanding Themes
5. **Cultural Diffusion** What aspects of early Indian empires have had a lasting impact on India and the rest of the world?

Determining Cause and Effect

As you read a mystery novel, you may try to figure out which events or actions caused the main character to act in specific ways. Understanding history is a similar process. We try to find reasons behind people's actions. Looking for cause-effect relationships unlocks the mystery of history.

Learning the Skill

To identify cause-effect relationships in history, first select an event. Then examine the situation before this event. How was it different? Look for related problems and actions. These are likely causes of the event. Suppose you select the following event: Asoka's renunciation of war. What events preceded Asoka's decision? In earlier years, Asoka had led many brutal wars of conquest. Eventually, he was horrified by the bloody results of war. This combination of underlying and specific events caused him to renounce war altogether.

Now examine what happened after Asoka renounced war. He became a Buddhist, promoted Buddhist ideas of compassion, and passed laws

Buddha with halo, Gupta period

based on this philosophy. He also built hospitals and roads and worked to improve conditions for his people. These were direct and indirect effects of Asoka's change of direction.

Certain words and phrases often indicate cause-effect relationships; these include *because, due to, therefore, as a result of, led to, and brought about.* It can be hard to determine causes and effects of historical events. Facts may be missing. Moreover, we can't test our ideas as we can in science experiments. Instead, we must rely on logic and common sense.

Practicing the Skill

Read the paragraph below. Then answer the questions that follow.

> **66** Cattle were the basis of the Aryan diet and economy, even serving as money. Wealth was measured in cattle, and so the Aryans raided each other's herds. They were often at war.… Dozens of Aryan words describe cattle, indicating their continued prominence in Aryan life. Later, their herds would be considered so sacred that a ban was placed on eating meat. **99**

1. What were causes of conflict among Aryans?
2. How did the importance of cattle affect the culture and language of Aryans?

Applying the Skill

Reread Section 2, "Rise of Buddhism." Then describe causes of Buddhism's rise in India and its effects on India and other parts of the world.

For More Practice

Turn to the Skill Practice in the Chapter Review on page 217 for more practice in determining cause and effect.

Connections Across Time

Historical Significance The civilization that developed in India between 1500 B.C. and A.D. 500 produced two of the world's great religions: Hinduism and Buddhism. Hinduism became not only India's major faith but also its way of life. Buddhism rejected many Hindu social practices and affirmed a disciplined life to achieve peace and deliverance from suffering. The belief in nonviolence has influenced modern leaders in their struggle for peace and human rights. Over the centuries, the two religions have inspired magnificent achievements in architecture and the arts. Especially since the A.D. 1800s, Hindu and Buddhist ideas and art forms have influenced the West.

Using Key Terms

Write the key term that completes each sentence. Then write a sentence for each term not chosen.

a. ahimsa
b. dharma
c. epics
d. *jati*
e. karma
f. nirvana
g. rajah
h. reincarnation
i. stupas
j. *varnas*

1. The invading Aryans brought to the Indian subcontinent a system of four main social classes, or _____.
2. Hindus believe in _____, a process of rebirth in which the soul resides in many bodies before it finally unites with Brahman Nerguna, or the universal spirit.
3. A person's _____ determines whether he or she will be closer to the universal spirit in the next life.
4. For purposes of prayer, Buddhist architects built large elaborate ____ over the remains of holy people.
5. Each *varna* was made up of social groups called ____ that were defined and ranked by different occupations.

Technology Activity

Using a Word Processor Search the Internet or your local library to locate information about the following religions of India: Buddhism, Hinduism, Jainism, Sikhism, Christianity, and Islam. Use a word processor to organize your research into a fact sheet. Include headings such as religion, number of followers, basic beliefs, and major figures. Illustrate your chart with symbols of the different regions.

Using Your History Journal

Refer to a world almanac to determine how many Buddhists and how many Hindus live in each region of the world today. Build a graph or create a world map that illustrates this information.

Reviewing Facts

1. **History** Identify Chandragupta Maurya and his role in developing early Indian civilization.
2. **Culture** Explain in your own words the Four Noble Truths of Buddhism.
3. **Culture** Define *ahimsa* and describe how it is practiced in Indian society.
4. **Culture** Identify the *Bhagavad Gita*.
5. **Culture** Discuss the concept of dharma and how it affected Indian family life. What were the duties of husbands? Of wives?
6. **Science** List some of the achievements of Indian mathematicians during the Gupta Empire.
7. **History** Describe the achievements of Asoka's reign and their impact on Indian society.

Critical Thinking

1. **Apply** How could a person use the principle of nonviolence, or ahimsa, as a force for social change?
2. **Making Comparisons** In what ways are Buddhism and Christianity different? In what ways are they similar?
3. **Synthesize** What might have happened if Asoka had not been horrified while viewing the carnage after a fierce battle?

4. Analyze Here, two Brahman cattle stand in a street of Mumbai, India. Why do Hindus abstain from eating meat?

Understanding Themes

1. Movement How was India affected by the Aryan invasions?

2. Innovation What might make Buddhism attractive to people from different cultures?

3. Cultural Diffusion Why did Gupta achievements in science and the arts spread quickly to other parts of the world, both Eastern and Western?

Linking Past and Present

1. The *varna* system created a huge underclass that Europeans called "the untouchables." How do you think this system created problems for modern India?

2. Religion has always had a major part in Indian society. How have religious differences hindered Indian unity in modern times?

3. Early in the 1900s, India applied the Hindu principle of nonviolence to help win its independence from Great Britain. Do you think people can still use nonviolence effectively to win freedom and human rights?

Geography in History

1. Location What mountain range forms India's northern border?

2. Movement What routes did the Aryan invaders take to the interior of India?

3. Region What effect did the invasion of the Aryans have on the developing culture of India?

4. Human/Environment Interaction What physical features made it difficult for one empire to unify all of northern and southern India?

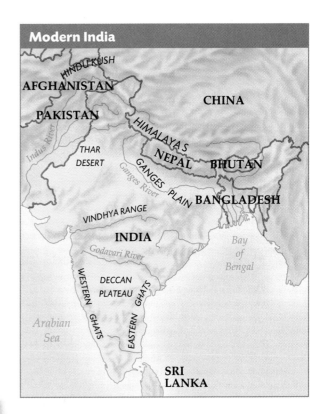

Modern India

Skill Practice

Reread the discussion of "The Gupta Empire" in Section 3. Then answer the following questions.

1. What caused the Gupta rulers to use spies and assassins?

2. The Guptas adopted Hinduism as India's religion. What effects did this have on art and architecture?

3. What were the effects of Gupta science and mathematics on world civilization?

4. What caused the breakup of the Gupta Empire?

China's Flourishing Civilization

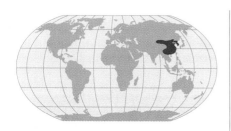

Chapter Themes

▶ **Uniformity** The Qin and Han dynasties establish and maintain a strong central government. *Section 1*

▶ **Innovation** The Chinese formulate ethical philosophies and make scientific and technological advances. *Section 2*

▶ **Cultural Diffusion** Traders carry ideas and products along the Silk Road. *Section 3*

The Storyteller

Whom do you agree with in the following conversation, dating from the 500s B.C.? What is right, or "straightness," in this case?

The Governor of She said to Confucius: "In our village there is a man nicknamed Straight Body. When his father stole a sheep, he gave evidence against him." Confucius answered, "In our village those who are straight are quite different. Fathers cover up for their sons, and sons cover up for their fathers...."

This conversation involves a conflict between law and family. Confucius's view—that family should always take precedence—reflects an attitude toward families that was dominant in Chinese culture for a long time.

Historical Significance

How did the ideas of Confucius and other Chinese thinkers affect behavior in Chinese society for centuries? How have their ideas influenced China's development and its relationship with other parts of the world?

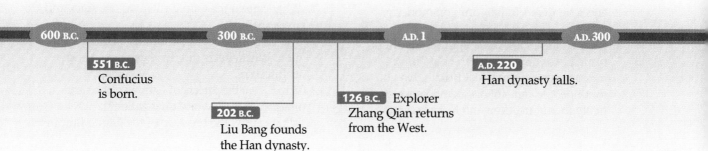

600 B.C.	300 B.C.	A.D. 1	A.D. 300

551 B.C. Confucius is born.

202 B.C. Liu Bang founds the Han dynasty.

126 B.C. Explorer Zhang Qian returns from the West.

A.D. 220 Han dynasty falls.

The Great Wall of China at Huang Ya Guan, a view of a section of the 4,000-mile-long wall

Your History Journal

Chinese inventions and discoveries include many "firsts" such as printed books, the compass, and gunpowder. Choose one Chinese invention or discovery reported in this chapter and write a short research report on its early history.

771 B.C. Zhou political power begins to decline.

221 B.C. Qin Shihuangdi founds the Qin dynasty.

141 B.C. Wudi becomes the sixth Han emperor.

Section 1

Three Great Dynasties

Setting the Scene

▶ **Terms to Define**
cavalry, civil service, mandarin

▶ **People to Meet**
Qin Shihuangdi, Liu Bang, Wudi, Zhang Qian

▶ **Places to Locate**
Great Wall of China, Silk Road

Find Out What major advances did China make under the Zhou, Qin, and Han dynasties?

The Storyteller

Seeing the Marquis Chao of Han asleep on the cold floor, the keeper of the royal hat covered him with a robe. Upon awakening, the marquis demanded to know who had covered him. Learning the keeper of the hat was responsible, the marquis punished the keeper of the robe for failing to perform his duty. Then he punished the keeper of the hat for undertaking tasks not his to perform. The trespass of one official upon the duties of another was considered a great danger.

—adapted from *Basic Writing of Mo Tzu, Hsün Tzu, and Han Fei Tzu,* reprinted in *The Global Experience: Readings in World History to 1500,* 1987

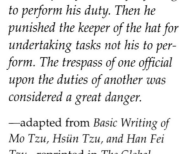

Late Zhou jade dragon

Around 1100 B.C., the Chinese people were fashioning ideas that would result in a unique civilization. From then until the A.D. 200s, the Chinese lived under three dynasties, or ruling families—the Zhou (JOH), the Qin (CHIN), and the Han (HAHN). The first of these, the Zhou, ruled the nation for more than 800 years, longer than any other Chinese dynasty.

The Enduring Zhou

The Zhou conquered the last Shang dynasty king around 1028 B.C., claiming the Mandate of Heaven, or heaven's approval. They called their king the Son of Heaven, saying that the Shang had lost the mandate by ruling poorly.

Eventually, the Zhou held a vast realm. To control their holdings, Zhou kings set up an agricultural system in which nobles owned the land and peasants worked it. They appointed their relatives to govern, giving each one a city-state.

Each local lord had total authority on his own lands and built his own army. At first all the lords pledged allegiance to the Son of Heaven. In time, though, some grew strong enough to challenge the king's authority.

In 771 B.C. the Zhou suffered a severe defeat in a conflict with their enemies. After that, political power fell increasingly to local nobles. In the next centuries, the nobles fought small wars until by the 200s B.C., several city-states were locked in a struggle that ended the Zhou era.

Even though Zhou rulers lost their power, the Zhou are remembered for many technological advances. During the Zhou period the Chinese built roads and expanded foreign trade. They obtained horses from western nomads, forming a

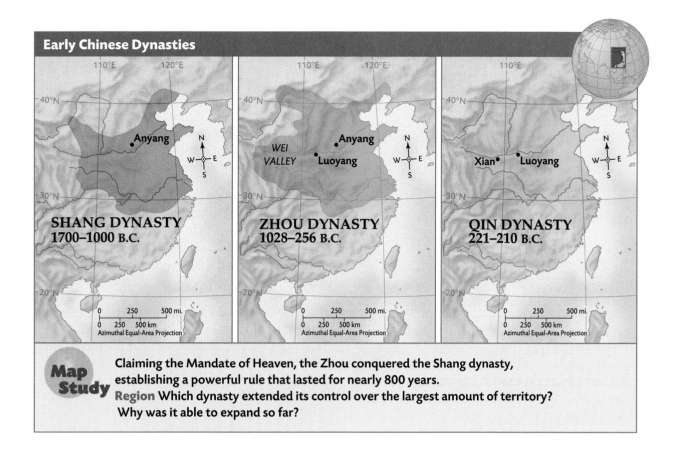

Early Chinese Dynasties

SHANG DYNASTY
1700–1000 B.C.

ZHOU DYNASTY
1028–256 B.C.

QIN DYNASTY
221–210 B.C.

Map Study Claiming the Mandate of Heaven, the Zhou conquered the Shang dynasty, establishing a powerful rule that lasted for nearly 800 years.
Region Which dynasty extended its control over the largest amount of territory? Why was it able to expand so far?

cavalry, or group of mounted warriors, along with horse-drawn chariots. The Zhou also added a deadly weapon: the crossbow. They further elaborated the system of picture writing begun by the Shang, a system that is the ancestor of modern Chinese writing. Under the Zhou, iron plows were invented, irrigation systems were developed, and flood-control systems were initiated. These and other advances led to population growth, and Zhou China became the world's most densely populated country.

The Mighty Qin

Meanwhile, several small states were struggling for control in China. Among them was a state on the western border ruled by the Qin. By 221 B.C., the Qin had wiped out the Zhou and conquered the rest of northern China, uniting much of the nation under a strong central authority for the first time. Westerners would later call the nation *China* after the Qin, whose first ruler added the title Shihuangdi (SHUR•HWONG•DEE), or First Emperor, to his name.

A tireless ruler, **Qin Shihuangdi** set out to create a government directly under his control. He reorganized the empire into military districts, appointing officials to govern them. This system prevented local lords from becoming strong enough to challenge the power of the central government—the problem that had led to the downfall of the Zhou.

The First Emperor made other changes to further centralize his control. He devised a system of weights and measures to replace the various systems used in different regions. He standardized coins, instituted a uniform writing system, and set up a law code throughout China.

Qin had grandiose plans for his empire, and he used forced labor to accomplish them. Gangs of Chinese peasants dug canals and built roads.

Footnotes to History

Court Magic
A court magician made a potion for Wudi, claiming that it would give immortality. Before the emperor got the potion, a scholar drank it. The scholar was immediately sentenced to death but told Wudi that, if the potion was genuine, Wudi would not be able to kill him. If the potion was a fake, he had done no harm. Wudi had to agree. Needless to say, the scholar had exposed a fraud.

The Great Wall

To Qin, one building project seemed especially urgent—shoring up China's defenses to the north. Earlier rulers had built walls to prevent attacks by nomadic invaders. Qin ordered those walls connected. Over several years some 300,000 peasants toiled—and thousands died—before the work was done. Eventually the wall stretched more than 4,000 miles (6,437 km). Rebuilt by later rulers, the **Great Wall of China** stands today as a monument to Qin's ambition and to the peasants who carried out their emperor's will.

Qin's Strict Rule

Qin Shihuangdi imposed a new order on China. He ended the power of the local lords by taking land from many of them and imposing a tax on landowners. He appointed educated men instead of nobles as officials to run his government.

Qin even imposed an early form of censorship, clamping down on scholars who discussed books and ideas. In 213 B.C. he ordered all books burned except those dealing with "practical" subjects like agriculture, medicine, and magic. In this way he hoped to break people's ties to the past. He agreed with his adviser, who said, "anyone referring to the past to criticize the present ... should be put to death." About 460 scholars resisted and were executed.

Qin's subjects saw him as a cruel tyrant who had lost the Mandate of Heaven. Nobles were angry because he had destroyed the aristocracy; scholars detested him for the burning of books; and peasants hated his forced-labor gangs. In 210 B.C. Qin died, and soon the dynasty itself came to an end. Even so, the rule of the Qin brought lasting changes. The most influential changes were new ways of organizing the nation, establishing foundations for the Chinese state that would last 2,000 years.

The Glorious Han

In 207 B.C. **Liu Bang** (LYOH BONG) overthrew the Qin government. A military official from a peasant background, Liu defeated his most powerful rival in 202 B.C. and declared himself the emperor of a new dynasty, the Han.

The Han governed China until A.D. 220, more than 400 years. The Han emperors used the same forms of centralized power that the Qin had set up, but without the harshness of Qin rule. Han China rivaled the Roman Empire in its power and achievement.

Advances Under Wudi

The Han dynasty reached its peak during the reign of **Wudi** (WOO•DEE), who ruled from 141 B.C. to 87 B.C. Wudi, one of the most talented and dynamic rulers in Chinese history, personally supervised all aspects of his government.

An ambitious ruler, Wudi extended his empire. He sent huge armies against the nomadic invaders and other non-Chinese peoples. He conquered lands to the north, including Korea and Manchuria, south into Southeast Asia, and west as far as northern India.

In 139 B.C. Wudi sent out an expedition led by **Zhang Qian** (JAHNG CHYEN), a general and explorer. Thirteen years later, Zhang staggered back. His troops had been nearly wiped out by barbarian attacks, and the general had endured more than 10 years of captivity.

Although he had made no conquests, Zhang brought back amazing tales he had heard on his travels. He told of a great empire to the west, with huge cities full of people "who cut their hair short, wear embroidered garments, and ride in very small chariots." Zhang, who was describing Rome, gave Han rulers their first hint of another civilization as advanced as their own.

Wudi's new interest in the West, fed by news of Zhang Qian's explorations, led to the expansion of trade routes later known as the **Silk Road**. Winding past deserts and through mountain passes, the Silk Road linked East and West. It allowed traders to exchange China's fine silk for Middle Eastern and European products, such as gold, glassware, and wool and linen fabrics.

Pax Sinica

Under the Han, China enjoyed a 400-year period of prosperity and stability, later referred to as the *Pax Sinica* (PAHKS SIH•nuh•kuh), the Chinese Peace. The *Pax Sinica* coincided with the *Pax Romana* in the West.

During the *Pax Sinica*, Wudi adopted an economic policy designed to prevent food shortages and high prices. Government agents stored surplus food during years of plenty and sold it when harvests were poor. Under this system, China was able to feed its growing population.

Before Wudi, emperors had chosen as their officials members of their families or of the aristocracy, a practice that led easily to corruption in government. Wudi wanted talented people to govern, and so he initiated changes. First, he asked people to recommend candidates for public posts. These candidates took long, difficult written examinations. After an official "graded" the tests, the emperor evaluated the results and appointed those with the highest scores.

Thomas J. Abercrombie

Silk Road

The Silk Route

National Geographic Publications
Art Division

A caravan of men and mules walk a trail that once formed part of the old Silk Road, a network of paths cutting across Asia from the Pacific coast of China to the Mediterranean Sea. The route, first traveled many years before the Christian era, was the passageway not only for Chinese silk but for a great range of products including jade and fruit, ideas and paintings. Today it is still possible to see how poles and rocks created the actual highway over which goods moved throughout many centuries—before ships, trains, buses, and airplanes replaced mules and packs.

You can trace the length of the trip on the accompanying map. A trader setting forth from the Chinese city of Nanjing would soon leave Chinese territory and enter a world of Muslim ethnic groups and treacherous terrain. The trail loops south and north of the scorching Takla Makan Desert and rises high through mountain passes across the Pamir Mountains. The whole trip was far too long for a single caravan to undertake. Instead, Chinese or Persian merchants dealt with central Asian middlemen from lands such as Afghanistan and Turkestan. ⊕

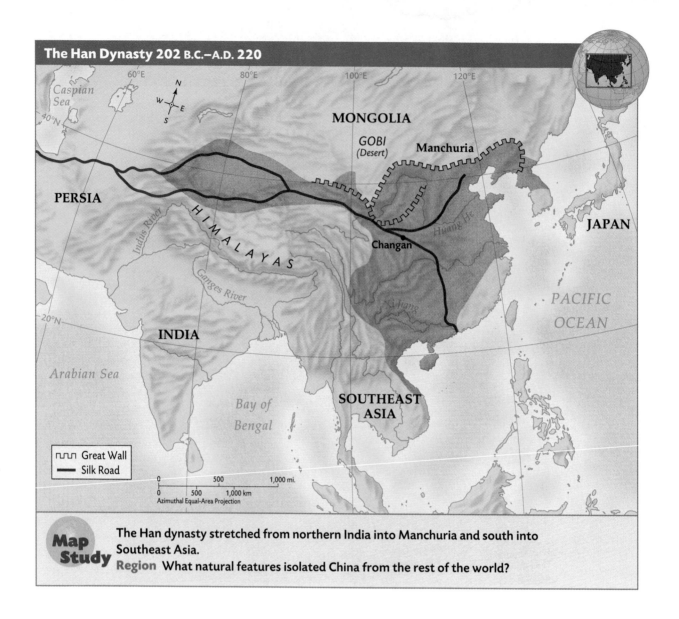

60°E 80°E 100°E 120°E

Caspian Sea

40°N

N
W E
S

MONGOLIA

GOBI (Desert)

Manchuria

PERSIA

H I M A L A Y A S

Indus River

Huang He

Changan

JAPAN

Ganges River

20°N

INDIA

Xi Jiang

Arabian Sea

Bay of Bengal

SOUTHEAST ASIA

PACIFIC OCEAN

ᄂᄀᄂ Great Wall
━━ Silk Road

0   500   1,000 mi.
0   500   1,000 km
Azimuthal Equal-Area Projection

Map Study The Han dynasty stretched from northern India into Manchuria and south into Southeast Asia.
Region What natural features isolated China from the rest of the world?

Wudi's examinations evolved into the civil service, a system that allowed anyone with ability to attain public office. At least, that was the theory. In practice, the system favored the wealthy, for education was expensive, and usually only the wealthy could afford to obtain enough education to pass the exams.

The civil service system made scholars the most respected members of Chinese society. A new class of well-educated civil servants, called mandarins, controlled the government, and they would continue to do so until the early 1900s.

After Wudi's reign, Han power declined until the dynasty eventually fell in A.D. 220. However, Han achievements in government, technology, science, and the arts were lasting.

SECTION 1 REVIEW

Recall
1. **Define** cavalry, civil service, mandarin.
2. **Identify** Qin Shihuangdi, Liu Bang, Wudi, Zhang Qian.
3. **List** two of the major achievements the Chinese people made under each dynasty—the Zhou, the Qin, and the Han.

Critical Thinking
4. **Analyzing Information** Did Wudi's civil service system offer equal opportunity to all Chinese? Explain.

Understanding Themes
5. **Uniformity** How did Qin Shihuangdi unify China?

500 B.C.   A.D. 1   A.D. 500

c. 522 B.C. Confucius begins to teach.

c. 500 B.C. Daoism emerges as a major Chinese philosophy.

c. A.D. 400 Buddhism becomes a popular religion in China.

Section 2

Three Ways of Life

Setting the Scene

▶ **Terms to Define**
ethics, filial piety, yin and yang

▶ **People to Meet**
Confucius (Kongfuzi), Laozi

Find Out What philosophic ideals shaped China's government, and how did they shape it?

The Storyteller

One of the duties of Prince Wei-hui's cook was to slaughter cattle for the royal table. When he performed this task, all his movements were harmonious, like a dance. The prince was amazed and asked his servant how he was able to do such heavy work so effortlessly. The cook explained, "What your servant loves is the Tao, which I have applied to the skill of carving. I work with my mind, and not with my eyes." In this way, the toughest cuts yielded easily before his skill. He had learned how to nurture his spirit while maintaining his livelihood.

—adapted from *A Source Book in Chinese Philosophy*, reprinted in *Lives and Times: A World History Reader*, James P. Holoka and Jiu-Hwa L. Upshur, 1994

Confucius

During the late Zhou era, scholars sought solutions to the problems of political breakdown and social disorder that were paralyzing China. Their efforts led to the rise of major philosophies, such as Confucianism, Legalism, and Daoism. These philosophies dealt very little with the supernatural or with eternal life; instead, they focused on life in this world and how it should be lived. By the latter part of the Han dynasty, between A.D. 50 and A.D. 100, Buddhism had reached China, and the Chinese blended its insights with those of Confucianism and Daoism.

TURNING POINT

Confucianism

China's most influential scholar was **Kongfuzi** (KOONG•FOO•DZUH), known in the West as **Confucius**. Born about 551 B.C. to a peasant family, Confucius at first sought a political post but later became a teacher. In his teachings, Confucius stated that social harmony and good government would return to China if people lived according to principles of ethics—good conduct and moral judgment. When a student asked Confucius for a single word that could serve as a principle for conduct, he responded: "Perhaps the word *reciprocity* will do. Do not do unto others what you would not want others to do unto you." This rule is similar to a familiar teaching of Judaism and Christianity, sometimes called the Golden Rule: "Do unto others as you would have others do unto you."

The Five Relationships

Confucius stressed the importance of moral behavior in five basic relationships: ruler and subject, parent and child, husband and wife, old and young, and friend and friend. A code of proper conduct governed each of these relationships. For example, rulers had a duty to rule justly and to set an example of right living. In return, subjects should be loyal and obey the law.

The most basic relationships, however, concerned the family. Confucius cared especially about filial piety, or children's respect for their parents and elders. For Confucius, the family represented society in miniature. He said:

> ❝The superior man spreads his culture to the entire nation by remaining at home…. The teaching of filial piety is a preparation for serving the ruler of the state; the teaching of respect for one's elder brothers is a preparation for serving all the elders of the community; and the teaching of kindness in parents is a training for ruling over people….When individual families have learned kindness, then the whole nation has learned kindness. ❞

After Confucius died in 479 B.C., his teachings were collected in a work called the *Analects*. During the Han dynasty, Confucian ethics provided the basis for the civil service system. They would continue to shape Chinese society and government until the early 1900s.

Legalism

Opposition to Confucian ideas, however, came from scholars known as Legalists. Legalism, as their philosophy was called, rejected the Confucian idea of learning by example. Instead, it emphasized the importance of strict laws and harsh punishments.

Legalism developed from the teachings of Hanfeizi (HAHN•FAY•DZEE), a scholar who lived during the 200s B.C. According to Hanfeizi, humans were by nature evil and required a strong, forceful government to make them attend to their duties. Because of its justification of force and power, Legalism was favored by many nobles and became the official policy of the Qin dynasty that unified China during the 200s B.C. Legalism later gave way to Confucianism. However, Legalism's influence was reflected in the harsh laws and punishments often inflicted on China's peasant population.

Daoism

In spite of their differences, Confucianism and Legalism both stressed the importance of an orderly society. Another philosophy called Daoism, however,

---

Measuring Earthquakes

People in Han China believed that earthquakes were caused by angry spirits expressing their displeasure with society. Scholars studied quakes closely in hope of finding a divine message.

In A.D. 132 Zhang Heng invented the world's first seismograph, an instrument for detecting and measuring earthquakes. Zhang's device resembled a domed, cylindrical urn. Each of eight dragons around the top held a ball in its jaws. At the base of the urn sat eight toads with upturned heads and open mouths, each directly under a dragon.

Zhang Heng's seismograph

When a tremor occurred, a mechanism caused one of the balls to fall into a toad's mouth. This action showed that somewhere an earthquake was taking place. The side of the seismograph where that toad was sitting indicated the quake's direction. As the ball popped into the toad's mouth, the loudness indicated the tremor's strength.

Today we know that shifting in the earth's crust causes earthquakes. This movement sends seismic waves across the earth's surface much as dropping a pebble in a pond sends ripples across water. Modern seismographs have sensors that can detect ground motions caused by seismic waves from both near and distant earthquakes. The sensors produce wavy lines that reflect the size of seismic waves passing beneath them. Impressions of the waves are registered on paper, film, or recording tape, or are stored and displayed by computers.

Linking Past and Present ACTIVITY

Contrast the workings of ancient and modern seismographs. Then, examine the differences in ancient Chinese and modern views about the causes of earthquakes.

---

emphasized living in harmony with nature. Daoism rejected formal social structures and the idea that people must fill specific roles in society.

Daoist Ideas

Daoism traced its origins to the teachings of a scholar named **Laozi** (LOW•DZUH), who is thought to have lived sometime around the 500s B.C. Laozi's ideas were recorded in the *Dao De Jing*, a Chinese classic. His followers, known as Daoists, believed that people should renounce worldly ambitions and turn to nature and the Dao, the universal force that guides all things. They used examples from nature to describe how one follows the Dao:

> **"** The highest good is like water.
> Water gives life to the ten thousand things
>   and does not strive.
> It flows in places men reject and so is like
>   the Dao.
> In dwelling, be close to the land.
> In meditation, go deep in the heart.
> In dealing with others, be gentle and kind.
> In speech, be true.
> In ruling, be just. **"**

By emphasizing harmony with nature, Daoists deeply influenced Chinese arts, particularly painting and poetry.

Daoist simplicity seems to oppose Confucian formalism, but a person could be both a Confucianist and a Daoist. Confucianism provided the pattern for government and one's place in the social order, and Daoism emphasized harmony within the individual attuned to nature. Because the emphasis of each was different, a person could easily be both.

Yin and Yang

A Chinese theory related to Daoist ideas was the concept of yin and yang, the two opposing forces believed to be present in all nature. Yin was cool, dark, female, and submissive, while yang was warm, light, male, and aggressive. Everything had both elements. For harmony the two elements had

History & Art Laozi on his buffalo. Guimet Museum, Paris, France. *How did the teaching of Laozi as recorded in the* Dao De Jing *influence Chinese arts and poetry?*

to be in balance. Human life and natural events resulted from the interplay between yin and yang.

The concept of yin and yang helped the Chinese reconcile seeming opposites—like Dao simplicity and Confucian formalism. It also helped them accept Buddhist ideas brought to China by monks and traders from India.

Buddhism

Buddhism reached China just as the Han Empire was collapsing, and its emphasis on personal salvation in nirvana appealed to many people seeking an escape from suffering. Confucianists could follow its Eightfold Path, and Daoists admired its use of meditation. By the A.D. 400s, Buddhism was widely embraced in China.

SECTION 2 REVIEW

Recall
1. **Define** ethics, filial piety, yin and yang.
2. **Identify** Confucius, Laozi.
3. **Explain** why Confucius believed the five relationships were important to Chinese

society. What was the goal of his philosophy?

Critical Thinking
4. **Making Comparisons** How would you compare Confucianists and Daoists in their ideas and also in their ways of life?

Understanding Themes
5. **Innovation** How did the concept of yin and yang help the Chinese people reconcile ideas in the thought of Daoism that seemed opposed to Confucianism?

1000 B.C. Chinese begin poems in the *Book of Songs*.

240 B.C. Chinese astronomers record appearance of Halley's comet.

c. 100 B.C. Chinese invent paper.

Section 3

Society and Culture

Setting the Scene

▶ **Terms to Define**

hierarchy, extended family, nuclear family, acupuncture

▶ **People to Meet**

Sima Qian

Find Out How was early Chinese society organized, and what scientific and technological breakthroughs took place in early China?

The Storyteller

Wu Phu was a physician, trained by Hua Tho, an outstanding medical theorist. Hua Tho impressed upon his pupils the importance of physical exercise as a means of obtaining good health. He compared an exercised body to running water, which never became stale. "When the body feels ill," he counseled, "one should do one of these exercises. After perspiring, one will sense the body grow light and the stomach will manifest hunger." There was merit in those recommendations. Wu Phu had carefully followed his master's regimen, and although he was past ninety years of age, his hearing, vision, and even his teeth were all still excellent.

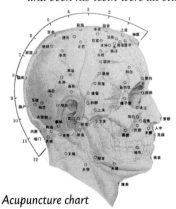

—adapted from "Hygiene and Preventive Medicine in Ancient China," reprinted in *Reflections on World Civilization*, edited by Ronald H. Fritze, James S. Olson, and Randy W. Roberts, 1994

Acupuncture chart

Confucian values governed all aspects of personal and social life in Han China. "With harmony at home, there will be order in the nation," Confucius had said. "With order in the nation, there will be peace in the world." And indeed, the family was supreme in Chinese society. It was the focus of life, bound together strongly by mutual love, loyalty, and dependence.

Family Life

The members of a Chinese family of the Han era lived and worked together. In an ideal family every member knew his or her role and the duties that went with it.

Relationships

Family members did not relate to each other as equals; instead, the family was a strict hierarchy, organized into different levels of importance. The oldest male in the home, usually the father, was dominant. Next in rank was the oldest son, followed by all the younger sons and all the females. The mother came before the daughters, and finally—at the bottom—the youngest daughter or childless daughter-in-law. Each family member expected obedience from those who were further down in the hierarchy, and each obeyed and respected those who were above.

Family Rules

Strict rules governed the relationships between husbands and wives, parents and grandparents, uncles and aunts, brothers and sisters, and other relatives. Each family member knew his or her place and understood its duties, and each was careful not to bring dishonor on the family by failing in those duties. Moreover, the duty to family members did not stop at death; all were expected to pay respect to departed ancestors.

Typical homes in Han China did not have the extended families, or families of many generations living together, that would later be typical. Rather, they had what we call today nuclear families, each consisting of parents and their children. The father assigned his children's careers, determined their education, arranged their marriages, meted out rewards or punishments, and controlled the family finances. The family also provided support for members who themselves could not contribute—the aged, the young, the sick, and even the lazy.

No doubt the system offered many opportunities for exploiting those further down in the hierarchy. Nevertheless, few fathers were tyrants. Like other family members, they practiced ethical principles of kindness and compassion, either from genuine love or from fear of the disapproval of others and the scorn of their ancestors.

Status of Women

Under the Confucian social system, women were subordinate to men. Confucius himself had little regard for women, saying, "Women and uneducated people are the most difficult to deal with."

Girls began life subservient to their fathers and brothers. Later their husbands and in-laws were their superiors, and eventually even a mother came under the authority of her own sons. Parents valued baby girls far less than baby boys. A poor family had to work hard to raise and support a child, and if that child was a daughter, she left home to become part of her husband's family as soon as she married.

Some women were able to gain respect in Chinese homes. With marriage and motherhood, they became revered. Other opportunities for women, such as education, were limited. In spite of Confucianism's predominance, women fared far better under the Han than they would in later centuries. They could inherit property, even own it after they married, and they could remarry after a husband's death.

Society and Economy

Chinese society consisted of three main classes: landowners, peasants, and merchants. Landowning families were wealthy. They lived in tile-roofed mansions with courtyards and gardens. They surrounded their homes with walls to protect them from bandits. They filled their rooms with fine furniture and adorned them with silk wall hangings and carpets. Wealthy families feasted on a rich variety of foods.

The landholders' wealth was generally limited, however, and families rarely kept their holdings for

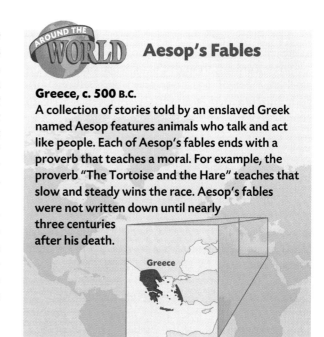

Aesop's Fables

Greece, c. 500 B.C.
A collection of stories told by an enslaved Greek named Aesop features animals who talk and act like people. Each of Aesop's fables ends with a proverb that teaches a moral. For example, the proverb "The Tortoise and the Hare" teaches that slow and steady wins the race. Aesop's fables were not written down until nearly three centuries after his death.

Greece

more than a few generations. When a family's land was divided, it went to all the sons, not just the oldest, with the result that in time individual landowners had less and less property.

Probably 90 percent of the Chinese people were peasants. The wealth that supported the lifestyles of the rich was gained from the hard labor of the peasants who cultivated the land. Unlike Western farmers, who usually lived on the land they farmed, most Chinese peasants lived in rural villages and worked fields outside their mud walls. Their homes were simple, and they ate a plain diet that featured millet, rice, beans, turnips, and fish.

The peasants raised livestock and toiled long hours in the grain fields. They faced constant threats from floods and from famines. As rent for the land, peasants turned over part of their produce to the landowner. The government required them to pay taxes and to work one month each year on public works projects such as road building. In times of conflict, peasants were drafted into the army as soldiers.

At the bottom of the social hierarchy were merchants—a group that included shopkeepers, traders, service workers, and even bankers. The merchants lived in towns and provided goods and services for the wealthy. In spite of the great wealth that many merchants accumulated, Chinese society generally held them in contempt. Confucianism taught that the pursuit of profit was an unworthy pastime for the "superior" individual. Merchants were not allowed to take the civil service examinations and enter government service.

For all the people in Han society except merchants, the civil service system provided opportunities for advancement, though the expense of education blocked most of the poor from competing. Still, poor but talented individuals sometimes rose to positions of power and influence.

Literature

Although the Qin burned thousands of books, many survived in royal libraries and secret private collections. Particularly prized was a collection of books called the Five Classics, some of which were written before Confucius. All candidates for the civil service were required to master them. No better example is recorded of the Chinese reverence for history.

The oldest of the Five Classics, the *Book of Songs*, preserves 305 of the earliest Chinese poems, written between 1000 B.C. and 600 B.C. The poems deal with political themes, ritual, and romance. Many seem modern, with their everyday topics and simple, concrete imagery—this one, for example:

> Near the East Gate
> Young women go
> Like so many clouds all day.
> Like drifting clouds
> A thought of them
> Soon blows away.
>
> There. White robe
> and a blue scarf—
> she makes my day.
>
> Near the Great Tower and Wall
> Go slender girls
> Like reeds by river's edge:
> Like bending reeds
> A thought of them
> Soon passes by.

The *Book of Documents* records political speeches

Images
of the Times

Han China

The Han dynasty was a golden age of Chinese history. Important political, economic, and cultural changes took place.

Wudi's examinations developed into a civil service system, leading to a wealthy class of mandarins who controlled the government.

and documents from early in the Zhou dynasty, including the earliest statement of the Mandate of Heaven. The *Book of Changes* presents a complex system for foretelling the future and choosing a course of action. In *Spring and Autumn Annals* Confucius reported major events that occurred in the state of Lu between 722 B.C. and 481 B.C.

The Five Classics were thought to carry solutions to most problems. Officials studied them closely to find support for their positions, such as the conduct of political leaders. Accounts of solar eclipses, meteor showers, and droughts were used to show what terrifying events and disasters could befall poor political leaders.

Another great collection of books, the Thirteen Classics, included the *Analects*—Confucius's sayings compiled by his students after his death. Many appeared as answers to questions. For example, Confucius was asked about the gentleman, or the "superior man." Among other replies he gave this one: "What the gentleman seeks, he seeks within himself; what the small man seeks, he seeks in others."

The Han Chinese encouraged literary pursuits and made literature available to everyone. An especially valuable work produced during the Han dynasty period was the *Historical Record*. Written by **Sima Qian** during the reign of Wudi, it is the first true history of ancient China.

Science and Technology

Besides literature and philosophy, China made major contributions in science and technology. By the 300s B.C., Chinese astronomers had calculated the length of the solar year as $365\frac{1}{4}$ days. They gazed through bronze tubes equipped with a device that divided the sky into measured segments, allowing them to make accurate measurements. They kept valuable records of solar and lunar eclipses and comet sightings. In 240 B.C. Chinese astronomers recorded the appearance of the object that would later be called Halley's comet—many centuries before Halley's birth.

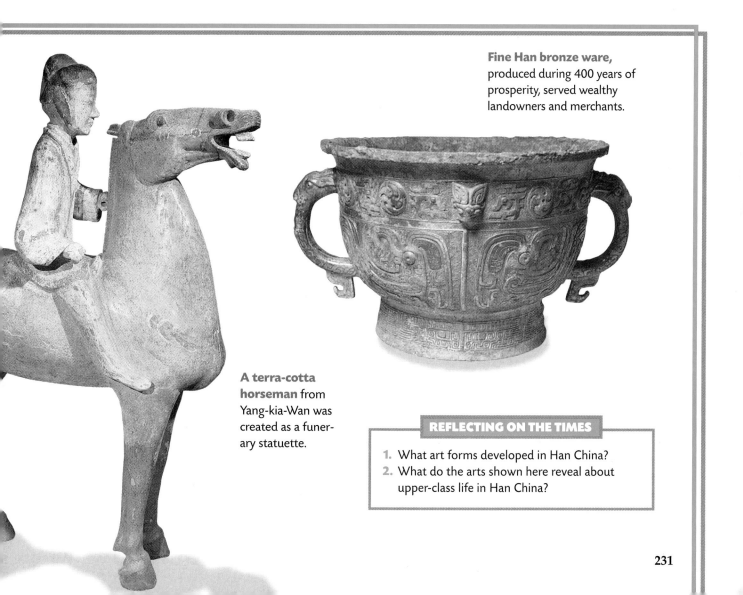

Fine Han bronze ware, produced during 400 years of prosperity, served wealthy landowners and merchants.

A terra-cotta horseman from Yang-kia-Wan was created as a funerary statuette.

REFLECTING ON THE TIMES

1. What art forms developed in Han China?
2. What do the arts shown here reveal about upper-class life in Han China?

Women prepare newly woven silk. Han weavers created beautiful damasks of many colors. *How did Chinese arts and inventions spread to other civilizations?*

Medicine

Chinese physicians recognized nutrition as vital and realized that some diseases resulted from vitamin deficiencies. Although they did not identify vitamins as such, they discovered and prescribed foods that would correct some problems. They also understood that many herbs had medicinal value.

Chinese doctors treated ailments and relieved pain with acupuncture, a technique in which the skin is pierced with thin needles at vital points. They believed acupuncture restored the balance between yin and yang in a person's body.

Farming and Transport

Under the Han, many improvements occurred in agriculture and transportation. Complex irrigation systems drained swamps and diverted rivers to quench parched fields. Advances in fertilizing crops helped farmers produce enough to feed China's growing population. Veterinary medicine helped save many farm animals. New canals and improved roadways reduced the cost of distributing food and permitted ideas to spread more rapidly.

Inventions

Many inventions in ancient China were especially vital to Chinese life and the economy. Made by the Chinese since prehistoric times, silk was in great demand as a trade item; its worth was attested to by the name of one of history's greatest trade routes—the Silk Road. Caravans carried the precious cargo as far as Rome.

Paper was probably invented by 100 B.C., although it was officially credited to an inventor of about 200 years later. Artisans pounded tree bark, hemp, or rags into a pulp. By treating it with gelatin, they discovered that they could then make paper. Used first for wrapping and clothing, paper was soon recognized as an ideal writing material.

The invention of paper benefited the bureaucratic Han government. Its centralized structure resulted in an explosion in the number of documents. Most were written on strips of wood, which were fragile and cumbersome to work with. The use of paper had many obvious advantages.

Other inventions improved mining and construction. Miners, using iron drill bits driven by workers on seesaw-like levers, drilled boreholes to obtain salt from the earth. Another invention was the wheelbarrow, which was first used on building sites around 100 B.C.

These are only a few examples from a list of Chinese "firsts," which also includes the first printed books, the earliest technologies for casting bronze and iron, the suspension bridge, the compass, and gunpowder. Such achievements caused China to remain far ahead of Europe in science and technology until the A.D. 1300s.

SECTION 3 REVIEW

Recall
1. **Define** hierarchy, extended family, nuclear family, acupuncture.
2. **Identify** the Five Classics, *Spring and Autumn Annals*, the *Analects*, Sima Qian.
3. **Explain** how families and government during the Han era reflected the Confucian idea of order.

Critical Thinking
4. **Making Comparisons** Compare a typical Han Chinese family with families you consider typical of America today.

Understanding Themes
5. **Cultural Diffusion** What ideas and products from ancient China have become popular in the West in recent years? What factors account for their popularity among Western thinkers and consumers?

Identifying Central Issues

The saying "He can't see the forest for the trees" refers to someone so focused on separate details that he cannot see the entire situation. Sometimes we face this problem when studying history. It is easy to focus on details such as names, dates, and places, thus losing sight of the bigger picture. To avoid this, it is important to identify the central issues. Central issues are the main ideas of historical material.

Learning the Skill

First, skim the material to identify its general subject. Look for headings and subheadings; often they highlight central issues. A central issue may also appear in the topic sentence of a paragraph. The other sentences in the paragraph usually explain and support the central issue.

When looking for central issues, ask yourself these questions: What is the general topic of this material? What ideas have the greatest emphasis? What main idea holds the details together? If I had to summarize this material in one sentence, what would it be? If you can answer one or more of these questions, you can identify central issues.

Practicing the Skill

Read the passage about the *Book of Changes* and answer the questions that follow.

❝ The *Book of Changes*—*I Ching* in Chinese—is unquestionably one of the most important books in the world's literature…. Nearly all that is greatest and most significant in the three thousand years of Chinese cultural history has either taken its inspiration from this book, or has exerted an influence on the interpretation of its text…. Indeed, not only the philosophy of China but its science and statecraft as well have never ceased to draw from the spring of wisdom in the *I Ching*…. Even the commonplaces of everyday life in China are saturated with its influence. In going through the streets of a Chinese city, one will find, here and there at a street corner, a fortune teller sitting behind a neatly covered table, brush and tablet at hand, ready to draw from the ancient book of wisdom pertinent counsel and information on life's minor perplexities…. ❞

1. What is the general subject of the passage?
2. Which idea has the greatest emphasis?
3. What are some details that support this idea?
4. Which sentence states the central issue of the passage?

Applying the Skill

Find a newspaper or magazine article that interests you. Identify the central issues in this article and summarize them in your own words.

For More Practice

Turn to the Skill Practice in the Chapter Review on page 235 for more practice in identifying central issues.

Connections Across Time

Historical Significance Confucian ideas have had a major impact on China's development. On the negative side, some historians point to the Confucian denial of women's rights and its stress on total obedience to authority. On the positive side, others state that the Confucian emphasis on stability helped early China build a strong government and that Confucius's ideas about relationships resulted in a more compassionate society. Confucius also left a revolutionary legacy. He considered it a society's duty to overthrow an unjust ruler and to ensure a fair distribution of wealth.

Using Key Terms

Write the key term that completes each sentence. Then write a sentence for each term not chosen.

a. acupuncture
b. civil service
c. extended family
d. hierarchy
e. ethics
f. mandarin
g. yin and yang
h. filial piety
i. cavalry
j. nuclear family

1. An _____ consists of parents, children, grandparents, and other relatives living together in one household.
2. Chinese doctors treated ailments and relieved pain with _____, a technique in which the skin is pierced with thin needles at vital points.
3. A Chinese theory related to Daoism was the concept of _____, the two opposing forces believed to be present in all of nature.
4. Confucius taught that individuals should live according to principles of _____.
5. The Chinese cared especially about _____, or children's respect for their parents.

Using Your History Journal

Many of Confucius's sayings compiled after his death are similar to proverbs. Write a set of your own proverbs about everyday decisions and situations.

Technology Activity

Building a Database The teachings of the ancient Chinese teacher Confucius date back to 479 B.C. Many of his teachings are still practiced in China today. Search the Internet or your local library for additional information about Confucius. Build a database of collected Confucian sayings, or analects. Organize analects by headings reflecting different categories according to Confucius's principles or ethics. Examples of categories would be a person's conduct or filial piety.

Reviewing Facts

1. **Culture** Identify Confucius and his ideas.
2. **Government** Explain how Mandarins came to shape China's government.
3. **Culture** List the five relationships in Chinese society that were identified by Confucius.
4. **Culture** Describe the *Book of Songs*, the *Spring and Autumn Annals*, and the *Historical Record*.
5. **History** Explain why Qin Shihuangdi ordered the construction of the Great Wall of China.
6. **Culture** Identify three groups in Han China.
7. **Government** List the characteristics of China's government and politics under the Zhou, Qin, and Han dynasties.
8. **Government** Analyze how Confucius applied the idea of filial piety to governments.
9. **Culture** Explain why Qin rulers strongly opposed the teachings of Confucius, though Han rulers like Wudi promoted Confucianism.
10. **Technology** List three Chinese inventions and state how they changed Chinese life.

Critical Thinking

1. **Synthesize** Create a time line showing major events in China from the Zhou to the Han dynasties.

2. Evaluate Was a strong family structure a positive or a negative influence on Chinese society?

3. Apply How does your society make use of the Han concept of appointing officials by ability?

4. Synthesize How would you respond if your government adopted the social policies of the Qin dynasty?

5. Compare How is Confucianism different from Christianity and Judaism? How is it similar?

6. Synthesize Think about how merchants were viewed in Han society and why. How might the United States be different if we felt that way about merchants?

Geography in History

1. Movement Refer to the map below. Buddhism came to China from which area of the world?

2. Location What cities became major Buddhist sites in China?

3. Region What large area was a major stronghold of Daoism?

4. Region What Daoist concepts made it possible for much of China to accept the teachings of Confucius, Laozi, and the Buddha into a unified belief system?

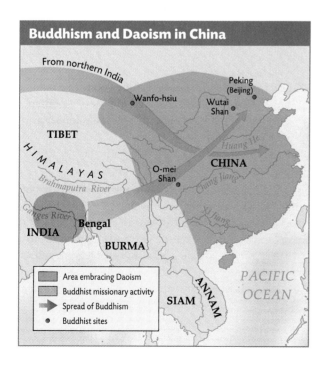

Buddhism and Daoism in China

From northern India

Wanfo-hsiu

Peking (Beijing)

Wutai Shan

TIBET

HIMALAYAS

Brahmaputra River

O-mei Shan

CHINA

Huang He

Chang Jiang

Xi Jiang

Ganges River

Bengal

INDIA

BURMA

SIAM

ANNAM

PACIFIC OCEAN

- ▢ Area embracing Daoism
- ▢ Buddhist missionary activity
- ➜ Spread of Buddhism
- • Buddhist sites

Understanding Themes

1. Uniformity What methods did Qin Shihuangdi use to unify China? What was their impact?

2. Innovation How did the ethical philosophy of Confucius influence Chinese society?

3. Cultural Diffusion How did Buddhism reach China?

Linking Past and Present

1. The Qin tried to control people's ideas by limiting the books they could read. Provide an example of a modern government that limits the information its people receive.

2. All candidates for China's civil service were required to master the Five Classics. Can you think of literature from our own culture that everyone should know? Why would it be difficult for Americans to agree on five classics?

Skill Practice

Read the passage below and answer the questions that follow.

❝Females should be strictly grave and sober, and yet adapted to the occasion. Whether in waiting on her parents, receiving or reverencing her husband, rising up or sitting down, when pregnant, in times of mourning, or when fleeing in war, she should be perfectly decorous. Rearing the silkworm and working cloth are the most important employments of the female; preparing food for the household and setting in order sacrifices follow next, each of which must be attended to. After that, study and learning can fill up the time. ❞

Book of Changes (I Ching)

1. What is the general topic of this passage?
2. What details are offered on this topic?
3. Which sentence, if any, states the central issue of this passage?
4. State the central issue in your own words.

ABCNEWS INTERACTIVE™

Turning Points in World History

Democracy in Greece

Setting up the Video

Work with a group of your classmates to view "Democracy in Greece" on the videodisc *Turning Points in World History*. The foundation of present-day democracy can be traced almost 2,500 years ago to ancient Greece. Athenians developed the idea of a democratic government in which the majority rules but the minority still has rights. This program takes a look at the origins of democracy and how it has influenced modern governments and cultures.

Side One,
Chapter 5

View the video by scanning the bar code or by entering the chapter number on your keypad and pressing Search. (Also available in VHS format.)

Hands-On Activity

Organize into cooperative groups. Write and perform five-minute skits about the importance of voting in a democratic society. Videotape skits to share with other classes.

Surfing the "Net"

African Artifacts

The African continent is rich with precious artifacts ranging from tools to jewelry. To find out more about African artifacts, look on the Internet.

Getting There

Follow these steps below to gather information about African artifacts on the Internet.

1. Go to a search engine. Type in the phrase *African artifacts*.
2. After typing in the phrase, enter words like those below to focus your search:
   - *jewelry*
   - *tools*
   - *pottery*
   - *countries*

3. The search engine should provide you with a number of links to follow. Links are "pointers" to different sites on the Internet and commonly appear as blue underlined words.

What to Do When You Are There

Click on the links to navigate through the pages of information and gather your findings. Design a bulletin board by printing images of African artifacts that you have located on the Internet. Use a word processor to create captions explaining what the artifacts are and where they are from. Include a map of Africa and label the countries where the various artifacts were found.

Unit 2 Digest

Chalices from the court of a wealthy Mycenaean king. *Besides the Mycenaeans, what other people influenced the development of early Greek civilization?*

From about 2000 B.C. to A.D. 500, major civilizations arose throughout the world. Although each civilization had unique traits, they all had common features, such as a stable political system, one or more major religions, and an interest in the arts and sciences. These civilizations produced many achievements that still influence the world today.

Chapter 4
The Rise of Ancient Greece

Although Greece's mountains protected against invaders, they also limited travel and communication among the Greeks and prevented them from uniting politically. Numerous harbors and closeness to the sea, however, encouraged the Greeks to become traders, and eventually they founded colonies around the Mediterranean Sea.

Greek civilization had its origins in the Minoan civilization on the Mediterranean island of Crete and the Mycenaean civilization on the European mainland. The Greeks provided a record of their legends and early history in two epic poems, the *Iliad* and the *Odyssey*. These epics taught such values as courage, dignity, and love of beauty. The Greeks worshiped gods and goddesses—who were both humanlike and superpowerful—and imitated their deities by themselves striving for excellence.

The polis—the Greek city-state—served as the center of Greek life. The two major Greek city-states were Sparta and Athens. Sparta was a military society that emphasized physical strength and service in the army. Athens built a much freer society that stressed education and public service. It also introduced the Western concept of democracy.

During the 400s B.C., the Greeks defeated the Persians in a series of wars. A golden age of cultural achievement in Athens followed the Persian conflicts. Later, resentment against Athenian power led to the Peloponnesian War between a Sparta-led alliance of city-states and Athens. The war brought defeat for Athens and a decline for the Greek city-state system.

Chapter 5
The Height of Greek Civilization

During the 400s B.C., Athens became the center of Greek civilization. Its classical style of art, architecture, and literature have endured in Western civilization. The Athenians expressed their love of beauty and harmony in such buildings as the Parthenon. They decorated their pottery with paintings and created masterpieces of sculpture. The Greeks were the first to write and perform plays—comedies and tragedies.

Greek thinkers believed in the power of reason to explain all things, a belief that became a basic principle of science. Socrates constructed a way of teaching known as the Socratic method. His student Plato studied human behavior and wrote the first book on political science. Aristotle wrote on logic and poetry, among other topics. The Greeks also produced the first true historians, Herodotus and Thucydides, and the father of medicine, Hippocrates.

By 330 B.C., a new political leader named Alexander of Macedonia had defeated the Persians and conquered an area from Egypt to India. His goal was to combine the best of Greek and Persian cultures into one civilization. After Alexander's death, his empire was divided among three of his generals.

Although Greek political unity had vanished, Greek culture spread and mixed with Middle Eastern cultures to form the Hellenistic civilization. This new civilization, which excelled in the sciences, developed in newly built cities, such as Alexandria, Egypt.

Chapter 6
Ancient Rome and Early Christianity

In the 500s B.C. the Romans set up a republic ruled by the upper classes but increasingly influenced by the common people. To protect their republic, the Romans formed a powerful army and began to expand their territory. By 264 B.C., Rome had conquered the entire Italian Peninsula. It then fought the Punic Wars against Carthage, finally defeating the North African city-state in 146 B.C

Rome's military conquests brought the Roman Republic wealth but also substituted slave labor on large estates for small, independent citizen-farmers. Mounting social tensions led to civil war and an increased political role for the army. In 45 B.C, the general Julius Caesar came to power and set up a dictatorship. In 27 B.C. his grandnephew Octavian, or Augustus, became the first Roman emperor.

About this time, the Roman Empire entered a long period of peace and prosperity known as the *Pax Romana*. The Romans of this era developed their system of laws and built roads, aqueducts, and public buildings. Great literary figures included the poets Horace and Virgil and the historians Livy and Tacitus.

During the *Pax Romana*, Christianity—based on the life and teachings of Jesus—began as a part of Judaism but quickly spread through the Roman world as a new religion. At the heart of early Christian preaching was the belief that Jesus was the Son of God and the way of salvation. After periodic persecutions, Christianity became the official religion of the empire in A.D. 392.

By the A.D 300s, political chaos, economic crisis, and Germanic invasions had led to the decline of the Roman Empire. Reform efforts by Emperors Diocletian and Constantine helped preserve the eastern part of the empire but only delayed the downfall of the western part of the empire until the late A.D 400s.

Visualizing History

Octavian, known as Augustus, preferred to be called "first citizen." *What was the period that began with his reign called?*

Chapter 7
Flowering of African Civilizations

Africa's diverse geography influenced the development of its civilizations. In areas of scarce rainfall, settlements arose near lakes or rivers, such as the Nile. Trading civilizations, such as Kush and Axum in eastern Africa, exchanged ideas and goods with places as far away as Rome and India. Movement of peoples, such as the Bantu migrations, spread culture to other parts of Africa.

In West Africa, a series of kingdoms arose and prospered between A.D. 300 and A.D. 1500. Ghana, the first of these territories, traded salt for gold brought by Arab traders. Mali, a nation that broke away from Ghana, also became powerful. Its king, Mansa Musa, created a rich trading empire through his contacts with the Middle East. Islamic culture spread throughout Africa. Songhai, the last of the great West African kingdoms, expanded its territory and developed a strong legal system based on the religion of Islam.

Trade contacts also brought power and wealth to city-states along the coast of East Africa. There Arab traders brought cotton, silk, and Chinese porcelain from India and Southeast Asia to exchange for ivory and metals from Africa's interior. Meanwhile, powerful kingdoms thrived in Southern Africa. These inland areas mined rich deposits of copper and gold. Traders from the East African coast made their way to the southern African kingdoms and began an active trade there.

Chapter 8
India's Great Civilization

About 1500 B.C. Aryan invaders conquered northern India and created a new society. Early Indian religious writings—the *Rig-Veda*, the *Mahabharata*, and the *Upanishads*—taught the principles of Hinduism, India's major religion. Hinduism includes belief in many deities and the concept of an eternal spirit, reincarnation, and the obligation to perform the duties of one's social group.

During the 500s B.C., Siddhartha Gautama founded Buddhism, which later spread from India to East Asia and Southeast Asia. Known as the Buddha, or Enlightened One, Gautama taught that people can free themselves from suffering by eliminating desire and by following rules of behavior, the Eightfold Path. Buddhism, as well as Hinduism, had a profound influence on the literature, arts, and architecture of Asia.

The Mauryas, who ruled from 321 B.C. to 184 B.C., founded an empire in northern India, and the Mauryan ruler Asoka helped spread Buddhism. About 500 years later, the Guptas reunited India, and their empire lasted from A.D. 320 to A.D. 600. Under the Guptas, scholars made numerous advances—including the development of algebra, the numbers 1 to 9, and the concept of zero.

Chapter 9
China's Flourishing Civilization

Under the Zhou dynasty, which ruled from about 1000 B.C. to 256 B.C., China made many technological advances and grew in population. Later the Qin and Han dynasties set up powerful central governments that brought stability, expanded Chinese territory, and increased foreign trade. Two notable achievements were the building of the Great Wall to protect against invaders and the creation of a civil service system in which officials were appointed on the basis of examinations.

Visualizing History A treasure of 6,000 terra-cotta soldiers from the Qin dynasty was uncovered in Shensi Province. *What other large structure was built during this time?*

Two major philosophies—Confucianism and Daoism—developed in early China. Founded by Confucius (Kongfuzi), Confucianism stressed basic moral rules in human relationships and the ideal of a courteous, well-educated individual. Daoism emphasized living in harmony with nature.

Chinese society consisted of landowners, peasants, and merchants. The Chinese family, dominated by the oldest male, played an important role. It functioned as an economic unit to which all members gave their earnings and which supported the old, the young, and the sick.

In addition to many literary works, the Chinese made great contributions in science and technology. These include the first printed book and the development of paper and gunpowder.

SURVEYING UNIT 2

1. **Chapter 4** How did the people of Athens and Sparta differ in their general attitudes toward life?
2. **Chapter 5** In what ways did the ancient Greeks lay the foundation of the arts and sciences of the West?
3. **Chapter 6** How did Christianity begin and later develop?
4. **Chapter 7** Why was trade so important to early African kingdoms and city-states?
5. **Chapter 8** What mathematical advances did early India pass on to other parts of the world?
6. **Chapter 9** How did the people of early India compare with the people of early China in their religious beliefs?

Regional Civilizations

Then & Now

As this period opened, advanced civilizations began to develop in many regions of the world. Although some cultures were cut off from other regions, trade and migrations spread ideas across continents and among several different peoples. Emerging centers of trade and commerce brought more highly organized social structures and governments. These regional civilizations contributed many ideas that influenced the development of the modern world. Christianity, Islam, Confucianism, and Buddhism spread over wide areas. Scientific discoveries crossed cultures. Some contact between cultures caused conflict that lasted for decades or centuries.

A Global Chronology

	A.D. 500	A.D. 700	A.D. 900
Political	A.D. 527 Justinian becomes Byzantine emperor.	A.D. 638 Arabs conquer Jerusalem.	
Scientific/ Technological		A.D. 850 Arabs perfect the astrolabe.	A.D. 1000 Chinese invent gunpowder.
Social/Cultural		A.D. 622 Muhammad flees Makkah (Islamic Year 1).	

Mayan clay figurine of a man and a woman wrapped in a blanket, c. A.D. 700–1000. Campeche, Mexico

Portfolio Project

Americans share the benefits of foods, inventions, discoveries, and ideas from all over the world. Often we do not think about the cultures that contributed these things. Create a map on which you show some products or ideas that originated in each of the following areas: the Middle East, Asia, Africa, South America, or Europe.

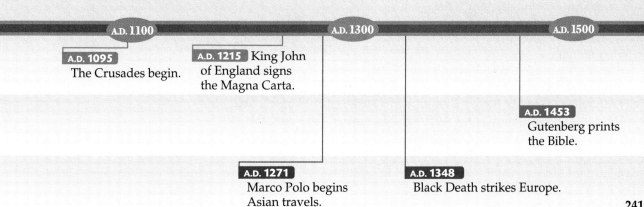

A.D. 1100

A.D. 1300

A.D. 1500

A.D. 1095
The Crusades begin.

A.D. 1215 King John of England signs the Magna Carta.

A.D. 1453
Gutenberg prints the Bible.

A.D. 1271
Marco Polo begins Asian travels.

A.D. 1348
Black Death strikes Europe.

241

The Spread of Ideas

Mathematics

*T*he invention of mathematics changed the course of civilization. Astronomers used mathematics to account for the movements of the sun and moon so they could mark the seasons. Geometry enabled people to calculate the volume of a cylindrical granary. Mathematics supported travel, from the earliest sea travel to the development of the space program. It all began with the Sumerians.

Sumerian cuneiform tablet

Indus Valley
The Use of Numerals

The Sumerians devised one of the world's earliest numbering systems. They used two wedge-like symbols for counting. One symbol stood for 1, the other for 10. But these symbols—and others to follow—basically came from the Sumerian cuneiform. The wedges served double-duty for symbolizing words and figures.

Other early peoples who invented numbering systems used letters from their alphabets. Then, around A.D. 500, Hindu people in the Indus River valley abandoned the use of letters. They created instead special number symbols to stand for the figures 1 to 9. Although modernized over time, these 9 Hindu symbols are the ones we use today.

The Middle East
The Rise of Algebra

Trade introduced people in the Middle East to the Hindu number system. About A.D. 825 an Arab mathematician, al-Khowarizmi of Baghdad, wrote a book recommending the new system to everyone. In a second book, al-Khowarizmi showed how the system could be used. He called the book *al-jabr w'al-muqabalah*, which roughly means "the art of bringing together unknowns to match a known quantity." The word *algebra* comes from the key word in the title—*al-jabr*, or "bringing together."

Persian astronomer

The wonder of the system caught Arab imaginations. Arabs especially liked the concept of zero—developed by the Hindus after they created the symbols for 1-9. In explaining this concept, one Arab mathematician wrote: "When [in subtraction] nothing is left over, then write the little circle so that the place does not remain empty." With the use of zero, mathematicians could build numbers of astronomical size using just 10 symbols.

The astrolabe was used by Muslim astronomers and navigators to observe and calculate the position of stars and other heavenly bodies.

Europe
The Triumph of Arabic Numerals

Muslims ruled in Spain from the A.D. 700s to the A.D. 1400s. Their presence opened the door for European use of the new Hindu-Arabic number system. At first, many Europeans rejected it. They clung instead to Roman numerals. The Italian city-state of Florence even passed a law banning the use of the Hindu-Arabic system.

Later, however, "Arabic numerals," as they were called, proved a more powerful conqueror than Arab soldiers. European merchants found knowledge of the symbols necessary for dealings with merchants in Muslim ports. Europeans who learned the new arithmetic also found it easier to do their tallies. By the A.D. 1400s, the numbers could even be found in popular art.

As you will read in this unit, Europeans began to adopt other practices from the Middle East as well. The pace of change quickened as wars and trade brought more people in contact with each other.

Book of Hours with Arabic numerals

LINKING THE IDEAS

1. How did the Hindu system of numbers differ from earlier systems?
2. What was the importance of the invention of zero?

Critical Thinking

3. **Cause and Effect** What was the role of conquest and trade in spreading the use of the Hindu-Arabic number system?

Byzantines and Slavs

Chapter Themes

▶ **Conflict** Byzantines fight off invaders and struggle over use of icons. *Section 1*
▶ **Innovation** Byzantines develop Eastern Orthodox theology and distinctive art forms. *Section 2*
▶ **Cultural Diffusion** Trade routes and invasions spread beliefs and ideas. *Section 3*

The Storyteller

The awestruck visitor arriving in A.D. 600 in the city of Constantinople in southeastern Europe scarcely knew where to turn. Splendid public buildings as well as simple private homes lined the streets; the scent of rare spices perfumed the air; people dressed in fine silk thronged the church of Hagia Sophia. "One might imagine that one has chanced upon a meadow in full bloom," the Greek historian Procopius wrote about the newly built church. "For one would surely marvel at the purple hue of some [columns], the green of others, at those on which the crimson blooms, at those that flash with white, at those, too, which nature, like a painter, has varied with the most contrasting colors." The church's grandeur reflected that of Constantinople, "city of the world's desire," capital of a prosperous empire that controlled east-west trade and laid the basis for the Greek and Slavic cultures of modern Europe.

Historical Significance

What cultural achievements did the Byzantines pass on to western Europe? How did their civilization affect the development of the peoples of eastern Europe?

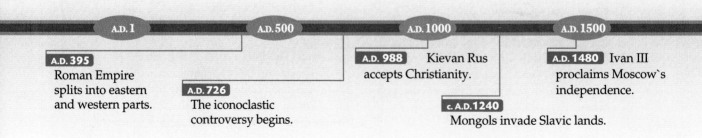

A.D. 1   A.D. 500   A.D. 1000   A.D. 1500

A.D. 395 Roman Empire splits into eastern and western parts.

A.D. 726 The iconoclastic controversy begins.

A.D. 988 Kievan Rus accepts Christianity.

c. A.D. 1240 Mongols invade Slavic lands.

A.D. 1480 Ivan III proclaims Moscow's independence.

The archangel Gabriel, an icon on wood, from the
Russian State Museum, St. Petersburg, Russia

Your History Journal

*Find out about a specific law in
Justinian's Code in an encyclopedia or a
book on the history of legal systems. Write
the law as an illuminated manuscript,
an art form described in this chapter.*

Section 1

The New Rome

Setting the Scene

▶ **Terms to Define**
   clergy, laity, icon, iconoclast, schism

▶ **People to Meet**
   Constantine, Justinian, Theodora, Leo III

▶ **Places to Locate**
   Byzantine Empire, Constantinople

 **Find Out** What made the Byzantine Empire rich and powerful?

The Storyteller

Byzantium [Constantinople] was in flames. A mob was screaming insults at Emperor Justinian and Empress Theodora. The emperor swiftly ordered the imperial treasury loaded onto ships to prepare for escape. Half crazed and without hope, Justinian held a final council of a few loyal friends; Theodora was present. After the military generals expressed their fears, Theodora suddenly rose and broke the silence. "I do not choose to flee," she said. "Never shall I see the day when

I am not saluted as the empress.... You have the money, the ships are ready, the sea is open. As for me, I shall stay." Hearing her, the others took heart. That day, Theodora saved Justinian's throne.

—adapted from *Theodora, Empress of Byzantium,* Charles Diehl, 1972

Theodora, detail of mosaic

After the Roman Empire was divided in A.D. 395, the eastern half became known as the **Byzantine Empire**. At its height in the A.D. 500s, the Byzantine Empire included most of the Balkan Peninsula, Italy, southern Spain, Asia Minor, Syria and North Africa. Its major population group, the Greeks, lived mainly in the central part of the empire. Also included in the empire were Egyptians, Syrians, Arabs, Armenians, Jews, Persians, Slavs, and Turks. These varied peoples and cultures gave Byzantine civilization an international character.

Byzantine Foundations

The location of **Constantinople**, the Byzantine capital, reinforced this multicultural character. The city was located near the centers of early Christianity as well as on major trade routes.

A Strategic City

In A.D. 330 the Roman emperor **Constantine** built Constantinople at a strategic place where Europe and Asia meet. Located on a peninsula, Constantinople overlooked the Bosporus, the narrow strait between the Sea of Marmara and the Black Sea. A second strait, the Dardanelles, connects the Sea of Marmara and the Aegean Sea, which leads to the Mediterranean. These straits gave the occupiers of the peninsula control over movement between the Mediterranean and the Black Seas and, as a result, over the routes leading east to Asia and north to northern Europe. The site of Constantinople itself offered natural protection from attack at a time when Germanic invaders were assaulting Rome to the west. Water protected the city on three sides, and triple walls fortified the side open to attack by land. Eventually a huge chain was strung across the narrow mouth of the deep harbor on Constantinople's north side for still greater protection.

The straits also made the peninsula a natural crossroads for trade. By A.D. 400 the Byzantine capital had become the wealthiest part of the Roman Empire, handling rich cargoes from Asia, Europe, and Africa.

Cultural Blend

After Rome's fall, the Byzantine Empire was regarded as heir to Roman power and traditions. Constantinople was known as the New Rome because its emperors were Romans who spoke Latin and many of its wealthy families came from Rome. Despite these ties, the Byzantine Empire was more than a continuation of the old Roman Empire.

Lands once part of the Greek world formed the heart of the Byzantine Empire. The Byzantine people not only spoke Greek but also stressed their Greek heritage. Eventually Byzantine emperors and officials also used Greek rather than Latin. Religious scholars expressed their ideas in Greek and developed a distinct form of Christianity known today as Eastern Orthodoxy. In addition to the Byzantine Empire's classical Greek heritage and Christian religion came cultural influences from eastern civilizations such as Persia. This mixture of cultures created a distinct Byzantine civilization. Between A.D. 500 and A.D. 1200, this civilization was one of the most advanced in the world and had a higher standard of living than western Europe.

Justinian's Rule

At its height the Byzantine Empire was ruled by **Justinian**, the son of prosperous peasants from Macedonia in the western part of the empire. While a young man in the court of his uncle, Emperor Justin I, he worked late into the night at his studies. Justinian's enthusiasm for knowledge and hard work continued after he became emperor in A.D. 527, at age 44.

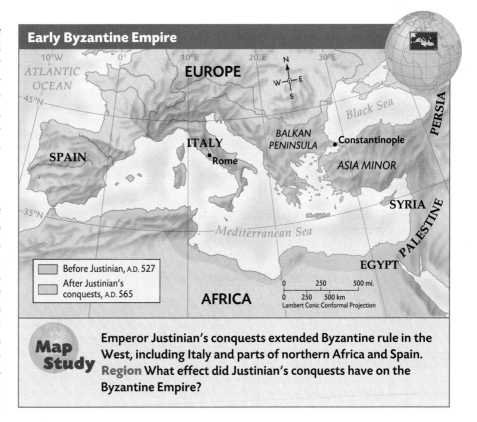

Early Byzantine Empire

Before Justinian, A.D. 527
After Justinian's conquests, A.D. 565

Map Study
Emperor Justinian's conquests extended Byzantine rule in the West, including Italy and parts of northern Africa and Spain. **Region** What effect did Justinian's conquests have on the Byzantine Empire?

Theodora's Support

Justinian's wife, **Theodora**, was beautiful, intelligent, and ambitious. Justinian had married her in spite of court objections to her occupation as an actress—a profession held in low esteem in the empire. A capable empress, Theodora participated actively in government, rewarding friends with positions and using dismissals to punish enemies.

Theodora was especially concerned with improving the social standing of women. She persuaded Justinian to issue a decree giving a wife the right to own land equal in value to the wealth she brought with her at marriage. This land gave a widow the income she needed to support her children without the assistance of the government.

In A.D. 532 Theodora's political talents helped save Justinian's throne. When a revolt of taxpayers in Constantinople threatened the government, Justinian's advisers urged him to leave the city. As flames roared through Constantinople and the rebels battered at the palace gates, Justinian prepared to flee. Theodora, however, persuaded him to remain in control.

Inspired by his wife's determination, Justinian reasserted his power. His army crushed the rebels, killing 30,000 people. From that time until his death in A.D. 565, Justinian ruled without challenge.

The Emperor Justinian, a mosaic from the A.D. 500s from Ravenna, Italy.
What architectural landmark did Justinian build?

Military Campaigns

During Justinian's reign, the Byzantines faced a serious military threat from the East. The Sassanian Empire of Persia, under Chosroes (kaz•ROH•eez) I, grew in strength and threatened to conquer the eastern provinces of the Byzantine Empire. The Byzantines rallied their forces and threw back the Persians. Justinian gained a brief period of security for the eastern borders by agreeing to pay tribute in return for peace.

Justinian dreamed of restoring the Roman Empire. In A.D. 533 he began the reconquest of Italy, North Africa, and Spain—Roman lands that had fallen to Germanic invaders. Under the general Belisarius, the Byzantine armies were strengthened and reorganized. Between A.D. 533 and A.D. 555, they fought a series of wars against the Vandals in North Africa, the Ostrogoths in Italy, and the Visigoths in southern Spain. The Byzantines conquered these Germanic groups and extended Byzantine rule in the west.

The successful reconquest, however, proved costly for the empire. The wars exhausted most of the Byzantine resources. Funds were low for defending the eastern borders, which faced attack by an expanding Persian Empire. Justinian's conquests did not last. Within a generation of his death, the empire lost many of its outlying territories.

Code of Laws

Justinian's legal reforms did last, affecting Western law even today. Shortly after becoming emperor, Justinian appointed a commission to codify, or classify, the empire's Roman laws. For centuries, these laws had accumulated without organization or classification.

The commission was made up of 10 scholars headed by a legal expert named Tribonian. For more than 6 years, the commission collected and organized vast numbers of laws. It threw out the ones that were outdated, simplified many, and put the remainder into categories. The commission's work was recorded in a collection of books known as the *Corpus of Civil Law*, or the Justinian Code. This massive work preserved Rome's legal heritage and later became the basis for most European legal systems.

The Arts

Under Justinian, Byzantine art and architecture

thrived and achieved their distinct character. The emperor ordered the construction of new roads, fortresses, aqueducts, monasteries, and other buildings. His most famous project was the church of Hagia Sophia, "Holy Wisdom," in Constantinople. The largest and most beautiful church in the empire, Hagia Sophia still stands today as one of the world's great architectural landmarks. ◗━

Byzantine Religion

Strong ties linked Byzantine emperors and the Church. The emperors were regarded as God's representatives on earth. Starting in the A.D. 400s, Byzantine emperors and empresses were crowned by the patriarch of Constantinople and took an oath to defend the Christian faith.

Church and State

Byzantine emperors frequently played a major role in church affairs. They appointed church officials, defined the style of worship, and used the wealth of the Church for government purposes.

Justinian strengthened this control over the

Church by intervening in disputes over church beliefs. He also tried to unify the empire under one Christian faith, a practice that sometimes led to persecution of Jews and non-Greek Christians.

Religious Controversy

Both Byzantine clergy—church officials such as priests and bishops—and laity—church members who were not clergy—were intensely interested in religious matters. In their homes, markets, and shops, Byzantines often engaged in heated religious discussions. Visitors to Constantinople saw shoppers in the marketplaces having lively discussions about such topics as the exact relationship of Jesus the Son to God the Father. Such arguments often became political issues and led to fights and riots.

In the A.D. 700s, a dispute broke out over the use of icons (EYE•KAHNZ), or religious images, in worship. Although Christians had disagreed about this practice since the A.D. 400s, the use of icons in churches became a political issue by the A.D. 700s.

Those who objected to the use of icons in Christian worship argued that the Bible, in the Ten Commandments, prohibited such images. Defenders stressed that icons were symbols of

Byzantine Architecture

Hagia Sophia, completed in A.D. 537, was built to symbolize both Christianity's importance in the Byzantine Empire and the Byzantine emperor's authority. It also represented the beginning of what became known as the Byzantine style of architecture.

Early Byzantine churches featured a central dome on a flat roof supported by four arches springing from columns or piers. Often the dome was pierced by windows and covered with glittering mosaics. Light streamed into the church from all directions and reflected off the decorated surfaces.

The Byzantine style eventually spread to other lands, such as Ukraine and Russia, that accepted Eastern Christianity. Architects in these lands modified the original Byzantine model to suit their own needs. For example, the Russians, who lived in a cold climate with a

lot of snow, replaced the flat roof and large central dome with sloping roofs and onion-shaped domes.

Today, Eastern Christians throughout the world still use some form of the Byzantine style. In cities and towns of North America, the descendants of Eastern Christian immigrants who came during the late 1800s and early 1900s have sometimes combined traditional Byzantine architectural principles with modern ones in their churches.

Hagia Sophia

Linking Past and Present ACTIVITY

Examine a church or other building in your community that is built in the Byzantine style. What elements of its architecture do you think reflect the basic Byzantine model? What elements do you think are modern or come from other cultural traditions?

Simplified Alphabet Becomes Popular

Japan, A.D. 860

The Japanese alphabet, hiragana, became popular around A.D. 860. It consisted of characters developed by simplifying the Chinese alphabet. Hiragana was popularized by women of the Heian court, who used the system in writing poetry, diaries, and novels. It was called "letters of women" because men continued to use kanji, or the Chinese system.

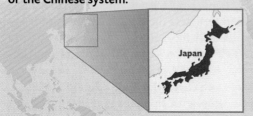

Japan

God's presence in human affairs. The leading champion of icons was the Byzantine theologian John of Damascus. Although a resident of the Islamic Empire, he wrote many religious articles defending the use of icons.

Believing that icons encouraged superstition and the worship of idols, in A.D. 726 Emperor **Leo III** ordered all icons removed from the churches. The emperor's supporters—mostly military leaders, government officials, and many of the people in Asia Minor—became known as iconoclasts, or image breakers.

Church leaders and other Byzantines resisted the order, and were supported by the Church in Rome, which was as important a center of Christianity as Constantinople. The Roman pope's involvement in the controversy strained relations between the Eastern and Western Churches.

Feeling his authority was being challenged, Leo asserted his power and suppressed demonstrations in favor of icons. Although several later emperors followed Leo's lead, they were not supported by

the people. In A.D. 787 a church council at Nicaea approved the use of icons. Soon after, the Empress Irene—the first woman to hold the Byzantine throne in her own right—allowed the use of icons as long as they were not given the worship due to God. The Eastern Church further settled the issue in A.D. 843, allowing the use of pictures, but not statues, in worship.

Conflict With Rome

Since the A.D. 300s, the Eastern and Western Churches had disagreed on a number of religious and political issues. As centuries passed, the disagreements intensified.

The iconoclastic controversy was but one of many reasons that divided the two churches. The most serious issue concerned the source of religious authority. The pope in Rome and the patriarch of Constantinople did not agree on their roles in the Christian Church. The pope stated that he was supreme leader of the Church; the patriarch of Constantinople opposed this claim. The two church leaders also disagreed over points of doctrine. They challenged each other for control of new churches in the Balkan Peninsula.

Relations between Eastern and Western Churches worsened in the A.D. 700s when the Germanic Lombards invaded central Italy. When the Byzantine emperor refused to give the pope in Rome military protection, the pope turned to the Franks, a Germanic Catholic people in western Europe. After the Franks defeated the Lombards, the pope gave the Frankish leader, Charlemagne, the title of emperor—a title which only the Byzantine ruler could legally grant. This action made the Byzantines even more bitter toward the pope and the Western Church.

By A.D. 1054 doctrinal, political, and geographical differences finally led to a schism (SIH•zuhm), or separation, of the Church into the Roman Catholic Church in the West and the Eastern Orthodox Church in the East. The split further weakened the Byzantine Empire, which had faced attacks from numerous peoples since its founding.

SECTION I REVIEW

Recall
1. **Define** clergy, laity, icon, iconoclast, schism.
2. **Identify** Constantine, Justinian, Theodora, Leo III.
3. **Locate** Constantinople on the map on page 247. Why was Constantinople's location significant?

Critical Thinking
4. **Analyzing Information** How were Byzantine emperors and the Christian Church linked?

Understanding Themes
5. **Conflict** How did religious disputes, such as the iconoclastic controversy, affect Byzantine political affairs?

Section 2

Byzantine Civilization

Setting the Scene

▶ **Terms to Define**
theology, regent, mosaic, illuminated manuscript, monastery, missionary

▶ **People to Meet**
Cyril, Methodius, the Seljuk Turks, the Ottoman Turks, Tiridates III, Tamara

▶ **Places to Locate**
Venice, Armenia, Georgia, Bulgaria, Serbia

 **Find Out** What role did Christianity play in Byzantine and neighboring societies?

The Storyteller

A bishop from Italy wrote home describing the Byzantine court: "In the audience-hall sat the Emperor on a throne before which stood an artificial tree, all gilded, on whose branches mechanical birds perched, singing. To either side of the throne stood a mighty lion, which, as the visitor approached, lashed the ground with its tail and from whose open jaws ... there came a terrifying roar." The visitor threw himself to the ground three times, and looking up beheld the Emperor raised by an invisible mechanism to the roof of the hall, where he sat glittering among his jewels.

—adapted from *Istanbul*, Martin Heurlimann, 1958

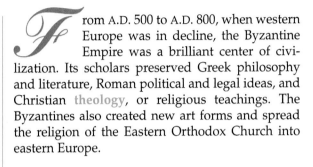

Emperor Constantine IX

From A.D. 500 to A.D. 800, when western Europe was in decline, the Byzantine Empire was a brilliant center of civilization. Its scholars preserved Greek philosophy and literature, Roman political and legal ideas, and Christian theology, or religious teachings. The Byzantines also created new art forms and spread the religion of the Eastern Orthodox Church into eastern Europe.

Byzantine Life

Byzantine society was divided into a hierarchy of social groups. Yet, there were few barriers to prevent a person from moving from one group to another. This flexibility brought variety and change to Byzantine life.

Family Life

The family was the center of social life for most Byzantines. Both the Church and the government supported marriage as a sacred institution. Divorce was difficult to obtain, and the Church generally forbade more than one remarriage.

Byzantine women were expected to live partly in seclusion, and so rooms in homes and churches were set aside for their sole use. Nevertheless, women had gained some rights through Theodora's efforts. Like the empress herself, some women became well educated and influential in the government. Several governed as regents, or temporary rulers, and a few ruled in their own right as empresses.

The Economy

Most Byzantines made a living through farming, herding, or working as laborers. Farmers paid heavy taxes that supported the government.

Although the base of the Byzantine economy was agricultural, commerce thrived in cities such as Constantinople, which was the site of a natural crossroads for trade. Byzantine ships loaded with cargo sailed between the Mediterranean and Black Seas by way of the Bosporus and Dardanelles. At the eastern shore of the Black Sea, goods could be shipped overland through Asia. Rivers such as the Dnieper, which flows from the Baltic region south to the Black Sea, provided access to northern Europe.

Merchants traded Byzantine agricultural goods and furs and enslaved people from northern Europe for luxury goods from the East. To Constantinople's busy harbor, called the Golden Horn, ships brought cloves and sandalwood from the East Indies; pepper, copper, and gems from India and Ceylon (present-day Sri Lanka); and silk from China.

The major Byzantine industry was weaving silk. It developed after A.D. 550, when Justinian sent two monks to China, the center of the silk industry.

On a visit to a silk factory the monks stole some silkworm eggs, hid them in hollow bamboo canes, and smuggled their precious cargo out of China. Brought to Constantinople, the silkworms fed on mulberry leaves and spun the silk that made the empire wealthy.

Byzantine Art and Learning

Among the products of Byzantine culture were beautiful icons, jewel-encrusted crosses, and carved ivory boxes for sacred items. These art forms were adopted by eastern Europe and also influenced western Europe and the Middle East.

Art

Religious subjects were the sources of most Byzantine art. Icons, the most popular art form, portrayed saints and other religious figures. Icons were displayed on the walls of churches, homes, and shrines. Magnificent churches were

Images of the Times

Byzantine Art

Byzantine art reflected the strong influence of Christianity.

The crucifix was a familiar Byzantine icon both in churches and in homes.

The Byzantine church of St. Kosmas at Loukas, Greece, displays a colorful mosaic.

embellished with gold and silver, polished and carved marble, ivory, and jewels, as well as icons and other religious images.

The Byzantines also excelled in the art of mosaic, or pictures made of many tiny pieces of colored glass or flat stone set in plaster. The most masterly mosaics captured the finest gradations of skin tones and textures of clothing—a skill even painters found difficult to master. Byzantine emperor Constantine VII, historian, painter, and author, described one mosaic:

> ❝ As you move, the figures seem to move, too. You could swear that their eyes are turning and shining and that their garments are rustling … the Byzantine mosaicist has succeeded in creating the illusion that his jig-saw puzzle has come to life. ❞

Religious scholars of the Byzantine Empire created another art form, the illuminated manuscript.

These were books decorated with elaborate designs, beautiful lettering, and miniature paintings. The brilliantly colored paintings portrayed religious themes as well as scenes of Byzantine daily life. Adopted in western Europe, the art of illuminating manuscripts provided a vivid record of daily life between A.D. 300 and A.D. 1200.

Education

Schools and learning also played an important role in Byzantine culture. The government-supported University of Constantinople, established in A.D. 850, trained scholars and lawyers for government jobs; the Eastern Orthodox Church provided religious schools to train priests and theological scholars. Beyond the religious subjects that reflected the primary role of the Church, areas of study included medicine, law, philosophy, arithmetic, geometry, astronomy, grammar, and music. Wealthy people sometimes hired tutors to instruct their children, particularly their daughters, who were usually not admitted to schools and universities.

Beautiful illuminated manuscripts, such as this from St. Catherine's Monastery at Sinai, were the work of religious scholars. Monasteries were financed by the emperor and by wealthy citizens.

REFLECTING ON THE TIMES

1. How do these images reveal the prosperity of the Byzantine Empire?
2. Who paid to have much of the religious art at churches and monasteries created?

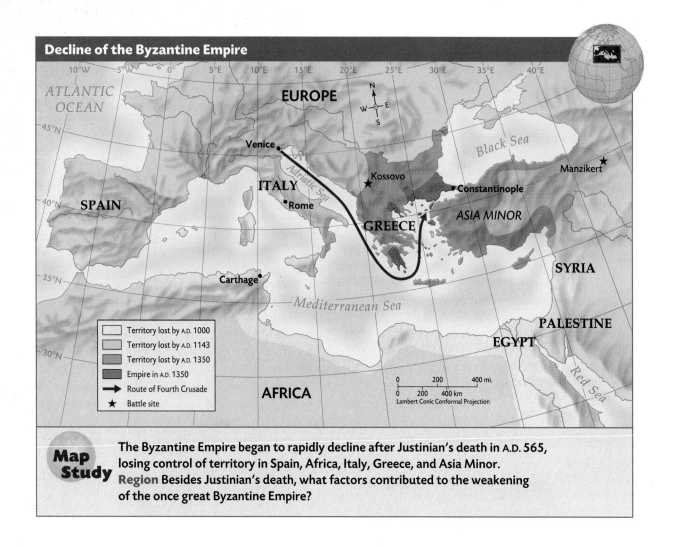

Decline of the Byzantine Empire

Map Study The Byzantine Empire began to rapidly decline after Justinian's death in A.D. 565, losing control of territory in Spain, Africa, Italy, Greece, and Asia Minor. **Region** Besides Justinian's death, what factors contributed to the weakening of the once great Byzantine Empire?

Byzantine literature focused on salvation of the soul and obedience to God's will. Writers composed hymns and poems in praise of Christ and his mother, Mary. Instead of popular fiction, Byzantine authors wrote books about the lives of the saints, which provided readers with moral lessons as well as accounts of the saints' miracles and adventures.

The foremost occupation of Byzantine scholars, however, was copying the writings of the ancient Greeks and Romans. By preserving ancient works on science, medicine, and mathematics, the Byzantines helped spread classical knowledge to the Western world.

Spread of Christianity

Near the end of the A.D. 300s, devout Christians throughout the Byzantine Empire formed religious communities called monasteries. In the monasteries, men called monks sought to develop a spiritual way of life apart from the temptations of the world. At the same time, they could help other people by doing good deeds and by setting an example of Christian living. Christian women who did the same were called nuns and lived in quarters of their own known as convents.

Monasteries and convents soon played an important role in Byzantine life. They helped the poor and ran hospitals and schools for needy children. They also spread Byzantine arts and learning. Monasteries also sent missionaries—people who carry a religious message—to neighboring peoples to convert them to the Christian faith.

Footnotes to History

Greek Fire

In fighting their enemies, the Byzantines used a terrifying weapon known as Greek fire, one of the earliest uses of chemicals in warfare. This chemical mixture exploded when it came into contact with fire or water. The formula remains a mystery; it probably included highly flammable oil, pitch, quicklime, sulfur, and resin.

Among the most successful missionaries were the brothers **Cyril** and **Methodius**. They reasoned that Christianity would be more acceptable to the Slavic peoples who lived north of the empire if it were presented in their own language. About A.D. 863 Cyril devised an alphabet for the Slavic languages. Known today as the Cyrillic (suh•RIH•lihk) alphabet in honor of its inventor, this script is still used by Russians, Ukrainians, Bulgarians, and Serbs. When Cyril and Methodius presented the Slavs with Cyrillic translations of the Bible and church ceremonies, they won many converts.

Decline and Fall

From its founding, the Byzantine Empire suffered frequent attacks by invading armies. Among them were Germanic Lombards, Slavs, Avars, Bulgars, Persians, and Arabs.

Unending Attacks

After Justinian died in A.D. 565, the Germanic Lombards took over most of Italy, the Avars attacked the northern frontier, Slavic peoples moved into the Balkans, and the Persians resumed their attacks in the east. By A.D. 626 the Slavs were at the walls of Constantinople. Although a brilliant counterattack stopped their advance, a new enemy—the Arabs from the Middle East—entered the scene. Followers of the new religion of Islam, the Arabs sought to spread their faith and acquire wealth. By the A.D. 630s, they occupied Syria and Palestine and had expanded into Persia and across North Africa. The Byzantines stopped the Arabs at Constantinople, but could not regain the lost territories in the Middle East and North Africa.

By A.D. 700 the Byzantine Empire was reduced to the territories that were primarily Greek. The loss of the non-Greek lands actually helped strengthen the empire because it now had one religion, one language, and one culture.

Christian Conquest

In A.D. 1071 northern European people called Normans seized the Byzantine lands in southern Italy. **Venice**, an Italian trading city on the Adriatic Sea, agreed to help the Byzantines' effort to regain the lands in return for trading privileges in Constantinople. The attempt failed, however, and the Byzantines soon lost control of trade, badly weakening an economy already strained by war.

In the same year, **the Seljuk** (SEHL•JOOK) **Turks**, who had come from central Asia and converted to Islam, defeated the Byzantines at the town

Visualizing History St. Jacob holding script in the Cyrillic alphabet, a modified form of the Greek alphabet. *What peoples use the Cyrillic alphabet today?*

of Manzikert. As the invaders advanced, the Byzantine emperor asked the pope's help in defending Christianity. Expeditions sent by the pope against the Islamic forces were more interested in taking over Palestine.

In A.D. 1204 Christian soldiers from western Europe agreed to help the Venetians attack Constantinople. For three days the attackers burned and looted the city, stealing and destroying priceless manuscripts and works of art. Their actions were so brutal that Pope Innocent III publicly condemned them:

❝ These defenders of Christ, who should have turned their swords only against the infidels [followers of Islam], have bathed in Christian blood. They have respected neither religion, nor age, nor sex.… It was not enough for them to squander the treasures of the Empire and to rob private individuals, whether great or small....

They have dared to lay their hands on the wealth of the churches. They have been seen tearing from the altars the silver adornments, breaking them in fragments, over which they quarrelled, violating the sanctuaries, carrying away the icons, crosses, and relics. **99**

The western Christians established "a Latin empire" in Constantinople. The Byzantine people resisted this rule successfully and reestablished their own culture in A.D. 1261.

Fall of Constantinople

The years of fighting had severely weakened the Byzantine Empire. Soon Serbs and Bulgars took over Balkan territory. New invaders from central Asia, **the Ottoman Turks**, attacked the eastern provinces. By the late A.D. 1300s, the Byzantine Empire consisted of only Constantinople and part of Greece.

About 100,000 people still lived in the capital; food was scarce, and wealth was gone. In A.D. 1453 the Ottomans laid siege to Constantinople. For six weeks their huge cannon blasted away at the city's walls. The Byzantines fought fiercely until their last emperor was killed.

For a thousand years, the Byzantine Empire had protected the Christian lands to its north. With the fall of Constantinople, central Europe lay open to attack by Islamic forces. Despite the empire's fall, the Byzantine heritage lived on in the civilization developed by the Eastern Slavs.

Neighboring Kingdoms

During the time of the Byzantine Empire, four neighboring kingdoms went through periods of prosperity and decline. Northeast of the empire, and south of the Caucasus Mountains between the Black and Caspian Seas, lay the kingdoms of **Armenia** and **Georgia.** Northwest of Byzantine territory, in Europe's Balkan Peninsula, arose two other realms—**Bulgaria** and **Serbia.**

Armenia

Located at a crossroads between Europe and Asia, Armenia struggled against foreign invasions. Settling the area in the 700s B.C., the Armenians within 300 years had become part of the Persian Empire. When Alexander the Great conquered Persia in the 330s B.C., his armies acquired Armenia but allowed it some freedoms. King Tigran II, who came to power about 95 B.C., built an independent Armenian kingdom stretching from the Caspian Sea to the Mediterranean Sea. The Romans, however, defeated Tigran in 69 B.C., and Armenia became part of the Roman Empire.

In the early A.D. 300s, the Armenians, under King **Tiridates** (TEER•uh•DAH •teez) **III**, accepted Christianity. This decision made Armenia the first officially Christian country in the world. Christianity gave Armenians a sense of national identity. Mesrob (MEH•zrohb), an Armenian scholar-monk, developed the Armenian alphabet in the early A.D. 400s. In A.D. 451, the Armenians successfully

Portrait of Sultan Mahmet II, who conquered Constantinople and renamed it Istanbul. *How long did the Byzantine city hold out against the sultan's siege?*

defended their Christian state against the Persians in the Battle of Avarair (ah•vah•RAHR).

Arab armies invaded Armenia in the A.D. 600s, but they failed to conquer the entire country. An independent Armenian kingdom eventually arose in the northern region. In the A.D. 1000s the Seljuk Turks swept into Armenia, followed by the Ottoman Turks in the A.D. 1400s. Within 300 years, Armenia had became a battlefield among the Ottomans, Persians, and Russians. During the A.D. 1800s, it was divided between the Russian and Ottoman empires.

Georgia

Like Armenia, Georgia continually faced waves of foreign invasions. Ancient Georgia consisted of two kingdoms known as Colchis and Iberia. Both realms came under Roman rule in 65 B.C. The Roman conquerors built new roads and introduced their laws and customs to the region. The Silk Road, which passed through the Caucasus Mountains, allowed the Georgians to prosper from trade between Europe and Asia. Caravans of silk cloth, spices, and other goods reached ports on Georgia's Black Sea coast and continued on to the Middle East and Europe.

Georgia accepted Christianity in the A.D. 300s. Georgian tradition states that a Christian woman named Nino was responsible for converting the Georgians. Meanwhile, newly Christianized Georgia was attacked by rival Persian and Byzantine armies.

During the A.D. 1100s and early A.D. 1200s, Georgia enjoyed a golden age of freedom and culture under Queen **Tamara** (tah•MAH•rah). However, from the late A.D. 1200s to the A.D. 1700s, the Georgians again faced a series of conquerors, including the Mongols, the Persians, and the Ottomans. Turning northward to the Russians for military aid, Georgia by the early A.D. 1800s had become part of the Russian Empire.

Bulgaria

The Balkan Peninsula also underwent upheavals. Conquered by Roman armies, the region that is present-day Bulgaria became part of the Roman Empire in the A.D. 40s. When Rome fell about 400 years later, Slavs from east central Europe and Bulgars from central Asia settled Bulgaria, where they eventually intermarried to become the Bulgarians.

Influenced by Byzantine culture and religion, the first Bulgarian state arose in the A.D. 600s. It reached its peak 300 years later under King Simeon I, and finally fell prey to Byzantine conquest in A.D. 1018. Byzantine decline, however, enabled the Bulgarians to regain their freedom. This second Bulgarian kingdom survived from the late A.D. 1100s to the late A.D. 1300s, when Ottoman invaders from central Asia conquered the territory. Ottoman rule of Bulgaria lasted more than 500 years.

Serbia

Northwest of Bulgaria was the Slavic kingdom of Serbia. During the A.D. 500s and 600s, groups of Slavs settled in the Balkan Peninsula. By the 1100s, the Serbs, one of the most powerful of these groups, had accepted Eastern Orthodox Christianity and the Cyrillic alphabet. They also formed a state. The Serbian kingdom enjoyed its greatest period of prosperity in the A.D. 1300s under Stefan Dusán (STEH•fahn doo•SHAHN), who assumed the title of emperor of the Serbs. Dusán's armies successfully fought the Byzantines, expanding Serbian rule throughout much of the Balkans.

After Dusán's death in 1355, his heirs lacked the skills to keep the Serbian kingdom united. The Serbs valiantly fought the Ottomans but were eventually defeated in 1389 in the Battle of Kosovo. Almost 500 years of Ottoman rule followed, but the desire to reverse the shame of Kosovo helped keep alive Serbian national pride.

SECTION 2 REVIEW

Recall
1. **Define** theology, regent, mosaic, illuminated manuscript, monastery, missionary.
2. **Identify** Cyril, Methodius, the Seljuk Turks, Manzikert, the Ottoman Turks, Tiridates III, Tamara.

3. **Explain** why the Bosporus and the Dardanelles are strategic waterways.

Critical Thinking
4. **Analyzing Information** Examine how the doctrinal and cultural split between the Roman Catholic Church and the Eastern Orthodox Church

contributed to the Byzantine Empire's decline.

Understanding Themes
5. **Innovation** How did Christianity affect culture in the Byzantine Empire and in neighboring kingdoms? What was the role of art and religion in these lands?

Section 3

The Eastern Slavs

Setting the Scene

▶ **Terms to Define**
steppe, principality, boyar, czar

▶ **People to Meet**
the Slavs, Rurik, Olga, Vladimir, Yaroslav, the Mongols, Alexander Nevsky, Ivan III

▶ **Places to Locate**
Dnieper River, Kiev, Novgorod, Moscow

 **ind Out** How did the Eastern Slavs develop separate cultures from those of western Europe?

The Storyteller

As a pagan prince, Vladimir behaved kindly; once he became a Christian, his generosity became unlimited. Beggars assembled in his courtyard every

Eastern Orthodox church

day for food, drink, clothing, and money. For the sick and weak, supply wagons were loaded up and driven around the city of Kiev. Once, when his friends showed disgust at having to eat with plain wooden spoons, Vladimir laughed and had silver ones cast for them. He was also the first Kiev prince to mint gold and silver coins. The first of these, made by inexperienced Russian crafts workers, were slightly lumpy and uneven, but bore Vladimir's picture and the inscription, "Here is Vladimir on his throne. And this is his gold."

—from *Vladimir the Russian Viking*, Vladimir Volkoff, 1985

fter the fall of Constantinople in A.D. 1453, the leadership of the Eastern Orthodox world passed from the Byzantines to **the Slavs**. The Slavs were among the largest groups living in eastern Europe. Because of their location, the Slavs had been in close contact with the Byzantines since the A.D. 900s.

This relationship made a lasting mark on the development of Slavic history. The Slavs, especially those living in the areas that are today the Balkan Peninsula, Ukraine, Belarus, and Russia, borrowed much from the Byzantines. On the basis of Byzantine religion, law, and culture, the Slavs built a new civilization. They also borrowed heavily from western European and Asian cultures. As a result of these different influences, Russia—the farthest north and east of the Slavic lands—never became a completely European or completely Asian country.

The Setting

One of the Byzantine trade routes ran north across the Black Sea and up the **Dnieper River**, then overland to the Baltic Sea. From trading posts along the river grew the roots of early Slavic civilization.

The Steppe

North of the Black Sea are vast plains, thick forests, and mighty rivers. Much of the land is an immense plain called the steppe. Ukrainian author Nikolay Gogol vividly captures its spirit in his *Cossack Tales*:

❝ The farther the steppe went the grander it became … one green uninhabited waste. No plow ever furrowed its immense wavy plains of wild plants; the wild horses, which herded there, alone trampled them down. The whole extent of the steppe was nothing but a green-gold ocean, whose surface seemed besprinkled with millions of different colored flowers. ❞

Although the steppe has rich black soil, the harsh climate makes farming difficult and crop failures common. Too far inland to be reached by moist ocean breezes, the steppe often has scanty rainfall. In addition, most of the land lies in the same latitudes as Canada and has the same short growing season. During the long, hard winter, blasts of Arctic air roar across the land and bury it deep in snow.

Forests and Rivers

North of the steppe stretch seemingly endless forests of evergreens, birch, oak, and other hardwoods. North–south flowing rivers such as the Dnieper, Dniester, and Volga cross the steppe and penetrate the forests, providing the easiest means of transportation. Yet travel is difficult for much of the year. In winter, deep drifts of snow cover the ground, and in the spring thaw the land turns to knee-deep mud.

The People

Historians know little about the origin of the first Slavic peoples. Some believe the Slavs came from present-day eastern Poland. Others think they may have been farmers in the Black Sea region. It is known that by about A.D. 500 the Slavs had formed into three distinct groups and had settled in different parts of eastern Europe.

Slavic Groups

One group, known as the West Slavs, lived in the marshlands, plains, and mountains of east-central Europe. They successfully fought the Germans to the west and the Scandinavians to the north for control of territory. Today the descendants of the West Slavs are the peoples of Poland, the Czech Republic, and Slovakia. Their religious ties came to be with the Roman Catholic Church, and their cultural ties were with western Europe.

Another group, known as the South Slavs, settled in the Balkan Peninsula, and had frequent contacts with the Byzantines. Today, their descendants are the Serbs, Croats, and Slovenes, whose languages and cultures were shaped by both the Roman Catholic West and the Orthodox East. One group of South Slavs—the Bosnians—were influenced by the religion of Islam from the Middle East.

The third and largest Slavic group, the Eastern Slavs, includes those now known as Ukrainians, Russians, and Belarussians. They lived north of the Black Sea between the Dnieper and Dniester Rivers and traded with the Byzantine Empire and northern Europe. From A.D. 500 to A.D. 800, some Eastern Slavs moved eastward toward the Volga River.

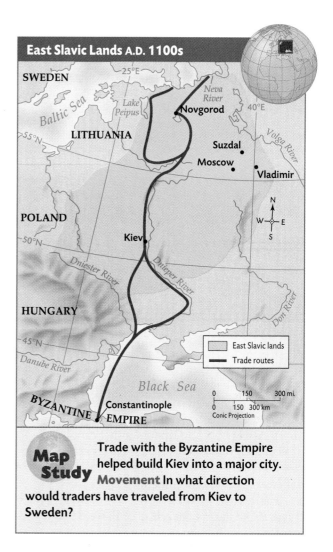

East Slavic Lands A.D. 1100s

Map Study Trade with the Byzantine Empire helped build Kiev into a major city. **Movement** In what direction would traders have traveled from Kiev to Sweden?

Early Ways of Life

The early Eastern Slavs lived in villages made up of related families. They were farmers who hunted wild game and birds to supplement the wheat, rye, and oats they grew. In the forests they cleared land by cutting and burning trees and scattering the ash to enrich the soil. On the steppes they ignited a "sea of flame" to burn off the grass for planting.

Most farm homes were sturdy log houses. With knife, chisel, and ax the peasants skillfully shaped the logs, notching them so that they would fit together without nails. Many log houses had wooden gables and window frames decorated with painted carvings of flowers and animals. Skilled artisans also used wood to make furniture, cooking utensils, musical instruments, boats, and images of favorite deities.

The Eastern Slavs used the many rivers in their region for transportation and trade. They set up trading towns along the riverbanks. By the A.D. 800s, a trade route ran from the Baltic Sea in the north to the Black Sea in the south.

Visualizing History This log house in Russian Siberia's Lake Baikal region evidences the decorative style of Eastern Slav houses. *How did these people build without nails?*

Kievan Rus

The early Eastern Slavs were not warlike. During the late A.D. 800s, they relied on Vikings, a group of warriors and traders from Scandinavia, to protect their trade routes. The Vikings not only provided military aid, they also helped to lay the foundations of Slavic government.

The arrival of the Vikings is recorded in the *Primary Chronicle*, a collection of Eastern Slavic history, tales, and legends written around A.D. 1100. According to the *Chronicle*, in about A.D. 860 the Slavic people from the northern forest village of Novgorod asked Vikings from Scandinavia for aid: "Our land is great and rich, but there is no order in it. Come to rule and reign over us." The Viking leader **Rurik** accepted the invitation. The Slavs called the Vikings and the area they controlled *Rus*; the word *Russia* is probably derived from this name.

Rise of Kiev

In about A.D. 880, Rurik's successor, Prince Oleg, conquered the fortress-village of **Kiev** (Kyiv in Ukrainian) to the south. Built high on a bluff where the forest meets the steppe, Kiev prospered because it lay on the Dnieper River trade route. Some still call it the mother of Eastern Slavic cities.

Control of Kiev enabled Oleg to dominate the water trade route. Towns along the route were brought together under his leadership. Kiev soon became the major city of a region of Slavic territories known as Kievan Rus. The rulers of Kiev, known as Grand Princes, conducted raids against Constantinople. They were attracted by the wealth and civilization of the Byzantine capital. In A.D. 911 a treaty ended these raids and established trade between the Byzantines and the Eastern Slavs. During the summer months, Slavic merchants carried furs, honey, and other forest products by boat to Constantinople. There they traded their goods for cloth, wine, weapons, and jewelry.

Kievan Government

By A.D. 900, Kievan Rus had organized into a collection of city-states and principalities, or territories ruled by princes. Each region enjoyed local self-government; however, they all paid special respect to the Grand Prince of Kiev. The Grand Prince collected tribute from the local princes to support his court and army. The major duties of these princes were to administer justice and to defend the frontiers. The princes were assisted by councils of wealthy merchants and landed nobles, who were known as boyars. Assemblies represented all free adult male citizens. They handled daily affairs and had the power to accept or remove princes.

These three institutions—the princely office, the council, and the assembly—varied in power from region to region. In the northeastern territories, the prince wielded a great deal of political power. In the southeastern areas, the boyars had the greatest political influence. In Novgorod and a few northern trading towns and cities, the assemblies overshadowed both princes and boyars. In these areas, the assemblies came close to establishing a tradition of representative government in the Eastern Slavic lands. However, later princes limited the powers of the assemblies.

Jim Brandenburg

Rurik the Rus

This 19th-century statue of Kievan Rus's ruler Rurik stands in the center of the Russian city of Novgorod. The bronze Rurik, a mighty Prince, holds symbols of military might and political power: a shield and sword. His fur cape sweeps proudly over his shoulders. Founder of nations, the Viking warrior proclaims a glorious past.

Rurik and his Viking warriors came from Scandinavia to what is now Russia and Ukraine in the A.D. 800s, perhaps invited there by native Slavic tribes constantly warring with each other. The Eastern Slavs during the A.D. 800s had little political stability, which made farming and commerce difficult. The Vikings changed that. Trading with the strong, plundering the weak, they moved south from Novgorod to Kiev, where they founded a political state, and from there they moved on to Odessa on the shores of the Black Sea. It took them two centuries to complete their expansion. By then the Vikings had lost their Scandinavian ways and had become assimilated into the local cultures. ⊕

Arrival of Christianity

Before the late A.D. 900s, the Eastern Slavs honored nature spirits and ancestors, and worshiped many deities. The most popular gods were Perun, god of thunder and lightning, and the Great Mother, goddess of the land and harvest. Images of the deities were built on the highest ground outside the villages.

Vladimir's Conversion

Because of contact with the Byzantine Empire, many Eastern Slavs were influenced by Eastern Orthodoxy. **Olga**, a princess of Kiev, became the first member of the Kievan nobility to accept the faith. Her grandson, Prince **Vladimir** of Kiev, decided to abandon the old beliefs and to adopt a new religion that he thought would help the Eastern Slavs become a more powerful civilization. An old Slavic legend states that Vladimir sent observers abroad to examine Judaism, Roman Catholicism, Eastern Orthodoxy, and Islam. Only the beautiful ceremony in the splendid Byzantine church of Hagia Sophia impressed the observers. In A.D. 988, after his own conversion to Eastern Orthodoxy, Vladimir ordered a mass baptism in the Dnieper River for his people.

Visualizing History This ancient monastery stands as a symbol of the influence of Byzantine Christianity. *How was Eastern Orthodoxy introduced in Kievan Rus?*

Effects of Conversion

The conversion to Eastern Orthodoxy brought Byzantine culture to Kievan Rus. Byzantine priests and bishops introduced the Eastern Slavs to colorful rituals and taught them the art of painting icons. The Eastern Slavs also learned to write their language in the Cyrillic alphabet. Schools were established in the towns for the sons of boyars, priests, and merchants. Byzantine architects arrived in Kiev to build stone churches with magnificent domes. Monasteries also were founded in the towns and countryside, and attracted many new converts.

Acceptance of Eastern Orthodoxy, however, tended to isolate the Eastern Slavs from the outside world. Following the split between the Eastern and Western Churches, Kievan Rus was separated from western Europe. Its people lost contact with developments that took place in that area after A.D. 1200. At the same time, the Byzantine practice of translating the Bible and Orthodox church services into local languages had an important impact. Because Kievan scholars had translations of some classical and Christian writings in their own language, they did not learn Greek or Latin. As a result, they did not deepen their knowledge of the heritage of western European civilization. Instead, they turned for inspiration to the traditions of their own local culture.

Kiev's Golden Age

Vladimir, who ruled from A.D. 980 to A.D. 1015, was one of the most important grand princes of Kiev. Known for his skills as a warrior, he successfully defended Kievan Rus's eastern frontiers against nomadic invaders. He also expanded its western borders by capturing lands in Poland and near the Baltic Sea.

Yaroslav's Reign

After a time of dynastic conflict, Vladimir's son **Yaroslav** became Grand Prince in A.D. 1019. Under Yaroslav's rule, Kievan culture reached its height. Yaroslav encouraged the spread of learning by establishing the first library in Kiev. Yaroslav also organized the Kievan legal system, drawing from Justinian's Code. Written primarily for the princes and merchants, the code treated crimes against property as well as against persons.

A skilled diplomat, Yaroslav arranged for his daughters and sisters to marry kings in Norway, Hungary, France, and Poland. To the Europeans, who were just arising from the isolation and disorder of the early Middle Ages, Kiev was a glittering capital whose culture outshone that of any in western Europe.

Kiev's Decline

After Yaroslav's death, Kiev declined in power and wealth for several reasons. First, Yaroslav began the practice of dividing up his lands among all his sons instead of willing them to one heir. Since no law established a clear line of succession, the heirs battled one another over control of Kiev. Second, the Latin Christian state created in Constantinople disrupted trade with the Byzantines and weakened Kiev's economy. Finally, in A.D. 1240 Mongol invaders from central Asia captured Kiev and completely destroyed it.

Mongol Rule

The Mongols, or Tatars, as the Slavs called them, defeated the armies of the Eastern Slavic princes and conquered most of the country except for Novgorod. They sacked towns and villages and killed thousands. Mongols sought to tax the peoples they conquered, rather than impose their culture. The Slavs were allowed to practice their Christian faith, but the Mongols required allegiance to the Mongol ruler and service in the Mongol army.

For two centuries, Mongol rule isolated most of the Eastern Slavs from European civilization. Although the occupation helped unify the Eastern Slavs, it also further distanced them from ideas and trends of the Western world.

Rise of Moscow

As city life in the south declined after the fall of Kiev, many Eastern Slavs—led by monks, farmers, and artisans—moved into the remote northern forests to escape Mongol rule. By the late A.D. 1200s, Vladimir–Suzdal and **Novgorod** were the strongest Eastern Slavic principalities.

Alexander Nevsky

The Mongols had never advanced as far north as Novgorod because the spring thaw turned the land into a swamp they could not cross. Instead, the city faced attacks in the Baltic Sea area from Swedes and Germans who wanted to convert the Eastern Slavs to Roman Catholicism. In a ferocious battle on the Neva River in A.D. 1240, Alexander,

Visualizing History Alexander Nevsky, ruler of Novgorod, fought the German Teutonic Knights in A.D. 1242. *Why did the Germans and Swedes attack the Eastern Slavs?*

prince of Novgorod, defeated the invading Swedes. This victory earned him the nickname **Alexander Nevsky**, Alexander "of the Neva," and his victory established Novgorod as a strong, independent principality.

Moscow's Beginnings

Daniel, the youngest son of Alexander Nevsky, became ruler of **Moscow**, a small but prosperous town located near vital land and water routes. Using war and diplomatic marriages, the princes of Moscow gradually expanded their state's territory. Moscow's importance grew in A.D. 1325 when the metropolitan, or leader of the Orthodox Church in the Eastern Slavic lands, was transferred there. By about A.D. 1350, Moscow had become the most powerful city. Cooperation with Mongol policies had kept it free from outside interference. Daniel's son, Prince Ivan I, became known as Money Bag because the Mongols even trusted him to collect taxes for them.

Muscovite forces defeated the Mongols at the Battle of Kulikovo in A.D. 1380. The tide had turned in favor of Moscow. Over the next hundred years, the Eastern Slavs steadily drove out the Mongols. In A.D. 1480 during the rule of **Ivan III**, Moscow

Gold-domed spires of the Church of the Annunciation reach toward the sky behind the Kremlin's walls. *What was the original purpose of the Kremlin?*

1472 when Ivan III married Sophia, niece of the last Byzantine emperor, he took the title czar, or "caesar," the title used by the Roman and Byzantine emperors. Ivan also made the two-headed Byzantine eagle the symbol of his rule.

In A.D. 1493 Ivan added the title Sovereign of All Russia. The lands he ruled, eventually known as Russia, were a hundred times as large as the original Muscovite state. The people spoke one language, and the princes served one czar. The Russian Orthodox Church, which identified its interests with those of the Muscovite ruler, proclaimed that Moscow was the Third Rome. The Church regarded Ivan as both the successor of the Byzantine emperor and protector of the Eastern Orthodox Church, a claim all succeeding Russian czars would also make.

Moscow's Culture

Eastern Orthodoxy shaped the development of Moscow's culture. Its leaders stressed the importance of obedience to the czar and the government. The Church taught the people that submission to authority was a Christian duty. Joseph Sanin, an influential church leader during Ivan III's reign, wrote that "although the [ruler] was like other men in his physical characteristics, in his power he was similar to God in heaven."

Although western European influences reached Russia, they were transformed by local Russian styles and tastes. Instead of using Greek, Latin, or other classical languages, the Church used an early Slavic language in its worship and writings. Russia's religious leaders and political rulers also encouraged the development of a unique national style of icon painting and building construction. Ivan III had western European and Russian architects rebuild the Moscow Kremlin, or fortress. In spite of Western influences on its construction, the Kremlin became known for the typically Russian splendor of its beautiful onion-domed churches and ornately decorated palaces. Today the Kremlin in Moscow is still a center of government, religion, and culture for Russia.

finally refused to pay taxes to the Mongols. The long submission to the Asian rulers was over. Today, Ivan is known as Ivan the Great because he was able to bring many of the Eastern Slavic principalities under his rule. His major gain was Novgorod, which controlled territory all the way east to the Ural Mountains, the traditional division between Europe and Asia.

The Third Rome

Other factors helped to strengthen the power of Moscow's rulers. After Constantinople fell to the Ottoman Turks in A.D. 1453, Moscow stood alone as the center of the Eastern Orthodox Church. In A.D.

SECTION 3 REVIEW

Recall
1. **Define** steppe, principality, boyar, czar.
2. **Identify** the Slavs, Rurik, Olga, Vladimir, Yaroslav, the Mongols, Alexander Nevsky, Ivan III.
3. **Locate** Kiev on the map on page

259. Why did Kiev prosper?

Critical Thinking
4. **Making Comparisons** Compare Kievan Rus with Moscow. How was each dependent on geography? What role did the Orthodox Church play in each?

Understanding Themes
5. **Cultural Diffusion** What traditions that had originated with Rome became part of Russian culture? How did Russian culture differ from the civilization of western Europe? Why?

Distinguishing Between Fact and Opinion

Imagine that you are watching two candidates for President debate the merits of the college loan program. One candidate says, "In my view, the college loan program must be reformed. Sixty percent of students do not repay their loans on time."

The other candidate replies, "College costs are skyrocketing, but only 30% of students default on their loans for more than one year. I believe we should spend more money on this worthy program."

How can you tell who or what to believe? First, you must learn to distinguish between fact and opinion.

Learning the Skill

A fact is a statement that can be proved to be true or false. In the example above, the statement "Sixty percent of students do not repay their loans on time" is a fact. By reviewing statistics on the number of student loan recipients who repay their loans, we can determine whether it is true or false. To identify facts, look for words and phrases indicating specific people, places, events, dates, times.

An opinion, on the other hand, expresses a personal belief, viewpoint, or emotion. Because opinions are subjective, we cannot prove or disprove them. In the opening example, most statements by the candidates are opinions.

Opinions often include qualifying words and phrases such as *I think, I believe, probably, seems to me, may, might, could, ought, in my judgment*, or *in my view*. Also, look for expressions of approval or disapproval such as *good, bad, poor*, and *satisfactory*. Be aware of superlatives such as *greatest, worst, finest*, and *best*. Notice words with negative meanings and implications such as *squander, contemptible*, and *disgrace*. Also, identify generalizations such as *none, every, always*, and *never*.

Practicing the Skill

For each pair of statements below, determine which is fact and which is opinion. Give a reason for each choice.

1. (a) The Byzantine Empire came to a pitiful end at the hands of the savage Turks.
   (b) The Byzantine Empire ended when Constantine XI died while defending Constantinople from invading Turks in A.D. 1453.
2. (a) The alliance with the Byzantine Empire made Kiev a major trading link between Europe and Asia and between Scandinavia and the Middle East.
   (b) In the A.D. 900s Kiev was the most isolated, uncivilized place and possessed little in the way of culture.
3. (a) The Byzantine culture was more advanced than any other of its day.
   (b) Vladimir's conversion to Eastern Orthodoxy brought Byzantine culture to Kievan Rus.

Applying the Skill

In a newspaper, find a news article and an editorial on the same topic or issue. Identify five facts and five opinions from these sources.

For More Practice

Turn to the Skill Practice in the Chapter Review on page 267 for more practice in distinguishing between fact and opinion.

Connections Across Time

Historical Significance As a crossroads of trade, the Byzantine Empire was a center for cultural diffusion. Its scholars transmitted Roman law and classical and Christian learning to western Europe. The Byzantine Church spread Christianity by sending missionaries to convert the Slavs and other neighboring peoples.

In addition, the Byzantines were cultural innovators who made a lasting impact. Their icons and mosaics became part of the Christian artistic heritage of Europe, and their architecture inspired building styles in eastern Europe and the Middle East.

Using Key Terms

Write the key term that completes each sentence. Then write a sentence for each term not chosen.

a. boyar
b. clergy
c. mosaic
d. iconoclasts
e. monasteries
f. illuminated manuscripts
g. missionary
h. regent
i. schism
j. laity
k. czar
l. steppe

1. Wanting to prevent superstition and idol worship, _____, or image breakers, supported the removal of all images from churches.
2. North of the Black Sea are thick forests, mighty rivers, and a vast plain known as the _____.
3. In A.D. 1054 doctrinal, political, and geographic differences led to a _____ between the Roman Catholic Church in the West and the Eastern Orthodox Church in the East.
4. In Kievan Rus, wealthy nobles and landowners who assisted the princes were called _____.
5. In A.D. 1472 the Muscovite ruler Ivan III took the title _____, the title used by the Roman and Byzantine emperors.

Technology Activity

Using the Internet Locate a Web site dealing with the history of the Cyrillic written language. Focus your search by using phrases such as *Cyrillic language* and *Slavic languages*. Create a bulletin board showing examples of Cyrillic words with their English translations. When possible, include illustrations.

Using Your History Journal

Write a short story describing a fictional case that may have come before an official of Justinian's court. Base the story on the law you described in Your History Journal at the beginning of this chapter.

Reviewing Facts

1. **Government** Explain the significance of Justinian's Code to later generations.
2. **Culture** Describe three major art forms that developed in the Byzantine Empire. What are the leading themes in Byzantine arts?
3. **Culture** Analyze how the Byzantine Empire promoted Christianity.
4. **Culture** Discuss the role of women in Byzantine society, especially in family life.
5. **Culture** Explain the contribution that Nino made to the development of Georgia.
6. **Geography** State the ways the early Eastern Slavs made use of their environment.
7. **History** Explain why the reign of Yaroslav is considered a golden age for Kievan Rus.
8. **History** Explain the effects of the Mongol invasions on Kievan Rus.
9. **History** Describe how Moscow's rise affected the Eastern Slavs.

Critical Thinking

1. **Analyze** Was the title of New Rome suitable or unsuitable for the city of Constantinople? Explain.

2. Evaluate Why was the preservation of Greek and Roman learning a significant contribution of Byzantine civilization?

3. Analyze What do these Byzantine coins reveal about the level of development of Byzantine civilization?

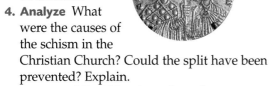

4. Analyze What were the causes of the schism in the Christian Church? Could the split have been prevented? Explain.

5. Evaluate Would Justinian have been an effective ruler if he had not married Theodora? Explain.

6. Analyze How did trade affect the Byzantine Empire?

7. Synthesize What were the three parts of Kievan government? Why did representative government not develop in the East Slavic lands?

8. Synthesize Imagine you are a Russian boyar under Ivan III. Would you resist calling him Czar? Explain.

Understanding Themes

1. Conflict How does conflict—such as the iconoclastic controversy in the Byzantine Empire—weaken a government?

2. Innovation Using Byzantine civilization as an example, explain how one civilization's ideas can be adapted to other societies.

3. Cultural Diffusion How can two societies be enriched by sharing cultural aspects? Give examples from the cases of Kievan Rus and Moscow.

1. Investigate the role the Bosporus played in World War I and World War II.
2. Explain the historical reasons why Russia has a continuing interest in the affairs of eastern European nations.
3. Investigate the historical roots of religious controversies in modern societies, such as Bosnia and Northern Ireland.

Skill Practice

Read the following statements. Determine which are facts and which are opinions. Give a reason for each choice.

1. The *Primary Chronicle* states that in A.D. 911 Grand Prince Oleg agreed on a peace treaty with the Byzantine emperors Leo and Alexander.
2. The Volga River is longer than the Danube River.
3. The Russian Orthodox Church is the most spiritually uplifting faith in the world.
4. Nomads wandered aimlessly throughout the steppes and lived in flimsy shelters.

Geography in History

1. Location Refer to the map below. By what year had the area around the Volga River been added to Moscow's holdings?

2. Place What geographic factors enabled the princes of Moscow to expand their territory?

3. Region By A.D. 1493 Moscow's ruler claimed to be "Sovereign of All Russia." About how far did Moscow's territory stretch from north to south in A.D. 1462?

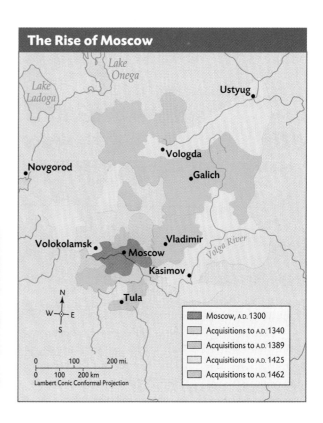

Chapter

11

A.D. 600–1300

Islamic Civilization

Chapter Themes

▶ **Innovation** The faith and principles of Islam become the basis of a new civilization. *Section 1*
▶ **Movement** Armies and merchants spread Islam through the Middle East and North Africa, and into Spain and Asia. *Section 2*
▶ **Cultural Diffusion** Contributions from many cultures and peoples enrich the Islamic state. *Section 3*

The Storyteller

"I was in Makkah at last," writes a devout Muslim woman about her pilgrimage to Makkah, the holiest city of the religion of Islam. She continues, "Before me was the Kaaba, a great black cube partly submerged in a torrent of white-robed pilgrims circling round and round. Around us, like a great dam containing the torrent, stood the massive walls and the seven slim minarets of the Sacred Mosque. High above, the muezzin began the evening call to prayer: 'Allahu Akbar! ... God is Most Great!'...

"Around the Kaaba ... repeating the customary prayers, swirled men and women of every race and nation, from every corner of the earth...."

All believers of Islam hope to share in this event at least once in their lives. Since the A.D. 600s, it has been one of the unifying celebrations for all Muslims.

Historical Significance

What are the basic beliefs and principles of Islam? What contributions has Islamic civilization made to world knowledge and culture?

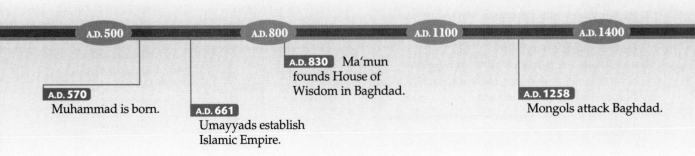

A.D. 500   A.D. 800   A.D. 1100   A.D. 1400

A.D. 830 Ma'mun founds House of Wisdom in Baghdad.

A.D. 570 Muhammad is born.

A.D. 661 Umayyads establish Islamic Empire.

A.D. 1258 Mongols attack Baghdad.

Apocryphal Life of Ali, from the *Kharar-nama*, late A.D. 1400s

Your History Journal

Choose a topic from the text headings on astronomy and geography, chemistry and medicine, or art and architecture in the Muslim world. Research the subject in a library and write a short report.

A.D. 600		A.D. 625		A.D. 650

A.D. 610	A.D. 622	A.D. 630	A.D. 632
Muhammad has his first revelation.	Muhammad and followers depart on the *Hijrah*.	The people of Makkah accept Islam.	Muhammad dies at Madinah.

Section 1

A New Faith

Setting the Scene

▶ **Terms to Define**
sheikh, revelation, *shari'ah*, mosque, imam, hajj

▶ **People to Meet**
Muhammad

▶ **Places to Locate**
Arabian Peninsula, Makkah

Find Out What are the basic beliefs and practices of Islam?

The Storyteller

(Allah) Most Gracious!
It is He Who has taught the Qur'an.
He has created man:
He has taught him speech (and Intelligence)
The sun and the moon follow courses (exactly)
computed; And the herbs and the trees–both
(alike) bow in adoration.
And the Firmament has He raised high and He has set up the balance (of Justice) In order that you may not transgress (due) balance. So establish weight with justice and fall not short in the balance. It is He Who has spread out the earth for (His) creatures: Therein is fruit and date-palms producing spathes (enclosing dates): Also corn with (its) leaves and stalk for fodder and sweet-smelling plants.

—from *The Quran,*
Chapter 55

Abu-Zayd preaching in the Mosque of Samarkand

South of Asia Minor lies the **Arabian Peninsula**, home of the Arabs. This location placed the Arabs at the margins of the great Middle Eastern civilizations. Like the ancient Israelites, Phoenicians, and Chaldeans, the Arabs were descended from Semitic tribes. Archaeologists have traced Arab civilizations in the Arabian Peninsula to at least 3000 B.C.

Arab Life

The relative geographic remoteness of the Arabian Peninsula kept the empires in the northern part of the region from invading Arab lands. Their isolation allowed the Arabs to create their own civilization.

The Setting

The Arabian Peninsula is a wedge of land of about 1 million square miles (2.6 million sq. km) between the Red Sea and the Persian Gulf. It is made up of two distinct regions. The southwestern area, across from the northeast coast of Africa, has well-watered valleys nestled between mountains. The rest of the peninsula, however, consists of arid plains and deserts.

Yet the peninsula is not entirely forbidding. Grass grows quickly during the showers of the rainy season, and oases, the fertile areas around springs and water holes, provide a permanent source of water for farmers, herders, and travelers. For centuries, nomadic herders and caravans have crisscrossed the desert, traveling from oasis to oasis.

Lives of the Bedouin

In ancient times many of the Arabs were bedouin (BEH•duh•wuhn), nomads who herded sheep, camels, and goats and lived in tents made of felt from camel or goat hair. They ate mainly fresh or dried dates, and they drank milk from their herds; on special occasions they also ate mutton.

The bedouin lived in tribes, each made up of related families. Arabs valued family ties because they ensured protection and survival in the harsh desert environment. Leading each tribe was a sheikh (SHAYK), or chief, appointed by the heads of the families. A council of elders advised the sheikh, who ruled as long as he had the tribe's consent. Warfare was part of bedouin life. The Arab tribes went on raids to gain camels and horses and battled one another over pastures and water holes, the most precious resources in the desert. To protect their honor and their possessions, the bedouin believed in retaliation—"an eye for an eye, and a tooth for a tooth."

For entertainment the bedouin enjoyed many activities. Camel and horse races and other games sharpened the men's abilities as warriors, and then everyone enjoyed an evening of storytelling around the campfires. Poets composed and recited poems about battles, deserts, camels and horses, and love. In these lines an Arab sheikh states his view of war:

> 66 From the cup of peace
>   drink your fill;
>   but from the cup of war
>   a sip will suffice. 99

Growth of Towns

By the A.D. 500s, many tribes had settled around oases or in fertile valleys to pursue either farming or trade. Groups of merchants soon founded prosperous market towns. The most important of these towns was **Makkah**, a crossroads of commerce about 50 miles (80 km) inland from the Red Sea.

People from all over the Arabian Peninsula traveled to Makkah to trade animal products for weapons, dates, grain, spices, jewels, ivory, silk, and perfumes. Enormous caravans from the fertile southwest passed through Makkah en route to Syria, Iraq, and as far away as China. Arabs also visited Makkah to worship at the peninsula's holiest shrine, the Kaaba, which contained statues of the many Arab deities. The business the pilgrims brought to Makkah made its merchants wealthy.

Signs of Change

As business ties replaced tribal ties in the trading towns, the old tribal rules were no longer adequate. At the same time, the Byzantine and Persian Empires were threatening to take over Arab lands. The Arabs had a common language, but they lacked a sense of unity and had no central government to solve these new problems.

Religious ideas were also changing. Contacts with the Byzantines, the Persians, and the

Heraclius Recaptures the True Cross

Jerusalem, A.D. 630

In A.D. 622 the Emperor Heraclius set out from Constantinople to recapture what was believed to be the "True Cross" on which Christ died. The cross had been taken by the Persians when they conquered Jerusalem. Heraclius advanced on the Persian capital of Ctesiphon, demanding the return of the cross. In A.D. 630, a triumphant Heraclius restored the True Cross to the Church of the Holy Sepulchre in Jerusalem.

Ethiopians introduced the teachings of the monotheistic religions of Judaism and Christianity. Moreover, a number of Christian and Jewish Arabs lived in the peninsula. Dissatisfied with their old beliefs, many idol-worshiping Arabs searched for a new religion. Holy men known as hanifs (hah•NEEFS) denounced the worship of idols and believed in one god. They rejected Judaism and Christianity, however, preferring to find a uniquely Arab form of monotheism.

This ferment in Arab religious life contributed to the emergence of the religion known as Islam, which means "submission to the will of Allah (God)." This faith would bring the Arabs into contact with other civilizations and change Arab history.

Muhammad and His Message

The prophet of Islam, **Muhammad**, was born in the bustling city of Makkah around A.D. 570. Muslim traditions state that Muhammad was orphaned at an early age and raised by an uncle.

Life of Muhammad

During his teens, Muhammad worked as a caravan leader on a trade route. His reputation as an exceptionally honest and able person prompted his employer, a wealthy widow of 40 named Khadija (kuh•DEE•juh), to put him in charge of her business affairs. When Muhammad was about 25 years old, Khadija proposed marriage to him.

Muhammad's marriage to Khadija relieved

him of financial worries and gave him time to reflect on the meaning of life. Muhammad was troubled by the greed of Makkah's wealthy citizens, the worship of idols, and the mistreatment of the poor. Seeking guidance, Muhammad spent time alone praying and fasting in a cave outside the city.

Revelation

Islamic tradition holds that, in A.D. 610, Muhammad experienced a revelation, or vision. He heard a voice calling him to be the apostle of the one true deity—Allah, the Arabic word for God. Three times the voice proclaimed, "Recite!" When Muhammad asked what he should recite, the voice replied:

> **"** Recite in the name of your Lord,
> the Creator,
> Who created man from clots of blood.
> Recite! Your Lord is the most bountiful
> One
> Who by the pen has taught mankind
> things they did not know. **"**

A second revelation commanded Muhammad to "rise and warn" the people about divine judgment. Although Muhammad had doubts about the revelations, he finally accepted his mission and returned to Makkah to preach.

In A.D. 613 Muhammad began sharing his revelations with his family and friends. He preached to the people of Makkah that there was only one God and that people everywhere must worship and obey him. He also declared that all who believed in God were equal. Therefore the rich should share their wealth with the poor. Muhammad also preached that God measured the worth of people by their devotion and good deeds. He told the people of Makkah to live their lives in preparation for the day of judgment, when God would punish evildoers and reward the just.

Muhammad made slow progress in winning converts. Khadija and members of Muhammad's family became the first Muslims, or followers of Islam. Many of the other converts came from Makkah's poor, who were attracted by Muhammad's call for social justice.

Opposition to Islam

Most Makkans rejected Muhammad's message. Wealthy merchants and religious leaders were upset by the prophet's attacks on the images at the Kaaba. They feared that monotheistic worship would end the pilgrimages to Makkah. Wealthy Makkans believed that this development would ruin the city's economy and lead to the loss of their prestige and wealth. Driven by these fears, the merchants persecuted Muhammad and the Muslims.

Muhammad persisted in his preaching until threats against his life forced him to seek help outside the city. He found it in Yathrib, a small town north of Makkah. In A.D. 622 Muhammad sent about 60 Muslim families from Makkah to Yathrib; soon after, he followed them in secret. His departure to Yathrib is known in Muslim history as the *Hijrah* (HIH•jruh), or emigration. The year in which the *Hijrah*

Visualizing History Nineteenth-century Turkish decorative tile with inscription "Allah is Great." The Ottoman Turks built an Islamic state that lasted until 1918. *What was the command Muhammad received in the second revelation?*

took place, A.D. 622, marks the beginning of the Islamic era and is recognized as the first year of the Muslim calendar.

POINT

The Islamic Community

Yathrib accepted Muhammad as God's prophet and their ruler. As the center of Islam, it became known as Madinat al-Nabi, "the city of the prophet," or Madinah (muh•DEE•nuh).

Origin of the Islamic State

Muhammad was a skilled political as well as religious leader. In the Madinah Compact of A.D. 624, Muhammad laid the foundation of an Islamic state. He decreed that all Muslims were to place loyalty to the Islamic community above loyalty to their tribe. Disputes were to be settled by Muhammad, who was declared the community's judge and commander in chief. All areas of life were placed under the divine law given to Muhammad and recorded in the Quran (kuh•RAHN), the holy scriptures of Islam. Muhammad also extended protection to Jews and Christians who accepted Islam's political authority.

Acceptance of Islam

Eventually the Makkans invaded Yathrib, forcing the Muslims to retaliate in self-defense. In the resulting battles, the Muslims defeated the Makkans, and the Muslims won the support of many Arab groups outside Madinah.

When Muhammad and his followers entered Makkah in A.D. 630, they faced little resistance. The Makkans accepted Islam and acknowledged Muhammad as God's prophet. The Muslims destroyed the idols in the Kaaba and turned the shrine into a place of worship believed to have been built by the prophet Abraham. Makkah became the spiritual capital of Islam, and Madinah remained its political capital.

The Muslims also expanded into new areas. By A.D. 631 their state included the entire Arabian Peninsula and was supported by a strong army representing each of the Arab tribes.

After a brief illness, Muhammad died at Madinah in A.D. 632. He left behind two major achievements. The first achievement was the formation of a religious community based on carefully preserved sacred writings. The second was the example of his life as an interpretive guide for Muslims to follow.

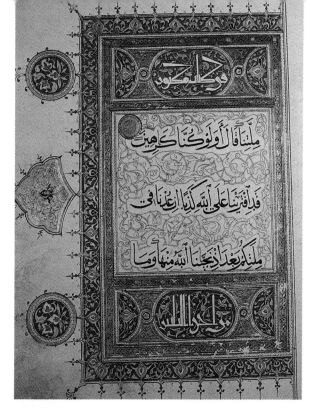

Visualizing History Because the Quran was written in Arabic, Muslims of many cultures adopted Arabic as a universal language. *What does the name "Quran" mean?*

Beliefs and Practices of Islam

Muhammad established beliefs and practices for his followers based on his revelations. In spite of social and political changes, these Islamic beliefs and practices have remained remarkably stable through the centuries.

The Quran

According to Muslim tradition, the angel Gabriel revealed divine messages to Muhammad over a 22-year period. Faithful Muslims wrote down or memorized these messages, but they were not compiled into one written collection until after Muhammad died. Then his successor, Abu Bakr, ordered Muslims to retrieve these messages from wherever they could be found, from the "ribs of palm-leaves and tablets of white stone and from the breasts of men." It took 20 years before the messages were compiled into the Quran, whose name means "recital." For all Muslims, the Quran is the final authority in matters of faith and lifestyle.

Written in Arabic, the Quran is believed to contain God's message as revealed to Muhammad. This message is expressed in stories, teachings, and exhortations. Some of the stories—such as Noah's

Lynn Abercrombie

Tower Mosque

In Samarra, Iraq, modern Muslim worshippers make their way up the spiral of a mosque built in the A.D. 800s. Some of the women, clothed from head to foot in black, are in purdah, or fully veiled from the public eye.

After Muhammad's death in A.D. 632, Islam spread through the Middle East, into Africa and Europe, and to the borders of India and China. This mosque was built during Islam's golden age, after the Abbasid caliphs assumed power over the Muslim Empire in A.D. 750. The new rulers shifted the capital of the still expanding Muslim Empire to the brand-new city of Baghdad and ended the legal distinctions between Arab Muslims and non-Arab Muslims, a division that had long deprived the non-Arabs of many legal rights. The peoples of the empire were now given greater freedom, and the Abbasids ruled over a period of great cultural flowering, peace, and order. ⊕

ark and Jonah in the belly of the whale—are variations of those found in the Bible.

Values

The Quran presents the basic moral values of Islam, which are similar to those of Judaism and Christianity. Muslims are commanded to honor their parents, show kindness to their neighbors, protect orphans and widows, and give generously to the poor. Murder, stealing, lying, and adultery are condemned.

The Quran also lays down specific rules to guide Muslims in their daily activities. It forbids gambling, eating pork, or drinking alcoholic beverages. It also contains rules governing marriage, divorce, family life, property inheritance, and business practices.

Law

Law cannot be separated from religion in Islamic society. Islam has no ranked order of clergy. Instead, generations of legal scholars have organized Islamic moral principles into a body of law known as the *shari'ah* (shuh•REE•uh). Based on the Quran and the Hadith (huh •DEETH), or sayings of Muhammad, the *shari'ah* covers all aspects of Muslim private and public life.

Five Pillars of Islam

The Quran presents the Five Pillars of Islam, or the five essential duties that all Muslims are to fulfill. They are the confession of faith, prayer, almsgiving, fasting, and the pilgrimage to Makkah.

Faith

The first pillar is the confession of faith: "There is no god but God, Muhammad is the messenger of God." It affirms the oneness of an all-powerful, just, and merciful God. All Muslims are required to submit to God's will as given in the Quran.

The confession stresses Muhammad's role as a prophet; he is not considered divine. Believing that at no time are humans without knowledge of God's will, Muslims view Muhammad as the last and greatest of several prophets whom God has sent to different peoples. Taking their lead from Muhammad, devout Muslims see their lives as a preparation for the Day of Judgement, when people will rise from death and be judged according to their actions. If they were faithful, they will be rewarded with eternal happiness in paradise. If they were not faithful, they will be condemned forever in hell.

To Muslims, Allah is the same god as the God of the Jews and the Christians. Adam, Abraham, Moses, and Jesus are considered prophets in the divine chain of messengers ending with Muhammad. As a result, Muslims have a great respect for the Bible, Judaism, and Christianity. They call Jews and Christians "People of the Book." Muslims believe the Arabs are descendants of Abraham through his son Ishmael and the Jews are descendants of Abraham through his son Isaac. The Quran also states that Jesus transmitted God's message and performed miracles.

Prayer

Muslims express their devotion in prayers offered five times each day—sunrise, noon, afternoon, sunset, and evening. Worshipers pray while facing Makkah, always using the same set of words and motions—kneeling, bowing, and

Visualizing History **A Turkish pulpit tile from the A.D. 1600s depicts the plan of the Kaaba at Makkah.** *What is the fifth pillar of Islam?*

Islamic mosque lamp from the Sulmaniyeh Mosque in Istanbul,
Turkey *What are the various uses that a mosque may serve in an Islamic community?*

Alms

The third pillar of Islam is the giving of alms, or charity. It reflects the Islamic view that the wealthy should assist the poor and weak. Almsgiving is practiced privately through contributions to the needy and publicly through a state tax that supports schools and aids the poor.

Fasting

The fourth pillar of Islam, fasting, occurs in the month of Ramadan (RAH•muh•DAHN), the ninth month in the Muslim calendar. During Ramadan, Muhammad received the first revelation. From sunrise to sunset Muslims neither eat nor drink, although they work as usual. Children, pregnant women, travelers, and the sick are exempt from fasting. At sunset the call for prayer—and in large cities the sound of a cannon—announces the end of the fast. Muslims then sit down to eat their "evening breakfast." In the cool evening hours, people stream out into the streets to greet their friends. At the end of Ramadan, there is a three-day celebration for the end of the fast.

Pilgrimage

The fifth pillar of Islam is the annual pilgrimage, or hajj, to Makkah. Every able-bodied Muslim who can afford the trip is expected to make the pilgrimage at least once in his or her lifetime. Those who perform the hajj are especially honored in the community.

The hajj takes place two months and ten days after the Ramadan fast and involves three days of ceremony, prayer, and sacrifice. Today, hundreds of thousands of Muslims come together to worship at the Kaaba and other shrines of Islam in Makkah and Madinah. The hajj is more than a religious pilgrimage. A visible expression of Muslim unity, the hajj allows a continuing exchange of ideas among the peoples of Africa, Europe, Asia, and the Americas who follow Islam.

touching one's forehead to the ground as a sign of submission to God.

Muslims can offer their daily prayers outside or inside, at work or at home. At noon on Fridays, many Muslims pray together in a mosque, a building that may serve as a place of worship, a school, a court of law, and a shelter.

An imam (ih•MAHM), or prayer leader, guides believers in prayer, and a sermon sometimes follows. Any male Muslim with the proper religious education can serve as an imam.

SECTION 1 REVIEW

Recall
1. **Define** sheikh, revelation, *shari'ah*, mosque, imam, hajj.
2. **Identify** Arabian Peninsula, Makkah, Muhammad, Muslims, *Hijrah*, Madinah Compact, Quran.
3. **Explain** What made life possible in the harsh environment of the Arabian Peninsula?

Critical Thinking
4. **Analyzing Information** In what ways was Islam a unique religion? In what ways was it similar to other religions that were also founded in this region—Judaism and Christianity?

Understanding Themes
5. **Innovation** Describe the Five Pillars of Islam and the Madinah Compact, and tell how they changed life in the Arabian Peninsula.

A.D. 600   A.D. 800   A.D. 1000   A.D. 1200

A.D. 632
Abu Bakr becomes the first caliph.

A.D. 732
Muslims and Christians fight the Battle of Tours.

A.D. 750
The Abbasid dynasty comes to power.

c. A.D. 1050 The Abbasids enter period of decline.

Section 2

Spread of Islam

Setting the Scene

▶ **Terms to Define**
caliph, jihad

▶ **People to Meet**
Abu Bakr, Ali, Mu'awiyah, Husayn, the Sunni, the Shiite, Harun al-Rashid

▶ **Places to Locate**
Damascus, Baghdad

Find Out How did the Islamic state expand, and how did it affect a variety of cultures?

The Storyteller

From the far reaches of the Mediterranean to the Indus River valley, the faithful approached the holy city. All had the same objective—to worship together at the holiest shrine of Islam, the Kaaba in Makkah. One such traveler was Mansa Musa, king of Mali in western Africa. Musa had prepared carefully for the long journey he and his attendants would take. He was determined to go, not only for his own religious fulfillment, but also for recruiting teachers and leaders, so that his land could learn more of the Prophet's teachings.

—adapted from *The Chronicle of the Seeker*, Mahmud Kati, reprinted in *The Human Record*, Alfred J. Andrea and James H. Overfield, 1990

Pilgrimage to Makkah

When Muhammad died in A.D. 632, he had left no clear instructions about who was to succeed him as the leader of Islam. Muslims knew that no one could take Muhammad's place as the messenger of God. They realized, however, that the Islamic community needed a strong leader who could preserve its unity and guide its daily affairs. A group of prominent Muslims met and chose a new type of leader, whom they called *khalifah* (kuh•LEE•fuh) or caliph (KAY•luhf), meaning "successor."

"The Rightly Guided Caliphs"

The first four caliphs were chosen for life. All were close friends or relatives of Muhammad. The first caliph was Muhammad's father-in-law and close friend, **Abu Bakr** (uh•BOO BA•kuhr). The last, his son-in-law Ali, was married to Muhammad's daughter Fatimah (FAH•tuh•muh). The first four caliphs followed Muhammad's example, kept in close touch with the people, and asked the advice of other Muslim leaders. For these reasons, Muslims have called them "the Rightly Guided Caliphs."

Early Conquests

The Rightly Guided Caliphs sought to protect and spread Islam. Their military forces carried Islam beyond the Arabian Peninsula. In addition to religious motives, the Arabs were eager to acquire the agricultural wealth of the Byzantine and Persian Empires to meet the needs of their growing population.

Arab armies swept forth against the weakened Byzantine and Persian Empires. By A.D. 650, these armies had acquired Palestine, Syria, Iraq, Persia, and Egypt. The conquests reduced the Asian part of the Byzantine Empire to Asia Minor and the Constantinople area and brought the Persian Empire completely under Muslim control.

Chapter 11 *Islamic Civilization* **277**

The Arab armies were successful for several reasons. First, they were united in the belief that they had a religious duty to spread Islam. The Islamic state, therefore, saw the conquests as a jihad (jih•HAHD), or holy struggle to bring Islam to other lands. In addition, continual warfare between the Byzantines and the Persians had weakened both of their empires and made them open to Arab attacks. Still another factor was the attempt of Byzantine and Persian rulers to impose religious unity on their peoples. Because of persecution, members of unofficial religions in both empires readily accepted Muslim rule.

Divisions Within Islam

While Muslim armies were achieving military success, rival groups fought for the caliphate, or the office of caliph. The struggle began when **Ali**, Muhammad's son-in-law, became the fourth caliph in A.D. 656. One of Ali's powerful rivals was **Mu'awiyah** (moo•UH•wee•uh), the governor of Syria. Mu'awiyah carried out conquests in Egypt

and Iraq, steadily weakening Ali's hold on the caliphate. In A.D. 661, Ali was murdered by a disillusioned follower, and Mu'awiyah became the first caliph of the powerful Umayyad (oo•MY•uhd) dynasty. Ali's son **Husayn** (hoo•SAYN), however, refused to accept Umayyad rule and continued the struggle. In A.D. 680, Husayn and many of his followers were massacred by Umayyad troops in a battle at Karbala in present-day Iraq.

The murders of Ali and Husayn led to a significant division in the Islamic world. The majority of Muslims, known as **the Sunni** (SU•nee), or "followers of the way," believed that the caliph was primarily a leader, not a religious authority. They also claimed that any devout Muslim could serve in the office with the acceptance of the people. However, **the Shiite**, the smaller group of Muslims who followed Ali and Husayn, believed that the caliphate should be held only by descendants of Muhammad through his daughter Fatimah and her husband Ali. Shiite Muslims stressed the spiritual, rather than political, aspects of Islamic leadership. Because of

Images *of the* Times

Islamic Art and Architecture

Inspired by their faith, artists and architects of Islam created unequaled geometric designs, floral patterns, and calligraphy.

Carpets and other textiles were turned into fine art pieces by the skilled hands of Islamic weavers.

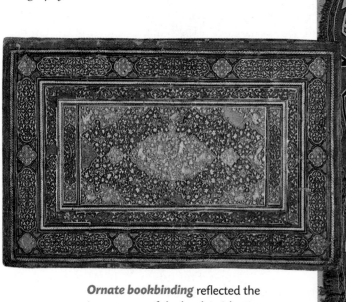

Ornate bookbinding reflected the importance of the book in Islamic civilization.

278

their conflicts with Sunni leaders, the Shiite also came to regard suffering and martyrdom as signs of their devotion to Islam.

The split between Sunni and Shiite Muslims had a profound impact on Islam and has lasted into modern times. Today, about 90 percent of Muslims are Sunnis; the minority Shiites live primarily in Iran, Iraq, and Lebanon. The Shiite movement itself has divided into several groups. In spite of differences, all Sunni and Shiite Muslims believe in the oneness of God, regard the Quran as sacred scripture, and make the hajj, or the yearly sacred pilgrimage to Makkah.

During the struggle for the caliphate, other Muslims, dissatisfied with the worldliness of the Umayyads, developed a mystical form of Islam known as Sufism. The Sufis, as the followers of this movement were called, sought direct contact with God through prayer, meditation, fasting, and spiritual writing. In addition to their devotional activities, many Sufis carried out missionary work that helped in spreading Islam to remote areas of India, Central Asia, Turkey, and North Africa.

The Islamic State

The Umayyad dynasty, which was founded by Mu'awiyah, ruled from A.D. 661 to A.D. 750. The Umayyads moved the capital from Madinah to **Damascus**, Syria, which was more centrally located in the expanding state.

Umayyad Conquests

In the next century, Umayyad warriors carried Islam east, to the borders of India and China. In the west, they swept across North Africa and into Spain, the southernmost area of Christian western Europe.

By A.D. 716 the Muslims ruled almost all of Spain. They advanced halfway into France before the Frankish leader Charles Martel stopped them at the Battle of Tours in A.D. 732. This battle halted the spread of Islam into western Europe.

Life in the Umayyad State

The Umayyads built a powerful Islamic state that stressed the political, rather than the religious,

Court of the Myrtles, Alhambra, Granada, Spain, remains as a striking example of intricate Islamic architectural design.

REFLECTING ON THE TIMES

1. What details characterize the interior walls of the Court of the Myrtles?
2. Why do you think the decorative arts flourished in the Islamic world during this period?

279

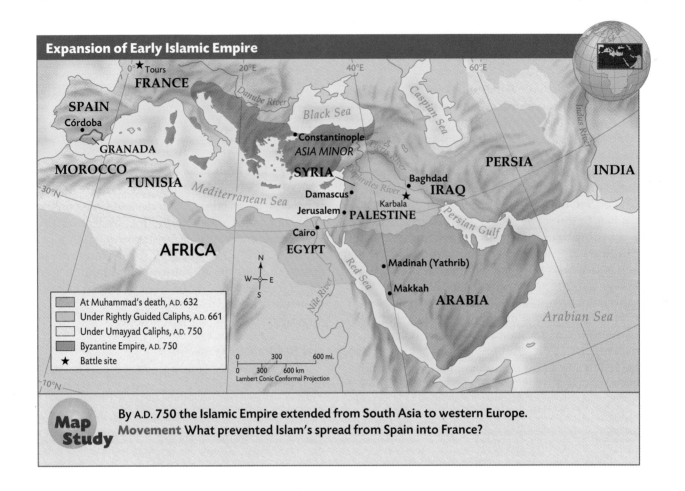

Expansion of Early Islamic Empire

Legend:
- At Muhammad's death, A.D. 632
- Under Rightly Guided Caliphs, A.D. 661
- Under Umayyad Caliphs, A.D. 750
- Byzantine Empire, A.D. 750
- ★ Battle site

0   300   600 mi.
0   300   600 km
Lambert Conic Conformal Projection

Map Study By A.D. 750 the Islamic Empire extended from South Asia to western Europe. **Movement** What prevented Islam's spread from Spain into France?

aspect of their office. As time went by, they ruled more like kings and less like the earlier caliphs.

The Umayyads did, however, help to unite the lands they ruled. They made Arabic the official language, minted the first Arabic currency, built roads, and established postal routes. Their administration depended on a civil service made up of well-trained bureaucrats who had served as officials in the Byzantine and Persian Empires.

Umayyad rule also improved conditions for many, particularly Jews and non-Greek Christians, who had often suffered under Byzantine rule. They had to pay a special tax, but they were tolerated because they believed in one God. The great Arab commander Khalid ibn al-Walid, who had led the conquest of Syria and Persia, described Muslim policy:

❝ In the name of Allah, the compassionate, the merciful, this is what Khalid ibn al-Walid would grant to the inhabitants of Damascus.... He promises to give them security for their lives, property and churches. Their city wall shall not be demolished, neither shall any Muslim be quartered in their houses. Thereunto we

give to them the pact of Allah and the protection of His Prophet, the Caliphs and the believers. So long as they pay the tax, nothing but good shall befall them. ❞

Opposition to Umayyad Rule

Despite this enlightened outlook, Umayyad rule caused dissatisfaction among non-Arab Muslims. They paid higher taxes, received lower wages in the army and government, and were discriminated against socially. Discontent was particularly strong in Iraq and Persia, the center of the Shiite opposition to Umayyad rule.

The Abbasids

In the year A.D. 747, the anti-Umayyad Arabs and the non-Arab Muslims in Iraq and Persia joined forces, built an army, and, in three years of fighting, overwhelmed the Umayyads. The new caliph, Abu'l-'Abbas, was a descendant of one of Muhammad's uncles. He established the Abbasid (uh•BA•suhd) dynasty, and his successor, al-Mansur, had a new city, **Baghdad**, built on the banks of the Tigris River. By the A.D. 900s, about 1.5 million people lived in Baghdad.

Baghdad lay at the crossroads of the land and

water trade routes that stretched from the Mediterranean Sea to East Asia. The city was shaped like a circle and surrounded by walls. Highways led from Baghdad's center to different parts of the empire and divided the city into districts. At Baghdad's heart stood the great mosque and the caliph's magnificent palace, where he ruled in splendor like the Persian rulers. Surrounding areas contained the luxurious homes of court members and army officials. Outer districts of the city were made up of the homes of the common people.

Abbasid Diversity

The Abbasid Empire reached its height under Caliph **Harun al-Rashid** (ha•ROON ahl•rah •SHEED), who ruled from A.D. 786 to A.D. 809. During this time, the Abbasids developed a sophisticated urban civilization based on the diversity of the empire's peoples. Harun and his successors worked to ensure equality among all Muslims, Arab and non-Arab. They set up a new ruling group that included Muslims of many nationalities. Persians became the dominant group in the government bureaucracy, while the Turks became the leading group in the army. Arabs, however, continued to control religious life and administration of law.

Breakup of the Islamic State

The Abbasids ruled the Islamic state from A.D. 750 to A.D. 1258; during this time, however, many of the lands that had been won by the Umayyads broke free from Baghdad. In central Asia, during the A.D. 800s, Persian Muslims set up the Samanid dynasty in the city of Bukhara (boo•KAHR•uh). Under Samanid rule, Bukhara and other central Asian cities, such as Samarkand and Tashkent, became major commercial, religious, and educational centers. Their wealth was based on caravans that traveled through the region, bringing silk, spices, and animal products from East Asia to European areas as far north as the Baltic Sea.

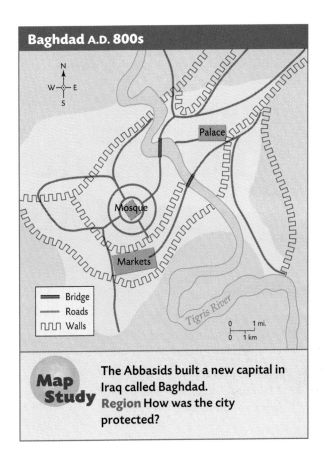

Baghdad A.D. 800s

Bridge
Roads
Walls

Map Study
The Abbasids built a new capital in Iraq called Baghdad.
Region How was the city protected?

Independent states also emerged in other parts of the crumbling Abbasid Empire. One of the last Umayyad princes fled to Spain and continued Umayyad rule there. The Egyptian dynasty, the Fatimids, gained control over areas in North Africa and the Middle East, rivaling Baghdad for power. Much of Persia also came under the control of rival rulers. By the A.D. 1000s, the Abbasids ruled little more than the area around Baghdad.

During the next 200 years, Baghdad and its Abbasid rulers came under the control of the Seljuk Turks and later, the Mongols. In their ferocious assault on the city in A.D. 1258, the Mongols burned buildings and slaughtered 50,000 inhabitants, among them the last Abbasid caliph.

SECTION 2 REVIEW

Recall
1. **Define** caliph, jihad.
2. **Identify** Abu Bakr, Ali, Mu'awiyah, Husayn, the Sunni, the Shiite, the Umayyads, the Abbasids, Harun al-Rashid.
3. **Locate** the cities of Damascus and Baghdad on the map on page 280. Why did the caliphs move the capital of the Islamic state to each of these cities?

Critical Thinking
4. **Evaluating Information** What were the strengths and weaknesses of Umayyad rule?

Understanding Themes
5. **Movement** How did expansion affect the ethnic diversity of the Islamic Empire? How did expansion affect the empire's stability?

c. A.D. 635
The Quran is compiled.

c. A.D. 830 Baghdad reaches its height as a major center of learning.

c. A.D. 910
Arab chronicler al Tabari writes a history of the world.

A.D. 1135
The Jewish philosopher Maimonides is born.

Section 3

Daily Life and Culture

Setting the Scene

▶ **Terms to Define**
   madrasa, bazaar, calligraphy, arabesque, chronicle

▶ **People to Meet**
   Ma'mun, al-Razi, Ibn Sina, Omar Khayyám, Moses Maimonides, Ibn-Khaldun

Find Out What were the achievements of Islamic civilization, and how did they spread to other parts of the world?

The Storyteller

One hundred and twenty camels were required to transport Ismail's books as he prepared to move from Baghdad to Cairo. It was not that he would be unable to obtain books in Cairo. That city, like Baghdad, was lavishly supplied with both public and private libraries whose collections numbered in the tens of thousands. Like many scholars in the Muslim world, Ismail had amassed a collection of works on topics from poetry, history, and law to medicine, mathematics, and astronomy. Now it would take a major effort to move them.

—adapted from *The Mind of the Middle Ages*, Frederick B. Artz, 1990

An astrolabe

In the Abbasid state, the arts and learning flourished despite political disunity. The time of conquest had ended, and the people had enough leisure to enjoy cultural activities. Because Arabic was the language of the Quran, it became the common language. Its widespread use enabled scientists, rulers, and writers from different lands to communicate with one another. This blend of people and ideas gave the Islamic state a new multicultural character and created a golden age.

Family Life

Islam set the guidelines for the way people lived. It laid down rules for family life and business as well as for religious practices.

Role of Women

Early Islam stressed the equality of all believers before God; however, as in the case of contemporary Christian and Jewish communities, in Islamic communities men and women had distinct roles and rights. The Quran told Muslims that "men are responsible for women." A woman's social position was therefore largely defined by her relationship as wife, mother, daughter, or sister to the male members of her family.

Islam did, however, improve the position of women. It forbade the tribal custom of killing female infants and also limited polygamy (puh•LIH•guh•mee), or the practice that allowed a man to have more than one wife. A Muslim could have as many as four wives, but all were to be treated as equals and with kindness. Also, a woman had complete control over her own property. If she were divorced, she could keep the property she had brought with her when she married. A woman could also inherit property from her father and remarry.

Most women's lives revolved around family and household. Other roles, however, were available to Muslim women, especially among the upper classes. Scholarship was a prominent way for women to win recognition, and many important teachers of Islamic knowledge were women. Women often used their control over property for investment in trade and in financing charitable institutions. The lists of Muslim rulers include a number of prominent women, both as members of the court and as leaders in their own right.

Many Muslim women made contributions in the arts, and several women in the caliph's court were renowned for their poetry. Some of them were not always happy with their lives, though, as indicated by this poem written by Maisuna, the bedouin wife of Mu'awiyah. Her comments made Mu'awiyah so furious that he sent her back to the desert: ← slave owners

66 The coarse cloth worn in the serenity
    of the desert
  Is more precious to me than the luxurious
    robes of a queen;
  I love the bedouin's tent, caressed by the
    murmuring breeze, and standing amid
    boundless horizons,
  More than the gilded halls of marble in
    all their royal splendor.
  I feel more at ease with my simple crust,
  Than with the delicacies of the court;
  I prefer to rise early with the caravan,
  Rather than be in the golden glare of
    the sumptuous escort.
  The barking of a watchdog keeping away
    strangers
  Pleases me more than the sounds of the
    tambourine played by the court singers;
  I prefer a desert cavalier, generous and
    poor,
  To a fat lout in purple living behind closed
    doors. 99
                    —Najib Ullah, *Islamic Literature*

Role of Men

In addition to politics and the army, Muslim men worked at a variety of businesses or in the fields. For leisure they visited public baths and meeting places where they relaxed and talked. Men also played chess and practiced gymnastics.

When Muslim boys reached age seven, they entered mosque schools, which cost little and were open to all boys. Wealthier families paid tuition, but many poor children were admitted without charge.

Being able to speak Arabic fluently and to write with grace and ease were skills that Muslims valued. For all but the sons of the wealthy, however, schooling ended with learning to read and write. Some young men continued their studies at *madrasas*, or theological schools. Those who were to become leaders in Muslim society studied the classical literature of Islam, memorized poetry, and learned to compose original verses.

City and Country

Most Arabs lived in rural or desert places. The leadership of the Islamic state, however, came from the cities.

Many cities, such as Damascus, in Syria, developed as trading centers even before the rise of Islam. Others, such as Kufa, in Iraq, developed from military towns set up during the early conquests. Muslim cities were divided into distinct business and residential districts. A maze of narrow streets, often covered to protect pedestrians from the scorching sun, separated the closely packed buildings.

Urban Centers

City homes were designed to provide maximum privacy and to keep the occupants cool in the blazing heat. Houses were centered around courtyards; in wealthy homes, these courtyards had fountains and gardens. Thick walls of dried mud or brick and few windows kept the interior dim and cool.

The interiors of most Muslim homes were plain with few pieces of furniture. They were decorated with beautiful carpets and small art objects. Most people sat on carpets or leaned on cushions or pillows. At mealtime, household members sat in a circle and ate from large trays of breads, meats, and fruits.

Footnotes to History

Magic Carpets
The magic carpet gliding through the air is a familiar form of transportation in *The Arabian Nights*. The real magic of Islamic carpets, however, is their glowing colors and intricate designs. During the Islamic Empire, carpets adorned both caliphs' palaces and shepherds' tents. Today, carpets from the Islamic world still give their magic to modern walls and floors.

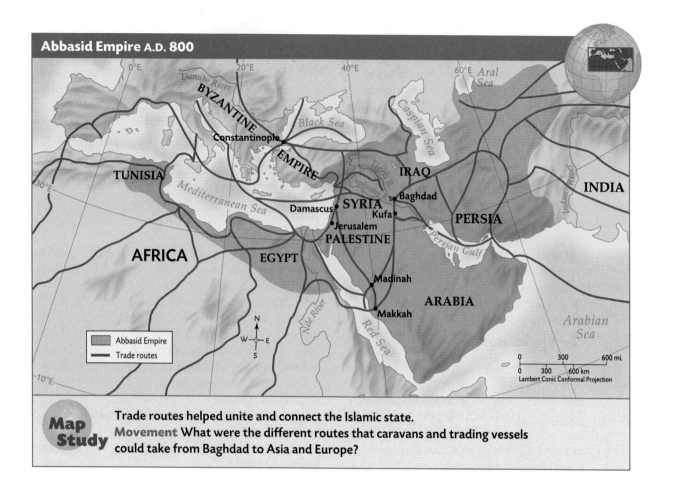

Map Study

Trade routes helped unite and connect the Islamic state.

Movement What were the different routes that caravans and trading vessels could take from Baghdad to Asia and Europe?

The main religious, government, and business buildings were at the center of the city. Dominating the skyline were graceful mosques and their slender minarets, or towers from which people were called to prayer. Mosques usually included a prayer hall where worshipers gathered on Fridays. At one end of this hall a mihrab, or niche, marked the direction of Makkah. Often mosques included schools and shelters for travelers.

Trade and the Bazaar

Muslim merchants dominated trade throughout the Middle East and North Africa until the A.D. 1400s. Caravans traveled overland from Baghdad to China. Muslim traders crossed the Indian Ocean gathering cargoes of rubies from India, silk from China, and spices from Southeast Asia. Gold, ivory, and enslaved people were brought from Africa, Asia, and Europe. From the Islamic world came spices, textiles, glass, and carpets.

The destination of these goods were the city bazaars, or marketplaces. In major cities, such as Baghdad, Damascus, and Cairo, the bazaars consisted of mazes of shops and stalls, often enclosed to shut out the glare of the sun. Buyers at the major bazaars included Europeans who purchased Asian goods,

shipped them across the Mediterranean Sea to Italy and then on to other parts of Europe. Men also met at the bazaars for conversation as well as business. Nearby were large warehouses and lodging houses that served traveling merchants.

Rural Areas

Because of the dry climate and the scarcity of water, growing food was difficult in many areas of the Islamic state. Farmers, however, made efficient use of the few arable areas. They produced good yields by irrigating their fields, rotating crops, and fertilizing the land. Most productive land was held by large landowners who received grants from the government. They had large estates and employed farmers from nearby villages to work the land. Muslim farms produced wheat, rice, beans, cucumbers, celery, and mint. Orchards provided almonds, blackberries, melons, apricots, figs, and olives. Farmers also cultivated flowers for perfume.

After Arab irrigation methods were introduced into Spain, Muslims there could cultivate valuable new crops, including cherries, apples, pears, and bananas. Seville, Córdoba, and other Spanish Islamic cities grew rich from the produce they sold in international trade.

Islamic Achievements

The use of Arabic not only promoted trade but also encouraged communication among the different peoples in the Islamic state. From these peoples the Islamic state built a rich storehouse of knowledge and scientific discovery.

Between the A.D. 800s and A.D. 1300s, Islamic scientists made important contributions in several scientific areas, such as mathematics, astronomy, chemistry, and medicine. They based their work on two main intellectual traditions. The first, and most important, was that of Greece. The second was that of India, which came to the Arabs by way of Persia.

The House of Wisdom

The Islamic world experienced a scientific awakening under the Abbasids. During the A.D. 800s, Baghdad became a leading intellectual center.

According to Muslim tradition, the Abbasid caliph **Ma'mun** (mah•MOON) founded the House of Wisdom at Baghdad in A.D. 830. This research center specialized in the translation into Arabic of Greek, Persian, and Indian scientific texts. Ma'mun staffed the institute with Christian, Jewish, and Muslim scholars who shared ideas from different intellectual traditions. They performed scientific experiments, made mathematical calculations, and built upon the ideas of the ancients. The House of Wisdom, therefore, sparked many of the mathematical and scientific achievements in the Islamic world.

Muslim science involved more than just theory; it was put to practical use. For example, mathematics was used to solve daily problems in business and agriculture. Astronomy was used to determine the hours of prayer and the time period of celebrations.

Mathematics

As you read in Chapter 7, Gupta mathematicians in India devised the numerals we know as Arabic numerals and the concept of zero. Muslim mathematicians adopted these numerals and used them in a place-value system. In this system, today used worldwide, a number's value is determined by the position of its digits. The place-value system made possible great achievements in mathematics.

Muslim mathematicians invented algebra and expressed equations to define curves and lines. Their work in geometry led to the development of trigonometry, which was used to calculate the distance to a star and the speed of a falling object. Mathematicians also were interested in practical applications, such as devising pumps and fountains and applying their skills to building and surveying.

Astronomy and Geography

At Ma'mun's observatory in Baghdad, astronomers checked the findings of the ancient Greeks, made observations of the skies, and produced physical and mathematical models of the universe. They accurately described solar eclipses and proved that the moon affects the oceans.

Muslim astronomers improved on a Greek device called the astrolabe, with which they determined the positions of stars, the movements of planets, and the time. The astrolabe made navigation easier and safer. It was also useful in religious practices, enabling Muslims to ascertain the direction of Makkah, the beginning of Ramadan, and the hours of prayer.

Using the astrolabe, Muslim geographers measured the size and circumference of the earth with accuracy unmatched until the 1900s. From such studies, geographers concluded that the earth was round, although most continued to accept the Greek theory that heavenly bodies revolve around the earth.

By the A.D. 1100s, Muslim geographers had determined the basic outlines of Asia, Europe, and North Africa and had produced the first accurate maps of the Eastern Hemisphere. They also traveled widely to gain firsthand knowledge of the earth's surface, its climates, and its peoples.

Chemistry and Medicine

Muslims developed alchemy, the branch of chemistry that attempted to change lead into gold. Although alchemists never succeeded in their goal, they did develop the equipment and methods that are still used in modern chemistry.

The renowned chemist and physician **al-Razi** (ahl•RAH•zee), who lived from A.D. 865 to A.D. 925, classified chemical substances as animal, mineral, or vegetable, a classification system that remains in use today. Al-Razi also made invaluable contributions to medicine. Among his nearly 200 works are a medical encyclopedia that describes the origin of disease and a handbook identifying the differences between smallpox and measles.

In the A.D. 900s, the doctor **Ibn Sina** (IH•buhn SEE•nuh) produced the *Canon of Medicine*, a monumental volume that attempted to summarize all the medical knowledge of that time. It described the circulation of the blood and the functions of the kidneys and the heart. It also offered diagnosis and treatment for many diseases.

Muslim physicians founded the science of optics, or the study of light and its effect on sight. Ibn al-Haytham, the founder of optics, discovered that the eye sees because it receives light from the object seen. Earlier physicians had believed the opposite: that the eye sees because it produces rays that give light to the object seen. Muslim medicine, in fact, was centuries ahead of the medicine practiced in the West.

Art and Architecture

Like mathematics and science, Islamic art and architecture benefited from the cultural diversity of the Islamic Empire. Opposed to idol worship, Muslim scholars discouraged artists from making images or pictures of living creatures. Instead, artists used calligraphy (kuh•LIH•gruh•fee), or the art of elegant handwriting, to decorate the walls of mosques and other public buildings with passages from the Quran. Often the beautiful script of written Arabic was accompanied by geometric designs entwined with plant stems, leaves, flowers, and stars. These arabesques (AR•uh•BEHSKS) decorated books, carpets, swords, and entire walls.

Islamic architects and artists did their best work in architecture, particularly in building and decorating mosques. Gardens and water, both precious in the arid Islamic lands, became artistic objects. Sun-drenched courtyards in mosques, palaces, and wealthy homes had trees to provide cool shade and flowers to delight the eye and nose; splashing fountains and running water refreshed both eye and ear.

Literature

Until the A.D. 600s, Arabic literature consisted mostly of poetry passed orally from one generation to the next. After the rise of Islam, religion had much influence in the creation of Arabic literature. The Quran, the first and greatest work in Arabic prose, was familiar to every Muslim, and its style influenced Islamic writing.

During the A.D. 700s, nonreligious prose appeared that both taught and entertained. The most famous of these writings was *Kalila and Dimna*, a collection of animal fables that presented moral lessons.

During the Abbasid period, Islamic literature blossomed as a result of contact with Greek thought, Hindu legends, and Persian court epics.

CONNECTIONS

Science and Technology

At the Doctor's

Today we take it for granted that the doctor can make us better when we get sick. In A.D. 765, however, the caliph al-Mansur was not so fortunate. His personal physicians—the best in Baghdad—could find no remedy for his chronic indigestion.

The caliph had heard that physicians in a Persian medical school based their practices on rational Greek methods of treatment. Traditional Arab medicine was based mainly on magic or superstition.

When the caliph asked the medical school for help, the chief physician, a Christian named Jurjis ibn Bakhtishu, cured al-Mansur. This encouraged other Muslim doctors to practice medicine based on the methods of the Greeks and Persians. Muslim doctors were the first to

Medicinal herb from an Islamic manuscript

discover the functions of internal organs and to diagnose illnesses such as meningitis. They also advanced surgery, carrying out head and stomach operations with the aid of anesthetics such as opium.

Believing that medicine required long training, Muslim doctors studied in hospitals and medical schools. Doctors based their treatments upon careful observation of their patients rather than superstition. They also diagnosed diseases such as measles and smallpox, prescribed treatments, and performed surgery. Such practices were unknown in the West until the A.D. 1100s and A.D. 1200s, when Islamic knowledge reached western Europe.

Linking Past and Present ACTIVITY

Explain why Islamic medicine was far ahead of Western medicine during the Middle Ages. Then, research sources and list five new methods of treatment developed by doctors in the past 50 years.

The upper classes valued elegant speech and the ability to handle words cleverly. Reading and appreciating literature became the sign of a good upbringing; every wealthy person took pride in having a well-stocked library. Córdoba, the Umayyad capital in Spain, had 70 libraries and more than half a million books. In contrast, the largest library in the Christian monasteries, at that time the center of European learning, held only a few hundred volumes.

In the A.D. 1000s, Persian became a second literary language in the Muslim world. Persian authors wrote epics about warrior-heroes, religious poetry, and verses about love. One of the best known works of this period is the *Rubaiyat* of **Omar Khayyám** (OH•MAHR KY•YAHM), a Persian mathematician and poet. You may also have heard some of the stories found in *A Thousand and One Nights*, also known as *The Arabian Nights*—stories such as "Sinbad the Sailor," "Aladdin and His Lamp," and "Ali Baba and the Forty Thieves." Originating in Arabia, India, Persia, Egypt, and other lands, the tales reflect the multinational character of the Islamic state.

Philosophy and History

Muslim philosophers tried to reconcile the Quran with Greek philosophy. They believed that religious truths could be analyzed and defended using logic. Many of their works were translated into Latin and later brought a new understanding of philosophy to western Europe. Ibn Sina, known in Europe as Avicenna, wrote numerous books on logic and theology as well as medicine. Ibn-Rushd, a judge in Córdoba, was the most noted Islamic philosopher. Christian schol-

ars in western Europe called him Averroës and used his commentaries on Aristotle.

Moses Maimonides (my•MAH•nuh•DEEZ), a Spanish Jew born in A.D. 1135, fled to North Africa to escape persecution from Spanish Christians. Maimonides became a leader in the Jewish community and a doctor to the Egyptian ruler. Like several Muslim scholars, Maimonides attempted to reconcile his faith with the teachings of Aristotle.

One of Maimonides' major contributions was the *Mishne Torah*, a 14-volume work on Jewish law

History & Art Turkish miniature depicting angels, from the *Ajac, ib Mahlukat* by Sururi, A.D. 1500s. British Museum, London, England *What cultural influences shaped the development of Islamic arts?*

Visualizing History A modern Islamic mosque in Isfahan, Iran, one of the most magnificent cities in the early Muslim world. *What kind of writings traced the early historical events of Islam?*

and tradition, written in Hebrew. His other major religious work, *The Guide of the Perplexed,* was written in Arabic and later translated into Hebrew and Latin. After his death in A.D. 1204, Maimonides was recognized as one of the world's great philosophers.

Like Judaism and Christianity, Islam traces its origins to historical events. Therefore, Islamic scholars were interested in writing history. At first they wrote chronicles, or accounts in which events are arranged in the order in which they occurred. The most famous of the Islamic chroniclers was al Tabari (al tah•BAH•ree), who in the early A.D. 900s wrote a multivolume history of the world, and Ibn

al-Athir (IH•buhn ahl•ah•THEER), who wrote an extensive history during the early A.D. 1200s.

Later, historians began to organize their accounts around events in the lives of rulers and others. The first Muslim historian to examine history scientifically was a North African diplomat named **Ibn-Khaldun** (IH•buhn KAL•DOON). He looked for laws and cause-and-effect relationships to explain historical events. Ibn Khaldun believed that history was a process in which human affairs were shaped by geography, climate, and economics, as well as by moral and spiritual forces. His work later influenced European historical writing.

SECTION 3 REVIEW

Recall
1. **Define** *madrasa,* bazaar, calligraphy, arabesque, chronicle.
2. **Identify** Ma'mun, House of Wisdom, al-Razi, Ibn Sina, Omar Khayyám, Moses Maimonides, Ibn-Khaldun.
3. **Locate** on the map on page

284 the major trade routes used by Muslim merchants. What features gave the Islamic state its multicultural character?

Critical Thinking
4. **Evaluating Information** Most Muslim scholars objected to the portrayal of living beings, but some Islamic art—such as

the painting on page 287—does show figures. Why is this so?

Understanding Themes
5. **Cultural Diffusion** What examples of cultural diffusion in the Islamic state can you find in these areas: (a) art, (b) mathematics, (c) commerce, and (d) literature?

Interpreting Demographic Data

Demographic data are statistics about a population, or group of people. Demographic data can tell us a great deal about where and how people live.

Learning the Skill

Demographers measure populations in different ways. Sometimes they simply count the number of people living in a country or region. By comparing these numbers, we can determine which countries have more people than others.

Suppose, however, that country A and country B each has five million people, but country A has five times more land area than country B. Country B would be more crowded, or more densely populated, than country A. Population density measures the number of people living within a certain area. Demographers also measure the population distribution, or the pattern of settlement within a country. For example, in Egypt most people live in the fertile Nile River valley and few people live in the desert.

Demographic data also describe population growth. Zero population growth occurs when births equal deaths. If births exceed deaths, the population is growing; if deaths exceed births, the population is shrinking. Population growth is expressed as a percentage rate. Demographers use growth rates to predict the future size of a population. A population pyramid is a graph showing the age distribution of a population. If the pyramid is wider at the bottom than at the top, the population is growing. If a pyramid is smaller at the bottom, the population is shrinking.

Practicing the Skill

The graphs on this page show demographic data for seven countries in the modern Islamic world. Use the graphs to answer these questions.

1. What kind of demographic data appears in each graph?
2. Which four countries have the largest total populations?
3. Which four countries are growing fastest?
4. How is population size related to growth rates in the graphs of these countries?

Applying the Skill

At the library, find demographic data about your city or county and illustrate it in a table, graph, or map. You could show population increase or decrease, population distribution, population growth rates, or age distribution. Write a short paragraph or pose questions that can help in interpreting your data.

For More Practice

Turn to the Skill Practice in the Chapter Review on page 291 for more practice in interpreting demographic data.

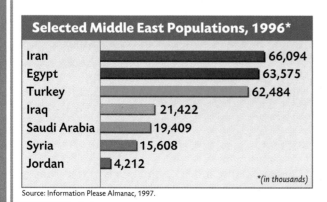

Selected Middle East Populations, 1996*

Iran	66,094
Egypt	63,575
Turkey	62,484
Iraq	21,422
Saudi Arabia	19,409
Syria	15,608
Jordan	4,212

(in thousands)

Source: Information Please Almanac, 1997.

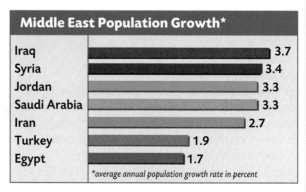

Middle East Population Growth*

Iraq	3.7
Syria	3.4
Jordan	3.3
Saudi Arabia	3.3
Iran	2.7
Turkey	1.9
Egypt	1.7

average annual population growth rate in percent

Connections Across Time

Historical Significance From Muhammad's revelations in the A.D. 600s grew the religion of Islam, which now includes more than a billion worshippers and ranks as one of the world's leading faiths. Today, Muslims predominate in the Middle East, Central Asia, Southeast Asia, and parts of Africa. Other areas of the world have significant numbers of Muslims.

During the Islamic Empire, Muslims preserved much ancient knowledge and made advances in the arts and sciences. Their achievements have enriched the cultures of the world.

Using Key Terms

Write the key term that completes each sentence. Then write a sentence for each term not chosen.

a. arabesques
b. caliph
c. chronicle
d. hajj
e. imam
f. jihad
g. *madrasa*
h. bazaars
i. revelations
j. calligraphy
k. *shari'ah*
l. sheikh
m. mosque

1. Islamic scholars and theologians organized Islamic moral rules into the _____, or code of law.
2. Islamic artists used the beautiful script of Arabic in _____ , or the art of elegant handwriting.
3. After Muhammad's death in A.D. 632, a group of prominent Muslims chose a _____ to head the Muslim community.
4. Muslims believed they had a religious duty to struggle for their faith through conquests known as _____.
5. Islamic geometric designs entwined with plant stems, leaves, flowers, and stars that decorate walls, books, and various objects are known as _____.

Technology Activity

Building a Database Search a library or the Internet to find information about different modern Islamic countries. Build a database collecting information about all Islamic countries of the world. Include information about beliefs, practices, and demographics of each country. Include a world map and label all countries that have a large Muslim population.

Using Your History Journal

Calligraphy, an elegant form of handwriting, is still used as an art form. Look at samples of calligraphy in an encyclopedia. Then, in calligraphy, reproduce the beginning page of your short report on Muslim life.

Reviewing Facts

1. **History** Identify the changes in the Arabian Peninsula during the A.D. 600s.
2. **Government** Explain how the Madinah Compact formed the basis for the Islamic state.
3. **Government** Discuss how disputes were resolved in the early Islamic community.
4. **Citizenship** Explain why some Muslims revolted against the Umayyads.
5. **Culture** Describe the role of women in the Islamic Empire.
6. **Science** Discuss some Islamic achievements in science and the changes they produced.
7. **Culture** Describe the career of Moses Maimonides. In what ways did he reflect the multicultural character of the Islamic Empire?
8. **Culture** Name the work in which a person would find tales such as "Sinbad the Sailor" and "Ali Baba and the Forty Thieves."
9. **History** Describe the change in writing history that was introduced by Ibn-Khaldun.

Critical Thinking

1. **Contrast** How did bedouin society differ from the society that formed under Islam?

2. **Apply** Would there have been a struggle for the caliphate if Muhammad had named a successor before his death?
3. **Analyze** Why do you think Abu Bakr wanted to compile Muhammad's revelations into one written collection?
4. **Synthesize** If the hajj was not among the Five Pillars of Islam, how might its omission have affected the Islamic state?
5. **Evaluate** How did Muslim scholars contribute to the world's knowledge?
6. **Contrast** How did the Islamic Empire under the Abbasids differ from the early Islamic community under Muhammad?

Geography in History

1. **Movement** Refer to the map below. Identify how far the Abbasid Empire had spread by A.D. 800 by naming the areas that it encompassed.
2. **Place** What was the capital city of the Abbasid Empire, and where was it located?
3. **Location** How did the city of Baghdad fortify itself against invasion?

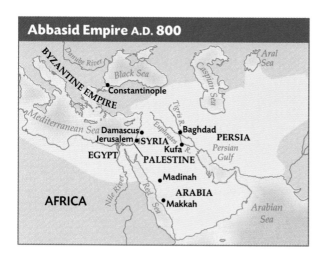

Abbasid Empire A.D. 800

Understanding Themes

1. **Innovation** What changes did the religion of Islam bring to the peoples of the Arabian Peninsula and the rest of the Middle East?
2. **Movement** How was the Umayyads' decision to move the nation's capital from Madinah to Damascus a result of Islamic expansion?

3. **Cultural Diffusion** How did the failure of the Umayyad government to embrace non-Arab Muslims destroy Umayyad rule?

Linking Past and Present

1. What evidence can you find in today's world of the split between the Sunni and the Shiite?
2. How have students today benefited from the work done at the House of Wisdom?
3. What words in the English language have their origins in the Arabic language?

Skill Practice

Study the population pyramid below and then answer these questions.

1. What is the general shape of the graph?
2. What percentage of the female population is between 0 and 19 years old?
3. Are there equal numbers of males and females in this population? How can you tell?
4. What conclusion can you draw about the growth rate in this population? On what data do you base this conclusion?

Age Distribution in Jordan

Age	% of Pop'n	Male	Female	% of Pop'n	Age
70+	0.8%			0.8%	70+
60-69	1.2%			1.1%	60-69
50-59	2.4%			2.2%	50-59
40-49	3.8%			3.4%	40-49
30-39	4.5%			4.2%	30-39
20-29	8.1%			7.3%	20-29
10-19	13.9%			12.4%	10-19
0-9	17.6%			16.3%	0-9

640   320   0   320   640

Total Population: 4,212,000
Total Male Population: 2,161,000
Total Female Population: 2,051,000
Life Expectancy (Male): 71 years
Life Expectancy (Female): 74 years
Sources: Broderbund Software, Inc, CIA World Factbook 1996.

The Rise of Medieval Europe

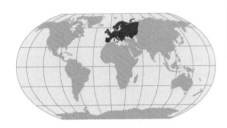

Chapter Themes

▶ **Movement** Invasions by Vikings, Magyars, and Muslims influence medieval Europe. *Section 1*

▶ **Cooperation** Nobles, church officials, and peasants develop ties of loyalty and service to one another. *Section 2*

▶ **Uniformity** The Catholic Church affects every aspect of medieval life. *Section 3*

▶ **Conflict** European kings, feudal lords, and popes struggle for political dominance. *Section 4*

Storyteller

It was tournament day. As trumpets flourished, the marshal shouted, "In the name of God and St. Michael, do your battle!" Knights on horseback thundered toward each other and met with a deafening clash. Lords and ladies cheered as their favorite unhorsed his opponents. The victor was awarded a prize from the lady whose colors he wore.

Such tournaments provided more than just entertainment. They also trained soldiers for combat. After the fall of Rome, wars were frequent. A professional warrior class—the knights—led the new, vigorous, competitive society that would reshape western Europe.

Historical Significance

How did Christianity, the classical heritage, and Germanic practices combine to form a new European civilization? How did this civilization develop and lay the foundation for modern European life?

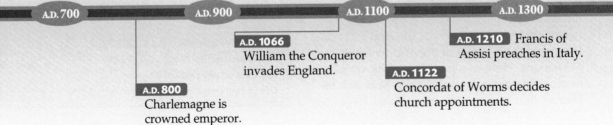

A.D. 700   A.D. 900   A.D. 1100   A.D. 1300

A.D. 1066 William the Conqueror invades England.

A.D. 1210 Francis of Assisi preaches in Italy.

A.D. 800 Charlemagne is crowned emperor.

A.D. 1122 Concordat of Worms decides church appointments.

 Apparition Before the Chapter of Arles by Giotto di Bondone. San Francesco, Assisi, Italy

Your History Journal

Monarchies and representative assemblies arose in medieval Europe. Draw a time line of key events in the development of these institutions.

Section 1

Frankish Rulers

Setting the Scene

▶ **Terms to Define**
   mayor of the palace, count

▶ **People to Meet**
   Clovis, Charles Martel, Pepin the Short, Charlemagne, the Vikings

▶ **Places to Locate**
   Frankish Empire, Scandinavia

 **Find Out** What made Frankish rulers, such as Charlemagne, exceptional rulers for their time?

The Storyteller

The men of medieval times, including Charlemagne, loved hunting. It was a cruel sport, but at least it provided meat for the royal tables. When Charlemagne sat down to dinner, the main course was usually a roast of game from the morning hunt. During the meal, one of the poets of the royal court might rise to read aloud a poem—to the dismay of the king's soldiers, who sometimes clapped their hands over their ears and glared at the poet until Charlemagne scolded them. With dinner, the king enjoyed "the wine of learning."

—freely adapted from *Charlemagne*, Richard Winston, 1968

Charlemagne

By A.D. 500, Germanic invasions had all but destroyed the urban world of the Roman Empire. Trade declined. Cities, bridges, and roads fell into disrepair and disuse. Law and order vanished, and education almost disappeared. Money was no longer used. For most people, life did not extend beyond the tiny villages where they were born, lived, and died.

Western Europe was so backward because of this decline that the early part of this period was once called "the Dark Ages." Scholars later combined the Latin terms *medium* (middle) and *aevum* (age) to form the term *medieval*, recognizing that this period was an era of transition between ancient and modern times. Out of this violent medieval period, or Middle Ages, a dynamic civilization arose. It combined elements of classical and Germanic cultures with Christian beliefs.

Merovingian Rulers

During the A.D. 400s the Franks, who settled in what is now France and western Germany, emerged as the strongest Germanic group. Their early rulers, known as Merovingian (MEHR•uh •VIHN•jee•uhn) kings for the ruler Merowig, held power until the early A.D. 700s.

Clovis

In A.D. 481 a brutal and wily warrior named **Clovis** became king of the Franks. Fifteen years later, Clovis became the first Germanic ruler to accept Catholicism. Clovis's military victories and his religious conversion gave his throne stability.

A century later the Frankish kingdom began to decline. Frankish kings had followed the custom of dividing the kingdom among their heirs. Heirs became rivals and fought each other for land. By A.D. 700 political power had passed from kings to government officials known as mayors of the palace.

Charles Martel

In A.D. 714 **Charles Martel**, or "Charles the Hammer," became mayor of the palace. When Muslim forces threatened Europe in A.D. 732, Charles led the successful defense of Tours, in France. This victory won him great prestige. As you read in Chapter 11, the victory ensured that Christianity would remain the dominant religion of Europe.

Pepin the Short

In A.D. 752, with the backing of nobles and church officials, **Pepin the Short**, the son of Charles Martel, became king of the Franks. The pope anointed, or put holy oil on, Pepin, making him a divinely chosen ruler in the eyes of the people.

In return for the Church's blessing, Pepin was expected to help the pope against his enemies. In A.D. 754 Pepin forced the Lombards, a Germanic people, to withdraw from Rome. He then gave the pope a large strip of Lombard land in central Italy. In appreciation, the pope cut his political ties to the Byzantine Empire and looked to the Franks as his protector. As a result, the fortunes of western Europe and Catholicism were bound more closely together.

Charlemagne's Empire

In A.D. 768 Pepin's son, **Charlemagne**, became the Frankish king. Charlemagne, or Charles the Great, was one of Europe's great monarchs. In Latin his name is written *Carolus Magnus*, which gave the name Carolingian to his dynasty. The king cut an imposing figure. His biographer, a monk named Einhard, described him this way:

> ❝Charles was large and strong, and of lofty stature, though not disproportionally tall … nose a little long, hair fair, and face laughing and merry…. He used to wear the national, that is to say, the Frankish, dress—next his skin a linen shirt and linen breeches, and above these a tunic fringed with silk; white hose fastened by bands covered his lower limbs and shoes his feet, and he protected his shoulders and chest in winter by a close-fitting coat of otter or marten skins. Over all he flung a blue cloak, and he always had a sword girt about him. ❞

Charlemagne nearly doubled the borders of his kingdom to include Germany, France, northern Spain, and most of Italy. His enlarged domain became known as the **Frankish Empire**. For the

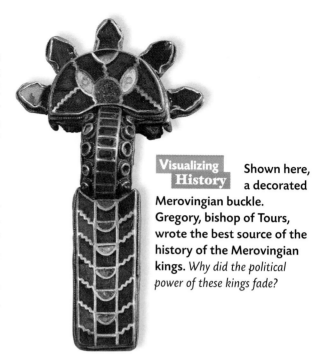

Visualizing History Shown here, a decorated Merovingian buckle. Gregory, bishop of Tours, wrote the best source of the history of the Merovingian kings. *Why did the political power of these kings fade?*

first time since the fall of Rome, most western Europeans were ruled by one government.

Because few western Europeans could read and write, Charlemagne wanted to revive learning. He set up a palace school at Aachen, his capital, to educate his officials. Alcuin (AL•kwihn), a scholar from England, ran the school and developed a program of study based on the Bible and Latin writings. Under Alcuin's direction, scholars preserved classical learning by copying ancient manuscripts. Charlemagne's school helped provide western Europeans with a common set of ideas.

A Christian Realm

One of the ideas that united western Europeans was the creation of a Christian Roman Empire. Church leaders believed that Charlemagne could turn this idea into reality. In A.D. 800 Charlemagne came to Rome to militarily defend Pope Leo III against the Roman nobles. To show his gratitude, Leo crowned Charlemagne the new Roman emperor. As protector of the Church and ruler of much of western Europe, Charlemagne wanted the title, but he had misgivings about receiving it from the pope. By crowning a monarch, the pope seemed to be saying that church officials were superior to rulers.

In spite of his concern, Charlemagne accepted his duties as emperor and worked to strengthen the empire. Because the central bureaucracy was small, he relied on local officials called counts to assist him. Each count was carefully instructed in the duties of office. The counts solved local problems, stopped feuds, protected the weak, and raised

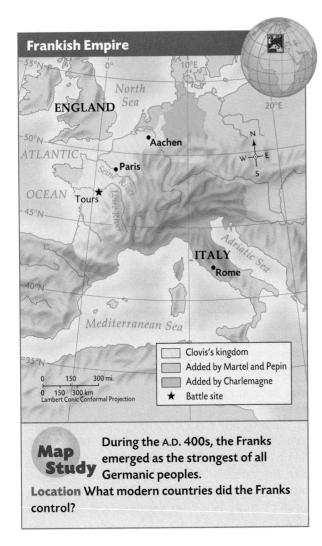

Frankish Empire

ENGLAND
North Sea
Aachen
ATLANTIC
Paris
Seine River
OCEAN
Tours ★
Loire River
Adriatic Sea
ITALY
Rome
Mediterranean Sea

0   150   300 mi.
0   150 300 km
Lambert Conic Conformal Projection

☐ Clovis's kingdom
☐ Added by Martel and Pepin
☐ Added by Charlemagne
★ Battle site

Map Study

During the A.D. 400s, the Franks emerged as the strongest of all Germanic peoples.

Location What modern countries did the Franks control?

armies for the emperor. Each year royal messengers, the *missi dominici*, went on inspections in which they informed Charlemagne about the performance of the counts and other local administrators. The emperor also traveled throughout the empire observing the work of his officials firsthand.

Collapse of Charlemagne's Empire

More than anything else, Charlemagne's forceful personality held his empire together. His death in A.D. 814 left a void that his only surviving son, Louis the Pious, could not fill. After Louis's death, Charlemagne's three grandsons fought one another for control of the empire.

In A.D. 843 the three brothers agreed in the Treaty of Verdun to divide the Carolingian lands. Charles the Bald took the western part, which covered most of present-day France. Louis the German acquired the eastern portion, which today is Germany. Lothair, who became the Roman emperor, took a strip of land in the middle of the empire stretching from the North Sea southward to Italy.

Invasions Increase Disunity

While internal feuding weakened the Carolingian kingdoms, outside invasions nearly destroyed them. Muslims from North Africa seized parts of southern Italy and gained control of the western Mediterranean. The Slavs marched out of the east to invade central Europe. From Asia a new group of fierce nomads called Magyars galloped west, leaving a trail of destruction. The most threatening attacks, however, came from **the Vikings**, raiders from **Scandinavia** to the north.

Viking Invasions

In medieval Scandinavian, to go *a-viking* means to fight as a warrior. Viking warriors traveled in long, deckless ships with one sail that were designed to slide swiftly through the water propelled by long oars. These boats were sturdy enough to cross the Atlantic Ocean, shallow enough to navigate Europe's rivers, and light enough to be carried past fortified bridges. The Vikings became known for surprise attacks and speedy retreats. What they could not steal they burned. No place in Europe was safe from attack.

Boasting names like Eric Bloodax and Harald Bluetooth, the Vikings sought riches and adventure. In the A.D. 800s they left their overpopulated homeland, which later became the kingdoms of Norway, Denmark, and Sweden. Viking warriors fought ferociously and showed their victims no mercy.

Viking Trade

The Vikings, however, were more than just raiders. They were also explorers and settlers. Skilled in sailing and trading, they moved along the Atlantic and Mediterranean coasts of Europe. The Norwegians settled the North Atlantic islands of Greenland and Iceland, and even reached North America. The Danes temporarily held England and established the Viking state of Normandy in northwestern France. The Swedes settled in present-day Ukraine and Russia.

Viking Culture

In Scandinavia and their new homelands, the Vikings worshiped many deities. They were proud of their gods and told stories of the gods' great deeds. These stories became written poems called *Eddas*. The Vikings also made up sagas, or long tales. At first, storytellers recited them at special feasts. After A.D. 1100 the Vikings wrote down their sagas. By this time they had converted to Christianity. With their acceptance of the new religion, the Vikings began to write their languages with Roman letters.

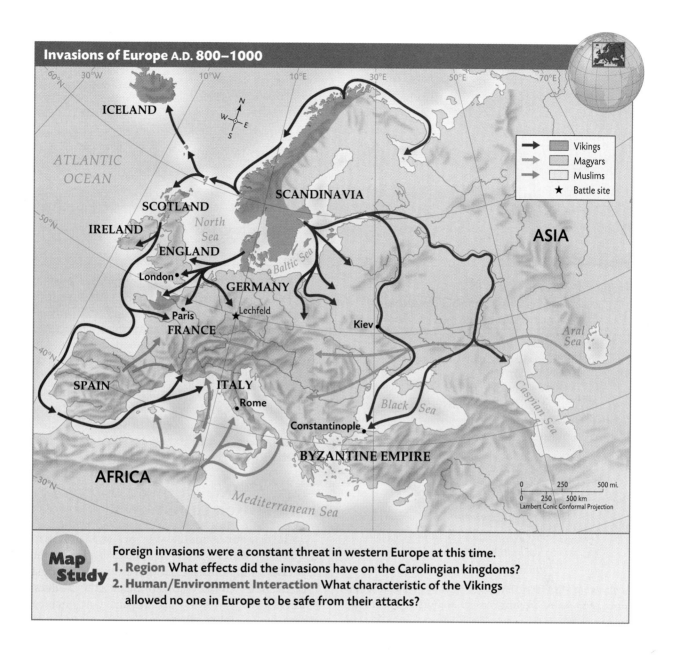

Invasions of Europe A.D. 800–1000

Legend:
- → Vikings
- → Magyars
- → Muslims
- ★ Battle site

Map Study

Foreign invasions were a constant threat in western Europe at this time.
1. **Region** What effects did the invasions have on the Carolingian kingdoms?
2. **Human/Environment Interaction** What characteristic of the Vikings allowed no one in Europe to be safe from their attacks?

A New Europe

The people of western Europe suffered at the hands of Vikings and other invaders. These raids isolated communities and severely weakened the central authority of monarchs. Trade declined, and many areas faced economic collapse. As a result of royal weakness, nobles and local officials took over the local defense. Beginning in the A.D. 900s, a new political and social system brought more stability to western Europe.

SECTION I REVIEW

Recall

1. **Define** mayor of the palace, count.
2. **Identify** Clovis, Charles Martel, Pepin the Short, Charlemagne, Treaty of Verdun, the Vikings.
3. **Explain** what problem resulted when Charlemagne was crowned by the pope.

Critical Thinking

4. **Making Comparisons** How did Charlemagne work to achieve European unity? How are European leaders trying to achieve the same goal in Europe today?

Understanding Themes

5. **Movement** Why did the Vikings, the Magyars, and the Slavs leave their homelands and invade western Europe?

A.D. 700

c. A.D. 750 Charles Martel grants warriors landed estates with peasants.

A.D. 900

c. A.D. 900 Feudalism takes hold in northern France.

A.D. 1100

c. A.D. 1000 Peasants begin to use three-field system in farming.

Section 2

Medieval Life

Setting the Scene

▶ **Terms to Define**

feudalism, fief, vassal, homage, tournament, chivalry, manorialism, serf

▶ **People to Meet**

knights, lords, ladies, peasants

ind Out How were loyalties maintained in a divided and often violent Europe?

The Storyteller

Medieval law laid down rules for marriage. When a young woman arrived at marriageable age, one of her brothers or male relatives had to find her a suitable husband. If he did not, she could register a complaint, and her relative could be called to the king's court and given a year and a day to find her one. The husband had to be suited to her social status and property. If the relative did not do this, the king would step in and assign the woman a part of the family inheritance. Then she could marry whomever she wished.

—from *Women's Lives in Medieval Europe, A Sourcebook*, edited by Emile Amt, 1993

Medieval tournament

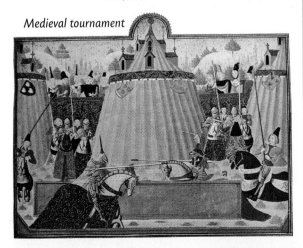

With the weakening of central government, a new political system known as feudalism developed in western Europe. Feudalism was a highly decentralized form of government that stressed alliances of mutual protection between monarchs and nobles of varying degrees of power. The system was based on giving land to nobles in exchange for loyalty and military aid. With the land came peasants to farm it and many powers usually reserved for governments. Feudalism took hold in northern France around A.D. 900 and spread through the rest of western Europe by the A.D. mid-1000s.

Feudal Relationships

The tie between military service and land ownership that characterized feudalism began in the A.D. 700s. At that time, Charles Martel was fighting the Muslims. Unlike the Europeans, the Muslim soldiers used saddles with stirrups that enabled them to fight on horseback, using a sword or lance. Charles wanted to adopt the stirrup and develop a cavalry. However, the cost of keeping such a force required a new type of military system. To support the cavalry, Martel began granting warriors fiefs, or estates with peasants. From these fiefs, warriors got the income to buy horses and battle equipment.

Frankish kings later enlarged this system by giving fiefs to counts and local officials. In time, such nobles assumed many of the powers usually held by government: raising armies, dispensing justice, and in some cases even minting coins. In return, the nobles swore an oath of loyalty and pledged military support to the king.

By the A.D. 900s, such arrangements among nobles and monarchs emerged as feudalism. Lords who had been granted fiefs were allowed to pass their lands on to their heirs. In return, these nobles were to provide **knights**, or mounted warriors, for the royal army.

In theory, feudal relationships were like a pyramid. The king was at the top. In the middle were various ranks of lords. Each lord was a vassal—a noble who served a lord of the next higher rank. At the bottom were the knights. In practice, however, a noble might be both a lord and a vassal, since a noble could pledge his allegiance to more than one lord. In fact, one German warrior, Siboto of Falkenstein, was vassal to 20 different lords. Of course, conflicts of loyalty arose if one of a vassal's lords went to war with another.

Feudal Obligations

Ties between a lord and a vassal were made official in a solemn ceremony known as homage. In return for a fief, the vassal pledged to perform certain duties. The most important obligation was military service. The vassal agreed to provide his lord with a certain number of knights for battle during a period of 40 to 60 days each year. In addition, the vassal agreed to serve in the lord's court, to provide food and lodging when the lord came visiting, and to contribute funds when the lord's son became a knight or when his oldest daughter married. Vassals also pledged to pay ransom in the event of the lord's capture in battle.

Castles for Defense

Because of the lack of a strong central government, warfare occurred frequently in feudal society. As a result, every noble built a castle, or fortified manor house, for defense against enemies. The first castles were wooden buildings with high fences of logs or mounds of hard-packed earth around them. By the A.D. 1100s castles were built of stone, with thick walls and turrets, or small towers. Each castle was built on a hill or mound surrounded by a deep moat. Castles had a square tower called a keep. The keep, located in the strongest part of the castle, contained many rooms, a hall, and a dungeon. Surrounding the keep was a large open area called a bailey. Within the bailey were various buildings, including barracks, storerooms, workshops, and a chapel.

Life of the Nobility

Lords, ladies, and knights made up the nobility of the Middle Ages. Although the nobles lived much easier lives than the peasants who worked for them, their lives can hardly be called luxurious or glamorous. Castles were built for security, not comfort, and were largely cold, dingy, and damp places.

Within his fief, a **lord**, or nobleman, had almost total authority. He collected rents in goods from

Visualizing History An illustration from the *Trés Riches Heures du Duc de Berry* shows peasants at work outside a castle. *Why did feudal lords need castles?*

peasants and settled disputes between his vassals. Any outside attempt to seize the land or control the inhabitants of his fief was met with violent resistance.

In contrast, a **lady**, or noblewoman, had few, if any, rights. A noblewoman could be wed as early as her twelfth birthday to a man her father selected. Her primary duties lay in bringing up children and taking care of the household. Noblewomen took pride in their needlework, turning out cloth and fine embroidery. They also learned to make effective medicines from plants and herbs. Some women shared the supervision of the estate with the lord and took over their husband's duties while the men were away at war.

Entertainment

Nobles looked forward to tournaments—mock battles between knights—as a show of military

1–Moat; 2–Drawbridge; 3–Guardroom; 4–Latrine; 5–Armory; 6–Soldiers' quarters; 7–Kitchen garden;
8–Storerooms and servants' quarters; 9–Kitchen; 10–Great hall; 11–Chapel; 12–Lord and lady's quarters; 13–Inner ward

Harry Bliss

Life in the Castle

The medieval castle was both fortress and home. The first castles, raised in the A.D. 900s, were square towers encircled by wooden ramparts. By the A.D. 1100s, castles had become mighty stone fortresses. From the towers and walls archers took aim and soldiers dumped boiling liquids on attackers. The castle was surrounded by a moat—a body of water encircling the castle—that could be crossed when a drawbridge was let down.

Inside it was crowded, smelly, dirty, and damp. The animals ate and slept with the people, and the smell of animal and human waste was everywhere. The occupants of the castle had to contend with cold earthen or stone floors, drafty halls, smoky rooms, and windows without glass that let in cold and heat along with light. Not even the lord and lady had their own private room. Grand but never comfortable, the castle's main purpose was military security. ⊕

skills. They also loved to hunt, and both men and women learned the art of falconry and archery. A dinner featuring several dishes of game and fish might follow. In a castle's great hall, nobles and their guests ate while being entertained by minstrels, or singers.

Becoming a Knight

A nobleman's son began training for knighthood at age 7. Beginning as a page, or assistant, in the house of a lord, he learned manners and the use of weapons. At 15, the page became a squire who assisted a knight and practiced using weapons. Once he proved himself in battle, the squire was knighted in an elaborate ceremony.

The behavior of knights was governed by a code of chivalry. This code called for knights to be brave in battle, fight fairly, keep promises, defend the Church, and treat women of noble birth in a courteous manner. Chivalry eventually became the basis for the development of good manners in Western society.

The Manorial System

The wealth of a feudal lord came from the labor of the **peasants** who lived on and worked the lord's land. Since the last years of the Roman Empire, many peasants had worked for large landowners, in part because they could not afford their own land and in part for protection. By the Middle Ages, economic life across Europe centered around a system of agricultural production called manorialism. It provided lords and peasants with food, shelter, and protection.

Manors, or estates, varied in size from several hundred to several hundred thousand acres. Each manor included the lord's manor house, pastures for livestock, fields for crops, forest areas, and a

Visualizing History **A suit of armor made of steel, brass, and leather belonging to an English knight, Master Jacobe.** *What knightly code became the basis of good manners in Western society?*

village where the peasants lived. While feudalism describes the political relationships between nobles, manorialism concerns economic ties between nobles and peasants.

Work on a Manor

In return for the lord's protection, the peasants provided various services for the lord. Chief among the obligations were to farm the lord's land and to make various payments of goods. For example, each time a peasant ground grain at the lord's mill, he was obligated to leave a portion for the lord. If he baked in the lord's oven, he left a loaf behind for the lord. In addition, peasants were obligated to set aside a number of days each year to provide various types of labor, such as road or bridge repair.

Warfare and invasions made trade almost impossible, so the manor had to produce nearly everything its residents needed. Most of the peasants farmed or herded sheep. A few worked as skilled artisans, for each manor needed a blacksmith to make tools, a carpenter for building, a

Footnotes to History

Identifying a Knight
To identify themselves, knights had individual designs painted on their shields and tunics. His particular design became known as the knight's coat of arms. In noble families, coats of arms were passed down from one generation to the next. The flags of some modern countries are based on the system of designs that were developed by the knights.

shoemaker, a miller to grind grain, a vintner to make wine, and a brewer to make beer. Peasant women made candles, sheared sheep, spun wool, and sewed clothing.

Peasants rarely left the manor. Most were serfs, people who were bound to the manor and could not leave it without permission. But the serfs were not slaves—they could not be "sold" apart from the land they lived on.

Increased Production

The manorial system normally produced only enough food to support the peasants and the lord's household. However, a number of improvements gradually boosted productivity and eased the threat of famine.

The first improvement was the development of a new, heavier type of plow. The new plow made deeper cuts in the ground and had a device called a mould-board that pushed the soil sideways. The heavier plow meant less time in the fields for peasant farmers. As a result, farmers developed a better method of planting.

Instead of dividing plots of land into two fields, one of which lay fallow, or unsown, each year, farmers in the A.D. 1000s began to use a three-field system. One field might be planted with winter wheat, a second with spring wheat and vegetables, and a third left fallow. The next year, different crops were planted in the fallow field. One of the two remaining fields was planted, and the other one was left fallow until the next year. This system produced more crops than the old system and helped to preserve the soil.

Peasant Life

Poverty and hardship characterized peasant life, and few serfs lived beyond the age of 40. Famine and disease were constant dangers. In times of war, the peasants were the first and hardest hit. Invading knights trampled crops and burned villages, causing famine and loss of life. To support the war, their lord might require additional payments of crops or labor. A monk of Canterbury described an English serf's account of his day:

> ❝ I work very hard. I go out at dawn, driving the oxen to the field, and I yoke them to the plough; however hard the winter I dare not stay home for fear of my master; but, having yoked the oxen and made the ploughshare and coulter fast to the plough, every day I have to plough a whole acre or more. ❞
>
> —Aelfric, *Colloquy*, A.D. 1005

Serfs like this man lived in tiny, one-room houses with dirt floors, no chimney, and one or two crude pieces of furniture—perhaps a table and stools. People slept huddled together for warmth. Coarse bread, a few vegetables from their gardens, and grain for porridge made up their usual diet. Meat was a rarity.

In spite of hardships, peasants were able to relax on Sundays and holy days. They enjoyed dancing, singing, and such sports as wrestling and archery. In addition, there were other amusements, such as religious plays, pageants, and shows by minstrels.

Despite the obvious differences between serfs and nobles, the two groups did share a common interest in the land. Medieval Europeans believed that every person was equal in the "eyes of God." In practice, however, society was viewed as a hierarchy with ranked leaders from top to bottom. Each person—no matter what his or her place might be in the hierarchy—had certain duties that were attached to his or her position in life. In general, people did not question their standing or obligations. Although the manorial system seemed to lack freedom and opportunity for most of the people involved in it, it did create a very stable and secure way of life during a time that was generally violent and uncertain.

SECTION 2 REVIEW

Recall
1. **Define** feudalism, fief, vassal, homage, tournament, chivalry, manorialism, serf.
2. **Identify** knight, lord, lady, peasant.
3. **Describe** the role of women in medieval Europe and male attitudes toward women.

Critical Thinking
4. **Making Comparisons** Compare and contrast the feudal class structure in medieval Europe with the *varna* system in early India discussed in Chapter 8.

Understanding Themes
5. **Cooperation** Diagram the ways nobles, knights, and peasants cooperated during the medieval period.

A.D. 529 Benedict introduces
rule for monasteries.

c. A.D. 650
Irish missionaries
win converts in
western Europe.

A.D. 1073 The monk
Hildebrand becomes
Pope Gregory VII.

A.D. 1232
The Inquisition begins.

Section 3

The Medieval Church

Setting the Scene

▶ **Terms to Define**
sacrament, abbot, abbess, cardinal, lay
investiture, heresy, excommunication, friar

▶ **People to Meet**
Benedict, Gregory I, Gregory VII,
Innocent III, Francis of Assisi, Dominic

▶ **Places to Locate**
Monte Cassino, Cluny

 How did the Catholic Church shape
the development of medieval Europe?

The Storyteller

*Alcuin, a Benedictine monk, arose to begin
his day. The day's work in a monastery depended
on sunlight hours, for candles were expensive and
no one in medieval times had access to cheap artificial light. Because it was winter, Alcuin had to
get up at 2:30 A.M., and go to bed at 6:30 P.M.*

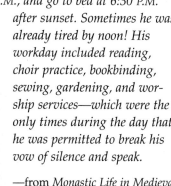

*after sunset. Sometimes he was
already tired by noon! His
workday included reading,
choir practice, bookbinding,
sewing, gardening, and worship services—which were the
only times during the day that
he was permitted to break his
vow of silence and speak.*

—from *Monastic Life in Medieval
England*, J.C. Dickinson, 1962

*Ancient monastery in
Glendalough, Ireland*

uring the Middle Ages, the Catholic
Church was the dominant spiritual influence in western Europe. For most peo-
ple, the Church was the center of their lives. A small
number of Europeans, however, were Jews, Muslims, or non-Catholic Christians.

The Medieval Church

Although the Church's primary mission was
spiritual, the decline of Rome in the A.D. 400s led the
Church to assume many political and social tasks.
During this time, the bishop of Rome, now called
the pope, became the strongest political leader in
western Europe. The pope claimed spiritual authority over all Christians, basing this claim on the belief
that Peter the Apostle, Rome's first bishop, had been
chosen by Jesus to lead the Church.

Religious Role

The Catholic Church taught that all people
were sinners and dependent on God's grace, or
favor. The only way to receive grace was by taking
part in the sacraments, or church rituals: baptism,
penance, eucharist, confirmation, matrimony,
anointing of the sick, and holy orders. One of the
most important sacraments was the eucharist, or
holy communion, which commemorated Christ's
death. People shared in the eucharist at a mass, or
worship service. At each mass, the priest blessed
wheat wafers and a cup of wine that stood on an
altar. According to Catholic teaching, the priests
and the worshippers received Jesus' invisible presence in the forms of the bread and the wine.

During the Middle Ages, people generally had
a limited understanding of church rituals. Masses
were said in Latin, a language few people understood. Also, many priests were poorly educated

and did not preach effectively. Moreover, few worshippers could read or write. What the average person learned about the Christian faith came from the statues, paintings, and later the stained glass windows that adorned most medieval churches.

Church Organization

The church hierarchy, which was described in Chapter 6, remained largely the same during the Middle Ages. The contact most people had with the Church was through parish priests, who conducted services and oversaw the spiritual life of the community. Occasionally bishops visited a parish to supervise the priests.

The pope, bishops, and priests formed what is called the secular clergy because they lived *in saeculo,* a Latin phrase that means "in the world." Other clergy, known as regular clergy, lived by a *regula,* or rule. Regular clergy included monks and nuns who lived apart from society. These Christians played an important role in strengthening the medieval Church.

Benedict's Rule

In A.D. 529 a Roman official named **Benedict** founded a monastery at **Monte Cassino** in Italy. His monastery became a model for monks in other communities. Benedict drew up a list of rules that provided for manual work, meditation, and prayer. According to the Benedictine rule, monks could not own goods, must never marry, and were bound to obey monastic laws. Their life was one of poverty, chastity, and obedience to the directives of an abbot, or monastery head.

Monastic Life

Monks dressed in simple, long robes made of coarse material and tied at the waist by a cord. They ate one or two plain meals each day. Most monasteries had a rule of silence; monks could not converse with one another except for a short time each day. In some monasteries total silence was the rule. During meals, one monk might read passages from

Images *of the* Times

Monastic Life

Although monasteries were closed religious communities, they profoundly influenced European culture during the Middle Ages.

An illustrated page from a book copied by monks shows the careful, artistic writing that became the manuscript before printing was developed.

St. Benedict and his monks, like all those who lived at the monasteries, ate together in a refectory.

Mont St. Michel presents a view of the beautiful old monastery's lower ramparts.

the Bible while the others meditated.

Women took part in monastic life by living in a convent under the direction of an abbess. Known as nuns, they wore simple clothes and wrapped a white cloth called a wimple around their face and neck. They alternated prayer with spinning, weaving, and embroidering items such as tapestries and banners. They also taught needlework and the medicinal use of herbs to the daughters of nobles.

Influence of Monastics

Although monks and nuns lived apart from society, they were not completely isolated. Indeed, they played a crucial role in medieval intellectual and social life. Since few people could read or write, the regular clergy preserved ancient religious works and the classical writings. Scribes laboriously copied books by hand, working in a small drafty room with only a candle or small window for light. Illuminated manuscripts decorated with rich colors and intricate pictures indicate that, although the task was tedious, it was lovingly done.

Monasteries and convents provided schools for young people, hospitals for the sick, food for the needy, and guest houses for weary travelers. They taught peasants carpentry and weaving and made improvements in agriculture that they passed on to others. Some monks and nuns became missionaries who spread Christian teachings to non-Christians.

Missionary Efforts

Pope **Gregory I** was so impressed with the Benedictine Rule that he adopted it to spread Christianity in Europe. In A.D. 597 he sent monks to England, where they converted the Anglo-Saxons to Catholicism. From England, missionaries carried Christianity to northern Germany. During the A.D. 600s, monasteries in Ireland sent missionaries throughout the North Atlantic and western Europe. Although the Irish were isolated from the pope in Rome, their missionaries won many converts. By the A.D. mid-1000s, most western Europeans had become Catholics.

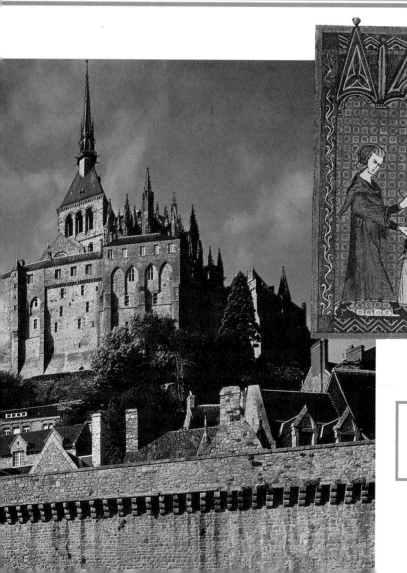

A father who has bought a place for his son in a monastery presents the youngster to an abbot.

305

Power of the Church

The medieval Catholic Church helped to govern western Europe. It had its own laws and courts that dealt with cases related to the clergy, doctrine, and marriage and morals. Disobedience to church laws resulted in severe penalties for a common person and ruler alike. For example, a lord or king who violated Church law could face an interdict, which banned an entire region or country from receiving the sacraments necessary to salvation.

The Church also had feudal ties that boosted its wealth and political power but often undermined its spiritual vitality. Many high church officials were nobles and held land from kings in return for military service. Because their religious duties prevented them from fighting, these church leaders gave some of their land to knights who would fight for them. The Church also received donations of land and money from nobles wanting to ensure their salvation. Nobles, however, began to influence church policies, especially by having relatives appointed to church positions. Many of these appointees had little devotion to their spiritual calling.

Visualizing History A young boy, having obtained the office of bishop, carries sacred church relics. *How did Pope Gregory try to stop the selection of church officials by secular rulers?*

Church Reform

By the A.D. 900s, many devout Christians were calling for reform. The reform movement began in the monasteries and spread throughout much of western Europe. Most famous was the monastery at **Cluny** in eastern France, whose monks won respect for leading lives of pious simplicity. The abbots of Cluny sent representatives to other monasteries to help them undertake similar reforms.

Other church leaders tried to free the Church from the control of feudal lords. They wanted the Church, not the state, to be the final authority in Western society. In A.D. 1059 a church council declared that political leaders could no longer choose the pope. Instead, the pope would be elected by a gathering of cardinals—high church officials in Rome ranking directly below the pope. In addition, the reformers insisted that the pope, not secular rulers such as lords and kings, should be the one to appoint bishops and other officials to church offices.

In A.D. 1073 the cardinals elected a reform-minded monk named Hildebrand as Pope **Gregory VII**. Gregory believed that the pope should have complete jurisdiction over all church officials. He especially criticized the practice of lay investiture, in which secular rulers gave the symbols of office, such as a ring and a staff, to the bishops they had appointed.

Fighting Heresy

Innocent III, one of the most powerful popes, also tried to reform the Catholic Church. In A.D. 1215 he convened a council that condemned drunkenness, feasting, and dancing among the clergy. The council also laid down strict rules for stopping the spread of heresy, or the denial of basic church teachings. Heresy had increased as corruption and scandal had rocked the Church. In the Middle Ages, heresy was regarded as seriously as the crime of treason is viewed today.

At first, the Catholic Church tried to convert heretics, or those who challenged its teachings. When that failed, however, heretics were threatened with excommunication, or expulsion from the Church. An excommunicated person was not allowed to take part in the sacraments and was also outlawed from any contact with Christian society. Since receiving the sacraments was considered to be essential for salvation, banishment was an especially severe penalty.

Early in the A.D. 1200s, for example, the Church became concerned about a group of heretics in France known as Albigensians (AL•buh•JEHN •shuhnz). The Albigensians believed that the material world was evil and rejected church sacraments. To end this heresy, Pope Innocent III sent French knights to crush the group.

The Inquisition

In order to seek out and punish people suspected of heresy, the Church set up a court in A.D. 1232 known as the Inquisition. Those brought before the court were urged to confess their heresy and to ask forgiveness. Often, however, Inquisition officials accused people without sufficient proof; sometimes they even used torture to obtain confessions. The Church welcomed back those who repented, but those who did not repent were punished. Punishment ranged from imprisonment to loss of property and even execution. According to church officials, these punishments were needed to save the souls of the heretics.

Friars Inspire Reform

Other reformers of the Church during the early A.D. 1200s were friars, or wandering preachers. At a time when church leaders were criticized for their love of wealth and power, the friars lived simply, owned no possessions, and depended on gifts of food and shelter to survive.

The friars followed monastic rules but did not isolate themselves from the rest of the Christian community. Instead, they lived in towns and preached Christianity to the people. The best-known friars were the Franciscans and the Dominicans. Because they were well known and liked, the friars kept many people loyal to the Catholic Church.

Francis of Assisi, the son of a wealthy Italian cloth merchant, founded the Franciscan friars about A.D. 1210. Francis and his followers sought to follow the simple life of Jesus and his disciples. They became known for their cheerful trust in God and their respect for nature as a divine gift.

A Spanish priest named **Dominic** organized the Dominican friars in A.D. 1215. Like the Franciscans, the Dominicans lived a life of poverty, simplicity, and service. In addition, they were well-educated, persuasive preachers who could reply to the arguments of heretics.

The Jews

As the Church's power increased in medieval Europe, the position of the Jews worsened. In the early Middle Ages, Jews and Christians had lived peacefully together in most of Europe. Many Jews had become merchants, artisans, or landowners, and their contributions to society were valued by their Christian neighbors.

By the 1000s, however, many Christians increasingly saw the Jews as outsiders and a threat to society. They unfairly blamed the Jews for plagues, famines, and other social problems. Such false accusations gave mobs the excuse to attack and kill thousands of Jews.

The most powerful source of anti-Semitism, or hatred of the Jews, came from interpretations of Christian doctrine. Many church leaders and laity blamed the Jews for Jesus' death and resented the Jews' refusal to become Christians. With church approval, political leaders required Jews in certain areas to wear badges or special clothes that identified them as Jews. Jews were also forced to live in separate communities that became known as ghettos. They also lost the right to own land and to practice certain trades. To earn a living, many Jews became peddlers or money-lenders, jobs despised by medieval Christians.

Beginning in the late 1200s, rulers in England, France, and certain parts of central Europe even expelled their Jewish subjects. Many of the expelled Jews settled in eastern Europe, especially Poland, where they received protection. Over the centuries, the Jews of eastern Europe developed thriving communities based on their religious traditions.

SECTION 3 REVIEW

Recall
1. **Define** sacrament, abbot, abbess, cardinal, lay investiture, heresy, excommunication, friar.
2. **Identify** Benedict, Gregory I, Gregory VII, Innocent III, Francis of Assisi, Dominic.
3. **Explain** how the Catholic Church provided the link between the ancient world and the medieval world.

Critical Thinking
4. **Synthesizing Information** Imagine that you are a religious, but superstitious, peasant living during the Middle Ages. Invent an explanation for the famine that has struck your village.

Understanding Themes
5. **Uniformity** How effective were the actions of the Catholic Church in trying to make all western Europeans believe and practice one faith?

Section 4

Rise of European Monarchy

Setting the Scene

▸ **Terms to Define**
    common law, grand jury, petit jury, middle class

▸ **People to Meet**
    Alfred the Great, William the Conqueror, Henry II, Thomas à Becket, Eleanor of Aquitaine, Philip Augustus, Henry IV

▸ **Places to Locate**
    England, France, Germany

 **ind Out** What were the achievements of medieval European monarchs?

The Storyteller

The English throne was at stake as the Battle of Hastings approached. William decided to provoke Harold to fight in single combat and called on him to spare the blood of his followers. Under Norman law, personal combat decided difficult cases, looking for the judgment of God to settle the matter. Harold refused because he knew the cause was not personal, but national. It would take a full-scale invasion to decide who would wear the English crown.

—adapted from *William the Conqueror*, Edward A. Freeman, 1927

William the Conqueror

After the decline of Rome, central authority in western Europe disappeared. Except for Charlemagne's reign in the late A.D. 700s, kings were rulers in name only, their lands and power gradually lost to nobles. However, in the A.D. 1100s, many European monarchs began to build strong states.

England

After the Romans abandoned Britain in the A.D. 400s, the island was invaded by Germanic Angles, Saxons, and Jutes. These groups took over much of Britain from the native Celts (KEHLTZ) and set up several kingdoms. In the late A.D. 800s, the Danish Vikings from Scandinavia posed another threat. King Alfred of Wessex, known as **Alfred the Great**, united the Anglo-Saxon kingdoms and defeated the Danes in A.D. 886. His united kingdom eventually became known as "Angleland," or **England**.

The Anglo-Saxons

Alfred ruled Anglo-Saxon England from A.D. 871 to A.D. 899. Like Charlemagne, he was interested in the revival of learning. The English king founded schools and hired scholars to translate many books from Latin to Anglo-Saxon. He also had the scholars write a history of England, known as the *Anglo-Saxon Chronicle*.

The kings who followed Alfred were weak rulers. When the last Anglo-Saxon king, Edward the Confessor, died in A.D. 1066, three rivals claimed the throne.

The Norman Conquest

One of the claimants to the throne was William, the Duke of Normandy. A cousin of the late English king and vassal of the French king, William had a feudal stronghold in northwestern France. Gathering a force of several hundred boats and some 6,000 soldiers, he invaded England in A.D. 1066. At the Battle of Hastings, William defeated Harold Godwinson, the king chosen by the Anglo-Saxon nobles. The victory won William the English crown and the name **William the Conqueror**.

As king, William kept tight control over the government. He took Anglo-Saxon lands, kept some of the land for himself, and gave the rest to his Norman vassals in return for military service. He later made all landowners swear direct loyalty to him. William also set up a council of nobles to advise him and named local officials called sheriffs to collect taxes. To determine taxable wealth, William carried out the first census in western Europe since Roman times. Every person, manor, and farm animal became an entry in the *Domesday Book*.

Royal Power

Although William's court and nobles were French-speaking, England's population remained largely Anglo-Saxon. Over the next 300 years, however, Norman French and Anglo-Saxon ways blended to form a new English culture. During this time, William's successors further strengthened the monarchy. Henry I, William's son who ruled from A.D. 1100 to A.D. 1135, created a royal exchequer, or treasury, to collect taxes and gave royal courts greater authority. Henry's grandson, **Henry II**, set up a system of common law, using traveling judges to apply the law equally throughout the land. In each community, the judges met with a grand jury that submitted the names of suspects. A petit jury soon developed to establish the guilt or innocence of the accused.

Henry's plan to try clergy in the royal courts brought him into conflict with **Thomas à Becket**, the archbishop of Canterbury. In A.D. 1170 four of Henry's knights, who believed they were acting on the king's command, murdered Becket in his cathedral.

At the height of his power, Henry ruled western France as well as England. His wife, **Eleanor of Aquitaine**, once married to the French king, owned vast lands in southwestern France. Although Henry's relations with Eleanor soured, Eleanor continued to influence royal policies through their sons, Richard I (the Lionhearted) and John.

CONNECTIONS — The Arts

Tapestries

The Bayeux Tapestry, made between A.D. 1073 and A.D. 1083, is a remarkable example of medieval art. It is a work of embroidery, a band of linen upon which pictures and patterns are stitched in colored wool. Twenty inches high and 230 feet long, it probably once decorated the walls of an entire room.

The 72 scenes on the tapestry illustrate William the Conqueror's invasion of England in A.D. 1066. Probably the work of William's wife, Matilda, and the ladies of her court, the tapestry tells the story of the invasion in a series of individual scenes, much as a story is told in a comic book today. The images are lively and simple and give a sense of movement and vitality. The tapestry even includes words to reveal what is happening in each scene.

The popularity of tapestries among the European nobility continued into the A.D. 800s and then declined. However, since World War II, interest in this art form has revived. Artists today experiment with materials and weaving to create many new kinds of wall tapestry. One of the most famous modern tapestries, "Christ in Glory," was done in 1962 by the English artist Graham Sutherland and hangs above the high altar in England's new Coventry Cathedral.

Bayeux Tapestry (detail)

Linking Past and Present ACTIVITY

Visit an art museum in your community that has medieval and modern tapestries. Compare and contrast the tapestries of both time periods in terms of their themes, techniques, and the materials used to make them.

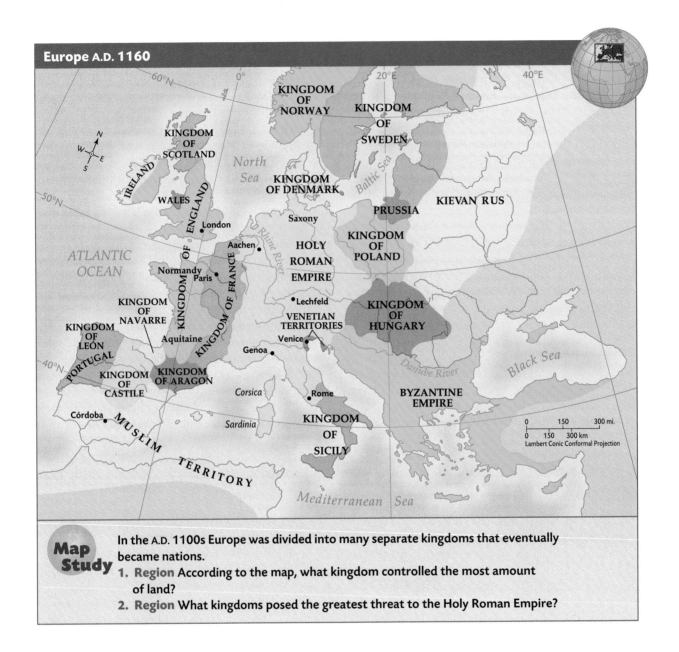

KINGDOM OF NORWAY

KINGDOM OF SWEDEN

KINGDOM OF SCOTLAND

IRELAND

North Sea

Baltic Sea

KINGDOM OF DENMARK

KIEVAN RUS

WALES

PRUSSIA

KINGDOM OF ENGLAND

London

Saxony

KINGDOM OF POLAND

ATLANTIC OCEAN

Aachen

Rhine River

HOLY ROMAN EMPIRE

Normandy

Paris

KINGDOM OF FRANCE

Lechfeld

KINGDOM OF NAVARRE

VENETIAN TERRITORIES

KINGDOM OF HUNGARY

Aquitaine

Venice

KINGDOM OF LEÓN

Genoa

PORTUGAL

KINGDOM OF CASTILE

KINGDOM OF ARAGON

Corsica

Rome

BYZANTINE EMPIRE

Danube River

Black Sea

Córdoba

MUSLIM TERRITORY

Sardinia

KINGDOM OF SICILY

| 0 | 150 | 300 mi. |
| 0 | 150 300 km | |

Lambert Conic Conformal Projection

Mediterranean Sea

Map Study In the A.D. 1100s Europe was divided into many separate kingdoms that eventually became nations.

1. **Region** According to the map, what kingdom controlled the most amount of land?

2. **Region** What kingdoms posed the greatest threat to the Holy Roman Empire?

The Magna Carta

During his reign, John lost some English land to France and became unpopular when he increased taxes and punished his enemies without trial. Alarmed at the loss of their feudal rights, a group of nobles met at Runnymede in A.D. 1215. They forced John to sign the Magna Carta, or Great Charter, one of the most important documents in the history of representative government.

The Magna Carta placed clear limits on royal power. The charter prevented the king from collecting taxes without the consent of the Great Council. It also assured freemen the right of trial by jury. Article 39 stated:

❝No freeman shall be taken, or imprisoned, or disseized [dispossessed], or outlawed, or exiled, or in any way harmed—nor will we go upon or send upon him—save by the lawful judgment of his peers [equals] or by the law of the land.❞

The nobles intended the Magna Carta to protect their feudal rights. Over time, however, it guaranteed the rights of all English people.

Rise of Parliament

During the reign of John's son, Henry III, an increase in population encouraged the growth of towns. A new social class—the middle class—was emerging. The middle class did not fit in the medieval social order of nobles, clergy, and peasants. Its income came from business and trade, not from the land. This group played an increasingly important role in government.

Recognizing the towns' growing power, Henry III added knights and burgesses, or important townspeople, to the Great Council that advised the king. By that time the Great Council was called Parliament, the name by which it is still known.

In A.D. 1295 Henry's son, Edward I, called into session the Model Parliament, which included representatives from the clergy, nobility, and burgesses. As England's government became more representative, Edward encouraged members of Parliament to advise him on business matters, submit petitions to him, and meet frequently.

By A.D. 1400 Parliament had divided into two chambers. Nobles and clergy met as the House of Lords, while knights and burgesses met as the House of Commons.

France

Like England, **France** developed a strong monarchy in the Middle Ages. The type of government that emerged in France, however, differed considerably from the increasingly representative government in England.

Beginnings of Central Government

After Charlemagne's death, the Frankish lands disintegrated into separate territories governed by feudal lords. These lords defended their own lands and were virtually independent rulers.

In A.D. 987 a noble named Hugh Capet seized the French throne from the weak Carolingian king. Capet controlled only the city of Paris and a strip of land between the Seine and Loire Rivers in northern France. The Capetian (kuh•PEE•shuhn) dynasty he established, however, lasted for more than three centuries. By the A.D. 1100s Capetian kings had established the principle of the eldest son inheriting the throne. The Capetians strengthened the power of the monarchy and brought French feudal lords under royal control.

As in England, the number of towns in France increased during the A.D. 1100s. Louis VI, who became king in A.D. 1108, used the townspeople to strengthen the royal government at the expense of the nobles. Louis awarded both the townspeople and the clergy positions on his court of advisers and also granted self-government to towns, freeing them from obligations to feudal lords. These measures led local officials to be loyal to the monarch rather than to feudal lords.

Strengthening the Monarchy

Philip II, known as **Philip Augustus**, ruled France from A.D. 1180 to A.D. 1223. Barely 15 when he succeeded to the throne, Philip was determined to strengthen the monarchy. During his 43-year reign Philip doubled the area of his domain, acquiring some territory through marriage and recapturing French land from England. By appointing local officials who were loyal to the king and forming a semipermanent royal army, Philip further weakened the power of feudal lords.

A Saintly Ruler

Philip's grandson became King Louis IX in A.D. 1226. Louis made royal courts dominant over feudal courts and decreed that only the king had the right to mint coins. Bans on private warfare and the bearing of arms further promoted the French monarch.

A very religious man, Louis was regarded as the ideal for his chivalry and high moral character. His advice to his son reveals these characteristics:

❝ [Have] a tender pitiful heart for the poor … [and] hold yourself steadfast and loyal toward your subjects and your vassals, without turning either to the right or to the left, but always straight, whatever may happen. And if a poor man have a quarrel with a rich man, sustain the poor rather than the rich, until the truth is made clear, and when you know the truth, do justice to them. ❞

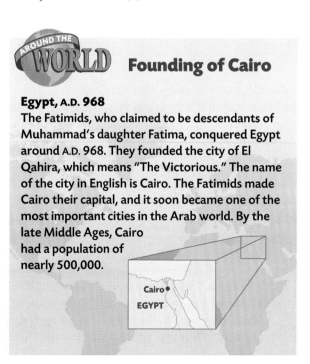

Founding of Cairo

Egypt, A.D. 968
The Fatimids, who claimed to be descendants of Muhammad's daughter Fatima, conquered Egypt around A.D. 968. They founded the city of El Qahira, which means "The Victorious." The name of the city in English is Cairo. The Fatimids made Cairo their capital, and it soon became one of the most important cities in the Arab world. By the late Middle Ages, Cairo had a population of nearly 500,000.

Cairo•
EGYPT

Signs of a Strong Monarchy

Louis IX's grandson, Philip IV, was so handsome he was nicknamed Philip the Fair. The blond, blue-eyed Philip increased France's territory and trade by defeating both England and Flanders in war. To pay for the wars, he raised taxes and taxed new groups, such as the clergy. Although Pope Boniface VIII opposed taxing the clergy, he could not force Philip to back down.

Before he died in A.D. 1314, Philip summoned the Estates-General, an assembly of nobles, clergy, and townspeople. He wanted to use the assembly to raise taxes on a national level rather than locally. The assembly, however, never became as powerful as Parliament in England. French kings kept a firm hand on government affairs.

The Holy Roman Empire

While monarchs in England and France were building strong central governments, rulers in **Germany** remained weak and often powerless. Among the major reasons were their disputes with the pope and with powerful German nobles.

"Emperor of the Romans"

During the A.D. 1000s and A.D. 1100s, German kings posed the biggest threat to the pope's authority. King Otto I, or Otto the Great, of Germany tried to restore Charlemagne's empire. After defeating the Magyars at the Battle of Lechfeld in A.D. 955, King Otto set his sights on Italy. In A.D. 962 Pope John XII sought Otto's help against Roman nobles who opposed the pope. In return for the German king's help, the pope in Rome crowned Otto Holy Roman emperor.

Problems of the Holy Roman Empire

Otto and his successors claimed the right to intervene in the election of popes, and Otto himself appointed and deposed several popes. The pope, as you have read, claimed the right to anoint and depose kings. These two conflicting claims led to centuries of dispute between the Holy Roman emperors and the Roman Catholic popes.

Powerful German lords also prevented the Holy Roman emperors from building a strong, unified state. Their challenges to imperial power caused several civil wars. Numerous wars with the Slavic states—Poland and Bohemia—and with Hungary also weakened the Holy Roman emperor's power.

Emperor and Pope Collide

During the rule of **Henry IV**, a major quarrel broke out with Pope Gregory VII. In A.D. 1073 the pope condemned lay investiture, hoping to free the Church from secular control. Since the bishops supported Henry in his struggle with feudal lords, the emperor refused to halt the practice.

The pope promptly proclaimed Henry deposed and urged the German nobles to elect another ruler. Henry gave in. In A.D. 1077 he made his way southward in bitter January weather across the snowy mountains to Canossa, Italy. There he sought forgiveness from the pope. He showed his repentance by standing before the gate of the castle begging for mercy for three days.

Gregory pardoned Henry, but the struggle between the Holy Roman emperor and the pope resumed later. Finally, in A.D. 1122, church officials and representatives of the Holy Roman emperor reached a compromise at the German city of Worms. This agreement, known as the Concordat of Worms, allowed the emperor to name bishops and grant them land. It also gave the pope the right to reject unworthy candidates.

Popes and monarchs would continue to struggle over power and territory in the coming years. The increasing strength of Europe's monarchies not only threatened the authority of the Church, but it also paved the way toward other changes on the European scene.

SECTION 4 REVIEW

Recall
1. **Define** common law, grand jury, petit jury, middle class.
2. **Identify** Alfred the Great, William the Conqueror, Henry II, Thomas à Becket, Eleanor of Aquitaine, Magna Carta, Philip Augustus, Henry IV.

3. **Explain** what factors account for the differences in the way French and English monarchs built strong states.

Critical Thinking
4. **Evaluating Information** Judge the importance of the Magna Carta and the English Parliament in the development of representative government.

Understanding Themes
5. **Conflict** Why did conflicts develop between popes and monarchs? Could their disputes have been resolved peacefully?

Critical Thinking SKILLS

Making Inferences

Just as you leave home to catch your school bus, you hear a news flash. Firefighters are battling a blaze near the bus garage. Your bus arrives 45 minutes late. Though no one told you directly, you know that the fire disrupted the bus schedule.

Learning the Skill

In the situation above, you made an *inference*. That is, from the limited facts at hand, you formed a conclusion. You knew that the fire was near the garage. From past experience, you knew that fire trucks often create traffic jams. By combining immediate facts and general knowledge, you inferred that the fire trucks delayed your bus.

To make accurate inferences, follow these steps:

- Read or listen carefully for stated facts and ideas.
- Then review what you already know about the same topic or situation.
- Use logic and common sense to form a conclusion about the topic.
- If possible, find specific information that proves or disproves your inference. In the example above, you could determine whether your inference was correct by asking the bus driver why she was late. Or you could read news reports describing the fire and its consequences.

Practicing the Skill

Read the passage about Pepin the Short and then answer the questions that follow.

❝ Charles's son, Pepin the Short, succeeded his father and became mayor of the palace in A.D. 741. Pepin … wished to be named king of the Franks. Since he had no blood claim to the throne, Pepin used his influence with the Frankish bishops and the pope to bring about a change in dynasties. In a show of support, the pope journeyed to France and anointed King Pepin I with holy oil.

In return for the Church's blessing, Pepin was to defend the pope against his enemies. In A.D. 754 the new king forced the Lombards, a Germanic people, to withdraw from Rome. Pepin seized a large tract of Lombard territory around Rome and gave it to the pope. ❞

1. What facts are stated about Pepin the Short's acquisition of the title King of the Franks?
2. Using these facts, what inference can you make about the pope's power in Europe at this time?
3. What facts are stated about Pepin's actions on behalf of the pope?
4. Using these facts, what inference can you make about the Lombards' relations with the pope and with the Franks?

Applying the Skill

Review the sections on "Monastic Life" and the "Influence of Monastics" on pages 304-305. Many men and women adopted the monastic lifestyle during the Middle Ages. What inferences can you make about their motivations? Also, do you think motivations were the same for men and women? How might you prove or disprove these inferences?

Ancient monastery

For More Practice

Turn to the Skill Practice in the Chapter Review on page 315 for more practice in making inferences.

Connections Across Time

Historical Significance Many of today's European nations, such as Great Britain and France, as well as many of the Western world's legal procedures and forms of government, trace their origins to the political struggles of medieval times.

The medieval Catholic Church wove Christianity into the fabric of Western culture and laid the basis for modern scholarship by preserving and transmitting the learning of the ancient world. Debates today concerning the relationship of Church and state have their echoes in the contest of medieval popes and monarchs for political supremacy.

Using Key Terms

Write the key term that completes each sentence. Then write a sentence for each term not chosen.

a. counts
b. cardinals
c. chivalry
d. fief
e. feudalism
f. friars
g. heresy
h. manorialism
i. abbess
j. common law
k. excommunication
l. sacraments
m. serfs
n. vassal

1. _____ are formal church rituals, such as baptism, eucharist, confirmation, marriage, anointing of the sick, and holy orders.
2. During the Middle Ages, economic life in Europe centered around a system of agricultural production called _____.
3. Peasants in medieval Europe often were _____, people who were bound to the manor.
4. In place of old feudal rules, Henry II of England established a _____ that applied throughout his kingdom.
5. The code of _____ called for knights to be brave in battle, fight fairly, keep promises, defend the Church, and treat noblewomen courteously.

Technology Activity

Using a Word Processor Use the draw program on your word processor, or software, to illustrate the layout of a typical medieval manor and surrounding fields. Include the lord's manor house, pastures for livestock, fields for crops, forest areas, and a village where peasants lived. Use a word processor to create a short story from a peasant's point of view, describing a typical day on a medieval manor.

Using Your History Journal

The Church had a significant role in medieval life. Imagine living as a monk or a nun. Write a short diary entry called "Today at the Monastery" or "Today at the Convent," describing the life of a monk or a nun.

Reviewing Facts

1. **History** List the invading groups that attacked the Carolingian Empire.
2. **History** Describe the major characteristics of feudalism and manorialism.
3. **History** Describe how medieval and ancient Roman life were similar and different.
4. **Culture** Outline briefly how missionaries carried Christianity across Europe.
5. **History/Culture** Describe the organization of the medieval Catholic Church.
6. **Culture** List the factors that helped maintain religious uniformity during medieval times.
7. **Culture** List several services that monasteries and convents provided for the community in medieval times.
8. **History** Explain why historians consider A.D. 1066 an important date.
9. **Culture** Describe the role of Eleanor of Aquitaine in medieval English history.

Critical Thinking

1. **Apply** Until the 1970s, "good manners" required a man to help a woman with her coat,

and push in her chair. How do these customs relate to chivalry?

2. **Evaluate** Every society has to develop ways to deal with ignorance, ill health, hunger, and homelessness. How did feudal society handle these problems compared to the way modern society handles them?

3. **Compare** How did medieval Europe treat its Jewish population? How have Europe's Jews fared in modern times?

Geography in History

1. **Place** Refer to the map below. Where did Leif Eriksson's journey lead him?

2. **Movement** What reasons did Vikings have for leaving Scandinavia and venturing out into the Atlantic?

3. **Human/Environment Interaction** Why did the Vikings sail across the far northern part of the Atlantic rather than through the warmer waters to the south?

4. **Location** After leaving Scandinavia, which landmasses did the Vikings explore?

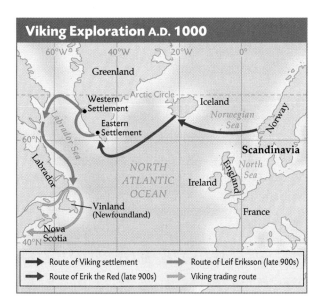

Viking Exploration A.D. 1000

Understanding Themes

1. **Movement** How can the movement of people both have created and crippled Frankish society?

2. **Cooperation** How were lords and peasants mutually dependent?

3. **Uniformity** How is uniformity implied in the term *regular clergy*?

4. **Conflict** How did the conflict between King John and the nobles, resolved in the Magna Carta, eventually have positive results for all English people?

Linking Past and Present

1. Common law, developed in England during the A.D. 1100s, later crossed the Atlantic Ocean and shaped the legal system of the United States. How does the American legal system today reveal the influence of English common law?

2. People often cherish a romantic view of medieval life: for example, medieval Europeans lived in elegant castles, wore beautiful clothes, and enjoyed festivals. Is such a view justified by historical evidence?

3. Improvements changed farming in Europe around A.D. 1000. What improvements today will increase farm productivity? What far-reaching effects will they have?

Skill Practice

Read the passage about knights. Use stated facts and your knowledge to answer the questions that follow.

❝ A knight cannot distinguish himself in [war] if he has not trained for it in tourneys. He must have seen his blood flow, heard his teeth crack under fist blows, felt his opponent's weight bear down upon him as he lay on the ground and, after being twenty times unhorsed, have risen twenty times to fight. ❞

1. From this passage, what can you infer about the physical appearance of many European knights?

2. What fact(s) or observations helped you make this inference?

3. What can you infer about the average length of a knight's career?

Chapter

13

A.D. 1050–1500

Medieval Europe at Its Height

Chapter Themes

▶ **Cultural Diffusion** The Crusades increase European contact with other areas. *Section 1*
▶ **Innovation** Advances in commerce, learning, and the arts change Europe. *Section 2*
▶ **Conflict** England and France battle while their monarchs gain power. *Section 3*
▶ **Conflict** The Church faces a split from within and opposition from without. *Section 4*

The Storyteller

"Well-beloved father," wrote a medieval student, "I have not a penny, nor can I get any save through you, for all things at the University are so dear: nor can I study in my [law books], for they are all tattered. Moreover, I owe ten crowns in dues to the [university administrator], and can find no man to lend them to me.

"Well-beloved father, to ease my debts ... at the baker's, with the doctor ... and to pay ... the laundress and the barber, I send you word of greetings and of money."

This letter from a medieval student sounds very much like something a modern student might write. At that time, however, the university was something new. It was part of the cultural awakening that took place in the High Middle Ages.

Historical Significance

What features of modern Western civilization had their beginnings during the height of the Middle Ages in western Europe? What new developments changed European society during the High Middle Ages?

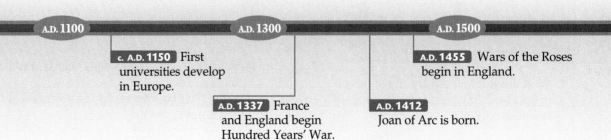

A.D. 1100

A.D. 1300

A.D. 1500

c. A.D. 1150 First universities develop in Europe.

A.D. 1337 France and England begin Hundred Years' War.

A.D. 1455 Wars of the Roses begin in England.

A.D. 1412 Joan of Arc is born.

316

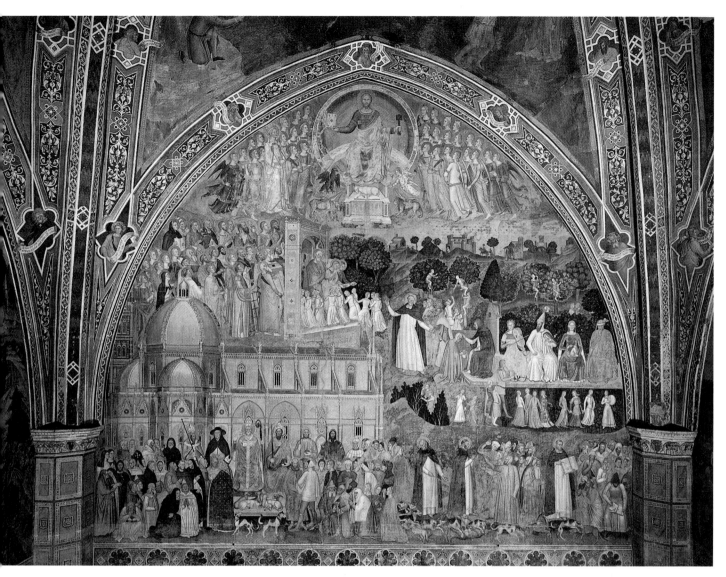

The Church Militant and Triumphant, a fresco from the A.D. 1300s by Andrea de Bonaiuto. The Spanish Chapel in Santa Maria Novella, Florence, Italy

Your History Journal

Medieval literature contains epics that were put into writing for the first time. Read an excerpt from Beowulf, *the* Song of Roland, *or* The Canterbury Tales *and take notes about life in Europe at the time.*

A.D. 1050

A.D. 1150

A.D. 1250

A.D. 1095 Pope Urban II calls for First Crusade.

A.D. 1147 Second Crusade begins.

A.D. 1204 Crusaders sack Constantinople.

A.D. 1212 Children's Crusade begins.

Section 1

The Crusades

Setting the Scene

▶ **Terms to Define**
the Crusades

▶ **People to Meet**
the Seljuk Turks, Pope Urban II, Saladin, Richard I

▶ **Places to Locate**
Jerusalem, Constantinople

 How did the Crusades begin, and what were their results?

Storyteller

Geoffrey de Renneville was footsore, thirsty, and covered with dust. He had joined the Crusade as an adventure. The Crusaders had traveled for weeks and were beset by flies, bandits, disease, poor food, and limited drink. The cavalcade stopped and the weary men dropped into an uneasy slumber. Suddenly, they were startled awake by the cry "Help for the Holy Sepulchre!" One by one the knights took up the cry. Shouting with the others, Geoffrey was reminded of the Crusade's purpose.

—adapted from *The Dream and the Tomb*, Robert Payne, 1984

Leaving for the Crusades

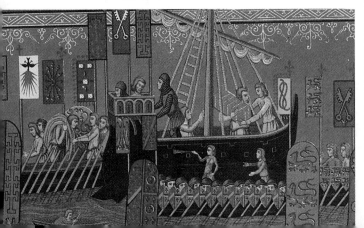

Life in the Early Middle Ages was characterized by decentralized government, warfare, cultural isolation, famine, and wretched living conditions. Trade was sparse, and agricultural production—the mainstay of the European economy—was inefficient.

By A.D. 1100, however, conditions in Europe had begun to improve. Some European monarchs succeeded in building strong central governments. Better farming methods led to larger crop yields and a growth in population. Towns and trade began to reappear. The Church held a powerful sway over the emotions and energies of the people. Changes in religion, society, politics, and economics made the High Middle Ages—the period between A.D. 1050 and A.D. 1270—a springboard for a new and brilliant civilization in western Europe.

The transformation of medieval society began with a holy war over the city of **Jerusalem**. European Christians undertook a series of military expeditions—nine in all—to recover the Holy Land from the Muslims. These expeditions were called the Crusades, from the Latin word *crux*, meaning "cross." Those who fought were called Crusaders because they vowed to "take up the cross."

POINT

Call for a Crusade

Jerusalem was a holy city for people of three faiths. Jews treasured it as Zion, God's own city, and as the site of Solomon's temple. To Christians, the city was holy because it was the place where Jesus was crucified and resurrected. Muslims regarded Jerusalem as their third holiest city, after Makkah and Madinah. According to Muslim tradition, Muhammad ascended to heaven from Jerusalem.

Jerusalem and the entire region of Palestine fell to Arab invaders in the A.D. 600s. Mostly Muslims, the Arabs tolerated other religions. Christians and

Jews were allowed to live in Jerusalem as long as they paid their taxes and followed certain regulations. European traders and religious pilgrims traveled to Palestine without interference.

In the late A.D. 1000s, **the Seljuk Turks**—a Muslim people from central Asia—took Jerusalem. Their conquest left Palestine in chaos, and the hazards of pilgrimage increased. Meanwhile, the Seljuks threatened the Byzantine Empire, especially **Constantinople**. The Byzantine emperor wrote to the pope in A.D. 1095 requesting military aid from the West. Concerns about the safety of Christian pilgrims gave added urgency to the emperor's request.

First Crusade

On a cold November day in A.D. 1095, **Pope Urban II** mounted a platform outside the church at Clermont, France. His voice shaking with emotion, he addressed the assembled throng, asking for a volunteer army to take Jerusalem and Palestine from the Seljuks:

> **❝** I exhort you … to strive to expel that wicked race from our Christian lands…. Christ commands it. Remission of sins will be granted for those going thither…. Let those who are accustomed to wage private war wastefully even against believers go forth against the infidels…. Let those who have lived by plundering be soldiers of Christ; let those who formerly contended against brothers and relations rightly fight barbarians; let those who were recently hired for a few pieces of silver win their eternal reward. **❞**

"Deus vult!" (God wills it!) shouted the crowd in response to the pope's plea. Knights and peasants alike vowed to join the expedition to the Holy Land. For knights, the Crusade was a welcome chance to employ their fighting skills. For peasants, the Crusade meant freedom from feudal bonds while on the Crusade. All were promised immediate salvation in heaven if they were killed freeing the Holy Land from non-Christians. Adventure and the possibility of wealth were other reasons to join the Crusade. In preparation for the holy war, red crosses of cloth were stitched on clothing as a symbol of service to God.

This First Crusade heightened already existing hatred of non-Christians and marked the onset of a long period of Christian persecution of the Jews. During the First Crusade, which began in A.D. 1096, three armies of Crusader knights and volunteers

Visualizing History **Pope Urban II arrives at the Council of Clermont.** *What did the pope ask the people to do?*

traveled separately from western Europe to the eastern Mediterranean. On the way, many of them killed Jews and sometimes massacred entire Jewish communities.

Led by French nobles, the three armies finally met in Constantinople in A.D. 1097. From there the Crusaders made their way to Jerusalem, enduring the hardships of desert travel as well as quarrels among their leaders. In June A.D. 1099, the Crusaders finally reached the city. After a siege of almost two months Jerusalem fell. Crusaders swarmed into the city and massacred most of its Muslim and Jewish inhabitants.

The success of the First Crusade reinforced the authority of the Church and strengthened the self-confidence of western Europeans. The religious zeal of the Crusaders soon cooled, however, and many knights returned home. Those who stayed set up feudal states in Syria and Palestine. Contact between the Crusaders and the relatively more sophisticated civilizations of the Byzantines and the Muslims would continue for the next 100 years and become a major factor in ending the cultural isolation of western Europe.

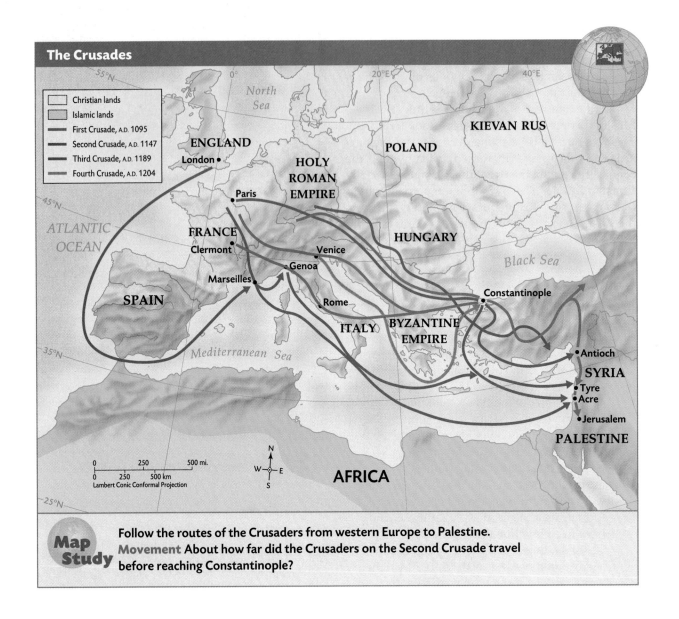

The Crusades

Legend:
- Christian lands
- Islamic lands
- First Crusade, A.D. 1095
- Second Crusade, A.D. 1147
- Third Crusade, A.D. 1189
- Fourth Crusade, A.D. 1204

0 250 500 mi.
0 250 500 km
Lambert Conic Conformal Projection

Map Study Follow the routes of the Crusaders from western Europe to Palestine. **Movement** About how far did the Crusaders on the Second Crusade travel before reaching Constantinople?

Second Crusade

Less than 50 years after the First Crusade, the Seljuks conquered part of the Crusader states in Palestine. Pope Eugenius IV called for a Second Crusade to regain the territory. Eloquent sermons by the monk Bernard of Clairvaux (KLAR•VOH) persuaded King Louis VII of France and Holy Roman Emperor Conrad III to lead armies to Palestine. The Second Crusade, which lasted from A.D. 1147 to A.D. 1149, was unsuccessful. Louis VII and Conrad III quarreled constantly and were ineffective militarily. They were easily defeated by the Seljuks.

Third Crusade

A diplomatic and forceful leader named **Saladin** (SA•luh•DEEN) united the Muslim forces and then captured Jerusalem in A.D. 1187. The people of western Europe were stunned and horrified. Holy Roman Emperor Frederick Barbarossa of

Germany, King Philip Augustus of France, and King **Richard I** of England assembled warriors for the Third Crusade. This "Crusade of Kings" lasted from A.D. 1189 to A.D. 1192 and was no more successful than the Second Crusade. Frederick Barbarossa died on the way to Palestine, and his army returned home. Philip Augustus returned to France before the army reached Jerusalem. Richard continued the struggle alone.

Although his army defeated the Muslims in several battles, Richard could not win a decisive victory over Saladin's well-trained and dedicated forces. After three years of fighting, Richard signed a truce with the Muslims and tried to persuade Saladin to return Jerusalem to the Christians. "Jerusalem," he wrote to the Muslim leader, "we are resolved not to renounce as long as we have a single man left." Saladin's reply to Richard showed his equal determination to keep the city:

> To us Jerusalem is as precious, aye and more precious, than it is to you, in that it was the place whence our Prophet made his journey by night to heaven and is destined to be the gathering place of our nation at the last day. Do not dream that we shall give it up to you.... It belonged to us originally, and it is you who are the real aggressors. "

Although Saladin refused to turn over Jerusalem, he allowed Christian pilgrims access.

Other Crusades

Other Crusades followed in the A.D. 1200s, but none succeeded in winning permanent Christian control of Palestine. By this time, western Europeans had lost sight of the religious goal of the Crusades. They were now more concerned about political and economic gain.

In the Fourth Crusade of A.D. 1204, Crusaders put aside their goal of marching to Jerusalem and instead attacked the Christian city of Constantinople. They burned libraries, destroyed churches, and stole valuable treasures. Their actions left a lasting bitterness between the Eastern Orthodox world and western Europe. The Fourth Crusade seriously weakened the Byzantine Empire, making possible a later Muslim advance into eastern Europe.

Effects of the Crusades

Although Western Europeans failed to gain control of Palestine, the Crusades helped to speed the pace of changes already underway in western Europe. They helped break down feudalism and increase the authority of kings. European monarchs levied taxes, raised armies, and cooperated on a large scale. Some nobles died in battle without leaving heirs, and their lands passed to kings. To raise money for weapons and supplies, many lesser nobles sold their estates or allowed their serfs to

History & Art *Return from the Crusade* by Karl Friedrich Lessing. Rheinland Museum, Bonn, Germany *How did the Crusades help to break down feudalism?*

buy their freedom to become freeholders on the land or artisans in the towns.

During the Crusades contact with the more advanced Byzantine and Muslim civilizations broadened European views of the world. The European presence in the East heightened demand at home for Eastern luxury goods: spices, sugar, melons, tapestries, silk, and other items. Commerce increased in the eastern Mediterranean area and especially benefited Italian trading cities, such as Venice and Genoa.

From the Muslims the Crusaders learned how to build better ships, make more accurate maps, use the magnetic compass to tell direction, and improve their weaponry. Religious military orders of knights primarily aided pilgrims, but they were also bankers for both princes and merchants.

The Crusades had less impact on the Muslims. Crusader states were relatively weak in an area divided among powerful Muslim rivals. The arrival of the Crusaders, however, helped unite the Muslims against a common enemy.

SECTION I REVIEW

Recall
1. **Define** the Crusades.
2. **Identify** the Seljuk Turks, Pope Urban II, Saladin, Richard I.
3. **Explain** why both Christians and Muslims of the A.D. 1000s and A.D. 1100s felt that Jerusalem should belong to them.

Critical Thinking
4. **Analyzing Information** In what ways were the Crusades a success? In what ways were they a failure? Could Christians and Muslims have resolved their differences peacefully? Explain.

Understanding Themes
5. **Cultural Diffusion** Describe how the Crusades contributed to cultural diffusion.

A.D. 1000   A.D. 1200   A.D. 1400

c. A.D. 1000 Europe's economy begins to revive.

c. A.D. 1150 French architects begin to build in the Gothic style.

c. A.D. 1348 The Black Death spreads throughout Europe.

c. A.D. 1386 Geoffrey Chaucer begins writing *The Canterbury Tales.*

Section 2

Economic and Cultural Revival

Setting the Scene

▶ **Terms to Define**

money economy, guild, master, apprentice, journeyman, charter, scholasticism, troubadour, vernacular

▶ **People to Meet**

Thomas Aquinas, Dante Alighieri, Geoffrey Chaucer

▶ **Places to Locate**

Venice, Flanders, Champagne, Bologna

 **ind Out** How did the growth of towns affect the society of medieval Europe?

The Storyteller

To help rebuild the cathedral, people for miles around brought their goods. So that the church might rise swiftly, larger and more beautiful than any they had seen, peasants, skilled workers, and even nobles pulled heavy carts filled with wood and stone. Religious fervor motivated the people, and the reward was a renewed spirit in the community. Perfect harmony reigned. During the night, the workers formed a camp with their wagons, and by the light of candles, they sang canticles and psalms. Everyone was doing penance and forgiving their enemies.

—adapted from *Chronique*, Robert de Torigni, in *Chartres*, Emil Mâle, translated by Sarah Wilson, 1983

Cathedral at Reims, France

The Crusades accelerated the transformation of western Europe from a society that was crude, backward, and violent—showing little cultural and technological advancement—to a civilization that exhibited some early features of modern Western civilization. Towns grew, trade expanded, and learning and the arts thrived.

Economic Expansion

The economy of western Europe had begun to show vigor around A.D. 1000. Agricultural production increased. Expanding opportunities in trade encouraged the growth of towns, and the lively atmosphere of the towns in turn stimulated creative thought and innovations in art.

Agricultural Advances

Plows during the Early Middle Ages were light and did not cut much below the surface of the soil. The invention of a new, heavier plow made it possible to cut through the rich, damp soils of northwestern Europe. This plow enabled farmers to produce more and to cultivate new lands, increasing food production. Nobles and freeholders—peasants not bound to the land—migrated to new areas, clearing forests, draining swamps, and building villages. In one of the largest migrations of the time, the Germans moved to areas of eastern Europe, doubling the territory they controlled.

About the same time, the collar harness replaced the ox yoke. Horses were choked by the ox yoke, but the new harness shifted weight off the neck and onto the shoulders, allowing farmers to replace oxen with horses. Horses pulled the plow faster than oxen, allowing farmers to plant and plow more crops.

As you read in Chapter 12, the three-field system of planting also made the land more productive. As the land began to feed more people, the population naturally increased.

Expansion of Trade

The revival of towns caused a rapid expansion of trade. Soon the sea-lanes and roads were filled with traders carrying goods to market. Important sea and river routes connected western Europe with the Mediterranean, eastern Europe, and Scandinavia. The repaired and rebuilt Roman road system carried international traders to and from Europe.

Italian towns, such as **Venice**, Pisa, and Genoa controlled the Mediterranean trade after A.D. 1200, bringing silks and spices from Asia to Europe. **Flanders,** a region including present-day northern France and southern Belgium, became the center of trade on Europe's northern coast. Textiles produced there were sent by way of an eastern route to the Black Sea and then traded at Middle Eastern markets for porcelain, silk, and silver. Towns along the Baltic coast formed the Hanseatic League, which controlled trade between eastern Europe and the North Atlantic.

The merchandise for sale in a town was varied and seemingly endless. This was especially true during trade fairs. Each year hundreds of traders met at large trade fairs in places convenient to land and water routes. Feudal lords charged the merchants fees, charged taxes on goods, and offered protection to the merchants. The most famous fair was at **Champagne** in eastern France, located in almost the exact center of western Europe. For four to six weeks each year, Champagne was a distribution point for goods from around the world.

Banking

Early merchants used the barter system, trading goods without using money. Before long, however, merchants found this system impractical. Moreover, some of the merchants who supplied luxury goods such as silk would only accept money in payment. European merchants therefore needed a common medium of exchange.

The rise of a money economy, or an economy based on money, had far-reaching consequences. Initially, it led to the growth of banking. Since traders came from many countries, they carried different currencies with different values. Moneychangers—often Jews or Italians—determined the value of the various currencies and exchanged one currency for another. They also developed procedures for transferring funds from one place to another, received deposits, and arranged loans, thus becoming the first bankers

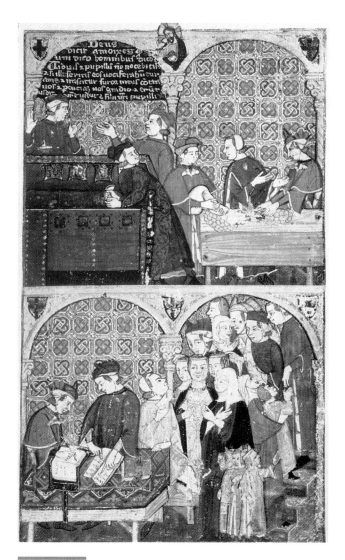

Visualizing History Italian bankers, from *Treatise on the Seven Vices: Avarice*. **The Church viewed lending with the intent to charge interest as evil.** *What is the origin of the term "bank"?*

in Europe. Indeed, the word *bank* comes from the *banca*, or bench, that the moneychangers set up at fairs.

As the money economy grew, it put the feudal classes in an economic squeeze. Kings, clergy, and nobles became dependent on money from banks to pay their expenses. To pay off their loans, they had to raise taxes, sell their lands, or demand money in place of traditional feudal services. As serfs became able to buy their freedom, the feudal system declined.

Growth of Towns

The number of towns in western Europe grew tremendously in the A.D. 1000s and A.D. 1100s. Many grew up beside well-traveled roads or near waterways. Although warfare had declined, settlements still faced bandits. To protect themselves, townspeople built walls around their towns. At first these enclosures were simple wooden fences. As the population grew, stone walls were built, with guard towers at the gates.

Inside the walls narrow, winding streets bustled with people, carts drawn by horses and oxen, and farm animals on the way to market. A din of noise and overpowering smells attacked the senses. Church bells chimed the hours; carts piled high with goods creaked and rumbled through streets that were little more than alleys. Shops lined the streets at ground level, and the shop owners often lived in quarters above. Most buildings were of wood and had thatch roofs, making fire a constant hazard.

Medieval towns had almost no sanitation, and a constant stench assailed the people from the garbage and sewage tossed into the streets. These conditions caused the rapid spread of diseases such as diphtheria, typhoid, influenza, and malaria. In crowded towns such diseases often turned into epidemics and took many lives. The worst of these epidemics—the bubonic plague—ravaged Europe between A.D. 1348 and 1350, killing one-third of the population and earning the name the Black Death.

Guilds

During the A.D. 1100s, merchants and artisans organized themselves into business associations called guilds. The primary function of the merchant guild was to maintain a monopoly of the local market for its members. To accomplish this end, merchant guilds severely restricted trading by foreigners in their city and enforced uniform pricing. The following regulations from Southampton, England, indicate the power of the merchant guilds:

❝ And no one shall buy honey, fat, salt herrings, or any kind of oil, or millstones, or fresh hides, or any kind of fresh skins, unless he is a guildsman; nor keep a tavern for wine, nor sell cloth at retail, except in market or fair days … ❞

Images of the Times

Medieval Life

The recovery of commerce and the beginnings of industries stimulated the growth of European towns.

Market scene in a medieval town is the subject of this fresco from Castello de Issogne, Val d' Aosta, Italy.

Craft guilds, by contrast, regulated the work of artisans: carpenters, shoemakers, blacksmiths, masons, tailors, and weavers. Women working as laundresses, seamstresses and embroiderers, and maidservants had their own trade associations.

Craft guilds established strict rules concerning prices, wages, and employment. A member of the shoemakers' guild could not charge more (or less) for a pair of shoes than other shoemakers, nor could he advertise or in any way induce people to buy his wares. Although the guilds prohibited competition, they set standards of quality to protect the public from shoddy goods.

Craft guilds were controlled by masters, or artisans who owned their own shops and tools and employed less-skilled artisans as helpers. To become a master at a particular craft, an artisan served an apprenticeship, the length of which varied according to the difficulty of the craft. Apprentices worked for a master without pay. An apprentice then became a journeyman and received pay. However, a journeyman could only work under a master. To become a master, a journeyman submitted a special sample of his work—a masterpiece—to the guild for approval. If the sample was approved, the journeyman became a master and could set up his own shop.

Aside from business activities, guilds provided benefits for their members such as medical help and unemployment relief. Guilds also organized social and religious life by sponsoring banquets, holy day processions, and outdoor plays.

Rise of the Middle Class

The medieval town, or burg, created the name for a new class of people. In Germany they were called *burghers*; in France, the *bourgeoisie* (BURZH•WAH•ZEE); and in England, *burgesses*. The name originally referred to anyone living in a town. Gradually it came to mean the people who made money through the developing money economy. They were a middle class made up of merchants, bankers, and artisans who no longer had to rely on the land to make a living.

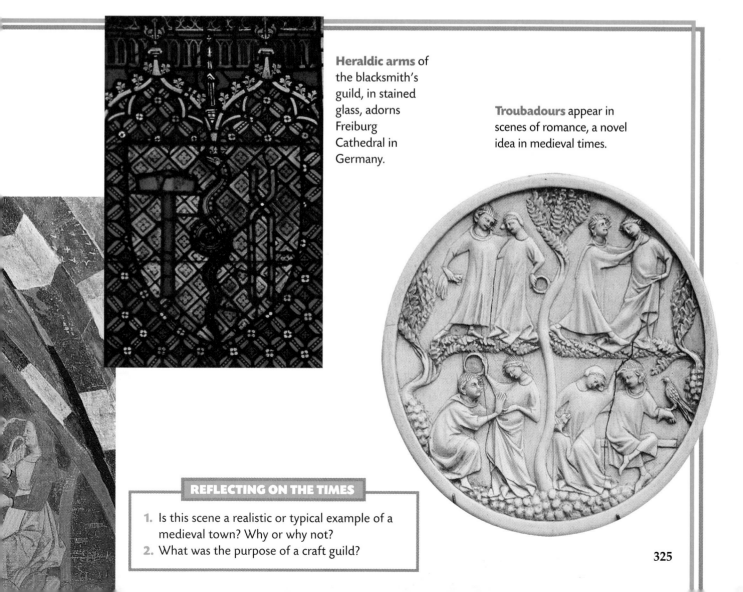

Heraldic arms of the blacksmith's guild, in stained glass, adorns Freiburg Cathedral in Germany.

Troubadours appear in scenes of romance, a novel idea in medieval times.

REFLECTING ON THE TIMES

1. Is this scene a realistic or typical example of a medieval town? Why or why not?
2. What was the purpose of a craft guild?

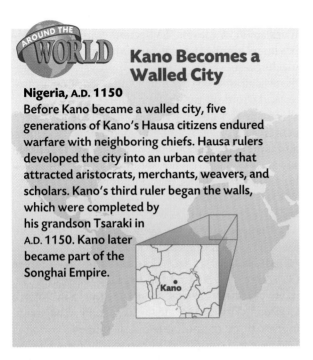
The middle class helped turn towns into organized municipalities. Businessmen created councils to administer town affairs and gained political power for themselves. As the money economy spread, kings began to depend on the middle class for loans and for income from the taxes they paid. The leading merchants and bankers became advisers to lords and kings.

Town Government

Conflict gradually developed between the feudal classes and the burghers. City dwellers did not fit into the feudal system; they resented owing taxes and services to lords. They wanted to run their own affairs and have their own courts and laws. At the same time, feudal lords feared the growing wealth and power of the middle class. To try to keep the burghers in line, the lords began to strictly enforce feudal laws.

The money economy gave the towns the income and power they needed to win the struggle against the lords. In the A.D. 1000s Italian towns formed groups called communes. Using the political power they gained from the growing money economy, the communes ended the power of feudal lords and made the Italian towns into independent city-states. In other areas of Europe, kings and nobles granted townspeople charters, documents that gave them the right to control their own affairs. At the same time, many towns remained a part of a kingdom or feudal territory.

Education

During the Early Middle Ages, most people were illiterate. Education was controlled by the clergy. In monastery and cathedral schools, students prepared for monastery life or for work as church officials. In addition to religious subjects, students learned grammar, rhetoric, logic, arithmetic, geometry, astronomy, and music.

As towns grew, the need for educated officials stimulated a new interest in learning. The growth of courts and other legal institutions created a need for lawyers. As a result, around A.D. 1150, students and teachers began meeting away from monastery and cathedral schools. They formed organizations that became known as universities.

Universities

At first the university was not so much a place as it was a guild of scholars organized for learning. Classes were held in rented rooms, churches, or outdoors. Because books were scarce, a teacher read the text and discussed it, while students took notes on slates. Classes did, however, meet regularly, and university rules set down the obligations of students and teachers toward each other. To qualify as a teacher, students had to pass an examination leading to a degree, or certificate of completion.

By the end of the A.D. 1200s, universities had spread throughout Europe. Most southern European universities were modeled after the law school at **Bologna** (buh•LOH•nyuh), Italy, and specialized in law and medicine. Universities in northern Europe, on the other hand, specialized in liberal arts and theology. These were generally modeled after the University of Paris.

New Learning

Medieval scholars studied Roman law, the works of Aristotle, and Muslim writings. Much of this knowledge reached Europe by way of Muslim and Jewish scholars in European Muslim strongholds, such as Spain and Sicily. European contact with Muslim scientific thought sparked an interest in the physical world that eventually led to the rise of Western science.

Many church leaders opposed the study of Aristotle's works, fearing that his ideas threatened Christian teachings. In contrast, some scholars thought the new knowledge could be used to support Christian ideas. They applied Aristotle's philosophy to theological questions and developed a system of thought called scholasticism. This new type of learning emphasized reason as well as faith in the interpretation of Christian doctrine. Scholastics sought to reconcile classical philosophy with the Church's teachings. They believed all knowledge could be integrated into a coherent whole.

One early scholastic teacher, Peter Abelard, taught theology in Paris during the early A.D. 1100s. In his book *Sic et Non* (Yes and No), he collected statements from the Bible and the writings of early Christian leaders that showed both sides of controversial questions. Abelard then had his students reconcile the differences through logic.

In the A.D. 1200s the most important scholastic thinker was **Thomas Aquinas** (uh•KWY•nuhs). In his work *Summa Theologica*, Aquinas claimed that reason was God's gift that could provide answers to basic philosophical questions. Reason, he said, existed in harmony with faith, both pointing to God and the orderliness of creation. The Catholic Church later accepted and promoted Aquinas's way of thinking.

Medieval Literature and Art

The spread of universities and the revival of intellectual endeavor stimulated advances in literature and the arts. Songs and epics of the Early Middle Ages were put in writing for the first time.

Epics and Romances

One of the earliest surviving literary works of the feudal world was the Anglo-Saxon epic *Beowulf*. A tale of grim battle and gloomy scenery, *Beowulf* reveals the harshness of life in northern Europe. Handed down by oral tradition for two centuries, it was finally written down in Old English (Anglo-Saxon) by an unknown poet in about A.D. 700. In colorful verses and exciting narrative, the epic describes how the Anglo-Saxon warrior Beowulf defeats a horrible monster named Grendel.

French epics called *chansons de geste*, or songs of high deeds, celebrated the courage of feudal warriors. The *Song of Roland*, written around A.D. 1100, gives an account of the chivalrous defense of Christianity by Charlemagne's knights.

Romances about knights and ladies were also popular. In southern France in the A.D. 1100s and A.D. 1200s, traveling poet-musicians called troubadours composed lyric poems and songs about love and the feats of knights. They helped define the ideal knight celebrated in the code of chivalry.

Geography

The Plague

The Black Death

The Black Death—known today as the bubonic plague—was the worst medieval epidemic. It began in China and spread across Asia. Trading ships carried the disease west to the Mediterranean and to Europe. During the worst phase of the plague—between A.D. 1348 and A.D. 1350—nearly 25 million Europeans died. Not until the early 1900s were rats carrying bacteria-infected fleas identified as the carriers of the plague.

The plague brought terror to many medieval Europeans, who saw it as God's punishment. As deaths increased, production declined, and prices and wages rose. To cut costs, many landowners switched from farming to sheep raising (which required less labor) and drove villagers off the land. Merchants in towns laid off workers and demanded laws to limit wages. These setbacks, as well as the fear of plague, sparked peasant and worker uprisings. It would take at least a century for western Europe to recover.

Today, plague occasionally occurs in developing areas of Asia, Africa, and South America. Knowledge of disease prevention and the development of vaccines, however, have largely isolated plague outbreaks and reduced their devastating impact on societies.

 **ACTIVITY**

Examine the effects of disease on medieval and modern societies. How is the spread of disease related to human movement?

Interior of a Gothic cathedral at Reims, France. *How did the Gothic style differ from the Romanesque?*

Vernacular Literature

Most medieval literature was written in the vernacular, or language of everyday speech. Instead of using Latin, people spoke the language of their own country—English, French, German, Italian, or Spanish. These languages gave each kingdom a separate identity. Use of vernacular languages in writing made literature accessible to more people.

Major literary works in the vernacular appeared during the A.D. 1300s. **Dante Alighieri** (DAHN•tay A•luh•GYEHR•ee) wrote *The Divine Comedy*, an epic poem in Italian that describes an imaginary journey from hell to heaven. In England, **Geoffrey Chaucer** produced *The Canterbury Tales* from about A.D. 1386 to A.D. 1400. These narrative poems describe a varied group of pilgrims who tell stories to amuse one another on on their way to Thomas à Becket's shrine at Canterbury.

Medieval Art

Early medieval churches were built in a style called Romanesque, which combined features of Roman and Byzantine structures. Romanesque churches had thick walls, columns set close together, heavy curved arches, and small windows. About A.D. 1150, French architects began to build in a new style called Gothic. They replaced the Romanesque heavy walls and low arches with flying buttresses. These stone beams, extending out from the walls, took the weight of the building off the walls. This allowed the walls to be thinner, with space for stained-glass windows. The ceiling inside was supported by pointed arches made of narrow stone ribs reaching out from tall pillars. These supports allowed architects to build higher ceilings and more open interiors.

Medieval painters, by contrast, turned their attention to a much smaller art form, the illuminated manuscript. Adorned with brilliantly colored illustrations and often highlighted with gold leaf, these works were miniature masterpieces whose beauty has endured to the present day.

Talented writers were also found among women in convents and at royal courts. The German abbess Hildegard of Bingen, known for her spiritual wisdom, wrote about religion, science, and medicine. She was also a noted composer of music. Another abbess, Herrad of Landsberg, assisted by her nuns, compiled the *Garden of Delights*, an encyclopedia of world history. Christine de Pisan, who grew up at the French royal court, authored numerous love poems.

SECTION 2 REVIEW

Recall

1. **Define** money economy, guild, master, apprentice, journeyman, charter, scholasticism, troubadour, vernacular.
2. **Identify** Peter Abelard, Thomas Aquinas, *Beowulf*, Dante Alighieri, Geoffrey Chaucer.

3. **Explain** why membership in a guild was advantageous for a medieval artisan. Why was it disadvantageous?

Critical Thinking

4. **Synthesizing Information** Create an imaginary medieval town. Briefly explain its physical characteristics. Then describe what a typical day for an artisan working there would be like.

Understanding Themes

5. **Innovation** Choose one of the following and trace its effect on medieval society: three-field system, money economy, guilds.

A.D. 1300	A.D. 1400	A.D. 1500

A.D. 1346 France and England fight the Battle of Crécy.

A.D. 1469 Ferdinand of Aragon and Isabella of Castile marry.

c. A.D. 1485 Henry VII founds England's Tudor dynasty.

Section 3

Strengthening of Monarchy

Setting the Scene

▶ **Terms to Define**
    cortes

▶ **People to Meet**
    Joan of Arc, Louis XI, Richard III, Henry VII, Ferdinand of Aragon, Isabella of Castile

▶ **Places to Locate**
    Crécy, Agincourt, Burgundy, Castile, Aragon

 **Find Out** How did European monarchs strengthen their powers during the Middle Ages?

The Storyteller

A popular legend in English history is the story of the first Prince of Wales. Edward, King of England, desired to make the proud chieftains of Wales acknowledge his power. He campaigned against them, soon controlling their lands. The Welsh chiefs refused to accept Edward as their prince. They agreed, however, to serve a prince whom Edward would choose— provided he was noble and spoke neither English nor French. Edward accepted these terms and showed them their prince, his newborn son, who was indeed of noble birth and could speak neither language. The chiefs accepted the baby as their lawful lord, the Prince of Wales.

—adapted from *The Three Edwards*, Thomas Costain, 1964

The Tower of London

During the late Middle Ages, Europe's monarchs set up stronger central governments. They won the loyalty of their people and began to limit the powers of clergy and nobles. Gradually educated common people and laymen became royal advisers. At the outset, however, violent warfare engulfed western Europe.

The Hundred Years' War

Between A.D. 1337 and A.D. 1453, England and France fought a series of conflicts, known as the Hundred Years' War. For centuries, England's rulers had fought hard to keep the French lands inherited from the Normans. France's kings, however, wanted to unite these lands to their kingdom. In 1337 warfare began anew when England's Edward III laid claim to the French crown.

Major Battles

At first, the English were victorious—at **Crécy** in 1346 and **Agincourt** in 1415. Their success was primarily due to their weapons: a firearm that was the forerunner of the cannon and the longbow. About as tall as a man, the longbow could shoot arrows capable of piercing heavy armor at 300 yards (274 km). French historian Jean Froissart described the impact of the longbow at Crécy:

❝ Then the English archers stept forth one pace and let fly their arrows so wholly [together] and so thick, that is seemed snow. When the [French soldiers] felt the [arrows piercing through heads, arms, and breasts, many of them cast down their cross-bows and did cut their strings and [retreated]… ❞

History & Art *"La Pucelle!" Jeanne d' Arc Leads Her Army* by Franck Craig, 1907. Musée d' Orsay, Paris, France *What did the "Maid of Orléans" accomplish for the French?*

Joan of Arc

Just as French fortunes had sunk to their lowest, a young woman helped bring about a dramatic reversal. In A.D. 1429, 17-year-old **Joan of Arc** appeared at the court of France's King Charles VII. She told the king that heavenly voices had called her to save France. With Charles's support, she inspired a French army to victory at Orléans, a town that had been placed under siege by the English. Soon after her triumph, Joan fell into English hands, was tried for witchcraft, and burned at the stake. Her courage, however, led the French to rally around their king and to gradually drive the English out of France. When the war ended in A.D. 1453, the port of Calais was the only French territory still in English hands.

Effects of the War

The Hundred Years' War deeply affected the peoples of France and England. France had suffered more severely than England, since the fighting had occurred on French soil. Yet victory gave the French a new sense of unity. England had been spared destruction, but its defeat led to bitterness among the nobles who had lost French lands. For the rest of the A.D. 1400s, England was divided by social conflict. In the long run, however, England's departure from France contributed to its unity and enabled the English to focus on problems at home.

The Hundred Years' War also hastened the decline of feudalism. The use of the longbow and firearms made feudal warfare based on castles and mounted knights outdated. Monarchs replaced feudal soldiers with national armies made up of hired soldiers. Maintaining these armies, however, was expensive. Monarchs turned to townspeople and the lower nobility for new sources of revenue. These groups willingly paid taxes and made loans in return for security and good government.

France

During the late 1400s, France's monarchy won much power and prestige. **Louis XI**, son of Charles VII, strengthened the bureaucracy, kept the nobles under royal control, and promoted trade and agriculture. Above all, he worked to unite all French feudal lands under his crown. Louis especially desired **Burgundy**, one of Europe's most prosperous areas. Burgundy's ruler, Charles the Bold, however, wanted to make his territory independent. Rather than fight Charles openly, Louis encouraged quarrels between Burgundy and the neighboring Swiss. After Charles's death in battle with the Swiss in A.D. 1477, Burgundy was divided between his daughter Mary and the French king.

Adam Woolfitt

Cathedral of Chartres

The cathedral stands out against a lowering sky. The old town of Chartres, France, crowds the foreground, where artisans, merchants, bakers, and stonemasons once lived, clustered near the great church. At the center of the photograph, the rose window provides a perfect example of medieval stained glass. The two towers, one ornate, the other plain, were finished in different periods. They pierce the sky—giving form to the faith and spirit of Europe's Middle Ages.

The cathedral reflects the technology of the High Middle Ages. Built before A.D. 1300, Chartres Cathedral, located about 50 miles southwest of Paris, is one of many works of Gothic architecture expressing both the fervor of the medieval era and the revival of the European economy, beginning around A.D. 1000. The growth of towns such as Chartres was a result of such changes. The combination of new building techniques, financial resources, and professional skills enabled the construction of the great cathedrals of Europe. ⊕

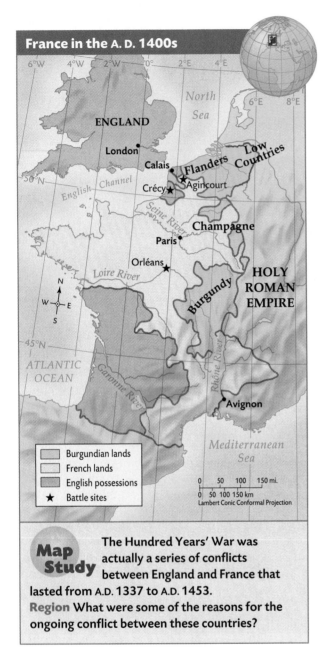

ENGLAND

London

Calais

Flanders

Low Countries

Crécy

Agincourt

Champagne

Paris

Orléans

Loire River

Seine River

North Sea

Burgundy

HOLY
ROMAN
EMPIRE

ATLANTIC
OCEAN

Garonne River

Rhône River

Avignon

Mediterranean Sea

English Channel

Burgundian lands
French lands
English possessions
★ **Battle sites**

0   50   100   150 mi.
0 50 100 150 km
Lambert Conic Conformal Projection

Map Study The Hundred Years' War was actually a series of conflicts between England and France that lasted from A.D. 1337 to A.D. 1453.
Region What were some of the reasons for the ongoing conflict between these countries?

England

During the Hundred Years' War, the English monarchy's power was limited by Parliament, which had won the right to levy taxes, approve laws, and provide advice. Royal authority further eroded as a result of a struggle among the nobility for control of the throne. Begun in A.D. 1455, this conflict became known as the Wars of the Roses because of the symbols of the rival families involved. The royal house of Lancaster bore the red rose; its rival, the house of York, a white rose.

During the Wars of the Roses, Edward, duke of York, overthrew the weak Lancaster dynasty and became King Edward IV. As king, Edward worked

to strengthen royal government and to promote trade. His death in A.D. 1483 brought uncertainty to England. The heirs to the throne were the late king's two sons. Edward's brother, Richard, however had himself proclaimed king and locked his young nephews in the Tower of London, where they were probably murdered. **Richard III** tried to rule well but lacked widespread support. He finally fell to the forces of Henry Tudor, a Lancaster noble, on Bosworth Field in A.D. 1485.

Henry became **King Henry VII**, the first Tudor king. Henry eliminated royal claimants to the throne, avoided costly foreign wars, and increased royal power over the nobles. As a result, the English monarchy emerged from the Wars of the Roses strengthened and with few challengers.

Spain

During the late A.D. 1400s, Spain emerged as a leading European power. Even before Pope Urban's call for the Crusades, the Christian rulers of northern Spain had been fighting the *Reconquista* (RAY•kohn•KEES•tuh), or "reconquest," of Muslim areas in Spain. By A.D. 1250, the Iberian Peninsula consisted of three Christian realms: Portugal in the west, **Castile** in the center, and **Aragon** on the Mediterranean coast. Only Granada in the south remained in the hands of the Moors, or Spanish Muslims.

In A.D. 1469 **Ferdinand of Aragon** and **Isabella of Castile** were married. Their two kingdoms, however, maintained separate governments, and royal power was limited by local interests. Christians settling in formerly Muslim areas, as well as large Jewish and Muslim communities in Castile and Aragon, had their own laws and officials. Special royal charters allowed many towns to keep their courts and local customs. Finally, assemblies known as cortes, in which nobles were powerful, had the right to review royal policies.

In Castile, however, the two monarchs worked to strengthen royal power. They sent out officials to govern the towns and set up special courts in the countryside to enforce royal laws. In A.D. 1492 their armies forced the surrender of the last Moorish stronghold at Granada. Shortly afterward, Ferdinand and Isabella ended religious toleration. To unite Spain, they wanted all Spaniards to be Catholic. Spanish Jews and Moors were ordered to convert or to leave Spain. The persecution and departure of many Jews and Moors, known for their banking, business, and intellectual skills, weakened Spain's economy and culture.

The Spanish monarchy also set up the Spanish Inquisition to enforce Catholic teaching. The Inquisition believed that Jews and Moors who had converted to Catholicism were still practicing their old religions in secret. It tortured, tried, and punished anyone suspected of heresy. The fear created by the Inquisition further strengthened the power of Spanish monarchs over their people.

The Holy Roman Empire

During the Middle Ages, the Holy Roman Empire, made up largely of German, Italian, and Slavic lands, was Europe's largest political unit. Despite its size, the Empire was far from achieving unity under a strong monarch. While most European rulers came to power through family ties, the Holy Roman emperor was elected by a diet, or assembly of mostly German princes who governed their local territories as independent rulers. The princes had the right to reject or accept the emperor's requests for taxes and soldiers.

In A.D. 1356 the number of princes taking part in imperial elections was limited to seven. Whenever an emperor died, these seven electors chose as his successor a politically weak noble with small landholdings. In the early 1400s, they began choosing emperors from the Hapsburgs, a family of nobles based in Austria. Once in power, Hapsburg emperors could not control the princes and unify the empire. Yet they were able to increase their prestige by securing other areas of Europe.

One of the most ambitious Hapsburg emperors was Maximilian I. Elected emperor in A.D. 1493, Maximilian married Mary of Burgundy and acquired the Low Countries (present-day Belgium, the Netherlands, and Luxembourg) as part of the Hapsburg inheritance. His grandson, Charles, born in A.D. 1500, eventually became king of Spain. German princes elected him Holy Roman emperor as Charles V. Under Charles, the Hapsburgs became the most powerful European royal family, ruling Spain, Austria, Germany, the Low Countries, and much of Italy.

Eastern Europe

The Middle Ages also saw the rise of kingdoms in the area of eastern Europe between present-day Germany and Russia. The largest and most powerful of these lands were Poland and Hungary.

Poland

Formed in the A.D. 900s by West Slavs, Poland had accepted Roman Catholicism and close ties with western Europe. About A.D. 1000, the Poles began fighting groups of German warriors known as the Teutonic Knights for control of areas of Poland near the Baltic Sea.

During the A.D. 1300s, Poland enjoyed a golden age under King Casimir III, who reduced the power of local nobles and formed a strong central government. In A.D. 1386, one of Casimir's successors, Queen Jadwiga (yahd•VEE•gah) married Wladyslaw Jagiello (vwah•DIHS•wahv yahg•YEH•loh), duke of neighboring Lithuania. Their marriage led to a union of Poland and Lithuania, creating one of the largest states in medieval Europe. With the added strength of the Lithuanians, Polish forces were finally able to defeat the Teutonic Knights at the Battle of Tannenburg in A.D. 1410.

Hungary

South of Poland, the kingdom of Hungary was made up of Magyars, Germans, and Slavs. In A.D. 1000 King Stephen I became a Roman Catholic and introduced his people to western European ways. His reign marked the beginning of a strong Hungarian monarchy.

In A.D. 1241 Mongols from central Asia invaded Hungary and caused widespread destruction. They soon withdrew, however, and the kingdom was able to rebuild. During the A.D. 1400s and A.D. 1500s, Hungary faced periodic attacks from the Ottoman Turks. In A.D. 1526 Hungary's King Louis II was defeated by the Ottoman ruler Suleiman I at the Battle of Mohacs (MOH•hahch). Most of Hungary came under the Ottomans; the rest was ruled by the Hapsburg emperors.

SECTION 3 REVIEW

Recall
1. **Define** *cortes*.
2. **Identify** Joan of Arc, Louis XI, Richard III, Henry VII, Ferdinand of Aragon, Isabella of Castile.

3. **Explain** the causes and effects of the Hundred Years' War.

Critical Thinking
4. **Applying Information** Relate how one European monarchy

changed during the Middle Ages.

Understanding Themes
5. **Conflict** Explain the reasons for the struggles between the various European monarchies.

A.D. 1300   A.D. 1400   A.D. 1500

A.D. 1309 Pope's court moves to Avignon, France.

A.D. 1378 Great Schism in the Church occurs.

A.D. 1415 Church authorities burn Jan Hus as a heretic.

A.D. 1436 Compromise reached between the Church and Hussites.

Section 4

The Troubled Church

Setting the Scene

▶ **Terms to Define**
pilgrimage, simony

▶ **People to Meet**
Pope Clement V, John Wycliffe, the Lollards, Jan Hus

▶ **Places to Locate**
Avignon, Bohemia

**ind Out**   Why was the Church under pressure to reform?

Storyteller

The situation was intolerable, Nicholas of Clèmanges thought angrily. The Church was increasingly corrupt. Greed, pride, and love of luxury prevailed in place of humility and charity. Comparing the current priests and bishops with the holy leaders of antiquity, he reflected, was like comparing mud to gold. What would come of such ills? "So great a flood of evils must assuredly be crushed and utterly

destroyed by God's most righteous judgment. It does not seem possible in any other way to chasten it." Nicholas prayed that the Church might be spared from complete destruction—that a little seed might remain in the world.

—adapted from *On the Ruin and the Repair of the Church*, Nicholas Clèmanges, reprinted in *Readings in Western Civilization*, 1986

The Church besieged by evil forces

During the upheavals of the Late Middle Ages—caused by warfare, the plague, and religious controversy—many people turned to the Church for comfort and reassurance. Religious ceremonies multiplied, and thousands of people went on religious pilgrimages, or journeys to holy places. In spite of this increase in religious devotion, the temporal authority of the Church was weakening due to the influence of strong monarchs and national governments. A growing middle class of educated townspeople and a general questioning of the Church's teachings also contributed to this decline.

Babylonian Captivity

During the early A.D. 1300s, the papacy came under the influence of the French monarchy. In A.D. 1305 a French archbishop was elected **Pope Clement V.** A few years later, Clement decided to move his court from Rome to **Avignon** (A•veen•YOHN), a small city in southern France, to escape the civil wars that were disrupting Italy. While in France, the pope appointed only French cardinals. Pope Clement V and his successors—all French—remained in Avignon until A.D. 1377.

This long period of the exile of the popes at Avignon came to be known as the Babylonian Captivity, after the period of the exile of the Jews in Babylon in the 500s B.C. For centuries, Rome had been the center of the western Church. With the pope in France, people feared that the papacy would be dominated by French monarchs. Others disliked the concern the Avignon popes showed for increasing church taxes and making church administration more efficient. They believed the popes had become corrupted by worldly power and were neglecting their spiritual duties. The Italian poet Petrarch complained:

❝ Here reign the successors of the poor fishermen of Galilee; they have strangely

forgotten their origin. I am astounded …
to see these men loaded with gold and
clad in purple, boasting of the spoils of
princes and nations. **"**

The Great Schism

Finally, in A.D. 1377, Pope Gregory XI left
Avignon and returned to Rome. After his death,
Roman mobs forced the College of Cardinals to
elect an Italian as pope. The cardinals later declared
the election invalid, insisting they had voted under
pressure. The cardinals then elected a second pope,
who settled in Avignon. When the Italian pope
refused to resign, the Church faced the dilemma of
being led by two popes.

This controversy became known as the Great
Schism because it caused serious divisions in the
Church. The Great Schism lasted from A.D. 1378 until
A.D. 1417 and seriously undermined the pope's
authority. People wondered how they could regard
the pope as the divinely chosen leader of Christianity
when there was more than one person claiming to be
the single, unquestioned head of the Church.

Calls for a Council

Many kings, princes, and church scholars
called for a reform of church government. The most
popular remedy was a general church council.
However, this solution posed many problems. First,
such councils were traditionally called by popes.
No pope was willing to call a council that would
limit his authority. However, the legality of a council would be questionable if it did not receive papal
approval. Second, different rulers in Europe supported particular popes for political reasons. Such
political divisions made it almost impossible to
reach agreement on even the site of a council, let
alone to reach agreement on the deeper and more
important issues involved.

By A.D. 1400 many western Europeans were
committed to the idea of a church council. In A.D.
1409 a council met at Pisa, Italy, to unite the Church
behind one pope. It resulted in the election of a
third pope, since neither the pope at Rome nor the
pope at Avignon would resign. Finally, in A.D. 1414,
another council met at Constance, Germany. It
forced the resignation of all three popes and then
elected Pope Martin V, ending the Great Schism.
The long period of disunity, however, had seriously weakened the political influence of the Church.
Moreover, many Europeans had come to feel a
greater sense of loyalty to their monarchs than to
the pope.

Calls for Reform

Church authority was also weakened by people's dislike of abuses within the Church. The clergy used many unpopular means to raise money.
Fees were charged for almost every type of service
the Church performed. Common people especially
disliked simony—the selling of church positions—
because the cost of buying these positions was
passed on to them. The princely lifestyles of the
clergy further eroded regard for the Church. Many
Europeans called for reform. Two of the clearest
voices belonged to an English scholar and a
Bohemian preacher.

John Wycliffe

John Wycliffe (WIH•KLIHF), a scholar at
England's Oxford University, criticized the
Church's wealth, corruption among the clergy, and
the pope's claim to absolute authority. He wanted
secular rulers to remove church officials who were
immoral or corrupt.

Wycliffe claimed that the Bible was the sole
authority for religious truth. He began to translate
the Bible from Latin into English so people could
read it themselves. Since church doctrine held that
only the clergy could interpret God's word in the
Bible, this act was regarded as revolutionary. Some
of Wycliffe's followers, known as **the Lollards**,
angrily criticized the Church. They destroyed
images of saints, ridiculed the Mass, and ate communion bread with onions to show that it was no
different from ordinary bread.

Widespread antipapal feelings made it difficult
for the English government to suppress Lollards.
Wycliffe was persuaded to moderate his views and
received only a mild punishment. He died peacefully in A.D. 1384, but his ideas spread.

Among those who supported the Lollards was
Bohemian-born Queen Anne, the wife of King

Silver Spoons
During the Middle Ages,
pewter spoons became
common utensils for eating. In the A.D. 1400s silver "apostle spoons," bearing the image of a
child's patron saint, were favored gifts for new-
borns in Italy. Only the wealthy could afford such
a luxury. From these apostle spoons came the saying that a privileged child is "born with a silver
spoon in his or her mouth."

John Wycliffe Reading His Translation of the Bible to John of Gaunt by Ford Madox Brown. *Why was Wycliffe's translation of the Bible revolutionary?*

Richard II. Anne sent copies of Wycliffe's writings to her homeland in the Holy Roman Empire, where they influenced another great religious reformer.

Jan Hus

During the late A.D. 1300s and A.D. 1400s, the Slavs of **Bohemia**, known as Czechs, became more aware of their own national identity. They wanted to end German control of their country and backed sweeping reforms in the Catholic Church in Bohemia, which had many German clergy. Their religious and political grievances combined to produce an explosive situation.

The Czechs produced religious pamphlets and copies of the Bible in Czech and criticized the corruption of leading church officials, many of whom were German. The leader of the Czech religious reform movement was **Jan Hus**, a popular preacher and professor at the University of Prague. When Hus and his works were condemned by the Church and political leaders, a violent wave of riots swept across Bohemia.

Faced with a possible full-scale rebellion against the Church, in A.D. 1415 the council at Constance demanded that Hus appear before them to defend his views. The Holy Roman emperor promised Hus safe conduct to Constance, Germany, but this guarantee was ignored. Hus was burned at the stake as a heretic, but his heroic death caused many Czechs to rally around their new martyr.

From A.D. 1420 to A.D. 1436, Hus's supporters, called Hussites, resisted the Church and the Holy Roman emperor, and the Church launched five crusades against the Hussites. All five failed. Using firearms and the tactic of forming movable walls with farm wagons, the Hussites defeated the crusading knights.

In A.D. 1436 representatives of the pope and the Holy Roman emperor reached a compromise with the Hussite leaders. They gave the Hussites certain religious liberties in return for their allegiance to the Church. The ideas of Jan Hus, however, continued to spread throughout Europe to influence later and more radical reformers. While this agreement gave the appearance that the Church had successfully met the challenges to its authority, the basic spiritual questions raised by Hus and others did not go away.

SECTION 4 REVIEW

Recall
1. **Define** pilgrimage, simony.
2. **Identify** Pope Clement V, Babylonian Captivity, Great Schism, John Wycliffe, the Lollards, Jan Hus, the Hussites.
3. **Explain** the effects of the Babylonian Captivity and the Great Schism on the Church.

Critical Thinking
4. **Synthesizing Information** Imagine you are a follower of Jan Hus just after his execution. How would you feel about carrying on his work?

Understanding Themes
5. **Conflict** Explain the rise of dissent among many devout Europeans. Why were they against the Church and its leadership?

Analyzing Historical Maps

When you walk through your town, you may see changes in progress. Perhaps a new restaurant has opened, or an old factory has been torn down. Change also takes place on a larger scale across nations and continents. Historical maps illustrate political, social, and cultural changes over time.

Learning the Skill

To analyze a historical map, first read the title to identify its theme. Then identify the chronology of events on the map. Many historical maps show changes in political boundaries over time. For example, the map below of the Frankish Empire uses colors to show land acquisitions under three different rulers. On the other map, however, colors represent areas controlled by different rulers at the same time. Read the map key, labels, and captions to determine what time periods and changes appear on the map.

To compare historical maps of the same region in different time periods, first identify the geographic location and time period of each map. Then look for similarities and differences. Which features have remained the same and which have changed? What groups control the area in each map? Has the country grown larger or smaller

over time? Have other features changed?

After analyzing the information on historical maps, try to draw conclusions about the causes and effects of these changes.

Practicing the Skill

The two maps on this page show the same region in different time periods. Study both maps and answer these questions.

1. What is the time period of each map?
2. How did the Frankish Empire change from A.D. 500 to A.D. 800?
3. Did France grow larger or smaller between A.D. 800 and A.D. 1400?
4. What other changes appear on these maps?

Applying the Skill

Compare a map of Europe today with a map of Europe in 1985 or earlier. Identify at least five changes that have occurred since the early 1980s.

For More Practice

Turn to the Skill Practice in the Chapter Review on page 339 for more practice in analyzing historical maps.

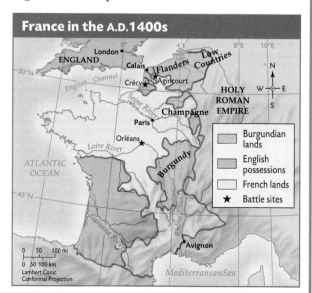

Frankish Empire A.D. 481–814

Legend:
- Clovis's kingdom
- Added by Martel and Pepin
- Added by Charlemagne
- ★ Battle site

France in the A.D.1400s

Legend:
- Burgundian lands
- English possessions
- French lands
- ★ Battle sites

Connections Across Time

Historical Significance Many features of modern Western civilization arose during the Middle Ages. The medieval history of Europe can still be seen in great cathedrals and in the rituals of the Roman Catholic Church. Modern labor unions and institutions of higher learning are related to medieval guilds and universities. Today's national languages in Europe first appeared during the Middle Ages. Finally, the middle class, which plays an important role in the world today, also had its beginnings during this period.

Using Key Terms

Write the key term that completes each sentence. Then write a sentence for each term not chosen.

a. apprentice
b. *cortes*
c. charter
d. scholasticism
e. Crusade
f. guilds
g. vernacular
h. simony
i. money economy
j. pilgrimages
k. master
l. troubadours

1. Church scholars developed a system of thought known as _____ that sought to reconcile faith and reason.
2. The rise of a _____ led to the growth of banking and put the feudal classes in an economic squeeze.
3. In Spain, assemblies known as _____ at first had the right to review the policies of Spanish monarchs.
4. In medieval France, traveling poet-musicians called _____ composed lyric poems and songs about love and the feats of knights.
5. During the Middle Ages, the rise of _____ languages gave each kingdom of Europe a separate identity.

Technology Activity

Using E-mail Locate an E-mail address for your local historical society or chamber of commerce. Write a letter requesting information about various styles and influences of medieval architecture found in your area. Using your response, create an illustrated tourist pamphlet of information about area structures. Include a map.

Using Your History Journal

From your notes on Beowulf, *the* Song of Roland, *or* The Canterbury Tales, *write a short description of the manners, customs, and values of the Europeans described in the work.*

Reviewing Facts

1. **History** List the various medieval Crusades and their results.
2. **Technology** Describe several agricultural improvements in the Middle Ages.
3. **Culture** Discuss the contributions made by women to the society of the Middle Ages.
4. **History** List the key events in the Hundred Years' War.
5. **Culture** Identify two church reformers and a major event in the life of each.
6. **Culture** Describe a typical medieval town.
7. **Economics** Identify the bourgeoisie and state their role in late medieval Europe.
8. **History** Discuss the impact of the Black Death.
9. **Government** Explain why townspeople and the lower nobility supported the rise of strong monarchies in western Europe.
10. **Culture** List the problems that the Catholic Church faced at the end of the Middle Ages.
11. **Government** State how Louis XI strengthened the French monarchy.
12. **History** Discuss the major result of the Wars of the Roses.
13. **History** Identify the *Reconquista*. How did it contribute to the unity of Spain?
14. **Economics** List new business methods that developed in Europe by the A.D. 1400s. How did they change European life?

Critical Thinking

1. **Apply** How did the medieval middle class change European society?
2. **Analyze** What various forces led to Europe's economic growth during the Middle Ages?
3. **Evaluate** How would Europe be different today if there had been no Crusades?
4. **Apply** How did European monarchies change during the Middle Ages? What were the effects of this change on culture, religion, and politics in Europe?

Geography in History

1. **Place** Refer to the map "Trade Routes A.D. 1400s." Name the major trading cities in western Europe during the 1400s.
2. **Human/Environment Interaction** Why did most European traders avoid overland routes whenever possible?
3. **Location** With which two areas to the east did the cities of Europe most want to trade?
4. **Movement** How did the desire for luxuries from the East lead to changes in transportation in the West?

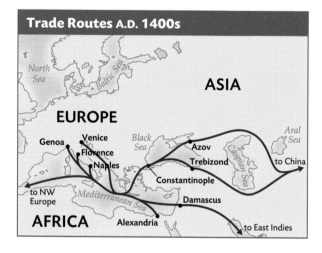

Trade Routes A.D. 1400s

Understanding Themes

1. **Cultural Diffusion** How did a mix of cultures affect medieval Europe?
2. **Innovation** Choose one medieval innovation and describe its influence on medieval society.

Do the same for a modern innovation and modern society.
3. **Conflict** How did continual conflict between England and France strengthen the monarchies of those countries?
4. **Conflict** Why was there religious dissent in the Catholic Church of the Late Middle Ages?

Linking Past and Present

1. The Crusades were a series of "holy wars" conducted by Christians against Muslims. Can you find examples of holy wars in modern times?
2. Compare the rise of towns in medieval Europe with the rise of towns in America.
3. How do medieval European universities compare to today's higher educational institutions?

Skill Practice

Study the map "Spread of the Black Death" and answer the questions below.

1. What is the topic and time period of this map?
2. What does color represent?
3. When and where did the Black Death begin?
4. In which direction did the Black Death spread? How does the map show this?
5. What factor do you think caused this pattern of the epidemic?`

Spread of the Black Death

East and South Asia

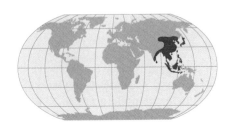

Chapter Themes

▶ **Movement** The Mongols of central Asia conquer China and parts of Europe. *Section 1*

▶ **Uniformity** A centralized government, a state religion, and a common language maintain China's cultural continuity. *Section 2*

▶ **Cultural Diffusion** The civilizations of Southeast Asia reflect the influences of India and China. *Section 3*

▶ **Innovation** Japan and Korea produce innovations from a blend of Chinese and local traditions. *Section 4*

The Storyteller

In China, in the year A.D. 1200, a lone student sat behind a desk in a room furnished only with a lamp, some paper, a writing brush, and an inkstone. He labored over a grueling government exam designed to test his knowledge of Confucian texts. He worried because examiners could fail a person for even a single misquotation. If he passed, he would be one of the Song emperor's officials. If he failed, he would have to hawk cheap goods in the streets.

Civil service examinations helped ancient China to maintain a consistent government no matter which dynasty was in power. Later, the neighboring countries of Korea and Japan adopted these civil service examinations as well as other aspects of Chinese culture.

Historical Significance

How did the civilizations of East and South Asia influence each other and the rest of the world?

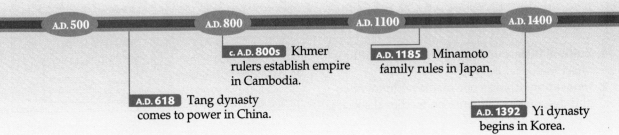

A.D. 500	A.D. 800	A.D. 1100	A.D. 1400

c. A.D. 800s Khmer rulers establish empire in Cambodia.

A.D. 1185 Minamoto family rules in Japan.

A.D. 618 Tang dynasty comes to power in China.

A.D. 1392 Yi dynasty begins in Korea.

A partial view of the summer palace constructed under
Emperor Ch'ien Lung. Bibliothèque Nationale, Paris, France

Your History Journal

*Consult an atlas and create a map of
East Asia. As you read the chapter, place
10 to 20 key events on your map in the
countries or areas where they occurred.
Include the dates of these events.*

Section 1

Central Asia

Setting the Scene

▶ **Terms to Define**
   clan, yurt, *yasa*, khan

▶ **People to Meet**
   the Seljuk Turks, the Mongols, Genghis Khan, Timur Lenk (Tamerlane)

▶ **Places to Locate**
   Mongolia

 **ind Out** How did the Mongols acquire the world's largest land empire?

The Storyteller

The caravan halted for the night. Chaghatai, the leader, before retiring posted a sign and fastened bells around the animals' necks. Maffeo, a young foreigner, wondered at these precautions. Chaghatai explained that strange things may happen in the Desert of Lop. "When a man is riding by night through this desert and something happens to make him … lose touch with his companions ... he hears spirits talking…. Often these voices make him stray from the path…. For this reason bands of travellers make a point of keeping very close together…. And round the necks of all their beasts they fasten little bells, so that by listening to the sound they may prevent them from straying from the path."

—adapted from *The Travels of Marco Polo*, Marco Polo, translated by Ronald Latham, 1958

Porcelain figure on camel

From the A.D. 1000s to the A.D. 1400s, invaders from the steppe of central Asia conquered territories in eastern Asia, the Middle East, and eastern Europe. Originally nomads, the invaders settled in many of the conquered areas. They adapted to the local cultures, advanced trade, and encouraged the exchange of goods and ideas.

The Steppe Peoples

At the beginning of the A.D. 1000s, large numbers of nomadic groups roamed the steppe of central Asia. Loosely organized into clans, or groups based on family ties, they depended for their livelihood on the grazing of animals. To protect their pastures and provide for a growing population, they organized under powerful chiefs. The chiefs formed cavalry units of warriors armed with bows and arrows. The nomadic peoples became a military threat to neighboring territories that were more culturally developed. They carried out a series of invasions that transformed the cultures of eastern Asia, the Middle East, and eastern Europe.

The Seljuk Turks

The first people of the steppes to engage in conquest were the Turks. Around A.D. 800, weak Abbasid rulers centered in Baghdad hired Turkish warriors to fight in their armies. As a result, the Turks became powerful and soon controlled the Abbasid government. Later, about A.D. 1000, a group of Muslim Turks called **the Seljuk Turks** moved from central Asia into the Middle East. There they formed settlements and restored the Sunni caliphate. The Seljuks also gained control of the main trade routes between eastern Asia, the Middle East, and Europe. They benefited from this trade and used their wealth to build an empire.

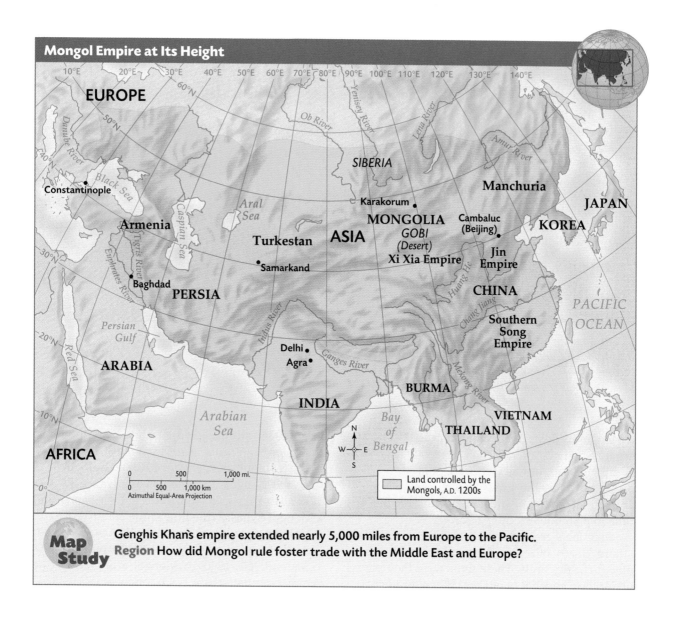

Mongol Empire at Its Height

EUROPE

SIBERIA

Constantinople

Armenia

Karakorum

Manchuria

JAPAN

MONGOLIA

Cambaluc
(Beijing)

KOREA

Turkestan

ASIA

GOBI
(Desert)

Samarkand

Xi Xia Empire

Jin
Empire

Baghdad

PERSIA

CHINA

Southern
Song
Empire

PACIFIC
OCEAN

Delhi

Agra

Ganges River

ARABIA

BURMA

INDIA

Bay
of
Bengal

VIETNAM

THAILAND

AFRICA

0   500   1,000 mi.
0   500   1,000 km
Azimuthal Equal-Area Projection

Land controlled by the
Mongols, A.D. 1200s

Map Study

Genghis Khan's empire extended nearly 5,000 miles from Europe to the Pacific.
Region How did Mongol rule foster trade with the Middle East and Europe?

Seljuk warriors also invaded the plains and highlands of Asia Minor. There they defeated the Byzantines at the Battle of Manzikert in A.D. 1071. The Byzantine emperor Alexius I Comnenus feared the loss of Byzantine territory to the Seljuks and appealed to the pope and the monarchs of western Europe for aid. About 20 years later, the Seljuk conquest of Palestine led to Pope Urban II's calling of the First Crusade.

Though the Seljuks were skilled warriors, they were unable to develop a well-organized government to rule their territories. Seljuk rulers lacked strong traditions of government administration and had difficulties holding the empire together. Local officials ignored the central government and acted like independent rulers. They began to fight each other for control of land. Weakened by internal upheavals, the Seljuks became prey to new nomadic invaders from central Asia.

The Mongols

During the late A.D. 1100s, **the Mongols** became the dominant nomadic group in central Asia. Their homeland was **Mongolia**, a region of forests and steppe northwest of China. In this wild and isolated area, they wandered from pasture to pasture with their herds of sheep, horses, and yaks, or long-haired oxen. Because of their nomadic life, the Mongols lived in movable tents called yurts. Their principal foods were meat and mare's milk. In a few fertile areas, Mongol farmers established small communities. There women raised grains while men herded animals.

Genghis Khan

Like other nomads, the Mongols at first were divided into clans. They were expert fighters on horseback, using bow and arrow. About A.D. 1206

Visualizing History Some people in Mongolia still live in yurts, circular domed tents of skins or felt stretched over a lattice frame. *Why did ancient Mongols choose this kind of housing?*

a Mongol leader named Temujin (teh•MOO•juhn) organized the scattered clans under one government. He brought together Mongol laws in a new code known as the *yasa*. Under Temujin's guidance, an assembly of tribal chiefs met for the first time to plan military campaigns.

Temujin's greatest achievement was in military affairs. He organized the Mongol armies into disciplined cavalry units. These units were then placed under the command of officers chosen for their abilities and not for their family ties. These changes made the Mongols the most skilled fighting force in the world at that time. As a result of his efforts, Temujin was recognized as khan, or absolute ruler. Now called **Genghis Khan** (JEHN•guhs KAHN), or "universal ruler," Temujin set out to create a large empire.

Mongol Conquests

The Mongol armies under Genghis Khan first conquered the other steppe peoples, most of whom were Turks. These victories brought tribute money to the Mongol state as well as new recruits for the Mongol armies. By A.D. 1211 the Mongols were strong enough to attack major civilizations. In that year, 100,000 Mongol horsemen invaded China. While fighting against the Chinese, the Mongols learned Chinese techniques of siege warfare. Using

gunpowder, storming ladders, and battering rams, they won significant victories against their opponents. In spite of Genghis Khan's death in A.D. 1227, the Mongols continued their advance. By A.D. 1279 all of China's territory was in their hands, and a Mongol dynasty ruled the entire country.

Under Ogadai (OH•guh•DY) Khan, the other Mongol forces moved westward. During the A.D. 1230s and A.D. 1240s, a Mongol army led by the commander Batu (bah•TOO) conquered East Slavic lands and then crossed the Carpathian Mountains into eastern and central Europe. Upon hearing of Ogadai's death, Batu's army returned to Russia. There they awaited the selection of a new khan. Meanwhile, Ogadai's widow ruled the Mongols.

During the same period, other Mongols invaded the Middle East. Using terror to subdue the region, the Mongols destroyed cities and killed many people. In A.D. 1258 the commander Helagu (heh•lah•GOO) captured Baghdad, the old Abbasid capital, and enslaved its inhabitants. The destruction of Baghdad represented a major setback to Islamic civilization. However, the Mongol advance was finally halted by the Mamluks, a Muslim military group that ruled Egypt.

The Mongol Empire

The Mongols created the largest land empire in history. Their territories extended from China to the frontiers of western Europe. Many of the great trade routes between Europe and Asia passed through Mongol lands. During the A.D. 1200s Mongol rule brought peace to the region. This advanced the growth of trade and encouraged closer cultural contacts between East and West.

The Mongols respected the highly advanced culture of conquered groups and learned from them. In China, Mongol rulers gradually adopted Chinese ideas and practices. In Persia and central Asia, Mongol settlers converted to Islam and intermarried with the local Turkish population. Turkish became the principal language of the region. The Mongols of Russia, however, kept their traditional customs and lived apart from the Slavs. They settled in the empty steppe region north of the Caspian Sea. From there, they controlled the Slavic principalities located in the northern forests.

The unity of the Mongol Empire did not last long. All Mongols gave allegiance to the khan in Mongolia. However, local rulers became increasingly independent. By the end of the A.D. 1200s, Mongol territories in Russia, central Asia, Persia, and China had developed into separate and independent domains.

Timur Lenk

About 100 years later, another powerful nomadic force emerged from central Asia. In the A.D. 1390s a Turkish-Mongol chief named **Timur Lenk** (in English, Tamerlane) rose to power in the region. As a youth, Timur was known for his athletic abilities, especially in horse riding. He began his rise as leader of a small nomadic tribe and extended his rule through numerous wars with neighboring tribes.

A devout Muslim, Timur hoped to spread Islam to new areas. His religious zeal also made him oppose Muslims who differed with his understanding of Islam. Claiming descent from Genghis Khan, Timur united the Turkish-Mongols by conquest and eventually extended their rule over much of the Middle East.

Although Timur was ruthless, the people under

Visualizing History Timur Lenk, or Tamerlane, devoted much of his life to conquest, from India to Russia to the Mediterranean. *What city was the center of his empire?*

his rule created important centers of civilization in central Asia. The most influential city in the region was Samarkand. A wealthy trading and craft center, it became known for its beautifully decorated mosques and tombs.

In A.D. 1402 Timur and his armies swept into Asia Minor, defeating another Turkish group—the Ottomans—at Ankara. However, Timur's effort to gain territory in Asia Minor never succeeded. In A.D. 1405 Timur died and was buried at Samarkand. The huge empire that he had created soon collapsed. The Ottomans were then able to regain their lost lands and began the building of their state.

SECTION 1 REVIEW

Recall
1. **Define** clan, yurt, *yasa*, khan.
2. **Identify** the Seljuk Turks, the Mongols, Genghis Khan, Batu, Helagu, Timur Lenk.
3. **Explain** why the empire of the

Seljuk Turks declined quickly.

Critical Thinking
4. **Synthesizing Information** What factors led the steppe peoples to expand their territories and to create empires?

Understanding Themes
5. **Movement** How did the Mongol conquests contribute to the spread of culture and ideas throughout Asia and parts of Europe?

A.D. 600   A.D. 1000   A.D. 1400

c. A.D. 649 Empress Wu begins to control the Chinese Empire.

A.D. 907 Tang dynasty ends.

A.D. 1260 Kublai Khan begins reign.

A.D. 1368 Yuan dynasty collapses.

Section 2

China

Setting the Scene

▶ **Terms to Define**
meritocracy, mandarin

▶ **People to Meet**
Tai Cong, Empress Wu, Xuanzang, Duo Fu, Li Bo, Zhao Kuangyin, Kublai Khan, Marco Polo

▶ **Places to Locate**
Changan, Hangzhou

 **Find Out** What were the significant achievements of the Tang, Song, and Yuan dynasties?

The Storyteller

Thoughtfully, Gui Xi considered the civil service examination. He was to select a single line of poetry and, using his finest calligraphy, write it on a silk scroll. Then he must create a painting linked to the chosen text, filling the scroll. To pass this vital test a man needed to be able to read, drawing conclusions and inferences. He also needed to demonstrate proficiency in the brush arts, a discipline requiring many years to master. Gui Xi recollected the steps essential to writing and painting. One must first find the spirit, rhythm, and thought, then one could seek to control the scenery, brush, and ink. For good work to result, mental and physical aspects must balance.

—adapted from *Record of Brush Methods: Essay on Landscape Painting*, Ching Hao, reprinted in *Varieties of Visual Experience*, 1991

Chinese calligraphy

For more than 350 years after the collapse of the Han dynasty in A.D. 220, Chinese kingdoms and invaders from the north rivaled each other for control of China. Then in A.D. 589, a northern official named Yang Jian (YAHNG JYEN) united China by conquering both the north and the south. Yang Jian took the title Emperor Wen and founded the Sui (SWAY) dynasty. Emperor Wen renewed many of the goals and traditions that had been accepted during the reign of the Han dynasty. He organized public works projects such as the rebuilding of the former Han capital city at **Changan** (CHONG•ON), the repair of the Great Wall, and the construction of a Grand Canal to link northern and southern China. However, to accomplish these projects Emperor Wen used crews of forced laborers, which made him quite unpopular with the peasants.

The Tang Dynasty

In A.D. 618 peasant uprisings against the Sui dynasty enabled a rebellious lord named Li Yuan (LEE YOO•AHN) to take control of the country and proclaim himself emperor. He established the Tang (TONG) dynasty, which lasted from A.D. 618 to A.D. 907. Under the Tang, the Chinese Empire expanded its borders to include new territories.

Government and Society

The military genius behind the early Tang expansion was a son of Li Yuan who took the name **Tai Cong** (TIE TSOONG). Not only was Tai Cong a warrior, but he was also a shrewd administrator. By restoring a strong central government in China, he maintained control of his enormous empire while continuing to expand it.

To obtain a position in the Tang government, candidates had to pass civil service examinations. Under Tang rule, these tests measured the degree to which candidates had mastered Confucian principles. According to Confucianism, an individual was expected to obey the emperor just as a son was expected to obey his father.

Because almost any male could take these examinations, the Chinese government claimed that it was a meritocracy—a system in which people are chosen and promoted for their talents and performance. But in practice it did not meet that ideal. Few boys from poor families could afford to pay tutors to help them prepare for the exams. Most could not spare the time away from their labor to study on their own.

Nevertheless, some peasants benefited from the Tang dynasty's rule. The Tang government gave land to farmers and enforced the peace that enabled them to till their land. In the Chang Jiang (Yangtze River) region, farmers were able to experiment with new strains of rice and better methods for growing it—both of which led to greater crop yields. With more food available, the Chinese population increased as well.

Foreign Influences

Tang rulers also devoted resources to the construction of roads and waterways. These routes made travel within China and to neighboring countries much easier. New and improved routes helped government officials to perform their duties. They also enabled Chinese merchants to increase trade with people from Japan, India, and the Middle East.

Chinese luxury goods, such as silk and pottery, passed through central Asia along the Silk Road. Beginning in central China, traders' camel caravans traveled north to the Great Wall and then headed west, crossing into central Asia just north of the Tibetan plateau. Some traveled as far west as Syria. These caravans brought Chinese goods and ideas to other cultures and returned with foreign products and new ideas as well. The Buddhist, Christian, and Islamic religions came to China by way of the Silk Road. During the Tang dynasty, Buddhism especially became very popular in China.

As trade increased the wealth of the empire, the Tang capital at Changan grew into the largest city in the world. Dazzling tales attracted merchants and scholars from countries throughout Asia to this city of 2 million people. Visitors to Changan spoke of wide, tree-shaded avenues and two vast market squares where merchants sold goods from Asia and the Middle East. They said that acrobats, jugglers, and dancers performed in the streets and that wealthy Chinese—including women—played the Persian games of chess and polo.

The Arts

In A.D. 649 Gaozong (GOW•DZOONG) succeeded Tai Cong as emperor of China. But Gaozong's wife, **Empress Wu**, actually ruled the empire. She expanded the bureaucracy and strengthened China's military forces.

History & Art *Four Travelers on Horseback,* porcelain figures from the Tang dynasty **Chinese potters discovered how to make porcelain in the A.D. 800s by firing pieces at very high temperatures.** *What constructions helped merchants trade fine Chinese wares with other countries?*

In A.D. 712 Empress Wu's grandson, **Xuanzang** (SEE•WAHN•DZONG), became emperor of China. Because Xuanzang welcomed artists to his splendid court, the arts flourished during his reign. Tang artisans made porcelain, a fine translucent pottery that became a prized commodity known in the West as "china."

Two of China's greatest poets, **Duo Fu** (DWA FOO) and **Li Bo** (LEE BWAW), produced their works in Xuanzang's court. Scholars compiled encyclopedias, dictionaries, and official histories of China. Writers popularized stories about ghosts, crime, and love. And while European monks were still slowly and laboriously copying texts by hand, Chinese Buddhist monks invented the more efficient technique of block printing. They carved the text of a page into a block of wood. Then they reproduced the page by inking the wood and pressing a piece of paper onto it.

Tang Decline

For a time the cultural splendor of Xuanzang's court masked its military weakness. However, the Tang ruler's vulnerability to attack was revealed in A.D. 755, when Turkish armies in central Asia successfully revolted against China. They cut off China's trade routes to the Middle East, and they put an end to the thriving exchange of goods and ideas along the Silk Road. Border wars with the Tibetans and rebellions in famine-stricken provinces plagued the Tang from A.D. 766 on. In A.D. 907 this turmoil finally caused the fall of the Tang dynasty.

The Song Dynasty

From A.D. 907 to 960, China was ruled by military dynasties. Then a military general named **Zhao Kuangyin** (JOW KWONG•YIN) seized the throne and established the Song (SOONG) dynasty.

Footnotes to History

Pasta

Almost everyone associates noodles, or pasta, with Italy. But, according to tradition, the Chinese were the first to make noodles, and their recipes were brought to Italy in the A.D. 1200s by the Polos. Some recent historians, however, claim that pasta actually originated in Persia and from there spread east and west.

Song emperors kept peace with a group of Mongols in the north, the Khitan, by paying them generously in silver. But in A.D. 1127 the Jurchen, a nomadic people, captured the Song capital of Kaifeng (KIE•FUHNG). The Song rulers set up their royal court in the southern city of **Hangzhou** (HONG•JOH).

Cultural Contributions

Song scholars, resentful of foreign influences, produced an official state philosophy called neo-Confucianism. This philosophy combined Confucian values with elements of Buddhism and Daoism.

Song rulers also more firmly entrenched the civil service system that the Tang had resurrected. They made determining one's knowledge of Confucian curriculum the main focus of these tests. The scholars who had passed the tests eventually formed a wealthy elite group, called mandarins by Westerners.

Rich and Poor

During the Song dynasty, China experienced unprecedented economic growth, partly because Song rulers used tax revenues to fund several public-works projects that benefited the economy. For example, they used these revenues to fund the digging of irrigation ditches and canals, which in turn helped farmers increase their crop yields.

The introduction of new crops from Southeast Asia, such as tea and a faster-growing rice plant, further boosted China's farming economy. The new crops also led to an increase in China's trade with India and Southeast Asia. With farming, trade, and commerce all thriving, urban centers prospered.

The urban wealthy lived in spacious homes and enjoyed going to teahouses, restaurants, and luxurious bathhouses. The capital of the dynasty, Hangzhou, grew to nearly 1 million residents.

Of course, the country still had many urban poor. The urban poor lived in flimsy houses. To survive they hawked cheap goods in the streets, worked as manual laborers, begged, or stole.

Song Arts and Sciences

Song achievements in the arts and sciences were many. The cuisine which people recognize today as distinctively Chinese originated during the Song dynasty. Experts regard Song porcelain as the best ever made. Landscape painting reached its peak during Song rule. Song inventors perfected the compass, a tool that enabled Chinese sailors to navigate on journeys far offshore. They also produced gunpowder that was first used in fireworks. Bamboo-tube rocket launchers charged with gunpowder made the Song army a powerful fighting force.

The Bodleian Library, Oxford, Ms. Bodl. 264, fol.219R

Kublai Khan and Marco Polo

This medieval English manuscript shows the Chinese emperor Kublai Khan presenting golden tablets to Marco Polo and his family to ensure their safe passage back to the West. In A.D. 1297 Marco Polo wrote an account of a trip he claimed to have made to China, and his book eventually became popular with the small literate class in Europe. The painter who embellished this manuscript had never met Marco Polo nor had he ever seen a picture of an Asian. Maybe that's why the emperor looks European rather than Asian.

The Mongol rulers of China put the country in closer touch with the Middle East and Europe. The Mongolian khans were outsiders who distrusted, and were distrusted by, their Chinese subjects. The khans turned to outsiders to help them rule, especially after Kublai Khan moved the Chinese capital to Beijing. The Polos (Marco Polo's father and uncle accompanied him to China) were but three of hundreds of European and Muslim merchants and artisans who moved in and out of China. But Marco Polo became famous, both in his time and in ours, because he wrote a book about his adventures. The Polos may have brought Chinese noodles back to Europe, and other European and Muslim travelers brought Chinese inventions such as gunpowder and the compass back to the West. This transfer of technology had a major impact on the history of Europe. ⊕

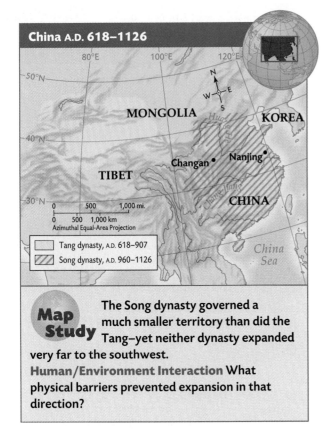

80°E 100°E 120°E

50°N

40°N

MONGOLIA   KOREA

Changan • Nanjing •

TIBET

30°N

0   500   1,000 mi.
0   500   1,000 km
Azimuthal Equal-Area Projection

CHINA

China
Sea

☐ Tang dynasty, A.D. 618–907

▨ Song dynasty, A.D. 960–1126

Map Study The Song dynasty governed a much smaller territory than did the Tang—yet neither dynasty expanded very far to the southwest.
Human/Environment Interaction What physical barriers prevented expansion in that direction?

China's enemies, however, were eventually able to obtain the secrets of Song military technology. Thus, using the Song Empire's own technology against it, the Mongols were able to completely capture northern China in A.D. 1234 and bring about the fall of the Song dynasty in southern China in A.D. 1279.

The Yuan Dynasty

During the A.D. 1200s, the Mongols invaded China and overthrew the Jurchen and Song rulers. They established the Yuan (YOO•AHN), or Mongol, dynasty. They became the first conquerors to rule most of the country.

Kublai Khan

The first great Mongol emperor of China was **Kublai Khan** (KOO•BLUH KAHN). A grandson of Genghis Khan, Kublai ruled from A.D. 1260 to A.D. 1294. Kublai Khan extended Mongol rule beyond China's borders. He conquered Korea in the north and part of Southeast Asia. He made two attempts to invade Japan, using Chinese and Korean ships. Both efforts failed because the Mongols were not skilled in naval warfare.

Although Kublai complied with some Chinese traditions to better control the Chinese, he tried to maintain Mongol culture. Government documents were written first in Mongolian, then translated into Chinese. Moreover, the highest positions in the emperor's court were given to Mongols or foreigners.

The most famous of these foreigners may have been a Venetian named **Marco Polo**. Polo claimed to have arrived in China about A.D. 1271 and to have stayed 17 years, traveling through Mongol territory on the Khan's missions. Whether true or not, Polo's tales of the splendor of Chinese civilization astounded Europeans.

Mongol Peace and Decline

Travel throughout China greatly improved because the Mongols enforced a relatively stable order. Merchants could safely travel the roads built by the Mongols. Mongol rule thus fostered trade and connections with Europe.

Through contact with the Middle East, Russia, and Europe, the Chinese obtained enslaved people as well as products such as glass, hides, clothes, silver, cotton, and carpets. In return, Europeans got exotic products such as silk, porcelain, and tea.

After Kublai Khan died in A.D. 1294, a series of weak successors took over the throne. The Chinese, still resentful of foreign rule, began to stage rebellions against these rulers. Finally, in A.D. 1368, a young Buddhist monk named Zhu Yuanzhang (JOO YOO•AHN•JAHNG) led an army against the capital and overthrew the Yuan dynasty.

SECTION 2 REVIEW

Recall
1. **Define** meritocracy, mandarin.
2. **Identify** Tai Cong, Empress Wu, Xuanzang, Duo Fu, Li Bo, Zhao Kuangyin, Kublai Khan, Marco Polo.
3. **Locate** the city of Changan in central China on the map above. Describe the capital city's human and physical characteristics.

Critical Thinking
4. **Evaluating Information** Do you think the Tang and Song systems of government were true meritocracies? Explain.

Understanding Themes
5. **Uniformity** What methods did the rulers of the Tang, Song, and Yuan dynasties use to unite China?

A.D. 800	A.D. 1100	A.D. 1400

A.D. 802 The Khmer people establish capital at Angkor.

A.D. 938 The Vietnamese defeat the Chinese in the Battle of Bach Dang River.

c. A.D. 1200s The Mongols destroy Burman city of Pagan.

A.D. 1350 The Thai establish kingdom of Ayutthaya.

Section 3

Southeast Asia

Setting the Scene

▶ **Terms to Define**
archipelago, animism

▶ **People to Meet**
the Khmer, Suryavarman II, Trung Trak, Trung Nhi, Ngo Quyen, Ramkhamhaeng

▶ **Places to Locate**
Angkor Wat, Pagan, Sukhothai, Ayutthaya, Melaka

Find Out How were Southeast Asians influenced by the cultures of China and India?

The Storyteller

The situation was a general's nightmare, T'u Sui thought despairingly. His lord, the Chinese emperor, was determined to subjugate the land of Yueh [Vietnam]. T'u Sui had gladly accepted the command of five hundred thousand men of ability to complete the task. However, when he attacked the Yueh fled into the mountains and forests where it was impossible to fight them or even to find them. Gradually, the troops grew weary of their duties. The Yueh would then attack, inflicting great losses upon the powerful Chinese army.

—from *Huai Nan Tzu*, reprinted in *Ancient Vietnam*, Keith W. Taylor

Mountains of Vietnam

Although China was the most culturally diverse and influential society in Asia from about A.D. 220 until A.D. 1400, other Asian civilizations were creating distinct and influential cultures of their own at the same time. Southeast Asian cultures were among these new societies.

Crossroads of Asia

South of China and east of India is the region known as Southeast Asia. Southeast Asia includes the present-day countries of Myanmar (Burma), Thailand, Vietnam, Laos, Cambodia, Malaysia, Singapore, Brunei, Indonesia, and the Philippines. Located in the tropics, many of these countries have fertile soils, warm climates, and abundant rainfall. Geographically, Southeast Asia is divided into mainland and maritime Southeast Asia. The latter includes more than 10,000 islands of the Philippine and Indonesian archipelagos, or chains of islands.

During the A.D. 100s, an exchange of goods and ideas began between India and Southeast Asia. This exchange led Southeast Asia to adopt many elements of Indian culture. For instance, at that time, traveling Indian traders and scholars introduced to Southeast Asia the Sanskrit language and the religions of Hinduism and Buddhism. Indian epics such as the *Ramayana* were interwoven with Southeast Asian stories and legends. Indian architecture, law codes, and political ideas also deeply influenced the cultures of the region. As contact with India increased, Indian culture gradually spread throughout Southeast Asia.

Southeast Asians nevertheless retained many of their own traditions. They continued to perform the art of shadow puppetry, to make intricately patterned cloth called batik, and to play their own unique instruments and music. They also believed in animism, the idea that spirits inhabit living and nonliving things.

The Khmer

In A.D. 802 **the Khmer** (kuh•MEHR) people of the mainland Southeast Asian country of Cambodia established a great Hindu-Buddhist empire with its capital at Angkor. The Khmer Empire reached its height during the A.D. 1100s, when it conquered much of the land that now includes Laos, Thailand, and Vietnam.

The empire's wealth came primarily from its rice production. Elaborate hydraulic engineering projects enabled the Khmer to irrigate and produce three crops of rice a year. With the wealth from this bountiful harvest, Khmer rulers subsidized mammoth construction projects. Adapting Indian building techniques to create their own distinctive architecture, the Khmer built hundreds of temples that glorified Hindu and Buddhist religious figures. They also constructed roads, reservoirs, irrigation canals, harbors, and hospitals. Khmer rulers were known for the splendor of their court. Borrowing from the Indian idea of kingship, Khmer rulers presented themselves as incarnations of the Hindu gods or as future Buddhas, which served to enhance their power. They bedecked themselves in elaborate finery and filled their palaces with ornate thrones and beautiful furnishings. A Chinese traveler named Zhou Dakuan (JOH DAH•KWON) described the splendor of a Khmer king in dress and manner:

> 66 His crown of gold is high and pointed like those on the heads of the mighty gods. When he does not wear his crown, he wreathes his chignon [hair gathered in a bun] in garlands of sweet-scented jasmine. His neck is hung with ropes of huge pearls (they weigh almost three pounds); his wrists and ankles are loaded with bracelets and on his fingers are rings of gold set with cats' eyes. He goes barefoot—the soles of his feet, like the palms of his hands, are rouged with a red stuff. When he appears in public he carries the Golden Sword. 99

Images of the Times

Angkor Wat

Angkor Wat (meaning "temple of the capital") was built in the A.D. 1100s by the Khmer ruler Suryavarman II. Suryavarman believed he was the incarnation of the Hindu god Vishnu.

The temple complex at Angkor Wat is encircled by a three-mile moat. The temples and monuments within the complex honored the god-king Suryavarman II and impressed visitors with their size and detailed ornamentation.

A bas–relief of the Bayon depicts a battle between the Khmer and the Chams.

Seen through a doorway, the pavilion and the central sanctuary reveal a five-headed Naga serpent.

During the A.D. 1100s, under the rule of King **Suryavarman** (soor•yah•VAHR•mahn) **II**, the Khmer kingdom reached the height of its power. Having expanded Cambodia by conquest to include parts of areas known today as Laos, Vietnam, and Thailand, the king decided to glorify both the Hindu god Vishnu and himself. He ordered the construction of **Angkor Wat**, a temple complex covering nearly a square mile. Carvings depicting the Hindu gods cover the walls of Angkor Wat, and, at the center of the complex, the sanctuary stands 130 feet (40 m) high. Angkor Wat also was used as an astronomical observatory.

The Khmer king poured so much of the empire's wealth into building Angkor Wat, however, that he severely weakened the kingdom. This excess, along with rebellions against Khmer rule and infighting between members of the royal family, further crippled the empire. In A.D. 1431 the Thai, a neighboring Southeast Asian people, captured the capital city of Angkor, bringing an end to Khmer rule there.

Vietnam

East of Cambodia and south of China lies the area of present-day Vietnam. Because of Vietnam's proximity to China and because the Chinese dominated Vietnam for more than 1,000 years, Vietnam's culture in some ways came to resemble that of China.

The Vietnamese absorbed elements of Chinese belief systems such as Confucianism, Daoism, and Buddhism. The Vietnamese also adopted Chinese forms of writing and government. Just as in China, Vietnamese officials were selected through civil service exams based on Confucian principles.

The Vietnamese retained many of their own traditions, however. They adopted Chinese religions and beliefs, but they continued to believe in animism. The Vietnamese built a *dinh*, or spirit house, in each village. This tiny house served as the home for the guardian spirit of a village. The Vietnamese wore their hair long and tattooed their skin. They wrote and spoke their own Vietnamese

A stone bas–relief of elephant and gods helps tell the story of the ancient Khmer civilization.

REFLECTING ON THE TIMES

1. What values of the Khmer are reflected in these images?
2. How did Suryavarman attempt to impress upon visitors that he was an incarnation of Vishnu?

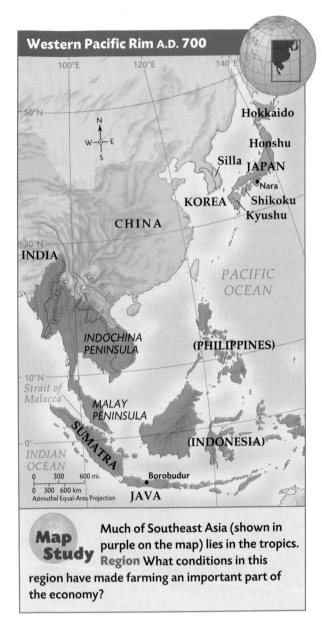

100°E   120°E   140°E

50°N

Hokkaido

Honshu

Silla   JAPAN
•Nara
KOREA   Shikoku
Kyushu
CHINA

30°N

INDIA

Red River

PACIFIC
OCEAN

Irrawaddy

Mekong River

INDOCHINA
PENINSULA
(PHILIPPINES)

10°N
Strait of
Malacca

MALAY
PENINSULA

SUMATRA

0°
INDIAN
OCEAN

(INDONESIA)

0   300   600 mi.

Borobudur

0 300 600 km
Azimuthal Equal-Area Projection   JAVA

Map Study   Much of Southeast Asia (shown in purple on the map) lies in the tropics. **Region** What conditions in this region have made farming an important part of the economy?

language, although in writing it they used Chinese characters. Even though the Chinese controlled Vietnam almost continuously from about 200 B.C. to A.D. 939, the Vietnamese fought hard to retain—and then to regain—their independence.

> The Viets [Vietnamese] were very difficult to defeat. They did not come out to fight, but hid in their familiar mountains and used the jungle like a weapon. As a result, neither side could win.... The Viets would raid suddenly, rob and get away fast, so that just as our army obtained its supplies from the home base, the Viets obtained theirs from our army.
>
> —Chinese general, c. 200 B.C.

In A.D. 39 two Vietnamese sisters, **Trung Trak** and **Trung Nhi**, clad in armor and riding atop elephants, led a successful revolt against the Chinese. For two years Vietnam was independent of China. Then the Chinese returned in greater numbers and defeated the Vietnamese. Rather than surrender to the Chinese, the Trung sisters are said to have drowned themselves in a river.

During the confusion after the overthrow of the Tang dynasty, the Vietnamese took advantage of China's disunity to revolt again. The Chinese sent a fleet of warships to Vietnam to try to subdue the rebels. In A.D. 938, however, under the leadership of **Ngo Quyen** (noo chu•YEHN), the Vietnamese defeated the warships in the Battle of the Bach Dang River. Although Emperor Tai Cong countered this defeat by launching an invasion of Vietnam, the Vietnamese date their independence from the battle, because Tai Cong's invasion failed.

After the Song dynasty gained control of China, the Song emperor threatened the Vietnamese with invasion. To keep peace with China, the Vietnamese agreed to send tribute—gifts—to the Chinese emperor. In return, China agreed not to invade Vietnam. From then on, the Vietnamese ruler called himself emperor at home, but in his messages to the Chinese court he referred to himself merely as a king.

Myanmar

The westernmost area of mainland Southeast Asia today includes the country of Myanmar (Burma). The first peoples to extensively settle most of present-day Myanmar were the Mons and the Tibeto-Burmans. From 200 B.C. to A.D. 100, these two groups gradually occupied different parts of the country. The Mons established villages in southern Burma, while the Tibeto-Burmans lived along the Irrawaddy (IHR•uh•WAH•dee) River in the northern part of the country. Although they developed their own traditions, the Mons and the Tibeto-Burmans accepted Buddhism and other aspects of Indian culture from visiting South Asian sailors and traders.

During the A.D. 500s, the Tibeto-Burmans became the dominant group and pushed the Mons southward. In A.D. 849 they set up a capital city called **Pagan** (pah•GAHN), which eventually became a center of Buddhist learning and culture. By the A.D. 1200s, skilled architects had transformed Pagan from a small settlement into a city of elaborate Buddhist temples and monasteries.

During the A.D. 1200s, the Mongol armies of Kublai Khan captured Pagan and ended its glory. To escape Mongol rule, many Burmans moved into the southern part of Myanmar. There they founded fortified towns along the rivers between their ruined capital and the Andaman Sea. Although Burman culture was preserved, a united kingdom did not arise again in Myanmar until the A.D. 1500s.

The Thai

More than four out of every five people who live in the Southeast Asian country of Thailand today belong to the ethnic group called Thai. They are descendants of people who began migrating south from China about A.D. 700. About A.D. 1238 the Thai established their first kingdom at **Sukhothai** (SOO•kah•TY) in the north-central part of the country.

Sukhothai

The Sukhothai kingdom lasted only about 100 years, but it was known for its wise leaders. The kingdom's greatest monarch, King **Ramkhamhaeng** (rahm•KAHM•hong), ruled from A.D. 1275 to A.D. 1317. He made Sukhothai into a center of learning and the arts. During Ramkhamhaeng's reign, the Thai developed an alphabet and writing system based on the Khmer script. Artisans from China taught the making of porcelain, and Buddhist monks from South Asia won most of the Thai people to Buddhism. Beautiful Buddhist temples, with many levels of roofs, rose gracefully above the skyline of Sukhothai. Even during Ramkhamhaeng's lifetime, the Thai saw his reign as a golden age. A stone pillar erected in A.D. 1292 and still standing has the following words engraved on it:

66 This Sukhothai is good. In the water there are fish. In the fields there is rice. The king does not levy a [tax] on his people.... Who wants to trade in elephants, trades. Who wants to trade in horses, trades. Who wants to trade in gold and silver, trades.... 99

Ayutthaya

In A.D. 1350 a prince named Ramathibodi (rah•MAH•thee•BOH•dee) overthrew the last Sukhothai ruler and founded a new kingdom known as **Ayutthaya** (ah•YOO•thy•yuh). He set up his capital south of Sukhothai and up the Chao Phraya River (chow PRY•uh) from where Bangkok, the present Thai capital, is today.

Visualizing History Wat Mahathat, an ancient Buddhist temple now restored, is in Sukhothai Historic Park, which was opened to the public in 1980. *What was accomplished in Sukhothai's golden age?*

The Ayutthaya kingdom lasted for about 400 years, with a succession of 33 kings. At its height, it held control over large areas of Southeast Asia, including parts of Myanmar and the Malay Peninsula. Like Sukhothai, Ayutthaya was an important center of Buddhist learning and culture. Economically prosperous, Ayutthaya carried on trade in teakwood, salt, spices, and hides with China and neighboring Asian kingdoms.

Seafaring Kingdoms

Many kingdoms in early Southeast Asia developed around strategic ports. The Indonesian islands became a crossroads in the expanding international trade that stretched from the Arabian Peninsula to China. Merchants of many lands— Arabs, Chinese, Indians, and Persians—traded such products as porcelain, textiles, and silk for Southeast Asian spices and valuable woods.

The Srivijaya (SHREE•vih•JAY•uh) Empire arose on the islands of Java and Sumatra in present-day Indonesia. Lasting from about A.D. 600 to A.D. 1100, the Srivijaya Empire was one of the region's

The Hindu temple of Pura Ulun Danau on Lake Bratan in the Central Mountains of Bali has a typical thatched roof. *How is Bali's religious heritage different from that of the rest of Indonesia?*

great seafaring powers. It controlled shipping along the Strait of Malacca that separates Sumatra from the Malay Peninsula. By the end of the A.D. 1100s, Srivijaya was reduced to a small kingdom, and the Majapahit (mah•jah•PAH•heet) kingdom began to dominate the Indonesian islands.

From the A.D. 400s to the A.D. 1400s, Buddhism and Hinduism were the dominant religious influences that affected maritime Southeast Asian life. During the early A.D. 1200s Muslim traders from the Arabian Peninsula and India brought Islam to the peoples of the Malay Peninsula and Indonesia.

The first major center of Islam in Southeast Asia was **Melaka**, a port kingdom on the southwestern coast of the Malay Peninsula.

From Melaka, Islam spread throughout the Indonesian islands. The only island to remain outside of Muslim influence was Bali, which has kept its Hindu religion and culture to the present day.

During the A.D. 1500s, a number of Muslim trading kingdoms competed for control of the Indonesian islands. European explorers, beginning with the Portuguese in A.D. 1511, gradually won control by setting local rulers against each other.

SECTION 3 REVIEW

Recall
1. **Define** archipelago, animism.
2. **Identify** the Khmer, Suryavarman II, Trung Trak, Trung Nhi, Ngo Quyen, Ramkhamhaeng.
3. **Locate** mainland Southeast Asia on the map on page 354.

Why would the mainland, and not the Indonesian and Philippine archipelagos, be more likely to come under the influence of India and China?

Critical Thinking
4. **Synthesizing Information** How might Buddhism or

Confucianism complement a belief in animism?

Understanding Themes
5. **Cultural Diffusion** What were some of the ways in which the cultures of China and India influenced the peoples of Southeast Asia?

Making Generalizations

Have you heard statements such as "Only tall people play basketball well" or "Dogs make better pets than cats"? Do you consider the validity of such statements? Or do you accept them at face value?

Learning the Skill

These statements, called generalizations, are broad statements about a topic. To be valid, a generalization must be based on accurate information. Let's examine the generalization "Only tall people play basketball well." Is this accurate? We can find many examples of tall basketball players. However, there are also many shorter players who excel at this sport.

In this case, we began with a generalization and looked for facts to support or disprove it. In other cases, you will make a generalization from a group of facts about a topic. To make a valid generalization, first collect information relevant to the topic. This information must be accurate facts, not opinions.

Suppose that you want to make a generalization about the relative danger of air and automobile travel. First, you would collect accident statistics involving airplanes and cars. Then classify the information into categories. Look for relationships between these categories. For example, you might put the airplane and automobile statistics in separate categories. You might also categorize the number of accidents and the number of fatalities. Finally, make a generalization that is consistent with most of the information.

Practicing the Skill

Read the passage about literature in the Tang dynasty and answer the questions that follow.

❝ Xuanzang welcomed artists to his splendid court…. Two of China's greatest poets, Duo Fu and Li Bo, produced their works in Xuanzang's court. Scholars compiled encyclopedias, dictionaries, and official histories of China. Writers popularized stories about ghosts, crime, and love. And while European monks were still slowly and laboriously copying texts by hand, Chinese Buddhist monks invented the more efficient technique of block printing. ❞

1. What facts about literature in the Tang dynasty are presented?
2. Organize these facts into categories.
3. How does the invention of block printing relate to the other facts?
4. What generalization can you make about literature during the Tang dynasty?

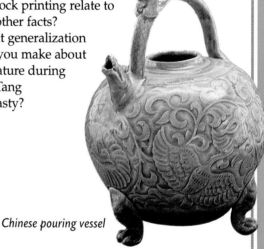

Chinese pouring vessel

Applying the Skill

Review the information in the chapter about religion in China, Cambodia, Vietnam, Korea, and Japan. Write a generalization about religion in East and Southeast Asia. Then support your generalization with at least five facts.

For More Practice

Turn to the Skill Practice in the Chapter Review on page 371 for more practice in making generalizations.

c. A.D. 400 Yamato clan founds Japanese imperial dynasty.

A.D. 668 The Silla kingdom conquers all of Korea.

A.D. 1274 Mongols make first attempt to invade Japan.

A.D. 1336 The Ashikaga family rules in Japan.

Section 4

Korea and Japan

Setting the Scene

▶ **Terms to Define**
   shamanism, shogun, shogunate, samurai, daimyo

▶ **People to Meet**
   Sejong, Yi-Sun-shin, Prince Shotoku, Lady Shikibu Murasaki, Yoritomo Minamoto

▶ **Places to Locate**
   Heian (Kyoto)

Find Out How did the Koreans and the Japanese accept China's culture?

The Storyteller

Zeami Motokiyo was adamant as he lectured his students. "Actors are not thoughtless mimics incapable of intellectualism or philosophy. We seek excellence, as do courtiers and men of letters." Motokiyo had been developing a new form of drama, the Noh play, that had uplifting stories and moral lessons, aspects that appealed to the educated upper classes. "Actors must always bear in mind the correct balance between mental and physical actions. An actor, using his intelligence, will make his presentation seem beautiful." Motokiyo wanted his actors to think as well as to rehearse.

—adapted from *Sources of Japanese Tradition*, Ryusaku Tsunoda, reprinted in *Sources of World History*, Volume 1, edited by Mark A. Kishlansky, 1994

Noh theater mask

Like the nations of Southeast Asia, Korea and Japan adopted elements of Chinese culture. But also like these other nations, they retained their own rich traditions.

Korea

A glance at Korea on the map on page 354 will reveal why a Korean proverb describes the country as "a shrimp between whales." Korea forms a peninsula on the east coast of Asia, extending south toward the western tip of Japan. Thus, it acts as a bridge between its two neighbors, China and Japan.

Early History

By legend, the Koreans claim descent from Tangun, the son of a bear and a god who supposedly founded the first Korean kingdom 5,000 years ago. Historians believe that the first Korean people were immigrants from northern Asia. These settlers lived in villages, grew rice, and made tools and other implements of bronze. They were animists who practiced shamanism, a belief that good and evil spirits inhabit both living and nonliving things. Shamans, or priests, interceded between the spirit world and humans.

In 109 B.C. China first invaded Korea, putting Korea under the control of the Han dynasty. From 109 B.C. until the fall of the Han dynasty in A.D. 220, Korea was dominated by China. But after the fall of the Han dynasty, Koreans regained control of their peninsula and, by A.D. 313, eventually formed three kingdoms—Silla, Paekche (pah•EHK•chee), and Koguryo. During the Three Kingdoms period, from A.D. 313 to A.D. 668, the Koreans adopted many elements of Chinese culture. Among these were Confucianism, Buddhism, calligraphy, and ideas about government.

Koreans also used Chinese knowledge of arts and sciences to make their own unique creations. For example, in the A.D. 300s, Koguryo artists produced mammoth cave art murals. In Silla, Queen Sondok built an astronomical observatory that still stands today and is the oldest observatory in Asia.

In A.D. 668 the kingdom of Silla conquered all of Korea, ushering in a period of peace, prosperity, and creativity. Korean potters produced superb porcelain decorated with flower designs. Koreans also created a unique mask dance that expressed sentiments of shamanism and Buddhism, which had been adopted as the state religion in A.D. 528. Over a 16-year period, Korean scholars compiled the *Tripitaka Koreana*, the largest collection of Buddhist scriptures in the world today. The *Tripitaka* has 81,258 large wooden printing plates.

The Yi Dynasty

In A.D. 1392 a dynasty called the Yi came to power in Korea. The Yi called their kingdom Choson and built Hanyang—today the city of Seoul—as their capital. They opened schools to teach Chinese classics to civil service candidates and made neo-Confucianism the state doctrine.

The adoption of Korean neo-Confucianism deeply affected people's roles and relationships. According to Korean Confucian doctrine, the eldest son in each family was bound by duty to serve his parents until their death. Korean women—who had been accorded high status under shamanism and Buddhism—were given much lower standing under Korean Confucianism. In fact, women from the higher ranks of society had to stay indoors until nightfall, when a great bell signaled the closing of the city gates. Even then, to go out they had to obtain permission from their husbands.

One of the greatest Yi rulers, King **Sejong**, had two significant accomplishments. He ordered bronze instruments to be used in measuring rain. As a result, Korea now has the oldest record of rainfall in the world. He and his advisers made a greater contribution by creating simplified writing to spread literacy. Together they devised *hangul*, an alphabet that uses 14 consonants and 10 vowels to represent Korean sounds. Although scholars continued to write with Chinese characters after the invention of *hangul*, writers began using *hangul* to transcribe folk tales and popular literature.

Although the Japanese tried to capture Korea in A.D. 1592, the Yi dynasty managed to successfully rebuff the Japanese invaders, mainly because of an invention created by Korea's Admiral **Yi-Sun-shin**. The admiral's ironclad warships, or "turtle ships," devastated the Japanese fleet. The Koreans won the war. However, in the years that followed, they increasingly avoided contact with the outside world and isolated themselves so totally that Korea became known as the Hermit Kingdom.

Japan

Just 110 miles (204 km) east of Korea lies the Japanese archipelago. As the map on page 354 shows, Japan consists of four large islands—Honshu, Shikoku, Kyushu, and Hokkaido—and many smaller ones.

Visualizing History Shown here is the world's oldest astronomical observatory in Asia. It was built at Silla, Korea, from 365 stones. *How much territory did the kingdom of Silla hold by A.D. 668?*

Mount Fuji and Lake Ashi at Hakone, Japan. *How did the physical beauty of the land affect Japanese art?*

Island Geography

Because of its island geography, Japanese culture formed mostly in isolation from mainland Asian cultures, except for that of China. Although the Japanese borrowed from Chinese civilization, their customs and traditions were different from those of most other Asian peoples.

The geography of these islands influenced the formation of Japanese culture in other ways as well. Because much of the land is mountainous—less than 20 percent of it is suitable for farming—the Japanese learned to get most of their food from the sea. They also learned to rely on the sea for protection from invaders—being a natural barrier to invasion from the mainland—and yet to regard it as a route of transport between the islands. The physical beauty of the land inspired deep reverence for nature in works by many Japanese painters and poets. Because these islands are located in an area where earthquakes, typhoons, floods, and volcanic eruptions are frequent, the Japanese long ago created a myth that helped to explain the stormy weather there.

Creation Myth

An ancient Japanese creation myth is the oldest explanation for the origins of Japan, its turbulent weather, and its first emperor. According to the myth, brother and sister gods Izanagi and Izanami dipped a spear into the churning sea. When they pulled it out, the drops of brine that fell upon the water's surface became the islands of Japan. The two gods then created the sun goddess Amaterasu, and because they loved her best of all their children, they sent her to heaven to rule over the world. Next they created Tsuki-yumi, the moon god, and Susanowo, the storm god, to be her companions.

Amaterasu gave life to everything around her. But Susanowo, who had a fierce temper, ruined his sister's rice crop and so frightened her that she hid in a cave. Without her in heaven, the world became dark. The other gods placed a jewel and a mirror on a tree outside the cave to coax Amaterasu back outside. When she came out and told them why she had hidden, the other gods banished Susanowo to the earth.

According to the myth, Susanowo's descendants were the first inhabitants of Japan. Amaterasu sent her grandson, Ninigi, to govern these descendants on the island of Honshu. So that all would acknowledge his divine power, she sent with him her mirror, her jewel, and a great sword. According to legend, Ninigi's grandson, Jimmu, conquered the rest of Susanowo's descendants in 660 B.C., becoming the first emperor of Japan.

By tradition, each successive emperor has received Amaterasu's three gifts: a mirror, a jewel, and a sword. Also by tradition, each emperor—until Hirohito—has claimed to be Amaterasu's descendant. In 1945, after the Japanese defeat in

World War II, Emperor Hirohito announced that he did not possess divine status.

Early Inhabitants

Among the first people to inhabit the Japanese islands were hunter-gatherers who came there from the mainland more than 10,000 years ago. These people had developed the technology to make pottery but not to make bronze or iron. When Koreans and others from mainland Asia invaded Japan during the 200s B.C. and 100s B.C., they were easily able to defeat the early inhabitants by using iron and bronze weapons.

The invaders introduced the islanders to agricultural methods, such as how to grow rice in flooded paddies. Heavy summer rains in Japan made it the ideal place to grow rice, which soon became Japan's most important crop.

Between A.D. 200 and A.D. 300, another influx of mainlanders came to Japan. According to scholars, these armor-clad warriors who fought on horseback were probably the ancestors of the aristocratic warriors and imperial family of Japan referred to in the creation myth.

In early Japan, though, even before there was an emperor or an imperial family, separate clans ruled their own regions. Clan members practiced a form of animism called Shinto, meaning "the way of the gods." Each clan included a group of families descended from a common ancestor, often said to have been an animal or a god. The clan worshiped this ancestor as its special *kami*, or spirit. Practitioners of Shinto believed that *kami* dwelled within people, animals, and even nonliving objects such as rocks and streams. To honor this *kami*—and the *kami* of their ancestors—they held festivals and rituals. Often these ceremonies were conducted by the chief of the clan, who acted as both military leader and priest.

The Yamato Clan

By about A.D. 400, the military skill and prestige of the Yamato clan, which claimed descent from Amaterasu, enabled it to extend a loose rule over most of Japan. Although other clans continued to rule their own lands, they owed their loyalty to the Yamato chief. In effect, he became the emperor.

Initially, the emperor had a great deal of political power. By the A.D. mid-500s, however, the emperor had become more of a ceremonial figure who carried out religious rituals. The real political power was held by the members of the Soga

Samurai Arts

Kiyomatsu, a samurai hero

In the A.D. 1100s the rise of military rule in Japan brought in a new style of art. Supported by daimyo and samurai, artists created paintings highlighting the skill and bravery of soldiers. These works show warriors in richly patterned clothing, riding magnificent horses and wielding long swords. The expressions of the riders and their horses often convey wild—but controlled—emotions.

Today in Japan the samurai artistic tradition is most prominent in movies and television. Many popular Japanese films are samurai tales set in feudal times and filled with action and adventure. Akira Kurosawa, one of the world's renowned directors, has made a number of samurai movies. His film *The Hidden Fortress*—about a brave general who leads an endangered princess to safety—helped inspire American director George Lucas to create the epic film *Star Wars*.

Linking Past and Present   ACTIVITY

Study a painting with a samurai theme. What values are expressed in the painting? You might want to view the films *The Hidden Fortress* and *Star Wars*. In what ways do you think these films reflect samurai values? In what ways do you think they do not?

family. The emperors kept their position as heads of Japan because people believed that only they could intercede with the gods. But the Soga family controlled the country.

Chinese Influences

In A.D. 552 a Korean king sent a statue of the Buddha and some Buddhist texts to the Japanese court. The king wrote, "This religion is the most excellent of all teachings" and suggested that the emperor make Buddhism the national religion. Buddhism had come to Korea from China, and its introduction to Japan made the Japanese open to Chinese culture. This curiosity about China was especially strong among Japan's nobles and scholars.

Through a kind of cultural exchange program that lasted four centuries, the Japanese learned much from the Chinese. Not only did they learn about the teachings of the Buddha, they also learned a great deal about Chinese art, medicine, astronomy, and philosophy. They incorporated much of this knowledge into Japanese culture. For instance, the Japanese adopted the Chinese characters for writing to create their own writing system.

Prince Shotoku was responsible for much of this cultural exchange. When he became the leading court official in A.D. 593, he instituted programs that encouraged further learning from Chinese civilization. He ordered the construction of Buddhist monasteries and temples and sent officials and students to China to study. When Shotoku heard about the Chinese Confucian ideas of government, he wrote a constitution for Japan in which he set forth general principles that explained how government officials should act.

After Shotoku's death, the Fujiwara family seized power in the name of the emperor and began to urge him to pattern the government more closely on that of China. China had a strong central government at that time.

In A.D. 646 government officials instituted the Taika reforms, or "Great Change." These reforms proclaimed that all the land was the property of the emperor rather than clan leaders. Clan leaders could oversee the peasants working the land, but they could no longer assign them land or collect taxes from them. Instead, government officials were to allocate plots to peasants and collect part of their harvest in taxes for the emperor.

In modeling their government on China, however, the Japanese did not always adopt Chinese ways. For example, civil service examinations were never accepted; instead officials gained their posts through family ties. Also, even after the Taika reforms, much of Japan remained under the control of regional clan leaders.

The Nara Period

Greater government centralization did not take place until A.D. 710, when Japan built its first permanent capital at Nara. A smaller version of China's Changan, Nara had an imperial palace, broad streets, large public squares, rows of Chinese-style homes, and Buddhist temples.

With the completion of the colossal Todaiji Temple at Nara in A.D. 752, Buddhist fervor in Japan reached its peak. Buddhism, however, did not replace Shinto, for each religion met different needs. Shinto linked the Japanese to nature and their homeland. Buddhism promised spiritual rewards to the good. Therefore, people practiced both.

During the Nara period, the Japanese also produced their first written literature. Scribes wrote histories of ancient Japan that combined the creation myths with actual events. Other writers compiled collections of Japanese poems.

The Heian Period

In A.D. 794 the Japanese established a new capital in **Heian,** later called **Kyoto.** For more than 1,000 years, this city remained the capital of Japan.

A century after the city was founded, Japan stopped sending cultural missions to China. In the period that followed, a small group of about 3,000 Japanese aristocrats, calling themselves "dwellers among the clouds," created Heian culture.

The focus of Heian court life was the pursuit of

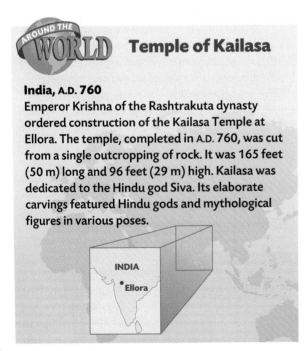

WORLD Temple of Kailasa

India, A.D. 760
Emperor Krishna of the Rashtrakuta dynasty ordered construction of the Kailasa Temple at Ellora. The temple, completed in A.D. 760, was cut from a single outcropping of rock. It was 165 feet (50 m) long and 96 feet (29 m) high. Kailasa was dedicated to the Hindu god Siva. Its elaborate carvings featured Hindu gods and mythological figures in various poses.

INDIA
• Ellora

The Lady Fujitsubo Watching Prince Genji Departing in the Moonlight by A. Hiroshige and U. Toyokuni, A.D. 1853. *What was a major theme of the Heian novel,* The Tale of Genji?

beauty. It pervaded all of life's activities, from wrapping presents to mixing perfumes and colors. People devoted hours each day to writing letters in the form of poems. Calligraphy was as important as the poem itself, for a person's handwriting was taken to be an indication of his or her character. People were even said to fall in love upon seeing each other's handwriting.

During the Heian period, women were the creators of Japan's first great prose literature. About A.D. 1010 **Lady Shikibu Murasaki** wrote *The Tale of Genji*, which some believe to be the world's first novel. The novelist chronicles the life and loves of a fictional prince named Genji. Filled with poems about the beauty of nature, *The Tale of Genji* quickly became very popular.

The Heian aristocrats were so deeply involved in their search for beauty, however, that they neglected tasks of government. Order began breaking down in the provinces. Warlike provincial leaders started running their estates as independent territories, ignoring the emperor's officials and refusing to pay taxes. Thus the Heian aristocrats eventually lost control of the empire completely.

The Way of the Warrior

As Heian power faded, two powerful court families, the Taira and the Minamoto, struggled for control. The families fought a decisive battle in A.D. 1185 in which the Taira were defeated. To **Yoritomo Minamoto**, head of the Minamoto family, the emperor then gave the title shogun, or "general," and delegated to him most of the real political and military power. While the emperor remained with his court in the capital of Kyoto carrying on ritual tasks, Yoritomo and his soldiers ran a shogunate, or military government, from Kamakura near present-day Tokyo.

The shogunate proved to be quite strong. Even though Kublai Khan tried twice to invade Japan— once in A.D. 1274 and again in A.D. 1281—he did not succeed. On the first occasion, Japanese warriors and the threat of a storm forced the Mongols to withdraw. On the second occasion, 150,000 Mongol warriors came by ship, but a typhoon arose and destroyed the fleet. The Japanese thought of the storm as the *kamikaze*, or "divine wind," and took it to be confirmation that their islands were indeed sacred.

In A.D. 1336 the Ashikaga family gained control of the shogunate. But the family failed to get control of regional warriors. Japan soon broke into individual warring states, leaving the shogun and the emperor as mere figureheads.

The powerful landowner-warriors in the countryside were called samurai. The most powerful samurai became daimyo (DY•mee•OH), or lords. Like the medieval knights of feudal Europe who pledged their loyalty to lords, samurai pledged their loyalty and military service to their daimyo. There were many samurai and many daimyo. Poor

Friends mourn the death of the Buddha in this Japanese painting.

How was Buddhism introduced to Japan?

rice farmers paid high taxes for the right to farm a daimyo's lands. In return, that daimyo provided the farmers with protection. The system in which large landholders give protection to people in exchange for their services is called feudalism. Japanese feudalism was similar to European feudalism as described in Chapter 12.

The samurai fought on horseback with bows, arrows, and steel swords. They dressed in loose-fitting armor. The samurai followed a strict code of honor called Bushido, meaning "the way of the warrior." Bushido stressed bravery, self-discipline, and loyalty. It demanded that the samurai endure suffering and defend his honor at all costs. If a samurai was dishonored or defeated, he was expected to commit suicide.

Japanese women too could be warriors. This passage from *The Tale of the Heike* describes a female Minamoto samurai:

❝ Tomoe had long black hair and a fair complexion, and her face was very lovely; moreover she was a fearless rider whom neither the fiercest horse nor the roughest ground could dismay, and so dexterously did she handle sword and bow that she was a match for a thousand warriors and fit to meet either god or devil. Many times

had she … won matchless renown in encounters with the bravest captains, and so in this last fight, when all the others had been slain or had fled, among the last seven there rode Tomoe. ❞

—*The Tale of the Heike*, A.D. 1200s

Growth of a Merchant Class

Despite the political turmoil during its feudal period, Japan developed economically at this time. Workshops on daimyo estates produced arms, armor, and iron tools. Each region began to specialize in goods such as pottery, paper, textiles, and lacquerware. Trade increased between regions.

The increasing trade led to the growth of towns around the castles of the daimyos. Merchants and artisans formed guilds to promote their interests—just as they did in medieval Europe. These guilds, called *za* in Japan, benefited their members in many ways. A *za* might pay a fee to exempt its members from paying tolls for shipping their goods. Over a long period of time, this exemption would save the members quite a bit of money.

Japanese merchants began to trade with Chinese and Korean merchants. Chinese copper coins became the chief means of exchange. The Japanese exported raw materials such as lumber, pearls, and gold, as well as finished goods such as swords and painted fans. The Japanese imported items such as medicines, books, and pictures.

Religion and the Arts

By the A.D. 1200s Buddhism had spread from the nobles to the common people. The opening words of *The Tale of the Heike* describe the Buddhist sentiments that were prevalent in Japan during its feudal period:

❝ In the sound of the bell of the Gion Temple echoes the impermanence of all things. The pale hue of the flowers of the teak tree show the truth that they who prosper must fall. The proud do not last long, but vanish like a spring-night's dream. And the mighty ones too will perish in the end, like dust before the wind. ❞

During Japan's feudal age, Buddhist teachings were simplified and gave rise to many religious groups. The new varieties of Buddhism all taught about a personal afterlife in paradise. The way to paradise, they stated, was through simple trust in the Buddha. With salvation so easily available, the influence of priests, monks, and nuns declined. For

Visualizing History Zen Buddhist monks sit in a meditation garden at Ryoanji Temple in Kyoto, Japan. *To a Zen Buddhist, what is the purpose of meditation?*

the first time, the common people began to play an important role in Buddhist life. With widespread support, Japanese Buddhist groups linked religion with patriotism. Some believed that Japanese Buddhism was the only true Buddhism and that Japan was the center of the universe.

While the common people turned to new forms of Buddhism, the samurai followed a form of Buddhism called Zen. The Japanese scholar Eisai had brought Zen to Japan from China late in the A.D. 1100s. Zen taught that the individual had to live in harmony with nature and that this harmony could be achieved through a deep religious understanding called enlightenment. The followers of Zen rejected book learning and logical thought, embracing instead bodily discipline and meditation. They believed that by meditation a student could free his mind and arrive at enlightenment.

Zen was particularly useful for warriors because it taught them to act instinctively, and thinking was a hindrance to action. Samurai could improve skills such as archery by freeing their minds from distractions to better concentrate on the object or target.

Zen also perfected art forms and rituals such as ikebana, or flower arranging, meditation gardens, and the tea ceremony. Ikebana grew out of the religious custom of placing flowers before images of the Buddha. The Zen practice of meditation gave rise to meditation gardens, consisting of carefully placed rocks surrounded by neatly raked sand.

Meditation also sparked the tea ceremony, an elegant, studied ritual for serving tea. One tea master said of the ceremony that it was intended to "cleanse the senses ... so that the mind itself is cleansed from defilements." These and other arts and rituals derived from Buddhism are still popular in Japan today.

SECTION 4 REVIEW

Recall
1. **Define** shamanism, shogun, shogunate, samurai, daimyo.
2. **Identify** Sejong, Yi-Sun-shin, Amaterasu, Jimmu, Shinto, Prince Shotuku, Taika reforms, Lady Shikibu Murasaki, Yoritomo Minamoto, Bushido.

3. **Explain** What is traditionally given to each new emperor of Japan? Why?

Critical Thinking
4. **Evaluating Information** Which would you prefer to follow, the ideals of the Heian court or the samurai code of Bushido? Why? What effects

do you think each viewpoint might have had on the people of Japan?

Understanding Themes
5. **Innovation** Identify one Chinese innovation that the Koreans or Japanese borrowed, and describe how they made it their own.

from

Four Poems

by Li Bo

*L*i Bo was born in A.D. 701 in western China. People began praising his beautiful poems even before he reached adulthood. Throughout his life he traveled extensively in China, amazing people with his ability to compose insightful, touching poems. He usually wrote about the world around him, the people he met, and the emotions he felt. By the time of his death in A.D. 762, he was regarded as one of China's greatest poets, a distinction he still holds today.

*I*n the following poem, Li Bo comments on an experience everyone faces at some time: parting with a close companion.

Taking Leave of a Friend

Blue mountains to the north of the walls,
White river winding about them;
Here we must make separation
And go out through a thousand miles
    of dead grass.

Mind like a floating wide cloud,
Sunset like the parting of old acquaintances
Who bow over their clasped hands at a distance.
Our horses neigh to each other
    as we are departing.

*T*he following poem is a favorite of many Chinese citizens who have left their homeland and settled in the United States or elsewhere.

On a Quiet Night

I saw the moonlight before my couch,
And wondered if it were not the frost
    on the ground.
I raised my head and looked out on the
    mountain moon;
I bowed my head and thought of my
    far-off home.

*L*i Bo used extensive symbolism in his writing. In the following poem, he compares life to a traveler on a journey.

Hard Is the Journey

Gold vessels of fine wines,
    thousands a gallon,
Jade dishes of rare meats,
    costing more thousands,

I lay my chopsticks down,
    no more can banquet,
And draw my sword and stare
    wildly about me:

Ice bars my way to cross
    the Yellow River,
Snows from dark skies to climb
    the T'ai-hang Mountains!

At peace I drop a hook
    into a brooklet,
At once I'm in a boat
    but sailing sunward …

    (Hard is the Journey,
    Hard is the Journey,
    So many turnings,
    And now where am I?)

So when a breeze breaks waves,
    bringing fair weather,
I set a cloud for sails,
    cross the blue oceans!

Visualizing History *Dawn Over Elixir Terrace* **depicts a tranquil river scene.** *How do the river and mountains present obstacles to the traveler in the poem?*

*S*ince Li Bo spent much of his time traveling, he was often separated from his family. He wrote and sent the following poem to his children.

Letter to His Two Small Children Staying in Eastern Lu at Wen Yang Village Under Turtle Mountain

Here in Wu Land mulberry leaves are green,
Silkworms in Wu have now had three sleeps:

My family, left in Eastern Lu,
Oh, to sow now Turtle-shaded fields,
Do the Spring things I can never join,
Sailing Yangtse always on my own—

Let the South Wind blow you back my heart,
Fly and land it in the Tavern court
Where, to the East, there are sprays and leaves
Of one peach-tree, sweeping the blue mist;

History & Art *Landscape of the Four Seasons* by **Shen Shih-Ch'ung.** *In what season did Li Bo write the above poem?*

Visualizing History This winter scene is a detail from the Ming dynasty painting *Landscape of the Four Seasons.* How many winters have passed since the author was at home?

This is the tree I myself put in
When I left you, nearly three years past;
A peach-tree now, level with the eaves,
And I sailing cannot yet turn home!

Pretty daughter, P'ing-yang is your name,
Breaking blossom, there beside my tree,
Breaking blossom, you cannot see me
And your tears flow like the running stream;

And little son, Po-ch'in you are called,
Your big sister's shoulder you must reach
When you come there underneath my peach,
Oh, to pat and pet you too, my child!

I dreamt like this till my wits went wild,
By such yearning daily burned within;
So tore some silk, wrote this distant pang
From me to you living at Wen Yang....

RESPONDING TO LITERATURE

1. In "On a Quiet Night," why is the person unhappy?
2. In "Hard Is the Journey," what do the gold vessels and jade dishes symbolize?
3. What types of images did Li Bo use in each of his poems included here?
4. **Supporting an Opinion** Which poem do you like best? Explain why.

Connections Across Time

Historical Significance Contacts among the civilizations of Asia led to an exchange of ideas and practices. The Chinese acquired tea and faster-growing rice plants from the Southeast Asians. The Mongols became an even more powerful fighting force once they learned to use Chinese gunpowder. The Khmer people of Cambodia acquired architectural skills from India and built huge temples. Japan and Korea adopted features of China's system of government.

Today, because of technological advances, cultural diffusion occurs on a global scale. Thus, Westerners learn a great deal from the peoples of Asia, and Asians, likewise, benefit from their encounters with Westerners.

Using Key Terms

Write the key term that completes each sentence. Then write a sentence for each term not chosen.

a. yurts
b. *yasa*
c. daimyo
d. meritocracy
e. samurai
f. shamanism
g. shogun
h. shogunate
i. archipelago
j. mandarins
k. clans

1. The Mongol warrior Temujin, later known as Genghis Khan, developed a code of law known as the _____.
2. The early Koreans practiced _____, a belief that priests could intercede between humans and spirits.
3. The Japanese _____ consists of four large islands and many smaller ones.
4. Because of its examination system, the Chinese government claimed that it was a _____, or a system in which people are chosen and promoted for their talents and performance.
5. In return for protection, Japanese farmers farmed the lands of powerful landowner-warriors known as _____.

Technology Activity

Creating a Multimedia Presentation Search a computerized card catalog or the Internet to locate information about Genghis Khan. Using multimedia tools, create a presentation about the reign of Genghis Khan. Incorporate images from the Internet in your presentation. Cite all electronic resources used.

Using Your History Journal

Choose one country from your map of East Asia. Draw that country on a separate sheet of paper. From the section of Chapter 14 that provides information on your chosen country, list 5 to 10 important facts or events beside your map.

Reviewing Facts

1. **History** Identify Tai Cong and name his important political achievements.
2. **Science/Culture** List the scientific and artistic accomplishments of the Song dynasty.
3. **History** Explain the significance of the Battle of the Bach Dang River to the Vietnamese.
4. **History** Discuss the importance of the *kamikaze*, the "divine wind," in early Japanese history.
5. **Culture** Describe examples of female leadership in early East and South Asia.

Critical Thinking

1. **Apply** How did civil service examinations aid in the development of a strong central government in China?
2. **Analyze** Why did China's economy expand during Song rule?
3. **Synthesize** Do you think the strengths of Mongol society would benefit a nation today? Why or why not?
4. **Evaluate** In what ways did Chinese innovations change the cultures of Korea and Japan?

5. Analyze Japanese gardens show a love for nature and order. How did the geography of the islands influence Japanese arts and gardening?

Japanese garden

Linking Past and Present

1. How has Japan's possession of Heian and samurai values helped it to become a world leader in industry today?
2. Confucianism spread to many East and South Asian countries. How do Confucian values benefit these countries today?

Skill Practice

Read the passage below and answer the questions that follow.

❝ Indian traders and scholars introduced to Southeast Asia the Sanskrit language and the religions of Hinduism and Buddhism. Indian epics such as the *Ramayana* were interwoven with Southeast Asian stories and legends. Indian architecture, law codes, and political ideas also deeply influenced the cultures of the region.... In A.D. 802 the Khmer people of Cambodia established a great Hindu-Buddhist empire.... Borrowing the Indian idea of kingship, Khmer rulers presented themselves as incarnations of the Hindu gods or as future Buddhas.... ❞

1. What facts are presented about India's influence on Southeast Asia in general?
2. What generalization can you make based on these facts?

Understanding Themes

1. **Movement** The Mongols were able to conquer a vast territory, but their empire survived for a relatively short time. Provide a hypothesis that might explain this situation.
2. **Uniformity** What elements of Chinese society remained the same during the Tang, Song, and Yuan dynasties? What effect did this stability have on China's culture?
3. **Cultural Diffusion** What are some of the similarities between Southeast Asian cultures and Chinese culture?
4. **Innovation** Identify one Chinese discovery and explain some of the ways in which it has been used by the Chinese and others. Name things in our culture that derive from this innovation.

Geography in History

1. **Place** Refer to the map below. What river formed a natural border between China and the kingdom of Koguryo?
2. **Region** How did geography contribute to Korea's becoming known as the Hermit Kingdom?

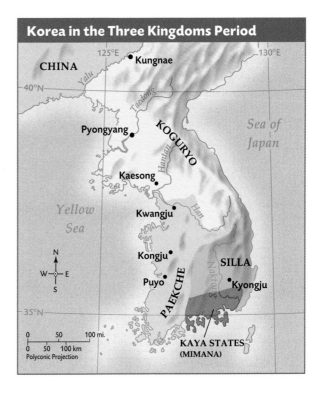

Korea in the Three Kingdoms Period

The Americas

Chapter Themes

▶ **Relation to Environment** Native Americans in North America adapt to a variety of environments. *Section 1*

▶ **Innovation** The Mesoamerican civilizations develop an understanding of astronomy and mathematics. *Section 2*

▶ **Change** The Aztec and the Inca conquer neighboring territories and establish powerful empires in Mexico and South America. *Section 3*

The Storyteller

In the Andes Mountains of South America, an Inca boy begs to hear how the Inca came to be. "The sun was unhappy with the world," the storyteller begins, "for he saw people living like wild beasts among the mountains and cliffs. He decided to send his son and daughter to teach them to adore the sun as their god. He gave special instructions: 'Each day that passes I go around all the world … to satisfy [men's] needs. Follow my example: Do unto all of them as a merciful father would do unto his well-beloved children; for I have sent you on earth for the good of men, that they might cease to live like wild animals.'"

This legend describes what the Inca people believed about the beginnings of their empire. Close to nature and deeply religious, the Inca were only one of a number of Native American groups who built powerful civilizations in the Americas.

Historical Significance

What were the achievements of Native Americans? How did Native American traditions shape the development of the Americas?

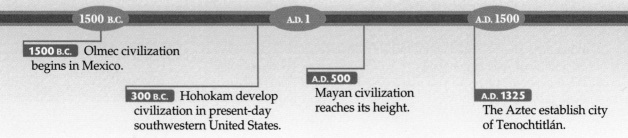

1500 B.C.		A.D. 1		A.D. 1500

1500 B.C. Olmec civilization begins in Mexico.

300 B.C. Hohokam develop civilization in present-day southwestern United States.

A.D. 500 Mayan civilization reaches its height.

A.D. 1325 The Aztec establish city of Tenochtitlán.

 Aztec turquoise mosaic of double-headed serpent, Mexico

Your History Journal

Using dates from section time lines and each section narrative, build a time line of important dates in Native American civilizations between 1500 B.C. and A.D. 1500.

5000 B.C.	2500 B.C.	A.D. 1	A.D. 2500

c. 5000 B.C. Hunter-gatherers first plant maize in the highlands of Mexico.

c. 3000 B.C. Native Americans make use of stone axes and digging sticks for farming.

c. A.D. 1500 Eastern Woodland peoples form the Iroquois League.

Section 1

The Early Americas

Setting the Scene

▶ **Terms to Define**
maize, weir, potlatch, confederation

▶ **People to Meet**
the Kwakiutl, the Hohokam, the Pueblo, the Apache, the Navajo, the Plains peoples, Mound Builders

▶ **Places to Locate**
Mexico, Great Plains

Find Out How did early Native Americans make use of their environment?

The Storyteller

A Navajo tale describes the origin of the twelve months of the year: First Man and First Woman built a hogan in which to live. Turquoise Boy and White Shell Girl came from the underworld to live with them. "It is not unwise that we plan for the time to come, how we shall live," said First Man. First Woman and First Man whispered together during many nights. They planned that there should be a sun, and day and night. Whenever Coyote, called First Angry, came to make trouble and asked them what they were doing, they told him: "Nothing whatsoever." He said, "So I see," and

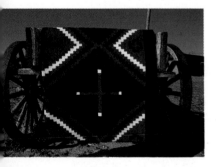

went away. After he had gone, they planned the twelve months of the year.

—adapted from *The Portable North American Indian Reader*, edited by Frederick W. Turner III, 1974

Navajo rug

When did the earliest humans come to the Americas? Until recently, archaeologists believed that humans arrived in the Western Hemisphere about 12,000 years ago. The theory was that tribes migrated from Asia to North America, following herds of bison and other game across the then-exposed land bridge that today is the Bering Strait.

New evidence, however, challenges this old theory. Archaeologists working in North America and South America have found sites that indicate the presence of humans as early as 40,000 years ago. New theories argue that humans arrived in more than one migratory wave. Some early humans may also have traveled by boat along the Pacific coast from Siberia to Alaska, then to South America.

Once in the Western Hemisphere, the peoples dispersed throughout North America and South America. As they adapted to particular environments, they developed distinct ways of life. Some remained nomadic, while others settled and developed complex civilizations.

The First Americas

Hunter-gatherers in the Americas used the resources of their environments for food, clothing, and shelter. People living along seacoasts collected mussels and snails. Those inland hunted game or fished in rivers and streams. Archaeologists have unearthed evidence of these ways of life in artifacts, such as rounded stones for grinding seeds, bone hooks for fishing, and heaps of shells at campsites.

By about 5000 B.C., a group of hunter-gatherers in a highland area of present-day **Mexico** had discovered that the seeds of maize, or corn, and other native plants could be planted and harvested, providing a reliable source of food. As this discovery spread from Mexico into the southwestern United States, groups of early people began to settle in permanent villages. About 3000 B.C. farmers made use of stone axes to clear their fields and pointed digging sticks to plant improved varieties of maize, beans, and squash.

As the food supply improved, the population of the Americas grew. By the time Europeans arrived in North America around A.D. 1500, about 30 million to 100 million Native Americans belonging to more than 2,000 different groups were inhabiting the two continents. About 15 to 20 million of these early inhabitants lived in the present-day United States and various parts of Canada.

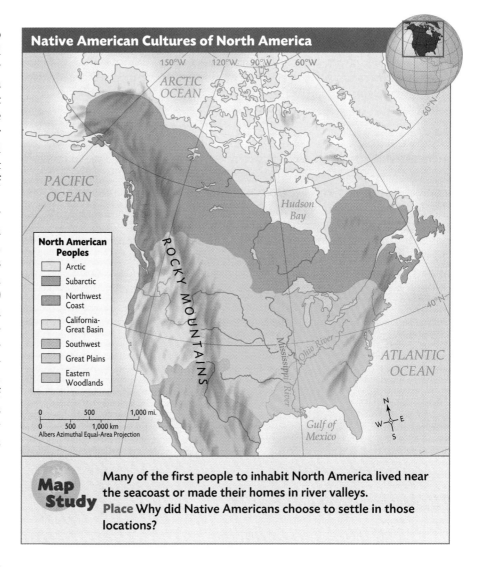

Native American Cultures of North America

North American Peoples
- Arctic
- Subarctic
- Northwest Coast
- California-Great Basin
- Southwest
- Great Plains
- Eastern Woodlands

0   500   1,000 mi.
0   500   1,000 km
Albers Azimuthal Equal-Area Projection

Map Study Many of the first people to inhabit North America lived near the seacoast or made their homes in river valleys. **Place** Why did Native Americans choose to settle in those locations?

North Americans

Much of what we know about the early people of northern North America comes from the work of archaeologists. Archaeological digs have uncovered homes, burial mounds, pottery, baskets, stone tools, and the bones of people and animals in the Arctic and Northwest, California and the Great Basin, the Southwest, the Great Plains, and the Eastern Woodlands. By studying these artifacts, archaeologists discovered that there were distinct regional differences. People who settled in a particular region developed a common culture. Gradually the arts and crafts and religious customs of each region grew to be distinct from those of other regions, a pattern historians call cultural differentiation. In each region, culture reflected the local geography and natural resources.

The Arctic and Northwest

The early people of the Arctic lived in the cold northern regions of present-day Canada and Alaska. The severe climate of this region prohibited

farming. Thus, small bands of extended families moved about, hunting and fishing. By 6500 B.C. some Arctic people were living in small villages of pit houses, covered with dome-shaped roofs of whalebone and driftwood. Villagers hunted whales, sea lions, seals, and water birds. They ate the meat and used the skins to make warm, protective clothing.

In contrast to the cold and snow of the Arctic, the thickly forested seacoast of the Pacific Northwest had a milder climate. Rainfall was plentiful, and mild winters and warm ocean currents kept rivers and bays free of ice. Like the people of the Arctic, those who settled along the Pacific Coast—**the Kwakiutl,** for example—hunted whales, fish, and other sea animals as their main source of food. Forests of the Northwest provided additional sources of food—small forest animals and acorns. After about A.D. 500 the people of the Northwest used other resources from the surrounding forests and rivers. With stone and copper woodworking tools they split cedar, fir, and redwood trees into planks to make houses and large canoes. They also developed ways to harvest salmon with fiber nets, stone-tipped spears, and elaborate wooden traps called weirs.

Society among the Kwakiutl and other Northwest peoples was organized into lineages, each of which claimed to be descended from a mythical ancestor. A lineage group lived together in a single large house and owned the right to use or display special designs, songs, ceremonies, or prized possessions, such as patterned sheets of copper. A lineage maintained exclusive use of its own fishing area and berry-picking grounds. The wealth of each lineage was displayed and given away as gifts at festive gatherings called potlatches. At a potlatch a chief might give away canoes, blankets, and other goods. In turn, guests might bring the chief deerskins and food.

To obtain items they themselves could not make, some people of the Northwest developed trading networks with people living farther south. Traders paddled redwood canoes along the coast, stopping at villages along the shore to exchange goods. Trade networks stretched from southern Alaska to northern California.

California–Great Basin

Native Americans living along the California coast enjoyed a warm climate and an abundance of food resources. Many communities lived on diets of abalone and mussels. Near San Francisco Bay, archaeologists have found evidence of this diet in heaps of discarded shells that date from 2000 B.C. In addition to shellfish, the first Californians fished for sea bass, hunted seals, and gathered berries and nuts. Having such abundant resources made food gathering easier for the people living in this region.

Like other Native Americans, they developed elaborate religious ceremonies designed to worship nature spirits believed to inhabit all of the natural world, but especially those spirits related to animals or plants used for food. The Chumash, who

Images of the Times

Native Americans

A variety of peoples have inhabited North America for thousands of years. Some mysteries of the earliest cultures have yet to be revealed.

Georgia's Etowa Mounds sheltered these two-foot high marble images of a man and a woman more than 500 years ago.

lived in the area of present-day southern California, would gather together at harvest festivals to celebrate the goodness of the earth. Villagers participated in dances and games.

Compared with those living along the coast, people living farther inland scratched their living from a harsh desert and mountain environment. Great Basin people moved about in small bands, living in windbreak shelters and eating seeds, grasshoppers, and small animals.

Southwest

People who settled in the high desert regions of present-day Arizona, New Mexico, southern Colorado and Utah, and northern Mexico had fewer resources than those who settled along the Pacific Coast. Nevertheless, the people of the Southwest adapted to their harsh environment by inventing techniques of irrigation to farm the land. For example, around 300 B.C., **the Hohokam** living in the area of present-day Arizona dug an irrigation canal 3 miles (4.8 km) long to draw the waters of the Gila and Salt Rivers onto fields planted with maize, kidney beans, and squash.

Farther north the Anasazi and their descendants, **the Pueblo**, grew maize on flat-topped hills or on the plains. They built two- or three-story dwellings of adobe, a sun-dried brick. Some of these peoples constructed their villages under ledges on the sides of cliffs to shade residents from the desert sun and to make the villages easier to defend.

Religious leaders governed these villages. In underground chambers called kivas, they held ceremonies to ensure harmony with the spiritual world. They believed that, if harmony existed, the spirits would provide rain for crops.

Another Southwest group known as **the Apache** lived in areas that were unsuitable for farming. They hunted wild birds and rabbits and gathered plants. Sometimes they raided Pueblo fields; other times they traded meat and hides with Pueblo villagers for maize and other food supplies. A neighboring people, **the Navajo**, did manage to

The **Great Serpent Mound** of the Adena culture (about 1000 B.C.), unlike other mounds, contains no graves or artifacts. The enormous serpent is about to swallow a huge oval. What does this mean? The builders left no clue.

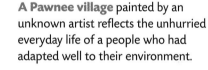

A **Pawnee village** painted by an unknown artist reflects the unhurried everyday life of a people who had adapted well to their environment.

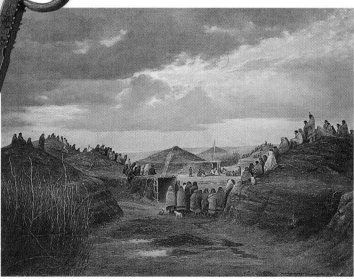

An **Iroquois condolence cane** was carved to record the attendance of chiefs at a memorial ceremony for a deceased Iroquois chief.

REFLECTING ON THE TIMES

1. How do researchers today try to discover information about early Native American cultures?
2. Why was the lifestyle of the Pawnee much different from that of the Iroquois?

377

Visualizing History In the Northwest a totem represented a bond of unity and was the symbol and protector of the group. *What does this totem reveal about Northwest Native Americans?*

one abundant resource—the great herds of bison, or buffalo, that roamed the plains. From earliest times, the Kiowa, Crow, Blackfoot, and other peoples of the plains followed the herds from one grazing ground to another. They used every part of the bison for their food, clothing, shelter, and tools.

Eastern Woodlands

Unlike the Plains peoples who depended on the bison, Native Americans of the woodlands east of the Mississippi River hunted deer, turkey, and other small game for food and clothing. Like the Plains peoples, Eastern Woodlands peoples made use of every part of the animals they killed. They ate deer meat, wore deerskin clothing, and made tools out of animal bones and antlers. Because of the warm summers, abundant rainfall, and fertile soil, the Woodlands peoples lived in farming villages and grew corn, squash, beans, and tobacco.

In the Ohio and Mississippi Valleys, groups of Native Americans known as **Mound Builders** erected large earthen mounds. Archaeologists today believe the mounds were ceremonial centers or tombs for leaders. A number of mounds were made in the shape of animals. The largest ceremonial center was Cahokia, in present-day Illinois. It had about 40,000 people and was probably a political and commercial as well as a religious settlement.

Native Americans living in the northeastern forests cleared the land and built fenced-in villages of long houses, made of poles covered with tree bark. While the women farmed, the men hunted, warred, and governed. During the A.D. 1500s, five groups allied to form the Iroquois League—a confederation, or loose union. A council of male representatives from each group discussed and resolved disputes, but every clan had an elderly female known as a "clan mother," who named and deposed chiefs and council members. When Europeans invaded Native American land, they met strong resistance from the Iroquois League.

raise a breed of sheep that could live on the sparse desert vegetation.

Great Plains

In contrast to the sparse Southwestern environment, vast grasslands covered the **Great Plains**, stretching from the Rocky Mountains to the Mississippi River. This environment provided a different challenge for the early people who inhabited the region. Native Americans adapting to life on the plains needed a reliable source of food. Farming in the region was difficult, as the thick plains sod was hard to plow. Moreover, maize needs more water than is naturally available on most parts of the Great Plains.

Although some farming was done along streams, most of **the Plains peoples** depended on

---

SECTION 1 REVIEW

Recall
1. **Define** maize, weir, potlatch, confederation.
2. **Identify** the Kwakiutl, the Hohokam, the Pueblo, the Apache, the Navajo, the Plains peoples, Mound Builders, Iroquois League.

3. **Describe** farming methods developed by early Native Americans of Mexico and the Southwest.

Critical Thinking
4. **Analyzing Information** Compare the structure of the Iroquois League with that of

the United States government.

Understanding Themes
5. **Relation to Environment** How did Native American peoples within the seven regions of North America depend on their environment and natural resources?

Section 2

Early Mesoamerican Cultures

Setting the Scene

▶ **Terms to Define**
  jaguar, slash-and-burn farming, obsidian

▶ **People to Meet**
  the Olmec, the Maya, the Teotihuacános, the Toltec

▶ **Places to Locate**
  San Lorenzo, La Venta, Yucatán Peninsula, Teotihuacán, Tula

 **Find Out** How did trade encourage the growth of city-states and kingdoms in the areas of present-day Mexico and Central America?

The Storyteller

How did the world begin? According to Mayan myth, "All was in suspense, all calm, in silence; all motionless, still.... There was nothing standing; only the calm water, the placid sea, alone and tranquil. Nothing existed. There was only silence in the darkness, in the night. Only the Creator[s] were there. By nature they were great thinkers. They decided: when day dawned for the first time, the human being must appear. Thus they spoke. "Let there be light, let there be dawn in the sky and on the earth."

—adapted from *Sources of World History*, edited by Mark A. Kishlansky, 1995

Chichén Itzá temple figure

Between 1500 B.C. and A.D. 1200, a series of sophisticated civilizations emerged in the areas of present-day Mexico, Guatemala, Honduras, El Salvador, and Belize. Amid volcanic mountains, cool valleys, dense rain forests, and dry forested plains, early farmers developed methods that produced plentiful harvests and supported large populations. Maize was their basic crop.

Ruins of ancient cities reveal an astonishing way of life. Ideas from earlier civilizations were adopted and modified by later ones. Although each culture had unique features, they shared common elements. Archaeologists have labeled them together as Mesoamerican civilizations. The prefix *meso-* means "middle" and refers to the fact that these people lived in the middle land area that joins North America and South America. Descendants of the early Mesoamericans continue to live in this region and maintain many of their early traditions.

The Olmec

About 150 years before Tutankhamen ruled Egypt, **the Olmec** emerged as one of the earliest Mesoamerican civilizations. Between 1500 B.C. and 400 B.C., the Olmec flourished in the swampy, lowland river valleys near the Gulf of Mexico. Our knowledge of the Olmec way of life and Olmec beliefs has come primarily from excavations of two principal Olmec sites, **San Lorenzo** and **La Venta**, discovered in the late 1930s. Until then, Olmec culture had been buried by centuries of accumulated layers of earth and rain forest.

Among the objects unearthed at San Lorenzo and La Venta were enormous stone heads carved from basalt, a volcanic rock. Some were more than 9 feet (2.7 m) tall and weighed as much as 40 tons.

This jade ceremonial ax in the form of a feline monster is from the pre-Columbian Olmec culture. *Why do archaeologists believe that religion played an important role in Olmec life?*

These heads are believed to be portraits of rulers, and may have been part of larger monuments. Without the aid of wheels or beasts of burden, but perhaps using river rafts, the Olmec had moved the heads some 60 miles (97 km) from the mountains to the sites where they were discovered.

Evidence suggests that San Lorenzo and La Venta each had populations of only about 1,000 at their peak. Yet there was clearly organization, planning, and a division of labor. A hilltop at San Lorenzo was sheared off to create a central plaza for market and ceremonial purposes. Stone drains were built to direct water during the rainy season. Early forms of hieroglyphic writings were developed as well as an early calendar.

From jade carvings, figurines, and carved stone murals, archaeologists infer that religion played an important role in the lives of the Olmec. Many carvings show the Olmec god, a being with a human body and the catlike face of a jaguar, the large spot-

ted wild cat that roamed the region. The Olmec believed the jaguar-god controlled their harvests.

Early Olmec farmers practiced what is known as slash-and-burn farming. To clear land, farmers cut down trees, let them dry, and then burned them. They planted maize among the fertile ashes. Since the soil became exhausted after a few years, farmers shifted fields and repeated the cycle on other lands.

Trade with other parts of Mesoamerica was common. Olmec artifacts have been found throughout the region, and Olmec ideas were echoed in later Mesoamerican civilizations.

The Maya

As early as 900 B.C., **the Maya** began to settle the **Yucatán Peninsula** of present-day Mexico. Mayan civilization reached its peak between A.D. 300 and A.D. 900. Mayan ruins can be found throughout the region in diverse terrains: highlands, lowlands, and coastal plains. The Maya adapted to their various environments, developing different farming practices, languages, and governments. The Maya were not unified in one empire. Instead, the patchwork of city-states and kingdoms were linked by culture, political ties, and trade.

Religion

Religion was at the center of Mayan life. The Maya believed in two levels of existence. One level was the daily physical life they lived. The second level was the Otherworld, a spiritual world peopled with gods, the souls of ancestors, and other supernatural creatures. The two levels were closely intertwined. Actions on each level could influence the other. Mayan myths explained the workings of this world and the Otherworld.

Mayan kings were spiritual leaders as well as political leaders. They were responsible for their people's understanding of the Otherworld and for their behaving in ways that would keep the gods pleased. Rulers performed rituals and ceremonies to satisfy the gods. In their great cities, the Maya constructed plazas, temples, and huge pyramids—symbolically sacred mountains—where thousands of people could gather for special religious ceremonies and festivals.

Images on Mayan temples, sacred objects, and pottery provide clues about Mayan beliefs and practices. The rain god, Chac, appears frequently. Images depict other gods in the form of trees, jaguars, birds, monkeys, serpents, reptiles, fish, and shells. Mythical creatures that combine parts of several animals are also shown.

Blood symbols also appear. Human sacrifices and bloodletting rituals were part of Mayan practice. These ceremonies were considered important to appease the gods and to maintain and renew life.

Some festivals also included a ceremonial ball game called *pok-a-tok*. For this game, the Maya invented the use of solid rubber balls about the size of basketballs. Players wearing protective padding batted the balls back and forth across a walled court. These games recalled games played by mythical Mayan heroes.

Sciences

Like the ancient Greeks, the Maya believed that the movements of the sun, moon, and planets were journeys of gods across the sky. Since the gods controlled nature—including harvests—charting the movements of the celestial bodies was essential.

To do this charting, Mayan priests became excellent mathematicians and astronomers. The Maya built on the earlier work of the Olmec. The Maya developed a system of mathematics using the base 20. They used three symbols to represent numbers. A dot stood for the number one; a bar was five; and a shell figure symbolized zero. Rather than expressing place value with the highest place to the left, the Maya expressed their numbers vertically with the largest place at the top. The Maya also developed accurate calendars, a 260-day sacred calendar and another 365-day calendar. The calendars were used to predict eclipses, schedule religious ceremonies, and determine times to plant and harvest.

Economy

The Mayan economy was based on agriculture and trade. In addition to maize, farmers grew beans, squash, pumpkins, chili peppers, and tomatoes. Slash-and-burn farming continued in some areas. Elsewhere the Maya produced larger harvests by intensively farming raised plots surrounded by canals.

Perhaps as often as every five days, farmers brought surplus crops to the open-air markets of the major cities. Maize and other produce were traded for cotton cloth, jade ornaments, pottery, fish, deer meat, and salt.

Mayan merchants participated in long-distance trade throughout Mexico and Central America. Traders transported their cargoes by canoes on rivers and coastal waterways. Overland, goods were carried by humans, for wheeled vehicles and beasts of burden to haul them were unknown.

CONNECTIONS The Arts

Mayan Architecture

Mayan temple-pyramids were the religious and political centers of Mayan cities. Built of stone, these vast stepped structures were mainly platforms for religious ceremonies. Stone temples at the summit of the pyramids were erected to memorialize dead rulers by associating them with the gods. Religious sacrifices conducted by priests took place outside the temple on top of the pyramid platform.

Archaeologists believe the stepped levels of the pyramids may have represented the harmonious layers of the universe. Mayan astronomers and priests held high administrative positions. Much of a priest's power was in his ability to predict the movements of stars and planets. Thus, a priest would consult with astronomers before projects were undertaken to see when the heavens would favor such actions.

Since the mid-1900s, Mexican architects have combined Mayan and other Native American designs with modern construction methods. Their work includes the buildings of the University of Mexico and the National Museum of Anthropology in Mexico City, as well as many resorts along Mexico's Caribbean and Pacific coasts.

Temple-pyramid at Chichén Itzá

Linking Past and Present **ACTIVITY**

What purpose did the Mayan temple-pyramids serve? How might you compare Mayan temple-pyramids with public buildings today?

Louis S. Glanzman

Serious Sport

In this illustration of an ancient Mayan game a rubber ball bounces off the leather pad on the player's chest. The object was to drive the ball through a stone ring, but players could not throw or bat the ball. They had to hit it off a leather pad on their elbow, wrist, torso, or hip. Making a goal was so rare that when a player scored, crowds rewarded the hero with all their clothing and jewelry—unless they could first flee.

Scholars believe that these games were played not only for sport but also on special holidays as ritual reenactments of Mayan raids. Large cities contained numerous walled courts lined with images of warfare and sacrificial victims. According to Mayan religious beliefs, ordinary humans could never outwit death, and so the Mayan ball court became a symbolic meeting ground—a kind of threshold between earth and the underworld. ⊕

Writings

The Maya were one of the first Native American peoples to develop a writing system. They wrote in accordion-folded books made of flattened bark covered with a thin layer of plaster. Four of these books have survived. They also carved inscriptions in clay, and on jade, bone, shells, and large stone monuments. Only within the past 25 years have linguists made major breakthroughs in translating Mayan writing. Linguists discovered that some inscriptions are phonetic syllables, while others represent full words. The Maya recorded the genealogy of their kings and royal families, mythology, history, ritual practices, and trade.

Collapse

By A.D. 900 the Maya in the lowlands showed signs of collapse. They stopped building and moved elsewhere. Why this happened is unclear. There is evidence of increasing conflict and warfare among Mayan royal and nonroyal families. Outsiders were also attacking. Agricultural breakdown, perhaps caused by warfare or by erosion and over-farming, may have produced rising malnutrition, sickness, and death rates.

Visualizing History The Teotihuacáno rain god Tlaloc is shown in an *incensario* (container for burning incense) from A.D. 400–700. *Where was the Teotihuacáno civilization located?*

Other Mesoamericans

In a high fertile valley 30 miles (48 km) northeast of present-day Mexico City, **the Teotihuacános** (TAY•oh•TEE•wuh•KAHN•ohs) flourished for about 750 years. By A.D. 100, they dominated the centrally located Mexican Plateau. At its height their main city, **Teotihuacán**, had an estimated 120,000 to 200,000 inhabitants.

Teotihuacán was laid out on a grid. The most important buildings were built along the north-south axis. Excavations of the ruins have revealed 600 pyramids, 2,000 apartment compounds, 500 workshop areas, and a huge marketplace. A valuable source of obsidian was found near Teotihuacán. Obsidian, a volcanic glass, was used for sharp-edged tools, arrow points, and other objects. It was easily traded, because Teotihuacán lay on the trade routes east to the Gulf of Mexico.

Teotihuacán declined about A.D. 750. Historians still are uncertain about the reasons for its decline. Drought may have been the cause, or invasion by **the Toltec**, a people from the north.

With a powerful army, the Toltec conquered land as far south as the Yucatán Peninsula. The Toltec capital of **Tula** was the center of a powerful mining and trading empire. Their gods Quetzalcoatl (ket•suhl•KWAH•tuhl), the "plumed serpent" god of the air, and Tezcatlipoca (tehz•KAHT•lee•POH•kuh), the god of war, would be adopted by the Aztec, a later Mesoamerican group. When invaders destroyed Tula in A.D. 1170, the Toltec Empire collapsed.

SECTION 2 REVIEW

Recall
1. **Define** jaguar, slash-and-burn farming, obsidian.
2. **Identify** the Olmec, the Maya, the Teotihuacános, the Toltec, Quetzalcoatl.
3. **Use** the map on page 390 to locate the area settled by the Maya. What large city did the Maya establish? On what landform was it located?

Critical Thinking
4. **Synthesizing Information** What common features linked the Mesoamerican civilizations?

Understanding Themes
5. **Innovation** What were some of the major achievements of the Mesoamerican civilizations?

The Maya

Some 2,000 years ago, the lowland Mayan civilization of what is now Central America flourished. A society dating to 1200 B.C., the Maya developed the most complex writing system in the Americas, built majestic temple-pyramids and palaces, and mastered astronomy and mathematics. Then suddenly, in the A.D. 800s, the record of life in the region fell silent: The people stopped erecting monuments, carving hieroglyphic texts, and making pottery. Their cities lay in ruins, their fields and villages were abandoned to the jungle, and the great civilization of the Maya vanished.

What happened to end the golden age of the Maya more than a thousand years ago? To answer that question, in 1989 an international team of archaeologists, sponsored in part by the National Geographic Society and Vanderbilt University, went to the Petexbatún rain forest of northern Guatemala. Amid the ruins of the ancient city of Dos Pilas, the team set to work on one of archaeology's greatest mysteries.

Enrico Ferorelli

Enrico Ferorelli

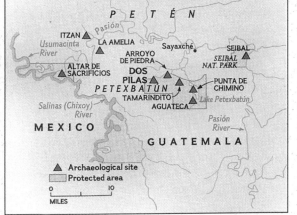

NGS Cartographic Division

After setting up a fully functioning camp complete with a computer lab and drafting workstations, scientists began their task. They studied thousands of potsherds, scores of monuments, bone fragments, spearheads, trash heaps, and miles of fortifications of Dos Pilas—built by renegades from the great Mayan center of Tikal—and nearby cities.

One spectacular find that told the fate of the Maya was a hieroglyphic stairway. Five limestone steps, about 20 feet wide, each with two rows of glyphs carved on the risers, climb to the base of the royal palace near the main plaza at Dos Pilas. Experts at deciphering glyphs were on hand to translate each glyph as it was uncovered. The story on the steps gives an account of the battles of the first ruler of the Petexbatún (referred to as Ruler 1) against his brother at Tikal, some 65 miles northeast of Dos Pilas.

One of the epigraphists summed up the inscription: "It begins by talking about the 60th birthday of

▨ *A Mayan warrior-king is portrayed on a stela carved in A.D. 731. Discoveries at Dos Pilas have led to new theories on the collapse of the Mayan civilization along the border of Guatemala and Mexico.*

▨ *A stairway of five long steps (top) came to light during excavations at the Dos Pilas site.*

Enrico Ferorelli

 As Vanderbilt graduate student Stacy Symonds excavated a defensive wall, she discovered the hieroglyphic stairway beneath it. Here she records information about the glyphs.

Ruler 1, that he danced a ritual dance. As you read down the steps, the glyphs give a historical sequence to his reign. We think Ruler 1 left Tikal and started a splinter kingdom at Dos Pilas. There's an emblem glyph——which is like a political title —for Tikal, and both brothers claimed it. Ruler 1 was defeated, but then there was another war. This time Dos Pilas won."

Although the glyphs told archaeologists about the origin of a dynasty, what was even more intriguing was a stone wall built on top of the stairs during the kingdom's fall. Less than a hundred years after memorializing their founder, the people of Dos Pilas threw a wall up over his monument in what must have been a desperate attempt to

protect themselves. Why did the people of Dos Pilas build defensive walls, which are rarely found at Mayan sites?

The second and third rulers of Dos Pilas changed traditional warfare when they set forth on campaigns of expansion. Digging a 30-foot shaft into the burial temple of Ruler 2, archaeologists discovered hieroglyphs on fine pottery that offered more clues. These glyphs suggest that Ruler 2, who reigned from A.D. 698 to A.D. 726, expanded the influence of Dos Pilas and gained control of other cities through marriage and political alliances.

Ruler 3 went on to wed a royal lady from the city of Cancuén and to dominate the entire region. He traveled to the cities of Tamarindito, Aguateca, Seibal, and others to perform ceremonies and quell unrest. After Ruler 3 died in A.D. 741, Ruler 4 took control, living mostly at Aguateca—by then a twin capital— which rests on a limestone bluff high above Lake Petexbatún.

In A.D. 761 something went wrong. According to hieroglyphs, the kings of the Petexbatún had overextended their domain. There had been hints of trouble for more than a decade: Ruler 4 had spent much of his 20-year reign racing from one end of the realm to the other, performing bloodletting rituals, leading battles, and contracting alliances. He used every technique to sustain the kingdom, but to no avail.

Then the city of Tamarindito threw off the yoke of Dos Pilas. Hieroglyphs at Tamarindito tell us that its warriors attacked the capital and killed Ruler 4.

About that time the citizens of Dos Pilas made a valiant last stand. In desperation they ripped stones from temples and monuments, including the tomb of Ruler 2 and the hieroglyphic stairway. They tore

down much of the royal palace to build two walls around the central palaces and temples.

The surviving nobles deserted their citizens and fled to Aguateca, proclaiming themselves the new rulers of the kingdom. They chose Aguateca as its final capital because of its defensive location. The people of Aguateca held out for about 50 years, but disappeared in the early A.D. 800s

⚓

IN A SPAN of only a few hundred years the kingdom rose, expanded, and collapsed as a succession of kings moved from limited conflict to widespread warfare. Scholars have argued that the Mayan civilization simply outgrew its environment, exhausting the soil and creating environmental and economic stress. But another possibility is that intensive warfare forced the Maya, at least in the Petexbatún area, to move close to fortresses such as Aguateca, where they would have soon run out of fertile land. Perhaps farmers were limited to fortified areas near cities that could provide protection, forcing them to forsake traditional agricultural practices that had sustained them for hundreds of years. The wars must have disrupted trade, upset population distribution, destroyed crops, and killed young farmer-warriors, exacting a huge price.

Scholars have added greatly to our view of Mayan society. Once regarded as a network of ceremonial centers ruled by peaceful priestkings, Mayan civilization is no longer seen that way. Battle and human sacrifice were aspects of life. Perhaps siege warfare was ultimately too costly for the Maya. For years to come, scientists will study the ruins in the Petexbatún rain forest researching changes that may have contributed to the collapse of the lowland Mayan civilization.

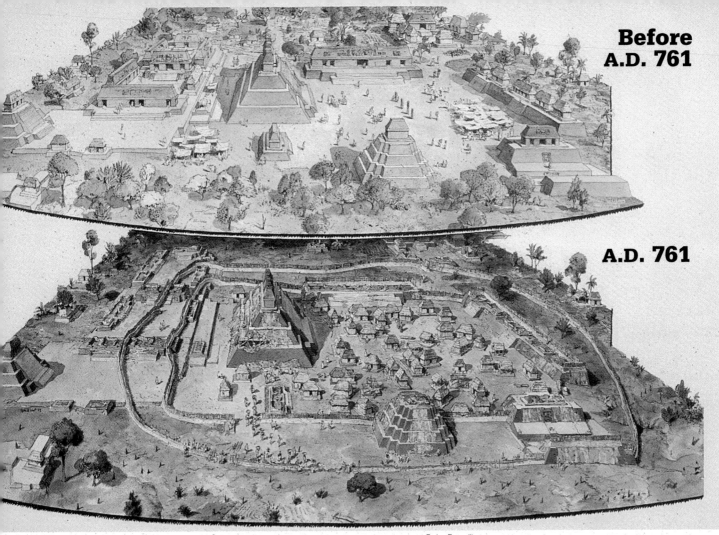

Enrico Ferorelli

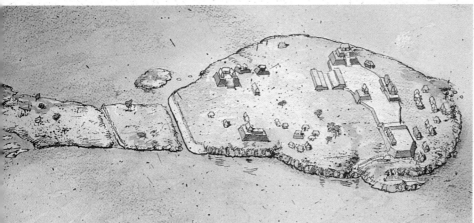

Enrico Ferorelli

◈ In proper Mayan style Dos Pilas's ceremonial precinct (above, top) featured palaces for rulers and temples to the gods. But an apparent golden age came to an abrupt end in A.D. 761 (above, bottom). After the killing of Ruler 4, warfare consumed the region. Residents tore down facades of temples and palaces to raise two walls. A cleared area between the walls likely served as a killing alley. Seeking refuge, farmers moved into the plaza and erected huts. Soon the city was abandoned.

◈ A peninsula became an island (left, top and bottom) as defenders of the Lake Petexbatún port dug three moats across the neck of land. At the tip of the island, a walled wharf protected a canoe landing. Perhaps the enemy proved too strong or conditions too harsh, for the outpost was abandoned.

Chapter 15 *The Americas* 387

A.D. 1300   A.D. 1400   A.D. 1500

A.D. 1325 The Aztec found their capital, Tenochtitlán.

A.D. 1438 The Inca emperor Pachacuti comes to power.

c. A.D. 1500 The Aztec control all of central and southern Mexico.

Section 3

The Aztec and Inca Empires

Setting the Scene

▶ **Terms to Define**
chinampas, hierarchy, quinoa

▶ **People to Meet**
the Aztec, the Inca, the Moche, Pachacuti

▶ **Places to Locate**
Tenochtitlán, Cuzco

Find Out What factors led to the rise and decline of the Aztec and the Inca Empires?

The Storyteller

Cortés captured many Aztec cities. This Aztec song remembers how it was:
"Broken spears lie in the roads;
we have torn our hair in our grief.
The houses are roofless now, and their walls
are red with blood....
We have pounded our hands in despair against
the adobe walls, for our inheritance, our
city, is lost and dead.
The shields of our warriors
were its defense, but they
could not save it.
We have chewed dry twigs
and salt grasses;
We have filled our mouths
with dust and bits of
adobe; we have eaten
lizards, rats and
worms...."

—from *Sources of World History,*
edited by Mark A. Kishlansky, 1995

Aztec Stone of the Sun calendar

Like other Native American groups, **the Aztec of Mexico and Central America and the Inca** of South America lacked metal tools, large work animals, and a practical use of the wheel. Yet they were able to develop centralized governments, raise armies and conquer empires. Both civilizations, however, came to sudden ends in the early A.D. 1500s, when they were overwhelmed and destroyed by Spanish invaders from Europe.

The Aztec Empire

The early Aztec were hunters and warriors who moved from the north into central Mexico during the A.D. 1200s. In A.D. 1325 they founded a city in central Mexico named **Tenochtitlán** (tay•NAWCH•teet•LAHN), today the site of Mexico City. According to Aztec legend, Aztec priests told their people to settle in the area where they would find an eagle sitting on a cactus and holding a snake in its beak. After much wandering, the Aztecs finally saw on an island in Lake Texcoco what the priests had described. There, they established Tenochtitlán.

Tenochtitlán

The Aztec turned Tenochtitlán into an agricultural center and marketplace. Since land for farming was scarce on the island, they built *chinampas*, or artificial islands, by piling mud from the bottom of the lake onto rafts secured by stakes. These became floating gardens where farmers grew a variety of crops, including corn and beans. With a plentiful food supply, the population grew and people moved outside the city to the mainland. A network of canals, bridges, and causeways was built to connect the mainland with the capital city.

Empire

Strengthened by early alliances with neighboring city-states, the Aztec then conquered more distant rivals. By A.D. 1500 their empire stretched from north-central Mexico to the border of Guatemala, and from the Atlantic Ocean to the Pacific Ocean. Conquered peoples had to pay heavy tribute in the form of food, clothing, raw materials, and prisoners for sacrifice.

As the Aztec Empire expanded, Tenochtitlán prospered. Estimates of the city's population by A.D. 1500 range from 120,000 to 200,000. Goods and tribute came to the city from all parts of the empire.

Government and Society

The Aztec civilization was organized as a hierarchy—divided into levels of authority, each level more powerful than the level below it. At the top was the emperor. His power came from his control of the army and was reinforced by religious beliefs.

The Aztec social order had four classes: nobility, commoners, serfs, and slaves. Land could be owned by noble families and commoners. Commoners included priests, merchants, artisans, and farmers. Serfs were farmworkers tied to noble lands. The lowest class included criminals and debtors, as well as female and children prisoners of war. Male prisoners of war were sacrificed to the Aztec gods.

Religion and the Arts

Religion motivated the Aztecs to engage in war and sacrifice. Borrowing ideas from the Maya and the Toltec, the Aztecs believed that live human sacrifices were needed to keep the gods pleased and to prevent drought, floods and other natural disasters. The chief deity was the sun god Huitzilopochtli (wee•tsee•loh•POHKT•lee), whose giant pyramid-temple arose in the center of Tenochtitlán.

Priests used a 360-day religious calendar to determine appropriate days for activities, such as planting crops or going to war. The Aztec also had a 365-day solar calendar that consisted of 18 months of 20 days plus 5 extra days. One of the most famous surviving pieces of Aztec sculpture is a large, circular calendar stone that represents the Aztec universe, with carvings that stand for the days of the Aztec month.

Aztec artists decorated temple-pyramids with scenes of deities or battles. Writers glorified Aztec victories in their works. The empire, however, proved to be fragile. Revolts in outlying areas weakened Aztec control. In A.D. 1521 the rebels joined the Spaniards in destroying the Aztec heritage.

Chocolate Is Introduced to Europe

Spain, A.D. 1528

According to legend, the Aztec ruler Montezuma had served Hernán Cortés a beverage called *chocolatl*. When Cortés returned to Spain in A.D. 1528, he brought with him the beans of the cacao tree. Spaniards added sugar, vanilla, and cinnamon to sweeten the bitter drink. Chocolate became a favorite with the aristocracy and spread to Italy, France, Austria, and England.

Spain

The Inca Empire

Other Native American civilizations arose in western South America. One of the earliest was **the Moche**, who lived on the north coast of present-day Peru between A.D. 100 and A.D. 600. In A.D. 1987 archaeologists discovered a noble's tomb that revealed the Moche had a social order based on ranks, skilled artisans who made metal ornaments, and rituals that included sacrifices.

Rise of the Inca

The Inca began as one of many small tribes competing for scarce fertile land in the valleys of the Andes mountain ranges. Around A.D. 1200 the Inca settled in **Cuzco** (KOOS•koh), which became their capital. They raided other tribes and slowly established a powerful empire.

The decisive period of Inca expansion began in A.D. 1438, when **Pachacuti**, the ninth Inca ruler, came to power. He and his son, Topa Inca Yupanqui, have been compared to Philip and Alexander the Great of Macedonia. By persuasion, threats, and force, they extended Inca boundaries far to the north and south.

The Inca Empire eventually included all of present-day Peru, much of Chile, and parts of Ecuador, Bolivia, and Argentina. It stretched more than 2,500 miles (4,020 km) through coastal deserts, dry highlands, fertile river valleys, and rain forests. Most of the Inca lived in the Andes highlands and adjusted to high altitudes. Cuzco was 11,600 feet (3,560 m) above sea level.

Government and Society

Pachacuti created a strong central government to control the vast realm. He permitted local rulers to continue governing conquered territories as long as they were loyal. Rebellious peoples were resettled elsewhere where they could pose less of a threat. Pachacuti instituted a complex system of tribute collections, courts, military posts, trade inspections, and local work regulations to bind outlying territories to the center. To further unite the diverse peoples, the Inca established a common imperial language—Quechua (KEH•chuh•wuh).

The Inca emperor and his officials closely regulated the lives of the common people. As a divine ruler, the emperor owned all land and carefully regulated the growing and distribution of foods, such as potatoes and quinoa (keen•wah), a protein-rich grain. To make good use of the limited arable land, Inca farmers cut step terraces into hillsides and built irrigation systems in the dry coastal plain. After harvest, part of their crops went to the government as taxes. Under the emperor's direction, work crews built roads and woven fiber suspension bridges that linked the regions of the empire.

The Inca believed in many deities, including the creator god Viracocha and the sun god Inti. Priests offered food, animals, and sometimes humans as sacrifices to please the deities. In A.D. 1995 archaeologists discovered in the Andes the frozen, preserved body of a teenage Inca girl. Food and pottery remains seemed to indicate that she was a sacrificial victim. Priests also served as doctors, using herbs to treat illnesses and performing an early form of brain surgery.

Instead of developing a writing system, the Inca kept records by using *quipu*, a rope with knotted cords of different lengths and colors. Each knot represented a different item or number. They also observed the heavens to predict seasonal changes. They were able to perform certain mathematical calculations that they used to design their buildings and roads.

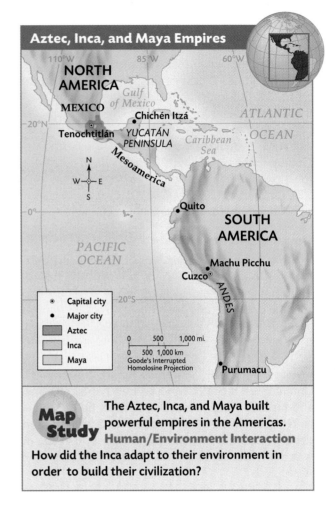

Aztec, Inca, and Maya Empires

NORTH AMERICA
MEXICO · Gulf of Mexico
Chichén Itzá
Tenochtitlán · YUCATÁN PENINSULA
Mesoamerica · Caribbean Sea
ATLANTIC OCEAN
Quito
SOUTH AMERICA
PACIFIC OCEAN
Machu Picchu
Cuzco
ANDES
Purumacu

◉ Capital city
● Major city
Aztec
Inca
Maya

0   500   1,000 mi.
0   500 1,000 km
Goode's Interrupted Homolosine Projection

Map Study The Aztec, Inca, and Maya built powerful empires in the Americas. **Human/Environment Interaction** How did the Inca adapt to their environment in order to build their civilization?

Inca Decline

The obedient, well-disciplined Inca would prove to be no match for the Spanish conquerors who arrived in South America in A.D. 1533. In spite of fierce resistance, the Inca Empire declined and eventually disappeared. Spanish forces slew those Inca who threatened their authority—an action that would be repeated in many parts of the Americas. Aspects of Inca culture, however, have survived among the Inca descendants living today in western areas of South America.

SECTION 3 REVIEW

Recall

1. **Define** *chinampas*, hierarchy, quinoa.
2. **Identify** the Aztec, the Inca, the Moche, Pachacuti.
3. **Use** the maps in the Atlas to describe the physical geography of Mexico and western South America. How did geography affect the early civilizations that arose in each of these two areas?

Critical Thinking

4. **Synthesizing Information** What do modern nations take as tribute after a war? How is this the same as or different from the tribute paid by Aztec people?

Understanding Themes

5. **Change** Contrast the methods used by the Aztec and the Inca to expand and administer their vast empires.

Analyzing Primary and Secondary Sources

You see a television interview with an eyewitness to a tornado. Later you read a newspaper account. Is one account more accurate than the other?

Learning the Skill

To determine the accuracy of an account, you must analyze its source. There are two main kinds of sources—primary and secondary. Primary sources are accounts or artifacts produced by eyewitnesses to events. Diaries, letters, autobiographies, interviews, artifacts, and paintings are primary sources. Secondary sources use information gathered from others. Textbooks and biographies are secondary sources. Because primary sources convey personal experiences, they often communicate the emotions and opinions of participants in an event. Secondary sources, written at a later time, often help us to understand events in a larger context.

Determine the reliability of the source. For a primary source, find out who wrote it and when. An account written during or immediately after an event is more reliable than one written years later. For a secondary source, look for good documentation. In a reliable account, researchers cite their sources of information in footnotes and bibliographies.

For both types of sources evaluate the author. Is this author biased? What background and authority does he or she have? Finally, compare two accounts of the same event. If they disagree, you should question their reliability.

Practicing the Skill

Read the sources and answer the questions.

❝ Finally the two groups met...When all was ready Moctezuma placed his feet, shod in gold-soled, gem-studded sandals, on the carpeted pavement and... advanced to an encounter that would shape both his own destiny and that of his nation....Moctezuma had servants bring forward two necklaces of red shells hung with life-size shrimps made of gold. These he placed around Cortés's neck. ❞

—from *Cortés* by William Weber Johnson, 1975

❝ When we had arrived at a place not far from the town, where several small towers rose together, the monarch raised himself in his sedan...Montezuma himself, according to his custom, was sumptuously attired, had on a species of half boot, richly set with jewels, and whose soles were made of solid gold.... Montezuma came up to Cortés, and taking him by the hand, conducted him himself into the apartments where he was to lodge, which had been beautifully decorated...He then hung about his neck a chaste necklace of gold, most curiously worked with figures all representing crabs. ❞

—from an account by Conquistador Bernal Díaz del Castillo, 1519

1. What is the general topic of the two sources?
2. Which is a primary source and which is a secondary source? How can you tell?
3. Though each quote deals with the same topic, what is a different technique each uses to approach that topic?

Applying the Skill

Find two accounts of a recent event or a historical event. Analyze the reliability of each. When were the accounts written? Is the author qualified to write on this topic? Is the account well-documented? Do the two accounts agree?

For More Practice

Turn to the Skill Practice in the Chapter Review on page 393.

Connections Across Time

Historical Significance Throughout the early history of the Americas, Native Americans established a variety of cultures and civilizations. The environment gave these peoples spiritual strength and economic support. Regarding the earth as sacred, they used the land's natural resources to develop agriculture, build ceremonial centers, and advance trade. Several Native American groups in Mesoamerica and South America formed vast empires that linked diverse peoples and spread new ideas and products.

The cultural aspects of these empires are still held by Native Americans living today in Mexico, Central America, and South America. In recent years, Native Americans in North America have reclaimed much of their heritage that had been suppressed with the advance of European civilization in the Americas.

Using Key Terms

Write the key term that completes each sentence. Then write a sentence for each term not chosen.

a. *chinampas*
b. weirs
c. quinoa
d. confederation
e. jaguar
f. maize
g. obsidian
h. potlatches
i. hierarchy
j. slash-and-burn farming

1. Around A.D. 1500 the Cayuga, Mohawk, Oneida, Onondaga, and Seneca formed a _____, or loose union.
2. Because of the scarcity of land to farm, the Aztec devised a way of making _____, or artificial islands.
3. Among Native Americans of the Pacific Northwest, the wealth of each lineage group was given away at _____.
4. The early Olmec practiced a form of agriculture known as _____.
5. By about 5000 B.C., hunter-gatherers in the highland area of present-day Mexico had discovered that the seeds of _____ could be planted.

Technology Activity

Using the Internet Access the Internet to locate a Web site about the Inca Empire. Use a search engine to help focus your search by using phrases such as *inca empire, mesoamerican civilizations,* or *native americans*. Create a bulletin board using the information found, and incorporate illustrations of Inca culture and artifacts.

Using Your History Journal

Parallel to your time line of important dates in Native American civilizations, add a time line of significant civilizations and achievements in Africa, Asia, and Europe. Use dates from the Unit 3 Digest on pages 395–397.

Reviewing Facts

1. **Geography** Explain how the food resources of Native Americans along the California coast differed from those of Native Americans living in the Great Basin.
2. **Geography** Discuss how the people of southwestern North America adapted to the desert.
3. **Culture** Identify the purposes of the mounds left by the Mound Builders.
4. **History** Name the two principal sites where excavations have revealed an ancient Olmec culture.
5. **Culture** Describe the four books that have survived from the Mayan civilization.
6. **History** Identify the events in the early A.D. 1500s that were responsible for the sudden end to the Inca and the Aztec civilizations.
7. **Science/Technology** Explain how mathematical, technical, and scientific innovations affected Native Americans.
8. **Geography** State what was unique about the location of the Aztec city of Tenochtitlán.
9. **Citizenship** Discuss the ways in which the Inca served their emperor and the empire.

Critical Thinking

1. **Analyze** How did the rise and decline of the Aztec and Inca Empires differ?
2. **Analyze** High in the Andes mountain ranges, the city of Machu Picchu was the last refuge of the Inca. Why did Inca rulers retreat to a city in such a remote location?

Ruins of Machu Picchu

Understanding Themes

1. **Relation to the Environment** How did Native Americans in the Eastern Woodlands differ from the Native Americans of the Great Plains? How were they similar?
2. **Innovation** What were some of the cultural achievements of the Mayan civilization?
3. **Change** How did Spaniards affect the Aztec and Inca civilizations?

Linking Past and Present

1. What impact do Native American traditions have on life in the Americas today? In what ways has modern civilization been affected by the early Native Americans?
2. Religion played an important role in early American and other ancient civilizations. What role does religion have in modern societies?

Skill Practice

Read the following excerpt and answer the questions.

❝ The things the Incas built were copied from the older civilizations that they conquered. In their cities, fortresses, roads, terraces, temples, they did only what had been done before by the people around them, but a great deal more of it. The ornamentation, the woven fabrics, the work in gold they pursued so avidly as a symbol of the Sun, all were adopted by their predecessors. ❞

— From *The Last Americans: The Indian in American Culture* by the American historian, William Brandon, 1974

1. What is the topic of the source?
2. Is this a primary or a secondary source? Explain your answer.
3. What authority does the author have?

Geography in History

1. **Movement** Refer to the map below. In the A.D. 1500s and A.D. 1600s Native American civilizations declined as the whole region came under the rule of powerful European nation-states. The triangular trade linked four continents between A.D. 1600 and A.D. 1760. How did trade change the population of the Caribbean Islands?
2. **Human/Environment Interaction** How did farming change when crops such as sugarcane began to be raised for trade?
3. **Movement** What positive and negative changes resulted from the cultural contact of peoples from four different continents?

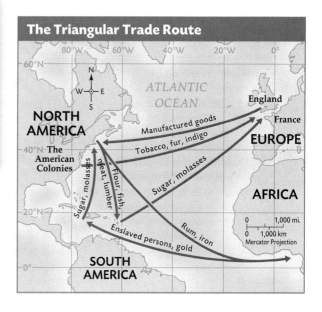

The Triangular Trade Route

 **Turning Points in World History**

The Crusades

Setting up the Video

Work with a group of your classmates to view "The Crusades" on the videodisc *Turning Points in World History*. The Crusades left lasting effects on the economic and political development of western Europe. Improvements abounded in the areas of new knowledge, trade, and technology. This program introduces the Crusades and the changes that occurred in European culture, art, and architecture.

Hands-On Activity

Create an oral history by interviewing a person about his or her experiences during a modern-day "crusade" (such as the civil rights or women's rights movements) that has left a lasting effect on our society. Create questions to ask this individual during a recorded interview. Share the results of your interview with the class.

Side One, Chapter 7

View the video by scanning the bar code or by entering the chapter number on your keypad and pressing Search. (Also available in VHS format.)

Surfing the "Net"

The Aztecs

The Aztecs held a vast empire until the early 1500s, when they were ultimately defeated by Spanish invaders from Europe. Their civilization was very advanced in areas such as building, agriculture and the creation of a highly centralized government. To learn more about the Aztecs, access the Internet.

Getting There

1. Go to a search engine. Type in the phrase *aztec culture*.
2. After typing in the phrase, enter words such as those below to focus your search:
   - *government*
   - *religion*
   - *innovations*
   - *contributions*

3. The search engine should provide you with a number of links to follow. Links are "pointers" to different sites on the Internet and commonly appear as blue underlined words.

What to Do When You Are There

Click on the links to navigate through the pages of information and gather your findings. Create a fact sheet of information about all aspects of Aztec culture. Include information such as type of government, agriculture, religion, and innovations. Include an accompanying map showing the Aztec Empire sphere of influence.

Unit 3 Digest

The period from A.D. 500 to A.D. 1500 was one of growth in many areas of the world. Expanded trade routes and missionaries' journeys spread intellectual, cultural, and religious beliefs from one people to another. Such contact between cultures caused conflict that lasted for decades, even centuries; yet at other times, ideas and ideals were peacefully adopted.

Chapter 10
Byzantines and Slavs

After the Roman Empire split in A.D. 395, the eastern half—at the crossroads of trade linking Europe, Asia, and Africa—developed into the Byzantine Empire. Primarily Greek, but populated by a diversity of peoples, the Byzantine Empire blended Greek and Roman thought, Christian belief, and cultural influences from Persia and other areas of the Middle East. The Byzantines continued the Roman tradition of rule by emperors and practiced their own form of Christianity. In A.D. 1054 most of Christianity split into two separate bodies: the Roman Catholic Church in western Europe and the Eastern Orthodox Church in the Byzantine Empire. This religious division heightened hostility between the Byzantines and the Christian kingdoms that had emerged in western Europe after the fall of the western Roman Empire. Throughout their history, the Byzantines held out against a series of invaders, including Persians, Arabs, and western European Christian Crusaders. In A.D. 1453 the Byzantine Empire finally came to an end when its capital, Constantinople, fell to the Ottoman Turks.

Byzantine culture, however, had a lasting effect on neighboring peoples, especially the Slavs of eastern Europe. Byzantine missionaries had converted many of the Slavic peoples to Christianity. Kiev, a Slavic fortress-town on the Dnieper River in present-day Ukraine, traded with Constantinople and became the first major center of Eastern Slavic civilization. Although Kiev declined after the A.D. 1200s, its cultural achievements became the foundation of the civilizations of Ukraine, Belarus, and Russia. The Russian city of Moscow became a leading center of Eastern Orthodox Christianity after the fall of Constantinople.

Visualizing History A Turkish pulpit tile from the A.D. 1600s depicts the plan of the Kaaba at Makkah. *What is the fifth pillar of Islam?*

Chapter 11
Islamic Civilization

While the Byzantines were building a Christian empire in the Mediterranean world, the Arabs of the Arabian Peninsula were spreading the religion of Islam. In A.D. 610 Muhammad, a merchant in the city of Makkah (Mecca), preached a message he claimed came from Allah (the Arabic name for God). Muhammad called for devotion to one God and for moral reform. From his revelations came the Quran, the holy book of Islam, and the Five Pillars: faith, prayer, almsgiving, fasting, and pilgrimage to Makkah.

Initially suffering persecution, Muhammad and other Muslims, or followers of Islam, finally created an Islamic state that placed divine law above local, tribal laws. After Muhammad's death, Islam divided into two separate groups, the Sunnis and the Shiites. However, the caliphs, or successors of Muhammad, spread Islam through a series of military victories over the Byzantine and Persian Empires. The Umayyad caliphs (A.D. 661-750) carried Islam eastward to India and China, as well as to North Africa and parts of southern Europe. They based their rule in Syria and created an Islamic empire that embraced many different peoples. Later, in the A.D. 800s, the Abbasid caliphs shifted the empire's center of power eastward to Iraq, where they set up Baghdad as the capital.

During the period of the Islamic empire, Muslim scholars preserved Greek philosophy and made advances in mathematics, astronomy, geometry, and medicine. Muslim artists, architects, and writers also made many contributions. In later centuries, western Europe, Africa, and parts of Asia would benefit from Islamic scientific and cultural achievements.

Chapter 12
The Rise of Medieval Europe

Historians today label the period from A.D. 500 to A.D. 1500 in western Europe as the Middle Ages, an age of transition between ancient and modern times. Compared with the Byzantine and Islamic societies of this period, western European culture was relatively backward. However, during the Middle Ages, Christianity, the Greek and Roman heritage, and the culture of Germanic invaders combined to create a new western European civilization.

Charlemagne, a Germanic king, became Holy Roman emperor in A.D. 800 and united western Europe for the first time since the fall of Rome. He also strengthened ties between his throne and the pope, the leading western European Christian leader based in Rome.

During the Middle Ages, the Roman Catholic Church exercised strong religious and political influence over western Europe. Devoutly religious men and women lived apart from society in communities known as monasteries. By preserving religious writings, establishing schools, and providing models of Christian living, they helped spread and strengthen Christianity in western Europe.

After Charlemagne's death, his empire divided, and western Europe entered a period of internal strife and external invasions. Feudalism, a new type of social organization, emerged to provide order and protection. It joined loyalty between higher and lesser nobles to ownership of land and military service. With the decline of central government and trade, estates owned by individual feudal nobles provided for most local needs. Most Europeans, however, were not warriors, but peasant farmers bound to the nobles' lands on which they worked.

European kings at this time were generally weak rulers, but they gradually created government bureaucracies and laid the foundations of Europe's modern nation-states. This strengthening of monarchy was especially advanced in England and France. In England, however, Parliament, an assembly that advised the king, placed limits on royal power and played a key role in passing laws. Meanwhile, the

Holy Roman Empire based in Germany saw its monarchy weakened by conflict between its emperors and various popes.

Chapter 13
Medieval Europe at Its Height

In the late A.D. 1000s, the Christians of western Europe began the first of a series of Crusades, or military expeditions, to win Palestine from Muslim rulers. The goal of making "the Holy Land" Christian did not succeed in the long run, but the Crusades did open Europe to Islamic and other ways of life and stimulated trade between European and Islamic peoples.

Around A.D. 1000, improvements in farming increased food production, and Europe's economy began to revive. As trade and the use of money expanded, towns grew up along trade routes. A new wealthy middle class emerged that sought political power and challenged the feudal system. Increased prosperity influenced the growth of art, literature, and learning based in universities.

During the A.D. 1300s and 1400s, French and English monarchs fought each other for control of French territory. Although England was eventually driven out of France, the conflict strengthened loyalty to royal authority in both countries. Meanwhile, Christian monarchs in Spain reconquered Muslim-ruled Spanish areas, and the Holy Roman emperor in Germany struggled for power with the pope. The increasing wealth of the clergy and the involvement of popes in political affairs damaged the Church's prestige.

Chapter 14
East and South Asia

Between A.D. 1000 and A.D. 1400, a series of steppe peoples from central Asia conquered vast areas of territory in Europe and Asia. The most important of these peoples were the Mongols, who ruled the world's largest land empire stretching from eastern Europe to China. Internal weaknesses, however, led to the breakup of the Mongol Empire into smaller units.

In China, the Tang dynasty, which ruled from A.D. 618 to A.D. 907, expanded Chinese borders and created a stable government. Trade with Japan and India increased, as well as overland trade to the Middle East along the Silk Road. The Tang capital,

Visualizing History This illuminated manuscript depicts Charlemagne's coronation as emperor in A.D. 800. *How did Charlemagne affect the history of medieval Europe?*

Changan, became the largest city in the world. Later weakened by rebellion and invasion, the Tang dynasty declined.

The Song dynasty then came to power, and with it a golden age of achievement in the arts, literature, science, and technology. Confucianism continued to exert an influence on the culture, resulting in social reforms. Great strides were made in economic growth, as well as science and technology, before China fell to the Mongols about A.D. 1270.

The Mongols became the first conquerors to control most of the country. They established a dynasty in China and enforced their peace. Under Mongol rule, China's trade increased with Europe, the Middle East, and Russia. By A.D. 1300, however, Mongol society in China had declined.

Meanwhile China's influence had extended to Korea and Japan and to parts of Southeast Asia. The Koreans were influenced by Chinese religion, government, and science. Japan, isolated from mainland Asia because of its island geography, had developed traditions different from those of other Asian countries. Yet, it too adopted certain Chinese ideas and practices. The Japanese later developed a feudal society of warrior landowners. Trade, however, increased and towns were established.

Chapter 15
The Americas

The earliest inhabitants on the North American continent came from Asia by way of the Beringia land bridge. They eventually settled as far as the southern tip of South America. As in other parts of the world, geography and climate influenced their ways of life.

A variety of Native American groups flourished in North America. Native Americans in the northeastern part of the continent had a high level of political organization. By the late A.D. 1500s, several groups had formed the Iroquois League to maintain peace. The Iroquois League's representative structure provided a flexible but stable system of government.

Powerful Native American empires emerged in the Americas, especially the Maya and Aztec in Mexico and Central America, and the Inca in South America. They built large ceremonial centers that included temple-pyramids, marketplaces, and palaces. Religion played a large role in daily life and in public ceremonies. These civilizations also developed an understanding of science, mathematics, and engineering.

SURVEYING UNIT 3

1. **Chapter 10** What cultural influences shaped the development of the Byzantine Empire?
2. **Chapter 11** How did Islamic civilization benefit western Europe, Africa, and parts of Asia?
3. **Chapter 12** Why did feudalism develop in western Europe during the Middle Ages?
4. **Chapter 13** How did Europe's economy change during the Middle Ages?
5. **Chapter 14** What areas of Asia were influenced by the spread of Chinese civilization?
6. **Chapter 15** What were the major achievements of the Native American empires?

Emergence of the Modern World

Then & Now

The Renaissance and Reformation changed European culture and created powerful political alliances. Europeans set out on uncharted seas to explore the world as powerful European monarchs competed for trade, influence, and territory. While the peoples of the Americas struggled against European invaders, civilizations in Asia reached pinnacles of cultural achievement.

Every time you use paper money or write a check, you are trusting in a system based on banking that originated during this period. As European trade and commerce increased, merchants turned to bankers for the capital to finance their ventures. Wealthy banking families even made loans to European monarchs. By the 1600s government-chartered banks began to replace family-owned banks. These banks issued banknotes and checks that made trading in heavy coins obsolete.

A Global Chronology

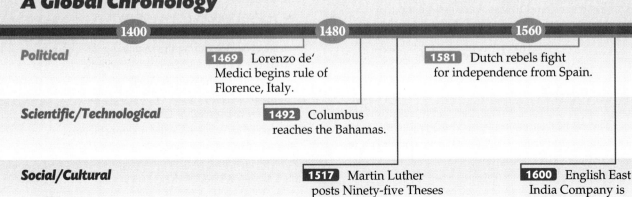

	1400	1480	1560
Political		**1469** Lorenzo de' Medici begins rule of Florence, Italy.	**1581** Dutch rebels fight for independence from Spain.
Scientific/Technological		**1492** Columbus reaches the Bahamas.	
Social/Cultural		**1517** Martin Luther posts Ninety-five Theses at Wittenberg Church.	**1600** English East India Company is established.

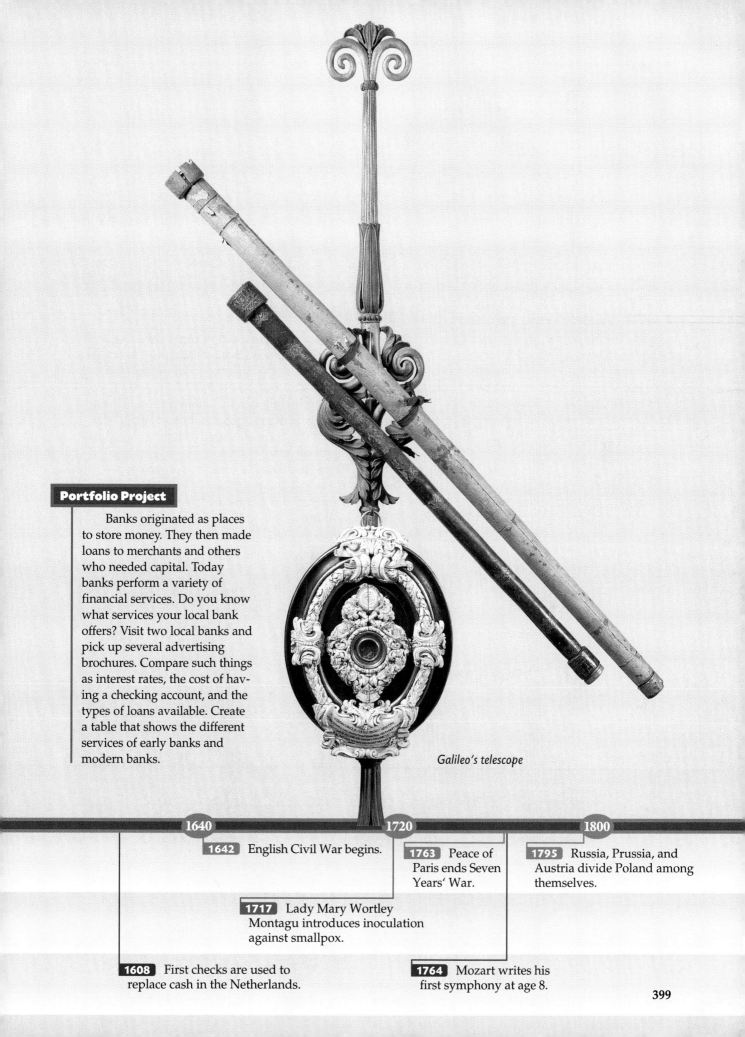

Portfolio Project

Banks originated as places to store money. They then made loans to merchants and others who needed capital. Today banks perform a variety of financial services. Do you know what services your local bank offers? Visit two local banks and pick up several advertising brochures. Compare such things as interest rates, the cost of having a checking account, and the types of loans available. Create a table that shows the different services of early banks and modern banks.

Galileo's telescope

1640

1642 English Civil War begins.

1717 Lady Mary Wortley Montagu introduces inoculation against smallpox.

1608 First checks are used to replace cash in the Netherlands.

1720

1763 Peace of Paris ends Seven Years' War.

1764 Mozart writes his first symphony at age 8.

1800

1795 Russia, Prussia, and Austria divide Poland among themselves.

Music

In the 1400s and 1500s, European ships edged into uncharted waters. These voyages set the stage for one of the greatest cultural exchanges in history, as people from Europe, Africa, and the Americas came face-to-face for the first time. One of the products of this exchange was the birth of "America music," a collection of styles deeply rooted in West Africa.

North America

The Caribbean

West Africa

West Africa
Traditional Rhythms

"We are almost a nation of dancers, musicians, and poets," recalled a West African named Olaudah Equiano. "Every great event ... is celebrated ... with songs and music suited to the occasion."

Equiano's words highlighted the importance of music to everyday life among the varied peoples of West Africa. Here musicians won fame for the skill with which they played complicated rhythms on drums, flutes, whistles, and stringed instruments. People added the sounds of their voices to a rhythm known as a call-and-response pattern. A leader would sing out a short piece of music, and people would sing it back to the beat of a drum.

African-style drum

North America
New Musical Forms

The musical heritage of West Africa traveled to the Americas aboard European slave ships. To endure the pains of slavery, West Africans kept alive musical patterns that reminded them of their ancestral homelands. Because most West Africans came as laborers, work songs took root first. The rhythmic patterns of these songs set the pace for repetitious tasks. West African laborers added field hollers—long calls by a worker in which other workers answered back. Outside the fields, enslaved Africans cried out for freedom in religious folk songs known as spirituals.

Over hundreds of years, these musical forms came together to create new styles. The blues grew out of the field songs and spirituals of slavery. Ragtime echoed the complicated rhythms of West African music. On these foundations grew yet other styles—jazz, rock 'n' roll, and rap.

Steel drums of the Caribbean

The Caribbean
Afro-Caribbean Beats

The sounds of West Africa could be heard wherever large enslaved African populations lived in the Americas. On islands in the Caribbean, the beat of bongos, the conga, the tambour, and other West African drums became the soul of Afro-Caribbean music. Added to the drums were European instruments such as the Spanish guitar and a variety of Native American instruments such as the marimba (xylophone), maraca, and wooden rhythm sticks called claves. Out of this blend of influences emerged a range of styles as diverse as the Caribbean islands themselves—reggae, calypso, salsa, and more.

Chicago 1955 by Ben Shahn

LINKING THE IDEAS

1. What are some of the features of West African music?
2. How did West African music influence musical styles in North America and the Caribbean?

Critical Thinking

3. **Evaluating Information** Which styles of music that you listen to at least once a week are influenced by West African musical patterns?

Renaissance and Reformation

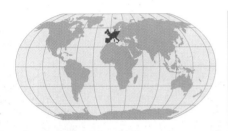

Chapter Themes

▶ **Innovation** The Renaissance leads to an artistic and intellectual awakening in Europe. *Section 1*

▶ **Cultural Diffusion** Renaissance ideas and artistic styles spread from Italy to northern Europe. *Section 2*

▶ **Conflict** Martin Luther's protests against the Catholic Church result in Protestantism. *Section 3*

▶ **Cultural Diffusion** Protestant religious groups spread reform through northern Europe. *Section 4*

▶ **Reaction** The Catholic Church enacts its own reform, the Catholic Reformation. *Section 5*

The Storyteller

Isabella d'Este, married in 1490 at the age of 16 to the Marquis of Mantua, played a vital role in ruling the Italian city-state of Mantua. A brilliant and well-educated young woman who loved Latin literature, Isabella gathered a fashionable assemblage of artists and statesmen in her sparkling court. In a room decorated with ornately carved woodwork and paintings that illustrated Greek myths, Isabella entertained her guests to her own lute recitals and poetry readings. Isabella was one of the many Italians of her time who rediscovered and repopularized Greek and Roman classics, educating their contemporaries to the glories of their classical past after a thousand years of neglect. The word Renaissance, *coming from the French word meaning "rebirth," was coined to refer to this rebirth of interest in classical ideas and culture.*

Historical Significance

What happened during the Renaissance that changed Europeans' outlook on the world? How did the Reformation shape the religious and political life of Europe?

1450	1500	1550	1600
	1469 Lorenzo de' Medici rules Florence.	**1517** Martin Luther promotes church reform.	**1563** Council of Trent ends.
	1508 Michelangelo begins painting the Sistine Chapel.		

Detail of *The Court* by Andrea Mantegna.
Palazzo Ducale, Mantua, Italy

Your History Journal

Choose a Renaissance sculptor, architect, or painter mentioned in this chapter. Research and write a short report on the work and influence of this person.

1436 Filippo Brunelleschi completes dome for Florence Cathedral.

c. 1490 Florence enjoys economic prosperity.

c. 1500 Rome becomes a major center of Renaissance culture.

Section 1

The Italian Renaissance

Setting the Scene

▶ **Terms to Define**
humanism, secular, individualism, sonnet, doge

▶ **People to Meet**
Niccolò Machiavelli, Lorenzo de' Medici, Michelangelo Buonarroti, Leonardo da Vinci

▶ **Places to Locate**
Florence, Rome, Venice

 Find Out What factors inspired the Renaissance?

The Storyteller

Michelangelo finished the Sistine Chapel in September 1512. Pope Julius came to see the completed work. One man had covered ten thousand square feet with the greatest wall painting in Italy. Michelangelo wrote to his father, "I have finished the chapel which I have been painting. The Pope is very satisfied.... Your Michelangelo, sculptor, in Rome." The artist, tired and in poor health, went home to Florence, hoping for rest and relaxation.

—adapted from *Michelangelo The Man*, Donald Lord Finlayson, 1935

Ancestors of Christ, detail from the Sistine Chapel

The Renaissance—the period from about 1350 until 1600 during which western Europeans experienced a profound cultural awakening—was in many ways a continuation of the Middle Ages, but it also signaled the beginning of modern times. The Renaissance caused educated Europeans to develop new attitudes about themselves and the world around them.

The Renaissance began first in the city-states of Italy. Unlike other areas of Europe, Italy had largely avoided the economic crisis of the late Middle Ages. Italian towns remained important centers of Mediterranean trade and boosted their production of textiles and luxury goods.

More than other Europeans, Italians were attached to classical traditions. The ruins of ancient Roman buildings, arches, and amphitheaters constantly reminded them of their heritage. Moreover, through trade Italian towns remained in close contact with the Byzantine Empire, where scholars preserved the learning of ancient Greece.

Humanism

Through renewed contact with the classics, Italian scholars improved their understanding of Greek and Latin, studied old manuscripts, and copied the classical writing style. This interest in classical learning, however, was more than just a fascination with ancient times. It led to a new intellectual movement known as humanism that focused on secular, or worldly, themes rather than on the religious ideas that had concerned medieval thinkers. Humanists—the scholars who promoted humanism—accepted classical beliefs and wanted to use them to renew their own society. Among the most important beliefs was individualism, an emphasis on the dignity and worth of the individual person.

Another was the idea of human improvement, that people should develop their talents through many activities: politics, sports, and the arts.

Education and Literature

Humanists believed that education could help people improve themselves. They opened schools that taught the *studia humanitas*, or humanities—Greek, Latin, history and philosophy, the subjects taught in ancient times. These schools became so popular that humanists began to replace the clergy as teachers of the sons of the wealthy.

Humanism also inspired new forms of literature written in the vernacular and focusing on personal feelings. During the 1300s, Francesco Petrarca, or Petrarch (PEE•TRAHRK), wrote sonnets, or short poems, that expressed his love for Laura, a woman who had died during the Black Death. His friend, Giovanni Boccaccio, in the work *Decameron*, described young people who tell stories to divert their attention from the plague's horrors.

As the Renaissance developed, writers also focused on the topics of individual ambition and success. During the 1500s, Benvenuto Cellini, a goldsmith and sculptor, glorified his achievements in one of the first modern autobiographies. In a popular manual, *The Book of the Courtier*, Baldassare Castiglione (bahl•dahs•SAHR•ray kahs•steel •YOHN•ay) gave advice to men and women on the Renaissance ideal of good behavior. Men were to be skilled in many activities; women were to be graceful, attractive, and courteous. The diplomat Niccolò Machiavelli (mak•ee•uh•VEHL•ee) wrote *The Prince*, a book that realistically analyzed the politics of Renaissance Italy. Rulers, Machiavelli said, should be ready to use force and deceit to hold power. Critics charged that *The Prince* justified immoral behavior in politics, but Machiavelli's book appealed to power-hungry Renaissance rulers. It also influenced the thought and actions of later political leaders.

Scholarship

Humanist scholars influenced more than just literature. With their independent thinking, they began to challenge long-accepted traditions, assumptions, and institutions. As they made all sorts of unsettling discoveries, it further validated their desire to challenge and question nearly everything—even long-standing church traditions. For example, in an exciting piece of Renaissance detective work, the scholar Lorenzo Valla determined that a document that supposedly provided the legal basis for the pope's supremacy over kings was actually a forgery.

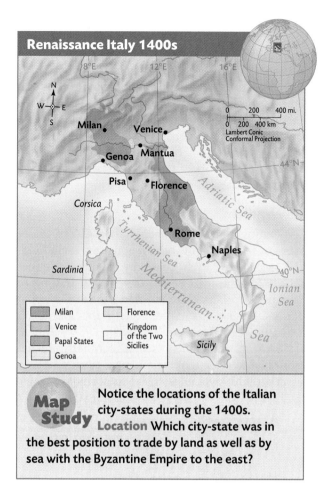

Renaissance Italy 1400s

Map Study Notice the locations of the Italian city-states during the 1400s. **Location** Which city-state was in the best position to trade by land as well as by sea with the Byzantine Empire to the east?

Through their teaching and writing, humanists reawakened the educated public to classical values. They also encouraged a ferment of new ideas that eventually spread from Italy throughout Europe and reshaped European civilization.

City Life

Town life was stronger in Italy than in other parts of Europe. As a result, Italians could easily discard feudalism and other medieval institutions that had their origins in the rural north. Italy did not become unified as did France and England. Wealthy and successful, most Italian communes, or communities, resisted the efforts of emperors, kings, and nobles to control them. They became independent city-states, each of which included a walled urban center and the surrounding countryside.

Social Groups

The Italian city-states fashioned a new social order in which wealth and ability mattered more than aristocratic titles and ownership of land. Wealthy merchants and bankers replaced the landed nobility as the most powerful social and political group—the upper class. Shopkeepers and artisans ranked below the wealthy merchants, forming a moderately prosperous middle class that employed large numbers of poor workers. Most of these workers—who were the majority of town dwellers—came to urban areas from the countryside. At the bottom of the social order were the peasants who worked on the country estates of the wealthy classes.

Government

During the Renaissance, Italy was not under one government, but instead consisted of individual city-states, each ruled by wealthy families whose fortunes came from commercial trading or banking. Workers often rebelled against the upper classes. Their demands for equal rights and lower taxes, however, were suppressed.

During the 1400s, social conflicts created upheaval so often that certain city-states felt it necessary to turn over all political authority to a single powerful leader to restore peace. These powerful political leaders were called signori (seen•YOHR •ee). Some signori ruled as dictators, using violence to maintain control. Others successfully ensured popular loyalty by improving city services, supporting the arts, and providing festivals and parades for the lower classes.

While dealing with internal unrest, city-states also fought with each other in territorial disputes. But the prosperous merchants and bankers, unlike the nobility they had supplanted, did not want to fight in these battles. Since military service would interfere with conducting business and trade, the signori chose to replace citizen-soldiers with hired soldiers known as condottieri (KAHN•duh•TYEHR•ee).

Hiring condottieri made wars very costly. To avoid this expense, signori began to seek territorial gain through negotiated agreements. To carry out this policy, they assembled the first modern diplomatic services. Permanent ambassadors were appointed to represent their city-states at foreign

Images of the Times

Art of the Italian Renaissance

The Italian Renaissance produced a host of great Italian artists and sculptors. Among the most notable of these were Michelangelo, Raphael, and Leonardo da Vinci.

Michelangelo created *David*, a gigantic marble sculpture, while at home in Florence between 1501 and 1504. A painter, architect, sculptor, and poet, he has had an unparalleled influence on Western art.

courts. The city-states also worked out an agreement among all the city-states that no one city-state would be allowed enough power to threaten the others. During the 1500s other European states adopted similar agreements with one another and also began to practice diplomacy.

Although the Italian city-states had much in common, each developed its own characteristic life. Three cities in particular played leading roles in the Renaissance: **Florence**, **Rome**, and **Venice**.

Florence

Originally a republic, Florence in the 1400s came under the control of a prominent banking family known as the Medici (MEH•duh•chee). Medici rulers helped to foster the spirit of humanism among the city-state's scholars and artists. With this spirit alive throughout the city, Florence became the birthplace of the Italian Renaissance.

Cosimo de' Medici gained control of Florence in 1434. He worked to end worker uprisings by introducing an income tax that placed a heavier burden on wealthier citizens. He used the tax revenues to make city improvements, such as sewers and paved streets, that benefited everyone. Cosimo also worked to establish peaceful relations between the city and its neighbors.

Cosimo's grandson **Lorenzo de' Medici** ruled Florence from 1469 to 1492, and he continued policies like those of his grandfather. He used his wealth to support artists, philosophers, and writers and to sponsor public festivals. As a result of the city's prosperity and fame, Lorenzo was known as "the Magnificent."

During the 1490s Florence's economic prosperity, based mostly on the banking and textile industries, began to decline with increasing competition from English and Flemish cloth makers. Tired of the Medici rule, discontented citizens rallied in support of a Dominican friar named Girolamo Savonarola (SA•vuh•nuh•ROH•luh). In fiery sermons before hundreds of people, Savonarola attacked the Medici for promoting ideas that he claimed were causing the downfall of Florence:

Leonardo da Vinci painted the *Mona Lisa* during a period of intensive study in Florence in 1503. His talent was also expressed in sculpture, architecture, and engineering.

Raphael painted the *School of Athens* for Pope Julius II. When Raphael died in Rome on his 37th birthday, the whole city mourned. His funeral mass was celebrated at the Vatican.

REFLECTING ON THE TIMES

1. What Renaissance values are reflected in the paintings and sculpture shown in this feature?
2. Why are there many similarities in style and subject matter among works of the Italian Renaissance?

Rome

During the 1500s Rome emerged as a leading Renaissance city. In Rome, the pope and the cardinals living in the Vatican made up the wealthiest and most powerful class.

Eager to increase their prestige, Renaissance popes rebuilt the ancient city. Architects constructed large churches and palaces, and artists created magnificent paintings and sculptures to decorate these buildings. Scholars came from all over Europe to study manuscripts and books in the Vatican Library.

Renaissance popes often placed political goals ahead of religious duties. In ruling Rome and its surroundings, they sent ambassadors to other lands, collected taxes, and fought wars. The most politically minded pope was Alexander VI. Elected pope in 1492, Alexander had bribed the College of Cardinals to vote for him. Once in office, he used the wealth of the Church to support his family, the Borgias. He especially encouraged his son Cesare, who raised an army and conquered much of central Italy.

After Alexander's death in 1503, his successors, Julius II and later Leo X, promoted artistic projects to beautify Rome. Their most notable effort was the rebuilding of St. Peter's Basilica, the largest church in the Christian world.

Venice

Another Renaissance center was Venice, the port city on the Adriatic Sea. Venice's economic power, enjoyed since the Crusades, was fading because of changing trade routes and Muslim invasions in the east. However, the city's role as a link between Asia and western Europe still drew traders from all over the world. Venetian shipyards also turned out huge galleys, and Venetian workshops produced high quality glass.

One benefit of Venice's prosperity was political stability. Venice's republican government was headed by an elected **doge**, (DOHJ), or leader. The doge officially ran the city, but the wealthiest merchants meeting in committee as the Council of Ten held the real power. This council passed laws, elected the doge, and even had to be consulted should the doge's son want to marry.

Influenced by Byzantine as well as western European culture, Venice was known for its artistic achievements. Painters, such as Titian, Tintoretto, and Giorgione, used brilliant oil colors to portray rural landscapes and classical and religious themes. Venetian architects, such as Sansovino and Palladio, erected buildings in the classical style.

History & Art **Brunelleschi's sculpture of the sacrifice of Isaac was a contest entry for the east doors of the Baptistry in Florence.** *Brunelleschi lost but is remembered for what architectural feat?*

❝ In the mansions of the great prelates and great lords there is no concern save for poetry and the oratorical art. Go … and see; [you] shall find them all with books of the humanities in their hands.… Arise and come to deliver [your] Church from the hands of the devils! ❞

So many people were won over by Savonarola that the Medici family was forced to turn over the rule of Florence to his supporters. On Savonarola's advice, the city's new leaders imposed strict regulations on public behavior. Gambling, swearing, and horse racing were banned. Savonarola urged his listeners to repent of their "worldly" ways. He had crowds make bonfires to burn books, paintings, fancy clothes, and musical instruments.

Savonarola soon aroused a great deal of opposition to his preaching. His criticism of church officials angered the pope. Many people in Florence disliked his strict ways. In 1498 Savonarola was hanged for heresy, and the Medici family returned to power. By this time, however, Florence's greatness had passed.

Renaissance Arts

What were the unique characteristics of Renaissance art? The humanists' emphasis on cultivating individual talent inspired Italian artists to express their own values, emotions, and attitudes. No longer content with creating symbolic representations of their subjects, artists made their subjects as lifelike and captivating as possible. Although much of the art was still devoted to religious subjects, it had more secular, or worldly, overtones. Interest in ancient Greece and Rome moved artists to include classical mythology as well as biblical themes in their works.

To make their creations lifelike and captivating, artists experimented with new techniques. For example, they learned to create a sense of perspective, which gave their paintings depth. They studied anatomy so they could portray human figures more accurately and naturally. Artists also learned to depict subtleties of gesture and expression to convey human emotions. Much of their work consisted of frescoes, or paintings done on damp plaster.

The public in Renaissance Italy appreciated works of art and hailed great artists as geniuses. Nobles and townspeople used art to decorate homes as well as churches. They lavishly rewarded artists and gave them a prominent place in society.

Architecture

During the Middle Ages, cathedral architects had pointed soaring arches and spires heavenward for the glory of God. During the Renaissance, however, Italian architects returned to the classical style. On churches, palaces, and villas they substituted domes and columns from classical Greek and Roman architecture for the medieval arches and spires. They sought both comfort and beauty in their buildings, adorning them with tapestries, paintings, statues, finely made furniture, and glass windows. Unlike the anonymous architects of the Middle Ages, Renaissance architects took credit for their fine buildings.

The most famous Italian Renaissance architect was Filippo Brunelleschi (BROO•nuhl•EHS•kee), best known for the dome he designed and completed in 1436 for the Cathedral of Florence. Until Brunelleschi submitted his design, no one had been able to come up with a way to construct a dome large or strong enough to cover the cathedral without the dome collapsing from its own weight. Brunelleschi's design—based on his own study of the domes, columns, and arches of ancient Rome—was considered to be the greatest engineering feat of the time.

Sculpture

Renaissance sculpture reflected a return to classical ideals. The free-standing statues of nude figures sculpted in bronze or marble during the Renaissance resembled ancient Greek and Roman sculptures of nude figures much more than they did medieval sculptures. Human figures in medieval sculptures had usually been portrayed in a stiff, stylized manner.

Some of the best-known Renaissance sculptors—Donatello, Michelangelo, and Ghiberti (gee•BEHR•tee)—came from Florence. There the Medicis opened a school for sculptors. Donatello was the first sculptor since ancient times to cast a large, free-standing nude statue. Although the sculptor **Michelangelo Buonarroti** later went to Rome to sculpt works for the pope, he learned his craft in Florence. Florentine sculptor Lorenzo Ghiberti took 21 years to create 10 biblical scenes on bronze doors for Florence's cathedral baptistry.

Painting

Italian Renaissance painters departed from the flat, symbolic style of medieval painting to begin a more realistic style. This change first appeared in the early 1300s when the Florentine artist-sculptor-architect Giotto (jee•AH•toh) effectively captured human emotions in a series of frescoes portraying the life of Francis of Assisi. In the 1400s Florentine

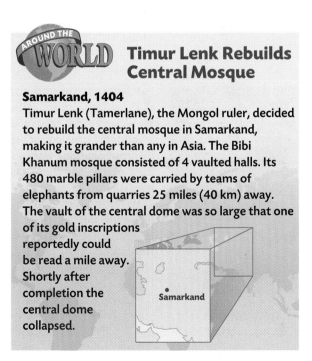

Timur Lenk Rebuilds Central Mosque

Samarkand, 1404
Timur Lenk (Tamerlane), the Mongol ruler, decided to rebuild the central mosque in Samarkand, making it grander than any in Asia. The Bibi Khanum mosque consisted of 4 vaulted halls. Its 480 marble pillars were carried by teams of elephants from quarries 25 miles (40 km) away. The vault of the central dome was so large that one of its gold inscriptions reportedly could be read a mile away. Shortly after completion the central dome collapsed.

Victor R. Boswell, Jr.

"The Last Supper"

Victor R. Boswell, Jr.

"One of you shall betray me," said Jesus, sitting amid the disciples gathered around in a flurry of worry, gossip, and fear. Between 1495 and 1497 Leonardo da Vinci painted *The Last Supper* on the walls of a monastery in Milan, Italy. Unstable paint and centuries of wear slowly destroyed the mural. In 1977 restoration of the painting began, as shown in the detail (above) depicting the apostles Matthew, Thaddeus, and Simon. The larger view of the master-

piece (left) shows visitors clustered around while restorers continue their work.

Da Vinci was one of the most famous painters of the Italian Renaissance. During the Renaissance the peoples of Europe began to see themselves as Europeans rather than as members of the kingdom of Christendom whose single passport was belief. The Renaissance was a period of upheaval and change in religion, politics, and economy. The arts flourished. Writers began using the language of their own nations instead of Latin. Painters, architects, and sculptors experimented with new techniques. Expressing his belief in the newfound power of paintings, da Vinci boasted that the painter could "even induce men to fall in love with a picture that does not portray any living woman." Indeed, people throughout the ages have fallen in love with *The Last Supper*. ⊕

artist Masaccio (muh•ZAH•chee•oh) employed lighting and perspective in his paintings to give depth to the human body and to set off his figures from the background. He thus created an even greater sense of realism than Giotto had.

One of the greatest Renaissance artists was **Leonardo da Vinci** (VIHN•chee). A citizen of Florence, he did much of his work in Milan and Rome. Da Vinci is best known for the *Mona Lisa*, a portrait of a strangely smiling young woman of Florence, and *The Last Supper*, a wall painting of Jesus' last meal with his disciples. In both works, da Vinci skillfully portrayed the subjects' personalities, thoughts, and feelings. He also made designs in notebooks on astronomy, mathematics, and anatomy. These drawings often pictured parachutes, flying machines, and other mechanical inventions far ahead of his time.

Another outstanding Renaissance artist—Michelangelo Buonarroti—began his career as a sculptor in Florence. There he did a famous marble statue of David, after the heroic biblical king. Later in Rome he sculpted *La Pietà* (PEE•ay•TAH), which shows the dead Jesus in the arms of his mother, Mary. Most of Michelangelo's sculptures were awesome in size and suggested controlled but intense emotions.

In 1508 Pope Julius II hired Michelangelo to work at the Vatican, painting the ceiling of the Sistine Chapel with scenes from the Bible. All of Michelangelo's painted figures resembled sculptures. They had well-formed muscular bodies that expressed vitality and power. Michelangelo ended his career by designing the dome of the new St. Peter's Basilica.

Like Michelangelo, the artist Raphael Santi worked at the Vatican. He completed a series of paintings on classical and religious themes for the pope's apartment. Raphael is most noted for his paintings of Mary, the mother of Jesus. These works were done in bright colors and reflected the Renaissance ideals of grace, harmony, and beauty.

History & Art *La Pietà* by Michelangelo Buonarroti. St. Peter's Basilica, The Vatican, Rome, Italy
What is the subject of La Pietà?

Women and the Arts

Although Renaissance women had few roles independent of men, some of them did contribute to the arts. These women were either daughters of artists who trained in their fathers' workshops or children of noblemen, who were expected to have literary, musical, and artistic skills. Among the most celebrated female artists were the portrait painters Lavinia Fontana and Sofonisba Anguissola (soh•foh•NIHZ•bah ahn•gwee•SOH•lah). An Italian noblewoman, Anguissola became a painter at the Spanish royal court of King Philip II.

SECTION I REVIEW

Recall
1. **Define** humanism, secular, individualism, sonnet, doge.
2. **Identify** Niccolò Machiavelli, Lorenzo de' Medici, Savonarola, Michelangelo Buonarroti, Leonardo da Vinci.
3. **Discuss** the meaning of the term "Renaissance." To what does it refer? What were its major characteristics?

Critical Thinking
4. **Making Comparisons** How does the role of female artists today compare with that of female artists in Renaissance times?

Understanding Themes
5. **Innovation** Identify one masterpiece in Renaissance literature or the arts. Explain how it reflects Renaissance ideals. Also state what subject is represented.

c. 1456 Johannes Gutenberg uses movable metal type in printing.

1494 Francis I of France invades Italy.

1509 Desiderius Erasmus writes *The Praise of Folly*.

Section 2

The Northern Renaissance

Setting the Scene

▶ **Terms to Define**
   châteaux

▶ **People to Meet**
   Johannes Gutenberg, François Rabelais, Desiderius Erasmus, Pieter Brueghel, Thomas More, William Shakespeare

▶ **Places to Locate**
   the Low Countries

 **Find Out** How did the Renaissance reach northern Europe?

The Storyteller

When Shakespeare's play Hamlet *opened in London, about 2,000 people crowded in to see the performance. Admission was one penny. Down in front of the stage, where it was standing room only, the crowd could be noisy. One writer complained: "Such heaving, and shoving, such pushing and shouldering— especially by the women! Such care for their clothes, that no one step on their dress;…. Such smiling and winking…. Never mind the stage—it is a comedy to watch them!"*

—freely adapted from *Shakespeare: Of an Age For All Time*, The Yale University Festival Lectures, edited by Charles Tyler Prouty, 1954

William Shakespeare

During the late 1400s, Renaissance art and humanist ideas—characterized by a revival of interest in classical antiquity— began to filter northward from Italy to France, England, the Netherlands, and other European countries. War, trade, travel, and a newly invented method of printing helped to promote this cultural diffusion. The people of the Northern Renaissance adapted ideas of the Italian Renaissance to their own individual tastes, values, and needs.

Spreading Ideas

War, as usual, helped spread ideas by furthering contact between people of different cultures. After France invaded Italy in 1494, French kings and their warrior-nobles became fascinated by Italian Renaissance art and fashions. In 1517 King Francis I brought Leonardo da Vinci to his court in France, thus helping to promote the entry of Renaissance ideas into northern Europe. Other European monarchs also developed an enthusiasm for the Renaissance. Kings and queens so eagerly supported scholars and artists that the number of humanists in the north grew rapidly along with the popularity of humanist ideas.

At the same time, Italian traders living in the north set an example for northern European merchants, who began to appreciate wealth, beauty, personal improvement, and other Renaissance values. These northern merchants—having only recently become successful enough to afford lifestyles based upon such values—began to spend their wealth on education, fine houses, and material goods. Some northern Europeans began to travel to Italy to study with Italian masters. Thus began the emergence of a newly educated middle class.

This spread of knowledge among the middle class was aided by the invention of the printing press. By the 1400s, German engravers had developed movable type, in which the type was set into adjustable molds, inked, and then pressed onto a sheet of paper. In 1456 **Johannes Gutenberg** printed a complete edition of the Bible using movable metal type. As a result of this invention, books were published more quickly and less expensively. Production of humanist texts could now begin to match the newfound desire for such works.

Although Italian Renaissance ideas became quite popular in the north, they were not merely transplanted there. Rather, northern scholars interpreted them according to their own individual ways of thinking. Furthermore, the people of each northern culture adapted these ideas to suit their own needs and traditions.

The French Renaissance

The French Renaissance had a character all its own. French architects blended medieval Gothic towers and windows with the classical arches used by Italian architects to create châteaux (sha•TOHZ), or castles, for Francis I and his nobles. These large country estates were erected primarily in the Loire River valley. The château of Chambord is a fine example.

Many French Renaissance writers borrowed extensively from the new literary forms of the Italian Renaissance. Inspired by Petrarch's sonnets, Pierre Ronsard (rohn•SAHR) wrote his own sonnets with common humanist themes such as love, the passing of youth, and the poet's immortality. Michel de Montaigne (mahn•TAYN) may have based his informal and direct style on Italian literary models. He cultivated the literary form called the personal essay, a short prose composition written to express clearly the personal view of a writer on a subject. In his essay "Of the Disadvantages of Greatness," Montaigne analyzed the authority of royalty:

> ❝ The most difficult occupation in the world, in my opinion, is to play the part of a king worthily. I excuse more of their faults than people commonly do, in consideration of the dreadful weight of their burden, which dazes me. It is difficult for a power so immoderate to observe moderation.... ❞

Physician-monk **François Rabelais** (RA•buh •LAY), France's most popular Renaissance author, wrote comic tales, satires, and parodies on a broad spectrum of contemporary life. He rejected the

Visualizing History *Erasmus* by Quentin Metsys. The "Prince of the Humanists" joined a love for the classics with respect for Christian values. *What reforms did Christian humanists promote?*

Middle Ages' focus on the afterlife and believed that people should enjoy life to the fullest. Exceptionally knowledgeable and gifted as a writer, he also wrote on such subjects as law, medicine, politics, theology, botany, and navigation.

Northern Europe

The Italian Renaissance was enthusiastically accepted by the wealthy towns of Germany and **the Low Countries** (present-day Belgium, Luxembourg, and the Netherlands). Universities and schools promoted humanist learning, and printers produced a large quantity of books. Latin was still the main scholarly language, but writers increased their use of German and Dutch.

Christian Humanism

Unlike in Italy, the Renaissance in northern Europe had a more religious tone. Groups of scholars, known as Christian humanists, wanted reforms in Catholicism that would eliminate abuses and restore the simple piety of the early Church. They believed that humanist learning and Bible study were the best ways to promote these goals.

The most famous Christian humanist, **Desiderius Erasmus** (dehz•ih•DEER•ee•uhs ih•RAZ•muhs), inspired his colleagues to study

Peasant's Dance by Pieter Brueghel the Elder. **The painting emphasizes the enjoyments of common people.** *What four subjects did northern European realistic artists paint?*

Greek and Hebrew so that they could understand older versions of the Bible written in these languages. Erasmus also used biting humor to make people take a more critical view of society. He specifically attacked the wealth of Renaissance popes. In his noted work, *In Praise of Folly*, he describes these popes, claiming that they were so corrupt they no longer practiced Christianity:

> 66 Scarce any kind of men live more [devoted to pleasure] or with less trouble.... To work miracles is … not in fashion now; to instruct the people, troublesome; to interpret the Scripture, [too bookish]; to pray, a sign one has little else to do … and lastly, to die, uncouth; and to be stretched on a cross, infamous. 99

Northern European Painters

Artists in northern Europe developed a style of painting that relied more on medieval than classical models. In the early 1400s, a group of Flemish painters, led by the brothers Jan and Hubert van Eyck (EYEK), painted scenes from the Bible and daily life in sharp, realistic detail. They developed the technique of painting in oils. Oils provided artists with richer colors and allowed them to make changes on the painted canvas. Painting in oils soon spread to Italy. Meanwhile, Italian Renaissance art reached northern Europe. Artists such as Albrecht Dürer and **Pieter Brueghel** (BROY•guhl) combined Italian technique with the artistic traditions of their homelands. They painted realistic portraits, religious themes, landscapes, and scenes of daily life.

The English Renaissance

Renaissance ideas did not spread to England until 1485, when the Wars of the Roses—bloody conflicts over who was the rightful heir to the throne—ended. Ultimately, the Tudor family defeated the York family, bringing the Tudor king Henry VII to power. Henry invited Italian Renaissance scholars to England, where they taught humanist ideas and encouraged the study of classical texts.

English humanists expressed deep interest in social issues. **Thomas More**, a statesman and a friend of Erasmus, wrote a book that criticized the society of his day by comparing it with an ideal society in which all citizens are equal and prosperous. The book, written in Latin, was called *Utopia*.

The English Renaissance was especially known for drama. The best-known English playwrights were **William Shakespeare** and Christopher Marlowe. They drew ideas for their works from medieval legends, classical mythology, and the histories of England, Denmark, and ancient Rome. Shakespeare dealt with universal human qualities such as jealousy, ambition, love, and despair so effectively that his plays are still relevant to audiences today.

SECTION 2 REVIEW

Recall

1. **Define** châteaux.
2. **Identify** Johannes Gutenberg, Michel de Montaigne, François Rabelais, Desiderius Erasmus, Jan and Hubert van Eyck, Pieter Brueghel, Thomas More, William Shakespeare.

3. **Describe** some elements of Italian Renaissance architecture used by French architects. How did they transform French architecture?

Critical Thinking

4. **Applying Information** Choose one writer or artist from the Northern Renaissance and explain how the works of this writer or artist reflected Renaissance ideas.

Understanding Themes

5. **Cultural Diffusion** How did Italian Renaissance ideas spread to northern Europe?

1517 Martin Luther preaches against indulgences.

1520 The Church condemns Luther's works.

c. 1550 Lutheranism spreads through northern Europe.

Section 3

The Protestant Reformation

Setting the Scene

▸ **Terms to Define**
   justification by faith, indulgences, vocation

▸ **People to Meet**
   Martin Luther, Pope Leo X

▸ **Places to Locate**
   Wittenberg, Worms

 **ind Out** How did Luther's religious reforms lead to Protestantism, a new branch of Christianity?

The Storyteller

In later years, Martin Luther remembered the fateful day he entered the monastery: "Afterwards I regretted my vow, and many of my friends tried to persuade me not to enter the monastery. I, however, was determined to go through with it.... I invited certain of my best men friends to a farewell party.... In tears they led me away; and my father was very angry ... yet I persisted in my determination. It never occurred to me to leave the monastery." Luther's break with the Church was an even bigger decision than the one to enter monastic life.

—adapted from *Luther and His Times*, E.G. Schweibert, 1950

Martin Luther

The Renaissance values of humanism and secularism stimulated widespread criticism of the Catholic Church's extravagance. By about 1500, educated Europeans began calling for a reformation—a change in the Church's ways of teaching and practicing Christianity. In Germany the movement for church reform eventually led to a split in the Church that produced a new form of Christianity known as Protestantism. The series of events that gave birth to Protestantism is known as the Protestant Reformation.

Martin Luther

The Protestant Reformation was begun by a German monk named **Martin Luther**, born in 1483, the son of middle-class townspeople. His father wanted him to become a lawyer, but Luther was interested in religion. In 1505 he was nearly struck by lightning in a thunderstorm. Terrified that the storm was God's way of punishing him, the law student knelt and prayed to Saint Anne. In return for protection, he promised to become a monk. Shortly thereafter, Luther entered a monastery.

As a young monk, Luther struggled to ensure his soul's salvation. He would confess his sins for hours at a time. Yet still he worried that God might not find him acceptable.

Then he read Saint Paul's Epistle to the Romans: "He who through faith is righteous shall live"—and Luther's worries dissolved. He interpreted this to mean that a person could be made just, or good, simply by faith in God's mercy and love. Luther's idea became known as justification by faith. Luther later stated that because of this discovery he felt as if he "had been born again and had entered Paradise through wide open gates."

Luther's Protest

Luther's ideas gradually matured and eventually brought him into conflict with the Church. At this time **Pope Leo X** was trying to raise money to rebuild St. Peter's Basilica in Rome. To this end, the pope sold church positions to his friends and also authorized sales of indulgences.

Indulgences were certificates issued by the Church that were said to reduce or even cancel punishment for a person's sins—as long as one also truly repented. People purchased indulgences believing that the document would assure them admission to heaven. John Tetzel, the Church's agent for selling indulgences in northern Germany, even went so far as to promise peasants that indulgences would relieve them of guilt for *future* sins. He also encouraged people to buy indulgences for the salvation of their dead relatives. Tetzel's sale of indulgences inspired a popular jingle: "Once you

hear the money's ring, the soul from purgatory is free to spring." (According to church teaching, purgatory is a place in the afterlife where people are made fit for heaven.)

Luther, a professor and priest in the town of **Wittenberg**, preached against the sale of indulgences. He also lectured against other church practices he believed were corrupt. Then, on October 31, 1517, Luther nailed on the door of the Wittenberg Church a placard with 95 theses, or statements, criticizing indulgences and other church policies.

Breaking With Rome

Printed copies of the Ninety-five Theses spread quickly all over Germany. Sales of indulgences declined sharply. Encouraged by this reaction, Luther published hundreds of essays advocating justification by faith and attacking church abuses.

Pope Leo X responded to the decline in indulgence sales by sending envoys to Germany to persuade Luther to withdraw his criticisms. But Luther refused. In 1520 the pope formally condemned Luther and banned his works. In 1521 Pope Leo X excommunicated Luther from the Church.

CONNECTIONS
Science and Technology

Printing

Before the 1400s books had to be copied by hand—a time-consuming method. Consequently, books were rare, owned and read only by scholars and the wealthy. Gutenberg's invention of movable type changed all that: books could be produced faster at lower cost; more people were able to buy books and expand their knowledge; and traditional ideas were questioned. German printers quickly adopted Gutenberg's invention and set up similar printing presses in other European countries.

Martin Luther was one of the first authors to benefit from the new technology. Since his books could be reproduced inexpensively and in large quantities, they could be easily obtained throughout Europe short-

Gutenberg's press

ly after Luther completed them. Thus, Luther was able to spread his ideas and gain widespread support before the Catholic Church could respond.

In the past few decades, more advances have been made in printing than in all the years since Gutenberg. Today high-speed machines and computer technology together have revolutionized the printing industry. Images are now transferred onto paper directly from computer files. The development of copy machines and laser printers has also made smaller printing jobs easier.

Linking Past and Present ACTIVITY

Describe how Gutenberg's printing press transformed European society during the 1400s and 1500s. How did Luther benefit from Gutenberg's invention? Explain how computer technology and other innovations have transformed printing and other means of communication today.

Shortly after Luther's excommunication, a diet, or council, of German princes met in **Worms**, Germany, to try to bring Luther back into the Church. They decided that Luther should take back his criticisms of the papacy. Meanwhile, Luther traveled to Worms as crowds of cheering people lined the road. Luther strode into the assembly hall and, when asked to take back his teachings, gave this reply: "I am bound by the Sacred Scriptures I have cited … and my conscience is captive to the Word of God. I cannot and will not recant [take back] anything.… God help me." Luther, condemned as a heretic and outlaw, was rushed out of Worms and hidden at a castle in Wartburg by a friend, Prince Frederick of Saxony.

While in hiding, Luther translated the New Testament into German. Earlier German translations of the Bible were so rare and costly that few people had them. With Luther's more affordable translation, most people could now read the Bible.

Lutheranism

After Worms, Luther laid the foundation of the first Protestant faith: Lutheranism. While Catholicism stressed faith and good works in salvation and the importance of church teaching as a spiritual guide, Lutheranism emphasized salvation by faith alone and the Bible's role as the only source of religious truth. Lutheran services centered on biblical preaching rather than ritual and were held in the language of the people instead of Latin. In this way people could understand and participate in the services. Luther and his followers also held that the Church was not a hierarchy of clergy, but a community of believers. All useful occupations, not just the priesthood, were vocations, or callings, in which people could serve God and neighbor.

Lutheranism brought a new religious message to Germany, but it also stirred social unrest among peasants wanting to end serfdom. When a major peasant revolt erupted in 1525, Luther, fearing social chaos, backed the princes against the peasants. The princes cruelly put down the uprising, killing thousands of people. Lutheranism became a more conservative movement as a result; however, it had already sown the seeds of more radical Protestant movements that would transform Europe's religious landscape.

SECTION 3 REVIEW

Recall

1. **Define** justification by faith, indulgences, vocation.
2. **Identify** Protestant Reformation, Martin Luther, Pope Leo X.
3. **Discuss** the religious changes brought by Luther's protest against the Catholic Church.

Critical Thinking

4. **Synthesizing Information** If you wanted to protest against something today, what medium would you use to communicate your cause? Why?

Understanding Themes

5. **Conflict** Why did the pope ask Luther to recant his beliefs and then excommunicate him when Luther would not do so?

Section 4

The Spread of Protestantism

Setting the Scene

▶ **Terms to Define**
   theocracy, predestination

▶ **People to Meet**
   Huldrych Zwingli, John Calvin, the Anabaptists, Henry VIII, Catherine of Aragon, Anne Boleyn, Mary, Elizabeth I

▶ **Places to Locate**
   Zurich, Geneva

Find Out What different forms of Protestantism emerged in Europe as the Reformation spread?

Storyteller

Mary Queen of Scots was a prisoner for seventeen long years. What was she to do, as she and her keeper's wife sat together all that time? She could sew. Over the years, she and her attendant ladies embroidered seas of fabric: tablecloths, cushions, and hangings, every piece scattered with coats of arms and emblems, every piece sprinkled with gold and silver spangles to catch the light. Some became gifts; but occasionally her presents were rudely refused. Her own son, King James VI, returned a vest his mother had embroidered for him because she had addressed it to "The Prince of Scotland."

—adapted from *Mary Queen of Scots*, Roy Strong and Julia Trevelyan Oman, 1972

Mary Queen of Scots

Although the Protestant Reformation spread throughout Europe in the 1500s, divisions began to appear within the movement soon after it had started. Not only did the Protestant reformers not believe in the same methods; they did not even agree on the same goals.

Swiss Reformers

After the rise of Lutheranism in Germany, many preachers and merchants in neighboring Switzerland separated from Rome and set up churches known as Reformed. **Huldrych Zwingli**, a Swiss priest who lived from 1484 to 1531, led the Protestant movement in Switzerland. Like Luther, Zwingli stressed salvation by faith alone and denounced many Catholic beliefs and practices, such as purgatory and the sale of indulgences. Unlike Luther, though, Zwingli wanted to break completely from Catholic tradition. He wanted to establish a theocracy, or church-run state, in the Swiss city of **Zurich**. By 1525 Zwingli had achieved this goal. But in 1531 war broke out over Protestant missionary activity in the Catholic areas of Switzerland. Zwingli and his force of followers were defeated by an army of Catholics.

In the mid-1500s **John Calvin**, another reformer, established the most powerful and influential Reformed group in the Swiss city of **Geneva**. Here Calvin set up a theocracy similar to Zwingli's rule in Zurich.

Born in 1509, Calvin grew up in Catholic France at the start of the Reformation. He received an education in theology, law, and humanism that prompted him to study the Bible very carefully and to formulate his own Protestant theology. In 1536 Calvin published his theology in *The Institutes of the Christian Religion*, soon one of the most popular books of its day, influencing religious reformers in Europe and later in North America.

The cornerstone of Calvin's theology was the belief that God possessed all-encompassing power and knowledge. Calvin contended that God alone directed everything that has happened in the past, that happens in the present, and that will happen in the future. Thus, he argued, God determines the fate of every person—a doctrine he called predestination.

To advance his views, Calvin tried to turn the city of Geneva into a model religious community. He began this project in 1541 by establishing the Consistory, a church council of 12 elders that was given the power to control almost every aspect of people's daily lives. All citizens were required to attend Reformed church services several times each week. The Consistory inspected homes annually to make sure that no one was disobeying the laws that forbade fighting, swearing, drunkenness, gambling, card playing, and dancing. It dispensed harsh punishments to people who disobeyed any of these laws. This strict atmosphere earned Geneva the title "City of God" and attracted reformers from all parts of Europe.

Visitors to Geneva helped to spread Calvinism, or John Calvin's teaching, throughout Europe. Because the Calvinist church was led by local councils of ministers and elected church members, it was easy to establish in most countries. Furthermore, the somewhat democratic structure of this organization gave its participants a stake in its welfare and inspired their intense loyalty.

The people of the Netherlands and Scotland became some of Calvin's most ardent supporters. John Knox, a leader of the Reformation in Scotland, and other reformers used Calvin's teachings to encourage moral people to overthrow "ungodly" rulers. They preached, as Calvin had, "We must obey princes and others who are in authority, but only insofar as they do not deny to God, the supreme King, Father, and Lord, what is due Him." Calvinism thus became a dynamic social force in western Europe in the 1500s and contributed to the rise of revolutionary movements later in the 1600s and 1700s.

Radical Reformers

Several new Protestant groups in western Europe, called **the Anabaptists**, initiated the practice of baptizing, or admitting into their groups, only adult members. They based this practice on the belief that only people who could make a free and informed choice to become Christians should be allowed to do so. Catholic and established Protestant churches, in contrast, baptized infants, making them church members.

Many Anabaptists denied the authority of local governments to direct their lives. They refused to hold office, bear arms, or swear oaths, and many lived separate from a society they saw as sinful. Consequently, they were often persecuted by government officials, forcing many Anabaptists to wander from country to country seeking refuge.

Although most Anabaptists were peaceful, others were fanatical in their beliefs. These zealots brought about the downfall of the rest. When in 1534 radical Anabaptists seized power in the German city of Münster and proceeded to burn books, seize private property, and practice polygamy, Lutherans and Catholics united to crush them. Together they killed the Anabaptist leaders and persecuted any surviving Anabaptist believers.

As a result, many Anabaptist groups left Europe for North America during the 1600s. In the Americas, the Anabaptists promoted two ideas that would become crucial in forming the United States of America: religious liberty and separation of church and state. Today, Protestant groups such as the Baptists, Mennonites, and Amish all trace their ancestry to the Anabaptists.

England's Church

Reformation ideas filtered into England during the 1500s. A serious quarrel between King **Henry VIII** and the pope, however, brought these ideas to the forefront.

The quarrel arose over succession to the throne. Although Henry's wife **Catherine of Aragon** had borne six children, only one child, Mary, survived. Henry wanted to leave a male heir to the throne so that England might not be plunged into another civil war like the Wars of the Roses. Believing that Catherine was too old to have more children, the king decided to marry **Anne Boleyn**. In 1527 Henry

Footnotes to History

King Henry VIII
Henry VIII was a typical Renaissance ruler who tried to excel in many areas. He enjoyed tennis, jousting, music, and discussions about religion and the sciences. He wrote a book of theology and composed several pieces of music, one of which may have been the song "Greensleeves."

Henry VIII, a portrait by Hans Holbein, shows the king's splendid royal attire, reflecting his authority. *Why did Henry seek Parliament's support in breaking with the Catholic Church?*

English Church instead of the pope. Despite this break with Rome, Henry was not a Protestant reformer. The new Church of England kept Catholic doctrines and forms of worship. Devout Catholics, however, opposed the king's rule of the Church. The most noted Catholic, the humanist scholar Thomas More, was beheaded for treason in 1535. Henry took other measures against supporters of the old religion. Between 1536 and 1540, he closed monasteries and convents, seized their land, and shared the gains with nobles and other high officials. In this way, the king filled his treasury and ensured influential support for his religious policies.

Henry also worked to strengthen the succession to the throne. He had the Church of England end his marriage to Catherine and then wed Anne Boleyn. Anne bore him a daughter, Elizabeth. In the years that followed, Henry married four more times but had only one son, Edward. When Henry died in 1547, 9-year-old Edward succeeded him to the throne. The young king was dominated by devout Protestant officials who introduced Protestant doctrines into the Church of England.

When Edward VI died in his teens, his Catholic half sister **Mary** became queen. Mary tried to restore Catholicism in England and ended up burning hundreds of Protestants at the stake. This persecution earned her the nickname of "Bloody Mary" and only served to strengthen her people's support for Protestantism.

After Mary's death in 1558, her Protestant half sister, **Elizabeth I**, became queen. To unite her people, Elizabeth followed a moderate course in religion. She made the English Church Protestant with some Catholic features. Anglicanism, as this blend of Protestant belief and Catholic practice was called, pleased most English people. However, radical Protestants known as Puritans wanted to "purify" the English Church of Catholic rituals. Although at first small in numbers, the Puritans gradually became influential both in the Church of England and the English Parliament.

asked the pope to agree to a divorce between himself and Catherine. But Catherine's nephew was the powerful Holy Roman Emperor Charles V, upon whom the pope depended for protection. Charles wanted Catherine to remain as queen of England in order to influence the country's policies in favor of his own interests. The pope refused Henry's request.

Henry would not be thwarted. With Parliament's support, he had a series of laws passed that separated the English Church from the pope. The most important law, the Act of Supremacy passed in 1534, made Henry head of the

SECTION 4 REVIEW

Recall

1. **Define** theocracy, predestination.
2. **Identify** Huldrych Zwingli, John Calvin, the Anabaptists, Henry VIII, Catherine of Aragon, Anne Boleyn, Edward VI, Mary, Elizabeth I.

3. **Explain** why divisions appeared among the different reformers within the Protestant movement.

Critical Thinking

4. **Making Comparisons** How did the Calvinists and Anabaptists differ in their attitudes

toward the government church members participating in government activities?

Understanding Themes

5. **Cultural Diffusion** Why did the Catholic Church want to stop the spread of Protestant ideas?

Critical Thinking SKILLS

Identifying Evidence

In a geography trivia game, you picked the following question: What is the longest river in the world? The game card says it is the Amazon River, but you think it is the Nile River. Your friends insist that you are wrong. How can you prove you are right?

You must identify evidence that will establish your claim. In the example above, you could consult an atlas, almanac, or encyclopedia to find the lengths of both rivers. In fact, you are correct! The Nile River is 4,160 miles long, while the Amazon is 4,000 miles long.

Learning the Skill

There are four basic kinds of evidence: 1) oral accounts (eyewitness testimony); 2) written documents (diaries, letters, books, articles); 3) objects (artifacts); and 4) visual items (photographs, videotapes, paintings). These kinds of evidence fall into one of two categories—primary evidence and secondary evidence.

Primary evidence is produced by participants or eyewitnesses to events. Eyewitness accounts or photographs of a fire are examples of primary evidence. Secondary evidence is produced later, by those who have not experienced the events directly. Textbooks and encyclopedias are examples of secondary evidence.

To identify evidence that proves a claim, first clearly define the claim. Search available information to find the kind of evidence that can prove or disprove the claim. Compare the pieces of evidence to see if they agree. Also, rate the objectivity of your evidence. In the example above, the sources you consulted—atlas, almanac, or encyclopedia—are all reliable sources of information.

However, if you are using primary sources such as letters, diaries, and news accounts, carefully assess which evidence is most reliable.

Practicing the Skill

Read the claim below. Then read each piece of evidence that follows. Decide which pieces of evidence prove the claim to be true and explain why.

Claim: *Humanism's emphasis on the value of the individual led to artistic flowering in the Renaissance.*

1. In Renaissance Italy humanist scholars opened schools to promote the study of history, philosophy, Latin, and Greek.
2. Renaissance artists used painting and sculpture to convey human emotions and values.
3. In Rome, the pope and cardinals made up the wealthiest and most powerful class of people.
4. In England, William Shakespeare wrote plays that dealt with universal human qualities such as jealousy, ambition, love, and despair.
5. The invention of the printing press spread knowledge of humanism throughout the newly emerging middle class.

Applying the Skill

Think about this claim: The humanist values of the Renaissance still dominate modern American culture. Find at least five pieces of evidence from newspapers, magazines, and other sources to prove or disprove this claim.

For More Practice

Turn to the Skill Practice in the Chapter Review on page 431 for more practice in identifying evidence.

Section 5

The Catholic Reformation

Setting the Scene

▶ **Terms to Define**
seminary, baroque

▶ **People to Meet**
Pope Paul III, the Jesuits, Ignatius of Loyola

▶ **Places to Locate**
Trent

Find Out How did the Catholic Church try to halt the spread of Protestantism?

The Storyteller

The Inquisition sometimes used "ordeals" to determine guilt or innocence, confident that God would give victory to an innocent person and punish the guilty. In the "Trial of the Cross," both parties, accuser and accused, stood before a cross with arms outstretched. The first to drop his arms was judged guilty. In the "Trial by Hot Water," the accused lifted a stone from the bottom of a boiling cauldron. If, after three days, his wound had healed, he was innocent. In the "Trial by Cold Water," the accused was tied up and lowered into water. If he sank, he was innocent. If he floated, he was guilty.

—from The Medieval Inquisition, Albert Clement Shannon, 1983

Trial of Books *(detail)*

Most of the people in Spain, France, Italy, Portugal, Hungary, Poland, and southern Germany remained Catholic during the Protestant Reformation. Nevertheless, Catholicism's power was threatened by Protestantism's increasing popularity in northern Europe. To counter the Protestant challenge, Catholics decided to enact reforms. The Catholic Church had had a history of periodic reform since the Middle Ages. Thus, in the movement that came to be known as the Counter-Reformation, or Catholic Reformation, the Church eliminated many abuses, clarified its theology, and reestablished the pope's authority over church members.

TURNING POINT

Reaffirming Catholicism

During the 1530s and 1540s, **Pope Paul III** set out to reform the Church and stem the Protestant advance. To establish the goals of the Catholic Reformation, he called a council of bishops at **Trent**, Italy, in 1545.

The Council of Trent

The Council of Trent, which met in several sessions until 1563, reaffirmed Catholic teachings that had been challenged by the Protestants. Salvation, it declared, comes through faith and good works, and church tradition is equal to the Bible as a source of religious truth. The Latin Vulgate translation of the Bible was made the only acceptable version of scripture.

The Council also put an end to many church abuses. It forbade the selling of indulgences. Clergy were ordered to follow strict rules of behavior. The

History & Art *The Council of Trent* by Titian. **Held off and on for about 20 years, this church council reaffirmed Catholic doctrine and introduced reforms.** *What Bible was made the only acceptable version?*

Council decided that each diocese had to establish a seminary, or theological school, to ensure a better-educated clergy.

The Inquisition

To deal with the Protestant threat, Pope Paul also strengthened the Inquisition. As you read in Chapter 12, the Inquisition was a church court set up to stamp out heresy. In addition to carrying out its traditional functions, the Inquisition in the 1500s introduced censorship to curtail humanist and Protestant thinking. In 1543 it published the Index of Forbidden Books, a list of works considered too immoral or irreligious for Catholics to read.

The Arts

The Church also used the arts to further the Catholic Reformation. The Council of Trent maintained the Church's elaborate art and ritual, and it declared that the Mass should be said only in Latin.

Church art and Latin ritual were to serve as sources of inspiration for educated and less educated Catholics alike. Many artists were influenced by the intensely emotional devotion of the Catholic Reformation. One of these was the Greek painter Domenikos Theotokopoulos, known in Spain as El Greco, or "The Greek." Residing in Spain, El Greco painted the saints in distorted figures that showed strong religious feelings.

As the Catholic Reformation spread through Europe, it helped spark a new style of art and architecture called baroque (buh•ROHK). The Renaissance arts had shown restraint, simplicity, and order, but the baroque arts stressed emotion, complexity, and exaggeration for dramatic effect. In painting, Peter Paul Rubens of Flanders was a master of the baroque style. He painted large altarpieces of emotional religious scenes as well as mythological subjects. Another master was the Spaniard Diego Velázquez, who painted portraits at the Spanish royal court. Among the most famous

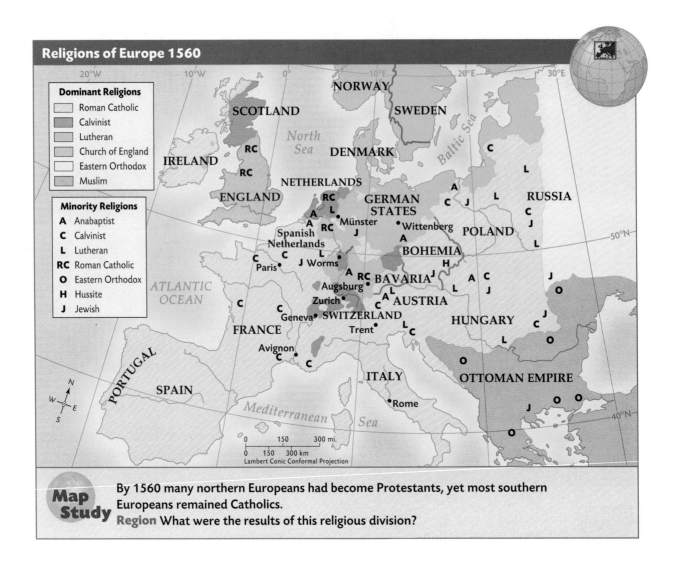

Religions of Europe 1560

Dominant Religions
- Roman Catholic
- Calvinist
- Lutheran
- Church of England
- Eastern Orthodox
- Muslim

Minority Religions
- A Anabaptist
- C Calvinist
- L Lutheran
- RC Roman Catholic
- O Eastern Orthodox
- H Hussite
- J Jewish

Map Study By 1560 many northern Europeans had become Protestants, yet most southern Europeans remained Catholics.
Region What were the results of this religious division?

baroque architects was the Italian artist Gian Lorenzo Bernini. His best known work is the public square of St. Peter's Basilica in Rome, which is enclosed by two great semicircles of columns.

Spreading Catholicism

The Church also set out to win converts and to strengthen the spiritual life of Catholics. Many religious orders and individuals in the Church became involved in these efforts.

Ignatius of Loyola

In 1540 the pope recognized a new religious order, the Society of Jesus, or **Jesuits**. Founded by **Ignatius of Loyola**, the Jesuits worked to spread Catholicism and combat heresy.

Ignatius was a Spanish noble whose military career had ended abruptly when he was wounded in battle. During a long recovery, he found comfort in the lives of the saints and vowed to serve God.

The outcome of his vow was the founding of the Jesuits, who followed a strict spiritual discipline and pledged absolute obedience to the pope.

The Jesuits wore the black robes of monks, lived simple lives, but did not withdraw from the world. They preached to the people, helped the poor, and set up schools. They also served as advisers in royal courts and founded universities. Jesuit centers of learning taught not only theology but also physics, astronomy, mathematics, archaeology, and other subjects.

As missionaries, the Jesuits helped strengthen Catholicism in southern Germany, Bohemia, Poland, and Hungary. They also carried their message to the Americas, Africa, and Asia. The Jesuit priest Matteo Ricci, for example, traveled to China and preached Christianity at the court of the Ming emperor. To make his message relevant to Chinese needs, Ricci learned to speak Chinese and dressed in Chinese clothing. Although he had little success in spreading his religious beliefs, Ricci shared with Chinese scholars his knowledge of European arts and sciences.

Teresa of Avila

Another supporter of Catholic renewal was the Spanish nun Teresa of Avila. Born to a noble family in 1515, Teresa entered a Carmelite convent. Daily life there, however, was not strict enough for the deeply religious Teresa, so she set up her order of Carmelite nuns. With the pope's approval, Teresa later opened many new convents throughout Spain. Made a saint after her death, Teresa became known for her spiritual writings that rank among the devotional classics of Christianity.

A Divided Europe

While Catholicism carried out reforms, the Catholic Holy Roman Emperor Charles V tried, but failed, to stem the spread of Protestantism in his domains. Finally, in 1555, Charles and the German princes signed the Peace of Augsburg, which allowed each prince—whether Catholic or Lutheran—to choose the religion of his subjects.

This treaty set the stage for the division of Europe into a Protestant north and a Catholic south, a division that remains to this day. Northern Germany and Scandinavia were Lutheran as a result of the efforts of monarchs and princes. Areas of southern Germany, Switzerland, the Netherlands, and Scotland—with their economic wealth based in towns—held to Calvinism. England set up its own Anglican Church, a blend of Protestantism and Catholicism under royal control.

There were many reasons why Europeans in large numbers supported Protestantism. One reason was undoubtedly religious conviction. However, nonreligious factors were also involved. German princes often favored Protestantism in order to increase their power. They made Protestantism the official religion of their territories, placing it under their control. They also seized lands and wealth owned by the Catholic Church. Townspeople also rallied to the new faith, which supported their business practices. Above all, northern Europeans saw Protestantism as a way to

Visualizing History Jesuit missionaries in Japan are depicted by a Japanese painter. *Who founded the Society of Jesus?*

defy an Italian-controlled Catholic Church that drew so much money from their homelands.

During the 1500s and early 1600s, religious wars engulfed Europe, bringing widespread killing and destruction. In France, a struggle for the monarchy heightened bitter fighting between French Protestants, or Huguenots, and the Catholic majority. Both sides carried out terrible atrocities. The most infamous event was the Saint Bartholomew's Day Massacre. On that day—August 24, 1572—violence erupted that led to the killing of 3,000 Huguenots.

Religious bigotry also brought hard times to European Jews caught in the middle of the Christian feuding. One exception to this pattern of intolerance was the Netherlands, which took in Jews driven out of other areas of Europe.

SECTION 5 REVIEW

Recall
1. **Define** seminary, baroque.
2. **Identify** Pope Paul III, the Jesuits, Ignatius of Loyola.
3. **List** the educational opportunities provided by the Jesuits.

Critical Thinking
4. **Analyzing Information** List any three of the reforms proposed by the Council of Trent. Beside each, give the Protestant viewpoint to which it responded.

Understanding Themes
5. **Reaction** Evaluate the actions the Church took to halt the spread of Protestantism and their effects. Which were successful, and which were not?

from

The Prince

by Niccolò Machiavelli

ike many other Renaissance thinkers, Niccolò Machiavelli (1469–1527) analyzed human actions rather than spiritual issues. Unlike many of his contemporaries, however, he focused on the selfish side of human nature more than on humanity's potential for progress. Machiavelli observed how successful politicians won and secured power. He sent his thoughts to an Italian prince, hoping to win a position as an adviser. His ruthlessly honest look at how politicians act both confirms and challenges the views we have toward our leaders.

*t is the custom of those who are anxious to find favor in the eyes of a prince to present him with such things as they value most highly or in which they see him take delight. Hence offerings are made of horses, arms, golden cloth, precious stones and such ornaments, worthy of the greatness of the Prince. Since therefore I am desirous of presenting myself to Your Magnificence with some token of my eagerness to serve you, I have been able to find nothing in what I possess which I hold more dear or in greater esteem than the knowledge of the actions of great men which has come to me through a long experience of present-day affairs and continual study of ancient times. And having pondered long and diligently on this knowledge and tested it well, I have reduced it to a little volume which I now send to Your Magnificence. Though I consider this work unworthy of your presence, nonetheless I have much hope that your kindness may find it acceptable, if it be considered that I could offer you no better gift than to give you occasion to learn in a very short space of time all that I have come to have knowledge and understanding of over many years and through many hardships and dangers. I have not adorned the work nor inflated it with lengthy clauses nor pompous or magnificent words, nor added any other refinement or extrinsic ornament wherewith many are wont to advertise or embellish their work, for it has been my wish either that no honor should be given it or that simply the truth of the material and the gravity of the subject should make it acceptable.…

As for the exercise of the mind, the prince should read the histories of all peoples and ponder on the actions of the wise men therein recorded, note how they governed themselves in time of war, examine the reasons for their victories or defeats in order to imitate the former and avoid the latter, and above all conduct himself in accordance with the example of some great man of the past.…

We now have left to consider what should be the manners and attitudes of a prince toward his subjects and his friends. As I know that many have written on this subject I feel that I may be held presumptuous in what I have to say, if in my comments I do not follow the lines laid down by others. Since, however, it has been my intention to write something which may be of use to the understanding reader, it has seemed wiser to me to follow the real truth of the matter rather than what we imagine it to be. For imagination has created many principalities and republics that have never been seen or known to have any real existence, for how we live is so different from how we ought to live that he who studies what ought to be done rather than what is done will learn the way to his downfall rather than to his preservation. A man striving in every way to be good will meet his ruin among the great number who are not good. Hence it is necessary for a prince, if he wishes to remain in power, to learn how not to be good and to use his knowledge or refrain from using it as he may need.…

Here the question arises; whether it is better to be loved than feared or feared than loved. The answer is that it would be desirable to be both

Visualizing History Machiavelli advised **Lorenzo de' Medici, who became the ruler of Florence in 1513, to be as cunning as his grandfather, Lorenzo the Magnificent, shown here.** *Why did Machiavelli believe it is better to be feared than loved?*

CAES · BORGIA · VALENTINV

Visualizing History This portrait of Cesare Borgia embodies the pride and confidence of the prince about whom Machiavelli wrote his political commentary. Borgia, the son of the controversial Pope Alexander VI, used his position as duke of Romagna to enhance papal political power. *When should a leader not keep his word, according to Machiavelli?*

but, since that is difficult, it is much safer to be feared than to be loved, if one must choose. For on men in general this observation may be made: they are ungrateful, fickle, and deceitful, eager to avoid dangers, and avid for gain, and while you are useful to them they are all with you, offering you their blood, their property, their lives, and their sons so long as danger is remote, as we noted above, but when it approaches they turn on you. Any prince, trusting only in their words and having no other preparations made, will fall to his ruin, for friendships that are bought at a price and not by greatness and nobility of soul are paid for indeed, but they are not owned and cannot be called upon in time of need. Men have less hesitation in offending a man who is loved than one who is feared, for love is held by a bond of

obligation which, as men are wicked, is broken whenever personal advantage suggests it, but fear is accompanied by the dread of punishment which never relaxes....

Hence a wise leader cannot and should not keep his word when keeping it is not to his advantage or when the reasons that made him give it are no longer valid. If men were good, this would not be a good precept, but since they are wicked and will not keep faith with you, you are not bound to keep faith with them....

So a prince need not have all the aforementioned good qualities, but it is most essential that he appear to have them. Indeed, I should go so far as to say that having them and always practicing them is harmful, while seeming to have them is useful. It is good to appear clement [merciful], trustworthy, humane, religious, and honest, and also to be so, but always with the mind so disposed that, when the occasion arises not to be so, you can become the opposite. It must be understood that a prince and particularly a new prince cannot practice all the virtues for which men are accounted good, for the necessity of preserving the state often compels him to take actions which are opposed to loyalty, charity, humanity, and religion. Hence he must have a spirit ready to adapt itself as the varying winds of fortune command him. As I have said, so far as he is able, a prince should stick to the path of good but, if the necessity arises, he should know how to follow evil.

A prince must take great care that no word ever passes his lips that is not full of the above mentioned five good qualities, and he must seem to all who see and hear him a model of piety, loyalty, integrity, humanity, and religion. Nothing is more necessary than to seem to possess this last quality, for men in general judge more by the eye than the hand; as all can see but few can feel. Everyone sees what you seem to be, few experience what you really are and these few do not dare to set themselves up against the opinion of the majority supported by the majesty of the state. In the actions of all men and especially princes, where there is no court of appeal, the end is all that counts. Let a prince then concern himself with the acquisition or the maintenance of a state; the means employed will always be considered honorable and praised by all, for the mass of mankind is always swayed by the appearances and by the outcome of an enterprise....

I am not ignorant of the fact that many have

Visualizing History

The Pier and the Ducal Palace (detail) by Luca Carlevaris.
According to the principles of Machiavelli, why should a ruler carefully maintain the exterior of the palace?

held and hold the opinion that the things of this world are so ordered by fortune and God that the prudence of mankind may effect little change in them, indeed is of no avail at all. On this basis it could be argued that there is no point in making any effort, but we should rather abandon ourselves to destiny. This opinion has been the more widely held in our day on account of the great variations in things that we have seen and are still witnessing and which are entirely beyond human conjecture. Sometimes indeed, thinking on such matters, I am minded to share that opinion myself. Nevertheless I believe, if we are to keep our free will, that it may be true that fortune controls half of our actions indeed but allows us the direction of the other half, or almost half....

RESPONDING TO LITERATURE

1. Describe in your own words Machiavelli's view of human nature.
2. Write a brief essay giving an example that explains whether today's politicians follow Machiavelli's advice.
3. Propose an alternative principle to Machiavelli's

view that "where there is no court of appeal, the end is all that counts."
4. **Making Judgments** Do you think individuals should follow Machiavelli's advice in dealing with their family, friends, and classmates? Why or why not?

Connections Across Time

Historical Significance During the Renaissance, Europeans focused less on religion and the afterlife and more on individual achievement and on worldly concerns. Like the ancient Greeks and Romans whom they admired, Europe's educated classes stressed human achievement and supported the arts—especially architecture, painting, and sculpture.

With a renewed interest in learning, Europeans began to question age-old traditions and called for church reforms. When changes did not take place, some Europeans broke away from Catholicism and formed Protestant churches. Protestantism—emphasizing individual salvation and the worthiness of ordinary occupations—profoundly influenced the lands and cultures of northern Europe.

Using Key Terms

Write the key term that completes each sentence. Then write a sentence for each term not chosen.

a. baroque
b. humanism
c. seminary
d. vocations
e. indulgences
f. predestination
g. justification by faith
h. theocracy
i. doge
j. sonnet
k. châteaux
l. secular
m. individualism

1. The Catholic Reformation made use of a new style of art known as _____.
2. _____, or the Renaissance interest in the ancient classical writings, sparked an interest in human creativity and fulfillment.
3. A _____ was a Renaissance form of writing that dealt with the theme of love.
4. _____ is the belief that a person could be made good simply by faith in God's mercy and love.
5. The Italian city of Venice had a republican style of government headed by an elected official called a _____.

Technology Activity

Using a Computerized Card Catalog Make use of a library's computerized card catalog to choose a Renaissance artist to research. Find information about the person's life and achievements. Using your research, create an oral history about that person by role-playing him or her. Have the class ask you questions about your life and your contributions to the Renaissance. Your responses should reflect your researched information.

Using Your History Journal

One effect of the Reformation was the migration of thousands of people to colonial America. Research and write a brief history of one religious group's migration. Create a map that shows the origin and destination(s) of that group.

Reviewing Facts

1. **Government/Culture** Explain how the city-states of Renaissance Italy were governed. What social classes were present in the typical city-state?
2. **Culture** Describe how the art and architecture of the Renaissance differed from the art and architecture of the Middle Ages.
3. **History** Discuss why the Protestant and Catholic Reformations were important turning points in the history of Europe.
4. **Culture** Explain why Henry VIII separated from the Catholic Church and created the Church of England.
5. **Culture** State how Ignatius of Loyola and Teresa of Avila helped to reform Catholicism.

Critical Thinking

1. **Apply** Why did the Medici rulers use tax revenues to fund public works projects that benefited all the citizens of Florence?
2. **Analyze** What were the causes of the Protestant Reformation? Could the Reformation have occurred without a reformer such as Luther?

3. **Evaluate** How did the religious reformations of the 1500s affect Europe? How might Europe's religious heritage affect efforts toward unity today?

4. **Analyze** Apollonio Giovanni, an Italian artist, painted the entry of a group of cavaliers into a town in the 1300s, shown below. In what ways does this painting show how Renaissance artists broke away from traditional forms?

Understanding Themes

1. **Innovation** Why did the Renaissance begin in Italy? How did the movement change European thought and culture?

2. **Cultural Diffusion** How did the people of northern Europe adapt Italian Renaissance ideas to their society?

3. **Conflict** Could the conflict between Luther and the pope have been resolved if either had reacted differently? Explain.

4. **Cultural Diffusion** What factors helped Protestant ideas to spread so rapidly?

5. **Reaction** In what ways could the Catholic Reformation be called the Counter-Reformation?

Skill Practice

Use the information in Chapter 16 to find evidence for each claim below. Then decide which claim you support.

1. Martin Luther was a sincere believer who only wanted to reform the Catholic Church.

2. Martin Luther was a rebel intent on splitting the Catholic Church.

Linking Past and Present

1. Do you think ancient Greek and Roman culture influences artists, architects, and writers as much today as it did during the Renaissance? Why or why not?

2. What ideas of the Protestant Reformation do you think affect the United States today?

Geography in History

1. **Location** What is the approximate location of the first Spanish bishopric in South America?

2. **Region** In what geographic region were most Spanish missions established during the 1500s?

3. **Human/Environment Interaction** Large areas of South America were unreached by missionaries in the first 200 years of Spanish, Portuguese, and French mission activity. What geographic feature contributed to this?

4. **Place** What river did Jesuit missionaries use as a means of gaining access to the interior of South America?

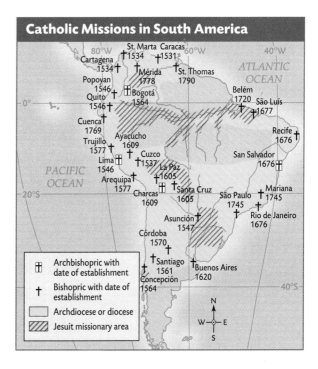

Catholic Missions in South America

Expanding Horizons

Chapter Themes

▶ **Innovation** European sailors borrow technological and navigational ideas from Asia. *Section 1*
▶ **Movement** European nations establish colonies in the lands they explore in Asia, Africa, and the Americas. *Section 2*
▶ **Change** The wealth of overseas colonies sparks the Commercial Revolution in Europe. *Section 3*

S*The*toryteller

On the night of October 11, 1492, Christopher Columbus scanned the horizon, praying that landfall was near. "About 10 o'clock at night, while standing on the sterncastle, I thought I saw a light to the west. It looked like a little wax candle bobbing up and down. It had the same appearance as a light or torch belonging to fishermen or travellers…."

The light flickered out, though, and the ship sailed on. The moon rose, but no land appeared. Two hours later, the boom of a cannon roared across the water. A sailor aboard the Pinta, *the fastest of the expedition's three ships, had sighted land. For Spain and other nations of Europe, the land that appeared in the darkness was part of a far greater treasure. As a result of Columbus's voyage, contacts increased among Europeans, Native Americans, Africans, and Asians.*

Historical Significance

How were Europe, Asia, Africa, and the Americas changed as the result of cross-cultural contacts from the 1400s to the 1700s?

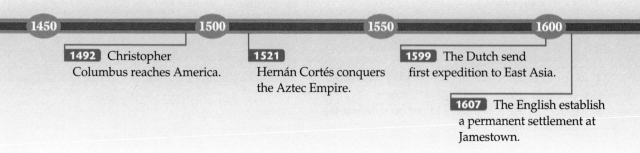

1450   **1500**   **1550**   **1600**

1492 Christopher Columbus reaches America.

1521 Hernán Cortés conquers the Aztec Empire.

1599 The Dutch send first expedition to East Asia.

1607 The English establish a permanent settlement at Jamestown.

Visualizing History This busy English port of the 1700s reveals England's position as one of Europe's major seafaring nations.

Your History Journal

Imagine crossing the Atlantic, the Pacific, or the Indian Ocean in the early 1600s. Compared to today, ships were small, and the journey was neither safe nor pleasant. Write a diary of a few days on such a voyage.

1400

1432 Prince Henry the Navigator's explorers reach the Azores.

1450

1488 Bartholomeu Dias of Portugal sails to the tip of Africa.

1500

1519 Magellan expedition sets sail from Seville, Spain.

Section 1

Early Explorations

Setting the Scene

▶ **Terms to Define**
cartographer, line of demarcation, circumnavigation

▶ **People to Meet**
Prince Henry the Navigator, Bartholomeu Dias, Vasco da Gama, Christopher Columbus, Ferdinand Magellan

▶ **Places to Locate**
Cape of Good Hope, Strait of Magellan

 **ind Out** Why did Europeans risk dangerous ocean voyages to discover sea routes to other parts of the world?

The Storyteller

Wealth was on everyone's mind when they thought about the New World. Ferdinand and Isabella wrote, "We have commanded [Columbus] to return … because thereby our Lord God is served, His Holy Faith extended and our own realms increased." The King and Queen offered financial incentives for accompanying Columbus: "Whatever persons wish to … dwell in … Hispaniola … shall pay no tax whatsoever and shall have for their own … the houses which they build and the lands which they work…." As a final enticement, Columbus insisted, "The Indians are the wealth of Hispaniola—for they perform all labor of men and beasts."

Spanish treasure

—adapted from *Ferdinand and Isabella*, Felipe Fernández-Armesto, 1975

In the 1400s European explorers tested uncharted oceans in search of a better trade route to Asia. They left their homelands filled with a desire for gold, glory, and for spreading Christianity. In just over 250 years, their ventures had destroyed and built empires at a great cost in human life. Their efforts, however, linked people of different cultures and ended forever the isolation of the world's major civilizations.

TURNING POINT

Age of Exploration

Europe in the 1300s had depended on spices from Asia. Such spices as pepper, cinnamon, and nutmeg were in great demand. Used chiefly to flavor and preserve meat, spices were also used for perfumes, cosmetics, and medicine.

The spice trade was controlled by Arab and Venetian merchants. Chinese and Indian traders sold spices to Arab merchants, who then shipped the cargoes overland to Europe and reaped huge profits in the sale of the spices to the Venetians. Europeans, eager to amass quick fortunes through direct trade with Asians, began to look for quicker routes eastward. Because the Mongols by the mid-1300s could no longer guarantee safe passage for traders on overland routes, Europeans were forced to consider the sea as a possible route to Asia.

Several motivations led Europeans into an era of exploration. Not only did merchants seek a profitable trade with Asia, but also church leaders sought to halt the expansion of Islam and to spread Christian teachings. Learning and imagination also played a part. Renaissance thinkers had expanded the European world view to include new possibilities for exploration and discovery.

Overseas voyages would end Europe's isolation and set it on the path of worldwide expansion.

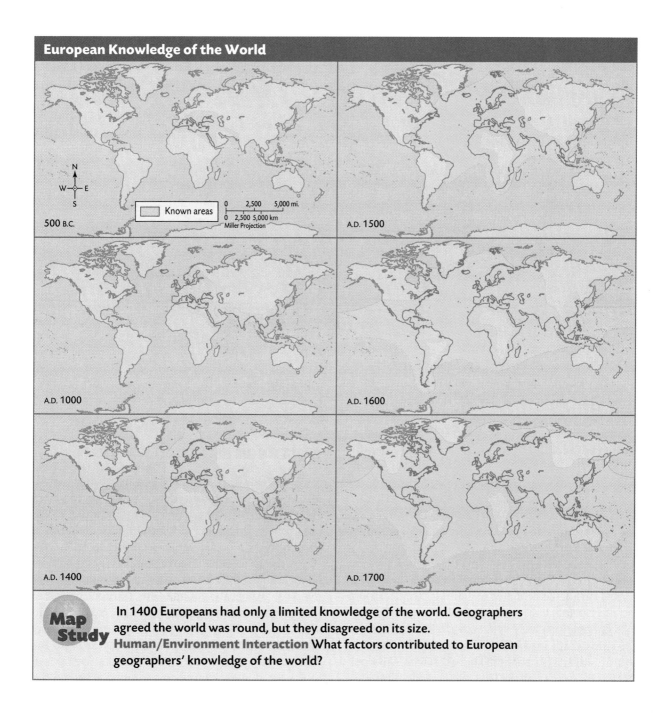

European Knowledge of the World

Known areas

0   2,500   5,000 mi.
0 2,500 5,000 km
Miller Projection

500 B.C.

A.D. 1500

A.D. 1000

A.D. 1600

A.D. 1400

A.D. 1700

Map Study In 1400 Europeans had only a limited knowledge of the world. Geographers agreed the world was round, but they disagreed on its size.
Human/Environment Interaction What factors contributed to European geographers' knowledge of the world?

They would also prepare the way for the rise of the world's first global age.

Technology of Exploration

Open-water ocean sailing—necessary to find a water route to Asia—required sailors trained in navigation, accurate maps, and oceangoing ships. For exploration to succeed, ships had to be able both to leave the coastal waters and sight of land and to return home. Ancient navigators stayed close to the coast, using landmarks to determine their position. Later, sailors who traveled beyond sight of land used the positions of stars and the sun

to determine in which direction they were traveling. Hourglasses told them how long they had traveled. Keeping track of speed, direction, and time theoretically enabled a captain to tell where the ship was. However, these calculations were very inaccurate.

The compass, of Chinese origin, enabled sailors to determine geographical direction. By 1100, sailors used the astrolabe—perfected by the Arabs—to determine the altitude of the sun or other heavenly bodies. But in practice, standing on the deck of a heaving ship, few ship captains had the skill and patience that the astrolabe required.

An astrolabe

Maps were another problem for early navigators. Most maps were wildly inaccurate, drawn from scattered impressions of travelers and traders. Cartographers, or mapmakers, filled their parchments with lands found only in rumor or legend.

Cartographers' skills gradually improved. By about 1300, coastal charts showed the Mediterranean coastline with a great degree of accuracy. During the Renaissance, works by the Hellenistic astronomer Ptolemy reappeared in Europe. His maps, improved over the centuries by Byzantine and Arab scholars, gave Europeans a new picture of the world. Ptolemy also introduced the grid system of map references based on the coordinates of latitude and longitude still in use today all over the world.

Innovations were also made in the construction of ships. Late in the 1400s, shipwrights began to outfit ships with triangle-shaped lateen sails perfected by Arab traders. These sails made it possible for ships to sail against the wind, not simply with it. Shipwrights also abandoned using a single mast with one large sail. Multiple masts, with several smaller sails hoisted one above the other, made ships travel much faster. In addition, moving the rudder from the ship's side to the stern made ships more maneuverable.

In the 1400s a European ship called a caravel incorporated all these improvements. The caravel was up to 65 feet (20 m) in length with the capability of carrying about 130 tons (118 metric tons) of cargo. Because a caravel drew little water, it allowed explorers to venture up shallow inlets and to beach the ship to make repairs. A Venetian mariner called the caravels "the best ships that sailed the seas." The caravels also carried new types of weapons—rifles and cannons.

Portugal Leads the Way

Portugal was the first European country to venture out on the Atlantic Ocean in search of spices and gold. Between 1420 and 1580, Portuguese captains pushed farther and farther down the west coast of Africa in search of a sea route to Asia.

Although **Prince Henry the Navigator**, son of King John I of Portugal, was not a sailor—never making an ocean voyage—he brought together mapmakers, mathematicians, and astronomers to study navigation. He also sponsored many Portuguese exploratory voyages westward into the Atlantic and southward down Africa's west coast. In the early 1400s Henry's explorers discovered the Azores, the Madeira Islands, and the Cape Verde Islands. These discoveries were the foundation of what in the 1500s became the Portuguese Empire.

In August 1487 **Bartholomeu Dias** left Portugal, intent upon finding the southern tip of Africa. In 1488 his expedition discovered the southern tip of Africa, which was later named the **Cape of Good Hope**. Dias's voyage proved that ships could reach East Asia by sailing around Africa.

In 1497 four ships led by **Vasco da Gama** sailed from Portugal for India. The expedition rounded the Cape of Good Hope, made stops at trading centers along the east coast of Africa, and landed at Calicut on the southwest coast of India in 10 months. There da Gama found Hindus and

Richard Schlecht

"Little Girl"

The *Niña*—"Little Girl"—was Christopher Columbus's favorite ship, a small, fast, sea-worthy vessel about 67 feet long. Descriptions of the *Niña* discovered in a Spanish document from the period have enabled historians to draw pictures of what the craft actually looked like. In this drawing the lines in red show the *Niña's* sails and riggings. The document also revealed that the *Niña* had four masts, not two or three, as previously believed. Columbus's beloved "Little Girl," the most technically advanced craft of her day, probably made three of his four voyages to the Americas.

The Europe of 1500 was on the brink of the modern era. Monarchs Isabella and Ferdinand of Spain could command Columbus and other explorers, who combined knowledge of sophisticated naval technologies with bravery and determination. In quick succession Columbus (1492), Vasco da Gama (1498), and Magellan (1519–21), among others, linked Europe with the rest of the world. The sea-sheltered Americas were invaded. The slave trade expanded and brought much of Africa into the shadow of the Americas. The Muslim peoples of Africa and Asia lost their central position as guardians of trade between Europe, Asia, and Africa. Within a few centuries, the whole world came within European explorers' reach. ⊕

Muslims trading fine silk, porcelain, and spices that made the glass beads and trinkets of the Portuguese appear shoddy.

Da Gama tried to persuade the ruler of Calicut and Muslim merchants in India to trade with the Portuguese. He had little success and returned home. In Portugal, however, da Gama was regarded as a national hero. He had pioneered a water route to India, and he had provided a glimpse of the riches that could come from direct trade with the East.

Spain's Quest for Riches

In the late 1400s Spain ended a long period of internal turmoil and wars against the Moors. Under King Ferdinand and Queen Isabella, Spain entered the race for Asian riches by backing the expeditions of an Italian navigator named **Christopher Columbus**.

Columbus Crosses the Atlantic

In 1492 Christopher Columbus approached Queen Isabella with an intriguing plan—to reach India by sailing west across the Atlantic. For years

Columbus Before the Queen by Peter Rothermel, 1842. National Museum of American Art, Washington, D.C. **Seven years of persistent pleading earned Spain's support.** *How many voyages did Columbus make seeking proof that he had discovered a new route to India?*

Columbus had tried unsuccessfully to persuade other European rulers to finance his voyage. With Queen Isabella his persistence paid off.

In August 1492 Columbus sailed from Spain with three small ships. He calculated the distance to India to be 700 leagues, about 2,200 nautical miles; he knew that the actual distance might be greater. To calm the crews' fears, he showed them a log that understated the distance they had sailed from home.

The days out of sight of land wore on and on, however, and the terrified sailors begged Columbus to turn back. After a false sighting of land, the crews began to talk of mutiny. Columbus reluctantly agreed to turn back if they did not reach land within three days.

After midnight on the second day, the expedition sighted land. In the morning Columbus and his men went ashore, becoming the first Europeans to set foot on one of the islands of the Bahamas. Columbus wrote of the inhabitants:

> 66 The islanders came to the ships' boats, swimming and bringing us parrots and balls of cotton thread … which they exchanged for … glass beads and hawk bells … they took and gave of what they had very willingly, but it seemed to me that they were poor in every way. They bore no weapons, nor were they acquainted with them, because when I showed them swords they seized them by the edge and so cut themselves from ignorance. 99

Believing he was off the coast of India, Columbus called the islanders "Indians." Columbus spent the next three months exploring the islands Hispaniola (present-day Haiti and the Dominican Republic) and Cuba in search of gold. Although he found enough gold to raise Spanish hopes, he saw no evidence of the great civilizations of Asia.

When Columbus returned to Spain, Ferdinand and Isabella gave him the title "Admiral of the Ocean Sea, Viceroy and Governor of the Islands he hath discovered in the Indies." Before he died in 1506, Columbus made three more voyages to the Caribbean islands and South America seeking proof that he had discovered a new route to Asia. He died certain that he had.

Even without sure proof, it was difficult for anyone to dispute Columbus's claim. Maps of the time did not show any landmass between Europe and Asia. It was not until 1507 that another Italian explorer, Amerigo Vespucci (veh•SPOO•chee), suggested that Columbus had discovered a "New World." In honor of Vespucci, the name *America* began to appear on maps that included the newly discovered lands.

Dividing the World

Both Spain and Portugal wanted to protect their claims in the Americas and turned to the pope for help. In 1493 the pope drew a line of demarcation, an imaginary line running down the middle of the Atlantic from the North Pole to the South Pole. Spain was to have control of all lands to the west of the line, while Portugal was to have control of all lands to the east of the line.

The Portuguese, however, feared that their line was so far to the east that Spain might take over their Asian trade. As a result, in 1494 Spain and Portugal signed the Treaty of Tordesillas (TAWR•duh•SEE•yuhs), an agreement to move the line of demarcation farther west. The treaty divided the entire unexplored world between just two powers, Spain and Portugal.

History & Art *Discovery of Magellan Strait* (artist unknown). **By this point in Magellan's voyage, one ship foundered on the rocks and another turned back.** *What did the journey prove?*

Voyage of Magellan

In 1519 an expedition led by **Ferdinand Magellan**, a Portuguese soldier of fortune, set sail from Seville under the Spanish flag to find a western route to Asia. The five ships and 260-man crew sailed across the Atlantic and made their way along the eastern coast of South America, searching every bay and inlet for this route.

Along the coast of Argentina, crews of three of the ships attempted a mutiny because Magellan had decided to halt the expedition until spring. Magellan executed the captain who had instigated the mutiny, regained control of the fleet, and resumed the expedition. Finally, near the southern tip of South America, the ships reached a narrow water passageway now called the **Strait of Magellan**. The ships threaded their way through the maze of rocky islands in the 350-mile- (504-km-) long strait. Strong currents and unpredictable gales separated one ship from the others, and its crew forced its return to Spain. Another was shipwrecked.

Magellan's ship and the two other remaining ships finally passed through the strait into the South Sea, which had been discovered and named six years earlier by Vasco Núñez de Balboa. Because the water was so calm, Magellan renamed it the Pacific Ocean. The fleet then sailed nearly four months before reaching land. Water and food ran out, and some sailors died. One of the crew wrote in his journal, "We ate biscuit, which was no longer biscuit, but powder of biscuits swarming with worms, for they had eaten the good."

At last the ships reached the present-day Philippines. Caught in a skirmish between a local chief and his enemy, Magellan was killed. The surviving crew escaped and sailed for Spain.

In 1522, after three years at sea, the last ship with its 18 survivors arrived at Seville, completing the first circumnavigation, or circling of the globe. The spices they brought back barely covered the cost of the voyage, but the expedition had a value far beyond money. It proved that the world was round and much larger than anyone had believed, that the oceans of the world were connected, and that the lands discovered by Columbus were not part of Asia.

SECTION 1 REVIEW

Recall
1. **Define** cartographer, line of demarcation, circumnavigation.
2. **Identify** Prince Henry the Navigator, Bartholomeu Dias, Vasco da Gama, Christopher Columbus, Ferdinand Magellan.

3. **Explain** why Portugal and Spain wanted to find a sea route to Asia.

Critical Thinking
4. **Synthesizing Information** Using the text as a resource, write a journal entry describing your experiences as a sailor on an expedition of Dias, Columbus, Magellan, or da Gama.

Understanding Themes
5. **Innovation** What sciences and new technologies led to voyages of exploration?

Section 2

Overseas Empires

Setting the Scene

▸ **Terms to Define**
conquistador, triangular trade, the Middle Passage

▸ **People to Meet**
Pedro Alvares Cabral, Hernán Cortés, Montezuma II, Francisco Pizarro, Atahualpa, Henry Hudson, Jacques Cartier, Samuel de Champlain, John Cabot

▸ **Places to Locate**
Brazil, Peru, West Indies, Quebec, Jamestown

 **Find Out** How did the Europeans exploit the lands and the peoples they found in Africa, Asia, and the Americas?

The Storyteller

John Sparke, who traveled with English admiral John Hawkins, wrote an account of the inhabitants of the Florida coast in 1589: "They have for apothecary [medicine] herbs, trees, roots, and gum, myrrh, and frankincense, with many others, whereof I know not the names…. Gold and silver they want [lack] not, for when the Frenchmen came, they offered it for little or nothing. They received for a hatchet two pounds of gold. The soldiers, being greedy, took it from them, giving them nothing for it. When the Floridians perceived that, they stopped wearing their gold ornaments, for fear that they would be taken away."

Native Americans digging gold

—from *The Hawkins Voyages*, edited by Clements R. Markham, reprinted in *The Annals of America*, 1968

The Treaty of Tordesillas claimed to divide the world between Spain and Portugal. Only Spain and Portugal, however, recognized the treaty. The Netherlands, France, and England soon joined them in a race to exploit wealth from the lands beyond Europe.

Portugal and Spain

Portugal's main interest lay in Africa and Asia, and in trade rather than colonization. When the Portuguese became the first Europeans to reach the Indian Ocean, they found themselves in waters already thoroughly explored by seafarers from Asian lands. Eager to seize control of the spice trade, the Portuguese reacted quickly to Vasco da Gama's voyage to India. In 1500, less than six months after da Gama's return, 13 ships were dispatched to Calicut. Led by **Pedro Alvares Cabral**, the Portuguese won a bloody trade war with Muslim merchants and defeated a large Arab fleet to establish Portuguese control of the Indian Ocean.

The Portuguese then built naval bases along the Indian Ocean—along the Persian Gulf and in Southeast Asia. They soon controlled shipping in the Indian Ocean. Next, they expanded eastward toward the Moluccas, or the Spice Islands. From the Spice Islands, the Portuguese established trading ports in China and Japan.

Portugal also colonized the area of present-day **Brazil**. Cabral claimed this territory as he swung west across the Atlantic to India in 1500. Because this area of South America juts east of the line of demarcation, it became Portuguese. The rest of South America had been claimed by Spain.

Settlers in Brazil grew income-producing crops such as sugarcane, tobacco, coffee, and cotton. Because the local population did not supply enough labor, enslaved people were brought from Africa. By the late 1500s, Brazil was one of Portugal's most important colonies.

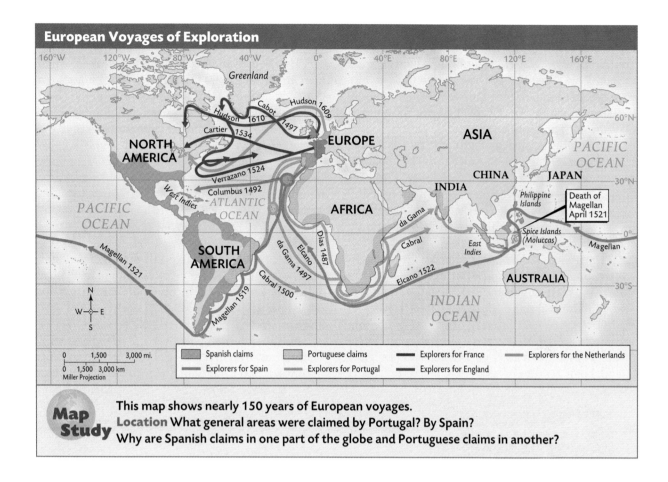

European Voyages of Exploration

This map shows nearly 150 years of European voyages.

Location What general areas were claimed by Portugal? By Spain? Why are Spanish claims in one part of the globe and Portuguese claims in another?

Map Study

Spain

Spanish conquistadors, or conquerors, came to the Americas "to serve God and his Majesty, to give light to those who were in darkness and to grow rich as all men desire to do."

One conquistador, **Hernán Cortés**, landed in Mexico in 1519 with about 600 men, 16 horses, and a few cannons. Guided by Malinche (mah•LIHN •chay), a Native American woman who learned Spanish, Cortés allied with local enemies of the Aztecs and journeyed inland to Tenochtitlán. Meanwhile, in the Aztec capital, messengers told the Aztec ruler **Montezuma II** that the approaching soldiers were "supernatural creatures riding on hornless deer, preceded by wild animals on leashes, dressed in iron." Thinking that Cortés might be the long-awaited god-king Quetzalcoatl returning from the east, Montezuma offered gifts of gold.

Tenochtitlán's riches were beyond anything the Spaniards had ever seen. Soon fighting broke out. With the advantage of horses and guns, the Spanish force ultimately slaughtered thousands of Aztec people. Within three years, Aztec resistance had ended and Cortés ruled Mexico.

In 1532 another conquistador, **Francisco Pizarro**, invaded the Inca Empire in present-day Peru. The Spaniards' arrival followed a conflict in which the Incan ruler **Atahualpa** (AH•tuh•WAHL •puh) won the throne from a brother. Aided by Native American allies, Pizarro captured Atahualpa and had thousands of Inca massacred. Although a ransom was paid for Atahualpa's release, the Spaniards killed him anyway. Inca resistance continued, but Spanish forces eventually conquered vast stretches of Inca territory in South America.

Building an Empire

By the 1600s, Spain's empire in the Americas included much of North America and South America as well as islands in the **West Indies**. Keeping close watch over their empire, Spanish monarchs named viceroys, or royal representatives, to rule local provinces with the advice of councils of Spanish settlers.

Spain had two goals for its American empire— to acquire its wealth and to convert Native Americans to Christianity. Farmers set up plantations, or large estates, for the growing of sugarcane; landowners drew gold and silver from mines. At the same time priests founded missions—settlements where many Native Americans lived, worked, and adopted European ways.

Under the encomienda system, Spanish monarchs granted landowners the right to use Native American labor. Native Americans, however, were enslaved and mistreated. Disease also took its toll. Exposed to diseases from Europe for the first time, millions of Native Americans died during the first 50 years of Spanish rule.

A few priests, such as Bartolomé de Las Casas, tried to protect the Native Americans. The Spanish government responded with laws meant to end abuses, but the laws were never enforced. In many cases, Native Americans resisted Spanish rule on their own by preserving their local cultures and by staging periodic revolts.

The decline in the Native American population led the Spaniards to bring over enslaved workers from Africa. As sugarcane production and profits soared, more and more Africans arrived to work in the fields and in various trades. In time, the coming together of African, Native American, and European peoples in Spain's American colonies gave rise to a new culture.

Colonies of the Netherlands

The Netherlands was also interested in expansion. In the late 1500s the Dutch won their independence from Spain. This small country on the North Sea had few natural resources and limited farmland. A large Dutch middle class saw commerce as the key to survival.

The period of the 1600s was the golden age of the Netherlands. Dutch ships were efficient, carrying more cargo and smaller crews than other ships. Amsterdam became the world's largest commercial city, and the Dutch enjoyed the world's highest standard of living.

The first Dutch expedition to East Asia returned in 1599. Three years later the Dutch chartered the Dutch East India Company to expand trade and ensure close relations between the government and enterprises in Asia.

In 1619 the company set up headquarters at Batavia on the island of Java in present-day Indonesia. Soon the Dutch controlled island trade

Images *of the* Times

The Dutch Republic

With no monarchy or aristocracy, the tastes and ideals of society as reflected in Dutch art were determined largely by the middle class.

The Flower Vendor and the Vegetable Vendor by Arnout de Muysor focuses on two important themes in Dutch painting of this period—middle-class life and trade.

The World Upside-down by Jan Steen, the son of a brewer, is representative of his earthy, humorous scenes of ordinary people.

in sugar, spices, coffee, and tea. Using Batavia as a base, the Dutch pushed the Portuguese and English out of Asian outposts. After taking Malacca from the Portuguese in 1641, the Netherlands controlled all trade with the Spice Islands. The Dutch also used force against local Muslim rulers to win lands and ports in the region.

At the same time, the Dutch set out for North America. An English navigator, **Henry Hudson**, claimed land for the Dutch along the Atlantic coast of North America, and in 1621 the government chartered the Dutch West India Company to establish colonies in the Americas. The company founded New Amsterdam on Manhattan Island at the mouth of the Hudson River. This settlement was soon a center for European and colonial trade.

The Dutch established a colony in Africa as well. In 1652 Dutch farmers known as Boers settled at the Cape of Good Hope to provide fresh food and water for sailing ships. By the 1700s, however, Dutch power was declining, and England had emerged as Europe's leading maritime nation.

French and English Colonies

The French and the English played only a small part in the early voyages of exploration. Religious conflicts and civil wars kept their interests focused at home. During the 1500s, however, France and England searched for overseas trading colonies.

Thwarted by the Portuguese and later the Dutch control of Asian markets, England and France turned toward North America and the Caribbean. In general, the French companies sought quick profits from trade rather than the long-term investment of farming. For the English, colonies could provide the raw materials—lumber, fish, sugarcane, rice, and wheat—they would otherwise have to purchase from other countries.

France

In 1524 the French hired an Italian captain, Giovanni da Verrazano, to find a Northwest Passage through America to Asia. Da Verrazano explored the North American coast from North

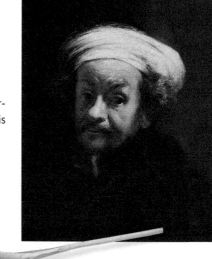

Rembrandt van Rijn, the celebrated Dutch painter, earned fame with his portraits of himself and of his family. Although he died poor and forgotten, his paintings were of more spiritual depth than those of his contemporaries.

REFLECTING ON THE TIMES

1. How does Dutch art compare with art from a nation like France that had a monarch and nobility?
2. Why did Rembrandt's work receive greater acclaim after he died?

Carolina to Maine without success. Ten years later the French navigator **Jacques Cartier** continued the search and sailed up the St. Lawrence River to the site of the present-day city of Montreal. He claimed much of eastern Canada for France.

In 1608 **Samuel de Champlain**, a French mapmaker, founded **Quebec**, the first permanent French settlement in the Americas. In 1673 missionaries Jacques Marquette and Louis Joliet explored the Mississippi Valley. Later, Robert Cavelier, known as Sieur de La Salle, claimed the entire inland region surrounding the Mississippi River for France.

Like the Spanish, the French sent Jesuit missionaries to convert Native Americans to Christianity. French explorers traded the Native Americans blankets, guns, and wine for animal skins. Trapping, fishing, and lumbering were also profitable.

Some French settlers went to the West Indies, where they claimed the islands of St. Kitts, Martinique, and Guadeloupe. The French brought enslaved Africans to work on sugar and tobacco plantations on the islands. Although most of their interests were in North America, the French also established trading posts in India.

England

England also showed an interest in overseas trade. In 1497 the Italian-born navigator **John Cabot** explored the coast of present-day Newfoundland. During the 1500s, English sea captains, such as Francis Drake, raided Spanish ships for gold and silver. English overseas expansion, however, did not begin until the founding of the English East India Company in 1600. This trading enterprise set up posts in India and Southeast Asia.

During the 1600s, the English also founded settlements in the Americas. On West Indian islands, such as Jamaica, they introduced sugarcane, worked by enslaved African labor. **Jamestown**, the earliest English settlement in North America, was founded in 1607 in present-day Virginia. In 1620 devout Protestants, calling themselves Pilgrims, sought religious freedom by establishing Plymouth in present-day Massachusetts. Before landing, the Pilgrims set down rules for governing Plymouth in the Mayflower Compact:

   ❝ We, whose names are underwritten…
   having undertaken for the glory of
   God, and advancement of the Christian faith…a voyage to plant [a]
   colony…do…enact, constitute, and frame
   …just and equal Laws…as shall be

thought most [appropriate] and convenient for the general good of the colony. **❞**

In the 1600s and 1700s, English settlements arose and thrived along the eastern coast of North America. In northern areas, family-operated farms emerged, while in southern areas, plantation farming based on African enslaved labor was established. Although English monarchs supervised these settlements by sending out governors, the English in North America enjoyed a large degree of self-government in their representative assemblies modeled on the English Parliament.

English settlement, however, pushed out the earlier inhabitants, the Native Americans. Concerned about land, the English had little desire to Christianize Native Americans, although they adopted Native American farming methods and foods, such as corn and beans. On the other side, Native Americans fought back to save their lands, but disease and food shortages had reduced their numbers. As the settlers expanded inland, they also came into conflict with the Dutch and the French. By 1765, after a series of wars, the English had emerged as the leading European power in much of North America.

Slave Trade

In the 1600s European territories in the Americas based their economies on agricultural products that required intensive labor. Enslaved Africans planted and harvested sugar, tobacco, and coffee crops. They also worked silver mines.

The Triangular Trade

The slave trade was part of what was called the triangular trade. Ships sailed the legs of a triangle formed by Europe, Africa, and the Americas. Typically, European ships left their home ports carrying manufactured goods—knives, swords, guns, cloth, and rum. In West Africa the ship captains traded their goods with local rulers for enslaved people, most of whom were war captives. During the second leg of the journey, the ships brought enslaved Africans across the Atlantic to various Caribbean islands or to mainland areas in North America and South America. The enslaved Africans were sold, and the money was used to buy sugar, molasses, cotton, and tobacco. Finally, the ships returned to Europe to sell the goods purchased in America.

The Middle Passage

An enslaved person's journey from the west coast of Africa to the lands of the Americas was a ghastly ordeal called the Middle Passage. This middle leg of the triangular trade originated from ports along a 3,000-mile (4,800-km) stretch on the west coast of Africa. Captured by other Africans, enslaved Africans were sold to European slave traders along the coast for transport to American plantations.

Because large cargoes brought large profits, the slave traders packed the captives as tightly as possible. Below deck, each African occupied a space only 4 or 5 feet (122 cm to 153 cm) long and 2 or 3 feet (60 cm to 92 cm) high. Chained together, they could neither stand nor lie at full length. In the darkness and stifling heat, many Africans suffocated or died of disease.

Estimates of the number of enslaved Africans brought to America range from 10 to 24 million. One in five who began the trip did not survive it. Because of the enormous value of their "cargo," however, slave traders made some effort to keep the enslaved people alive. Psychological torment may have been worse than physical conditions. Some Africans committed suicide by jumping overboard. Others simply lost the will to live and refused to eat. Enslaved people on hunger strikes were fed forcibly.

An Enslaved Person's Life

Africans who survived the long Middle Passage faced another terror when they arrived in American ports: the slave auction. Examined and prodded by plantation owners, most Africans were sold to work as laborers—clearing land, hoeing, planting, weeding, and harvesting. The work was hard, the hours long, and life expectancy short. Because many

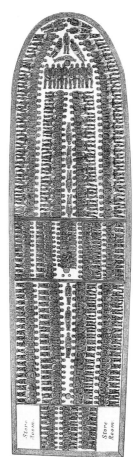

Visualizing History A deck plan shows tightly packed ranks of enslaved people on a ship bound from Africa to the Americas. *What did enslaved people experience on the Middle Passage?*

Europeans believed that Africans were physically suited to hard labor, especially in hot, humid climates, the enslaved people were viewed as nothing more than a unit of labor to exploit for profit.

Resistance

In addition to its inhumanity, the slave trade wrenched untold numbers of young, productive Africans from their homelands. This population loss at least temporarily weakened many African societies. As a result, many Africans tried to resist the slave trade. One of them was Affonso I, ruler of Kongo in central Africa. As a Christian, Affonso favored contact with Europeans but spoke out against the trade in human lives. The slave trading network, however, was too powerful for Affonso and other African opponents to end it.

Enslaved people also acted to obtain freedom. Despite heavy odds, a few escaped their masters and got far enough away to set up their own free communities. The ultimate weapon, however, was mass rebellion. In many areas of the Americas, enslaved people outnumbered free populations, who constantly feared uprisings. The most successful uprising occurred in the French-ruled West Indian island of Saint Domingue. There, a prolonged rebellion in the 1790s led to the creation of the republic of Haiti in 1804. By the early 1800s, humanitarian concerns and fear of uprisings both had fueled an anti-slavery movement that saw slavery as an evil bringing only violence, oppression, and suffering.

SECTION 2 REVIEW

Recall
1. **Define** conquistador, triangular trade, the Middle Passage.
2. **Identify** Pedro Alvares Cabral, Hernán Cortés, Montezuma II, Francisco Pizarro, Atahualpa, Henry Hudson, Jacques Cartier, Samuel de Champlain, Jacques Marquette, Louis Joliet, John Cabot.
3. **State** the goals that Spain had for its American empire.

Critical Thinking
4. **Making Comparisons** How did treatment of Native Americans differ in the colonies of Spain, France, and England?

Understanding Themes
5. **Movement** What motivated Europeans to move from their countries to the Americas?

1400	1500	1600

c. 1400s Increased trade leads to advanced banking methods.

c. 1500s The nation replaces the city and the village as Europe's primary economic unit.

c. 1600 Europe's population reaches 100 million.

Section 3

Changing Ways of Life

Setting the Scene

▶ **Terms to Define**
joint-stock company, entrepreneur, mercantilism, bullion, balance of trade

▶ **Places to Locate**
Florence, Augsburg

 How did increased trade and colonial expansion set the stage for a global economy?

Storyteller

The English and French considered piracy against Spain practically a religious crusade. Pirates sometimes held Holy Communion before starting a raid on a Spanish ship! The strangest pirate fleet of all, based in England, attacked Spaniards passing anywhere near, and openly sold their stolen cargo in the market. Even their Spanish prisoners were publicly auctioned for prices set by the ransom money each one might bring. Public opinion finally forced Elizabeth I to put a stop to all this: She declared the pirates public outlaws—"Rascals of the Sea."

—adapted from *The Pirate Picture*, Rayner Thrower, 1980

Pirate ship

he age of exploration brought far-reaching changes to global cultures. Overseas trade and the conquest of empires expanded Europe's economy. This search for wealth led to the rise of modern capitalism, an economic system in which money is invested in business to make profits.

The Commercial Revolution

By the 1600s the nation had replaced the city and village as the basic economic unit in Europe. Nations competed for markets and trade goods. New business methods were instituted for investing money, speeding the flow of wealth, and reducing risks in commercial ventures. These changes, which came to be known as the Commercial Revolution, formed the roots of modern financial and business life.

New Business Methods

Launching an overseas trading venture was a major undertaking. The financial backer of the voyage had to raise money for supplies and to hire a crew. Often several years passed before a fleet finished trading overseas and returned home. Only then could the initial investment be recovered. Governments and rich merchants alone had enough money to back such trading voyages, and even they needed financial assistance.

At first merchants turned to bankers for the money to finance their ventures. Families like the Medici of **Florence**, Italy, and the Fuggers of **Augsburg**, Germany, loaned money as part of their operations. By the 1500s these families were so wealthy that they accepted deposits, made loans, and transferred funds over long distances. Both banking families had branches in several European cities and also made loans to European monarchs.

Visualizing History This European port scene by Jan Griffier the Elder shows the mix of cultures that resulted from the increased trade between Europeans and the rest of the world. *How did merchants protect themselves against losses?*

By the 1600s, however, these banking families were beginning to be replaced by government-chartered banks. The banks accepted deposits of money and charged interest on loans. Before long the banks began to provide other services. They issued banknotes and checks, making large payments in heavy coins a thing of the past. They acted as money changers, exchanging currencies from other countries. The banks even provided official exchange rates for foreign currency.

Individual merchants who wanted to invest in exploration often raised money by combining their resources in joint-stock companies, organizations that sold stock, or shares, in the venture, enabling large and small investors to share the profits and risks of a trading voyage. If a loss occurred, investors would lose only the amount they had invested in shares. This sharing of risk provided a stable way of raising funds for voyages.

A few joint-stock companies became rich and powerful through government support. For example, the Dutch government gave the Dutch East India Company a monopoly in trade with Africa and the East Indies. It also gave the company the power to make war, to seize foreign ships, to coin money, and to establish colonies and forts. In return the government received customs duties, or taxes on imported goods, from the company's trade.

Increase in Money

As gold and silver flowed into Europe from abroad, the supply of coined money increased. This, in turn, led to inflation, or a dramatic rise in prices. Money, however, became more widely available for large enterprises, and ideas changed about the nature and goals of business. Gradually, a sys-

 **Footnotes to History**

Spanish Doubloons and Pieces of Eight

During the 1500s, Spanish ships called galleons sailed the seas loaded with gold doubloons and silver pieces of eight. Minted from the plunder of Central and South American mines, the coins were a favorite target for pirates of other nations. Today, marine archaeologists have explored a number of sunken galleons and recovered hundreds of doubloons and pieces of eight—still worth a fortune.

tem based on the belief that the goal of business was to make profits took shape. Individuals known as entrepreneurs combined money, ideas, raw materials, and labor to make goods and profits. Profits were then used to expand the business and develop new ventures.

An entrepreneur in the cloth industry, for example, would buy wool and employ spinners to make the wool into yarn. Weavers and dyers would also be hired to turn the yarn into cloth. The entrepreneur would then sell the cloth on the open market for a price that brought a profit. Of course, entrepreneurs took risks when they put up capital for businesses. They could lose their investment if prices fell or workers could not produce goods at a specified time or for a specific market.

In the 1600s the greatest increase in trade took place in the countries bordering the Atlantic Ocean—Portugal, Spain, England, and the Netherlands—in large part because they had the largest colonial empires. Italian cities such as Venice and Genoa, formerly the leading trade centers in Europe, found themselves cut out of overseas trade as trade routes and fortunes gradually moved westward toward the Atlantic Ocean and the Americas.

Mercantilism

A new theory of national economic policy called mercantilism also appeared. This theory held that a state's power depended on its wealth. Accordingly, the goal of every nation was to become as wealthy as possible.

Europeans believed that the measure of a nation's wealth was the amount of bullion, or gold and silver, it owned. One Venetian summed up the general feeling about bullion: "[It is] the sinews of all government, it gives it its pulse, its movement, its mind, soul, and it is its essence and its very life. It overcomes all impossibilities, for it is the master … without it all is weak and without movement."

Under mercantilism, nations could gain wealth by mining gold and silver at home or overseas. Thus, Spain sent conquistadors to the Americas to seize the silver and gold mines of the Aztec and Inca Empires. Governments could also gain wealth through trade. Nations sought to create a favorable balance of trade by exporting more goods than they imported. The gold and silver received for exports would exceed that paid for imports. This greater wealth meant greater national power and influence in the world.

CONNECTIONS

Economics

The Commercial Revolution

Queen Elizabeth opens the Royal Exchange

Europe's economic prosperity during the 1500s and 1600s made European merchants eager to increase their fortunes. Overseas trade, however, was costly and dangerous. Individual merchants found it impossible to take the entire burden on themselves. If a voyage failed, the merchant would lose everything.

This uncertainty led to the rise of joint-stock companies, which shared expenses, risks, and profits by selling stock to many investors. Joint-stock companies became so popular that stock exchanges, where investors could buy and sell stock, developed in western Europe.

Setting up a joint-stock company involved getting a charter from the monarch, who controlled merchant trade. Charters became important in the founding of settlements and trading ventures in the Americas. Also, with their emphasis on shared risk and gain, joint-stock companies were the forerunners of modern corporations. Today, the Hudson's Bay Company, chartered in 1670 to operate the fur trade in Canada, exists as a large retail corporation with many business interests.

Linking Past and Present **ACTIVITY**

Explain why joint-stock companies were popular among merchants. Compare and contrast the joint-stock company of the 1600s with the modern corporation.

Visualizing History Coffeehouses, such as this one depicted in London in 1668, were places to converse about the news of the day—fires, feasts, riots, weddings, plays, and scandals. *Besides coffee, what other foods and drinks were introduced to Europe in this period?*

To increase national wealth, governments often aided businesses producing export goods. They sold monopolies, or the right to operate free of local competition, to producers in certain key industries. They also set tariffs, or taxes on imported goods, to protect local industries from foreign competitors.

Colonies, or overseas territories ruled by a parent country, were highly valued in the mercantilist system. They were both the sources of raw materials as well as vital markets for finished goods provided by the parent country. The primary reason for having colonies was to help make the parent country self-sufficient.

European Daily Life

The Commercial Revolution had a noticeable impact on European society. Merchants prospered most from the expansion of trade and empire. They began to surpass the nobility in both wealth and power. Hereditary nobles had to rely on rents from their lands for wealth, but rents did not rise as fast as prices.

The newly rich entrepreneurs set trends in lifestyles. Coffeehouses became their favorite gathering places where business and gossip were exchanged. A Spaniard described a coffeehouse in Amsterdam in 1688:

> ❝ [They] are of great usefulness in winter, with their welcoming stoves and tempting pastimes; some offer books to read, others gaming-tables and all have people ready to converse with one; one man drinks chocolate, another coffee, one milk, another tea

and practically all of them smoke tobacco …In this way they can keep warm, be refreshed and entertained for little expense, listening to the news. ❞

Joseph de la Vega, *The Wheels of Commerce*, 1817

In the countryside, however, peasants lived as meagerly as they ever had. The French writer Jean de La Bruyère (LAH•broo•YEHR) remarked that European peasants worked like animals, lived in hovels, and survived on a diet of water, black bread, and roots.

A Global Exchange

During the Commercial Revolution, Europe's population grew rapidly. In 1450 Europe had about 55 million people; by 1650, Europeans numbered about 100 million. They also had become more mobile. Towns expanded outside their walls as more and more people left rural areas to be closer to centers of trade.

Europe's growing population demanded more goods and services. This demand was met by Europe's increasing contacts with the rest of the world. As Europe's trade expanded, it contributed to a worldwide exchange of people, goods, technologies, ideas, and even diseases that had profound consequences for the entire globe.

Known as the Columbian Exchange, after Christopher Columbus, the transfer of products from continent to continent brought changes in

History & Art *Man-o'-War Firing a Salute* by Jan Porcellis. **Building an empire called for military strength in this period of intense European rivalry.** *What caused many Europeans to venture to America?*

ways of life throughout the world. Europeans brought wheat, grapes, and livestock to the Americas. From Native Americans, Europeans acquired food items such as corn, potatoes, tomatoes, beans, and chocolate, which they brought back to Europe. Easy-to-grow food crops, such as the potato, fed Europe's growing population. Some foods, such as corn, also spread to Asia and Africa, boosting population growth there. From Asia and Africa, Europeans brought to Europe and the Americas tropical products—bananas, coffee, tea, and sugarcane—and luxury goods, such as ivory, perfumes, silk, and gems.

New global trading links increased the movement of people and cultures from continent to continent. Europeans, seeking wealth or fleeing economic distress and religious persecution, moved to the Americas and other parts of the world. They exchanged food, ideas, and practices with the peoples living in these areas. European influences profoundly affected local cultures. European traders spread European languages, and European missionaries taught Christianity and European values. Wealthy Europeans, in turn, developed an interest in the arts, styles, and foods of Asia, especially Chinese porcelain, Indian textiles, and Southeast Asian spices. At the same time, the drastic decline of the Native American populations and the forcible removal of Africans to the Americas revealed that European expansion often had a disruptive effect on cultures in other parts of the world.

SECTION 3 REVIEW

Recall
1. **Define** joint-stock company, entrepreneur, mercantilism, bullion, balance of trade.
2. **Identify** capitalism and discuss the changes of the Commercial Revolution that led to its rise.
3. **Discuss** the changes brought by European expansion to other parts of the globe.

Critical Thinking
4. **Synthesizing Information** Imagine that you are an entrepreneur of the 1700s. Invent a way for making profits by using your capital and talents. Appraise the potential risks and profits in your venture.

Understanding Themes
5. **Change** Decide which class of European society benefited most from the Commercial Revolution. Why?

Using a Computerized Card Catalog

By now you probably have been assigned several research reports. Skill in using a computerized card catalog will help you find the information you need to complete your assignment.

Learning the Skill

Go to the card-catalog computer in your school or local library. What information do you need? Type in the name of an author or performer (for tapes, cassettes, and CDs); the title of a book, videotape, audiocassette, or CD; or a subject heading. You will access the on-line, or computerized card catalog that lists all the library's resources for that topic. The computer will list on screen the title's author, or the information you requested.

The "card" that appears on screen will provide other information as well, including the year the work was published, who published it, what media type it is, and the language in which it is written or recorded. Use this information to determine if the material meets your needs. Then check to see if the item is available. In addition, find the classification (biography, travel, and so on) and call number under which it is shelved.

Practicing the Skill

This chapter discusses explorers. The following steps will help you use the computerized card catalog to find additional information on the subject "explorers":
1. Type "s/explorers."
2. From the list of subjects that appears on the screen, determine which might apply to European explorers from the 1400s to the 1700s.
3. Follow the instructions on the computer screen to display all the titles under each subject you selected. For example, the instructions might be to type the line number next to the subject and press RETURN.
4. Determine which of the books, videos, audiocassettes, and CDs now on the screen you want to learn more about.
5. What do the instructions on the screen tell you to do to find more details?
6. What do the instructions on the screen tell you to do if you want to find out how many copies of the title the library owns and if and where a copy is available?

Applying the Skill

Use the computerized card catalog in your school or local library to identify four resources—books, videotapes, CDs, or audiocassettes—you can use to write two reports. Write one report on French explorer Jacques Cartier, and the other report on technological advances in exploration from 1400 to 1700.

For More Practice

Turn to the Skill Practice in the Chapter Review on page 453 for more practice in using a computerized card catalog.

Connections Across Time

Historical Significance The period from the 1400s to the 1700s is often called the first global age. During this time, the peoples of Europe, Asia, Africa, and the Americas came into direct contact. Through exploration, the size and dimensions of the world and its oceans became known. Europeans established overseas empires, bringing prosperity to their homelands. However, the European process of establishing colonies often left a negative impact on the cultures that Europeans encountered. In the long run, the meeting of civilizations throughout the world laid the foundation of the global community that we know today, with its exchange of ideas and practices among different peoples.

Using Key Terms

Write the key term that completes each sentence. Then write a sentence for each term not chosen.

a. cartographers
b. circumnavigation
c. conquistadors
d. entrepreneurs
e. joint-stock companies
f. line of demarcation
g. Middle Passage
h. mercantilism
i. balance of trade
j. bullion
k. triangular trade

1. An enslaved person's journey from Africa to the Americas was known as the _____.
2. As a result of discoveries made by early European explorers, _____ were able to draw maps with greater accuracy.
3. In 1522 Ferdinand Magellan's crew arrived at Seville, Spain, completing the first _____, or circling of the globe.
4. _____, or organizations that sold stock in ventures, enabled large and small investors to share the risks and profits of a trading voyage.
5. The theory of _____ held that a nation's power rested on its accumulated wealth.

Using Your History Journal

Exploration brought people from Europe into contact with the cultures of Asia, Africa, and the Americas for the first time in this period. Imagine and describe such a meeting. Remember that these people did not, when meeting, understand each other's language or culture.

Technology Activity

Using a Spreadsheet Search the Internet or your local library for additional information about early European explorers and their achievements. Organize your information by creating a spreadsheet. Include headings such as name, regions of exploration, types of technology used, and contributions. Provide a map of the world labeling oceans, continents and the routes that European explorers took in discovering the world.

Reviewing Facts

1. **History** Identify the causes and effects of European expansion in the 1500s.
2. **Technology** Describe the improvements that shipbuilders incorporated in the caravel.
3. **Economics** Explain why the Dutch turned to commerce instead of agriculture in the late 1500s.
4. **Government** Identify the Mayflower Compact and discuss politics in England's colonies.
5. **Citizenship** Describe what the Middle Passage was like for enslaved Africans.
6. **History** Explain in what ways the French and the English differed in their aims for their colonies.
7. **Economics** State how a joint-stock company enabled small investors to profit from a major voyage.

Critical Thinking

1. **Apply** Why did Columbus's plan to reach Asia by a western route appeal to Spain?
2. **Analyze** Were the English and the Spanish justified in colonizing the Americas? Why or why not?

3. **Evaluate** How would the colonies have been different if Europeans had not used slave labor?

4. **Synthesize** Why is the era from the 1400s to the 1700s called the Age of Exploration? What are its major features? What was its impact?

5. **Evaluate** How did the influx of wealth from the colonies help bring about the Commercial Revolution in Europe?

6. **Analyze** What were the results of Ferdinand Magellan's circumnavigation?

7. **Apply** Why were the Dutch eager to establish overseas colonies?

Geography in History

1. **Place** What European city was the first to have potatoes for consumption?

2. **Movement** Why were potatoes introduced into Sweden and Finland so much later than they were in other nations?

3. **Human/Environment Interaction** How would new crops such as the potato affect agriculture?

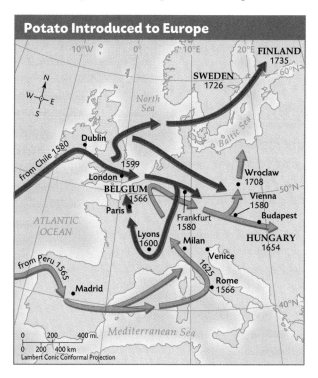

Understanding Themes

1. **Innovation** How did Chinese and Arab discoveries aid European voyages of exploration?

2. **Movement** How did the Columbian Exchange affect changes in world populations?

3. **Change** How did the Commercial Revolution encourage more European voyages of exploration and colonization?

Linking Past and Present

1. History books used to say that Columbus "discovered" America. What did they mean, and why do we no longer see his voyage in this way?

2. Making profits motivated early entrepreneurs. Is this still the goal of entrepreneurs today?

3. Compare and contrast modern space explorations with European voyages of exploration. Consider the technologies used, the ways explorations were funded, and the impact of these ventures on human knowledge.

Skill Practice

Use the card catalog computer in your school library to find out more about Spain's empire from the 1500s to the 1700s.

1. Type "s/Spain."

2. From the list of subjects that appears on screen determine which might apply to Spain's empire from the 1500s to the 1700s.

3. Follow the instructions on the computer screen to display all the titles under each subject you selected. Which book on the screen do you want to learn more about?

4. Who is the author and publisher of the book and in what year was the book published?

5. What is the call number of the book?

6. Is the book available?

7. Go back to the screen that displays all the titles under the subject you selected. Are there any videotapes, audiocassettes, or CDs listed? If so, which resource do you want to learn more about? What is the call number? Is the resource available?

Chapter
18
1350–1850
Empires of Asia

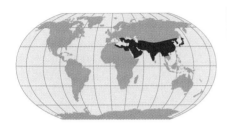

Chapter Themes

▶ **Movement** Muslim rulers govern empires that cover vast regions of Asia, North Africa, and Europe. *Section 1*

▶ **Cultural Diffusion** China is directly challenged by its contacts with western European cultures. *Section 2*

▶ **Reaction** Japan enforces isolationist policy to keep out Western influences. *Section 3*

▶ **Change** Southeast Asian lands face the growth of European trade and commerce in their region. *Section 4*

The Storyteller

Within the city walls of Vienna, Austria, people quaked as thundering cannonballs signaled the beginning of the Turkish siege of the city on September 27, 1529. Occupying the surrounding hills were 100,000 Turkish soldiers led by their skilled commander Suleiman.

By mid-October, Turkish troops twice had broken through part of Vienna's walls, but failed to capture the city as the Austrians and their allies rushed to plug the breaches. This clash between European and Asian armies was one of many encounters between different civilizations during the early modern period.

Historical Significance

What kinds of empires arose in Asia during the early modern period? How did they respond to the arrival of Europeans in their areas?

1300	1500	1700	1900

1368 Ming dynasty begins in China.

1453 The Ottomans capture Constantinople.

1587 Hideyoshi outlaws Christianity in Japan.

Voyage of the Emperor Qianlong (detail of a scroll), Qing dynasty.
Musée Guimet, Paris, France

Your History Journal

Research one of the following topics, make notes, and write an outline for a short paper: the Imam Mosque of Isfahan, the Taj Mahal, the Forbidden City, and the Imperial Palace of Tokyo.

1526 Babur founds the Mogul dynasty in India.

c. 1740 Nader Shah expands the empire of Safavid Persia.

1856 The Hatt-I Humayun decree sets out reforms for the Ottoman Empire.

Section 1

Muslim Empires

Setting the Scene

▶ **Terms to Define**
sultan, grand vizier, janissary, *millet*

▶ **People to Meet**
Suleiman I, Shah Abbas, Babur, Akbar

▶ **Places to Locate**
Istanbul, Isfahan, Delhi

Find Out How did Muslim rulers control and govern much of the Middle East, North Africa, and India between the 1500s and 1800s?

The Storyteller

On the day that Jahangir was crowned emperor of the Moghuls [Moguls], favorable omens abounded. His coronation was a scene of splendor, illuminated by nearly three thousand wax lights in branches of gold and silver. By his command, the imperial crown was brought to him. On each of the twelve points of this crown was a single diamond.... At the point in the center was a single pearl ... and on different parts of the same were set two hundred rubies. The Emirs of his empire, waiting for Jahangir's commands, were covered from head to foot in gold and jewels.

—adapted from *Memoirs of the Emperor Jahangir Written by Himself*, translated by David Price, reprinted in *The Human Record*, Alfred J. Andrea and James H. Overfield, 1990

Mogul warriors

Between the 1400s and the 1800s, three Muslim empires—the Ottoman Empire, the Persian Empire, and the Mogul Empire—conquered and controlled much of eastern Europe, central Asia, and India respectively. Strong leaders used powerful armies to amass territory that gave them economic control over major trade routes. As these empires spread into new areas, the religion and culture of Islam also expanded.

The Ottoman Empire

During the late 1200s, Turkish clans—calling themselves Ottoman Turks after their first leader, Osman—settled part of Asia Minor and began conquests to build an empire. They conquered much of Byzantine territory, making Constantinople their capital in 1453. Extending their Muslim empire even farther, by the 1500s the Ottomans controlled the Balkan Peninsula and parts of eastern Europe. By the end of their rule in the early 1900s, they had acquired much of the Middle East, North Africa, and the Caucasus region between the Black and Caspian Seas.

The Ottoman Empire maintained a strong navy in the Mediterranean to protect the lucrative trade they controlled there. Alarmed by the threat to their trade and to Christianity, Europeans under Philip II of Spain fought and defeated the Ottoman fleet at the Battle of Lepanto in 1571. But the Ottomans rebuilt their navy and remained a significant seapower until the 1700s.

Suleiman I

Suleiman I was one of the early Ottoman rulers who strengthened Muslim forces prior to the Battle of Lepanto. He was a multitalented man—a heroic military commander, a skillful administrator, and a patron of the arts. Ruling from 1520 to 1566, Suleiman received the name "The Lawgiver" for his work in organizing Ottoman laws.

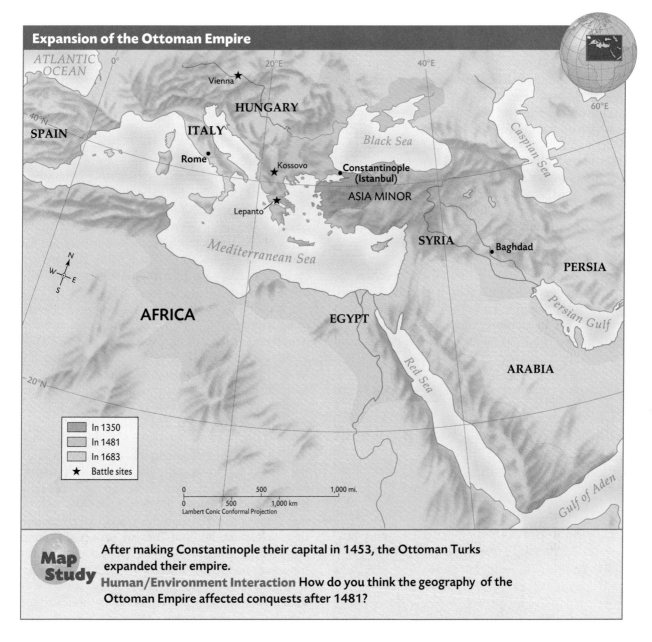

Expansion of the Ottoman Empire

ATLANTIC OCEAN

Vienna ★

HUNGARY

SPAIN

ITALY

Rome •

Kossovo ★

Constantinople (Istanbul)

ASIA MINOR

Black Sea

Caspian Sea

Lepanto ★

Mediterranean Sea

SYRIA

Baghdad •

PERSIA

Persian Gulf

AFRICA

EGYPT

ARABIA

Red Sea

Gulf of Aden

In 1350
In 1481
In 1683
★ Battle sites

0   500   1,000 mi.
0   500   1,000 km
Lambert Conic Conformal Projection

Map Study After making Constantinople their capital in 1453, the Ottoman Turks expanded their empire.

Human/Environment Interaction How do you think the geography of the Ottoman Empire affected conquests after 1481?

Suleiman acted as both the sultan, or political ruler, and the caliph, or religious leader; he enjoyed absolute authority. To rule effectively, however, Suleiman needed support from his personal advisers, the bureaucracy, a group of religious advisers known as the Ulema, and a well-trained army. A grand vizier, or prime minister, headed the bureaucracy that enforced the sultan's decisions throughout the empire. The Ulema made rulings on questions of Islamic law, and the army held much control within the empire by conquering and controlling new territories.

The Ottomans recruited officers from among the conquered peoples of their empire. An elite corps of officers called janissaries came from the Balkans, where Christian families were required by the Ottomans to turn over young boys to the govern-ment. Converted to Islam, the boys received rigorous training that made them a loyal fighting force.

Ottoman Law

Because the empire was so large, Ottoman Muslims ruled diverse peoples, including Arabs, Greeks, Albanians, Slavs, Armenians, and Jews. The population was divided into several classes: a ruling class made up of the sultan's family and high government officials; the nobility, which administered agricultural estates; and the largest class, the peasants who worked on those estates.

To accommodate these diverse populations, the government made special laws affecting those who did not practice Islam, the empire's official religion. Non-Muslims were allowed to practice their faith. Ottoman law also permitted the empire's diverse religious groups to run affairs in their own *millets*, or communities, and choose their own leaders to present their views to the Ottoman government.

The Ottoman Islamic civilization borrowed many elements from the Byzantine, Persian, and Arab cultures they had absorbed. Mosques, bridges, and aqueducts reflected this blend of styles. The Christian city of Constantinople was transformed into a Muslim one and renamed **Istanbul**. Ottoman architects renovated Hagia Sophia into a mosque and then planned new mosques and palaces that added to Istanbul's beauty. Ottoman painters produced detailed miniatures and illuminated manuscripts.

Decline of the Ottomans

By 1600 the Ottoman Empire had reached the peak of its power; thereafter it slowly declined. Even at its height, however, the empire faced enemies on its borders. Conquests ended as the Ottomans tried to fight both Persians and

Europeans. In 1683 Polish King John III Sobieski led European forces in ending an Ottoman siege of Vienna. This European victory dealt a decisive blow to the Ottoman Empire. When Ottoman military conquests ceased, massive poverty and civil discontent afflicted Ottoman lands.

Reform

By the 1700s, the Ottoman Empire had fallen behind Europe in trade and military technology. Russia and other European nations began taking Ottoman territory, and local rulers in North Africa gradually broke away from Ottoman control. In the 1800s uprisings in the Balkans led to freedom for the Greeks, Serbs, Bulgarians, and Romanians. Unsuccessful revolts in Armenia and Arabia were brutally crushed.

Wanting to halt Ottoman decline, Ottoman rulers during the 1800s used European ideas to reform and unify the empire. In 1856 Sultan Abdul-Mejid I issued the Hatt-I-Hamayun, a sweeping reform decree that created a national citizenship, reduced the authority of religious leaders, and opened government service to all peoples.

Reaction

Powerful resistance to change grew among the religious leaders, who had lost civil authority in their own communities. Although many Muslim, Jewish, and Christian leaders protested reform, merchants and artisans in the individual communities welcomed it. Non-Turkish groups, such as Armenians, Bulgarians, Macedonians, and Serbs, however, had little interest in any reform that would save the empire. They began to think of themselves as separate nationalities and wanted nation-states of their own.

After Abdul-Mejid's death in 1861, the reform movement lacked the strong leadership needed to guarantee its success. To gain public support, reformers known as the Young Ottomans overthrew the weak sultan Abdul-Aziz and replaced him with Abdul-Hamid II.

At first the new sultan went along with the reformers. In 1876 he proclaimed a new constitution. He affirmed the unity of the empire and promised individual liberties for his subjects. In 1877 the first Ottoman parliament met in Istanbul. But later that same year Abdul-Hamid II decided to resist reform. He suddenly dissolved the parliament and ended constitutional rule. The sultan believed that moving the Ottoman government toward liberalism would lead to ruin. To further protect the empire from change, he drove many of the Young Ottomans into exile. Then he imposed absolute rule.

Visualizing History **Portrait of Suleiman, "The Lawgiver,"** **from the late 1600s.** *What provision did the Ottoman law make for peoples of diverse religions?*

Safavid Persia

To the east of the Ottoman Empire lay Persia, a land that had once been part of the Islamic Empire, but which had broken away because of religious differences. In the 1500s Shiite Muslims, bitter enemies of the Ottoman Turks, conquered the land of present-day Iran. The Shiite leader, Ismail (ihs•MAH•EEL), conquered and unified the numerous people living there, declaring himself to be the founder of the Safavid (sah•FAH•weed) dynasty.

Safavid rulers required all of their Persian subjects to accept the Shiite form of Islam. Belief in the Shia branch of Islam distinguished people living in Persia from neighboring Sunni Muslim peoples—the Arabs and Turks.

Shah Abbas

The Safavid leader **Shah Abbas** came to the throne in 1587. His army regained some western territory lost to the Ottomans in previous years. Then the shah sought allies against the Ottomans even among such Christian states as England. The English used their alliance with Persia to seize the strategic Persian Gulf port of Hormuz in 1622, gaining control of the Persian silk and East Indian spice trade.

With his empire secure against the Ottoman forces, Shah Abbas set up his court in **Isfahan**, which became one of the most magnificent cities in the entire Muslim world. Towering above the city was the blue dome of the Imam Mosque, which was covered with lacy white decorations. Near the mosque, Abbas had a three-story palace built for his personal use. He also ordered beautiful streets and parks constructed throughout the city.

During the reign of Abbas, Persian spread as the language of culture, diplomacy, and trade in most of the Muslim world. Later the language spread to India. Urdu, spoken in Pakistan today, is partly based on Persian.

Nader Shah

After the death of Shah Abbas in 1629, inept Safavid rulers weakened the empire, bringing on its decline. In 1736, after the Safavid decline, Nader Shah came to power. He expanded the Persian Empire to its greatest height since Darius. But after his assassination in 1747, territory was lost and the country was divided.

In the late 1700s another Turkic group, the Qajar dynasty, seized the Persian throne and established a new dynasty in Tehran. The Qajars ruled Persia until 1925.

Visualizing History The Imam Mosque in Isfahan (in present-day Iran) was built by Shah Abbas during the early 1600s. *What cultural impact did Safavid Persia have on the Muslim world?*

The Mogul Empire

Even before the Ottomans and the Safavids built their empires, Islamic invaders from central Asia had conquered much of northern India by the 1100s. The invaders set up a sultanate, or Muslim kingdom, in **Delhi** in 1206. Once order was restored, northern India prospered economically and culturally. Traditional Hindu culture survived the invasions and blended with Islamic civilization.

Timur Lenk in India

By the late 1300s the Muslim Mongol ruler, Timur Lenk (Tamerlane), had conquered much of central Asia and made Samarkand the capital of his empire. Although a devout Muslim, Timur Lenk was also a ruthless leader. His forces sacked the city of Delhi in 1398, killing thousands and leaving the city in rubble. After Timur Lenk's death, his Islamic

Otis Imboden

Taj Mahal

The beauty of the Taj Mahal has awed visitors for centuries. A pear-shaped dome crowns the square central building, complete with a reflecting pool. The marble surface glitters with semiprecious stones: jade from China; turquoise from Tibet; lapis lazuli from Afghanistan; chrysolite from Egypt; and mother-of-pearl from the Indian Ocean. Inside all this wealth and beauty lies Mumtazi Mahal, wife of the Mogul emperor of India, Shah Jahan, who ruled from 1628 to 1658. He fell in love with Mumtazi at 16 and adored his queen throughout her life. In 1629, shortly after Shah Jahan's reign began, Mumtazi died in childbirth, after giving birth to their 14th child. Her death left him in black despair, and in his grief he decided to build the world's greatest tomb.

Or so goes the legend. Contemporary scholars argue that Shah Jahan built the Taj Mahal not only as a resting place for his well-loved wife—and later for himself—but also as a symbol of his power and wealth. The Moguls were Muslims—outsiders and conquerors who ruled India in an absolute monarchy. Their administration left India weak and, by the 1800s, vulnerable to British conquest. In their art and architecture they gave India a more lasting legacy. "The Taj Mahal," wrote Indian poet Rabindranath Tagore, is "like a solitary tear suspended on the cheek of time." ⊕

empire disintegrated; yet northern India would face other Muslim invasions.

Akbar the Great

In the early 1500s **Babur**, who was a descendant of Timur Lenk, led another attack on northern India. Using artillery and with cavalry riding elephants and horses, Babur conquered Delhi at the Battle of Panipat in 1526. Then he set up the Mogul dynasty, the Persian name for Mongol, which lasted three centuries in India. Unlike Timur Lenk, the Moguls encouraged orderly government, and they expanded the arts.

Babur's grandson, **Akbar**, was a benevolent ruler who brought peace and order to northern India. Recognizing that most of the people he ruled were Hindus, Akbar encouraged religious tolerance to end quarrels between Hindus and Muslims. Whereas Muslims believed in one God, Hindus worshiped many deities. Hindus and Muslims differed about sacred foods, social organization, and religious customs. To reduce tension among his people, Akbar repealed a tax on Hindus.

Extremely curious about all religions, Akbar invited religious scholars of other faiths to his court to learn about other religions. He concluded that all religions revealed the same divine truth, whatever their external practices were. He tried to set up a new religion that he called Divine Faith. The new religion included features of many of the world's religions such as Islam, Hinduism, and Christianity.

Mogul Civilization

Under Akbar's rule music, painting, and literature flourished in Mogul India. Mogul rulers made their lavish courts centers of art and learning. Although Akbar could not read, he understood the value of education and set up a large library, employing more than 100 court painters to illustrate the elegantly bound books.

Another Mogul ruler, Shah Jahan, created one of the world's most beautiful buildings—the Taj

History & Art *Akbar Hunting Tigers Near Gwalior* by Husain Haqqash, c. 1580, from the *Akbar-Nama*. Victoria and Albert Museum, London, England *How did Akbar encourage religious tolerance?*

Mahal at Agra—a magnificent example of Muslim architecture. Muslim architects introduced the arch and dome to India, and in trading contacts with China, Muslim merchants brought gunpowder, paper, and Chinese porcelain to Mogul India.

Mogul Decline

During the late 1600s, Mogul rulers, such as Shah Aurangzeb, abandoned religious toleration. They persecuted India's Hindu majority as well as the Sikhs, followers of Sikhism (SEE•KIH•zuhm), a new religion founded by the teacher Nanak in the 1500s. Sikhism holds to a belief in one God and teaches that good deeds and meditation bring release from the cycle of reincarnation. Today there are about 14 million Sikhs, most of whom live in the northern Indian state of Punjab. During the late 1600s, both Sikhs and Hindus rebelled against the Moguls and helped weaken Mogul authority. As Mogul central government declined, local rulers became more independent.

SECTION 1 REVIEW

Recall
1. **Define** sultan, grand vizier, janissary, *millet*.
2. **Identify** Suleiman I, Hatt-I Humayun, Shah Abbas, Babur, Akbar.
3. **Use** the map on page 457 to compare the Ottoman Empire's boundaries in 1481 to those in 1683. How did the growth of the Ottoman Empire lead to decline?

Critical Thinking
4. **Making Comparisons** How did Shah Abbas's patronage of the arts compare to that of a contemporary European monarch?

Understanding Themes
5. **Movement** How do you think the movement of Muslims into northern India affected the people already living there?

1405 China begins first seagoing expedition.

1644 The Manchus establish the Qing dynasty.

1800 China's population reaches 350 million.

Section 2

Chinese Dynasties

Setting the Scene

▶ **Terms to Define**
junk, queue, labor-intensive farming

▶ **People to Meet**
Hong Wu, Yong Le, Zheng He

▶ **Places to Locate**
Beijing, the Forbidden City

Find Out Why did China flourish and then decline during the Ming and Qing dynasties?

The Storyteller

The examination process for civil servants was riddled with corruption. "There are too many men who claim to be pure scholars and yet are stupid and arrogant," K'ang-hsi [Kangxi] fumed. Incompetent examiners were set on memorization instead of independent thinking. Candidate lists were manipulated to favor specific provinces.

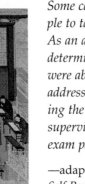

Some candidates even hired people to take the exams for them. As an active ruler K'ang-hsi was determined to have officials who were able and efficient. He addressed the problems by holding the exams under armed supervision and reading the exam papers himself.

—adapted from *Emperor of China: Self-Portrait of K'ang-hsi*, translated by Johnathan D. Spence, reprinted in *The Human Record*, Alfred J. Andrea and James H. Overfield, 1990

Han civil service exam

In 1368, after the Yuan dynasty fell, a new era of reform began. The Ming and the Qing dynasties built strong central governments that implemented agricultural and public works projects. As food production and trade increased, so did China's population. At the same time, China looked to earlier achievements to invigorate its culture. After years of prosperity, Chinese emperors isolated themselves from their people and the outside, resulting in government corruption, rebellions, and decline.

The Ming Dynasty

After 89 years of Mongol rule, a military officer named Zhu Yuanzhang (JOO YOO•AHN•JAHNG) led a rebellion that overthrew the Yuan dynasty. Born into a poor peasant family, Zhu had been a Buddhist monk before entering the army. In 1368 he became emperor, taking the name **Hong Wu** and establishing his capital at Nanjing. For the first time in more than 1,000 years, the Son of Heaven was of peasant origin. Hong Wu gave the name *Ming* ("brilliant") to his dynasty, which would rule China for nearly 300 years.

Peace and Stability

The Ming dynasty brought peace and stability to China. Hong Wu and the early Ming rulers imposed new law codes, reorganized the tax system, and reformed local government.

The new law codes were harsher than those of previous Chinese dynasties. Scholars, traditionally exempt from corporal punishment, had to endure public whippings if they displeased the emperor and his officials. Formerly, the saying was that "a gentleman could be ordered to die but should never be humiliated."

Visualizing History The Forbidden City in the heart of the city of Beijing contains hundreds of buildings. Many of these buildings housed the emperors of China and their imperial court from 1421 to 1911. *How did the Ming Emperor Yong Le contribute to Chinese scholarship?*

Chinese persons replaced Mongols in all civil service posts, and Confucianism again became the empire's official doctrine. The Ming dynasty restored the old examination system, making the tests even stricter than in earlier dynasties.

Strong rulers at the beginning of the dynasty enforced peace throughout the land. With peace and additional revenues from a reformed tax system, economic prosperity came to China. But northern China had been devastated by nomadic invaders. To encourage farmers to move there, the government offered free land, tools, seeds, and farm animals. Farmers reclaimed and restored much of the land in the north, and the policy helped secure the northern frontier from invaders.

With more land under cultivation, farmers could sell their surplus produce at local markets. Government workers repaired and maintained the canal system that connected local markets. Increased agricultural productivity also freed workers for nonfarming tasks. Artisans in larger numbers expanded the production of silk, textiles, tea, and porcelain to meet the demands of growing urban populations. Thus, trade within China

increased, enriching merchants in cities such as Shanghai and Guangzhou (GWONG•JOH).

As city merchants and artisans grew wealthier, they demanded more popular entertainments and learning. The third Ming emperor, **Yong Le**, ordered 2,000 scholars to compile a treasury of Chinese histories and literature. This massive library included neo-Confucian writings from the Song dynasty and also many Buddhist scriptures.

Ming writers preferred the novel to other forms of fiction. Their works were based largely on tales told over the centuries by storytellers. One of the most popular novels, *The Romance of the Three Kingdoms*, describes military rivalries at the end of the Han era.

POINT

Chinese Exploration

The early Ming emperors spent government money on a navy that could sail to foreign ports and collect tribute for the emperor. The ships, known as junks, usually traveled along the coastline, but they could also venture into open water.

From 1405 to 1433, emperors sent out seven seagoing expeditions. Their purpose was "glorifying Chinese arms in the remote regions and showing off the wealth and power of the [Middle] Kingdom." The leader of the voyages was a Chinese Muslim named **Zheng He** (JUNG HUH).

Zheng He took his first fleet to the nations of Southeast Asia. In later voyages he reached India, sailed up the Persian Gulf to Arabia, and even visited eastern Africa. Everywhere he went, he demanded that the people submit to the emperor's authority. If they refused, he applied force; rulers who accepted were rewarded with gold or silk.

Zheng He brought back trade goods and tribute from many lands. From Africa he returned home with animals for the emperor's zoo. As a result of Zheng He's voyages, Chinese merchants settled in Southeast Asia and India and spread Chinese culture.

Later Ming emperors, however, did not follow through: ocean voyages were costly, and in the early 1400s China concentrated its funds on military forces to combat threats from nomadic tribes to the north. The emperor's officials saw no great benefit in exploring expeditions and halted them. The government discouraged trade with foreign countries partly because Confucian philosophy regarded trade as the lowest of occupations. The emperor even forbade construction of seagoing vessels.

Inside the Forbidden City

To help defend the northern border, Yong Le shifted his capital from Nanjing to Cambaluc, renaming it **Beijing** (BAY•JING), which means "northern capital." He ordered the city completely rebuilt, modeled after the great Tang capital of Changan. For 16 years, from 1404 to 1420, workers labored on its construction. On the Chinese New Year's Day in 1421, the government moved to Beijing.

A visitor entering Beijing walked through the great gate in the 30-foot-(9-meter-) high southern wall. Government workers passed through the Gate of Heavenly Peace to the offices of the Imperial City.

Images of the Times

Chinese Life

Under the stable, centralized rule of the Ming and Qing dynasties, crafts, industry, and agriculture flourished.

Breeding the silkworm required patience, but the reward was income from trade.

The Gate of Supreme Harmony at Beijing's Forbidden City is guarded well by a centuries-old lion.

Farther north, across a moat and through the Meridian Gate, stood **the Forbidden City**, where the emperor and his family lived. The Forbidden City had two main sections: one for the emperor's personal use and another for state occasions. The main courtyard outside the gate held 90,000 people. The emperor sometimes appeared before guests here, but ordinary people stayed out or faced a penalty of death.

The residential section of the Forbidden City consisted of many palaces with thousands of rooms. Pavilions and gardens gave comfort to the imperial family, who spent their days in fabulous splendor. Later Ming emperors devoted much of their time to pleasure. In the last 30 years of one emperor's reign, he met with his closest officials only five times.

Corrupt officials, eager to enrich themselves, took over the country. As law and order collapsed, Manchu invaders from Manchuria attacked the northern frontier settlements. Revenues for military spending were limited by the expenses of the lavish court. The Manchus managed to conquer a weakened China.

The Qing Dynasty

In 1644 the Manchus set up a new dynasty, called the Qing (CHING), or "pure." For only the second time in history, foreigners controlled all of China. The Manchus slowly extended their empire to the north and west, taking in Manchuria, Mongolia, Xinjiang (SHIN•JEE•ONG), and Tibet. The offshore island of Taiwan became part of the empire in 1683. For almost 300 years the Qing dynasty ruled over the largest Chinese empire that ever existed.

Adapting Chinese Culture

The Manchus had already accepted Confucian values before invading China. Their leaders understood that these precepts benefited the ruling class. Ruling over an empire in which Chinese outnumbered Manchus by at least 30 to 1, the Manchu rulers controlled their empire by making every effort to adopt many of the native Chinese customs and traditions.

A Ming porcelain bowl painted in underglaze displays the familiar blue willow pattern.

Iron workers decorate this Chinese vase preserved in the Golestan Palace, Tehran, Iran.

REFLECTING ON THE TIMES

1. What artistic creation was done under the emperor's patronage?
2. How do these objects and scenes reflect life under the Ming and Qing dynasties?

Economics

Feeding China

During the Ming and Qing eras, China expanded its agricultural production. Rapid population growth, particularly in eastern China, made it necessary for farmers to grow more food. Terracing—the steplike areas that farmers dug out of hillsides—helped them make full use of their lands. To help farmers water their crops and transport them to market, the government continued building canal and irrigation systems.

Meanwhile, new crops from the Americas arrived in China on Chinese ships that traveled regularly to Southeast Asia. During the 1500s, Spanish ships brought sweet potatoes, maize, and peanuts as well as silver and gold from the Americas to the Philippines. There Chinese merchants exchanged silk or porcelain for the precious metals and exotic foods. All these factors helped make China's population the largest in the world.

Chinese irrigation

Today, China is still the world's most populous country, despite government efforts to limit population growth. Farm production also has significantly risen because of better opportunities for farmers to make profits on the open market. Electricity reaches many villages, and a few rural households now operate small factories and businesses. Dam construction, bridge building, and other public works have transformed rural China, while new products have come to China through increased trade with other parts of the world.

Linking Past and Present **ACTIVITY**

Discuss past and present ways used by the Chinese to expand food production. In doing so, how have they changed their environment? How have modern farming practices affected the environment in various parts of the world?

Manchus kept control by naming Manchus to the officer corps and by ensuring that most of the soldiers were Manchus. To control the Chinese civil service, Manchus reserved the top jobs in the government hierarchy for their people. Even Chinese officials in lower positions had a Manchu supervisor monitoring their work. Critical military and government positions thus remained loyal to the Manchu leadership.

In 1645 the Manchu emperor ordered all Chinese men to shave their heads leaving a single queue, or braid, at the back of their heads—or be executed. Among the people this order was known as "Keep your hair and lose your head" or "Lose your hair and keep your head." The upper classes had to adopt the Manchu tight, high-collared jacket and abandon their customary loose robes. But in spite of the many-layered controls, the Manchu rulers took on more elements of Chinese culture.

The Qing were fortunate in having able emperors in the first years of their rule. Emperor Kangxi, who ruled from 1661 to 1722, reduced taxes and undertook public works projects, such as flood control. Kangxi, himself a poet, also sponsored Chinese art. Other emperors secured new territory, extending the Qing Empire.

Daily Life

The Manchus made few changes in China's economy. The government-sponsored work projects and internal peace contributed to economic prosperity in the 1700s. Agricultural improvements increased food production, whereupon China's population exploded, from about 150 million in 1600 to 350 million in 1800. China was the most populous country in the world.

More than three-fourths of the Chinese people lived in rural areas. In the south where Chinese farmers worked as tenants, each family farmed its plot and paid rent to a landlord. In the north, more families owned their land. But because a family divided its land among its sons, over the generations the average peasant's share of land shrank.

As population increased, every inch of land had to be made productive. Although the Chinese had invented such simple machines as the wheelbarrow and paddle-wheel pumps, farmers depended on human labor for most farm tasks. In hill country, farm workers dug flat terraces into the hillsides where rice and other crops could be grown. Workers carried pails of water to fill the rice paddies. This labor-intensive farming, in which work is performed by human effort, contrasts with agriculture in which the hard work is done by animals or machinery.

Subsistence farming was not a year-round occupation during the Qing dynasty. Many farmers grew cash crops such as cotton, rather than just their own food. A writer in the 1700s described the life of farm families in one district:

> ❝ The country folk only live off their fields for the three winter months.... During the spring months, they ... spin or weave, eating by exchanging their cloth for rice.... The autumn is somewhat rainy, and the noise of the looms' shuttles is once again to be heard everywhere in the villages.... Thus, even if there is a bad harvest ... our country people are not in distress so long as the other counties have a crop of cotton [for them to weave]. ❞

Silk production provided extra income for farm families. They grew mulberry trees, whose leaves provided food for silkworms. From the leaves women and girls plucked the cocoons and carefully unwound them. Then the silk was ready for those who spun it into thread and others who wove it into silk cloth.

Internal trade flourished during the Qing period. There was a lively exchange of goods within and between the various regions of China. Great merchant families made fortunes trading rice, silk, fish, timber, cloth, and luxury goods. The growth of trade prompted specialization. Some regions were famous for textiles; others for cotton, porcelain, tea, or silk. At Jingdezhen, the emperor's porcelain factory employed thousands of workers. Artists painted delicate patterns or scenes on vases, bowls, and plates. Others made chemical glazes that formed a hard, shiny surface on the pottery after it was fired in a hot kiln.

Contacts With Europeans

European demand for Chinese goods such as silk and porcelain was high, attracting European ships to China's coast. The first Europeans arrived in China during the Ming dynasty. In 1514 Portuguese caravels landed near Guangzhou. The Chinese called Portuguese sailors ocean devils, and local officials refused to deal with them. Nonetheless, by 1557 the Portuguese had built a trading base at Macao.

Jesuit missionaries followed the Portuguese traders with the dream of converting China's huge population to Christianity. Although most Chinese officials were not interested in Christianity, the Jesuits' scientific knowledge impressed them. In 1611 the emperor placed a Jesuit astronomer in charge of the Imperial Calendar, and in years to come Jesuits gained other government positions. They also converted some court officials to Christianity. By the 1700s, however, Qing rulers worried that Jesuits were too involved in government affairs and forced the missionaries to leave. The Jesuits had failed to make China a Christian nation.

Qing Decline

During the 1700s corruption and internal rebellions forced the Qing dynasty into a slow decline. As the population grew, the government raised taxes to support public services. High-ranking officials, however, kept much of the revenue. Peasant rebellions followed.

By 1850 the Qing faced the Taiping Rebellion. The leader of this revolt came in contact with Christian missionaries and developed his version of Christianity. He organized many Chinese into a political movement to replace the Qing dynasty with a "Heavenly Kingdom of Great Peace." Lasting 14 years, the rebellion left much of southern China destroyed and the central government weakened. Thus undermined, the Qing faced new threats from foreign imperialistic powers.

SECTION 2 REVIEW

Recall
1. **Define** junk, queue, labor-intensive farming.
2. **Identify** Hong Wu, Yong Le, Zheng He, the Forbidden City, the Manchus.
3. **Use** the world map on pages A4 and A5 in the Atlas to determine the distance Chinese explorers traveled to reach the east coast of Africa. How does this record compare to Prince Henry's expeditions?

Critical Thinking
4. **Evaluating Information** How did the achievements of the Ming and Qing dynasties differ? Did the Qing build on the successes of the Ming, or did they create a completely new civilization?

Understanding Themes
5. **Cultural Diffusion** What might have happened if the Chinese had continued moving westward? Would China have colonized as Europeans did?

1600	1700	1800

1600 Tokugawa Ieyasu wins the Battle of Sekigahara.

1636 Act of Seclusion forbids Japanese to leave the country.

c. 1700s Japanese cities grow in size and population.

Section 3

The Japanese Empire

Setting the Scene

▶ **Terms to Define**
sankin-kotai, metsuke, geisha, haiku

▶ **People to Meet**
Oda Nobunaga, Toyotomi Hideyoshi, Tokugawa Ieyasu, Francis Xavier, Matsuo Basho

▶ **Places to Locate**
Edo, Nagasaki

 **Find Out** Why was Japan more adaptable to changes than China before the 1800s?

The Storyteller

Yamaga Soko bowed deeply. The shogun, Tokugawa Ieyasu, would determine if Yamaga was prepared to assume a samurai's responsibilities. "In peacetime, we should not be oblivious to the danger of war. Should we not then prepare ourselves for it?" asked Tokugawa. Yamaga understood that many considered the use of arms evil. "Beyond these military duties, we have other functions. We are examples for all society, leading simple and frugal lives," Yamaga responded. Not only would the samurai excel at death; they should also cultivate all aspects of life. Tokugawa spoke again, "A samurai's life calls for constant discipline. Are you, Yamaga Soko, prepared to devote yourself to this?"

—adapted from *Sources of Japanese Tradition*, reprinted in *The Human Record*, Alfred J. Andrea and James H. Overfield, 1990

Samurai in combat

While China enjoyed stability in the 1400s and 1500s, Japan experienced a period of turmoil. The shogun was a mere figurehead, and the emperor performed only religious functions. Daimyos, who controlled their own lands, waged war against their neighbors as feudal lords had done in Europe in the 1400s. "The strongest eat and the weak become the meat" was a Japanese expression of the time. Warriors showed no chivalry or loyalty. This time of local wars left Japan with a political system known as the Tokugawa shogunate that combined a central government with a system of feudalism.

Tokugawa Shogunate

Oda Nobunaga (oh•DAH noh•boo•NAH•gah) was the first military leader to begin uniting the warring daimyos. He announced his ambition on his personal seal: "to bring the nation under one sword." After winning control of a large part of central Japan, Nobunaga led his army against the capital city of Kyoto in 1568. Five years later, amid the chaos caused by the weak Ashikaga (ah•shee•KAH•gah) family, Nobunaga deposed the Ashikaga shogun. Meanwhile, his forces had moved against Buddhist military strongholds around Kyoto. After a 10-year siege, he won and so became the most powerful man in the country. In 1582, however, a treacherous soldier murdered him.

Toyotomi Hideyoshi

Power then shifted to Nobunaga's best general, **Toyotomi Hideyoshi** (toh•yoh•TOH•mee HEE•day•YOH•shee), who rose from a peasant family to his high position in the military. By 1590 Hideyoshi had forced Japan's daimyos to pledge their loyalty to him. Acting as a military dictator, Hideyoshi furthered his goal of unity by disarming the peasants to prevent them from becoming warriors. In 1588 he ordered the "great sword hunt," demanding that all peasants turn in their weapons. To stabilize the daimyo realms he controlled, he imposed laws that prevented warriors from leaving their daimyo's service to become merchants or farmers. The laws also prevented farmers and merchants from becoming warriors.

Hideyoshi, planning to expand Japan's power abroad, invaded Korea as a step toward conquering China. The invasion had another purpose—to rid the country of warriors who could start rebellions at home. However, as you learned in Chapter 14, Admiral Yi's Korean turtle ships thwarted Hideyoshi's conquest.

Tokugawa Ieyasu

After Hideyoshi's death in 1598, a third leader, **Tokugawa Ieyasu** (toh•kuh•GAH•wah ee•YAH•soo), completed the work of unification. At the Battle of Sekigahara (seh•kee•gah•HAR•ah) in 1600, Ieyasu defeated the last of his opponents. Three years later, Ieyasu asked the emperor to make him shogun. The Tokugawa family retained the shogunate for 250 years.

Tokugawa Rule

Ieyasu established his government headquarters at the fishing village of **Edo**, present-day Tokyo. There he built a stone fortress protected by high walls and moats. Today, the fortress is the Imperial Palace, but during the Tokugawa shogunate, the Japanese emperor continued to live in Kyoto. Although the emperor remained the official leader of Japan, the shogun exercised the real power.

After taking control, Ieyasu reassigned the daimyos' lands. He divided the daimyos into three groups: Tokugawa relatives, longtime supporters of the Tokugawa family, and those who came to the Tokugawa side only after the Battle of Sekigahara. He issued the most productive lands near Edo to the Tokugawa relatives. The others—potential enemies—received less desirable lands in outlying areas of Japan.

To ensure daimyo loyalty, Ieyasu set up a system called *sankin-kotai*, or attendance by turn. Each daimyo had to travel to Edo every other year, bringing tribute and remaining in the shogun's service for a full year. Thus, half the daimyos were directly under the shogun's control at any one time. Even when the daimyos returned to their estates, they had to leave their families at Edo as hostages.

The daimyos spent much of their income traveling to and from Edo and maintaining several households. They also had to get the shogun's permission to marry and to repair or build their castles. *Sankin-kotai* kept them weak, obedient to the

shogun, and less able to rebel against the government. Much like Louis XIV of France, the shogun turned his aristocracy into courtiers who were carefully watched and controlled.

Political System

The Tokugawa family and a select group of daimyos controlled the government. Together they made up the Council of Elders, the leading administrative body. Assisting the Council, as the "eyes and ears" of the state, was a group of officials known as the *metsuke*. The *metsuke* toured the country and reported on possible uprisings or plots against the shogun. A genuine bureaucracy began to develop, working on the principles of joint decision making and promotion based on talent and success.

Social Classes

Before 1600 there had been some social mobility between classes in Japan. Hideyoshi and Ieyasu

Visualizing History As a member of a professional class of women, a geisha might serve a samurai in song or dance, by playing a musical instrument, or engaging in stimulating conversation. *What were the symbols of authority permitted only to a samurai?*

had both risen to the top from lowly backgrounds. To maintain social stability and limit future rivals, they introduced measures that froze the Japanese social structure.

Under Tokugawa rule, the Japanese were divided into four social classes. At the top were the samurai, including the daimyos, who held all political power. They alone could wear symbols of authority: a sword and a distinctive topknot in their hair. The farmers, as major food producers, were the second-highest class. They were followed by artisans who made goods. Merchants were at the bottom of society, because they only exchanged goods and thus were not productive.

No one could change his social class or perform tasks that belonged to another class. One samurai recalled that his father took him out of school because he was taught arithmetic—a subject fit only for merchants. A character in a popular puppet play, written by the author Chikamatsu, described the proper order of society:

> 66 A samurai's child is reared by samurai parents and becomes a samurai himself because they teach him the warrior's code. A merchant's child is reared by merchant parents and becomes a merchant because they teach him the way of commerce. A samurai seeks a fair name in disregard for profit, but a merchant, with no thought to

his reputation, gathers profit and amasses a fortune. This is the way of life proper to each. This strict social order helped maintain peace and stability throughout Japan. 99

Tokugawa Ethics

Tokugawa ethics placed loyalty to the shogun above the family. Duty and honor became the central values. Individuals had to develop strict inner discipline to live up to the requirements of their assigned place in life. These values gradually spread from the samurai through all social classes in Japan.

Over the course of time, Tokugawa rules for personal conduct evolved into complex rituals and etiquette. Minute details came to have heavy symbolic meaning. They became a way to maintain conformity and control. This was important for a society that had a large population and only a small area of productive land.

Contacts With the West

The peace and order of the Tokugawa shogunate were interrupted when the first Europeans—the Portuguese—arrived in Japan in 1543. Although the Japanese looked upon Europeans as barbarians, the warrior society saw that European weapons meant power. They purchased muskets and cannon to defeat their opponents.

Roman Catholic missionaries soon followed the Portuguese merchants. **Francis Xavier**, the earliest of the Jesuit priests who came to Japan, admired the Japanese people. To convert them, the Jesuits adopted their customs. Jesuit missionaries learned the subtleties of conversing in polite Japanese and set up a tea room in their houses so that they could receive their visitors properly.

After Xavier won the support of some local daimyos, Christianity spread rapidly. Oda Nobunaga himself lent support to the Christians, for during this time he was moving against the Buddhist monasteries that were serving as military strongholds. Jesuits trained Japanese priests to create a strong Japanese Christian church. By 1614 the Jesuits had converted 300,000 Japanese.

Many Japanese welcomed the first contact with Westerners, whose customs and styles became widespread in Japanese society. Even for Japanese who had not converted to Christianity, Christian symbols became fashionable. A missionary described non-Christian daimyos who would wear "rosaries of driftwood on their breasts, hang a

Visualizing History In Tokugawa Japan, cities became leading centers of Japanese culture. Artisans began to produce goods for a growing urban market. *What social classes made up Tokugawa Japan?*

Merchants from the West arrive in Japan accompanied by Jesuit missionaries. *How did Christian missionary activity end under Tokugawa rule?*

crucifix from their shoulder or waist … they think it good and effective in bringing success in daily life."

Hideyoshi began to suspect that Christian influence could be harmful to Japan. He had heard of Spanish missionaries in the Philippines who had helped establish Spain's control over the islands. In 1587 Hideyoshi outlawed Christianity. Although some priests were crucified, Hideyoshi generally did not enforce his ban on the religion.

Tokugawa Ieyasu and his successors also feared that Christianity threatened their power and so continued to persecute Christians, killing them or forcing them to leave Japan. When Japanese Christians in the port city of **Nagasaki** defied authorities and refused to disband, the government attacked their community in 1637 and finally wiped them out in 1638.

Japan barred all Europeans except the Dutch. Unlike the Spanish and the Portuguese, the Dutch were interested only in trade, not conquest or religious conversion of the Japanese. For this reason, after 1641 the Tokugawa government confined the Dutch to a tiny island in Nagasaki harbor where they and a few Chinese carried on a tightly regulated trade. Through the Dutch traders, a trickle of information about the West continued to flow into Japan.

Despite Japan's geographic isolation and the Tokugawa policy of isolation, Japan's society and economy continued to change internally. During the early Tokugawa period, agriculture brought wealth to daimyos and samurai, who profited from the rice produced on their lands. Merchants, in turn, grew wealthy by lending money to daimyos and samurai.

Japan's Policy of Isolation

The Tokugawa rulers, deciding that contact with outsiders posed too many dangers, laid down edicts. Their seclusion policy lasted 200 years. The Act of Seclusion of 1636 forbade any Japanese to leave the country and added, "All Japanese residing abroad shall be put to death when they return home." The government banned construction of ships large enough for ocean voyages.

Footnotes to History

Karate

Karate is unarmed combat in which a person uses primarily the hands or feet to strike a blow at an opponent. This martial art began on the island of Okinawa near Japan. During the 1600s, Okinawa's Japanese conquerors forbade the local people to own weapons. In response, many Okinawans learned to turn their hands and feet into fighting instruments.

First Public Opera House Opens

Venice, Italy, 1637
The Teatro San Cassiano—the world's first public opera house—opened in Venice in 1637. Early baroque operas consisted of recitatives, or informational parts, sung by soloists accompanied by one or two instruments. The arias, or solos expressing a character's feelings, allowed opera singers to show off their vocal skills. By the late 1600s, operas were being written and performed in England, France, and Germany. Italian opera, however, remained the accepted style.

Venice

As the daimyos became a debtor class, the merchant class became more powerful.

The system of *sankin-kotai* also helped merchants to prosper and trade to increase, because merchants provided the goods and services that the daimyos needed on their twice-yearly trips to Edo. To smooth the daimyos' journey, the government built roads, which also made it easier for traders to take their goods to distant regions. Rest stations along the roads often grew into trading or administrative towns of considerable size.

At the same time, the demands for increased taxes led the daimyos to increase agricultural yields. As agriculture became more efficient, farming required fewer people. Unemployed farmworkers moved to prosperous towns and cities, seeking work as artisans. In urban centers such as Edo, Kyoto, and Osaka, social order began to break down and class distinctions became less rigid.

Social life in the cities converged on bathhouses, restaurants, and theaters. Japanese merchants and samurai could relax in the company of geishas, women who were professional entertainers. Geishas were trained in the arts of singing, dancing, and conversation. Urban amusement centers also provided employment for playwrights, artists, and poets. At this time a new form of theater known as Kabuki developed. Kabuki became popular for its portrayal of historical events and emotion-filled domestic scenes. Another form of drama that arose during this period was the elaborate Japanese puppet theater called Bunraku, in which three-man teams manipulated each puppet as a backstage chorus sang a story.

A popular form of art called ukiyo-e developed from the demand for prints of famous actors and their plays. At first, ukiyo-e prints were black-and-white, but soon ornate, brightly colored prints appeared in street stalls. Printed on delicate rice paper, they are highly prized collectors' items today.

A new form of poetry called haiku (HY•koo) also became popular among city people. In only 17 syllables, the haiku was to express a thought that would surprise the reader. **Matsuo Basho**, one of the great haiku masters, wrote this haiku:

> ❝In my new clothing
> I feel so different
> I must
> Look like someone else. ❞

As cities grew in size and population during the 1700s and 1800s, the ban on foreign contacts was gradually relaxed. Some Japanese began to study Western medicine in books that the Dutch brought to Nagasaki. Their interest in the so-called Dutch learning spread to Western science and technology. However, it would not be until the other Europeans arrived in the 1800s that Japan would begin to absorb other Western ideas.

SECTION 3 REVIEW

Recall
1. **Define** *sankin-kotai, metsuke,* geisha, haiku.
2. **Identify** Oda Nobunaga, Toyotomi Hideyoshi, Tokugawa Ieyasu, Francis Xavier, Matsuo Basho.
3. **Describe** how the *sankin-kotai* system affected the daimyos.

How did shoguns benefit from the system? How was the emperor affected?

Critical Thinking
4. **Synthesizing Information** Imagine that you lived in Japan during the Tokugawa shogunate. Which social class would you have wanted to

belong to? Explain.

Understanding Themes
5. **Reaction** Explain why Japan reacted to Western ideas by adopting a policy of isolation. How did this reaction to outside influences affect Japan's development over the next few centuries?

Using a Word Processor

There are several ways to create a professional looking printed document. You may use a word processor or a computer word processing software program. A word processor is a keyboard-operated terminal with a video display.

Learning the Skill

When you open most word processors, you are initially presented with a blank document. To create a new document, simply begin typing. Use the following tips to help you format the document to make it look the way you want:

1. Text fonts, or size and style of type, can be chosen. To choose font or size and style of type, click **Font** on your Standard toolbar.
2. Text can be made to appear **bold**, *italicized*, or underlined. To do this, first highlight the text (drag the cursor, or pointer, over the text with the left mouse button depressed). Then choose the modification mentioned above (the way you do this depends on the word processor you are using).
3. Press **Tab** to indent a paragraph. Press **Enter** to start a new paragraph.
4. To insert new text in a line, move the cursor to the point where you want the line to go and type. The word processing program moves the existing text to the right to make room for the new text.
5. When you finish typing, click the **Spell Check** button on the Standard toolbar to check the spelling of your document.

Practicing the Skill

This chapter focuses on the empires of Asia from 1350 through 1850. Create a newspaper article about an important event during one of these empires. Be sure to include a headline in your article. To use a word processor to create this document, complete the following steps.

1. Choose a font and the text size from the stan-

dard toolbar. Use a different text and size for your headline than you use for the rest of the text.
2. Type two or three paragraphs of copy about the event you chose for your article. As you type, make modifications to the text, such as bold, italics, or underlining.
3. Press **Tab** to indent a paragraph. Press **Enter** to start a new paragraph.
4. Insert new text in a line.
5. Use **Spell check** to check the spelling of your document.

Applying the Skill

Using a word processor, create an official-looking document that explains the Ottoman Laws described on pages 457–458 of this textbook.

For More Practice

Turn to the Skill Practice in the Chapter Review on page 479 for more practice in using a word processor.

1500		1700	1900

1511 Portuguese seize port of Melaka on the Malay Peninsula.

1565 Spaniards found a colony in the Philippines.

1767 Troops from Burma seize Ayutthaya.

1868 Chulalongkorn becomes king of Siam.

Section 4

Southeast Asia

Setting the Scene

▶ **Terms to Define**
   colony, *datus*, animism

▶ **People to Meet**
   Trailok, Phraya Chakkri, Mongkut, Chulalongkorn

▶ **Places to Locate**
   Manila, Java, Indochina, Bangkok

 **Find Out** How was the Thai kingdom able to keep its independence while other parts of Southeast Asia gradually came under European control?

The Storyteller

The century-old Bayon Temple of Angkor swarmed with workers. Huge stone faces with faint, haunting smiles gazed in all directions. A European merchant stepped closer to examine the temple and nearly collided with a monk. When asked about the faces, the monk replied, "This old Hindu shrine will become a Buddhist temple. Jayavarman, our king, has adopted the Buddhist religion and wishes to introduce its teaching throughout our land. Sculptors have been commissioned to create new images on the temple. Most important is the image of boddhisattva, a compassionate being who looks everywhere for souls to save."

—freely adapted from *World History*, Volume 1, William Duiker and Jackson Spielvogel, 1994

Relief from Bayon Temple of Angkor

By the mid-1400s, Southeast Asia was carrying on extensive trade with other regions. This was partly because of its location on the water route between India and China. In addition, Southeast Asia produced valuable spices and woods that people in other parts of the world wanted to buy.

European Influences

In the early 1500s the first European explorers reached Southeast Asia in search of new trade routes and products. With the coming of the Europeans, Southeast Asian kingdoms faced a growing challenge to their independence and traditional ways of life.

The Portuguese Spice Trade

Coming from India, the Portuguese were the first Europeans to reach Southeast Asia in the early 1500s. They set out to control the region's lucrative spice trade which, for many years, had been controlled by Muslim traders. In 1511 Portuguese soldiers captured the most important of the Muslim ports—Melaka, on the west side of the Malay Peninsula.

During the next 25 years, the Portuguese built a number of new trading posts in Southeast Asia. They patrolled the seas near the islands of present-day Indonesia to keep out the ships of other countries. The Portuguese also tried to spread Catholicism in maritime Southeast Asia. They had little success, however, because most Southeast Asian islanders resented Portuguese disregard for their traditional cultures.

Spanish Rule in the Philippines

The Spaniards were eager to find their own route to the spices of Southeast Asia. In 1519 Ferdinand Magellan, exploring for Spain, reached Southeast Asia by sailing westward around the

Visualizing History During the 1600s, the Netherlands reached its height as a seafaring power. Dutch merchant ships sailed the seas from the Caribbean region to the East Indies (Indonesia). *How did the Dutch win control of the Indonesian island of Java?*

southern tip of South America. Magellan and his crew landed in the Philippines, becoming the first Europeans to visit these islands.

In 1565 the Spanish founded a colony, or overseas territory ruled by a parent country, in the Philippines. Although the Spanish did not find spices in the Philippines, they did find fertile land and an excellent location for trade. Spanish soldiers and officials established a fortified settlement at **Manila** on the island of Luzon. Manila's magnificent harbor made the Philippines a valuable link in Spain's trade with Asia and the Americas.

The Spaniards gradually expanded their control to other parts of the islands. They persuaded many of the *datus*, or local rulers, to pledge loyalty to Spain in return for keeping their regional powers. Under Spanish rule, most of the people of the Philippines—largely of Malay and Chinese descent—accepted many Spanish customs as well as the Roman Catholic faith. Spanish Roman

Catholic clergy established missions, learned the local languages, taught the people European agricultural methods, and introduced new crops—such as maize (corn) and cocoa—from the Americas. Spain's control of the Philippines would last well into the late 1800s.

Dutch Traders in Indonesia

By the end of the 1500s, English and Dutch traders were also wanting a share in the Southeast Asian spice trade. After breaking Portuguese control of the trade, they began to fight each other. During the 1620s, the Dutch finally succeeded in forcing the English to leave the islands that now make up present-day Indonesia. A further step toward Dutch control of the islands came in 1677 when the ruler of Mataram, a kingdom on the island of **Java**, asked the Dutch to help him defeat a rebel uprising. In return for their assistance, the Dutch received important trading rights and

Javanese lands. Through similar agreements and by force, the Dutch had gained control of most of the other Indonesian islands by the late 1700s.

The French in Vietnam

The French were latecomers in the European pursuit of trade and colonies in Southeast Asia. Beginning in the 1600s, French traders based in India carried out only limited trade with the Vietnamese and other peoples in the Southeast Asian region of **Indochina**. Because of the weakness of this trade link, the Vietnamese and their Indochinese neighbors were able to keep the French from taking control of their area. Roman Catholic missionaries from France, however, converted many Vietnamese to Christianity.

By the early 1800s most of Indochina was ruled by local emperors who came from the region of Annam in present-day Vietnam. At this time, Indochina was predominantly Chinese in culture. Devoted to Confucian ideas, the Annamese emperors persecuted their Christian subjects and tried to keep Indochina closed to Europeans. Angered at the policies of the Annamese court, the French in 1858 returned to Southeast Asia in force. Their stated purpose was to protect local Christians from persecution. However, they also wanted Indochina's rubber, coal, and rice. In the 1860s the French began to colonize the region.

The Thai Kingdom

While European influence grew throughout Southeast Asia, the independent kingdom of Ayutthaya (ah•YU•tuh•yuh) continued to flourish in the area that is present-day Thailand. Under a series of powerful kings, the Thai people of Ayutthaya developed a rich culture based on Buddhism, Hinduism, and animism, the idea

Visualizing History This bronze bas-relief of the Buddha reveals the important role that Buddhism has played in unifying the Thai people and in supporting their rulers. *What other religious influences shaped the development of Thai culture?*

that both living and nonliving things have spirits or souls.

Trailok's Rule

One of the most powerful Ayutthaya monarchs was King **Trailok**, who ruled from 1448 to 1488. Trailok set up a strong central government with separate civil and military branches directly responsible to him. He also brought local leaders to Ayutthaya and put them in charge of new governmental offices. These officials were required to live in the capital where the king could easily oversee their work.

Trailok set up a rigid class system based on loyalty to the Thai monarchy. All male Thai were given the use of varying amounts of land according to their rank. Nobles and merchants were given as much as 4,000 acres (1,620 ha), while enslaved people, artisans, and other subjects with little status received 10 acres (4 ha) or less. Women were not included in this distribution of land.

Expansion

While the Ayutthaya kingdom set its internal affairs in order, Thai soldiers fought battles with neighboring peoples, such as the Khmer, Burmans, and Malays. Through conquests, the Ayutthaya kingdom grew to almost the size of present-day Thailand. In 1431 Thai soldiers from Ayutthaya captured Angkor Wat and destroyed it. They also overcame the Malays in the south as well as smaller Thai kingdoms in the north.

During the mid-1500s a border dispute led to war between the Ayutthaya kingdom and Burma (Myanmar). Soldiers from Burma briefly captured the city of Ayutthaya in 1569, but the Thai king Naresuan defeated Burma's ruler in the Battle of Nong Sarai in 1593.

European Contacts

The 1500s also saw the beginning of European contacts with Ayutthaya. The Portuguese and later the Dutch and the English sent delegations to the kingdom to encourage trade. For much of the 1600s, Thai rulers allowed Europeans the right to carry out trade in their territory. In 1612

British traders took a letter from King James I to the Thai monarch. They reported back that the city of Ayutthaya, with its palaces and Buddhist temples, was as large and awesome as London.

The Thai, however, became concerned that Europeans wanted to colonize as well as trade. In 1688 a Thai group that opposed European influences took over the kingdom. The new rulers expelled most of the Europeans except for a few Dutch and Portuguese traders. The kingdom closed its ports to the West until 1826.

The Bangkok Era

Free of European influence, Thai rulers hoped for a period of calm. Burma, however, wanted to resume the conflict with Ayutthaya that it had lost in the late 1500s. In 1767 an army from Burma defeated the Thai and sacked and burned the city of Ayutthaya. The Thai, however, soon rallied after the disaster. Phraya Taksin (PRY•uh tahk•SEEN), a Thai general, led his troops against Burma's army and drove it out of the region.

After proclaiming himself king, Taksin forced rival Thai groups to accept his rule. He reigned until 1782, when rebel leaders overthrew him. The rebels called on General **Phraya Chakkri** (PRY•uh SHAH•kree) to be the new Thai monarch. Chakkri founded the royal dynasty that still rules Thailand today. Chakkri built a new capital called **Bangkok** on the Chao Phraya River. Under Chakkri's rule, the reborn Thai kingdom became known as Siam.

Reforming Monarchs

By the mid-1800s Europeans were pressuring Thai rulers to widen trade opportunities in Siam. King **Mongkut** recognized the threat that Western colonial nations posed to the independence of his kingdom. He moved quickly to protect Siam by setting foreign nations against one another through competition.

Mongkut achieved this goal by allowing many Western nations to have commercial opportunities

Visualizing History King Mongkut ruled Siam from 1851 to 1868. He increased the powers of the monarchy while supporting social reforms to improve the conditions of his subjects. *How did Mongkut work to preserve Siam's independence?*

in the kingdom. The Thai king welcomed what he judged to be the positive influences of Western commerce on his country. He encouraged his people to study science and European languages with the Christian missionaries who had accompanied European traders to the kingdom.

After Mongkut's death in 1868, his son **Chulalongkorn** (choo•lah•LAHNG•kohrn) came to the throne. Like Mongkut, Chulalongkorn worked to modernize Siam while protecting the kingdom from European controls. He ended slavery, founded schools, encouraged his people to study abroad, and built railways and roads.

SECTION 4 REVIEW

Recall
1. **Define** colony, *datus*, animism.
2. **Identify** Melaka, Manila, Trailok, Phraya Chakkri, Bangkok, Mongkut, Chulalongkorn.
3. **Locate** Southeast Asia on the map on page 354, and explain why it attracted European explorers, traders, and missionaries during the 1500s and 1600s.

Critical Thinking
4. **Making Comparisons** How do you think the Spanish conquest of the Philippine Islands differed from the Portuguese conquest of the Indonesian islands?

Understanding Themes
5. **Change** How did the Thai kings Mongkut and Chulalongkorn respond to the growth of Western influence in their region?

Connections Across Time

Historical Significance From 1350 to 1850 many social and political changes came to Asia. Islam continued to expand and reached South Asia as a result of the Mogul invasions. Despite efforts at toleration, conflicts developed between Muslims and Hindus that still divide South Asia today.

During the early modern period, China turned inward instead of meeting the challenge of the West. Japan and Siam at first took the same route; however, they eventually introduced reforms that preserved their freedom. In Japan's case, reforms also enabled it to compete successfully with Western countries.

Using Key Terms

Write the key term that completes each sentence. Then write a sentence for each term not chosen.

a. geisha
b. grand vizier
c. haiku
d. janissaries
e. *sankin-kotai*
f. colony
g. labor-intensive farming
h. sultan
i. queue
j. *datus*
k. *millets*

1. The Ottoman leader Suleiman I acted as both the _____, or political ruler, and the caliph, or religious leader.
2. During the Manchu dynasty, the Chinese practiced _____ in which workers dug flat terraces into hillsides to grow rice.
3. Ottoman sultans maintained a special corps of soldiers known as _____ who were noted as a fierce and loyal fighting force.
4. Japanese writers developed _____, a form of poetry made up of 17 syllables, that became popular among city people.
5. Ottoman law allowed religious groups to run affairs in their own _____, or communities.

Technology Activity

Using a Computerized Card Catalog Use a computerized card catalog to locate sources about traditional Japanese customs that are practiced in Japan today. Write an essay discussing how political power, leadership, and loyalty in traditional Japan compare to how these characteristics are viewed in modern democracies. Share your opinions with the rest of the class.

Using Your History Journal

From your notes and outline write a three-page paper on one of the four sites listed on page 455. Discuss what that place reveals about the civilization that built it.

Reviewing Facts

1. **History** Name the three great Muslim empires in eastern Europe, central Asia, and India.
2. **Culture** Define the relationship between Sunni Muslims and Shiite Muslims living in the Ottoman Empire and the Persian Empire.
3. **Culture** Explain how the Moguls' religion brought them into conflict with the majority of India's people. Describe how Mogul rulers reacted.
4. **History** Explain the purpose of the voyages of Zheng He.
5. **History** List the steps taken by the Manchus to maintain their control over China.
6. **Culture** Describe the role of geishas in Japan.
7. **Culture** Discuss the effects of the shogunate's policies on Japan's Christian population.

Critical Thinking

1. **Apply** How did religious differences cause strife between Muslim empires?
2. **Evaluate** Would you consider Suleiman I a successful ruler? Why was he called "The Lawgiver" by the Ottomans?
3. **Analyze** How did Akbar's religious tolerance in India differ from that of the Manchus in China?

4. **Evaluate** Which government described in this chapter was most successful in meeting its people's needs? Why?

5. **Evaluate** How did the movement of Islamic peoples affect northern India? What impact did Islam have on religion in this part of India?

6. **Analyze** What factors led to China's growth in both land and population during the Qing dynasty? How did government policies contribute to this growth?

7. **Evaluate** Was the Ming dynasty's policy of isolationism beneficial to China? Explain.

8. **Analyze** How did new urban centers in Japan influence growth in the arts and entertainment?

Geography in History

1. **Region** Refer to the map below that shows the political divisions of Japan about 1560. For more than a century, feudal lords fought for control of territory. How many daimyo clans ruled in Japan during this period?

2. **Location** What is the relative location of the Takeda domains?

3. **Human/Environment Interaction** What geographic conditions helped make it possible for Japan to enforce a policy of isolation from the rest of the world in the 1600s?

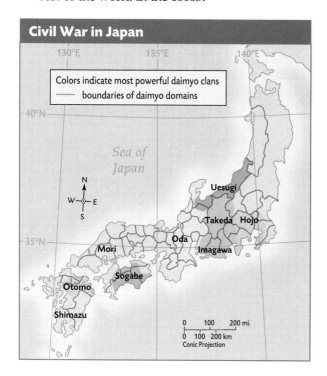

Civil War in Japan

Colors indicate most powerful daimyo clans
—— boundaries of daimyo domains

Sea of Japan

Uesugi
Takeda Hojo
Oda
Mori   Imagawa
Sogabe
Otomo
Shimazu

0   100   200 mi.
0 100 200 km
Conic Projection

Understanding Themes

1. **Movement** What areas of Asia came under the rule of the Muslim empires?

2. **Cultural Diffusion** How did Christianity spread to China? To Japan?

3. **Reaction** What good and bad effects resulted from Japan's policy of isolation?

4. **Change** What development was crucial in advancing Dutch control of the islands of Indonesia?

Linking Past and Present

1. Do you think it is possible for today's nations to follow a policy of isolation like Japan's in the early modern period? Have any tried to?

2. From the 1300s to the 1800s powerful Asian rulers took drastic measures to implement changes that they supported. Is a powerful ruler or a strong central government necessary today for technological advancement and economic prosperity? Give reasons to support your position.

Skill Practice

Using a word processor or a computer word processing software program, create a one-page professional-looking document using the subject of Japan's isolationist policy—The Act of Seclusion of 1636. For example, you might wish to create a letter written by the Tokugawa rulers to European rulers or create a handbill that was given out to European traders to warn them about the isolation policy. Be sure to complete the following steps while creating your document:

1. use more than one font and text size
2. use bold, italics, and underlining
3. include paragraph indents
4. run spell check
5. try other word processing techniques that help create a professional-looking document

19 1500–1750
Royal Power and Conflict

Chapter Themes

▶ **Conflict** Spanish and English monarchs engage in a dynastic struggle. *Section 1*

▶ **Change** Tudor monarchs bring stability and prosperity to England. *Section 2*

▶ **Uniformity** France's Louis XIV strengthens absolute monarchy in France and limits rights of religious dissenters. *Section 3*

▶ **Conflict** Dynastic and religious conflicts divide the German states. *Section 4*

▶ **Innovation** Peter the Great attempts to modernize Russian society. *Section 5*

The Storyteller

"We hunted all morning, got back around 3 o'clock in the afternoon, changed, went up to gamble until 7 o'clock, then to the play, which never ended before 10:30, then on to the ball until 3 o'clock in the morning.... So you see how much time I had for writing."

Princess Elizabeth-Charlotte, sister-in-law of France's King Louis XIV, described court life at the Palace of Versailles in a letter to a friend as an endless round of social activities. A man of tremendous energy and drive, Louis routinely devoted eight or nine hours daily to matters of state, regularly rode and hunted, ate with great enthusiasm, and expected courtiers, or members of his court, to do the same as well.

Historical Significance

How did monarchs build strong nation-states in early modern Europe? How did their efforts in national expansion contribute to Europe's legacy of territorial disputes and wars?

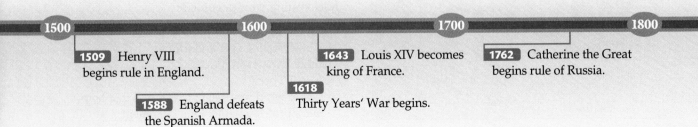

1500	1600	1700	1800

1509 Henry VIII begins rule in England.

1588 England defeats the Spanish Armada.

1618 Thirty Years' War begins.

1643 Louis XIV becomes king of France.

1762 Catherine the Great begins rule of Russia.

The vast palace and grounds of Versailles lie outside of Paris, France. Versailles was home to France's monarchs and the royal court during the late 1600s and most of the 1700s.

Your History Journal

Choose a country from this chapter. As you read the section, create a time line of important events between 1500 and 1750. Include the reigning monarchs, expansions of territory, laws, and conflicts.

1556 Philip II becomes king of Spain.

1588 The English defeat the Spanish Armada.

c. 1590s Aragon revolts against Castilian control.

1647 Plague kills thousands of Spaniards.

Section 1

Spain

Setting the Scene

▶ **Terms to Define**
absolutism, divine right, armada, inflation

▶ **People to Meet**
Philip II, the Marranos, the Moriscos, Charles II

▶ **Places to Locate**
Madrid

 Why did Philip II and other Spanish monarchs have difficulty ruling the Spanish Empire?

The Storyteller

The Duke of Alva's son, ten-year-old Alejandro, was ecstatic. He had been appointed as a page to King Philip—an excellent beginning to a career with the Spanish court. Alejandro would learn to fence and to perform feats of horseman-

Philip II

ship, as well as the rudiments of reading and writing. In five or six years, when he completed his education, Alejandro would become a member of His Majesty's court and would be expected to serve at arms. That position was the fulfillment of most young men's desires. If he proved himself truly outstanding, he might become one of Philip's personal attendants, a position usually reserved for the sons of princes.

—from Charles V and Philip His Son, Marino Cavalli, reprinted in The Portable Renaissance Reader, Mary Martin McLaughlin, 1977

In the 1500s and 1600s, European monarchs sought to create powerful kingdoms in which they could command the complete loyalty of all their subjects. This form of government, known as absolutism, placed absolute, or unlimited, power in the monarch and his or her advisers. The strength of absolutism rested on divine right—the political idea that monarchs receive their power directly from God and are responsible to God alone for their actions. An absolute monarchy, it was reasoned, would unify diverse peoples and bring greater efficiency and control.

During the age of absolutism, the Hapsburgs remained Europe's most powerful royal family. But their lands were too scattered for any one person to rule effectively. To remedy this problem, Charles V retired in 1556 and divided the empire, leaving the Hapsburg lands in central Europe to his brother, Ferdinand, who became Holy Roman emperor. He gave Spain, the Netherlands, southern Italy, and Spain's overseas empire to his son, **Philip II**.

Philip II

Philip II, who ruled from 1556 to 1598, was the most powerful monarch in Spanish history. A devout Catholic, Philip saw himself as the leading defender of the faith. His efforts to end Protestantism in his domains made him the enemy of all Protestants. Son of the Holy Roman Emperor Charles V and Isabella of Portugal, Philip worked to increase the Hapsburg family's power throughout Europe. This effort led Philip to involve Spain in a number of costly European wars.

Known as the Prudent King, Philip II was cautious, hardworking, and suspicious of others. He built a granite palace called El Escorial, which served as royal court, art gallery, monastery, and tomb for Spanish royalty. There Philip spent most of his time at his desk, carefully reading and responding to hundreds of documents from all over the empire. Bureaucrats advised him and handled routine matters, but he made all decisions and signed all papers that he received.

Unrest

Philip II faced many difficulties in ruling Spain. The Spanish kingdoms had united when Ferdinand of Aragon married Isabella of Castile in 1469. A uniform system of government for the entire country, however, had not been set up. Separate laws and local authorities remained in place, but the ways of Castile eventually came to dominate Spanish life. In the 1500s Castile had more territory, people, and wealth than any other part of Spain.

Philip II made Castile the center of Spain and the empire. **Madrid**, located in Castile, became the capital. The Castilian, or literary, form of Spanish was spoken at the royal court. Most of Philip's advisers came from Castile. Trade from the overseas empire was controlled by the Castilian city of Seville, and Castilian merchants benefited most from trade. Leaders in Aragon and other Spanish provinces resented the dominance of Castile, and in the 1590s Aragon revolted. The revolt was put down, but discontent continued into the 1600s.

Religious Policy

Philip had to deal with a number of troubling religious issues in his European domains. He was concerned about the loyalty of large religious minorities in Spain. These minorities included Protestants, **the Marranos** (Jews who had converted to Christianity), and **the Moriscos** (Muslims who had become Christians). Philip supported the Inquisition's efforts to uproot the heresies believed to exist among these groups. He personally attended several *autos da fé,* the elaborate public rituals of sentencing usually followed by executions. The Inquisition was so thorough that Protestantism never took hold in Spain. Its actions, however, led to a revolt by the Moriscos in 1569. The revolt was brutally crushed, and finally in 1609 the Moriscos were expelled from the country.

In 1567, when Philip had sought to impose Catholicism on the Netherlands, Dutch Protestants rebelled against his rule. This conflict proved to be long, bloody, and complex. The Dutch declared their independence in 1581, but the fighting continued. England gave support to the Dutch and to the English "sea dogs" who raided Spanish ships in their ports. Meanwhile, Philip extended his crusading zeal into the eastern Mediterranean, where in 1571 he defeated the Ottoman Turks in a naval battle at Lepanto off the coast of Greece.

Visualizing History The Spanish Armada entered the English Channel in late July, 1588. *What advantages did the English fleet have over the Spanish Armada?*

Spanish Armada

Catholic Spain faced a growing challenge from Protestant England. Philip at first had supported Elizabeth I as England's queen against the pope's wishes. When Elizabeth aided the Dutch, Philip decided to act against her.

In 1586 Philip laid plans to invade England. In May 1588 a force of 130 ships and 33,000 men, known as the Spanish Armada, sailed for the English coast. (An armada is a fleet of warships organized to carry out a mission.) Two months later, the Armada entered the English Channel in crescent formation. The English had faster, more maneuverable ships and longer-range cannons than did the Spaniards. Yet they were unable at first to block the Spanish formation. English fire ships, however, were able to separate the Spanish vessels. Running out of shot and short of water, the Spanish fleet retreated to the stormy North Sea. After circling the northern tip of Great Britain, a number of Spanish ships later sank near the rocky coasts of Scotland and Ireland.

The defeat of the Armada not only ended Philip's plan to invade England, it also marked the beginning of Spain's decline as a sea power. During the next two centuries, the Dutch Netherlands, England, and France would gradually reduce Spanish might in Europe and around the world.

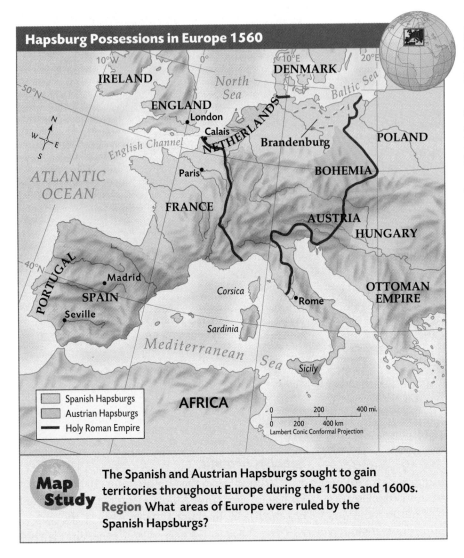

Map Study

The Spanish and Austrian Hapsburgs sought to gain territories throughout Europe during the 1500s and 1600s. **Region** What areas of Europe were ruled by the Spanish Hapsburgs?

presented a new kind of hero who did not conform to commonly accepted beliefs and practices.

Cervantes's novel also symbolized the steady decline of Spain as a European power. Despite Spain's resource-rich overseas empire, costly wars drained the national treasury, forcing the government to borrow money from foreign bankers. This, along with the flow of gold and silver from the Americas, led to inflation, an abnormal increase in currency resulting in sharp price rises. In addition, Spain's industry and agriculture declined. The government excessively taxed and weakened the industrious middle class. It also expelled the Muslims and Jews, many of whom were skilled artisans and merchants.

Philip II's successors lacked his political skills and turned the government over to corrupt and incompetent nobles.

Last of the Spanish Hapsburgs

The period from 1550 to 1650 is called Spain's cultural *siglo de oro*, or "golden century." Midway through this era, the Spanish author Miguel de Cervantes (suhr•VAN•teez) wrote *Don Quixote*, a novel about a landowner who imagines himself a knight called to perform heroic deeds. In making fun of medieval romances of chivalry, *Don Quixote*

Spain became involved in a series of European wars, and overtaxed citizens in various parts of the empire rebelled. **Charles II**, who became king in 1665, was the last of the Spanish Hapsburgs. No one expected him to rule long, since he was physically and mentally weak. Although Charles later married, he did not have any children. With no heirs to the throne of Spain, European monarchs plotted to control the succession to the Spanish throne.

SECTION 1 REVIEW

Recall
1. **Define** absolutism, divine right, armada, inflation.
2. **Identify** Philip II, El Escorial, the Marranos, the Moriscos, Spanish Armada, Charles II.
3. **Use** the map of the Hapsburg

domains above to locate Spain, Portugal, and the Netherlands. Why was the Netherlands opposed to Hapsburg rule?

Critical Thinking
4. **Analyzing Information** Why did Philip II send the Spanish

Armada against England? What was the outcome of this effort?

Understanding Themes
5. **Conflict** What were the reasons for internal unrest in the Spanish Empire under Philip II's rule? How did Philip respond?

1500　　　　　　　　　　1550　　　　　　　　　　1600

1547 Henry VIII dies.　**1558** Elizabeth I becomes queen of England.　**1597** Poor Law makes local areas responsible for care of the unemployed.

Section 2

England

Setting the Scene

▶ **Terms to Define**
 gentry, yeomen, balance of power

▶ **People to Meet**
 Henry VII, Henry VIII, Elizabeth I, William Shakespeare

▶ **Places to Locate**
 Scotland, Ireland

Find Out ▶ How did Tudor monarchs influence English and European affairs?

The Storyteller

On this day, Elizabeth would be crowned Queen of England. London was arrayed with pavilions and bright banners, and the city's fountains offered wine, not the usual brackish water. Alison Crisp eagerly awaited the royal procession to Westminster Abbey. Although only six years of age, she would present a costly gift to Elizabeth from the Orphans Home board of directors. When the procession neared, the queen commanded her coachmen to stop. Alison flawlessly presented the gift. As the queen prepared to move on, Alison surprised her with another gift, a bouquet of flowers she had picked. With Elizabeth's acceptance of the child's humble offering, the rapport between the queen and her people strengthened.

—from *Description of Elizabeth I's Coronation Procession in 1559*, John Hayward, in *The Past Speaks*, L.B. Smith and J.R. Smith, 1993

Elizabeth I

ngland, like Spain, developed a strong monarchy. Its Tudor dynasty, which ruled from 1485 to 1603, brought unity to the country after a long period of decline and disorder. Tudor monarchs were hardworking, able, and popular. They greatly expanded the power and authority of the Crown. They were not, however, as absolute in their rule as other European monarchs. Instead, institutions such as Parliament and the courts of law set bounds to the authority that Tudor monarchs could exercise.

Early Tudors

Henry VII, the first Tudor monarch, became king in 1485 after the Wars of the Roses. He used shrewd maneuvering to disarm his rivals and to increase the prestige of his family. Most of Henry's close advisers came from the gentry and merchant classes. Titles were given to these officials, who formed a new aristocracy dependent on the king.

Henry VII helped rebuild England's commercial prosperity. He encouraged the expansion of foreign trade, especially the export of finished woolens to the Netherlands, Germany, and Venice. He promoted the improved collection of taxes as well as careful government spending. In foreign policy Henry avoided war, using diplomacy and the arrangement of suitable royal marriages to strengthen England's interests abroad.

Henry VIII

The second Tudor to rule was **Henry VIII**, son of Henry VII and the most powerful of all Tudor monarchs. Unlike his father, Henry VIII fought wars on the European continent and began to make England a great naval power. His personal life, however, would have a lasting effect on English history. In his pursuit of a male heir, Henry married six times. He worked with Parliament to obtain his personal goals and to break with the Catholic

Church. As a result of this cooperation, the House of Commons increased its power during Henry VIII's reign. Henry, however, furthered support for his policies by seizing monastery lands and selling them to wealthy landowners.

Edward VI and Mary I

After Henry VIII's death in 1547, England entered a brief period of turmoil. Edward VI, Henry's son and successor, was only 9 years old when he became king. He died in 1553 after a short reign. Protestant nobles then plotted to prevent Edward's Catholic half sister, Mary, from becoming queen. The English people, however, supported Mary's claim to the Tudor throne.

Mary's Catholic policies soon offended the English. Despite strong opposition, Mary married Philip II of Spain in 1554. The next year, she restored Catholicism and had about 300 Protestants burned at the stake for heresy. At Philip's urging, Mary involved England in a war with France. As a result, England lost the port of Calais, its final foothold on the European continent. Many English people feared that England would be controlled by Spain. Before this fear could be realized, Mary died childless, and the throne then passed to her Protestant half sister, Elizabeth.

Elizabeth I

Elizabeth I became queen in 1558, when she was 25 years old. She was shrewd, highly educated, and had a forceful personality. With a sharp tongue she asserted her iron will, causing sparks to fly in exchanges with Parliament. Elizabeth, however, used her authority for the common good of her people. On frequent journeys throughout the kingdom Elizabeth earned the loyalty and confidence of her subjects. During her travels, Elizabeth stayed at the homes of nobles who entertained her with banquets, parades, and dances.

Elizabeth's reign was one of England's great cultural periods. Poets and writers praised

Images of the Times

Tudor England

Under Tudor monarchs, England enjoyed a period of stability and relative prosperity.

Mary I married Philip II of Spain in 1554, against the wishes of her Protestant subjects. This coat of arms represents the marital union of the two monarchs.

Elizabeth in their works. The theater flourished under playwrights such as **William Shakespeare**. During Elizabeth's reign, English was transformed into a language of beauty, grace, vigor, and clarity.

Marriage

People fully expected that Elizabeth would marry and that her husband would rule. The common attitude of the time was that only men were fit to rule and that government matters were beyond a woman's ability. Elizabeth, however, was slow in seeking a husband. She had learned from the lesson of her sister Mary: to marry a foreign prince would endanger England. At the same time, marrying an Englishman would cause jealousies among the English nobility. In the end, Elizabeth refused to give up her powers as monarch for the sake of marriage. To one of her suitors she stormed, "God's death! My lord, I will have but one mistress [England] and no master." Elizabeth's refusal to marry caused a great deal of speculation as to who would succeed her.

Court and Government

In matters of government, Elizabeth was assisted by a council of nobles. With her approval they drafted proclamations, handled foreign relations, and supervised such matters as the administration of justice and the regulation of prices and wages. These advisers were assisted by small staffs of professional but poorly paid bureaucrats.

Although Parliament did not have the power to initiate legislation, it could plead, urge, advise, and withhold approval. These powers gave Parliament some influence, especially when it was asked to consider tax laws.

The task of enforcing the queen's law was performed by unpaid respected community members known as justices of the peace. Most justices belonged to the rural landowning classes. They knew both the law and local conditions. They maintained peace, collected taxes, and kept the government informed of local problems. Their voluntary participation in support of the government was a key to its success.

The Court of Elizabeth I was known for its love of fashions and style. Noble men and women who served the queen wore elegant clothes and enjoyed music and the arts.

The Globe Theater in London was the site where many of William Shakespeare's plays—tragedies, comedies, and histories—were performed.

REFLECTING ON THE TIMES

1. Why is Elizabeth's reign considered one of England's great cultural eras?
2. Why was Mary I an unpopular ruler?

Social and Economic Policy

Elizabeth believed in the importance of social rank. During the late 1500s, English society was led by the queen and her court. Next were prominent nobles from the great landed families and a middle group of gentry, or lesser nobles, merchants, lawyers, and clergy. This group provided the source of Tudor strength and stability. The lowest social rank was comprised of yeomen, or farmers with small landholdings, and laborers.

Government laws and policies closely regulated the lives of the common people. The Statute of Apprentices of 1563 declared work to be a social and moral duty. It required people to live and work where they were born, controlled the movement of labor, fixed wages, and regulated apprenticeships. The Poor Laws of 1597 and 1601 made local areas responsible for their own homeless and unemployed. These laws included means to raise money for charity and to provide work for vagabonds.

Elizabeth inherited a monarchy that was badly in debt. Royal revenues, which came from rents of royal land, fines in court cases, and duties on imports, barely covered annual expenses. The queen, however, spent lavishly on court ceremonies to show the power and dignity of the monarchy. In other matters, she showed the greatest financial restraint, leading many to call her a "pinchpenny."

To raise funds without relying on Parliament, Elizabeth sold off royal lands, offices, licenses, monopolies, and the right to collect customs. These measures helped but could not solve the problem. England faced the costs of war and mounting inflation. Elizabeth was therefore forced to turn to Parliament for funds. When she ended her reign, England remained badly in debt.

Foreign Policy

By Elizabeth's time, England had lost all of its possessions on the European continent. France was too powerful for England to defeat in order to regain territories. Although England could not completely withdraw from continental affairs, it developed a foreign policy suitable for a small island nation with limited resources.

For security, the English relied on the English Channel to protect their island from European invaders. Building and maintaining a strong navy was therefore important in defending the nation. For that reason, Elizabeth continued the efforts begun by her Tudor predecessors to build such a navy.

History & Art *Elizabeth I* by George Glower, 1596. National Portrait Gallery, London, England **A woman of keen intellect, Elizabeth I was gifted in music, languages, and the arts. In addition, she was an excellent public speaker.** *What foreign policy strategy did England develop under Elizabeth I's reign?*

Spain and France posed the greatest naval threats to England. The attack of the Spanish Armada made England realize the dangers of an alliance between Spain and France. England might be able to defeat one power, but certainly not both. As a result, the English relied on diplomacy as well as sea power to protect their interests.

During Elizabeth's reign, England worked to balance the power of European nations. In international affairs, balance of power refers to the system in which each nation helps to keep peace and order by maintaining power that is equal to, or in balance with, rival nations. One nation cannot overpower another. If one nation becomes more powerful than the other, a third nation can reestablish the balance by supporting the second nation.

Under Elizabeth's rule, England operated as the third balancing nation. In the early part of Elizabeth's reign, England and Spain feared the power of the French. England cooperated with Spain in order to keep France out of the Netherlands. Later, when the Netherlands revolted against Philip II, the English supported the rebels and allied with the weaker power against the stronger one.

Scotland was largely Catholic and hostile toward England during the 1550s. Although part of **Ireland** was under English rule, the rest of the country resisted English armies. To protect English interests, Elizabeth sought to solidify her ties with Scotland and Ireland so they could not be used as bases for Spanish and French attacks on England.

In the 1560s, with Elizabeth's help, Scotland became Protestant and an ally of England. Mary Stuart, later known as Mary, Queen of Scots, was Elizabeth's cousin. She was forced to abdicate her position as queen of Scotland in 1567. She later fled to England, where her presence caused controversy. Mary was a Catholic and heir to the English throne. Many English Protestants feared she would try to replace Elizabeth. In 1586 Mary was accused of plotting with English and foreign Catholics against Elizabeth. Public fears of a Catholic monarchy were strong. In 1587 Elizabeth finally agreed to Mary's

Visualizing History Sir Francis Drake was one of England's most famous explorers and military leaders. After sailing around the world, Drake was knighted in 1581 by Queen Elizabeth I. His naval warfare later helped make England a major sea power. *What European nation was England's primary enemy during the time of Elizabeth I and Francis Drake?*

execution, although she was hesitant to sentence to death another monarch.

In the 1590s, England carried out military campaigns in Ireland to conquer the Irish. With Scotland and Ireland allied with England, a period of temporary peace came to the British Isles.

Elizabeth died in 1603 at the age of 69. With her death came the end of the Tudor dynasty. King James VI of Scotland, the Protestant son of Mary, Queen of Scots, became the new monarch of England. As James I, he founded the Stuart dynasty and united Scotland and England under a common ruler.

SECTION 2 REVIEW

Recall
1. **Define** gentry, yeomen, balance of power.
2. **Identify** Henry VII, Henry VIII, Edward VI, Mary I, Elizabeth I, William Shakespeare, Poor Laws, James I.
3. **Explain** England's foreign policy under Elizabeth I.

Critical Thinking
4. **Evaluating Information** Contrast the effect on English history of Henry's many marriages with the effect of Elizabeth I's refusal to marry.

Understanding Themes
5. **Change** How did the rule of the Tudor monarchs, especially the rule of Elizabeth I, affect the development of England?

Section 3

France

Setting the Scene

▶ **Terms to Define**
  intendant

▶ **People to Meet**
  Henry IV, Cardinal Richelieu, Louis XIV

▶ **Places to Locate**
  Versailles

Find Out ▶ What kind of monarchy developed in France under the Bourbon monarchs?

The Storyteller

A flourish of trumpets sounded. The crowd of courtiers bowed as King Louis entered the Grand Salon at Versailles, accompanied by his attendants. The Duke of Saint-Simon, one of many noblemen whose power Louis was systematically eclipsing, was nonetheless required to be present. He observed that the king "liked splendor, magnificence, and profusion in everything: you pleased him if you shone through the brilliancy of your houses, clothes, tables, equipages." Because everyone tried to emulate the king, a taste for extravagance and luxury was spreading through all classes of society.

—adapted from *The Memoires of the Duke of Saint-Simon*, reprinted in *Aspects of Western Civilization, Volume II*, Perry M. Rogers, 1988

Louis XIV's lavish court life

After a period of religious conflict, peace was restored to most of France when Henry of Navarre became King **Henry IV** in 1589. He founded the Bourbon dynasty, which ruled France with some interruptions until the early 1800s. During most of that time, Bourbon kings maintained an absolute monarchy that was imitated by monarchs throughout Europe.

Henry IV

Henry IV was a Protestant, but he converted to Catholicism to quiet his Catholic opponents. Believing that people's religious beliefs need not interfere with their loyalty to the government, Henry issued the Edict of Nantes in 1598 to reassure the Huguenots, the name given to France's Protestants. The edict allowed Protestant worship to continue in areas where the Protestants were a majority, but barred Protestant worship in Paris and other Catholic strongholds. The edict granted Huguenots the same civil rights as Catholics.

These actions ended religious strife and enabled France to rebuild itself. With the help of his minister of finance, Henry restored the Crown's treasury, repaired roads and bridges, and supported trade and industry. He also tried to restore discipline in the army and bring order to the government bureaucracy. All of these royal policies were put into effect without the approval of the Estates-General and thus laid the foundation for the absolute rule of later Bourbon monarchs.

Cardinal Richelieu

When Henry IV was assassinated in 1610, his 9-year-old son, Louis XIII, became king. Louis's mother, Marie de Medici, was regent for the next 7 years. In 1617 Louis gained the throne by force and exiled his mother from court. A few years later, he gave power to one of her advisers, **Cardinal Richelieu**.

Gradually Louis gave complete control of the government to the cardinal, who set out to build an absolute monarchy in France. To realize this goal, Richelieu had to reduce the power of the nobles and the Huguenots.

When Louis XIII came to the throne, the nobility was in control of the provinces. Nobles collected taxes, administered justice, appointed local officials, and even made alliances with foreign governments. To end the nobles' power, Richelieu destroyed their fortified castles and stripped them of their local administrative functions. The nobility retained social prestige, while authority in local government affairs was given to special agents of the Crown known as intendants. Non-nobles, Richelieu believed, would not assert themselves and challenge the king's authority.

Richelieu also sought to take away the military and territorial rights given to the Huguenots by the Edict of Nantes. The Huguenots were seen as a threat to the French state. In 1625 radical Huguenots revolted against Louis XIII. After the defeat of Protestant forces at the seaport of La Rochelle in 1628, Richelieu took away the Huguenots' right to independent fortified towns. The Huguenots were, however, allowed to keep their religious freedom.

Having weakened the monarchy's internal enemies, Richelieu sought to make France the supreme power in Europe. He strengthened the French army and took steps to build up the economy. In order to strengthen national unity, he supported French culture. Under Richelieu's direction, France's leading writers in 1635 organized the French Academy. The Academy received a royal charter to establish "fixed rules for the language … and render the French language not only elegant but also capable of treating all arts and sciences." In the following century, French became the preferred language of European diplomacy and culture.

Louis XIV

Louis XIV is recognized as the most powerful Bourbon monarch. He became king in 1643 at the age of 5. At first, France was ruled by his two regents—his mother, Anne of Austria, and Cardinal Mazarin, Richelieu's successor. When Mazarin died in 1661, Louis announced that he would run his own government. He was then 23 years old.

The 72-year reign of Louis XIV was the longest in European history. It set the style for European

Visualizing History Cardinal Richelieu strengthened France's economy by promoting the manufacture of luxury goods. He also gave charters to commercial companies for overseas trade. *How did Richelieu encourage the growth of French culture?*

monarchies during the 1600s and 1700s. During his own lifetime, Louis was known as the Sun King, around whom the royalty and nobility of Europe revolved. He set up a lavish court and surrounded himself with pomp and pageantry. Louis's monarchy had power as well as style. Although Louis relied on a bureaucracy, he was the source of all political authority in France. In one of his audiences, he is said to have boasted, *"L'état, c'est moi!"* ("I am the state!").

Absolute Rule

Louis emphasized a strong monarchy because of his fear of disorder without it. As a child, he had lived through the Fronde, a series of uprisings by nobles and peasants that occurred between 1648 and 1653. During the Fronde, royal troops lost control of Paris and mobs rioted in the streets. The young Louis and his regents were called to give an account of their actions before the *Parlement*, or supreme court of law, in Paris. The Fronde was crushed, but Louis never forgot this attempt to limit royal power. As king, he intended never to let it happen again.

Louis XIV's feelings about absolute monarchy were later supported by Jacques Bossuet (ZHAHK baw•SWAY), the leading church official of France during the 1600s. Bossuet's defense of the divine origins of monarchy became one of the most famous justifications of absolute rule. He wrote:

> ❝ What grandeur that a single man should embody so much! … Behold this holy power, paternal and absolute, contained in a single head: you see the image of God in the king, and you have the idea of royal majesty. ❞

According to Bossuet, subjects had no right to revolt even if the king was unjust. Kings need account to no one except God, but they should act with humility and restraint because "God's judgment is heaviest for those who command."

Court Life

After the Fronde, Louis made plans to live outside of Paris. He moved his court and government to a new palace that he built at **Versailles**. The Palace of Versailles was a large, splendid structure. No expense was spared, for Versailles was to demonstrate the wealth, power, and glory of France.

The palace had elegant royal apartments, sweeping staircases, mirrored halls, priceless tapestries, and lavish formal salons and dining rooms. There were offices for government bureaucrats as well as tiny, cramped rooms where officials lived. As many as 10,000 people lived at Versailles. Outside the palace were acres of formal gardens, filled with marble sculptures and fountains.

In this setting Louis felt secure from the danger of Parisian mobs. Here he had the nobility attend his court so that he could control them. Instead of using the nobles in government service, Louis had them wait on him in a round of daily court rituals. The nobility depended on the king's favor for pensions, court posts, and protection from creditors.

In exchange for ending the nobles' power, Louis freed them from taxation. To nobles and nonnobles alike, he sold many offices with salaries. The sale of offices provided needed royal income but became a long-term drain on the treasury.

Government Policies

Louis continued the efforts of Henry IV and Richelieu to strengthen the power of the monarch and the state. He followed the tradition of Richelieu and chose his top advisers not from the nobility, but from middle-class families. Sons often succeeded their fathers in government service.

Although Louis was an absolute monarch, he was not able simply to change the traditions of his country's feudal past. Legal systems varied throughout France. Private tolls and customs were levied on

History & Art *Louis XIV of France* by Hyacinthe Rigaud, c. 1701, The Louvre, Paris, France **Louis XIV worked six to eight hours a day at what he called "the business of being king."** *How does this painting reflect the monarchy of Louis XIV?*

goods moving from one province to another. Weights and measures were not uniform. There were separate authorities and districts for financial, judicial, religious, and administrative affairs.

If Louis had tried to change these practices, it would have disrupted the kingdom and endangered his throne. Instead, the king kept the traditional ways, but added to them new administrative offices and practices. Two key people aided Louis XIV in his efforts—Jean-Baptiste Colbert (kohl•BEHR) and François Michel Le Tellier, the Marquis de Louvois (loov•WAH). As economic and financial minister, Colbert followed mercantilist policies to promote trade and industry. Louvois served as minister of war and helped make France's army the strongest in Europe.

Taxation

While reforming some aspects of government practice, Louis failed to adjust the complicated and unjust tax system. The poor carried most of the tax burden, while nobles, clergy, and government officials were exempt from many payments. Independent tax collectors often made large profits from their work, but they were allowed to continue this practice since the money they provided was needed to support the army.

The unreformed tax system heightened the economic differences between the regions of France. Since any visible improvement in one's farm or household might lead to higher tax payments, there was little desire to improve one's output. The tax system encouraged people to move from heavily taxed regions to regions with lower taxes. As a result, heavily taxed regions became poorer.

Religious Policy

Louis regarded the Huguenots as a threat to his absolute monarchy. Many Huguenots were military leaders and prosperous merchants. They often controlled local commerce. In spite of their high social standing, the Huguenots faced mounting persecution from Louis's government. The king wanted the Huguenots to accept Catholicism. He believed that, in this way, they would prove their loyalty to the throne. In 1685 the Edict of Nantes was repealed. Huguenots could no longer practice their religion, and their children had to become Catholics.

The result of the king's policy was the emigration of about 200,000 Huguenots to such places as the Netherlands, England, and England's American colonies. Many of these talented people contributed to the economic growth and prosperity of the lands where they settled.

Expansion

Louis XIV pursued a bold and active foreign policy. His goal was to expand the glory and power of France. Other European rulers were fearful of Louis's desire for expansion, and as a result, allied in opposition to France.

At the end of Louis XIV's reign, Europe was concerned about the succession to the Spanish throne. It was expected that Charles II of Spain would die without an heir. Both France and Austria had claims to the throne. The rest of Europe was alarmed that the balance of power would be disrupted if France inherited Spain's vast empire. Prior to Spanish king Charles II's death, the European powers worked out a plan to divide the Spanish Empire. The will of Charles II upset this plan by stating that the entire empire should remain intact and pass to Louis XIV's grandson, Philip of Anjou. Louis XIV accepted the provisions of the will. When Charles II died in 1700, Philip of Anjou became King Philip V of Spain. As a result, Europe was plunged into a conflict known as the War of the Spanish Succession.

Conflict

The War of the Spanish Succession lasted from 1701 to 1713. During the conflict England, the Dutch Netherlands, and Austria led a Grand Alliance of European nations against France and Spain.

Peace was finally restored with the Treaty of Utrecht in 1713. England and the Dutch Netherlands recognized Philip V as king of Spain, on the condition that France and Spain never be united under one crown. England gained trade advantages with the Spanish colonial empire. France, however, was forced to surrender the North American provinces of Nova Scotia and Newfoundland to England. The War of the Spanish Succession drained the French treasury, brought increased poverty, and created opposition to Louis's rule.

Louis XIV's Legacy

France enjoyed one of its most brilliant cultural periods under Louis XIV. Builders and artisans designed and decorated palaces and churches. Artists and playwrights portrayed the daily life of the king's court, the nobility, and the lower classes. Louis's building projects and his wars, however, had left the country near financial ruin. The ways in which Louis weakened the French nobility also had their costs. The nobles lost their ability to govern, but not the desire for power. The peasants and the middle class resented the privileges and wealth of the nobles. After Louis XIV's death in 1715, the nobility sought to expand its power under Louis's great-grandson, Louis XV. Conflicts between the nobles and the middle and lower classes would bring France to the brink of revolution.

SECTION 3 REVIEW

Recall
1. **Define** intendant.
2. **Identify** Henry IV, Edict of Nantes, Cardinal Richelieu, Louis XIV, Treaty of Utrecht.
3. **Explain** how Henry IV tried to bring religious peace to France.

Critical Thinking
4. **Evaluating Information** What do you think were the successes and failures of Louis XIV's reign?

Understanding Themes
5. **Uniformity** What were Cardinal Richelieu's political goals? How did Richelieu reduce the power of the nobility? Of the Huguenots?

Section 4

The German States

Setting the Scene

▶ **Terms to Define**
   pragmatic sanction

▶ **People to Meet**
   Maria Theresa, Frederick II

▶ **Places to Locate**
   Austria, Prussia

Find Out ▶ How was the Thirty Years' War different from prior European wars?

The Storyteller

Thomas Taylor traveled slowly and cautiously from Dresden to Prague. He was overwhelmed by a harshness he had never witnessed in his native England. Life all around him was insecure and uncomfortable. Violent outlaws roamed the highways, torture was part of the judicial process, executions were horrible, famine and disease were evident in every town. Taylor detoured around public refuse heaps, swarming with rats and carrion crows. He dodged the bodies of executed criminals dangling from the gallows. Taylor had heard rumors of war. If the rumors were true, he judged it would be long, brutal and terrible.

—freely adapted from *The Thirty Years' War*, C.V. Wedgwood, 1961

The Thirty Years' War

While the Bourbons were building the strongest monarchy in Europe, the Hapsburgs of Austria were trying to set up their own absolute monarchy in central and eastern Europe. Their efforts renewed tensions between Europe's Catholics and Protestants. This eventually led to yet another conflict—the Thirty Years' War. Though most of the fighting took place in Germany, all the major European powers except England became involved.

The Thirty Years' War

Conflicts between Catholics and Protestants had continued in Germany after the Peace of Augsburg in 1555. These disputes were complicated by the spread of Calvinism, a religion that had not been recognized by the peace settlement. Furthermore, the Protestant princes of Germany resisted the rule of Catholic Hapsburg monarchs.

In 1618 the Thirty Years' War began in Bohemia, where Ferdinand of Styria had become king a year earlier. Ferdinand was also the Hapsburg heir to the throne of the Holy Roman Empire. An enemy of Protestantism who wanted to strengthen Hapsburg authority, Ferdinand began his rule by curtailing the freedom of Bohemian Protestants, most of whom were Czechs. In 1618 the Czechs rebelled and took over Prague. Soon the rebellion developed into a full-scale civil war—Ferdinand and the Catholic princes against the German Protestant princes. Philip III of Spain, a Hapsburg, sent aid to Ferdinand.

The Czech revolt was crushed by 1620 and, over the next 10 years, the Czechs were forcefully reconverted to Catholicism. Instead of ending, however, the war continued. Protestant Denmark now fought against the Hapsburgs, hoping to gain German territory. The Danes were soon defeated and forced to withdraw. Then Sweden entered the war to defend the Protestant cause. By this time the war had been going on for 12 years, and religious issues were taking second place to political ones. In 1635, under Cardinal Richelieu, Roman Catholic France took up arms against the Roman Catholic Hapsburgs to keep them from becoming too powerful.

For 13 more years the war dragged on—rival armies plundering the German countryside and destroying entire towns. Historians estimate that Germany lost about one-third of its people.

When the conflict finally ended in 1648, the outcome was the further weakening of Germany and the rise of France as Europe's leading power. The Peace of Westphalia ending the war recognized Calvinism among the official religions and divided the Holy Roman Empire into more than 300 separate states. The Hapsburgs still ruled Austria and Bohemia, but their control of the other German states was in name only, thus ending their hope of establishing an absolute monarchy over all of Germany.

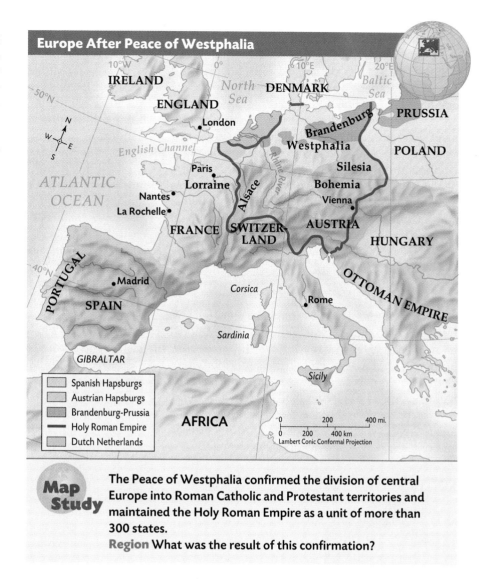

Europe After Peace of Westphalia

Legend:
- Spanish Hapsburgs
- Austrian Hapsburgs
- Brandenburg-Prussia
- Holy Roman Empire
- Dutch Netherlands

Map Study The Peace of Westphalia confirmed the division of central Europe into Roman Catholic and Protestant territories and maintained the Holy Roman Empire as a unit of more than 300 states.

Region What was the result of this confirmation?

Austria

After the Thirty Years' War, the Austrian Hapsburgs concentrated on building a strong monarchy in **Austria**, Hungary, and Bohemia. Austria was still the most powerful of the German states. In 1683 the Austrians, with the aid of the Poles, lifted an Ottoman siege of Vienna. By 1718, Austrian armies had regained territory in the Balkan Peninsula from the Ottomans. As a result of the War of the Spanish Succession, the Austrians received the Spanish Netherlands and acquired lands in Italy.

In 1740, 23-year-old **Maria Theresa** inherited the throne of Austria from her father, Holy Roman Emperor Charles VI. According to law and custom, women were not permitted to rule Austria. In 1718 Charles had convinced the monarchs of Europe to accept a pragmatic sanction, or royal decree having the force of law, by which Europe's rulers promised not to divide the Hapsburg lands and to accept

Footnotes to History

Tulip Mania

During the Thirty Years' War, western Europeans fell in love with tulips. Dutch traders brought tulip bulbs into Europe from Ottoman Turkey beginning in the 1500s, and gardeners in the Netherlands and other parts of Europe took a liking to the blossoms. This led to a public craze for tulips that reached a peak in the 1630s.

female succession to the Austrian throne.

Maria Theresa had not received any training in political matters, yet she proved to be a clever and resourceful leader. Overcoming the opposition of the nobility and most of her ministers, Maria Theresa greatly strengthened the Austrian central government. She reorganized the bureaucracy, improved tax collection, and furthered the building of roads. Understanding that the unity of her empire depended on a strong economy, Maria Theresa ended trade barriers between Austria and Bohemia and encouraged exports. She also used government funds to boost the production of textiles and glass.

Prussia

Maria Theresa faced a number of enemies in Europe. One of these was France, the traditional rival of the Hapsburgs. In the 1700s a new European rival rose to prominence in northeastern Germany. Brandenburg-Prussia was ruled by the Hohenzollern family, which had governed the territory of Brandenburg since the 1400s. During the Thirty Years' War, they gained control of **Prussia** and other widely scattered lands in Germany.

Great Elector

One of the greatest of the Hohenzollern monarchs was Frederick William. He held the title "Great Elector." After the Thirty Years' War, Frederick William increased the strength of Brandenburg-Prussia by creating a permanent standing army. To meet the cost of his army, he proposed raising taxes. The Junkers, or nobles, opposed this plan. Frederick William then worked out a compromise with them. He permitted only Junkers to be landowners, freed them from taxes, and gave them full power over the peasants. In return, the Junkers agreed that Frederick William could tax townspeople and peasants. These two groups were too weak to organize and oppose this increased burden. In 1663 the Junkers further strengthened their ties to the Hohenzollerns. They pledged allegiance to Frederick William. As a result of this alliance with the Junkers, Frederick William was able to become an absolute ruler.

Frederick William was succeeded by his son Frederick I. Frederick aided the Austrian Hapsburgs against Louis XIV in the War of the Spanish Succession. As a reward, Frederick was given the title of king. He was, however, a weak ruler who did little to strengthen his country.

CONNECTIONS

The Arts

The Sounds of Bach

Johann Sebastian Bach

Born in Eisenach, Germany, in 1685, Johann Sebastian Bach was one of the world's most talented composers. He wrote music for the Lutheran Church, wealthy nobles, and other musicians. Bach's work reflects the baroque style of music, which reached its height during the early 1700s. Baroque music was characterized by lively, complex dramatic compositions that appealed to the listener's mind and emotions.

Bach is especially known for two types of baroque music—counterpoint and fugue. In counterpoint, two or more melodies are combined. In the fugue, several instruments or voices play together, each playing the same melodies but with variations.

For about 50 years after Bach's death in 1750, his work was neglected. Today Bach is esteemed as a brilliant musician, and his influence has touched even modern popular music and film. Walt Disney had Mickey Mouse conducting Bach's *Toccata and Fugue in D Minor* in the 1940 movie classic *Fantasia*. Bach's style is at least hinted at in the rock song *A Whiter Shade of Pale* and in rock musician Jethro Tull's jazz-like arrangement of the *Bourrée* from the *E Minor Lute Suite*.

Linking Past and Present ACTIVITY

Explain why Johann Sebastian Bach's work is called "baroque." How was he regarded after his death? How is he regarded today? What impact has Bach had on modern music?

Frederick William I

Frederick William I, who ruled from 1713 to 1740, was a powerful leader. He centralized the Prussian government, uniting all functions into one bureaucracy under his direct control. He supported production and trade and brought more revenue into the government treasury. Known as the Royal Drill Sergeant, Frederick William devoted his life to the Prussian army and made it the most efficient fighting force in Europe. Royal agents recruited men from rural areas of Germany. Frederick William I especially delighted in recruiting tall soldiers. He formed a special "regiment of giants" that he drilled himself.

Frederick II

In 1740 **Frederick II**, Frederick William I's son, became king of Prussia. As a boy, Frederick preferred music and art to horseback riding and military drills. However, when he became king, Frederick adopted his father's military ways and set out to expand Prussian territory. Frederick the Great, as he became known, rejected Austria's pragmatic sanction and seized the Austrian province of Silesia.

Frederick's attack on Silesia began a conflict called the War of the Austrian Succession. Prussia's forces were stronger than those of Austria. In spite of Austria's disadvantage, the Austrian empress, Maria Theresa, decided to send her forces into battle. Spain and France backed Prussia, while Great Britain (formed in 1707 as the result of a union between England and Scotland) and the Dutch Netherlands supported Austria.

After seven years of fighting, in 1748 the European powers signed the Treaty of Aix-la-Chapelle, which officially recognized Prussia's rise as an important nation. Frederick was allowed to keep Silesia; Maria Theresa was able to hold the rest of her domain: Austria, Hungary, and Bohemia.

The Austrian ruler, however, was not satisfied with the treaty and was determined to recover Silesia. To this end, Maria Theresa changed her alliance from Great Britain to France. She also gained the support of Russia since Prussia's Frederick II was

The War of Jenkins' Ear

Caribbean Sea, 1739

The War of Jenkins' Ear was part of a series of conflicts among European nations in the 1700s. In the waters off Florida, an English smuggler named Robert Jenkins lost his ear in a fight with Spaniards in 1731. Jenkins' appearance in Parliament in 1738 further incited public opinion against Spain. The result was war, declared in June 1739, over possession of Georgia and commercial rivalry at sea. Within a year, the War of Jenkins' Ear had become part of the more serious War of Austrian Succession.

an archenemy of Empress Elizabeth of Russia. These alliances set the stage for further conflict.

The Seven Years' War—from 1756 to 1763—was a worldwide conflict in which Great Britain and France competed for overseas territory, and Prussia opposed Austria, Russia, France, and other nations. The war between Austria and Prussia erupted in 1756. After victories in Saxony—a German state and an ally of Austria—and after a later victory over the Austrians in Silesia, Frederick II signed a peace agreement that enabled him to retain most of Silesia.

The struggle between Great Britain and France in North America was known as the French and Indian War. The British and French also fought in India. At the Treaty of Paris in 1763, France gave up most of French Canada and its lands east of the Mississippi River to Great Britain. Great Britain also replaced France as the leading power in India. As a result of the Seven Years' War, Great Britain emerged as the strongest colonial empire and Prussia retained the province of Silesia.

SECTION 4 REVIEW

Recall
1. **Define** pragmatic sanction.
2. **Identify** Ferdinand of Styria, Peace of Westphalia, Maria Theresa, Frederick II, Silesia.
3. **State** what primary factor

caused the Thirty Years' War. What were the war's results?

Critical Thinking
4. **Analyzing Information** How did Maria Theresa strengthen the central government in Austria

and in her other domains?

Understanding Themes
5. **Conflict** How did the many conflicts among the German states affect the balance of power?

Section 5

Russia

Setting the Scene

▶ **Terms to Define**
    boyar, *dvorianie*, serf

▶ **People to Meet**
    Ivan IV, Peter I, Catherine II

▶ **Places to Locate**
    Poland, Siberia, St. Petersburg

Find Out How did the power of Russian czars differ from that of other European monarchs?

The Storyteller

When first posted, no one could believe the decree. Czar Peter had ordered all children from the nobility and clerical classes [clergy] to study mathematics and geometry. Those who refused were forbidden to marry until they mastered the material. Such commands seemed absurd and many scoffed at the czar's ability to enforce his demands. However, teachers arrived in each district and local taxes were increased for support. Priests likewise received notification and no priest dared solemnize a marriage without proper certification. Father Konstantin looked sadly at the couple before him and explained, "You do not have the proper certification. I cannot marry you."

Russian Orthodox Bishop

—adapted from *Decree on Compulsory Education of the Russian Nobility*, reprinted in *The Human Record, Volume 2*, Alfred J. Andrea and James H. Overfield, 1990

Between 1500 and 1800, Russia made tremendous territorial gains and became a major European power. Slavs elsewhere lost ground and were taken over by other powers.

In southeastern Europe, the Ottoman Turks ruled most of the Balkan Peninsula and the Serbs, Bosnians, and Macedonians who lived there. Under the Ottomans, some of these Slavs converted to Islam, while the rest remained Eastern Orthodox. Hungary ruled the Croats (KROH•ATZ), and Austria controlled the Slovenes (SLOH•VEENZ). Both these Slavic peoples remained Roman Catholic and oriented to western Europe.

In central Europe, Austria ruled the Slovaks and Czechs. Neighboring **Poland** had been an important European power from the late 1300s. Polish monarchs created one of the larger states of Europe, but by the 1600s Poland had gradually weakened. Ukrainian subjects rebelled against Polish rule in the mid-1600s and allied with Russia. By 1764 almost all of Ukraine was under Russian control. In the late 1700s Prussia, Austria, and Russia divided Poland among themselves. The Belarus region and its people, the Belarussians, passed from Polish to Russian control at this time.

Rise of Russia

From the 1200s to the early 1700s, Russia was isolated from western European developments, such as the Crusades, the Renaissance, and the Reformation. Russia developed its own civilization based on the values of the Eastern Orthodox Church and the Byzantine Empire. The Russian monarchy became all-powerful and easily crushed its opponents. The nobility, the established church, and the towns—all of whom had posed repeated opposition to royal power elsewhere in Europe— never posed the same challenge in Russia.

Ivan IV

The most powerful of the early czars was **Ivan IV**, who ruled from 1533 to 1584. Known as Ivan "the Terrible" or "the Awesome," he was at once learned, religious, and cruel. Ivan became czar at the age of three. While growing up, he was caught between rival groups of nobles who sought to rule the country. He witnessed much cruelty and was never able to rid himself of his early memories. As an adult, Ivan saw treason everywhere and arrested, exiled, or executed many of his closest advisers. In a fit of rage, he even killed his own son.

Ivan took many steps against the boyars (boh•YAHRZ), or nobles, to reduce their potential threat to his throne. He seized their scattered lands and placed them under his direct control. The former owners were uprooted and dispersed. On the seized land, which made up about one-half of the country, Ivan placed his own loyal people. They became a secret police force, the *oprichniki*, (aw•PREECH•nee•kee) and terrorized the rest of the country.

Ivan IV also increased Russia's trade with western Europe and worked to expand his borders. Despite Russia's vast size, it had few seaports free of ice throughout the year. Gaining more access to the sea for trade and security became a major goal of Russian rulers. During the late 1500s, Ivan conquered Mongol lands east and south of Moscow but waged unsuccessful war against Poland, Lithuania, and Sweden for territory near the Baltic Sea.

The Time of Troubles

After Ivan's death in 1584, Russia drifted toward chaos. During the "Time of Troubles," from 1598 to 1613, noble feuds over the throne, peasant revolts, and foreign invasions plagued the country. Finally in 1613, an assembly of clergy, nobles, and townsmen named 17-year-old Michael Romanov as czar. Michael began the Romanov dynasty that ruled Russia until 1917.

During the 1500s and 1600s, Russian society experienced many changes. Boyars became more closely tied to the czar's service, townspeople lost what little influence they had on government, and peasants were bound to the land as a virtually enslaved workforce. To escape, many peasants moved to borderlands south of Moscow. In Ukraine, some formed self-governing villages of warrior pioneers and their families and became known as Cossacks. Peasants, traders, and adventurers also moved into **Siberia**, the vast stretch of land east of European Russia.

Visualizing History **Peter the Great, a man of restless energy and sometimes hasty decisions, attempted many reforms.** *What reforms did he introduce to make Russia more like western European nations?*

Peter the Great

In 1689 **Peter I**, known as Peter the Great, came to the throne. He was a towering figure, nearly 7 feet (2 m) tall. Peter had boundless energy and volcanic emotions. During his reign, he sought to bring Russia into the mainstream of European civilization.

Encounter With the West

As a young man, Peter enjoyed practical subjects, such as mechanics, geography, and military strategy. He sought out tutors among the foreign community in Moscow to learn the basic skills of navigation and shipbuilding. He discovered that Russian knowledge of the outside world was quite limited. Most Russians were illiterate peasants; only a few nobles were well educated.

After becoming czar, Peter took an 18-month study tour of England and the Netherlands. He visited shipyards, factories, mills, and laboratories. He learned carpentry and developed enough skill in surgery and dentistry to want to practice on others.

Steve Raymer

Peter's Great City

G.D. Talbot

Where he first set foot on the Baltic coast, legend has it, Peter the Great proclaimed: "Here there shall be a town." On May 16, 1703, Russian workers laid the foundations for a fortress on the Baltic coast. The city of St. Petersburg soon spread out, and in 1712 Peter made it the new capital of Russia. A traveler in his youth, he was determined that his new capital would imitate the imposing European cities he had visited. St. Petersburg did not remain the capital of Russia, but the new city offered Peter the Great a chance to consolidate the power of the Russian central government and to drag Russia into the modern world. Many changes were inaugurated: He forbade men to wear beards or to dress in the traditional long robes called caftans. He simplified the Cyrillic alphabet. He was relentless. At times he even resorted to terror. But he transformed Russia and made his new city on the Baltic Sea a window to the West.

Today Peter's legacy is everywhere: in the shipyards, the research centers, and the architecture of ornate palaces such as the Winter Palace (center), completed during the reign of Catherine the Great in 1762. "I have a whole labyrinth of rooms ... and all of them are filled with luxuries," she wrote of the Winter Palace and the adjoining Hermitage, where Pavilion Hall (top) fills one small corner. 🌐

When he returned home, Peter forced the Russian nobility to adopt the ways of western Europe. He ordered members of the court to wear western European clothing. Men entering Moscow were forced to shave their beards or pay a fine. Women, who had always been excluded from social gatherings, were ordered to attend parties.

Peter sent Russians abroad to study shipbuilding, naval warfare, mathematics, and foreign languages. He invited foreign experts to train Russians. His greatest effort to open Russia to Europe was the building of a new capital, which he named **St. Petersburg**. Located at the mouth of the Neva River near the Baltic Sea, St. Petersburg became Russia's "window to the West."

Foreign Policy

Peter's goal was to make Russia a European power. He expanded Russia's borders in the south, east, and northwest. In 1689 Russia forced China to accept Russian control of Siberia. In the early 1700s, the Danish navigator Vitus Bering claimed for Russia what became known as the Bering Strait between Siberia and Alaska. Russian settlements eventually started in Alaska and even California.

During much of Peter's reign, Russia fought Poland, Sweden, or the Ottoman Empire. Russian failures to win warm-water ports on either the Baltic or Black Seas convinced Peter to modernize the military. His reforms paid off in 1721, when Russia defeated Sweden and won control of the eastern end of the Baltic region.

Government Administration

Peter made sweeping changes in the Russian government. Borrowing ideas from France, he introduced a central bureaucracy and placed local governments under its control. Peter brought the Eastern Orthodox Church under his direct authority. In place of a single independent church leader, Peter created the Holy Synod, a council of bishops responsible to the government.

Peter also created a new class of nobles called *dvorianie* (DVOH•ree•YAH•nee•YUH), who, in return for government service, were allowed to own hereditary, landed estates. A noble's duty to the czar started at age 15 and continued until death.

Peter used privileges and force to make the established nobility accept government service. Nobles were given full control over the serfs, or peasant laborers who worked the estates and were bound to the land. While freedom for peasants had gradually increased in western Europe, the opposite was true in Russia.

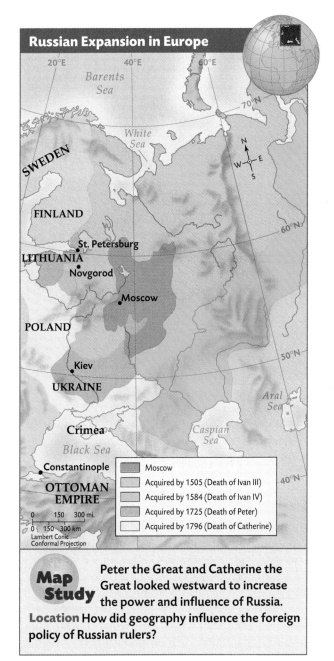

Russian Expansion in Europe

	Moscow
	Acquired by 1505 (Death of Ivan III)
	Acquired by 1584 (Death of Ivan IV)
	Acquired by 1725 (Death of Peter)
	Acquired by 1796 (Death of Catherine)

Map Study Peter the Great and Catherine the Great looked westward to increase the power and influence of Russia.
Location How did geography influence the foreign policy of Russian rulers?

Finally, Peter changed the tax laws to increase government income and efficiency. Under the plan, nobles paid no taxes. As in France, the tax burden fell on the poorest classes.

Economic Changes

To stimulate economic growth, Peter brought agriculture and craft production under strict government control. He gave incentives to increase production in favored areas such as mining and metalworking. New production centers were provided with land, money, and workers. Most of the workers were tied to their trades as the serfs were to the land.

Portrait of Catherine the Great by Alexandre Roslin. Musée des Beaux Arts, La Rochelle, France *What changed Catherine's mind about the equality of all people?*

Catherine the Great

After Peter's death in 1725, Russia was ruled by a series of weak or ordinary monarchs. The next notable ruler was **Catherine II**. In 1762, Catherine seized the throne from her weak husband, Peter III, and ruled as empress of Russia until 1796. Although born a German princess, Catherine easily adopted Russian ways and earned the respect of her people.

As monarch, Catherine was greatly influenced by leading western European thinkers. She studied their works and corresponded with a number of them. For a time, she believed that all people were born equal and that it was "contrary to the Christian faith and to justice to make slaves of them."

Early in her reign, Catherine considered freeing the serfs. A peasant rebellion that threatened her rule, however, made Catherine change her mind. To ensure the continued support of the nobles, she released them from the government service required by Peter I. Catherine also allowed the nobles to treat their serfs as they pleased. During Catherine's reign, more peasants were forced into serfdom than ever before, and their conditions worsened. The common people of Russia had fewer rights than those in any other part of Europe. When groups of them revolted, Catherine brutally crushed the uprisings.

A successful foreign policy earned her the name Catherine the Great. She significantly expanded Russia's borders to the south and achieved the goal of securing a warm-water port on the Black Sea. In making this gain, Russian armies defeated the Ottoman Turks. In the west, Catherine acquired territory from Poland. Prussia and Austria took the rest of Poland, which then ceased to exist until 1919.

Catherine was the last of the great absolute monarchs of the 1700s. By the time of her death in 1796, new ideas of liberty and equality had spread throughout western Europe. These new ideas directly challenged and questioned the age-old institution of monarchy.

Effects

Peter's reforms strengthened Russia's role in foreign affairs. In his own country, however, Peter had only limited success. His domestic policies broke the traditional Eastern Orthodox culture that had united nobles and peasants. With Peter's reign, a dangerous split developed between the few who accepted European ways and the many who clung to traditional values. An observer noted: "The tsar pulls uphill alone with the strength of ten, but millions push downhill." Many of Peter's reforms were incomplete and hasty. Yet his measures brought Russia into the mainstream of western European civilization.

SECTION 5 REVIEW

Recall
1. **Define** boyar, *dvorianie*, serf.
2. **Identify** Ivan IV, the Romanovs, Peter I, Catherine II.
3. **Locate** the cities of Moscow and St. Petersburg on the map on page 501. Why did Czar Peter the Great move the Russian capital from Moscow to St. Petersburg?

Critical Thinking
4. **Synthesizing Information** How did the reigns of Peter the Great and Catherine the Great affect the Russian nobility and the common people?

Understanding Themes
5. **Innovation** How did Peter the Great try to make Russia accept western European ideas and practices?

Recognizing a Stereotype

Emanuella asks her friend Ashley if she would date a football player. Ashley says, "No way. Football players are all muscle and no brains." Ashley has expressed a stereotype—an oversimplified description of a group. Because stereotypes may be both inaccurate and harmful, we must learn to recognize them in speaking, writing, and thinking.

Learning the Skill

A stereotype can describe any group—a gender, race, religion, country, region, city, neighborhood, school, or profession. Stereotypes blur or ignore the characteristics of individuals within the group. In the example above, Ashley may reject the friendship of a very considerate and intelligent person just because he plays football. While this is a negative stereotype, other stereotypes may have positive or neutral connotations. "Blondes have more fun," for example, is a positive stereotype. Negative stereotypes, however, are the least accurate and most harmful.

Stereotypes can influence not only our attitude about a group's members, but also can affect our behavior toward them. History is full of examples of oppression and persecution directed at particular groups of people. Negative stereotypes usually accompany and support these destructive acts.

Because stereotypes are so common, it is easy to ignore or accept them. Instead, learn how to recognize and evaluate them. Certain words, phrases, and thoughts signal the presence of stereotypes. In any kind of material, written or oral, first notice characteristics attributed to a particular group. Look for exaggerations, often indicated by words such as *all*, *none*, *every*, *always*, and *never*. Identify strong negative adjectives such as *lazy*, *sneaky*, *cruel*, and *corrupt*. Note a consistently positive or negative tone to the description.

Once you recognize a stereotype, then evaluate its accuracy. Think about whether the stereotype puts a positive or negative slant on the information concerning a specific group. Ask yourself: Does this stereotype agree or disagree with what I know about individual members of this group?

Practicing the Skill

Each statement below contains a stereotype held by people from the 1500s to the 1700s. Identify the stereotype in each statement. Identify any words or phrases that helped you recognize the stereotype, and tell whether it has a negative, positive, or neutral connotation.

1. England is an isle fouled by heretics and barbarians. *(Spain, 1554)*
2. It is against the law, human and divine, that a woman should reign and have empire above men. *(England, 1560)*
3. The Italians are so jovial and addicted to music that nearly every countryman plays on the guitar, and will commonly go into the field with a fiddle. *(England, 1600)*
4. Do not put such unlimited power into the hands of husbands. Remember all men would be tyrants if they could. [We ladies] will not hold ourselves bound by any laws in which we have no voice, or representation. *(United States, 1776)*

Applying the Skill

Identify three stereotypes about groups within your community. For each stereotype, write a paragraph evaluating its accuracy by recalling your own experiences with individual members of the group.

For More Practice

Turn to the Skill Practice in the Chapter Review on page 505 for more practice in recognizing a stereotype.

Connections Across Time

Historical Significance One of the results of the Age of Monarchy was the emergence of strong national states in Europe. Absolute monarchs centralized their governments and established powerful military forces to protect and to expand their countries' natural borders.

Monarchs plunged Europe into wars over territorial, religious, and economic issues. By forcefully asserting their power, monarchs created the national boundaries that would form the basis of modern Europe. Later wars would modify the boundaries but not change them completely. Today, monarchs reign but do not rule in several European democracies.

Using Key Terms

Write the key term that completes each sentence. Then write a sentence for each term not chosen.

a. absolutism
b. balance of power
c. intendants
d. serfs
e. divine right
f. boyars
g. armada
h. inflation
i. yeomen
j. pragmatic sanction
k. *dvorianie*

1. Ivan IV of Russia took steps against the _____ to reduce their potential threat to his throne.
2. In 1718 the Holy Roman emperor Charles VI convinced Europe's monarchs to accept a _____ in which they promised to accept Maria Theresa as the future Hapsburg monarch.
3. During Spain's decline as a European power, its economy suffered from _____, an abnormal increase in currency resulting in sharp price increases.
4. During the 1600s and the 1700s, European monarchs claimed to rule by _____, the theory that monarchs derive their power from God.
5. During Elizabeth I's reign, England worked for a _____ on the Continent to prevent one European power from becoming too strong.

Technology Activity

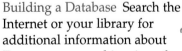 

Building a Database Search the Internet or your library for additional information about European monarchies since the early 1500s. Build a database collecting biographical information about European monarchies from the 1500s to present day. Include information such as name of monarchy, country, date of coronation, achievements, and names of heirs.

Using Your History Journal

Choose an event from the country time line you created. Write a short opinion paper on why you believe that this was the most significant development, person, or decision in that nation during the period 1500 to 1750.

Reviewing Facts

1. **History** List at least four European royal families and their countries during the period from about 1500 to about 1800.
2. **History** Identify major characteristics of Europe's age of absolutism.
3. **Government** Explain how England's Henry VIII strengthened support for his policies.
4. **Citizenship** State why Henry IV's issuing of the Edict of Nantes was a significant event.
5. **History** Identify the changes that Peter the Great brought to Russia.

Critical Thinking

1. **Analyze** How were the Hapsburg and Tudor monarchies of the 1500s similar? How were they different? Which one do you think was more successful?
2. **Synthesize** Imagine you are a soldier during the Thirty Years' War. Describe how you joined the army and what conditions were like during the war. What hopes do you have for the future?
3. **Evaluate** Consider the leadership style of Maria Theresa of Austria, who had no training in political matters. Can a person today be a successful political leader with no prior training or experience?

4. **Evaluate** Which of the monarchs described in this chapter do you most admire? Which one do you least admire? Explain your reasons.

5. **Evaluate** What does the portrait of Frederick the Great below reveal about the values and characteristics of the Prussian monarchy?

Understanding Themes

1. **Conflict** How did Spain's rivalry with England develop during the period from about 1500 to about 1750?

2. **Change** How did Tudor monarchs bring stability to England?

3. **Uniformity** How did Louis XIV try to strengthen French loyalty to his monarchy?

4. **Conflict** What dynastic and religious issues divided the German states?

5. **Innovation** Why did Peter the Great want to make innovations in government and society?

Skill Practice

The following lines from William Shakespeare's plays include stereotypes that were common in 16th-century England. Identify each stereotype and any words or phrases that helped you recognize it.

1. "Frailty, thy name is woman!"
2. "These Moors are changeable in their moods."
3. "This Hebrew will turn Christian; he grows kind."
4. "Today the French … all in gold, like heathen gods, shone down the English."

Linking Past and Present

1. European monarchs in the 1600s and 1700s resolved their territorial disputes and ambitions through war. How do present-day leaders resolve disputes? Explore the similarities and the differences between contemporary world leaders and monarchs in early modern Europe.

2. European monarchs in the 1600s and 1700s were powerful leaders who claimed to rule by divine right. What is the position of monarchs in Europe today? How is power exercised in modern European governments?

Geography in History

1. **Location** Refer to the map below. Along what body of water did Pomerania lie? What was the population loss over much of its area?

2. **Place** Of Bohemia, Saxony, and Silesia, which area had suffered the least population loss?

3. **Region** In general, what parts of the Holy Roman Empire retained the most population? Why do you think this was so?

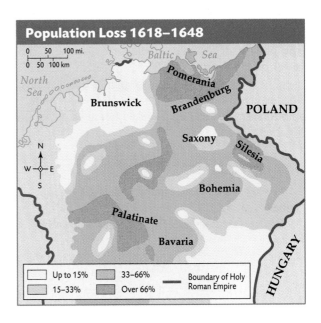

Population Loss 1618–1648

Turning Points in World History

Age of Exploration

Setting up the Video

Work with a group of your classmates to view "Age of Exploration" on the videodisc *Turning Points in World History*. The voyages of the age of exploration opened new doors for European explorers to gain new contacts for trade, expansion, and innovation that profoundly changed European culture. This program highlights the history of European exploration and speculates about future trends for modern explorers.

Side One, Chapter 9

View the video by scanning the bar code or by entering the chapter number on your keypad and pressing Search. *(Also available in VHS format.)*

Hands-On Activity

Research information about current discoveries that are taking place in space explorations. Using a word processor, write a minireport about the latest findings. Share your results with the rest of the class.

Surfing the "Net"

Sunken Treasures

During the 1500s, Spanish galleons were constantly searching for treasure to take back to Spain. Typically, the loot included precious stones, gold doubloons, and silver pieces of eight. Many treasure-laden vessels were sunk due to bad weather or pirates trying to steal the fortune in the midst of a battle. To find out more about recent discoveries of sunken treasures, access the Internet.

Getting There

Follow these steps to gather information about sunken treasure.
1. Go to a search engine. Type in the phrase *sunken treasure*.
2. After typing in the phrase, enter words such as the

following to focus your search:
- *spanish history*
- *florida keys*
- *location*

3. The search engine should provide you with a number of links to follow. Links are "pointers" to different sites on the Internet and commonly appear as blue underlined words.

What to Do When You Are There

Click on the links to navigate through the pages of information and gather your findings. Using a word processor, create a chart to organize your information. Include headings such as location of a sunken galleon, date of sinking, date of discovery, and treasure recovered from the galleon. Include a map labeling the location of discovered sunken ships.

Unit 4 | Digest

The Marriage of Giovanni Arnolfini and Giovanna Cenami by Jan van Eyck, 1434. National Gallery, London, England *What values were popular throughout Renaissance Europe?*

From 1400 to the mid 1700s, rulers in various parts of the world increased the power and prestige of their territories. In Europe two major movements—the Renaissance and the Reformation—encouraged Europeans to gain new knowledge, explore lands overseas, acquire new resources, and spread Christianity.

Religion, politics, and economic needs also spurred new developments in Asia. There, Muslim empires ruled over vast areas between the Mediterranean Sea and South Asia. Other parts of Asia—China, Japan, and Southeast Asia—developed their traditional cultures while facing growing challenges from European explorations. A new age dawned in which the world's different civilizations for the first time came into close contact with each other.

Chapter 16
Renaissance and Reformation

In the 1300s scholars in Italy revived the ancient Greek ideal of individual achievement. Their interest in the classics sparked a new era of European thought and art known as the Renaissance. For the first time since the fall of Rome, European artists and writers emphasized the value of human activities and feelings in their works. This represented a departure from the medieval concern with religion and spiritual values. During the Italian Renaissance, highly talented people—such as Michelangelo Buonarroti and Leonardo da Vinci—also created works of art that have been admired throughout the centuries for their technical skill and beauty.

From Italy the Renaissance spread to northern Europe, where it became more religious in its emphasis. Scholars such as Erasmus and Thomas More called for simpler forms of worship and other church reforms. Johannes Gutenberg's use of movable type in printing made an increasing number of books at cheaper prices available to more people. As a result, Renaissance ideas spread rapidly and challenged traditional religious and cultural beliefs.

Protests against church abuses soon led to a split in Western Christianity. Reformers such as Martin Luther and John Calvin criticized the pope's authority and many Catholic teachings and practices. Their two major ideas—that the Bible, rather than church tradition, was the source of authority and that salvation was by faith alone—won support throughout northern Europe and led to a new form of Christianity known as Protestantism. In England, the monarch replaced the pope as head of the Church in England. Later the English Church became Protestant with Catholic features.

To counter Protestantism, the Roman Catholic Church began its own reform movement to correct church abuses and to more clearly define its teachings. As part of this effort, the pope sent the Jesuits, a new religious order, as missionaries to Protestant areas in Europe and non-Christian areas in Asia.

Chapter 17
Expanding Horizons

During the 1400s, Muslims and Italians controlled the rich overland spice trade from Asia. Wanting to share in this wealth, European countries bordering the Atlantic Ocean sought a direct sea route to the spice-producing islands of Southeast Asia. Advances in navigation by Chinese and Muslim inventors made their oceangoing voyages possible. By the 1500s, Portugal had discovered a route to South Asia around the southern tip of Africa. Its traders followed the route and founded trading centers in India and Southeast Asia.

Portugal's rival, Spain, joined in the effort to reach Asia. By 1522, Columbus, Magellan, and other explorers under Spain's flag had reached the Americas or had circled the globe. The Spaniards later set up a large overseas empire that included Mexico, Central America, most of South America, and the Philippines.

France, England, and the Netherlands led the search for shorter routes to Asia, and they eventually surpassed Spain in overseas exploration. The Dutch acquired Portugal's spice trade in Southeast Asia. France traded with Native Americans in North America's interior lands. England set up colonies or trading posts in the Americas and South Asia.

European overseas expansion brought riches to European countries. However, the same expansion often had both a positive and negative impact on the cultures that Europeans encountered. Europeans brought new skills, beliefs, and goods to overseas areas. Peoples in Asia, Africa, and the Americas, however, saw their traditional cultures undermined by European expansion, and millions died of mistreatment or diseases brought by Europeans. Portugal, Spain, and England relied on enslaved people from Africa to work their plantations and mines in the Americas.

The slave trade became part of the larger trading network that was beginning to link Europe, Asia, Africa, and America. Gold and silver from the Americas to Europe increased trade between Europe and Asia, where demand for the precious metals was high. European manufactured goods flowed around the world, while agricultural products, such as corn, chocolate, yams, potatoes, coffee, and tea, came to Europe from Asia, Africa, and the Americas. All of these exchanges, both positive and negative, contributed to the rise of the global community that we know today.

Chapter 18
Empires of Asia

From the late 1400s to the 1700s, three Muslim empires—the Ottoman, the Safavid Persian, and the Mogul—ruled parts of Asia, Europe, and Africa. The Ottomans controlled the Middle East and much of North Africa and Europe's Balkan Peninsula. Suleiman I, who ruled from 1520 to 1566, strengthened government administration, but later military defeats at Lepanto (1571) and Vienna

Visualizing History During the 1500s and 1600s, European explorers, traders, and missionaries traveled the seas to Africa, the Americas, and Asia. *What earlier developments in European finance and business encouraged voyages of exploration?*

(1683) halted the Ottoman advance into Europe. To the east, the Safavid dynasty ruled Persia, or present-day Iran. Under Safavid leadership, Persia enjoyed a flowering of culture, and the Persian language became the language of culture, diplomacy, and trade in most of the Muslim world. Muslims from central Asia conquered northern India and set up the Mogul dynasty. Akbar, a Muslim ruler of the 1500s, fostered religious tolerance among Muslims and Hindus. Mogul rulers encouraged the arts—music, painting, and literature.

In China the Ming dynasty, which ruled from 1368 to 1644, encouraged the development of agriculture and sponsored overseas explorations that sailed as far as Africa and Arabia. Although the expeditions brought back rich tribute, the Chinese did not continue their voyages of discovery. In 1644 Manchu invaders conquered China and set up the Qing dynasty. Internal peace and government-sponsored improvements brought prosperity and increased population. During the 1700s, government corruption and internal revolts weakened the dynasty. Meanwhile, the Chinese faced new threats from European explorations in their part of the world.

In the 1500s Japan's warrior classes came under the rule of a military leader known as a shogun. During this period, Portuguese traders reached Japan, and European Catholic missionaries made many converts among the Japanese. Fearing this foreign influence, Japan's military leaders closed Japan's borders to all except a few Dutch traders.

Visualizing History The Ottoman ruler Selim I, who was crowned in 1512, fought wars of expansion against the neighboring Persians and Egyptians. *What areas eventually made up the territory of the Ottoman Empire?*

From the 1400s to the 1800s, large areas of Southeast Asia came under European influence. The Thai kingdom (Siam) was the only Southeast Asian area to remain free of European control. Thai kings built a strong central government and employed reforms that preserved their country's independence.

Chapter 19
Royal Power and Conflict

During the 1500s and 1600s, European monarchs strengthened their thrones and created powerful central governments. Their efforts paved the way for the rise of modern nation-states in Europe.

In Spain, Philip II sought national unity by using the Spanish Inquisition to force Protestants, Jews, and Muslims to accept Catholicism. His religious policy sparked revolts, especially among the Protestant Dutch in the Spanish-ruled Netherlands.

Protestant England supported the Dutch and challenged Spanish sea power. After the defeat of the Spanish Armada by the English in 1588, Spain began to lose much of its power. During the 1600s, the Spanish monarchy and economy declined, although Spain still held on to its overseas empire.

English Tudor monarchs, such as Henry VIII and Elizabeth I, brought England peace and stability. They increased royal power while allowing Parliament and other non-royal institutions to flourish. As the English economy prospered, the first steps were taken toward building an overseas empire based on trade.

Elsewhere in Europe, wars of religion between Protestants and Catholics shaped political boundaries and brought much hardship to Europe's people. When the Hapsburg monarchs of Austria tried to advance Catholicism and curtail Protestant liberties, war erupted among central Europe's Protestant and Catholic rulers. Other European nations, including Catholic France and Protestant Sweden, entered this conflict known as the Thirty Years' War. The Peace of Westphalia finally ended the war in 1648. By this time, the concerns of Europe's rulers had shifted from enforcing religious uniformity to extending their own political powers.

From 1600 to 1789, European monarchs wielded great power. They believed in the theory of absolute monarchy, which held that kings and queens ruled as representatives of God and were responsible to God alone, not to parliaments or citizens. In France, monarchs such as Louis XVI created a strong royal government that became the model for other European royal houses. Louis also sought to expand French territory in a series of wars that cost France thousands of lives and much wealth. During the 1700s, major wars between France and Great Britain (formed by a union in 1707 between England and Scotland) spread overseas to Europe's colonies. By the 1760s, France had lost much of its overseas empire to Great Britain.

Meanwhile, Russia, once largely isolated from European affairs, began to take on an international role under the rule of Peter the Great. Peter rebuilt the Russian state, enhanced its military power, and increased contacts with western Europe. His reforms, however, created a large gap between the Europeanized upper classes and the traditionally Russian lower classes.

SURVEYING UNIT 4

1. **Chapter 16** How did the use of movable type in printing affect developments in Europe during the 1500s?
2. **Chapter 17** What effect did European expansion have on Europeans? On peoples living in Asia, Africa, and the Americas?
3. **Chapter 18** Would the world be different if China had continued its voyages of exploration? Explain.
4. **Chapter 19** How did Ottoman, Mogul, or Ming rulers in Asia compare with monarchs in Europe during the period from the 1500s to the 1700s?

Epilogue

1700–Present

The Modern Era

Epilogue 1

The Age of Revolution (pages 512-525)

By challenging the authority of both the church and the state, the ideas of the Scientific Revolution and the Enlightenment triggered an era of enormous social and political upheaval in Europe and America. The English, American, and French revolutions, with their emphasis on rights, liberty, and popular government, brought forth new political systems and dramatically changed the relationship between people and their rulers.

Assault on the Bastille, artist unknown

Epilogue 2

Industry and Nationalism (pages 526-539)

The practical application of the scientific ideas of the Age of Revolution launched the industrial revolution. As factories were built, people seeking jobs migrated to the cities. A new way of life emerged, with its own distinct social groups and politics. Industrial technology, combined with the political ideas of the Age of Revolution, culminated in the development of an intense nationalism among the peoples of Europe and America. This led to the Age of Imperialism, as the industrial nations used their power and technology to spread their influence throughout the world.

Beirmeister and Wain Steel Forge by P.S. Kroyer

Epilogue 3
World In Conflict (pages 540-553)

The Age of Imperialism triggered several cataclysmic wars and revolutions. World War I destroyed the German and Russian empires. The war was one of the primary reasons for the communist revolution in Russia, the rise of Nazism in Germany, and the increase in militarism in Japan. These events led to World War II, and to the emergence of the United States and Soviet Union as superpowers. The rise of the Soviet Union spread communist ideas around the world, and encouraged civil war in China and Southeast Asia. Both world wars also helped to develop Asian and African nationalism.

American Troops Arriving in Paris July 14, 1918 by J.F. Foucher

Epilogue 4
The Contemporary World (pages 554-567)

After World War II, the United States and the Soviet Union engaged in a cold war that ended with the Soviet Union's collapse in 1991. In Asia and Africa, the ideas of communism and nationalism led to a series of independence movements that ended Europe's empires. After World War II, technological development also accelerated. Developments in the aerospace industry, in medicine, in communications and in computer technology transformed the world and increased the interdependence of its many societies.

The space shuttle in orbit

Age of Revolution

Focus On...

- **Scientific Revolution**
- **English and American Revolutions**
- **The French Revolution**

Then & Now

The discoveries and writings of the Age of Revolution ignited a fuse of knowledge that exploded in a scientific revolution so complete and far-reaching that the years from 1500 to 1830 are often called "the beginning of the modern age."

Every time you have your temperature taken with a mercury thermometer, receive medication through a fine-needled syringe, let a doctor listen to your heartbeat through a stethoscope, or have your tooth drilled by a dentist, you are seeing instruments invented during the Age of Revolution. When you study a cell through a microscope or a star through a telescope, you are using equipment developed to fill the needs of sixteenth- and seventeenth-century scientists for precise, accurate scientific instruments. Even the simple multiplication symbol × was proposed during this age of scientific revolution.

A Global Chronology

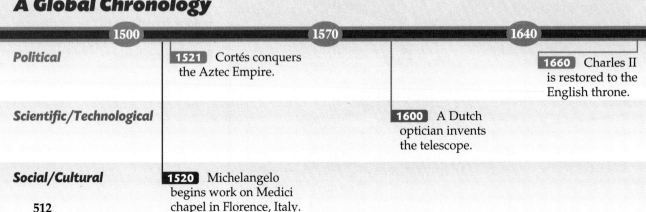

	1500	1570	1640
Political	**1521** Cortés conquers the Aztec Empire.		**1660** Charles II is restored to the English throne.
Scientific/Technological		**1600** A Dutch optician invents the telescope.	
Social/Cultural	**1520** Michelangelo begins work on Medici chapel in Florence, Italy.		

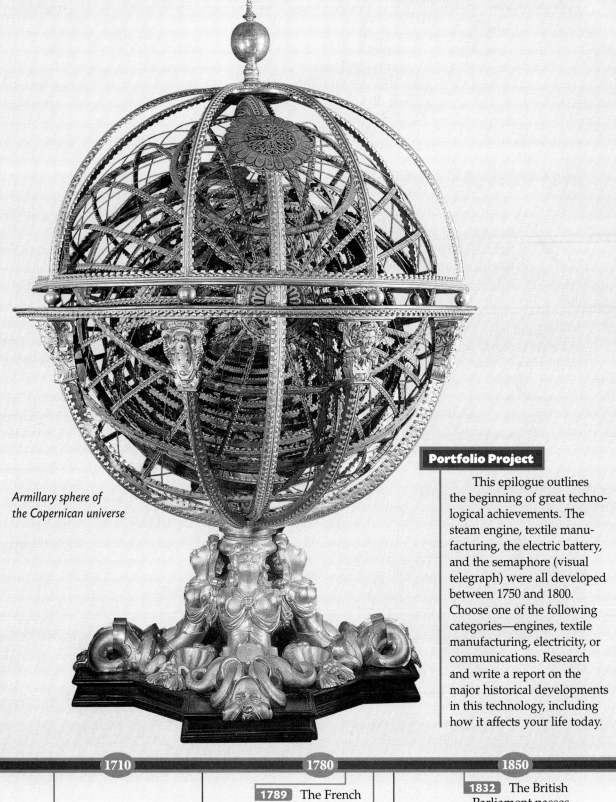

*Armillary sphere of
the Copernican universe*

Portfolio Project

This epilogue outlines the beginning of great technological achievements. The steam engine, textile manufacturing, the electric battery, and the semaphore (visual telegraph) were all developed between 1750 and 1800. Choose one of the following categories—engines, textile manufacturing, electricity, or communications. Research and write a report on the major historical developments in this technology, including how it affects your life today.

1710

1780

1850

1789 The French Revolution begins.

1832 The British Parliament passes the Reform Bill.

1687 Isaac Newton states the theory of gravity.

1799 Rosetta stone found in Egypt makes deciphering hieroglyphics possible.

1740 Frederick the Great introduces freedom of the press and of worship in Prussia.

1804 Ludwig van Beethoven composes his Third Symphony, the *Eroica*.

The Spread of Ideas

Revolution

In the 1600s and 1700s, revolution bounced back and forth across the Atlantic. The pattern started with the arrival of the first English colonists in North America. They carried with them ideals born of the English Revolution. They believed that governments existed to protect the rights and freedoms of citizens.

The United States
Revolutionary Ideas

In 1776 the colonists fought a revolution, making clear the principles of freedom and rights in the Declaration of Independence:

> *We hold these truths to be self-evident, that all men are created equal, that they are endowed by their Creator with certain unalienable rights, that among these are life, liberty, and the pursuit of happiness.*

These ideas bounced back across the Atlantic to influence the French Revolution. French rebels in 1789 fought in defense of *Liberté, Egalité, Fraternité* (Liberty, Equality, Fraternity). In drafting their declaration of freedom, French revolutionaries repeated the principles of the American Declaration of Independence: "Men are born and remain free and equal in rights."

Signing of the Declaration of Independence

Italy
The Age of Revolution

The spread of ideas—specifically, revolutionary ideas—forms the subject of Epilogue 1. The spark that sent the spirit of revolution flashing across Europe and the Americas began in the minds of six-teenth-century European scientists. These thinkers challenged established ideas defended by the Roman Catholic Church. Church officials tried to stop the spread of new scientific ideas. But once unleashed, the ideas respected neither authority nor geographic boundary. Defiance of one authority, in this case, the Church, soon led people to question other authorities as well. The result was the intellectual and political upheavals that historians call the Age of Revolution.

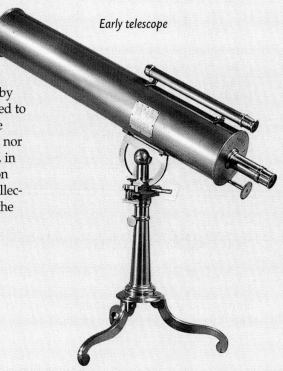

Early telescope

Haiti
Exporting Revolution

In 1791 the ideals of the American and French Revolutions traveled across the Caribbean and the Atlantic to the French-held island colony of Saint Domingue. Inspired by talk of freedom, enslaved Africans took up arms. Led by Toussaint-Louverture, they shook off French rule. In 1804 Saint Domingue, present-day Haiti, became the second nation in the Americas to achieve independence from colonial rule. "We have asserted our rights," declared the revolutionaries. "We swear never to yield them to any power on earth."

Toussaint-Louverture

LINKING THE IDEAS

1. What was the role of government according to the American colonists?
2. What ideals did the Americans and the French share?

Critical Thinking

3. **Cause and Effect** Why do you think revolutionary ideas respect neither authority nor geographic boundaries?

The Age of Revolution

From about 1600 to the early 1800s, people in the Western world lived through a time of revolution, or swift and far-reaching change. During this period, Western thinkers laid the foundation of modern science and developed new ideas about society and politics. The two most powerful ideas were democracy—the right of the people to take an active part in government—and nationalism—the right of people who share a common culture to have their own nation. In some areas, people influenced by the new ideas rebelled against monarchs in the hope of creating better societies.

Scientific Revolution

During the 1500s and 1600s, European thinkers began relying on their own reasoning rather than automatically accepting traditional beliefs. In their investigation of nature, they gradually developed the scientific method. They also developed new instruments, such as the telescope and microscope, to help them in their work. Over time, one discovery or invention led to others, creating an explosion of knowledge known as the Scientific Revolution.

The advance of science transformed the European understanding of the natural world. The work of scientists such as Galileo and Isaac Newton enabled Europeans to view the universe as a huge, orderly machine that worked according to definite laws that could be stated mathematically.

Triumph of Reason

Impressed by scientific findings in the natural world, many European thinkers came to believe that reason could also discover the natural laws governing human behavior. They claimed that once these laws were known, people could use the laws to guide their lives and to improve society. England was an early leader in this effort. There, philosophers such as Thomas Hobbes and John Locke applied scientific reasoning to the study of government. Locke's basic conclusions—that government's authority rested on the people, and that the people had the right to overthrow an unjust government—later were important in the development of democracy in Europe and North America.

During the 1700s Europeans boasted that they had entered an Age of Enlightenment, when the light of reason would free all people from the darkness of ignorance and superstition. They looked to France as the leading center of Enlightenment thought. Through the printed word and at public gatherings, French thinkers called philosophes claimed that science and reason could be used to promote progress in all areas of human life.

REVIEW

1. **Identifying Trends** How did the European view of the natural world change from the 1500s to the early 1800s?
2. **Analyzing Changes** Why did European political thinkers during the Enlightenment stress the importance of natural laws?

Visualizing History The Copernican model of the universe placed the sun at the center. Ptolemy's second-century model had the sun and the planets revolving around Earth. *The work of what two scientists enabled Europeans to view the universe as a huge, orderly machine?*

English and American Revolutions

While Europe experienced a revolution in science and ideas, its monarchs faced mounting opposition to their methods of rule. The first successful challenge to the power of monarchy came in England. There, during the early 1600s, a bitter quarrel divided the Stuart kings—James I and Charles I—and Parliament.

Monarch and Parliament

The monarchs were determined to impose their absolute rule on the country, while Parliament, under the control of Puritan landowners, wanted to bind royal authority to its will.

During the 1640s, a violent civil war was fought between the supporters of the monarchy and the supporters of Parliament. The conflict finally ended in 1640 with the monarchy's defeat and Charles I's execution—events that shocked the rest of Europe. A republic was then proclaimed under the leading parliamentary general, Oliver Cromwell. Although Cromwell brought reforms and efficient government, most English people grew to resent his strict Puritan rule. Cromwell's death in 1658 was followed two years later by the restoration of the monarchy under Charles II, the son of Charles I.

During Charles II's reign, the monarch and Parliament shared political power in an often uneasy relationship. When Charles died in 1685, his brother, James II, ascended the throne. James, a Roman Catholic, angered the English with his desire to restore Catholicism and absolute monarchy. In 1688 Protestant nobles in Parliament invited Mary, James's Protestant daughter, and William of Orange, her husband and ruler of the Netherlands, to invade England with Dutch troops.

In return for the English throne, William and Mary agreed to accept a Bill of Rights. This document assured the English people basic civil rights and made the monarch subject to the laws of Parliament. During the next 100 years, England developed into a constitutional monarchy. Under this political system, the monarch's powers were

Visualizing History **Mocking King George III,** *Horse Throwing His Master* **represented American colonists in revolt against the British monarchy.** *How did colonial economic interests help to ignite the American Revolution?*

gradually reduced, and Parliament became the major power in the government of England.

The American Republic

By the mid-1700s, Great Britain was trying to tighten its control over its recently acquired overseas empire, especially North America. Enjoying a large measure of self-government, the North American colonies opposed Parliament's efforts to enforce trade laws and impose taxes on them. They began to press for even more freedom from the home country.

History & Art *The Spirit of '76 by* Archibald Willard. Abbot Hall, Marblehead, Massachusetts
Revolution was romanticized in the art of the 1800s. *Why did the American colonies rebel?*

During the 1700s, relations between Great Britain and the North American colonies steadily worsened. The arrival of British troops in North America to put down colonial protests signaled the beginning of what became known as the Revolutionary War. In 1776, 13 of the colonies declared their freedom from British rule and became a new nation—the United States of America. Five years later, the American victory at Yorktown ended the war, and the British officially recognized the independence of their former colonies. From the 1700s to the present century, the success of the American Revolution has inspired colonial peoples struggling to escape from the hold of empires.

Following the Revolutionary War, the United States briefly functioned as a loose union of states with republican governments. In 1788 the nation ratified the United States Constitution. With its blend of European Enlightenment philosophy and American democratic ideals, the United States Constitution served as a model for people in other countries who wanted republican governments.

problems. When the monarch refused to reform voting methods, Third Estate delegates took the revolutionary step of meeting separately as the National Assembly. As the government of France from 1789 to 1791, the National Assembly ended the privileges of nobles and clergy, guaranteed basic human rights for all citizens, and established a constitutional monarchy. Louis XVI, however, was not content to rule under a constitution. He plotted with nobles and foreign monarchs to regain his absolute authority. In the summer of 1792, Austria and Prussia responded to Louis's appeals for help and invaded France. In response, angry revolutionaries in Paris arrested the king and called for a democratic government.

After the king's removal, a National Convention elected by all adult males proclaimed France a democratic republic and executed the king. The Convention then drafted a large army to push back the foreign invaders and to spread the revolution throughout Europe. To crush opposition at home, the leaders of the Convention put aside democratic practices and carried out a Reign of Terror, executing thousands of people. The Terror ended in 1794, and the wealthy middle

---

REVIEW

1. **Relating Ideas** How was Enlightenment thought reflected in the political events and the political changes that took place in North America during the 1700s?
2. **Analyzing Events** Why was William and Mary's acceptance of the Bill of Rights an important event in English history?

The French Revolution

The formation of the American republic had a profound impact on the French, who were becoming increasingly critical of their absolute monarchy. Under this system, France's few nobles and clergy—the First and Second Estates—enjoyed power and privilege, while the majority of the people—the Third Estate—paid most of the taxes and had almost no voice in running the nation's government. During the late 1780s, an explosive combination of social injustice, economic distress, and Enlightenment ideas led to the outbreak of the French Revolution.

The revolution began in 1789 when King Louis XVI called a meeting of the Estates-General to solve the government's deepening financial

Visualizing History Dr. Guillotin's invention of the guillotine, an instrument to make execution more humane, became a symbol of the terror and bloodshed of the revolution. *How did the radicals bring about King Louis XVI's execution?*

Battle at Eylau by Antoine Jean Gros **Severe November weather froze the French troops as they retreated from Moscow.** *What two factors brought about the downfall of Napoleon's empire?*

class came to power a year later under a new republican government called the Directory. Plagued by scandal and opposed by both conservatives and radicals, the Directory was overthrown by Napoleon Bonaparte in 1799.

Napoleon and Europe

Although Napoleon professed loyalty to the revolutionary ideals, he made himself emperor and imposed strict rule on France. He reformed French law by creating the Napoleonic Code. Although it placed the state above the individual, the new code preserved some revolutionary principles, such as the equality of all men before the law. The code did, however, curtail the rights of women and placed limits on freedom of speech. Napoleon also acknowledged the dominant role of Catholicism in French society but affirmed religious toleration for all.

With a powerful army, Napoleon deposed many foreign monarchs and brought a large part of the European continent under French rule. However, by 1814, Napoleon's empire was falling apart as a result of the combined military might of France's enemies and the growth of anti-French nationalism in the conquered lands.

After Napoleon's defeat, European leaders met in 1814 and 1815 at the Congress of Vienna to determine Europe's future. Opposed to democracy and nationalism, they sought to return to the political and social system that had existed before 1789. They restored monarchs ousted by Napoleon to their thrones and adjusted political boundaries so that France would no longer be able to dominate Europe. Although France never again ruled a European empire, the Congress failed in its efforts to restore absolute monarchy. Democracy and nationalism became powerful forces in the years after the Congress of Vienna and swept aside Europe's traditional social and political order.

REVIEW

1. **Understanding Cause and Effect** What two major factors led to the fall of Napoleon's empire?
2. **Making Comparisons** Compare the political revolutions in England, North America, and France. Which revolution was the most conservative? Which was the most radical? Explain your answers.

Turning Points in World History

The Scientific Revolution

Setting up the Video

Work with a group of your classmates to view "The Scientific Revolution" on the videodisc *Turning Points in World History*. The scientific revolution played a large role in shaping the world as we know it today. The seventeenth century changed dramatically from a reliance on faith and mysticism to include scientific thinking that led to many new inventions. This program examines the scientific revolution and its effects on civilization.

Hands-On Activity

Collect the following items for an invention you will create: two plastic spoons, one rubber band, two paper clips, a sheet of paper measuring 8x11, and a roll of scotch tape. Use all of the items to invent a gadget for practical use. Demonstrate your invention to the class.

Side One, Chapter 10

View the video by scanning the bar code or by entering the chapter number on your keypad and pressing Search. (Also available in VHS format.)

Surfing the "Net"

Napoleonic Code

One of Napoleon's greatest gifts to France was his contribution to French civil law. In the Napoleonic Code, he changed old feudal laws to laws that were consistent and included some revolutionary reforms. The Napoleonic Code was a compromise between the ideas of the French Revolution and older ideas. It gave new freedoms to the people, for example, but maintained the system of inheritance. To learn about the Napoleonic Code look on the Internet.

Getting There

Follow these steps to gather information about the Napoleonic Code.
1. Go to a search engine. Type in the phrase *napoleonic code*.

2. After typing in the phrase, enter words such as the following to focus your search:
   • *principles*   • *government*   • *law*
3. The search engine should provide you with a number of links to follow. Links are "pointers" to different sites on the Internet and commonly appear as blue underlined words.

What to Do When You Are There

Click on the links to navigate through the pages of information and gather your findings. Using a word processor, create a chart comparing the American Bill of Rights to the Napoleonic Code. Share your findings with the class.

Developing Multimedia Presentations

You have been assigned a research report to present to your class. You want to really hold the attention of your classmates. How can you do this? One way is to use a variety of media.

Learning the Skill

At its most basic, a multimedia presentation involves using several types of media. To discuss the Age of Enlightenment, for example, you might show photographs or slides of the art, play and listen to recordings of the music or literature, or present a video of a play written during this time period.

You can also develop a multimedia presentation on a computer. Multimedia as it relates to computer technology is the combination of text, video, audio, and animation in an interactive program.

In order to create multimedia productions or presentations on a computer, you need to have certain tools. These may include traditional computer graphic tools and draw programs, animation programs that make still images move, and authoring systems that tie everything together. Your computer manual will tell you which tools your computer can support.

Practicing the Skill

Epilogue 1 focuses on the Age of Revolution from 1500 to 1830. Ask yourself questions such as the following to develop a multimedia presentation on the politics of that era:

• Which forms of media do I want to include? Video? Sound? Animation? Photographs? Graphics? Other?

• Which of these media forms does my computer support?

• What kind of software programs or systems do I need? A paint program? A draw program? An animation program? A program to create interactive, or two-way, communication? An authoring system that will allow me to change images, sound, and motion?

• Is there a "do-it-all " program I can use to develop the kind of presentation I want?

Applying the Skill

Keeping in mind the four guidelines given above, write a plan describing a multimedia presentation you would like to develop. Indicate what tools you will need and what steps you must take to make the presentation an exciting reality.

from

Les
Misérables

by Victor Hugo

*As we have seen, litera-
ture can be a bridge to
the past, transporting
us to a world that may seem strange or
obscure at first, but that has much in
common with our own. Across the gap
between then and now we can see faces
that we recognize, situations that are
familiar, hopes that we share. The selection that follows was written by one of
France's most celebrated writers, Victor
Hugo. Hugo lived from 1802 to 1885, a
time of dramatic and violent change for
France. In this scene, Monsieur
Gillenormand snoops through the
belongings of his grandson, Marius.
Assisting the grandfather is Marius's
aunt. Marius's father has recently died.*

M. Gillenormand, who had risen early
like all the elderly who are in good
health, had heard [Marius] come in, and hurried
as fast as he could with his old legs, to climb to
the top of the stairs where Marius's room was,
to give him a kiss, question him while embracing him, and find out something about where
he had come from.

But the youth had taken less time to go
down than the old man to go up, and when
Grandfather Gillenormand went into the garret
room, Marius was no longer there.

The bed had not been disturbed, and on it
were trustingly laid the coat and the black
ribbon.

"I like that better," said M. Gillenormand.

And a moment later he entered the drawing
room [room for receiving guests] where Mlle.
Gillenormand the elder was already seated,
embroidering her carriage wheels.

The entrance was triumphant.

In one hand M. Gillenormand held the coat
and in the other the neck ribbon, and cried out,
"Victory! We are about to penetrate the mystery!
We shall know the end of the mystery, unravel
the wanton ways of our rascal! Here we are
right to the core of the romance. I have the portrait!"

In fact, a black shagreen box, rather like a
medallion, was fastened to the ribbon.

The old man took this box and looked at it
for some time without opening it, with that air
of desire, delight, and anger, with which a poor,

hungry devil sees an excellent dinner pass right under his nose, when it is not for him.

"For it is clearly a portrait. I know all about these things. They are worn tenderly against the heart. What fools they are! Some abominable floozy, probably enough to bring on the shudders! Young people have such bad taste nowadays!"

"Let's see, father," said the old maid.

The box opened by pressing a spring. They found nothing in it but a piece of paper carefully folded.

"More and more predictable," said M. Gillenormand, bursting with laughter. "I know what that is. A love letter!"

"Ah! Then let's read it!" said the aunt.

And she put on her spectacles. They unfolded the paper and read this:

"*For my Son.*—The emperor made me a baron on the battlefield of Waterloo. Since the Restoration contests this title I have bought with my blood, my son will take it and bear it. I need not say that he will be worthy of it."

The feelings of the father and daughter are beyond description. They felt chilled as by the breath of a death's head [skull]. They did not exchange a word. M. Gillenormand, however, said in a low voice, and as if talking to himself, "It is the handwriting of that bandit."

The aunt examined the paper, turned it over every which way, then put it back in the box.

At that very moment, a little rectangular package wrapped in blue paper fell out of the coat pocket. Mademoiselle Gillenormand picked it up and unwrapped the blue paper. It was Marius's hundred

[calling] cards. She passed one of them to M. Gillenormand, who read: *Baron Marius Pontmercy.*

The old man rang. Nicolette [the chambermaid] came. M. Gillenormand took the ribbon, the box, and the coat, threw them all on the floor in the middle of the drawing room, and said:

"Take those things away."

A full hour passed in complete silence. The old man and the old maid sat with their backs turned to one another, and were probably each individually thinking over the same things. At the end of that hour, Aunt Gillenormand said, "Pretty!"

A few minutes later, Marius appeared. He was just coming home. Even before crossing the

Visualizing History **A French salon displays the wealth of the bourgeoisie. With the end of the revolution, the return of social class distinctions accompanied the restoration of the monarchy.** *Why was Monsieur Gillenormand angry about Marius's calling cards?*

A republican club meets in Paris in 1848. Victor Hugo's concern for the common people underlies much of his writing. Social commentary and support for democratic movements mark his works in the 1850s and 1860s. *How does the character of Monsieur Gillenormand portray aristocracy?*

threshold of the drawing room, he saw his grandfather holding one of his cards in his hand; the old man, on seeing him, exclaimed with his crushing air of sneering bourgeois superiority, "Well! Well! Well! Well! Well! So you are a baron now. My compliments. What does this mean?"

Marius blushed slightly, and answered, "It means I am my father's son."

M. Gillenormand stopped laughing, and said harshly, "Your father; I am your father."

"My father," resumed Marius with downcast eyes and stern manner, "was a humble and heroic man, who served the Republic and France gloriously, who was great in the greatest history that men have ever made, who lived a quarter of a century in the camps, under fire by day, and by night in the snow, in the mud, and the rain, who captured colors [flags], who was twenty times wounded, who died forgotten and abandoned, and who had but one fault; that was to have too dearly loved two ingrates [ungrateful persons], his country and me."

This was more than M. Gillenormand could bear. At the word, "Republic," he rose, or rather, sprang to his feet. Every one of the words

Marius had just spoken, produced on the old royalist's face the effect of a blast from a bellows on a burning coal. From dark he had turned red, from red to purple, and from purple to flaming.

"Marius!" he exclaimed, "abominable child! I don't know what your father was! I don't want to know! I know nothing about him and I don't know him! But what I do know is that there was never anything but miserable wretches among them! That they were all beggars, assassins, thieves, rabble in their red bonnets! I say all of them! I say all of them! I don't know anybody! I say all of them! Do you hear, Marius? Look here, you are as much a baron as my slipper! They were all bandits, those who served Robespierre! All brigands who served Bu-o-na-parté! All traitors who betrayed, betrayed, betrayed! Their legitimate king! All cowards who ran from the Prussians and English at Waterloo! That's what I know. If your father is among them I don't know him, I'm sorry, so much the worse. Your humble servant, sir!"

In turn, it was Marius who now became the coal, and M. Gillenormand the bellows. Marius shuddered in every limb, he had no idea what to do, his head was burning. He was the priest who sees all his wafers thrown to the winds, the fakir [member of a Muslim religious order] seeing a passerby spit on his idol. He could not allow such things to be said before him. But what could he do? His father had just been trodden underfoot and stamped on in his presence, but by whom? By his grandfather. How could he avenge the one without outraging the other? It was impossible for him to insult his grandfather, and it was equally impossible for him not to avenge his father. On one hand a sacred tomb, on the other a white head. For a few moments he felt dizzy and staggering with all this whirlwind in his head; then he raised his eyes, looked straight at his grandfather, and cried in a thundering voice: "Down with the Bourbons, and that great hog Louis XVIII!"

Louis XVIII had been dead for four years; but that made no difference to him.

Scarlet as he was, the old man suddenly turned whiter than his hair. He turned toward a bust of the Duc de Berry that stood on the mantel and bowed to it profoundly with a sort of peculiar majesty. Then he walked twice, slowly and in silence, from the fireplace to the window and from the window to the fireplace, covering the whole length of the room and making the parquet creak as if an image of stone were walking over it. The second time, he bent toward his daughter, who was enduring the shock with the stupor of an aged sheep, and said to her with a smile that was almost calm, "A baron like Monsieur and a bourgeois like myself cannot remain under the same roof."

And all at once straightening up, pallid, trembling, terrible, his forehead swelling with the fearful radiance of anger, he stretched his arm towards Marius and cried out, "Be off!"

Marius left the house.

The next day, M. Gillenormand said to his daughter, "You will send sixty pistoles [old gold coins] every six months to that blood drinker, and never speak of him to me again."

RESPONDING TO LITERATURE

1. What political conflict of the period does the heated clash between Marius and his grandfather represent?
2. What sort of person is Monsieur Gillenormand?
3. If Marius's father had not been a hero at the Battle of Waterloo, do you think Marius still would have become a revolutionary? Explain your answer.
4. **Supporting an Opinion** Was the era of the French Revolution and Napoleon "the greatest history that men have ever made," as Marius claims? Support your answer with evidence.

Industry and Nationalism

Focus On...

- Age of Industry
- Cultural Revolution
- Democracy and Reform
- Reaction and Nationalism
- The Age of Imperialism

Then & Now

For centuries wealthy landowners in Europe controlled a static agricultural economy. Peasant families farmed strips of land, and small industries and trades met local needs. Then, in England in the late 1700s, innovations in farming made agriculture a profitable business. An agricultural revolution helped start a revolution in industry, beginning in textiles. The factory system expanded the power and wealth of the middle class. While scientific and medical advances improved life for many, in much of Europe the poor remained powerless.

How long would it take you to walk to school? The railroad began the revolution in transportation. When a German engineer redesigned the internal combustion engine to run on gasoline, the automobile took center stage. Within a few decades the automobile would transform society in every industrial country.

A Global Chronology

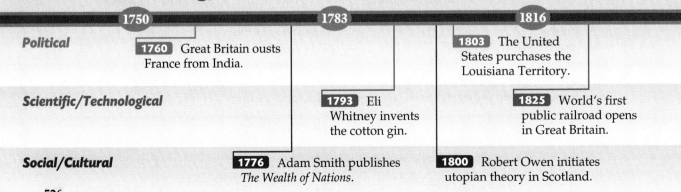

1750   **1783**   **1816**

Political

1760 Great Britain ousts France from India.

1803 The United States purchases the Louisiana Territory.

Scientific/Technological

1793 Eli Whitney invents the cotton gin.

1825 World's first public railroad opens in Great Britain.

Social/Cultural

1776 Adam Smith publishes *The Wealth of Nations.*

1800 Robert Owen initiates utopian theory in Scotland.

Steam locomotive and wood car

Graphs can show the dramatic changes caused by the Industrial Revolution. Create several graphs that illustrate these changes from the early 1800s to the 1900s. Subjects of your graphs for any industrializing nation or group of nations may include: population growth; spread of railroads; and production of goods such as cotton, steel, coal, and oil. Libraries and the Internet have good historical references for these statistics. After completing the graphs, write a list of questions that can be answered from the data shown in each graph.

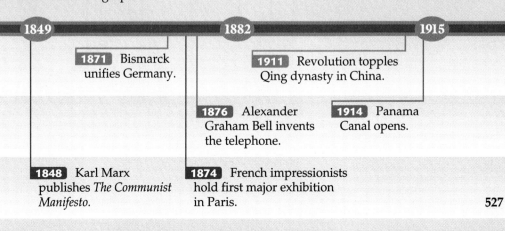

1849 **1882** **1915**

1871 Bismarck unifies Germany.

1911 Revolution topples Qing dynasty in China.

1876 Alexander Graham Bell invents the telephone.

1914 Panama Canal opens.

1848 Karl Marx publishes *The Communist Manifesto*.

1874 French impressionists hold first major exhibition in Paris.

The Spread of Ideas

Industrialization

*T*he rise of industry changed the world forever. So dramatic were the changes that historians have labeled the period the Industrial Revolution. Although the revolution began in Britain, it respected neither time nor place. The revolution traveled beyond Britain to touch every nation on earth.

Great Britain
Workshop of the World

The birth of industry needed certain preconditions: the science, incentive, and money capital to build machines; a labor force to run them; raw materials and markets to make the system profitable; and efficient farms to feed a new group of workers. At the start of the 1700s, Great Britain possessed all these conditions. Here industrialism first took root.

As with the development of agriculture, no one person can be credited with the invention of industry. Instead, it grew from the innovations of individuals who developed machines to do work formerly done by humans and animals. One inventor built on the ideas of another. In 1705, for example, Thomas Newcomen devised a crude steam engine to pump water out of coal mines. In 1769 James Watt improved upon Newcomen's work and built a more efficient steam engine. Other inventors adapted Watt's engine to run cloth-making machines. Business owners soon brought machines and workers together in a single place called a factory.

By the 1800s, industry had catapulted Great Britain into a position of world leadership. "[Britain has] triumphantly established herself as the workshop of the world," boasted one leader. It was impossible to monopolize this idea. Workshops began to hum in America.

James Watt

Watt's steam engine

The United States
The Revolution Spreads

Great Britain tried to keep the secrets of industry locked up. It forbade the export of industrial machines. It also barred the people who built and operated the machines from leaving the country. In 1787, however, a young factory supervisor named Samuel Slater found a way to escape. He disguised himself as a farm-hand and boarded a ship for New York.

Working entirely from memory, Slater built a mill in Pawtucket, Rhode Island. On December 20, 1790, the mill turned out the first machine-made cotton yarn produced in America.

Within two years, Slater had sales offices in Salem, New York City, Baltimore, and Philadelphia. As Slater's mills turned out cotton, the United States began churning out its own brilliant industrial inventors. They produced more than just machines. They came up with new industrial principles such as Eli Whitney's use of standardized parts and Henry Ford's use of the assembly line. Together these two ideas gave the world mass production—a concept that would revolutionize people's lives around the globe.

Samuel Slater's mill

Japan
The Search for Markets

In 1853, the Industrial Revolution traveled to Japan in the form of a fleet of United States steamships sent to open the island to trade. "What we had taken as a fire at sea," recalled one Japanese observer, "was really smoke coming out of their smokestacks."

The military power produced by United States industry shook the Japanese. Recalled the same observer, "What a joke, the steaming teapot fixed by America—Just four cups [ships], and we cannot sleep at night."

The Japanese temporarily gave in to American demands. But they also vowed that they too would possess industry. By the start of the 1900s, Japan had joined other industrial nations in the search for markets. By 1914 Japan's merchant fleet was the sixth largest in the world and their foreign trade had increased one hundred-fold in value in fifty years.

Matthew Perry's steamboat in Tokyo Bay

LINKING THE IDEAS

1. How was the idea for a cotton mill brought from Great Britain to the United States?
2. What feature of the American fleet most impressed the Japanese in 1853?

Critical Thinking

3. **Drawing Conclusions** Why did the British want to control the spread of an idea that made production of goods easier?

Industry and Nationalism

In the 1800s a new and vigorous spirit of change and progress enveloped the world. Great Britain led the way in the late 1700s, as inventors and industrialists helped to transform primarily rural, agricultural economies into industrial economies based on cites, factories, and manufactured goods. This swift advance of industry throughout western Europe and North America was accompanied by discoveries in science and medicine, as well as changing cultural and political attitudes. In many countries people were inspired to fight for political reform. At the same time, increasingly industrialized nations competed to establish themselves as world powers.

History & Art *The Gas Factory at Courcelles* by Ernest Jean Delahae. Musée du Petit Palais, Paris, France *How did increasing industrialization affect the social order?*

Age of Industry

Before the 1700s, long-established traditions ruled daily living in Europe, and change was slow. Most people lived in rural villages and farmed small tracts of land. They were generally self-sufficient farmers who grew the food or made the things their families needed.

Agricultural Improvements

In the late 1700s, however, great changes began to occur. Wealthy landowners took control of land that for centuries had been open to all villagers, forcing many small farmers to move to the cities to find work.

As landowners gained control of greater tracts of land, they worked to get the highest possible crop yield and devised such techniques as crop rotation and fertilization. The increased food supply enabled people to live healthier, longer lives. As a result, Europe's population grew dramatically.

The Industrial Revolution

A growing population looking for work in cities, coupled with abundant natural resources such as coal, iron, and water power, helped to ignite the Industrial Revolution in Great Britain, which eventually spread throughout the world. Power-driven machinery took the place of handwork done in the home. As industry came to dominate economies, inventors developed technology for industrialists to increase and speed production.

Expanding and increasingly complex industries led to a changing social order in the mid-1800s. As factory owners and managers prospered, a sizable middle class grew. Many workers, however, endured crowded and unsanitary living quarters and poor working conditions. In the late 1800s some workers joined to form labor unions in the hope of improving their lives.

REVIEW

1. **Identifying Trends** How did the Industrial Revolution transform European society in the 1800s?
2. **Relating Ideas** What social groups emerged as industry developed in Europe and North America?

Cultural Revolution

The Industrial Revolution brought about many changes in the social and cultural life of the West. In their daily lives, Western Europeans and North Americans were forced to grapple with the challenges posed by the new industrial society.

New Ideas

Economists such as Adam Smith and David Ricardo pointed out the basic principles of capitalism and held that businesses should operate without governmental interference. Other thinkers, including British philosophers Jeremy Bentham and John Stuart Mill, favored capitalism but called for government supervision and reforms to provide social justice. Still others, such as the German philosopher Karl Marx, opposed capitalism and supported socialism, believing that workers either by themselves or through the government should control industry.

Scientific Advances

The Age of Industry also saw many exciting scientific advances. In the 1850s British naturalist Charles Darwin proposed a theory of evolution to explain the origins of life. About the same time, medical pioneers such as Louis Pasteur used new scientific knowledge to conquer diseases such as smallpox and rabies that had plagued humankind for thousands of years.

Medical discoveries meant a better quality of life. Meanwhile, improved means of transportation enabled people to venture from their native lands to seek new opportunities in other parts of the world. Increased interest in education led to the spread of literacy as public schools and libraries were established throughout Europe and the United States.

The Arts

The rapid pace of social changes in Europe and North America was reflected in the arts. Painters and writers expressed a diversity of approaches. Romantics reacted to industrialization by glorifying nature, the emotional, the spiritual, and the ideal. Realists rejected the idealism of the romantics and vividly portrayed the lives of ordinary people and the problems of urban industrial life that they wanted to change. Impressionists and their artistic successors abandoned the rules governing traditional art and focused on colors, light, and the structure of objects.

REVIEW

1. **Making Comparisons** How did Adam Smith and Karl Marx differ in their views about the way economic affairs should be handled?
2. **Relating Ideas** What impact did industrial and scientific advances have on the daily lives of people?

Democracy and Reform

Economic and social transformation inspired the growth of democracy in various parts of the world. In some places, the political changes were gradual and peaceful; in other places, they were sudden and violent.

Great Britain

Great Britain was the world's strongest economic and imperial power during most of the 1800s. The British government moved slowly toward democracy as more people gained voting rights and election districts were redistributed to give equal representation. Electoral reform in Great Britain brought about the rise of political parties that represented certain well-defined beliefs.

While democracy evolved in Great Britain, the working class, women, and Irish Catholics often used pressure to speed up the reform process. Meanwhile, overseas colonies, such as Canada, Australia, and New Zealand, benefited from the era of reform and achieved self-rule within the British Empire.

France

In France, political changes did not come so easily. The 1800s was a century of turmoil, as the French government changed in form from monarchy to republic to empire to republic.

The Second Republic of France, created by a revolution in 1848, served as a stepping-stone from which Louis-Napoleon launched the Second Empire of France. The most striking achievement of the Second Empire was economic growth. The Second Empire collapsed as a result of French defeat in a war with Prussia. The Third Republic of France, created in 1875, lacked stability, but managed to survive several crises that threatened its collapse. The most enduring achievements of the Third Republic were its safeguards of civil liberties and educational reforms.

The United States

As the countries of Europe struggled with demands for reform, the United States in the early 1800s more than doubled in size. As new states entered the Union, the slavery issue began to divide public opinion. The South favored the protection and expansion of slavery, while the North argued for either limiting slavery to the South or abolishing it altogether.

The slavery debate drew the country into a bloody civil war in 1861. President Abraham Lincoln led the United States through this bitter conflict as he strove to save the Union. After the Civil War, the United States, once more reunited, began to develop into a strong industrial nation.

Latin America

Farther south, the Enlightenment ideas of freedom and equality influenced the peoples of Latin America. Beginning in the late 1700s, Latin American colonists began to fight for independence from Spanish or Portuguese rule. Dedicated leaders such as Simón Bolívar and José de San Martín helped Latin Americans achieve this goal by the mid-1820s.

The newly independent Latin American countries, however, lacked experience in self-government, and military dictators frequently came to power during the 1800s. Economic advancement was hampered by the huge social gap that divided wealthy landowners from impoverished farmers.

REVIEW

1. **Making Comparisons** How did Great Britain differ from France in the advance toward democracy?
2. **Relating Ideas** What ideas had an impact in promoting the cause of independence in Latin America?

Reaction and Nationalism

The desire for national independence, known as nationalism, became one of the most powerful forces in Europe during the 1800s. In some areas people struggled to unify small, individual states into one nation. In others people fought to break free from large empires.

Italy

Following the Congress of Vienna in 1815, a movement for Italian unity grew and spread across Italy. To achieve political unification, the Italians had to expel Austria from the Italian Peninsula and overcome the opposition of the pope. Giuseppe Mazzini, Giuseppe Garibaldi, and Count Camillo di Cavour were key figures in generating interest in the cause of unity and gained the military support needed to expel Austria and unite southern Italy with the rest of the peninsula. In 1861 Italy became a constitutional monarchy under the leadership of Sardinia.

Germany

A similar quest for political unification took place in the much larger area of central Europe known as Germany. The main figure in German political unification was Otto von Bismarck, the prime minister of Prussia. In the early 1860s Bismarck directed the development of a strong Prussian army. Prussia's military victories helped to win the support of Germans for the cause of unity.

In 1871 Germany finally became one nation under William I of Prussia, who served as kaiser, or emperor. Bismarck, however, discouraged the growth of democracy and tried in vain to destroy the Catholic and Socialist political parties. Conflict between Bismarck and the new kaiser, William II, led to Bismarck's resignation in 1890.

The Russian Empire

Russian czars generally resisted the forces of nationalism, democracy, and social change that were affecting the Russian Empire. As these forces transformed Europe during the 1800s, Russia's rulers strove to keep their absolute powers.

After 25 years of repressive rule by Nicholas I, Alexander II undertook major reforms, including the emancipation of serfs in 1861. For many liberals these reforms did not go far enough. When radicals assassinated Alexander II in 1881, political repression returned in full force under Alexander III, but revolutionary groups continued to grow.

Preservation of the old order was the objective of Alexander III's successor, Nicholas II. The urban working class, in spite of its small size, became a major political force during Nicholas' reign. Strikes and protests following Russia's defeat in the Russo-Japanese War forced limited political concessions from the czar.

Austria-Hungary

The Austrian Empire also tried to maintain its old order. As the empire's diverse nationalities rallied for independence and reform in 1848, Emperor Francis Joseph was able to retain power only by playing one national group against another. In 1867, after Austria's defeat in the Seven Weeks' War, Francis was forced to accept the dual monarchy that gave Hungary equal standing with Austria in the empire. Meanwhile, the Slavic peoples of the empire continued to push for greater political rights.

REVIEW

1. **Making Comparisons** How did the influence of nationalism on Italy in the mid-1800s differ from its influence on Austria-Hungary during the same period?
2. **Identifying Trends** How did Russian czars of the 1800s and early 1900s respond to the forces of change that were affecting their empire?

The Age of Imperialism

Three key factors led to the rise of imperialism in the 1800s. First, European nationalism prompted rival countries to engage in competition for overseas territory. Second, the Industrial Revolution created a great demand for more raw materials and new markets. Finally, feelings of cultural and racial superiority also influenced Europeans to impose their cultures on distant lands.

Imperialism in Africa and Asia

Africa was especially affected by the European zeal to found new colonies. Beginning around 1870, the major European powers divided the continent among themselves, established colonies, and exploited the continent's natural resources. By 1914 only two African nations—Liberia and Ethiopia—had managed to escape European control.

In India, the British East India Company established a strong hold over the subcontinent and its abundant resources in the 1700s. Following the Sepoy Rebellion in 1857, the British government took direct control of India's affairs. To quell further unrest in India, the British spent vast amounts of money on the country's economic development. Most Indians, however, still resented British rule. In 1885 the Indian National Congress was formed, signaling the start of the long struggle for independence.

Also during the 1800s, the major European powers began to intervene in the internal affairs of China. Using military power or the threat of it, they forced China to accept trade agreements that favored Western interests. These agreements allowed the Europeans to carve out economically valuable spheres of influence in China. When the Chinese fought back in the Boxer Rebellion of 1900, the Europeans quickly crushed the revolt. Eleven years later, Chinese revolutionaries overthrew the corrupt Qing dynasty and established a republic.

The United States forced Japanese leaders to open their doors to trade when it sent Commodore Matthew C. Perry to Japan in 1853. As a result, the Meiji leaders who took control of Japan in the late 1860s decided to make Japan a great power capable of competing with the West. They reformed Japan's government and began a program to modernize and industrialize the nation. Partly as a result of this program, Japan defeated Russia in 1905 in the Russo-Japanese War. By 1914 Japan had emerged as a modern industrial nation and world power.

The United States and Latin America

Like the European powers, the United States in the late 1800s wanted to exercise influence on world affairs. During these decades the United States used the Monroe Doctrine to oppose European involvement in Latin America. At the same time, the United States government and American businesses were becoming increasingly involved in the affairs of Latin American nations. This trend increased following the Spanish-American War and construction of the Panama Canal. Tension between Latin American nations and the United States grew as a result of the United States government's repeated interventions in the region during the first two decades of the 1900s.

Meanwhile, United States intervention was accompanied by an upsurge of nationalism in Latin America. A revolution swept Mexico from 1910 to about 1920. During this upheaval, the dictatorship of Porfirio Díaz was overthrown, and various rebel leaders competed for power. The final outcome of the struggle was a new constitution and social reforms.

Visualizing History The Boxers in China launched a series of attacks against foreigners in 1900. *What were "spheres of influence"?*

REVIEW

1. **Identifying Trends** What factors led to the growth of imperialism as a significant force in the world during the 1800s?
2. **Making Comparisons** How was the influence of imperialism in India different from the influence of imperialism in China?

ABCNEWS INTERACTIVE™ Turning Points in World History

The Industrial Revolution

Setting up the Video

Work with a group of your classmates to view "The Industrial Revolution" on the videodisc *Turning Points in World History*. The Industrial Revolution started in the late 1700s and changed the way people lived. The introduction of modern machines and the building of factories brought both technical advancement and its own set of problems. This program examines the social issues of the Industrial Revolution and where we are today within our own technological revolution.

Side Two, Chapter 3

View the video by scanning the bar code or by entering the chapter number on your keypad and pressing Search. (Also available in VHS format.)

Hands-On Activity

Using multimedia tools, create a presentation about present technology innovations and how these advancements are changing people's lives. Be sure to include some innovations that affect how most people live their daily lives.

Surfing the "Net"

Imperialism

During the Age of Imperialism, world powers lay claim to different parts of the world. Spheres of influence included the region of Latin America. Access the Internet to find out about the effects of imperialism on Latin American countries.

Getting There

Follow these steps to gather more information about the history of various Latin American countries.
1. Find a search engine. Type in the name of a Latin American country.
2. After typing in the name of a Latin American country, enter words such as these to focus your search:

- *history*
- *imperialism*
- *colonialism*
- *independence*

3. The search engine should provide you with a number of links to follow. Links are "pointers" to different sites on the Internet and commonly appear as blue underlined words.

What to Do When You Are There

Click on the links to navigate through the pages of information and gather your findings. Create a news report researching the specific country's history of colonialism, and how the country attained its independence. Videotape all news reports and show to other classes.

Technology

SKILLS

Using the Internet

Have you heard the expression, "surfing the Net?" This means you can search through the Internet to find information on many subjects. You won't get wet, but you sure can learn a lot and have fun!

Learning the Skill

The Internet is a global computer network that offers many features, including the latest news and weather, stored information, E-mail, and on-line shopping. Before you can connect to the Internet and use the services it offers, however, you must have three things: a computer, a modem, and a service provider. A service provider is a company that, for a fee, gives you entry to the Internet.

Once you are connected, the easiest and fastest way to access sites and information is to use a "Web browser," a program that lets you view and explore information on the World Wide Web. The Web consists of many documents called "Web pages," each of which has its own address, or Uniform Resource Locator (URL). Many URLs start with the keystrokes *http://*

Practicing the Skill

Epilogue 2 discusses the Age of Imperialism, when the Panama Canal and the Suez Canal were completed. Surf the Internet to learn about the history of these canals.

1. Log on the Internet and access one of the World Wide Web search tools, such as Yahoo at website http://www.yahoo.com *or* Lycos at http://www.lycos.com *or* WebCrawler at http://www.webcrawler.com
2. Search by category or by name. If you search by category in Yahoo, for example, click on *Social* Science. To search by name, type in *Panama Canal and Suez Canal.*

3. Scroll the list of Web pages that appears when the search is complete. Select a page to bring up and read or print it. Repeat the process until you have enough information you can use to develop a short report on the two major canals completed during the Age of Imperialism.

Applying the Skill

Go through the steps just described to search the Internet for information on the Sepoy Rebellion in India. Based on the information, write an article for your school newspaper or magazine about your topic.

from
The Beggar
by Anton Chekhov

Anton Chekhov, who died in 1904 at age 44, wrote several plays and short stories that became classics of Russian literature. The issue he confronts in the following excerpt—how to help those in need—remains a vital issue today. A wealthy lawyer, Skvortsoff, is angered by the lies a beggar tells to win sympathy and money from passersby. Skvortsoff complains to the beggar that "you could always find work if you only wanted to, but you're lazy and spoiled and drunken!"

"By God, you judge harshly!" cried the beggar with a bitter laugh. "Where can I find manual labor? It's too late for me to be a clerk because in trade one has to begin as a boy; no one would ever take me for a porter because they couldn't order me about; no factory would have me because for that one has to know a trade, and I know none."

"Nonsense! You always find some excuse! How would you like to chop wood for me?"

"I wouldn't refuse to do that, but in these days even skilled wood-cutters find themselves sitting without bread."

"Huh! You loafers all talk that way. As soon as an offer is made you, you refuse it. Will you come and chop wood for me?"

"Yes, sir; I will."

"Very well; we'll soon find out. Splendid—we'll see—"

Skvortsoff hastened along, rubbing his hands, not without a feeling of malice, and called his cook out of the kitchen.

"Here, Olga," he said, "take this gentleman into the wood-shed and let him chop wood."

The tatterdemalion [clothed in ragged garments] scarecrow shrugged his shoulders, as if in perplexity, and went irresolutely after the cook. It was obvious from his gait that he had not consented to go and chop wood because he was hungry and wanted work, but simply from pride and shame, because he had been trapped by his own words. It was obvious, too, that his strength had been undermined by vodka and that he was unhealthy and did not feel the slightest inclination for toil.

Skvortsoff hurried into the dining room. From its windows one could see the wood-shed and everything that went on in the yard. Standing at the window, Skvortsoff saw the cook and the beggar come out into the yard by the back door and make their way across the dirty snow to the shed. Olga glared wrathfully at her companion, shoved him aside with her elbow, unlocked the shed, and angrily banged the door.

"We probably interrupted the woman over her coffee," thought Skvortsoff. "What an ill-tempered creature!"

Next he saw the pseudo-teacher, pseudo-student seat himself on a log and become lost in thought with his red cheeks resting on his fists. The woman flung down an ax at his feet, spat angrily, and, judging from the expression of her lips, began to scold him. The beggar irresolutely pulled a billet [log] of wood toward him, set it up between his feet, and tapped it feebly with the ax. The billet wavered and fell down. The beggar again pulled it to him, blew on his freezing hands, and tapped it with his ax cautiously, as if afraid of hitting his overshoe or of cutting off his finger. The stick of wood again fell to the ground.

Skvortsoff's anger had vanished and he now began to feel a little sorry and ashamed of himself for having set a spoiled, drunken, perchance sick man to work at menial labor in the cold.

"Well, never mind," he thought, going into his study from the dining room. "I did it for his own good."

An hour later Olga came in and announced

Religious Procession in the Province of Kursk by Ilya Repin. Tretyakov Gallery, Moscow, Russia **Ilya Repin painted realistic scenes of everyday Russian life.** *How does Chekhov portray Russian life in his story "The Beggar"?*

Female Farmers by Kazimir Malevich. Russian State Museum, St. Petersburg, Russia **Malevich used modern painting techniques to portray the life of peasant women in rural Russia.** *What role does Olga play in Chekhov's story?*

that the wood had all been chopped.

"Good! Give him half a ruble [the Russian unit of currency]," said Skvortsoff. "If he wants to he can come back and cut wood on the first day of each month. We can always find work for him."

On the first day of the month the waif made his appearance and again earned half a ruble, although he could barely stand on his legs. From that day on he often appeared in the yard and every time work was found for him. Now he would shovel snow, now put the wood-shed in order, now beat the dust out of rugs and mattresses. Every time he received from twenty to forty kopecks [one kopeck equals one-hundredth of a ruble], and once, even a pair of old trousers were sent out to him.

When Skvortsoff moved into another house he hired him to help in the packing and hauling of the furniture. This time the waif was sober, gloomy, and silent. He hardly touched the furniture, and walked behind the wagons hanging his head, not even making a pretense of appearing busy. He only shivered in the cold and became embarrassed when the carters jeered at him for his idleness, his feebleness, and his tattered, fancy overcoat. After the moving was over Skvortsoff sent for him.

"Well, I see that my words have taken effect," he said, handing him a ruble. "Here's for your pains. I see you are sober and have no objection to work. What is your name?"

"Lushkoff."

"Well, Lushkoff, I can now offer you some

other, cleaner employment. Can you write?"

"I can."

"Then take this letter to a friend of mine tomorrow and you will be given some copying to do. Work hard, don't drink, and remember what I have said to you. Good-bye!"

Pleased at having put a man on the right path, Skvortsoff tapped Lushkoff kindly on the shoulder and even gave him his hand at parting. Lushkoff took the letter, and from that day forth came no more to the yard for work.

Two years went by. Then one evening, as Skvortsoff was standing at the ticket window of a theater paying for his seat, he noticed a little man beside him with a coat collar of curly fur and a worn sealskin cap. This little individual timidly asked the ticket seller for a seat in the gallery and paid for it in copper coins.

"Lushkoff, is that you?" cried Skvortsoff, recognizing in the little man his former wood-chopper. "How are you? What are you doing? How is everything with you?"

"All right. I am a notary [a clerk who certifies legal documents] now and get thirty-five rubles a month."

"Thank Heaven! That's fine! I am delighted for your sake. I am very, very glad, Lushkoff. You see, you are my godson, in a sense. I gave you a push along the right path, you know. Do you remember what a roasting I gave you, eh? I nearly had you sinking into the ground at my feet that day. Thank you, old man, for not forgetting my words."

"Thank you, too," said Lushkoff. "If I hadn't come to you then I might still have been calling myself a teacher or a student to this day. Yes, by flying to your protection I dragged myself out of a pit."

"I am very glad, indeed."

"Thank you for your kind words and deeds. You talked splendidly to me then. I am very grateful to you and to your cook. God bless that good and noble woman! You spoke finely then, and I shall be indebted to you to my dying day; but, strictly speaking, it was your cook, Olga, who saved me."

"How is that?"

"Like this. When I used to come to your house to chop wood she used to begin: 'Oh, you sot [drunkard], you! Oh, you miserable creature! There's nothing for you but ruin.' And then she would sit down opposite me and grow sad, look into my face and weep. 'Oh you unlucky man! There is no pleasure for you in this world and there will be none in the world to come. You drunkard! You will burn in hell. Oh, you unhappy one!' And so she would carry on, you know, in that strain. I can't tell you how much misery she suffered, how many tears she shed for my sake. But the chief thing was—she used to chop the wood for me. Do you know, sir, that I did not chop one single stick of wood for you? She did it all. Why this saved me, why I changed, why I stopped drinking at the sight of her I cannot explain. I only know that, owing to her words and noble deeds a change took place in my heart; she set me right and I shall never forget it. However, it is time to go now; there goes the bell."

Lushkoff bowed and departed to the gallery.

RESPONDING TO LITERATURE

1. Explain how the beggar Lushkoff's character and behavior change between the beginning of Chekhov's story and the conclusion of the story.
2. Contrast Skvortsoff's plan for helping Lushkoff improve his life and what actually helped Lushkoff.
3. What advice do you think Chekhov would give to people today who want to help the poor?
4. **Predicting an Outcome** What might have happened if Skvortsoff had found out immediately that Olga was chopping the wood for Lushkoff?

World in Conflict

Focus On...

- World War I
- Between Two Fires
- Nationalism in Asia, Africa, and Latin America
- World War II

Then & Now

Nationalism and imperialism had dire consequences for Europe and the world. When national pride and the scramble for overseas territories dictated foreign relations among industrial states, conflict was inevitable. Two world wars resulted. Never before in the history of civilization had the world endured devastation on such a massive scale.

When you climb aboard a jetliner, you may reflect on the technology of air travel developed in this period. After World War II, many people hoped that the refined instruments of war could be turned to peaceful purposes. The power of the atom could be used to produce energy rather than bombs. Airplanes, developed in World War I and refined in World War II, could become a major means of transportation.

A Global Chronology

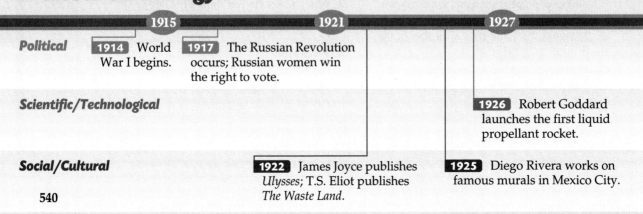

	1915	**1921**	**1927**
Political	**1914** World War I begins.	**1917** The Russian Revolution occurs; Russian women win the right to vote.	
Scientific/Technological			**1926** Robert Goddard launches the first liquid propellant rocket.
Social/Cultural		**1922** James Joyce publishes *Ulysses*; T.S. Eliot publishes *The Waste Land*.	**1925** Diego Rivera works on famous murals in Mexico City.

A 1938 Zenith console radio

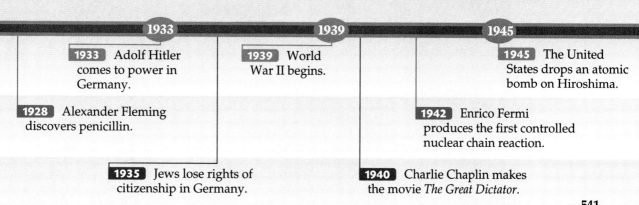

1933
1933 Adolf Hitler comes to power in Germany.

1928 Alexander Fleming discovers penicillin.

1935 Jews lose rights of citizenship in Germany.

1939
1939 World War II begins.

1940 Charlie Chaplin makes the movie *The Great Dictator*.

1945
1945 The United States drops an atomic bomb on Hiroshima.

1942 Enrico Fermi produces the first controlled nuclear chain reaction.

The Spread of Ideas

International Peacekeeping

*T*he 1900s taught people the meaning of world war. No previous century in history had ever seen conflicts that literally spanned the globe. In addition to numerous regional conflicts, the 20th century witnessed two world wars. As the scope of war grew, so did the commitment to collective security—the principle in which a group of nations join together to promote peace.

Europe
The League of Nations

As early as 1828, an American named William Ladd sought to establish a Congress of Nations to settle international disputes and avoid war. Nearly a century later, at the end of World War I, the victorious nations set up a "general association of nations" called the League of Nations.

By 1920 42 nations had sent delegates to the League's headquarters in Geneva, Switzerland. Another 21 nations eventually joined, but conspicuously absent was the United States. Opponents in the United States Senate had argued that membership in the League went against George Washington's advice against "entangling alliances."

When the League failed to halt warlike acts in the 1930s, these same opponents pointed to the failure of collective security. The League was a peacekeeper without a sword—it possessed neither a standing army nor members willing to stop nations that used war as a method of diplomacy.

UN distribution center in the Gaza Strip

Rwandan child at a refugee camp

The United States
The United Nations

Non-membership in the League did not protect the United States from the horrors of war. The Japanese air attack on Pearl Harbor, Hawaii, ended the notion that the United States could isolate itself from the rest of the world.

As World War II drew to a close, the United States hosted a meeting in San Francisco to create a new global peacekeeping organization. Here delegates from 50 nations hammered out the Charter of the United Nations. The document's Preamble sets forth a formula for international peace:

> *We the peoples of the United Nations, determined to save succeeding generations from the scourge of war, which twice in our lifetime has brought untold sorrow to mankind and to reaffirm faith in fundamental human rights ... and to promote social progress and to better standards of life and to promote our strength to maintain international peace and security, and to ensure ... that armed force shall not be used, save in the common interest ... have resolved to combine our efforts to accomplish these aims.*

In the years following, the United Nations (UN) attempted to eliminate the root causes of war. In 1946 it founded the UN Educational, Scientific, and Cultural Organization (UNESCO) and the UN Children's Fund (UNICEF). These agencies promoted global education and the well-being of children. Two years later, in 1948, United States delegate Eleanor Roosevelt convinced the UN to adopt The Universal Declaration of Human Rights. This committed the UN to the elimination of oppression wherever it existed.

South Africa
The Power of World Opinion

Like the League of Nations, the UN could be only as strong as its members were prepared to make it. The development of atomic weapons, however, was a powerful incentive for members to cooperate. By 1995, the UN had taken part in 35 peacekeeping missions—some successful, some failures. It also had provided protection for more than 30 million refugees.

The UN's ability to use world opinion to promote justice was perhaps best tested in South Africa. In 1977 the UN urged nations to use an arms embargo and economic sanctions against South Africa until apartheid was lifted. In 1994 South Africa held its first all-race elections. Many believed this was a major triumph for collective international action.

UN troops in Beirut, Lebanon

LINKING THE IDEAS

1. What factors made it difficult for the League of Nations to promote world peace?
2. What methods has the United Nations used to encourage peace?

Critical Thinking

3. **Forming Opinions** The United Nations Declaration of Human Rights sees injustice in one part of the world as a threat to peace in all parts of the world. Do you agree? Why or why not?

World in Conflict

wo destructive wars engulfed the world in the first half of the 1900s. World War I brought about the collapse of many European royal dynasties, triggered a Communist revolution in Russia, and left many countries in political and economic chaos. This turmoil, the bitterness created by the peace treaties that ended the war, and the worldwide economic depression that started in 1929 led to the rise of dictatorships in Germany, Italy, and Japan.

During the 1930s, the world once again was set on a course toward war. When it arrived, World War II proved to be the most destructive in history. At its end, European dominance of world affairs had ended, with many new nations arising from the ashes of the overseas European empires. Above all, two superpowers—the United States and the Soviet Union—were extending their power and struggling for global influence.

World War I

In the late 1800s, nationalism and imperialism created intense rivalries among European powers. To secure protection, the nations of Europe formed two rival alliances. France, Great Britain, and Russia formed the Triple Entente in the early 1900s to offset the Triple Alliance concluded in the late 1870s and early 1880s by Germany, Italy, and Austria-Hungary.

The Conflict

The conflict between the two armed camps began on June 28, 1914, when a member of a Serb nationalist group assassinated Archduke Francis Ferdinand, the heir to the Austro-Hungarian throne. Austria-Hungary thereupon declared war on Serbia, and bound by their alliances, the other European powers entered the conflict.

For four years war raged on land, at sea, and in the air. The belligerents used sophisticated new weapons, such as machine guns, tanks, airplanes, and poison gas. In the west the war quickly settled into a stalemate along two parallel lines of trenches stretching from Switzerland to the North Sea.

To try to win control of the seas and cut off Germany's supply lines, Great Britain blockaded all German ports. The Germans struck back, however, with U-boats, or submarines. After German U-boats sank four American merchant ships in 1917, President Woodrow Wilson asked Congress for a declaration of war. It was America's intervention that proved to be the turning point of the war, as the United States gave the Allies much-needed human and material resources. In November 1918, Germany finally surrendered.

The war changed the map of Europe. The Ottoman and the Austro-Hungarian empires ceased to exist, and new European nations rose from the breakup. The peace settlements signed at Versailles, moreover, made Germany responsible for the war and imposed a heavy financial penalty on its people.

The Russian Revolution

In Russia, the war brought about the fall of the czarist autocracy. The Russian people had endured great hardships in the war, and public anger against the government mounted. In early 1917 spontaneous demonstrations forced Czar Nicholas II to abdicate. Later that year the Bolsheviks, a Marxist political party led by Vladimir Ilyich Lenin, overthrew the provisional government that had replaced the czar. The Bolsheviks were eventually victorious in the civil war that followed, and Russia became a Communist state.

REVIEW

1. **Relating Ideas** What general factors led to the outbreak of World War I?
2. **Identifying Trends** What new inventions made World War I a more destructive conflict than previous wars?

Between Two Fires

World War I was an important turning point in the 1900s. It carried away the old political order, shattered traditions, and ushered in an era of experimentation in culture. The war also changed the way many people looked at the world, destroyed

Lenin guided the affairs of the Soviet state through civil war and economic collapse until his death in January 1924. *What changes did Lenin's successor, Joseph Stalin, bring to the Soviet Union?*

their faith in progress and creating feelings of disillusionment instead. In the postwar era, artists experimented with new styles and subject matter. Innovative forms of technology, such as the automobile and the radio, changed people's lives and brought the world closer together.

The Western Democracies

The United States came out of the war in far better shape than its allies. The 1920s were boom years for the American economy, and an atmosphere of exuberance and frivolity earned the decade the name "Roaring Twenties." But when the stock market crashed in 1929, the nation fell into a major economic depression that had worldwide repercussions.

Although the war and the depression had a terrible effect on Great Britain and France, democratic traditions in these nations were firmly entrenched. Their governments were able to survive assaults from the political extremists on the left and right. Great Britain, however, lost its privileged position in world trade and was no longer a leading economic power. France, too, faced severe economic problems after the war, and Communist, Fascist, and Socialist parties vied for power. In 1934, however, the Communists joined forces with the Socialists to thwart a Fascist takeover. While in power, the Popular Front, as it was called, instituted many social reforms.

The Rise of Dictators

World War I shattered the economies of Germany and Italy, but these countries did not have strong democratic traditions. Amid political and economic chaos in Italy, Benito Mussolini seized power and in 1922 established a Fascist dictatorship. In Germany Adolf Hitler and the Nazi party gained an audience by blaming the Communists and Jews for Germany's economic woes. In 1933 Hitler became German chancellor and moved quickly to crush his opponents and establish a dictatorship.

Dramatic changes were also occurring in the Soviet Union. Seven years of world and civil war had devastated the country. After seizing power, Lenin tried to quickly impose a new socialist order but faced widespread opposition. In 1921 he finally consolidated Communist power under the New Economic Policy (NEP) that allowed limited capitalism. After Lenin's death in 1924, Joseph Stalin won a political struggle with his rival, Leon Trotsky, and established a brutal dictatorship.

Beginning in the late 1920s, Stalin set about putting all Soviet industries and agriculture under state control. In a succession of purges in the 1930s, Stalin also eliminated suspected opponents from positions of leadership. Many ordinary Soviet citizens also suffered imprisonment, exile, and death during this grim period.

REVIEW

1. **Analyzing Ideas** Why is World War I considered an important turning point in the 1900s?
2. **Identifying Trends** What common problems did many nations face in the 1920s and 1930s? Why did democracy survive in Great Britain and France, while it collapsed in Italy and Germany?

Nationalism in Asia, Africa, and Latin America

In spite of the turmoil created by World War I, the European powers retained control of their colonial territories in the Middle East and Africa. But in the years following World War I, nationalist forces in these Middle Eastern and African territories began the long struggle for independence.

During the 1930s, Mexico's government broke up many estates and gave the land to peasant groups. *What action taken by the Mexican government at this time affected ties to the United States?*

The Middle East, Africa, and India

The old Ottoman Empire of Turkey, weakened by discord and external threats, crumbled during the war. After General Mustafa Kemal repulsed a Greek invasion in 1922, the Turks deposed the Ottoman sultan and formed the Republic of Turkey with Kemal as president. Persians, too, asserted their independence and gave Persia a new name—Iran.

Although Great Britain granted Egypt complete independence in 1936, it controlled neighboring Palestine and continued to rule African colonies, such as Kenya and Nigeria. Despite India's contributions to the British war effort, Great Britain refused to grant independence and moved to stifle a growing nationalist movement. As a result, Mohandas K. Gandhi and other nationalists organized nonviolent protests against British rule, including strikes and a refusal to buy British goods.

East Asia

In China the nationalist Guomindang army led by Chiang Kai-shek overthrew the local military leaders who had ruled the country since 1916. After acquiring power, Chiang turned on Chinese Communist allies, many of whom fled to the mountainous interior of China. When the Japanese invaded China in the 1930s, however, Chiang again joined with the Communists in an effort to repulse the invaders.

In Japan military leaders became a powerful force in the 1920s and 1930s. Believing that Japan could solve the problems of an expanding population and limited resources by acquiring new territories, these leaders launched a program of territorial expansion without their government's approval. By the late 1930s, Japan's government was controlled by the increasingly powerful military, and the Asian country was on a collision course with the Western powers.

Latin America

Although most Latin American countries had achieved political independence long before the 1920s, they remained economically dependent on the United States. They also faced United States military intervention whenever American economic interests were threatened by internal political discord. In the early 1930s President Franklin D. Roosevelt proclaimed the Good Neighbor policy and withdrew American troops from Nicaragua and Haiti, where they were protecting American business interests. This policy eased Latin America's fears of the United States, but tensions increased again in 1938 when Mexico took over foreign-owned oil industries.

REVIEW

1. **Identifying Trends** What kind of protest did Mohandas K. Gandhi direct against British rule in India?
2. **Relating Ideas** How did nationalism in Latin America differ from nationalism in other parts of the world?

World War II

The expansionist policies of the Fascist dictatorships that came to power in the 1920s and 1930s increasingly threatened world peace. The League of Nations, which had been formed after World War I to preserve peace, proved powerless to stop the drift toward war.

Failure of Appeasement

Adolf Hitler aimed to bring much of Europe under Nazi control. When the German leader threatened to invade Czechoslovakia in 1938, British Prime Minister Neville Chamberlain negotiated the Munich Agreement that gave Hitler the part of Czechoslovakia that he demanded. This policy of appeasement, or compromise with the dictatorships, only whetted Hitler's appetite. Six months later, he seized all of Czechoslovakia. Convinced that the West would do nothing to stop him, Hitler secured the help of the Soviet Union in attacking Poland in September, 1939. The Nazi assault on Poland led Britain and France to declare war on Germany.

Waging War

After taking control of Norway and Denmark in the spring of 1940, German troops invaded the Netherlands, raced through Belgium and northern France, and pushed the British and French forces to the English Channel. France surrendered in June, leaving the British to fight Hitler alone.

In the summer and fall of 1940, Great Britain won a crucial victory over Germany in the air conflict known as the Battle of Britain. In spite of widespread American sympathy for Great Britain, isolationists in the United States kept the nation out of the war. The American government was, however, supplying the British with equipment to fight the war. By 1941 Nazi Germany ruled large areas of Europe, and in June of that year, Germany invaded the Soviet Union.

To prevent the United States from interfering with its expansionist aims in East Asia and the Pacific, Japan engaged in an attack on the United States fleet at Pearl Harbor. This attack on Pearl Harbor brought the United States into the war. The United States joined with the Allies—Great Britain, the Soviet Union, the Free French, and other anti-Fascist governments and nations.

Allied Victory

Not until 1942 did the tide begin to turn in favor of the Allies. Americans defeated Japanese naval forces at the Battle of Midway. In 1943, Soviet forces repulsed a German offensive at Stalingrad, and British and American forces pushed the Germans out of North Africa. From there, the Allies launched an invasion of Sicily and the Italian Peninsula.

On June 6, 1944, Western Allied forces invaded Normandy in France and pushed toward Germany as Soviet troops advanced from the east. In April 1945 Western and Soviet Allies met at the Elbe River, and the following month Germany surrendered. When Japanese leaders refused to surrender, the United States dropped its new secret weapon, the atomic bomb, on Hiroshima and Nagasaki in August. Days later Japan surrendered.

World War II was over, but much of Europe and Asia lay in ruins, and tens of millions of people had died. The Allies divided Germany and its capital of Berlin into four sections, each of which was occupied by one of the powers. Tensions between the Soviet Union and the Western Allies increased, however, and the fragile wartime alliance began to unravel.

REVIEW

1. **Making Comparisons** How were the causes of World Wars I and II different? How were they similar?
2. **Relating Ideas** What were the major turning points of World War II?

Visualizing History After Pearl Harbor, San Francisco prepared for possible Japanese air attacks by sandbagging buildings. *Why was the Japanese attack on Pearl Harbor a significant event?*

Turning Points in World History

The Holocaust

Setting up the Video

Work with a group of your classmates to view "The Holocaust" on the videodisc *Turning Points in World History*. The Holocaust was a horrific period in history when the Nazi regime was responsible for murders and crimes against 6 million Jews. This program examines the impact on those who experienced Nazi control during the 1930s and 1940s.

Hands-On Activity

Using the Holocaust theme, create a haiku. The Japanese haiku is one of the shortest types of lyric poetry. The haiku is made up of 17 syllables arranged in three lines. The first line has 5 syllables, the second 7, and the third 5.

Side Two, Chapter 6 | **|||||||||** | *View the video by scanning the bar code or by entering the chapter number on your keypad and pressing Search. (Also available in VHS format.)*

Surfing the "Net"

Mohandas K. Gandhi and India

The early 1900s brought a great struggle for India concerning the issue of independence from Great Britain. Mohandas K. Gandhi provided leadership for independence by practicing active nonviolence. To learn more about Gandhi and the nonviolent movement, access the Internet.

Getting There

Follow these steps to gather information about Mohandas Gandhi.

1. Go to a search engine. Type in *mohandas gandhi*.

2. After typing in the phrase, enter words such as these to focus your search:
   - *india*
   - *soulforce*
   - *independence*

3. The search engine should provide you with a number of links to follow. Links are "pointers" to different sites on the Internet and commonly appear as blue underlined words.

What to Do When You Are There

Click on the links to navigate through the information and gather your findings. Organize into cooperative groups of three. Design large banners promoting peace and nonviolence for today's world. Share your banner with the other groups. Be sure to explain why you chose particular symbols, language, or colors for your banner.

Using a Spreadsheet

Electronic spreadsheets can help people manage numbers quickly and easily. You can use a spreadsheet any time a problem involves numbers that can be arranged in rows and columns.

Learning the Skill

A spreadsheet is an electronic worksheet. All spreadsheets follow a basic design of rows and columns. Each *column* (vertical) is assigned a letter or number. Each *row* (horizontal) is assigned a number. Each point where a column and row intersect is called a *cell*. The cell's position on the spreadsheet is labeled according to its corresponding column and row—Column A, Row 1 (A1); Column B, Row 2 (B2), and so on.

Spreadsheets use *standard formulas* to calculate the numbers. You create a simple mathematical equation that uses these standard formulas and the computer does the calculations for you.

Practicing the Skill

Suppose you want to know the population densities (population per square mile) of the countries in South Asia. Use these steps to create a spreadsheet that will provide this information.

1. In cell A1 type *Country*, in cell B1 type *Population*, in cell C1 type *Land Area (square miles)*, and in cell D1 type *Population per square mile*.
2. In cells A2-A5 respectively, type one of the following country's name: *India, Pakistan, Bangladesh*, and *Sri Lanka*. In cell A6, type the words *Total for South Asia*.
3. In cells B2-B5, enter the population area of each country shown in cells A2-A5.
4. In cells C2-C5, enter the land area (square miles) of each country shown in cells A2-A5.
5. In cell D2, create a formula to calculate the population per square mile. The formula for the equation tells what cells (B1 ÷ C1) to divide. Copy this formula into cells D3-D5.

6. Use the process in step 5 to create and copy a formula to calculate the total population of South Asia (B2 + B3 + B4 + B5) for cell B6; to calculate the total Land Area of South Asia (C2 + C3 + C4 + C5) for cell C6.
7. Use the process in step 5 to create and copy a formula to calculate the population per square mile of South Asia (B6 ÷ C6) for cell D6.

Applying the Skill

Use a spreadsheet to enter your test scores and your homework grades. At the end of the grading period, the spreadsheet can calculate your average grade.

from

Gifts of Passage

by Santha Rama Rau

antha Rama Rau, born in Madras, India, in 1923, spent her childhood in India, England, and South Africa. In each place, she closely watched the way people from different backgrounds related with one another. Advances in transportation and communication have sharply increased the interactions of people from different cultures. Today these interactions shape the world more than ever before. In the following excerpt, Rau recalls her early experiences at a school for English and Indian children in India.

t the Anglo-Indian day school in Zorinabad to which my sister and I were sent when she was eight and I was five and a half, they changed our names. On the first day of school, a hot, windless morning of a north Indian September, we stood in the head-mistress's study and she said, "Now you're the *new* girls. What are your names?"

My sister answered for us. "I am Premila, and she"—nodding in my direction—"is Santha."

The headmistress had been in India, I suppose, fifteen years or so, but she still smiled her helpless inability to cope with Indian names. Her rimless half-glasses glittered, and the precarious bun on the top of her head trembled as she shook her head. "Oh, my dears, those are much too hard for me. Suppose we give you pretty English names. Wouldn't that be more jolly? Let's see, now—Pamela for you, I think." She shrugged in a baffled way at my sister. "That's as close as I can get. And for *you*," she said to me, "how about Cynthia? Isn't that nice?"

My sister was always less intimidated than I was, and while she kept a stubborn silence, I said "Thank you," in a very tiny voice....

That first day at school is still, when I think of it, a remarkable one. At that age, if one's name is changed, one develops a curious form of dual personality. I remember having a certain detached and disbelieving concern in the actions of "Cynthia," but certainly no responsibility. ...

During the years of British rule, the Indian subcontinent had a wealthy upper class of princes and their families. This upper-class Indian family of the 1940s practiced traditional ways but was also familiar with the customs of the British aristocracy. *What are the British teachers' attitudes toward ordinary Indians in the story by Santha Rama Rau?*

Accordingly, I followed the thin, erect back of the headmistress down the veranda [porch] to my classroom feeling, at most, a passing interest in what was going to happen to me in this strange, new atmosphere of School.…

I can't remember too much about the proceedings in class that day, except for the beginning. The teacher pointed to me and asked me to stand up. "Now, dear, tell the class your name."

I said nothing.

"Come along," she said, frowning slightly. "What's your name, dear?"

"I don't know," I said, finally.

The English children in the front of the class—there were about eight or ten of them—giggled and twisted around in their chairs to look at me. I sat down quickly and opened my eyes very wide, hoping in that way to dry them off. The little girl with the braids put out her hand and very lightly touched my arm. She still didn't smile.

Most of the morning I was rather bored. I looked briefly at the children's drawings pinned to the wall, and then concentrated on a lizard clinging to the ledge of the high, barred window behind the teacher's head. Occasionally it would shoot out its long yellow tongue for a fly, and then it would rest, with its eyes closed and its belly palpitating, as though it were swallowing several times quickly. The lessons were mostly concerned with reading and writing and simple numbers—things that my mother had already taught me—and I paid very little attention. The teacher wrote on the easel blackboard words like "bat" and "cat," which seemed babyish to me; only "apple" was new and incomprehensible.

When it was time for the lunch recess, I followed the girl with braids out onto the veranda. There the children from the other classes were assembled. I saw Premila at once and ran over to her, as she had charge of our lunchbox. The children were all opening packages and sitting down to eat sandwiches. Premila and I were the only ones who had Indian food—thin wheat chapatties [a type of bread], some vegetable curry, and a bottle of buttermilk. Premila thrust half of it into my hand and whispered fiercely that I should go and sit with my class, because that was what the others seemed to be doing.…

I had never really grasped the system of competitive games. At home, whenever we played tag or guessing games, I was always allowed to "win"—"because," Mother used to tell Premila, "she is the youngest, and we have to allow for that." I had often heard her say it, and it seemed quite reasonable to me, but the result was that I had no clear idea of what "winning" meant.

When we played twos-and-threes that afternoon at school, in accordance with my training, I let one of the small English boys catch me, but was naturally rather puzzled when the other children did not return the courtesy. I ran about for what seemed like hours without ever catching anyone, until it was time for school to close. Much later I learned that my attitude was called "not being a good sport," and I stopped allowing myself to be caught, but it was not for years that I really learned the spirit of the thing.…

It was a week later, the day of Premila's first test, that our lives changed rather abruptly. I was sitting at the back of the class, in my usual inattentive way, only half listening to the teacher. I had started a rather guarded friendship with the girl with the braids, whose name turned out to be Nalini (Nancy, in school). The three other Indian children were already fast friends. Even at that age it was apparent to all of us that friendship with the English or Anglo-Indian children was out of the question. Occasionally, during the class, my new friend and I would draw pictures and show them to each other secretly.

The door opened sharply and Premila marched in. At first, the teacher smiled at her in a kindly and encouraging way and said, "Now, you're little Cynthia's sister?"

Premila didn't even look at her. She stood with her feet planted firmly apart and her shoulders rigid, and addressed herself directly to me. "Get up," she said. "We're going home."

I didn't know what happened, but I was aware that it was a crisis of some sort. I rose obediently and started to walk toward my sister.

"Bring your pencils and your notebook," she said.

I went back for them, and together we left the room. The teacher started to say something just as Premila closed the door, but we didn't wait to hear what it was.

In complete silence we left the school grounds and started to walk home. Then I asked Premila what the matter was. All she would say was "We're going home for good."…

When we got to our house the ayah [maid] was just taking a tray of lunch into Mother's room. She immediately started a long, worried questioning about what are you children doing back here at this hour of the day.

Mother looked very startled and very concerned, and asked Premila what had happened.

Premila said, "We had our test today, and she made me and the other Indians sit at the back of the room, with a desk between each one."

Mother said, "Why was that, darling?"

"She said it was because Indians cheat," Premila added. "So I don't think we should go back to that school."

Mother looked very distant, and was silent a long time. At last she said, "Of course not, darling." She sounded displeased.

We all shared the curry she was having for lunch, and afterward I was sent off to the beautifully familiar bedroom for my siesta. I could hear Mother and Premila talking through the open door.

Mother said, "Do you suppose she understood all that?"

Visualizing History These Indian women are dressed in the sari, a garment of several yards of material draped so that one end forms a skirt and the other a shoulder or head covering. *How do you think the two Indian girls in the story dressed for their classes at the British school?*

Premila said, "I shouldn't think so. She's a baby."

Mother said, "Well, I hope it won't bother her."

Of course, they were both wrong. I understood it perfectly, and I remember it all very clearly. But I put it happily away, because it had all happened to a girl called Cynthia, and I never was really particularly interested in her.

RESPONDING TO LITERATURE

1. Why did Santha and her sister leave school?
2. Explain why Santha was unable to tell the class her name.
3. When the headmistress gives Santha and her sister new names, what can you determine the headmistress thought of Indian culture?
4. **Demonstrating Reasoned Judgment** Explain why Santha's mother would or would not keep her children home permanently from the Anglo-Indian school.

The Contemporary World

Then & Now

International tension continued after World War II. Two blocs of nations aligned themselves behind the United States and the Soviet Union to dominate world politics. The two sides fought a cold war using economic powers, diplomacy, espionage, and the threat of nuclear war. When the cold war ended, leaders struggled to address the long-standing problems of nationalism, poverty in the developing nations, distribution of resources, and environmental damage.

The pace of scientific and technological change quickened. Satellite communications and computers linked in a global network offered undreamed of challenges and opportunities. When you turn on your computer, remember that it has been just a few years since this technology was invented. No one can guess the nature or degree of change it will bring to your future.

A Global Chronology

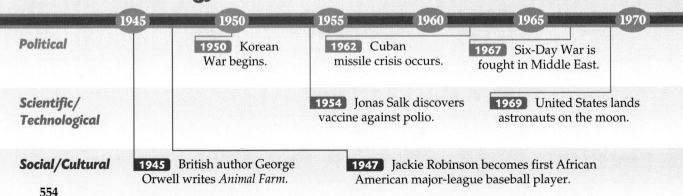

	1945	1950	1955	1960	1965	1970
Political		**1950** Korean War begins.	**1962** Cuban missile crisis occurs.		**1967** Six-Day War is fought in Middle East.	
Scientific/ Technological			**1954** Jonas Salk discovers vaccine against polio.		**1969** United States lands astronauts on the moon.	
Social/Cultural	**1945** British author George Orwell writes *Animal Farm*.		**1947** Jackie Robinson becomes first African American major-league baseball player.			

Computer Pentium chip

Portfolio Project

Choose an ongoing worldwide problem or situation such as ethnic wars or rivalries, the conflict between Arabs and Israelis, economic difficulties in former Soviet states, population growth in overcrowded cities, oil or other resource shortages, debt in developing nations, the spread of arms, hunger and homelessness, or terrorism. Collect and study news articles about this subject. Write a one-page essay offering suggestions for dealing with the issue.

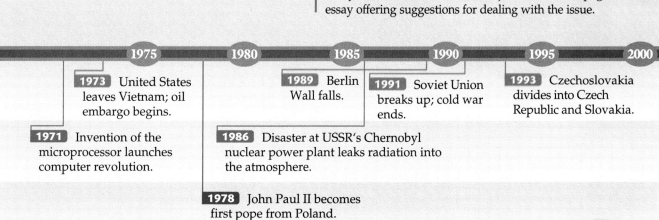

1975 **1980** **1985** **1990** **1995** **2000**

1973 United States leaves Vietnam; oil embargo begins.

1989 Berlin Wall falls.

1991 Soviet Union breaks up; cold war ends.

1993 Czechoslovakia divides into Czech Republic and Slovakia.

1971 Invention of the microprocessor launches computer revolution.

1986 Disaster at USSR's Chernobyl nuclear power plant leaks radiation into the atmosphere.

1978 John Paul II becomes first pope from Poland.

The Spread of Ideas

Communications

The invention of writing reshaped history. So did Johannes Gutenberg's use of movable type. Today, however, electronics technology is moving communications forward at a startling rate. Two of the biggest changes have been the linking of people around the world via satellite broadcasts and the creation of a vast computer network known as the "information highway."

The United States
Satellite Communications

In October 1957, a special announcement interrupted radio broadcasts across the United States. "Listen now ... for the sound which forever separates the old from the new," said the broadcaster. Then a voice from outer space—and eerie beep ... beep ... beep.

The former Soviet Union had taken the lead in space exploration by launching a tiny communications satellite named *Sputnik I*. A crudely simple device by today's standards, the first satellite could do little more than beam back radio signals. In the cold war era, however, it sent shock waves through American society.

Three years later, the United States launched *Echo* and *Courier*. Instead of beeps, these satellites relayed telephone calls between Europe and the United States. In 1962, the United States launched *Telstar*—the first satellite to relay live television programs from one place to another. By the 1980s people around the world with satellite dish antennas could tune in to hundreds of television programs. The effect was revolutionary. Repressive governments in Eastern Europe and elsewhere could not legislate against free speech beamed down from the skies.

Telstar

Scientist and Soviet Sputnik I

China
Satellite Dishes

In the 1990s, satellite dishes sprouted like mushrooms across the People's Republic of China. Star TV, a pan-Asian satellite service, boomed down Mandarin-speaking rappers out of Hong Kong, English broadcasts of CNN News, NFL football games, and movies from Japan. The uncensored broadcasts enraged government officials. However, a 1993 ban against satellite dishes proved nearly impossible to enforce. Even while officials tried to dismantle the thousands of large dishes, kits for smaller dishes were being smuggled into the country.

The example of China was repeated in other repressive nations. Iran, Myanmar (Burma), and other countries tried and failed to ban satellite reception. Even free governments, such as India, expressed concern about the "cultural invasion," but satellite television, a part of the information age, was here to stay.

Communications satellite

Africa
The Internet

A telephone line and a personal computer—that is all someone needs to jump on the information highway. Internet Web sites exist globally, putting individuals in touch with databases and other computer users on every continent.

In Africa, the least electronic continent, UNESCO is helping the Pan-African News Agency to link up with the Internet. The project will help Africans overcome one of the legacies of imperialism—a communications system that linked African nations with European capitals rather than with each other. The driving force behind the project, a Senegalese journalist named Babacar Fall, sees the Internet as one of the keys to unlocking Africa's economic potential. "Without information," explained Fall, "there can be no development."

High school students on the Internet

LINKING THE IDEAS

1. How did the revolution in satellite communications get its start?
2. How has this revolution affected nondemocratic political systems?

Critical Thinking

3. **Drawing Conclusions** How has the revolution in communications made our world more interdependent?

The Contemporary World

The period from 1945 to the present brought a major political realignment among the nations of the world. Weakened by World War II, European colonial nations withdrew from Asia and Africa. New nations arose from the remains of the European empires and struggled to establish their roles in the global community of nations.

The United States and the Soviet Union emerged from World War II as superpowers and became locked in a struggle for global influence known as the cold war. As the Soviet Union sought to spread communism worldwide, the United States tried to resist its spread and to promote democracy. For the most part, the cold war was not fought on battlefields, although armed conflicts did occur. The main weapons in this struggle were propaganda, espionage, diplomacy, and the threat of nuclear war.

By the 1980s, the Soviet Union and the Eastern European nations under its sway faced severe economic difficulties. Communism proved incapable

of reform, in spite of concerted efforts by Mikhail Gorbachev to introduce drastic changes and improve relations with the West. With the Soviet Union moving away from strict communism, popular uprisings succeeded in toppling Communist governments in Eastern Europe without the fear of Soviet intervention. The collapse of the Soviet Union itself and the emergence of new republics in 1991 signaled the end of the cold war. The complexities of the transition from communism to free enterprise soon became apparent, and hope for a new era of global cooperation faded as ethnic rivalries led to bloody conflicts in various parts of the world.

The Cold War

The World War II alliance quickly dissolved when conflict arose over the postwar reorganization of Europe. As a result, Europe was divided into the Eastern bloc, dominated by the Soviet Union, and the Western bloc, tied to the United States.

Communist governments emerged throughout Eastern Europe, either voluntarily or by force. The economies of Eastern European countries were government-controlled and tied to the Soviet Union. The Soviets regarded the Eastern bloc as a buffer zone against Western influences. In 1955 the Soviet Union created the Warsaw Pact to maintain its control in the region. Uprisings in Hungary and Czechoslovakia against Soviet domination were put down by force.

After World War II, the United States, as the leader of the non-Communist world, issued the Truman Doctrine, which promised aid to countries fighting Communist takeover. Western Europe's democratic nations rebuilt their shattered economies under the United States-sponsored Marshall Plan. With the United States and Canada, they formed the NATO alliance in 1949 for mutual defense against Soviet attack. Economic prosperity came to western Europe by 1960, and a movement for European unification led to the formation of a free trade area known as the Common Market.

The United States and Canada developed strong economies after World War II. The cold war

Visualizing History **The cold war led to an arms race between the United States and the Soviet Union. This Soviet rocket launcher was based in Ukraine.** *What major step did the Western allies take in 1949 to contain communism?*

affected American politics during the 1950s, when concern arose about Communist influences in American government and society. During the 1960s women, African Americans, Hispanic Americans, and Native Americans began to make advances in civil rights. The Vietnam War divided American society and led to a questioning of the United States's military role in world trouble spots.

REVIEW

1. **Relating Ideas** How did the cold war affect the continent of Europe?
2. **Analyzing Information** How did the United States largely view its role in world affairs after World War II?

Asia and the Pacific

The post–World War II period brought profound changes to the nations of Asia and the Pacific. Japan arose from the ashes of defeat to become one of the world's major economic and trading nations. European colonies became independent nations and faced the problems of building united societies and developing successful economies. In South Asia, ethnic and religious rivalries led to the creation of three new nations: India, Pakistan, and later, Bangladesh.

After World War II, China was torn by civil war between Nationalists and Communists. The Communist victory in 1949 established the People's Republic of China on the mainland, with the Nationalist government based on the island of Taiwan. Beginning in the 1970s, China maintained its Communist system while encouraging limited free enterprise and contacts with the West.

Korea and Vietnam, both divided into Communist and non-Communist states, became hot spots in the cold war. The Korean War, fought from 1950 to 1953, saw American-led United Nations forces fight back a Communist advance, but the conflict ended in stalemate, with Korea returning to its divided status at the 38th parallel. In Vietnam, however, Communist forces defeated American and anti-Communist Vietnamese forces and united the entire country under Communist rule. The Vietnam conflict lasted from the 1950s to the mid-1970s, with direct American military involvement beginning in the mid-1960s.

Visualizing History Since the 1960s, Taiwan has developed a booming economy that exports goods to other parts of the world. *How was Taiwan affected by events in China during the late 1940s?*

Since the Korean and Vietnam conflicts, economic prosperity has come to the nations along Asia's Pacific Rim, stretching from South Korea through Japan, Taiwan, and Hong Kong to Southeast Asia. Australia, New Zealand, and other South Pacific nations are increasingly involved in trade with their Asian neighbors.

REVIEW

1. **Relating Ideas** What impact did communism have in Asia after 1945?
2. **Identifying Trends** What area of Asia is entering a new era of economic prosperity?

Africa

World War II weakened Europe's hold on Africa and led to the rise of nationalist movements. From about 1956 to 1993, a number of new nations arose throughout the continent. Newly independent African nations worked to build stable governments, resolve ethnic conflicts, and create modern economies.

The legacy of colonialism, however, often interfered with these efforts. Some African countries, based on boundaries established by the European powers without regard to ethnic loyalties, experienced internal unrest. Others, forced by European colonial rulers to rely on a single crop or product, had difficulty protecting their economies from sharp declines in world commodity prices.

Many Africans sought to reestablish their cultural identity and began to throw off reminders of the colonial past. A movement for African unity created new political and economic links among the nations on the continent. Meanwhile, after years of struggle against racial segregation, South Africa in the mid-1990s became a full democracy open to all its races, especially the black majority.

Visualizing History **Israeli Prime Minister Yitzhak Rabin was assassinated in 1995 by a young Israeli opposed to the peace process.** *What did Israel agree to do as a result of the peace process?*

REVIEW

1. **Analyzing Information** How has the colonial legacy affected modern Africa?
2. **Identifying Trends** What change came to South Africa in the mid-1990s?

The Middle East

After 1945, fully independent nations arose in the Middle East as European influence declined. Huge oil reserves brought tremendous economic growth to some Middle Eastern nations, but the attractiveness of its oil wealth also drew the Middle East into the cold war struggle between the superpowers.

Arabs united in opposing the formation of the Jewish state of Israel in 1948. During the years of the Arab-Israeli conflict, the Israelis were able to preserve their independence and even extend their territory. A major issue related to the fighting was the status of the Palestinian Arabs, who claimed the land which Israel occupied.

After years of struggle, Israel and its Arab neighbors began to make peace in the 1970s and 1980s. With the end of the cold war, this task became somewhat less complicated. By the early 1990s, Israel had agreed to give back some of the territory it had taken in the 1967 war in return for guarantees of peace and security from the Arabs. The peace process, however, was often marred by violence from opponents of peace on both sides.

REVIEW

1. **Relating Ideas** What natural resource made the Middle East a place of confrontation between the superpowers during the cold war?
2. **Identifying Trends** How has the relationship between Israel and the Arab nations evolved since 1948?

Latin America

The nations of Latin America faced many challenges during the postwar period. Rapid industrialization brought new wealth to the region, but the population was sharply divided between rich and poor. Social inequality often led to political unrest and civil war.

In the late 1950s, Fidel Castro's revolution in Cuba brought communism and the influence of the cold war to the Western Hemisphere. To contain the spread of communism, the United States often supported military dictatorships in various Latin

American countries. During the 1970s and 1980s, civil wars developed in Central America and South America between military dictators calling for social order and left-wing forces supporting radical social reforms. Many civilians were killed either by repressive governments or guerrilla forces.

During the 1980s and 1990s, pro-democracy movements overturned dictatorships in several Latin American countries. Today the region faces rapid population growth and heavy foreign debt. Mexico especially has faced economic crisis and internal upheaval as it tries to integrate its economy with those of the United States and Canada.

Visualizing History This leftist mural in Bolivia reflects the political conflicts dividing many Latin American countries. *What two groups fought civil wars in Latin America during the 1970s and 1980s?*

REVIEW

1. **Analyzing Information** How has Latin America changed economically since 1945?
2. **Identifying Trends** How has democracy fared in Latin America in recent years?

The World in Transition

After a tense beginning in the early 1980s, superpower relations warmed considerably by the end of the decade, signaling the end of the cold war. In 1985 the new Soviet leader Mikhail Gorbachev departed from hard-line Communist rule and introduced the policies of glasnost (openness) and perestroika (restructuring) that set out economic and social reforms for the Soviet Union. This resulted in the collapse of the Soviet Union and the end of its Communist system in 1991. Russia's leader Boris Yeltsin and the other leaders of the now independent republics of the Commonwealth of Independent States (CIS) faced challenges from internal unrest as they attempted to move their economies toward free enterprise.

The reform movement spread to the countries of Eastern Europe, which threw off Soviet domination and launched new governments. East Germany and West Germany reunited in 1990. Meanwhile, the nations of western Europe moved forward toward economic and political unity as members of the European Union (EU).

During the mid-1990s, ethnic and national divisions affected peoples and governments in various parts of the world. In places such as Czechoslovakia and Canada, disputes split or nearly split countries in two. The bloodiest encounters took place along the southern borders of the former

Soviet Union and in the Balkans. Former Yugoslavia in the Balkans was torn apart by civil war, especially in the republic of Bosnia-Herzegovina, where Serbs, Croats, and Muslims fought for control of territory. In 1995 a peace agreement sent in a NATO-led peacekeeping force that included soldiers from the United States, Russia, and European Union countries.

As the world heads into the twenty-first century, the interdependence and common purpose of nations and peoples are gradually being recognized. Space exploration has permitted us to see the earth as a single unit with a shared environment. Advances in technology have enabled instantaneous communication across the globe, creating an electronic neighborhood of the world's people.

Such advances, however, are offset by rapid increases in world population and industrial growth. These trends have created critical environmental problems that now affect the entire world. It is now apparent that global cooperation is essential to protecting the future of the planet.

REVIEW

1. **Identifying Trends** Have the 1980s and 1990s seen a shift toward political freedom throughout the world? Explain, using examples from two continents.
2. **Relating Ideas** How have global environmental problems such as deforestation changed people's thinking about the political relationships among nations?

ABC NEWS INTERACTIVE™

Turning Points in World History

Fall of the Berlin Wall

Setting up the Video

Work with a group of your classmates to view "Fall of the Berlin Wall" on the videodisc Turning Points in World History. On New Year's Eve, 1990, the two Germanys celebrated reunification. Afterward, Germany was faced with many economic problems to address—such as high unemployment and the arrival of refugees from Eastern Europe that placed a strain on social services.

Hands-On Activity

Create an economic fact sheet about Germany's present economic status. Include information such as GDP, unemployment rate, imports, exports, rate of currency, and other related information.

Side Two,
Chapter 9

View the video by scanning the bar code or by entering the chapter number on your keypad and pressing Search. (Also available in VHS format.)

Surfing the "Net"

Human Rights

The protection of human rights has been a major priority for the United Nations since its creation in 1945. In 1948, the United Nations adopted an important human-rights document known as the Universal Declaration of Human Rights. This document addresses economic, social, and political rights. To find out about the content of the United Nations Universal Declaration of Human Rights document, look on the Internet.

Getting There

Follow these steps to gather in-depth information about the content of the Universal Declaration of Human Rights.

1. Go to a search engine. Type in *united nations.*

2. After typing in the phrase, enter terms such as the following to focus your search.
   - *human rights document*
   - *peace*
3. The search engine should provide you with a number of links to follow. Links are "pointers" to different sites on the Internet and commonly appear as blue underlined words.

What to Do When You Are There

Click on the links to navigate through the pages of information and gather your findings. Design a poster illustrating the different articles of the United Nations Declaration of Human Rights. Hang posters around your classroom.

Developing a Database

Do you have a collection of sports cards or CDs? Have you ever kept a list of the names, addresses, and phone numbers of friends and relatives? If you have collected information and kept some sort of list or file, then you have created a database.

Learning the Skill

An electronic database is a collection of facts that are stored in a file on the computer. The information is organized in fields.

A database can be organized and reorganized in any way that is useful to you. By using a database management system (DBMS)—special software developed for record keeping—you can easily add, delete, change, or update information. You give commands to the computer telling it what to do with the information, and it follows your commands. When you want to retrieve information, the computer searches through the file, finds the information, and displays it on the screen.

Practicing the Skill

Fidel Castro is one of the Latin American leaders discussed in this epilogue. Follow these steps to build a database of the political events that have taken place during his years as Cuba's leader.

1. Determine what facts you want to include in your database.
2. Follow instructions in the DBMS that you are using to set up fields. Then enter each item of data in its assigned field.
3. Determine how you want to organize the facts in the database—chronologically by the date of the event, or alphabetically by the name of the event.
4. Follow the instructions in your computer program to place the information in order of importance.

5. Check that the information in your database is all correct. If necessary, add, delete, or change information or fields.

Applying the Skill

Bring to class current newspapers. Using the steps just described, build a database of current political events in Latin American countries. Explain to a partner why the database is organized the way it is and how it might be used in this class.

Bridge to the Past
Literature

from
Modern Poems

by
Jaime Torres Bodet, Nazim Hikmet, and Gabriel Okara

*M*odern poets have continued to explore both universal themes, such as friendship and loneliness, as well as individual preferences for a particular place or group of people.

The following poem was written by one of Mexico's greatest writers, Jaime Torres Bodet, who was born in 1902 and was active in politics. Bodet served the government as an administrator and diplomat. In this poem, Bodet urges people to take risks in their lives. Bodet died in 1974.

The Window

Translated from Spanish by George Kearns

You closed the window, And it was the world,
the world that wanted to enter, all at once,
the world that gave that great shout,
that great, deep, rough cry
you did not want to hear—and now
will never call to you again as it called today,
asking your mercy!

The whole of life was in that cry:
the wind, the sea, the land
with its poles and its tropics,
the unreachable skies,
the ripened grain in the resounding wheat field,
the thick heat above the wine presses,
dawn on the mountains, shadowy woods,
parched lips stuck together longing for
cool water condensed in pools,
and all pleasures, all sufferings,
all loves, all hates,
were in this day, anxiously
asking your mercy …

But you were afraid of life,
And you remained alone,
behind the closed and silent window,
not understanding that the world calls to a man
only once that way, and with that kind of cry,
with that great, rough, hoarse cry!

*N*azim Hikmet, who lived from 1902 to 1963, often criticized the government of his native Turkey for serving only the wealthy. In 1951 he left Turkey, never to return, and settled in Europe. His sympathy for the peasants of his country, his love of nature, and his hope for humanity are all suggested in the following poem.

The World, My Friends, My Enemies, You, and the Earth

Translated from Turkish by
Randy Blasing and Mutlu Konuk

Nazim Hikmet

I'm wonderfully happy I came into the world,
I love its earth, its light, its struggle, and its bread.
Even though I know its dimensions from pole to pole to the
  centimeter,
and while I'm not unaware that it's a mere toy next to the sun,
the world for me is unbelievably big.
I would have liked to go around the world
and see the fish, the fruits, and the stars that I haven't seen.
However,
I made my European trip only in books and pictures.
In all my life I never got one letter
        with its blue stamp canceled in Asia.
Me and our corner grocer,
we're both mightily unknown in America.
Nevertheless,
from China to Spain, from the Cape of Good Hope to Alaska,
in every nautical mile, in every kilometer, I have friends and
    enemies.
Such friends that we haven't met even once—
we can die for the same bread, the same freedom, the same dream.
And such enemies that they're thirsty for my blood,
          I am thirsty for their blood.
My strength
is that I'm not alone in this big world.
The world and its people are no secret in my heart,
     no mystery in my science.
Calmly and openly
      I took my place
          in the great struggle.
And without it,
      you and the earth
        are not enough for me.
And yet you are astonishingly beautiful,
       the earth is warm and beautiful.

Gabriel Okara, born in 1921, is one of many Nigerian writers to achieve international acclaim since the 1960s. Others include Chinua Achebe, Christopher Okigbo, and Wole Soyinka. Some of Okara's poems deal with the problems of living in a country that is influenced by European culture. Others deal with family, friends, and daily life.

Once Upon a Time

Once upon a time, son,
they used to laugh with their hearts
and laugh with their eyes;
but now they only laugh with their teeth,
while their ice-block-cold eyes
search behind my shadow.

There was a time indeed
they used to shake hands with their hearts;
but that's gone, son.
Now they shake hands without hearts
while their left hands search
my empty pockets.

"Feel at home," "Come again,"
they say, and when I come
again and feel
at home, once, twice,
there will be no thrice—
for then I find doors shut on me.

So I have learned many things, son.
I have learned to wear many faces
like dresses—homeface,
officeface, streetface, hostface, cock-
tailface, with all their conforming smiles
like a fixed portrait smile.

And I have learned, too,
to laugh with only my teeth
and shake hands without my heart.
I have also learned to say, "Goodbye,"
when I mean, "Good-riddance";
to say "Glad to meet you,"
without being glad; and to say "It's been
nice talking to you," after being bored.

Visualizing History National unity has been difficult for Nigeria to achieve because of its diverse ethnic groups. *How does the author remember his childhood years before strife divided the country?*

But believe me, son.
I want to be what I used to be
when I was like you. I want
to unlearn all these muting things.
Most of all, I want to relearn
how to laugh, for my laugh in the mirror
shows only my teeth like a snake's bare fangs!

So show me, son,
how to laugh; show me how
I used to laugh and smile
once upon a time when I was like you.

RESPONDING TO LITERATURE

1. In your own words, define "the great struggle" that Hikmet refers to near the end of his poem.
2. Explain whether you think the poem by Bodet is written just to the people of Mexico or whether it applies to people throughout the world.
3. What is the main point of the poem by Okara?
4. **Demonstrating Reasoned Judgment** How does each poet view individuals who are willing to act boldly?

APPENDIX

Study and Writing Skills Handbook

Pavillion Hall at the Hermitage, St. Petersburg, Russia

Outlining

To sketch a scene, first you would draw the rough shape, or outline, of the picture. Then you would fill in this rough shape with details. Outlining written material is a similar process. You begin with the rough shape of the material and gradually fill in the details.

Learning the Skill

Outlining has two important functions. When studying written material, it helps you identify main ideas and group together related facts. In writing, it helps you put information in a logical order.

There are two kinds of outlines–formal and informal. An informal outline is similar to taking notes. You write only words and phrases needed to remember ideas. Under the main ideas, jot down related but less important details. This kind of outline is useful for reviewing material before a test.

A formal outline has a standard format. In a formal outline, label main heads with Roman numerals, subheads with capital letters, and details with Arabic numerals. Each level would have at least two entries and should be indented from the level above. All entries use the same grammatical form. If one entry is a complete sentence, all other entries at that level must also be complete sentences.

When outlining written material, first read the material to identify the main ideas. In textbooks, section heads provide clues to main topics. Then identify the subheads. Place details supporting or explaining subheads under the appropriate head.

Practicing the Skill

Study the outline below of Chapter 6, Section 1 and then answer these questions.
1. Is this an example of a formal or an informal outline?
2. What are the three main headings?

3. How do subheads under the heading "The Roman Republic" relate to this main idea?

I. The Settlement of Italy
   A. Greeks
   B. Indo-Europeans
   C. Etruscans
II. The Rise of Rome
   A. The Founding of Rome
      1. Romulus kills Remus
      2. Latins cooperate to build Rome
   B. Overthrow of the Etruscans
III. The Roman Republic
   A. Social Groups
      1. Rome has patricians and plebeians
   B. Political System
      1. Romans can only elect patricians to be their leaders
      2. The Senate and Assembly of Centurions make laws
      3. Rome is led by two consuls
      4. Plebeians want to elect their own leaders and an Assembly of Tribes is created
      5. Rome's law is codified into 12 tablets
   C. Religion
   D. Family
      1. The father is head of the household
      2. Women have few legal rights
      3. Roman values are thrift, discipline and loyalty to family

Applying the Skill

Write a formal outline for Section 2 of this chapter.

The Forum

Selecting and Using Research Sources

You have to write a report, so you head off to the library. There you are surrounded by bookshelves filled with books. Where do you begin?

Learning the Skill

Libraries contain many kinds of research sources. Understanding the content and purpose of each type will help you find relevant information more efficiently. Here are brief descriptions of important sources:

Reference Books Reference books include encyclopedias, biographical dictionaries, atlases, and almanacs.

An encyclopedia is a set of books with short articles on many subjects arranged alphabetically. General encyclopedias present a wide range of topics, while specialized encyclopedias have articles on a theme—i.e., an encyclopedia of music.

A biographical dictionary provides brief biographies listed alphabetically by last names. Each biography gives data such as the person's place and date of birth, occupation, and achievements.

An atlas is a collection of maps and charts for locating geographical features and places. An atlas can be general or thematic. An atlas contains an alphabetical index of place names that directs you to the map(s) where that place appears.

An almanac is an annually updated reference that provides current statistics together with historical information on a wide range of subjects.

Card Catalog The library's catalog, on computer or cards, lists every book in the library. Search for books by author, title, or subject. Each listing gives the book's call number and location. Computer catalogs also show whether the book is currently available.

Many libraries have joined networks. A library network usually has a single computer catalog listing all the books in the network. A patron can borrow any book in the system. Find out whether your library is part of a network.

Periodical Guides A periodical guide is a set of books listing topics covered in magazine and newspaper articles.

Computer Databases Computer databases provide collections of information organized for rapid search and retrieval.

If you have trouble finding the needed information, ask the librarian for help.

Practicing the Skill

Suppose you are going to Egypt and want to learn more about the historical sites before you go. Read the research questions below. Then decide which of the following sources you would use to answer each question and why.

a. encyclopedia
b. atlas
c. historical atlas
d. almanac
e. biographical dictionary
f. catalog entry: Egypt—travel
g. catalog entry: Egypt—archaeology
h. periodical guide

1. Where is each city on the trip itinerary located?
2. What are the places of interest in each city?
3. What have been the major discoveries in Egyptian archaeology since 1800?
4. Are there any modern historical sites you would want to visit?

Applying the Skill

Use research resources from your school or local library to research the following topic:

What medical expertise did the ancient Egyptians develop? Are any medical techniques of ancient Egypt similar to those used by doctors today? Make a list of the contributions ancient civilizations have made to medicine. List your sources.

Writing a Research Report

Writing a research report is similar to most other complex tasks. There are tools to use, skills to master, and steps to follow.

Learning the Skill

Select a topic that interests you. Brainstorming, skimming books and magazines, and talking with classmates can help.

Do preliminary research to determine whether your topic is too broad or too specific. Suppose you've chosen "The Fall of the Roman Empire." The library's computers list more than 100 books on this topic. A more manageable topic might be: "The Emperor Constantine's Reforms."

As early as possible, write a statement defining what you want to prove, discover, or illustrate in your report. For this topic, your statement might be: "Constantine's reforms helped preserve the eastern half of the Roman Empire for 1000 years."

- **Prepare to do research**. Formulate a list of main idea questions.
- **Research your topic and take notes**. At the library, use the computerized referral service to find suitable research sources. Note cards are a great tool for preparing a research report. They let you record and combine related facts and ideas from several sources. Prepare note cards on each main idea question listing the source information. Keep all the facts for each main idea together.
- **Organize your information**. Build an outline or another kind of organizer. Follow your outline or organizer in writing a rough draft.
- **Write a rough draft**. A research report should have three main parts: the introduction, the body, and the conclusion. The introduction briefly presents the topic and gives your thesis statement. In the body, follow your outline to develop the impor-

tant ideas in your argument. Connect these ideas with transitions. The conclusion summarizes and restates your findings.

In writing the rough draft write as quickly as possible without editing. Imagine that you are explaining your findings and ideas to an interested listener.

Revise the draft into a final report. Put it away for a day or so; then reread it with the cold, clear eye of an editor. Does the report have a clear structure—an introduction, a body, and a conclusion? Does the body contain all the main ideas arranged logically? Are there transitions to lead the reader from one thought to the next? If not, revise it and repeat the writing process. Correct spelling, punctuation, and grammar. Finally, make a clean copy.

Practicing the Skill

Suppose you are writing a report on the Great Wall of China. Answer the following questions about the writing process.
1. How could you narrow this topic?
2. What are three main idea questions to use?
3. Name three possible sources of information.
4. What are the next two steps in the process of writing a research report?

Applying the Skill

Choose a topic and prepare note cards. Continue your research on this topic, organize your information, and write a short report.

Preparing a Bibliography

In the previous skills exercise, you wrote a research report on some topic of interest. To complete your report, you have one more step—preparing a bibliography.

Learning the Skill

A bibliography is a list of sources used in a research report. These sources include: books; articles from newspapers, magazines, and journals; interviews; films, videotapes, audiotapes, and compact discs. Why do you need a bibliography? What purpose does it serve?

There are two main reasons to write a bibliography. First, those who read your report may want to learn more about the topic. Second, a bibliography supports the reliability of your report.

A bibliography should follow a definite format. The entry for each source must contain all the information needed to find that source: author, title, publisher information, and publication date. You should have this information already on note cards. If you neglected this step earlier, you must return to the library to find the sources again.

In a bibliography, arrange entries alphabetically by the author's last name. The following are accepted formats for bibliography entries, followed by sample entries. Note the form of punctuation used between parts of the entry.

Books
Author's last name, first name. <u>Full Title</u>. Place of publication: publisher, copyright date.
Oliver, Roland A. <u>Africa in the Iron Age, 500 B.C. to A.D. 1400</u>. New York: Cambridge University Press, 1975.

Articles
Author's last name, first name. "Title of Article." <u>Name of Periodical</u> in which article appears, Volume number (date of issue): page numbers.

Williams, Marie. "The Silk Road Through Pakistan." <u>PSA Journal</u>, Vol. 63 (March 1997): pp. 12-14.

Other Sources
For other kinds of sources, adapt the format for book entries.

Practicing the Skill

Review the sample bibliography below for a report on the Maya. Then answer the questions that follow.

Sharer, Robert J. Daily Life in Maya Civilization. Westport, Conn.: Greenwood Press, 1996.
Schele, Linda. <u>A Forest of Kings: the Untold Story of the Ancient Maya</u>. New York: Morrow, 1990.
"Cracking the Maya's Code: New Light on Dark History." <u>The Economist</u>, Vol. 341 (December 21, 1996): pp. 55-59.
La Bastille, Anne. "How the King of the Birds was Chosen: and Other Mayan Folktales." <u>International Wildlife</u>, (March-April, 1997) pp. 30-35.

1. Are the bibliography entries in the correct order? Why or why not?
2. What is missing from the first book listing?
3. What is missing from the second article listing?

Applying the Skill

Compile a bibliography for your research report. Include at least five sources, preferably a mix of books and articles. Exchange bibliographies with another student and check each other for proper format and arrangement.

A

abbess the director of a convent (p. 305)

abbot the head of a monastery (p. 304)

absolutism political system in which a monarch (or group) holds supreme, unlimited power or theory that supports such a system (p. 482)

acupuncture traditional technique of Chinese medicine using thin needles at vital body points (p. 232)

age set in traditional Africa, a group of males or females of similar age who learn skills and go through life stages together (p. 188)

ahimsa (uh•HIHM•sah) Hindu doctrine of nonviolence toward all living things (p. 207)

alphabet system of symbols or characters that represent the sounds of a language (p. 82)

amphora a tall, two-handled Greek vase (p. 131)

animism belief that spirits are found in both living and nonliving things (pp. 351, 476)

anthropologist (an•thruh•PAH•luh•jihst) scientist who studies physical and cultural characteristics of humans and their ancestors (p. 20)

apprentice person who works for a master to learn a trade, art, or business (p. 325)

aqueduct a channel built to carry water (p. 168)

arabesque (ar•uh•BEHSK) complex designs typical of Islamic art, combining intertwining plants and geometric patterns (p. 286)

"Arabic numerals" counting symbols (1-9) devised by mathematicians in Gupta India (p. 214)

archaeologist (ahr•kee•AHL•uh•jihst) scientist who studies earlier peoples and cultures (p. 20)

archipelago a group or chain of islands (p. 351)

aristocrat member of the nobility or the upper class (p. 113)

armada (ahr•MAH•duh) a fleet of warships (p. 483)

artifact a historic object made or used by humans, such as a tool, ornament, or pottery (p. 20)

artisan person skilled in a craft (p. 33)

B

balance of power the distribution of power among rival nations so that no one is dominant (p. 489)

balance of trade difference in value between what a nation imports and what it exports over a period of time (p. 448)

bard a poet who tells stories by singing (p. 108)

baroque (buh•ROHK) ornate, dramatic artistic style developed in Europe in the 1550s (p. 424)

barter a system of trade in which goods, not money, are exchanged (p. 82)

bazaar marketplace in an Islamic city (p. 284)

bishop a regional leader of the early Christian Church, with authority over a diocese and other clergy (p. 174)

boyar a landowning noble of early Russia (pp. 260, 499)

bullion gold or silver in the form of bars or plate (p. 448)

bureaucracy a group of government officials headed by an administrator (p. 48)

C

caliph (KAY•lihf) supreme leader of Islam, chosen as the "successor" of Muhammad (p. 277)

calligraphy the art of beautiful handwriting (p. 286)

cardinal high-ranking official of Roman Catholic Church, appointed by the pope (p. 306)

cartographer person who makes maps (p. 436)

cavalry soldiers mounted on horseback (p. 221)

charter formal document granting the right of self-rule (p. 326)

châteaux (sing., chateau [Fr.]) castles (p. 413)

chinampas artificial islands built by the Aztecs for use as gardens (p. 388)

chivalry code of conduct for medieval knights, based on ideals of honor and courtesy (p. 301)

chronicle an account that records events in the order in which they happened (p. 288)

circumnavigation sailing completely around something, such as the world (p. 439)

citizen in ancient Greece, a person who took part in the government of a city-state (p. 112)

city-state an independent state consisting of a city and the surrounding land and villages (p. 59)

civil service system by which government offices are given on the basis of examinations (p. 224)

civilization highly organized society marked by advanced knowledge of trade, government, arts, science, and often written language (p. 32)

clan group based on family ties (p. 342)

classical describing the artistic style of ancient Greece and Rome, characterized by balance, elegance, and simplicity (p. 130)

clergy persons, such as priests, given authority to conduct religious services (p. 249)

colony a settlement of people outside their homeland, linked with the parent country by trade and direct government control (pp. 82, 475)

comedy story or play intended to entertain and amuse, usually with a happy ending (p. 134)

common law body of English law based on tradition and court decisions, not specific laws (p. 309)

confederation a loose alliance or union of several states or groups (pp. 82, 378)

conquistador (kon•KEES•tuh•dohr) a Spanish "conqueror" or soldier in the Americas (p. 441)

constitution plan of government (p. 117)

consul in ancient Rome, one of two officials who headed the executive branch (p. 157)

cortes (KOR•tays) assembly of nobles, clergy, and town officials in medieval Spain; also, the parliament of modern Spain (p. 332)

count a noble who acted as a local official within the Frankish empire (p. 295)

covenant a solemn pledge or agreement (p. 83)

Crusades military expeditions by European Christians in the 11th–13th centuries to regain the Holy Land from the Muslims (p. 318)

cultural diffusion the exchange of goods, ideas, and customs among different cultures (p. 34)

culture the way of life of a given people at a given time, including language, behavior, and beliefs (p. 24)

cuneiform (kyoo•NEE•uh•fawrm) Sumerian system of writing using wedge-shaped markings (p. 60)

czar (from "caesar") title taken by rulers of Russia beginning in the late 1400s (p. 264)

D

daimyo (DY•mee•oh) a powerful local noble in feudal Japan (p. 363)

datus local rulers in the Philippines (p. 475)

deity a god or goddess (p. 31)

democracy form of government in which the citizens hold power (p. 114)

dharma duties and rights of members of each class in traditional Hindu society (p. 205)

Diaspora (dye•AS•pur•uh) term for the scattering of communities of Jews outside their original homeland after the Babylonian captivity (p. 86)

dictator in ancient Rome, a leader given temporary absolute power during a crisis (p. 157)

disciple an active follower of a teacher (p. 172)

divine right political theory that a ruler derives his or her power directly from God and is accountable only to God (p. 482)

doge (DOHJ) the elected leader of the republic in the city-states of Venice and Genoa (p. 408)

domain territory held by a ruler (p. 142)

domesticate to tame animals or plants to serve human needs (p. 30)

dvorianie (dvoh•ree•YAH•nee•yuh) new class of Russian landed nobility established by Peter the Great (p. 501)

dynasty a line of rulers who belong to the same family (p. 47)

E

economy system by which goods and services are produced and distributed to meet people's needs (p. 33)

empire group of territories or nations ruled by a single ruler or government (p. 49)

entrepreneur person who undertakes risks to establish a business (p. 448)

epic long poem celebrating the deeds of a legendary or historical hero (p. 203)

ethics a system of moral principles that guide behavior (p. 225)

excommunication formal exclusion from membership or participation in a church (p. 306)

exodus the departure of a large group of people (p. 84)

extended family family group including several generations as well as other relatives (p. 229)

F

feudalism medieval political system in which monarchs and lesser nobles made alliances based on exchanging land grants for loyalty (p. 298)

fief under feudalism, an estate with its peasant workers granted to a noble in exchange for loyalty and military help (p. 298)

filial piety children's respect for their parents, an important principle in Confucian ethics (p. 226)

friar member of a Catholic order who preached in towns and practiced poverty (p. 307)

G

geisha Japanese woman trained as a professional entertainer (p. 472)

gentry in Elizabethan England, the social group including minor nobility and landowners (p. 488)

ghana title of the ruler of a region in ancient Africa, later applied to the kingdom (p. 189)

grand jury in English law, group of people who decide whether the evidence of a crime justifies bringing a person to trial (p. 309)

grand vizier (vih•ZEER) prime minister to the sultan of a Muslim country (p. 457)

guild medieval business association of merchants or craftsworkers (p. 324)

H

haiku (HY•koo) Japanese poetry form with 17 syllables, usually in three lines (p. 472)

hajj pilgrimage to Makkah that every able-bodied Muslim is expected to make at least once (p. 276)

heresy disagreement with or denial of the basic teachings of a religion (p. 306)

hierarchy group of people organized according to levels of rank or importance (pp. 228, 389)

hieroglyphics ancient Egyptian writing system using picture symbols for ideas or sounds (p. 52)

homage formal ceremony establishing feudal ties between a lord and a vassal (p. 299)

hominid (HAH•muh•nihd) member of the group that includes human beings and earlier human-like creatures (p. 20)

humanism Renaissance movement based on the literature and ideas of ancient Greece and Rome, such as the worth of each individual (p. 404)

hygiene the science of good health (p. 138)

I

icon a Christian religious image or picture (p. 249)

iconoclast ("image breaker") an opponent of the use of icons in Byzantine churches, who thought they encouraged the worship of idols (p. 250)

illuminated manuscript book page decorated by hand with elaborate designs, beautiful lettering, or miniature paintings (p. 253)

imam (ih•MAM) a Muslim prayer leader (p. 276)

indemnity payment for damages or losses (p. 160)

individualism emphasis on the dignity and worth of the individual person (p. 404-05)

indulgence pardon sold by the Catholic Church to reduce one's punishment for sins (p. 416)

inflation situation in which prices rise quickly while the value of money decreases (pp. 176, 484)

intendant an agent representing the king of France in local government (p. 491)

J

jaguar spotted wild cat of Mesoamerica (p. 380)

janissary member of an elite corps of soldiers in the Ottoman Empire (p. 457)

jati groups based on occupation formed within larger social classes (varna) in ancient India, each with its own rules and customs (p. 204)

jihad (jih•HAHD) Muslim struggle to introduce Islam to other lands (p. 278)

joint-stock company trading venture that sold shares to divide costs and profits (p. 447)

journeyman craftsworker who has finished an apprenticeship and works for pay (p. 325)

junk a Chinese sailing ship (p. 464)

justification by faith Martin Luther's concept that faith alone is enough to bring salvation (p. 415)

karma in Hinduism, the idea that one's actions in life determine one's destiny and future (p. 207)

khan an absolute ruler of the Mongols (p. 344)

L

labor-intensive farming agriculture that relies on human labor, not animals or machines (p. 466)

labyrinth a complex, confusing series of connected passages (p. 107)

laity church members who are not clergy (p. 249)

lay investiture medieval practice in which secular rulers appointed and inaugurated church officials such as bishops (p. 306)

line of demarcation imaginary line in the Atlantic Ocean, drawn by the pope in 1493 to divide the world's lands between Spain and Portugal (p. 439)

logic the science of reasoning and establishing proof for arguments (p. 135)

M

madrasa Muslim school of theology and law (p. 283)

maize corn native to the Americas (p. 374)

mandarin member of the elite class of civil servants in Chinese government (pp. 224, 348)

mandate in ancient China, authority granted by heaven to deserving rulers, called the Mandate of Heaven (p. 71)

manorialism medieval economic system linking nobles and the peasants on their land (p. 301)

martyr person who suffers and dies for a belief (p. 173)

master skilled artisan who owned a shop and employed other craftsworkers (p. 325)

matrilineal tracing family descent through the mother and her ancestors (p. 187)

mayor of the palace Frankish official who, by A.D. 700, held real power in government (p. 294)

mercantilism economic policy of European nations in the 1600s, equating wealth and power (p. 448)

mercenary a soldier who serves a foreign country for pay (p. 124)

meritocracy system in which people gain success on the basis of ability and performance (p. 347)

messiah in Judaism, a savior promised by the Hebrew prophets, who would bring peace (p. 171)

metsuke group of officials who gathered information for the Tokugawa shoguns (p. 469)

middle class class of society that originally fell between nobility and peasants, earning their income from business and trade (p. 310)

Middle Passage middle section of the triangular trade, in which enslaved Africans were brought by ship to the Americas (p. 445)

millet community of non-Muslims within the Ottoman Empire (p. 458)

missionary person who travels to carry the ideas of a religion to others (p. 254)

monarchy rule by a king or a queen (p. 47)

monastery a community of men who have taken religious vows (p. 254)

money economy economic system in which money (not barter) is used to buy and sell (p. 323)

monopoly control of all (or almost all) trade or production of a given good (p. 194)

monotheism belief in one God (pp. 83, 189)

monsoon seasonal wind that affects climates and ways of life in southern Asia (p. 66)

mosaic picture made up of tiny pieces of colored glass, tile, or stone set in mortar (p. 253)

mosque a Muslim house of worship (pp. 191, 276)

multicultural representing several different cultural and ethnic groups (p. 195)

myth a traditional story that explains natural events (p. 35)

N

nirvana in Buddhism, a state of oneness with the universe, the end of the cycle of rebirth (p. 210)

nomad member of a group of people with no fixed home, who travel constantly to find food and water (p. 22)

nuclear family family group consisting only of parents and children (p. 229)

O

obsidian black volcanic glass (p. 383)

oligarchy form of government in which a small group holds political power (p. 114)

oral tradition the legends and history of a culture preserved by word of mouth (p. 184)

P

paleontologist (pay•lee•ahn•TAH•luh•jihst) scientist who studies fossil remains (p. 20)

patriarch in the early Christian Church, one of five powerful bishops in major cities (p. 174)

patrician a member of the wealthy aristocratic class of ancient Rome (p. 156)

perspective an artistic technique for showing relationships and space between objects (p. 131)

petit jury group of people who determine the guilt or innocence of a person on trial (p. 309)

phalanx in ancient Greece, a military formation in which foot soldiers stood so that their shields overlapped (p. 114)

pharaoh title of rulers of ancient Egypt (p. 49)

philosopher a thinker or lover of wisdom (p. 135)

pilgrimage journey to a holy place (p. 334)

plateau a relatively flat region of land higher than the surrounding area (p. 185)

plebeian (plih•BEE•uhn) a citizen of ancient Rome who was not an aristocrat (p. 156)

polis city-state of ancient Greece (p. 112)

polytheism worship of many gods (p. 52)

pope the bishop of Rome, later the head of the Roman Catholic Church (p. 174)

potlatch feast held by Native Americans of the Pacific Northwest to display their wealth (p. 376)

pragmatic sanction decree issued by a ruler on an important question (p. 495)

predestination doctrine of John Calvin that each person's fate is predetermined by God (p. 419)

prehistory time before written history (p. 20)

principality territory ruled by a prince (p. 260)

prophet a person who preaches or interprets what are thought to be messages from God (p. 83)

Q

queue (KYOO) single braid of hair at the back of the head (p. 466)

quinoa grain grown in the Andes (p. 390)

R

radiocarbon dating modern scientific method for telling the age of once-living material by measuring the amount of radioactive carbon remaining in it (p. 21)

rajah an Aryan tribal chief in ancient India; later the ruler of an Indian state (p. 202)

regent person who acts as a temporary ruler (p. 251)

reincarnation the rebirth of the soul or spirit in different bodies over time (p. 206)

republic a government in which citizens elect the leaders (p. 156)

revelation a vision of divine truth, such as those attributed to Muhammad (p. 272)

rhetoric art of effective public speaking (p. 119)

S

sacrament one of the established formal rituals of the Roman Catholic Church, such as baptism, holy communion, or matrimony (p. 303)

samurai class of landowning warriors in feudal Japan, who pledged loyalty to a daimyo (p. 363)

sanctuary building used for worship (p. 130)

sankin-kotai ("alternate attendance") in feudal Japan, system in which a daimyo had to spend every other year at the shogun's court (p. 469)

satrap governor of a Persian province (p. 91)

savanna a flat grassland, with few trees, in tropical or subtropical regions (p. 185)

schism (SIH•zuhm) the division of the Christian Church in 1054 that separated the Roman Catholic Church and the Eastern Orthodox Church (p. 250)

scholasticism medieval school of thought that tried to bring together Aristotle's philosophy and the teachings of Church scholars (p. 326)

sect a subgroup with distinct beliefs within a larger religious group (p. 171)

secular worldly, not overtly or specifically religious (p. 404)

seminary school for educating priests, as ordered by the Council of Trent (p. 423)

serf a peasant laborer legally bound to the lands of a noble (pp. 302, 501)

shamanism belief that spirits inhabit living and nonliving things, communicating with humans through priests called shamans (p. 358)

shari'ah (shuh•REE•uh) Islamic code of law that includes rules for all aspects of life (p. 275)

sheikh (SHAYK) chief of a bedouin tribe (p. 271)

shogun military ruler of feudal Japan (p. 363)

shogunate government established by a shogun's family and followers in feudal Japan (p. 363)

simony the selling of official positions in the medieval Roman Catholic Church (p. 335)

slash-and-burn farming farming method in which land for crops is cleared by cutting and burning trees to fertilize the soil (p. 380)

sonnet poetry form with 14 lines and a fixed pattern of rhyme and meter (p. 405)

steppe wide, grassy, semiarid plains of Eurasia, from the Black Sea to the Altai Mountains (p. 258)

stupa a dome-shaped Buddhist shrine built over relics or bones of a holy person (p. 210)

subcontinent landmass that is part of a continent but distinct from it, such as India (p. 66)

sultan political leader with absolute authority over a Muslim country (p. 457)

symposium in ancient Athens, a gathering of men that featured eating, drinking, entertainment, and intellectual discussions (p. 123)

T

technology the skills and knowledge used by people to make tools and do work (p. 24)

theocracy government headed by religious leaders or a leader regarded as a god (pp. 48, 418)

theology study of religious questions (p. 251)

tournament medieval sport in which knights competed to show their fighting skills (p. 299)

tragedy story or play in which the central character struggles against destiny but meets an unhappy end (p. 132)

triangular trade three-directional trade route between Europe, Africa, and America in the 1600s (p. 444)

tribune in ancient Rome, an official who represented the plebeians (p. 157)

triumvirate in ancient Rome, a three-person ruling group (p. 162)

troubadour poet-musician of the Middle Ages, who traveled from court to court (p. 327)

tyrant in ancient Greece, a person who seized power and established one-man rule (p. 114)

U V

varna one of four main social classes in Aryan society of ancient India (p. 203)

vassal in feudalism, a noble who held land from and served a higher-ranking lord (p. 299)

vernacular the language of everyday speech, not of scholars, in a country or region (p. 328)

vocation a calling from God to take up certain work (p. 417)

W X Y Z

weir net or trap placed across a river to catch fish (p. 376)

yasa Mongol law code of Genghis Khan (p. 344)

yeoman (YOH•mun) in English society, a farmer who owned land (p. 488)

yin and yang in Chinese thinking, the opposing principles present in all nature (p. 227)

yurt large, round, portable tent used by nomads of central Asia (p. 343)

A

abbess/abadesa superiora de un convento (pág. 305)

abbot/abad superior de un monasterio (pág. 304)

absolutism/absolutismo sistema político en el cual un monarca (o grupo) tiene poder supremo e ilimitado, o teoría que sustenta tal sistema (pág. 482)

acupuncture/acupuntura técnica tradicional de la medicina china que utiliza agujas finas en puntos vitales del cuerpo (pág. 232)

age set/grupo etario en el África tradicional, un grupo de varones o hembras de edad semejante que adquieren destrezas y siguen juntos a través de las distintas etapas de la vida (pág. 188)

ahimsa/ahimsa doctrina hindú de no-violencia hacia todo lo que tiene vida (pág. 207)

alphabet/alfabeto sistema de símbolos o caracteres que representan los sonidos de un lenguaje (pág. 82)

amphora/ánfora jarrón griego alto, de dos asas (pág. 131)

animism/animismo creencia de que los espíritus residen tanto en los seres vivos como en las cosas inanimadas (págs. 351, 476)

anthropologist/antropólogo científico que estudia las características físicas y culturales de los seres humanos y sus antecesores (pág. 20)

apprentice/aprendiz persona que trabaja para un maestro a fin de aprender un oficio, arte o negocio (pág. 325)

aqueduct/acueducto canal construido para conducir las aguas (pág. 168)

arabesque/arabesco complejos diseños típicos del arte islámico que combinaban plantas entrelazadas y patrones geométricos (pág. 286)

"Arabic numerals"/números arábigos símbolos de numeración diseñados por matemáticos en Gupta, India (pág. 214)

archaeologist/arqueólogo científico que estudia pueblos y culturas de la Antigüedad (pág. 20)

archipelago/archipiélago grupo o cadena de islas (pág. 351)

aristocrat/aristócrata miembro de la nobleza o de la clase alta (pág. 113)

armada/armada escuadra de buques de guerra (pág. 483)

artifact/artefacto histórico objeto fabricado o usado por los humanos, tal como una herramienta, adorno o artículo de alfarería (pág. 20)

artisan/artesano persona diestra en un arte manual (pág. 33)

B

balance of power/equilibrio de poder la distribución del poder entra naciones rivales de modo que ninguna predomine (pág. 489)

balance of trade/equilibrio comercial diferencia en valor entre lo que una nación importa y lo que exporta durante un período de tiempo (pág. 448)

bard/bardo poeta que narra cuentos por medio del canto (pág. 108)

baroque/barroco estilo artístico recargado y dramático, desarrollado en Europa a mediados del siglo XVI (pág. 424)

barter/trueque sistema de comercio en el cual se intercambiaban bienes y no dinero (pág. 82)

bazaar/bazar mercado público en una ciudad islámica (pág. 284)

bishop/obispo jefe regional de la Iglesia Cristiana primitiva, con autoridad sobre una diócesis y otros miembros del clero (pág. 174)

boyar/boyardo un noble propietario de tierras en la Rusia primitiva (págs. 260, 499)

bullion/lingote oro o plata en forma de barras o planchas (pág. 448)

bureaucracy/burocracia un grupo de funcionarios del gobierno encabezado por un administrador (pág. 48)

C

caliph/califa líder supremo de Islam, escogido como sucesor de Mahoma (pág. 277)

calligraphy/caligrafía el arte de escribir con letra hermosa (pág. 286)

cardinal/cardenal eclesiástico de alto rango en la Iglesia Católica designado por el Papa (pág. 306)

cartographer/cartógrafo persona que dibuja mapas (pág. 436)

cavalry/caballería cuerpo de soldados a caballo (pág. 221)

charter/carta constitucional documento formal que concede el derecho al gobierno propio (pág. 326)

chateaux/castillos un tipo de fortaleza (pág. 413)

chinampas/chinampas islas artificiales construidas por los aztecas para utilizar como jardines (pág. 388)

chivalry/caballería código de conducta de los caballeros medievales basado en ideales de honor y cortesía (pág. 301)

chronicle/crónica relación que registra eventos en el orden en que éstos sucedieron (pág. 288)

circumnavigation/circunnavegación viaje marítimo

completamente alrededor de algo, como por ejemplo, el mundo (pág. 439)

citizen/ciudadano en la antigua Gracia, persona que participaba del gobierno en una ciudad-estado (pág. 112)

city-state/ciudad-estado un estado independiente que consistía en una ciudad y las tierras y aldeas que la rodeaban (pág. 59)

civil service/servicio civil sistema mediante el cual puestos del gobierno son concedidos mediante exámenes (pág. 224)

civilization/civilización sociedad altamente organizada caracterizada por el conocimiento avanzado del comercio, gobierno, artes, ciencia y a menudo, lenguaje escrito (pág. 32)

clan/clan grupo unido por lazos familiares (pág. 342)

classical/clásico que describe el estilo artístico de las antiguas Gracia y Roma, caracterizado por el equilibrio, la elegancia y la simpleza (pág. 130)

clergy/clero personas, tales como los sacerdotes, que tienen autoridad para conducir servicios religiosos (pág. 249)

colony/colonia establecimiento de personas que están fuera de su país, enlazado a la madre patria por el comercio y el control directo del gobierno (págs. 82, 475)

comedy/comedia historia o representación que se propone entretener y divertir usualmente con un desenlace feliz (pág. 134)

common law/derecho consuetudinario sistema de leyes inglesas basadas en la tradición y decisiones de la corte, no en leyes específicas (pág. 309)

confederation/confederación alianza flexible o unión de varios estados o grupos (págs. 82, 378)

conquistador/conquistador aventurero o soldado español en las Américas (pág. 441)

constitution/constitución plan de gobierno (pág. 117)

consul/cónsul en la antigua Roma, uno de los dos magistrados que dirigían al poder ejecutivo (pág. 157)

cortes/cortes asamblea de los nobles, el clero y los funcionarios del pueblo en la España medieval; también, el parlamento en la España moderna (pág. 332)

count/conde noble que actuaba como funcionario local dentro del imperio de los francos (pág. 295)

covenant/convenio pacto o acuerdo solemne (pág. 83)

Crusades/Cruzadas expediciones militares por cristianos europeos en los siglos XI al XIII para con-quistar la Tierra Santa de manos de los musulmanes (pág. 318)

cultural diffusion/difusión cultural intercambio de bienes, ideas y costumbres entre diferentes culturas (pág. 34)

culture/cultura modo de vida de un pueblo en un tiempo determinado, que incluye su lenguaje, conducta y creencias (pág. 24)

cuneiform/cuneiforme sistema de escritura sumerio que utilizaba símbolos en forma de cuña (pág. 60)

czar/zar (de "caesar") título adoptado por los gobernantes de Rusia desde finales del siglo XV (pág. 264)

D

daimyo/daimyo poderoso noble local en el Japón feudal (pág. 363)

datus/datus gobernantes locales en las Filipinas (pág. 475)

deity/deidad un dios o diosa (pág. 31)

democracy/democracia forma de gobierno en la cual los ciudadanos ejercen el poder (pág. 114)

dharma/dharma deberes y derechos de los miembros de cada clase en la sociedad hindú tradicional (pág. 205)

Diaspora/Diáspora término que se refiere a la dispersión de las comunidades judías fuera de su patria original después de la Cautividad de Babilonia (pág. 86)

dictator/dictador en la antigua Roma, líder a quien se daba poder temporal absoluto durante una crisis (pág. 157)

disciple/discípulo activo seguidor de un maestro (pág. 172)

divine right/derecho divino teoría politica que mantiene que un gobernante deriva su autoridad directamente de Dios y es responsable de sus actos sólo ante Dios (pág. 482)

doge/dux líder electo de la república en las ciudades-estados de Venecia y Génova (pág. 408)

domain/dominio territorio perteneciente a un gobernante (pág. 142)

domesticate/domesticar adiestrar animales o adaptar plantas para satisfacer necesidades humanas (pág. 30)

dvorianie/dvorianie nueva clase de nobleza rusa dueña de tierras, establecida por Pedro I el Grande (pág. 501)

dynasty/dinastía sucesión de gobernantes que pertenecen a la misma familia (pág. 47)

economy/economía sistema por el cual bienes y servicios son producidos y distribuidos para satisfacer las necesidades del pueblo (pág. 33)

empire/imperio grupo de territorios o naciones regidos por un solo emperador o gobierno (pág. 49)

entrepreneur/empresario persona que corre riesgos para fundar un negocio (pág. 448)

epic/poema épico poema extenso que celebraba las hazañas de un héroe legendario o histórico (pág. 203)

ethics/ética sistema de principios morales que guían la conducta (pág. 225)

excommunication/excomunión exclusión formal de la membresía o de su participación en una iglesia (pág. 306)

exodus/éxodo emigración de un grupo numeroso de personas (pag. 84)

extended family/familia completa grupo familiar que incluye a varias generaciones así como a otros parientes (pág. 229)

F

feudalism/feudalismo sistema político medieval en el cual los monarcas y los nobles menores hacían alianzas basadas en el intercambio de concesiones de tierras por lealtad (pág. 298)

fief/feudo bajo el feudalismo, una tierra con sus labriegos concedida a un noble a cambio de lealtad y ayuda militar (pág. 298)

filial piety/piedad filial respeto de los hijos hacia sus padres, un principio importante en la filosofía moral de Confucio (pág. 226)

friar/fraile miembro de una orden religiosa católica que predicaba en los pueblos y practicaba la pobreza (pág. 307)

G

geisha/geisha mujer japonesa adiestrada profesionalmente para entretener (pág. 472)

gentry/gentry en la Inglaterra isabelina, el grupo social que incluía a la nobleza menor y a los terratenientes (pág. 488)

ghana/ghana título del gobernante de una región en el África antigua, que más tarde fue aplicado al reinado (pág. 189)

grand jury/gran jurado en la ley inglesa, grupo de personas que deciden si la evidencia de un crimen justifica llevar a una persona a juicio (pag. 309)

grand vizier/gran visir primer ministro del sultán de un país musulmán (pág. 457)

guild/gremio asociación comercial medieval de mercaderes o artesanos (pág. 324)

H

haiku/hai kai forma de poesía japonesa generalmente con tres versos de 17 sílabas (pág. 472)

hajj/hajj peregrinación a La Meca que todo musulmán en buenas condiciones físicas se supone realice por lo menos una vez en su vida (pág. 276)

heresy/herejía desacuerdo con la enseñanzas básicas de una religión o negación de las mismas (pág. 306)

hierarchy/jerarquía grupo de personas organizadas de acuerdo con niveles de rango o importancia (págs. 228, 389)

hieroglyphics/jeroglíficos sistema egipcio antiguo de escritura que utilizaba símbolos pictóricos para representar ideas o sonidos (pág. 52)

homage/homenaje ceremonia formal que establecía lazos feudales entre un señor y un vasallo (pág. 299)

hominid/homínido miembro del grupo que incluye a los seres humanos y a las criaturas primates primitivas (pág. 20)

humanism/Humanismo movimiento renacentista basado en la literatura e ideas de las antiguas Grecia y Roma, tales como el valor de cada individuo (pág. 404)

hygiene/higiene la ciencia de la buena salud (pág. 138)

I

icon/ícono imagen religiosa cristiana o cuadro que representa a un santo u otra persona sagrada (pág. 249)

iconoclast/iconoclasta ("destructor de imágenes") un opositor al uso de íconos en las iglesias bizantinas, que pensaba que éstos estimulaban la adoración de ídolos (pág. 250)

illuminated manuscript/manuscrito iluminado página de un libro, decorada con elaborados diseños, hermosas letras, o pinturas en miniatura (pág. 253)

imam/imán un guía de oraciones musulmanas (pág. 276)

indemnity/indemnización pago por daños y pérdidas (pág. 160)

individualism/individualismo énfasis en la aignidad de la persona (pág. 404–05)

indulgence/indulgencia perdón vendido por la Iglesia Católica para reducir el castigo de pecados (pág. 416)

inflation/inflación situación en la cual los precios suben rápidamente mientras que el valor del dinero disminuye (págs. 176, 484)

intendant/intendente agente que representaba al rey de Francia en el gobierno local (pág. 491)

J

jaguar/jaguar gato salvaje con manchas en la piel, de América Central (pág. 380)

janissary/jenízaro miembro del cuerpo más selecto de soldados del Imperio Otomano (pág. 457)

jati/jati grupos formados dentro de las mayores clases sociales *(varna)* en la antigua India según las ocupaciones de sus miembros y con sus propias reglas y costumbres (pág. 204)

jihad/jihad lucha mahometana para introducir el islamismo en otras tierras (pág. 278)

joint-stock company/compañía por acciones empresa comercial que vende acciones para dividir entre los participantes los costos y las ganancias (pág. 447)

journeyman/jornalero artesano que ha terminado su aprendizaje y trabaja por un jornal (pág. 325)

junk/junco embarcación china (pág. 464)

justification by faith/justificación por la fe concepto de Martín Lutero de que la fe por sí sola es suficiente para alcanzar la salvación (pág. 415)

K

karma/karma en el hinduismo, la idea de que las acciones de los hombres en la vida determinaban sus destinos y sus futuros (pág. 207)

khan/kan gobernante absoluto de los mongoles (pág. 344)

L

labor-intensive farming/agricultura manual intensiva agricultura que confía en el trabajo humano, no en animales o máquinas (pág. 466)

labyrinth/laberinto conjunto complejo y confuso de pasajes que se conectan (pág. 107)

laity/el estado seglar miembros de una iglesia que no pertenecen al clero (pág. 249)

lay investiture/investidura seglar práctica medieval en la cual las autoridades seglares designaban e investían a funcionarios de la iglesia tales como los obispos (pág. 306)

line of demarcation/línea de demarcación línea imaginaria en el Océano Atlántico, trazada por el papa en 1493 para dividir las tierras del mundo entre España y Portugal (pág. 439)

logic/lógica la ciencia del razonamiento y del establecimiento de pruebas en los debates (pág. 135)

M

madrasa/madrasa escuela musulmana de teología y leyes (pág. 283)

maize/maíz el maíz nativo de la América (pág. 374)

mandarin/mandarín miembro de la clase más selecta de funcionarios en el gobierno chino (págs. 224, 348)

mandate/mandato en la antigua China, la autoridad concedida por el cielo a gobernantes merecedores de ello, llamada el Mandato del Cielo (pág. 71)

manorialism/economía feudal sistema económico medieval que ataba a los nobles y a los campesinos a su tierra (pág. 301)

martyr/mártir persona que sufre y muere por una creencia (pág. 173)

master/maestro artesano hábil que era el propietario de un taller y empleaba a otros artesanos (pág.325)

matrilineal/línea materna que traza el origen de una familia a través de la madre y los ancestros de ésta (pág. 187)

mayor of the palace/jefe del palacio dignatario franco que, alrededor del siglo VIII d.C. tenía poder en el gobierno (pág. 294)

mercantilism/mercantilismo política económica de las naciones europeas en el Siglo XVII, que igualaba la riqueza al poder (pág. 448)

mercenary/mercenario soldado que sirve a un país extranjero por dinero (pág. 124)

meritocracy/sistema de ascenso por méritos sistema en el cual las personas obtienen éxito a base de su habilidad y actuación (pág. 347)

messiah/mesías en el judaísmo, el salvador prometido por los profetas hebreos, quien traería la paz (pág. 171)

metsuke/metsuke grupo de funcionarios que recolectaban información para los shogúnes de Tokugawa (pag. 469)

middle class/clase media clase social que originalmente estaba entre la nobleza y el campesinado, y que se ganaba la vida por medio de actividades comerciales (pág. 310)

Middle Passage/Paso Central sección intermedia del comercio triangular, en el cual los africanos esclavizados eran traídos a la América por barco (pág. 445)

millet/millet comunidad de los no-musulmanes dentro del imperio otomano (pág. 458)

missionary/misionero persona que viaja para llevar las principios de una religión a otras personas (pág. 254)

monarchy/monarquía gobierno de un rey o una reina (pág. 47)

monastery/monasterio comunidad de hombres que han tomado votos religiosos (pág. 254)

money economy/economía monetaria sistema económico en el cual se usa el dinero y no el trueque para comprar y vender (pág. 323)

monopoly/monopolio control de todo (o casi todo) el comercio o la producción de un producto determinado (pág. 194)

monotheism/monoteísmo creencia en un solo dios (págs. 83, 189)

monsoon/monzón viento periódico que afecta el clima y las formas de vida en el sur de Asia (pág. 66)

mosaic/mosaico cuadro hecho de pedazos de vidrio de colores, barro cocido o piedra unidos con mortero (pág. 253)

mosque/mezquita templo mahometano (págs. 191, 276)

multicultural/multicultural que representa varios grupos culturales y étnicos diferentes (pág. 195)

myth/mito relato tradicional que explica sucesos naturales (pág. 35)

nirvana/nirvana en el budismo, estado de unidad con el universo; el final del ciclo de renacimiento (pág. 210)

nomad/nómada miembro de un grupo de personas sin hogar fijo, que viajan constantemente para buscar comida y agua (pág. 22)

nuclear family/núcleo familiar grupo familiar que incluye sólo a padres e hijos (pág. 229)

O

obsidian/obsidiana cristal volcánico negro (pág. 383)

oligarchy/oligarquía forma de gobierno en la cual un grupo pequeño ejerce el poder político (pág. 114)

oral tradition/tradición oral las leyendas e historia de una cultura preservada de viva voz (pág. 184)

paleontologist/paleontólogo científico que estudia los fósiles (pág. 20)

patriarch/patriarca en la Iglesia cristiana primitiva, uno de los cinco obispos poderosos en las ciudades importantes (pág. 174)

patrician/patricio miembro de una clase aristocrática acaudalada en la antigua Roma (pág. 156)

perspective/perspectiva técnica artística que muestra las relaciones y el espacio entre los objetos (pág. 131)

petit jury/jurado menor grupo de personas que determinan la culpabilidad o la inocencia de una persona procesada (pág. 309)

phalanx/falange en la antigua Grecia, una formación militar en la cual soldados de infantería se colocaban de tal modo que sus escudos quedaban superpuestos (pág. 114)

pharaoh/faraón título de los gobernadores del antiguo Egipto (pág. 49)

philosopher/filósofo un pensador o un amante de la sabiduría (pág. 135)

pilgrimage/peregrinación viaje a un lugar sagrado (pág. 334)

plateau/altiplanicie región relativamente llana más elevada que el área circundante (pág. 185)

plebeian/plebeyo ciudadano de la antigua Roma que no era un aristócrata (pág. 156)

polis/polis ciudad-estado de la antigua Grecia (pág. 112)

polytheism/politeísmo adoración de varios dioses (pág. 52)

pope/papa el obispo de Roma, más tarde el jefe de la Iglesia Católica Romana (pág. 174)

potlatch festín celebrado por los americanos nativos del Noroeste del Pacífico (pág. 376)

pragmatic sanction/sanción pragmática decreto emitido por un gobernante sobre un asunto importante (pág. 495)

predestination/predestinación doctrina de John Calvin (fundador del calvinismo) que predicaba que el destino de una persona estaba predeterminado por Dios (pág. 419)

prehistory/prehistoria tiempo anterior a la historia escrita (pág. 20)

principality/principado territorio gobernado por un príncipe (pág. 260)

prophet/profeta persona que predica o interpreta lo que se cree son mensajes de Dios (pág. 83)

Q

queue/coleta trenza de pelo única en la parte posterior de la cabeza (pág. 466)

quinoa/quinua grano cultivado en los Andes (pág. 390)

R

radiocarbon dating/datación de carbono radioactivo método científico moderno para determinar la edad de un sustancia que tuvo vida, midiendo la cantidad de carbono que permanece en ella (pág. 21)

rajah/rajá jefe tribal ario en la antigua India; más tarde el gobernante de un estado indio (pág. 202)

regent/regente persona que actúa como gobernante temporal (pág. 251)

reincarnation/reencarnación el renacimiento del alma o el espíritu en diferentes cuerpos a través del tiempo (pág. 206)

republic/república gobierno en el cual los ciudadanos eligen a sus dirigentes (pág. 156)

revelation/revelación visión de una realidad divina, como las atribuidas a Mahoma (pág. 272)

rhetoric/retórica el arte de hablar en público de manera efectiva (pág. 119)

S

sacrament/sacramento uno de los rituales formales establecidos por la Iglesia Católica Romana, tales como el bautismo, la sagrada comunión o el matrimonio (pág. 303)

samurai/samurai clase de guerreros terratenientes en el Japón feudal que juraban lealtad a un *daimyo* (pág. 363)

sanctuary/santuario edificio considerado sagrado, usado para la adoración (pág. 130)

sankin-kotai/sankin-kotai ("presencia alterna") en el Japón feudal, el sistema en el cual un *daimyo* tenía que residir en años alternos en la corte de un shogún (pág. 469)

satrap/sátrapa el gobernador de una provincia persa (pág. 91)

savanna/sabana llanura cubierta de vegetación, con pocos árboles, en las regiones tropicales o subtropicales (pág. 185)

schism/Cisma de Oriente la división de la Iglesia cristiana en 1054, que separó a la Iglesia Católica Romana de la Iglesia Ortodoxa Oriental (pág. 250)

scholasticism/escolasticismo enseñanza medieval que trataba de combinar la filosofía de Aristóteles con las enseñanzas de los sabios de la Iglesia (pág. 326)

sect/secta subgrupo con sus propias creencias dentro de un grupo religioso mayor (pág. 171)

secular/seglar mundano, que no es abierta o específicamente religioso (pág. 404)

seminary/seminario escuela destinada para la enseñanza de los sacerdotes, según ordenó el Concilio de Trento (pág. 423)

serf/siervo campesino labrador que dependía de las tierras de un noble (págs. 302, 501)

shamanism/chamanismo creencia de que los espíritus habitan en cosas vivas y muertas, y que se comunican con los humanos a través de unos sacerdotes llamados chamanes (pág. 358)

shari'ah/shari ah código islámico de leyes que contiene reglas para todos los aspectos de la vida (pág. 275)

sheikh/jeque jefe de una tribu beduina (pág. 271)

shogun/shogún gobernador militar en el Japón feudal (pág. 363)

shogunate/shogunado gobierno fundado por la familia de un shogún y sus seguidores en el Japón feudal (pág. 363)

simony/simonía venta de cargos oficiales en la Iglesia Católica Romana medieval (pág. 335)

slash-and-burn farming/sistema de quema y siembra método de labranza en el cual la tierra cosechable se limpia talando y quemando los árboles para fertilizar el terreno (pág. 380)

sonnet/soneto composición poética de 14 versos y con un patrón de rima y métrica (pág. 405)

steppe/estepa llanuras de Eurasia, extensas, herbáceas, semiáridas, que se extienden desde el Mar Negro hasta los montes Altai (pág. 258)

stupa/estupa capilla budista con bóveda semiesférica, construida sobre las reliquias o los huesos de un santo (pág. 210)

subcontinent/subcontinente porción de tierra que es parte de un continente pero bien diferenciada del mismo, tal como la India (pág. 66)

sultan/sultán líder político con autoridad absoluta sobre un país mahometano (pág. 457)

symposium/simposio en la antigua Atenas, reunión que se celebraba con banquetes, entretenimiento y discusiones literarias (pág. 123)

technology/tecnología las habilidades y conocimientos empleados por las personas para fabricar herramientas y trabajar (pág. 24)

theocracy/teocracia gobierno encabezado por líderes religiosos o por un líder considerado como un dios (págs. 48, 418)

theology/teología el estudio de temas religiosos (pág. 251)

tournament/torneo deporte medieval en el cual los caballeros competían para mostrar sus habilidades en la lucha (pág. 299)

tragedy/tragedia historia o representación teatral en la que el personaje central lucha contra el destino pero que desemboca en un final trágico (pág. 132)

triangular trade/comercio triangular ruta de tres direcciones entre Europa, África y América en el Siglo XVII (pág. 444)

tribune/tribuna en la antigua Roma, magistrado que representaba a los plebeyos (pág. 157)

triumvirate/triunvirato en la antigua Roma, grupo de tres personas gobernando (pág. 162)

troubadour/trovador músico y poeta de la Edad Media que viajaba de corte en corte (pág. 327)

tyrant/tirano en la antigua Grecia, persona que usurpaba el poder y establecía un gobierno unipersonal (pág. 114)

varna/*varna* una de las cuatro clases sociales principales en la sociedad aria de la antigua India (pág. 203)

vassal/vasallo en el feudalismo, noble que ocupaba la tierra de un señor de más alto rango y le servía (pág. 299)

vernacular/vernáculo el lenguaje del habla diaria, no de los eruditos, en un país o región (pág. 328)

vocation/vocación llamado de Dios para asumir cierto trabajo (pág. 417)

weir/nasa red o trampa colocada a lo ancho de un río para coger peces (pág. 376)

yasa/*yasa* código de leyes de Gengis Kan (pág. 344)

yeoman/campesino propietario en la sociedad inglesa, un campesino que poseía tierras (pág. 488)

yin and yang/yin y yan en el pensamiento chino, los principios opuestos presentes en toda naturaleza (pág. 227)

yurt/yurta tienda de campaña portátil grande y redonda que usaban los nómadas del Asia central (pág. 343)

ACKNOWLEDGMENTS

Text

Grateful acknowledgment is given authors and publishers for permission to reprint the following copyrighted material.
58 W.G. Lambert, Shamash Hymn from Babylonian Wisdom Literature, Copyright © 1960. Reprinted by permission Oxford University Press; **72** Reprinted by permission of Houghton Mifflin Co. All rights reserved; **146** From "Antigone" in *Sophocles, the Oedipus Cycle: An English Version* by Dudley Fitts and Robert Fitzgerald, copyright 1939 by Harcourt Brace & Company and renewed 1967 by Dudley Fitts and Robert Fitzgerald, reprinted by permission of Harcourt Brace & Company. CAUTION: All rights, including professional, amateur, motion picture, recitation, lecturing, performance, public reading, radio broadcasting, and television are strictly reserved. Inquiries on all rights should be addressed to Harcourt Brace & Company, Permissions Dept., Orlando, FL 32887; **366** Li Bo, "On a Quiet Night" from *The Works of Li Bo the Chinese Poet*, translated by Shigeyoshi Obata. Published in 1965 by Paragon Book Reprint Corp.; **366** Li Bo, "Taking Leave of a Friend" from Personae by Ezra Pound. Copyright 1926 by Ezra Pound. Reprinted by permission of New Directions Publishing Corporation; **367** "Hard Is the Journey" and **368** Li Bo, "Letter to His Two Small Children Staying in Eastern Lu at Wen Yang Village Under Turtle Mountain" from Li Bo and Tu Fu, translated by Arthur Cooper. Translation copyright © 1973 by Arthur Cooper. Reprinted by permission of Viking-Dutton, Inc.; **388** from "The Broken Spears" by Miguel Leon-Portilla, Copyright © 1962, 1990 by Beacon Press, Reprinted by permission of Beacon Press; **426** Niccolò Machiavelli, *The Prince*, translated and edited by Thomas G. Bergin. Copyright © 1947 by F. S. Crofts & Co. Inc. Reprinted by permission of Viking-Dutton, Inc.; **522** From *Les Misérables* by Victor Hugo, translated by Lee Fahnestock and Norman MacAfee. Translation copyright © 1987 by Lee Fahnestock and Norman MacAfee. Used by permission of Dutton Signet, a division of Penguin Books USA Inc.; **536** "The Beggar" from *The Short Stories of Anton Chekhov* by Anton Chekhov, edited with introduction by Robert Linscott. Copyright © 1932 and renewed 1960 by The Modern Library, Inc. Reprinted by permission of Random House, Inc.; **550** From "By Any Other Name" from *Gifts of Passage* by Santha Rama Rau. Copyright © 1951 by Vasanthi Rama Rau Bowers. Copyright renewed. Reprinted by permission of HarperCollins Publishers, Inc. "By Any Other Name" originally appeared in The New Yorker; **564** Jaime Torres Bodet, "The Window," translated by George Kearns. Translation copyright © 1974, 1963 by the McGraw-Hill Book Company, Inc.; **565** "The World, My Friends, My Enemies, You, and the Earth" from *Things I Didn't Know I Loved* by Nazim Hikmet, translated by Randy Blasing and Mutlu Konuk, copyright © 1975 by Randy Blasing and Mutlu Konuk. Reprinted by permission of Persea Books, Inc.; **566** Gabriel Okara, "Once Upon a Time," from African Voices, edited by Howard Sergeant. Copyright © 1973 by Howard Sergeant. Used by permission of Evans Brothers Ltd, London.

Maps

Cartographic Services provided by Ortelius Design, and GeoSystems Global Corp.

Photographs

Cover i Egyptian National Museum, Cairo, Egypt/SuperStock; **iv** (l)Erich Lessing/Art Resource, NY; (t)Museo Capitolino, Rome/E.T. Archives, London/SuperStock; **v** (t)The British Museum, London/Bridgeman Art Library/SuperStock, (b)Laurie Platt Winfrey, Inc.; **vi** (l)The Metropolitan Museum of Art, Munsey Fund, (1932932.130.6), (t)Giraudon/Art Resource, NY; **vii** (l)Palazzo Ducale, Mantua, Italy/M. Magliari/SuperStock, (t)Scala/Art Resource, NY; **viii** (l)David David Gallery, Philadelphia/Superstock, (r)Heraklion Museum, Crete/Kurt Scholz/ Superstock, (b)Scala/Art Resource NY; **ix** (b)Christies, London/Bridgeman Art Library/SuperStock (t)The British Library, London/Bridgeman Art Library/SuperStock; **x** (b)The Metropolitan Museum of Art, The Michael C. Rockefeller Memorial Collection, Gift of Nelson A. Rockefeller, 1964 (1978.412.352). Photo by Schecter Lee; **xi** (l)Museum of Mankind/E.T. Archives, London/SuperStock; (b)Georgia Department of Natural Resources; **xii** (b)Michael Holford; (t)Robert Emmett Bright/Photo Researchers; **0** Lauros-Giraudon/Art Resource, NY; **2** NASA; **8** Simon Fraser/Science Photo Library/Photo Researchers; **10** (t)NASA, (b)Edna Douthout; **11** (t)Bosvieux/Explorer/Photo Researchers, (c)David R. Frazier, (b)Jeff Greenberg/Photo Researchers; **12** (tl) Robert Harding Picture Library, (tr)Fred Maroon/Photo Researchers, (cl, cr)Musee de Petit Palais, Paris/Bridgeman Art

Library/SuperStock, (b)NASA; **13** The Metropolitan Museum of Art, The Michael C. Rockefeller Collection, Gift of Nelson A. Rockefeller, 1972 (1978.412.310); **15** National Museum, Belgrade/E.T. Archives, London/SuperStock; **16-17** Anthony Howard/Woodfin Camp & Associates; **16** Heraklion Museum, Crete/Kurt Scholz/SuperStock; **17** (t)David David Gallery, Philadelphia/SuperStock, (b)National Museum, Lagos, Nigeria/Kurt Scholz/SuperStock; **19** Jean Clottes/Sygma; **20** Esias Baitel/Gamma-Liaison; **21** John Reader/Science Photo Library/Photo Researchers; **26** Boltin Picture Library; **27** John Reader/Science Photo Library/Photo Researchers; **28-29** Erich Lessing/Art Resource, NY; **28** Boltin Picture Library; **29** Scala/Art Resource, NY; **31** Ara Guler/Magnum; **32** Scala/Art Resource, NY; **33** Borromeo/Art Resource, NY; **35** Ira Block/The Image Bank; **36** Scala/Art Resource, NY; **45** The British Museum, London/Bridgeman Art Library/SuperStock; **46** Giraudon/Art Resource, NY; **47** (t)Sylvain Grandadam/Photo Researchers, (b)Erich Lessing/Magnum; **49** John Heaton/Westlight; **51** Michael Holford; **52** Boltin Picture Library; **58** Boltin Picture Library; **59** Ancient Art & Architecture Collection Ltd.; **60 through 62** Boltin Picture Library; **63** (l)Aleppo Museum, Syria/ E.T. Archives, London/SuperStock, (r)Museum of Baghdad, Iraq/ Silvio Fiore/SuperStock; **64** Musee de Louvre, Paris/E.T. Archives, London/SuperStock; **66** Borromeo/Art Resource, NY; **68** Scala/Art Resource, NY; **69** Courtesy the Institute of History and Philology; **70-71** Bridgeman/Art Resource, NY; **72 74 79** Michael Holford; **80** Giraudon/Art Resource, NY; **83** Laura Zito/Photo Researchers; **85** David Forbert/SuperStock; **86** SuperStock; **87** Brent Turner; **88** Boltin Picture Library; **90-91** SEF/Art Resource, NY; **90 91** Erich Lessing/Art Resource, NY; **93** H. Linke/SuperStock; **97** Jerry Bergman/Gamma-Liaison; **98** Scala/Art Resource, NY; **99** Laurie Platt Winfrey, Inc.; **101** Scala/Art Resource, NY; **102-103** Bettmann Archive; **103** Joseph Nettis/Photo Researchers; **105** Scala/Art Resource, NY; **106** Erich Lessing/Art Resource, NY; **107** SuperStock; **108** Alberto Incrocci/The Image Bank; **110** Museo Capitolino, Rome/E.T. Archives, London/SuperStock; **111** House of Masks, Delos, Greece/Bridgeman Art Library/SuperStock; **112** William Katz/ Photo Researchers; **113** Giraudon/Art Resource, NY; **115** Michael Holford; **116-117** Bill Bachmann/Photo Researchers; **116** Nimatallah/Art Resource, NY; **117** Art Resource, NY; **118** The Brooklyn Museum, Charles Wilbour Fund; **120 122** Scala/Art Resource, NY; **123** Foto Marberg/Art Resource, NY; **127** Bettmann Archive; **129** Scala/Art Resource, NY; **130** Scala/Art Resource, NY; **131** Werner Forman Archive/Art Resource, NY; **134** Museo Delle Terme, Rome/E.T. Archives, London/SuperStock; **135** Scala/Art Resource, NY; **136** Museo Capitolino, Rome/E.T. Archives, London/SuperStock; **138** Erich Lessing/Art Resource, NY; **140** Scala/Art Resource, NY; **141** Musee du Louvre, Paris/E.T. Archives, London/SuperStock; **142-143** Erich Lessing/Art Resource, NY; **142** (r)Staatliche Antikensammlung, Munich/Bridgeman Art Library/ Art Resource, NY, (l)The Metropolitan Museum of Art, Bequest of Walter C. Backer, 1972 (1972.118.95); **143** (l)Art Resource, NY, (r)Giraudon/Art Resource, NY; **144** Boltin Picture Library; **145** Eric Lessing/Art Resource; **146 147 148** Art Resource, NY; **153** Erich Lessing/Art Resource, NY; **154 through 159** Scala/Art Resource, NY; **160** Prenestino Museum, Rome/E.T. Archives, London/SuperStock; **161** Scala/Art Resource, NY; **162** Archaeological Museum, Venice/E.T. Archives, London/SuperStock; **164** Robert Emmett Bright/Photo Researchers; **166-167** Scala/Art Resource, NY; **166** (c)Villa of the Mysteries, Pompeii/Euramax/SuperStock, (l)The Metropolitan Museum of Art, Rogers Fund, 1903 (03.14.5); **167** Alinari/Art Resource, NY; **168 171** Scala/Art Resource, NY; **172** Erich Lessing/Art Resource, NY; **173** Werner Forman/Art Resource, NY; **174** Scala/Art Resource, NY; **175** Robert Frerck/Tony Stone Images; **176** (l)Erich Lessing/Art Resource, NY; **179** Scala/Art Resource, NY; **181** The Metropolitan Museum of Art, Fletcher Fund, 1924 (24/97.21ab) **183** Tassili N'Ajjer Plateau, Algeria/Holton Collection/SuperStock; **184** Roger K. Burnard; **185** Egyptian Expedition of The Metropolitan Museum of Art, The Rogers Fund, 1930 (30.4.21); **186** file photo; **189** The Metropolitan Museum of Art, The Michael C. Rockefeller Collection, Gift of Nelson A. Rockefeller, 1972 (1978.412.310); **190** The British Museum, London/Bridgeman Art Library/SuperStock; **190-191** The Elliott Elisofon Archives, Museum of African Art, The Smithsonian Institution; **191** The Metropolitan Museum of Art, The Michael C. Rockefeller Memorial Collection, Gift of Nelson A. Rockefeller, 1964 (1978.412.352). Photo by Schecter Lee; **194** H. von Meiss/Photo Researchers; **195** Dave G. Houser; **196** M.P. Kahl/Photo Researchers;

197 Mark Burnett; 199 The Metropolitan Museum of Art, The Michael C. Rockefeller Collection, Gift of Nelson A. Rockefeller, 1972 (1978.412.310); 201 Scala/Art Resource, NY; 202 Toby Molenaar/The Image Bank; 204 Robert Harding Picture Library; 204-205 B. Kapbor/SuperStock; 205 Art Resource, NY; 207 Victoria & Albert Museum, London/Art Resource, NY; 208 Christies, London/Bridgeman Art Library/SuperStock; 211 Ancient Art & Architecture Collection; 213 Gueorgui Pinkhassov/Magnum Photos, Inc.; 214 James P. Blair/National Geographic Image Collection; 215 Borromeo/ Art Resource, NY; 217 Jon Gardey/Robert Harding Picture Library Ltd.; 219 Tony Stone Images; 220 Bettmann Archive; 225 Bibliotheque Nationale, Paris/Bridgeman Art Library/SuperStock; 226 Michael Holford; 227 Giraudon/Art Resource, NY; 228 Paul Biddle & Tim Malyon/Science Photo Library/Photo Researchers; 230 Bibliotheque Nationale, Paris; 231 (l)Giraudon/Art Resource, NY, (r)Bettmann Archive; 232 Bettmann Archive; 233 Mark Burnett; 237 SuperStock; 238 Robert Emmett Bright/Photo Researchers; 239 Robert Harding Picture Library; 241 Jacksonville Museum of Contemporary Art, FL/SuperStock; 242 Erich Lessing/Art Resource; 243 (l)The Smithsonian Institution, (c)Archive Photos, (r)Ancient Art & Architecture Collection, 245 246 248 Scala/Art Resource, NY; 249 SuperStock; 251 Hagia Sophia, Istanbul, Turkey/E.T. Archives, London/SuperStock; 252 (l)Michael Holford, (r)Ancient Art & Architecture Collection; 253 255 Ancient Art & Architecture Collection; 256 SEF/Art Resource, NY; 258 Roy/Explorer/Photo Researchers; 260 Art Wolfe/Tony Stone Images; 262 263 Bettmann Archive; 264 Richard Bergman/Photo Researchers; 265 Michael Holford; 267 Ancient Art & Architecture Collection; 269 Bettmann Archive; 270 British Library, London/Bridgeman Art Library International Ltd; 272 AKG Berlin/SuperStock; 273 Ancient Art & Architecture Collection; 275 Werner Forman/Art Resource, NY; 276 Michael Holford; 277 Bibliotheque Nationale, Paris/The Bridgeman Art Library International Ltd; 278-279 Lerner Fine Art Collection/ SuperStock; 278 Courtesy of the Arthur M. Sackler Gallery, Smithsonian Institution, Washington, D.C.; 279 Ancient Art & Architecture Collection; 282 286 Bettmann Archive; 287 Michael Holford; 288 SuperStock; 293 San Francisco, Assisi/Canali PhotoBank, Milan/SuperStock; 294 Bettmann Archive; 295 Scala/ Art Resource, NY; 298 British Library, London/Bridgeman Art Library/SuperStock; 299 Ancient Art & Architecture Collection; 301 The Metropolitan Museum of Art, Munsey Fund, 1932(32.130.6); 303 Robert Smith/Ancient Art & Architecture Collection; 304-305 Art Resource, NY; 304 (l)Ronald Sheridan/Ancient Art & Architecture, (r)Abbey of Monteoliveto Maggiore, Sienna/E.T. Archives, London/SuperStock; 304-305 Art Resource, NY; 305 306 Ronald Sheridan/Ancient Art & Architecture Collection; 307 Museo del Prado, Madrid/E.T. Archives, London/SuperStock; 308 Ronald Sheridan/Ancient Art & Architecture Collection; 309 Erich Lessing/Art Resource, NY; 313 Robert Smith/Ancient Art & Architecture Collection; 317 Scala/Art Resource, NY; 318 Ancient Art & Architecture Collection; 319 Giraudon/Art Resource, NY; 321 Erich Lessing/Art Resource, NY; 322 O. Troisfontaines/SuperStock; 323 The British Library, London/Bridgeman Art Library/SuperStock; 324-325 Scala/Art Resource, NY; 325 Ancient Art & Architecture Collection; 327 Giraudon/Art Resource, NY; 328 Scala/Art Resource, NY; 329 British Library, London/E.T. Archives, London/SuperStock; 330 Erich Lessing/Art Resource, NY; 334 Ancient Art & Architecture Collection; 336 Bridgeman Art Library/Art Resource, NY; 341 Bibliotheque Nationale, Paris/AKG Berlin/SuperStock; 342 Laurie Platt Winfrey, Inc.; 344 J. Bertrand/Photo Researchers; 345 SEF/Art Resource, NY; 346 Naomi Duguid/Asia Access; 347 Laurie Platt Winfrey, Inc.; 351 Wolfgang Kaehler; 352-353 Ernest Manewal/ SuperStock; 352 (l)George Holton/Photo Researchers, (r)Frederick Ayer/Photo Researchers; 353 R. Rowan/Photo Researchers; 355 A. Hubrich/H. Armstrong Roberts; 356 Jim Steinberg/Photo Researchers; 358 T. Iwamiya/Photo Researchers; 359 Rick Browne/Photo Researchers; 360 Masao Hayashi/Dunq/Photo Researchers; 361 Bettmann Archive; 363 Private Collection/Bridgeman Art Library/ SuperStock; 364 Freer Gallery; 365 Paul Chesley/Tony Stone Images; 366 Mary Evans Picture Library; 367 The Metropolitan Museum of Art, Edward Elliott Family Collection. Purchase, the Dillon Fund Gift, 1982. !982.2.2; 368 369 Bettmann Archive; 371 file photo; 373 Boltin Picture Library; 374 Steve Smith/Westlight; 376-377 Mark Burnett; 376 Georgia Department of Natural Resources; 377 (l)Cranbrook Institute of Science, (r)Bettmann Archive; 378 J. Warden /SuperStock; 379 S. Vidler/SuperStock; 380 Museum of Mankind/E.T. Archives, London/SuperStock; 381 W. Bertsch/H. Armstrong Roberts; 383 Jacksonville Museum of Contemporary Art, FL/SuperStock; 388 Michael Zabe/Art Resource, NY; 391 Woodfin Camp & Associates; 393 Loren McIntyre/Woodfin Camp & Associates; 394 Mark Burnett; 395 Werner Forman/Art Resource, NY; 397 Giraudon/Art Resource, NY; 399 Scala/Art Resource, NY; 400 The British Museum; 401-402 Scala/Art Resource, NY; 401 Wolfgang Kaehler; 403 Palazzo Ducale, Mantua, Italy/M. Magliari/SuperStock; 404 Sistine Chapel, Vatican, Rome/Bridgeman Art Library/SuperStock; 406-407 Vatican Museums & Galleries, Rome/Fratelli Alinari/ SuperStock; 406 Galleria Dell'Academia, Florence/Scala/ SuperStock; 407 Erich Lessing/Art Resource, NY; 408 Scala/Art Resource, NY; 410 Victor R. Boswell, Jr.; 411 Vatican Museums & Galleries, Rome/Canali PhotoBank, Milan/SuperStock; 412 AKG, Berlin/ SuperStock; 413 Scala/Art Resource, NY; 414 Erich Lessing/ Art Resource, NY; 415 SuperStock; 416 Erich Lessing/Art Resource, NY; 417 (l)Erich Lessing/ Art Resource, NY, (r)National Museum, Copenhagen/E.T. Archives, London/SuperStock; 418 Mary Evans Picture Library/Photo Researchers; 420 Scala/Art Resource, NY; 421 Erich Lessing/Art Resource, NY; 422 Michael Holford; 423 Giraudon/ Art Resource, NY; 425 Werner Forman Archive/Art Institute of Chicago/Art Resource, NY; 426 through 429 Scala/Art Resource, NY; 431 Erich Lessing/Art Resource, NY; 433 National Maritime Museum; 434 Karen Kasmauski/Woodfin Camp & Associates; 436 (l)SuperStock, (r)Michael Holford; 438 National Museum of American Art, Washington DC/Art Resource, NY; 439 440 AKG, Berlin/SuperStock; 442-443 Alinari/Art Resource, NY; 442 Erich Lessing/Art Resource, NY; 443 (t)Scala/Art Resource, NY, (b)Brent Turner/BLT Productions; 445 Bettmann Archive; 446 447 SuperStock; 448 Bridgeman/Art Resource, NY; 449 Michael Holford; 450 Bridgeman/Art Resource, NY; 455 456 Giraudon/Art Resource, NY; 458 Art Resource, NY; 459 Adam Woolfitt/Woodfin Camp & Associates; 461 by courtesy of the Board of Trustees of the Victoria & Albert Museum, London/Bridgeman Art Library/ SuperStock; 462 Bibliotheque Nationale, Paris; 463 Dallas & John Heaton/Westlight; 464-465 Philadelphia Free Library/AKG, Berlin/SuperStock; 464 G. Hunter/SuperStock; 465 (l)Art Trade, Bonhams, London/Bridgeman Art Library/SuperStock, (r)SEF/Art Resource, NY; 466 D.E. Cox/Tony Stone Images; 468 Werner Forman Archive/Art Resource, NY; 469 Culver Pictures Inc./SuperStock; 470 Kita-In Saitumi/Werner Foreman Archive/Art Resource, NY; 471 Michael Holford; 473 Doug Martin; 474 George Holton/Photo Researchers; 475 SuperStock; 476 Scala/Art Resource, NY; 477 Bettmann Archive; 481 Giraudon/Art Resource, NY; 482 Bridgeman Art Library, London/SuperStock; 483 Bettmann Archive; 485 Victoria & Albert Museum/Art Resource, NY; 486 Michael Holford; 487 (l)Bridgeman/ Art Resource, NY, (r)National Portrait Gallery, London; 488 489 National Portrait Gallery, London/SuperStock; 490 Giraudon/Art Resource, NY; 491 Lauros-Giraudon/Art Resource, NY; 492 A&F Pears Ltd., London/ SuperStock; 494 Museum of Art History, Vienna/AKG, Berlin/ SuperStock; 496 AKG, Berlin/SuperStock; 498 Novosti from Sovfoto; 499 Michael Holford; 502 Giraudon/Art Resource, NY; 505 Bridgeman/Art Resource, NY; 507 National Gallery, London/ SuperStock; 508 Bridgeman/Art Resource, NY; 509 Giraudon/Art Resource, NY; 513 Scala/Art Resource, NY; 514 Architect of the Capitol, Washington D.C.; 515 Bettmann Archive; 516 (l)Stock Montage, (r)Scala/Art Resource, NY; 517 (t)Bettmann Archive, (b)Original painting hangs in the Selectmen's Meeting Room, Abbot Hall, Marblehead MA; 518 (l)Stock Montage, (r)Giraudon/Art; 519 Scala/Art Resource, NY; 522 Giraudon/Art Resource, NY; 523 The Metropolitan Museum of Art, Gift of Mrs. Herbert N. Straus, 1942(42.203.1) Photo by Derry Moore; 524 Mary Evans Picture Library/Photo Researchers; 527 L. Berger/SuperStock; 528 Stock Montage; 529 (t)Library of Congress, (b)Laurie Platt Winfrey, Inc.; 530 Musee de Petit Palais, Paris/Bridgeman Art Library/SuperStock; 533 Stock Montage; 536 Archive Photos; 537 Scala/Art Resource, NY; 538 Russian Sate Museum, St. Petersburg/Bourkatouskey/ SuperStock; 541 Aaron Haupt; 542 UPI/Bettmann Archive; 543 (t)AP/ Wide World Photos, (b)Lena Kara/SIPA; 545 B. Swersey/Gamma-Liaison; 546 Schalkwijk/Art Resource, NY; 547 AP/Wide World Photos; 550 UPI/Bettmann; 551 Laurie Platt Winfrey, Inc.; 553 Rudi Von Briel; 555 Chuck O'Rear/Westlight; 556 (l)UPI/Corbis-Bettmann, (r)Sovfoto/Eastfoto; 557 (l)T. Rosenthal/SuperStock, (r)NASA; 558 Epix/Sygma; 559 Adrian Bradshaw/SABA; 560 BlackStar; 561 David L. Perry; 565 AP/Wide World Photos; 567 Dennis Stock/Magnum.